A History *of* FLORENCE, ALABAMA

(with 1850 Census of Lauderdale County)

Compiled by:
Jill K. Garrett

Southern Historical Press, inc.
Greenville, South Carolina

This volume was reproduced
from a personal copy located in
the Publishers private library

Please direct all correspondence and book orders to:
SOUTHERN HISTORICAL PRESS, Inc.
1071 Park West Blvd.
Greenville, SC   29611

Originally printed Columbia, TN 1968
ISBN #978-1-63914-333-7
Printed in the United States of America

CONTENTS

A History of Florence, Alabama . . . . 1 - 77

Addendum 78

Footnotes 81

1850 Census of Lauderdale County, Alabama C1

Lauderdale County marriages, 1820 - 1825 . . . . C-138

Lauderdale County marriages, 1825 - 1833 . . . . C-144

Index . . . . C-155 or 239

INTRODUCTION

This is a companion study of "A History of Lauderdale County, Alabama," completed in 1964. As the history of Florence is so closely allied with the history of the county some repetition has been unavoidable. It is hoped that this has been kept to a minimum as new source material was used in the main part for this study. Events that were examined in detail in the initial study may not be mentioned in this study--or if so, only touched on briefly. Additional research has furnished some facts that were not available for the study of the county.

The 1850 census of Lauderdale County is included in this work. The spelling and information is as shown on that census. Some of the handwriting was most difficult to read, so allowance for error must be made for information from this census. If ages do not agree with family records, it is possible that the information on this census might have been given by someone not in the household. Questionable and confusing information will be underscored.

I should like to thank my mother, Iris Hopkins McClain, for permitting me the use of some of the Raymond Y. McClain papers. I should also like to express my appreciation to Mrs. Mary Threet Sharp for the current historical clippings which she has furnished me. Again, I have used material from the William L. McDonald papers, and I should like to thank Mr. McDonald for these papers. I am most grateful to Mrs. Willodyne J. Sloan of Alexander City, Alabama, for a gift set of Moore's History of Alabama, which was of great value in the research for this study.

The third, and final, work on Lauderdale County will be completed in the winter and distributed in 1969. This will be a study and listing of some of the cemeteries of Lauderdale County.

                   Jill K. Garrett

Columbia, Tennessee
November 1968

CHAPTER I

The Alabama Territory was created by an act of Congress on March 3, 1817; and William Wyatt Bibb of Georgia was appointed Territorial Governor by President James Monroe.

At the first session of the Alabama Territorial Legislature, meeting on January 19, 1818, in two rooms at the Douglas Hotel in St. Stephens, thirteen new counties were created, including Lauderdale County. St. Stephens, a village of some forty houses, was the territorial capital from 1817 to 1819, was located on the Tombigbee River in Washington County. In 1819 when the population in the territory had increased to the required number for statehood, Governor Bibb called the members of the Territorial Legislature to meet in Huntsville. Alabama was admitted to the Union on December 14, 1819.

This was not the first attempt in creating a county in this section. As early as 1783 a land company composed of William Blount, Governor of Tennessee, his brothers John and Thomas, General Joseph Martin, General Griffith Rutherford, Col. John Sevier, General Richard Caswell, and Colonel John Donelson, had been formed to acquire title to all land in the present state of Alabama north of the Tennessee River. As the state of Georgia claimed this land, these men petitioned Georgia to organize the region into a county. This commission was appointed and steps were taken toward organization. Houston County, Georgia, was organized and Valentine Sevier, Jr., was chosen to represent the county at the next meeting of the Georgia legislature. He was not seated, and the proposed county was rejected, but only by a small vote.[1]

Georgia claimed all the territory between her present boundary and the Mississippi River, and as far north as the southern line of the present state of Tennessee. This claim was disputed by South Carolina, who claimed a twelve mile wide strip as far west as the Mississippi, including what is now Lauderdale County. South Carolina's claims were based on a colonial charter.[2]

In March 1785 a company including John Donelson, John Peyton, and David Henry traveled through the wilderness from Nashville to the mouth of Elk River, expecting to meet the other commissioners there. Finding none, Donelson left five men, including Peyton, and returned to the Cumberland Settlements. He left only a few men as he believed only a few could successfully hide in the woods at the mouth of Elk River, which was a great resort for trading. These men stayed a week and as no others arrived, they returned to the Cumberland. In the spring of the following year, Turner Williams and Argalus Jeter came to Elk River for a stay of three days.[3]

When John Donelson and his flotilla floated down the Tennessee River in 1780, they encountered hostile Indians at both ends of the Muscle Shoals, and at the lower end had five of their party wounded.

The Indians had villages on the south side of the river, consisting of only a few rude huts, "inhabited by a refractory people who refused to be governed by the laws and customs of their nation." These renegades had been attracted to this area by the prospect of plundering the emigrants who might be stranded in their descent of the treacherous and dangerous rapids of the shoals.

As these renegades were too small in number and too far removed from the Cumberland Settlements, they were ignored. French traders from the Wabash had started trading with the Indians at Muscle Shoals about 1783, and the settlement here became important to French trade.

A town called Coldwater (also found as Cold Water) was established at the mouth of Coldwater Creek, which "takes its rise in the bold stream that gushes from beneath a bluff of limestone, at the present town of Tuscumbia, Alabama." The town remained a secret until 1787.

While the French trader, Monsieur Viez, traded with the Indians at Muscle Shoals, the Indians did not harass the Cumberland settlements. In 1784 or 1785, the trade fell into the hands of others who encouraged the Indians to molest the whites and even furnished ammunition for the sport.[4]

The existence of Coldwater was discovered by two Chickasaw warriors, who informed their chief, Piomingo, who in turn advised General James Robertson in Nashville. When Robertson's brother Mark was killed by marauders from Muscle Shoals, he determined to destroy Coldwater. As few settlers had ever penetrated the forests as far south as the Tennessee River, two Chickasaws were employed as guides. One of these was named Toka, and the expedition to destroy Coldwater is often called the Toka Expedition.

Robertson's expedition attacked and burned the town. According to one source, three Frenchmen, one French woman, and about twenty Indians were killed. Robertson had them buried on the spot.[5]

The name of Doublehead begins appearing in records about 1791. He was beyond question "the most cruel and bloodthirsty Indian in the Cherokee nation." Judge Haywood, a Tennessee historian, recorded that Doublehead shed with his own hands as much human blood as any man of his age in America![6] And as one local historian remarked, after reading of Doublehead's atrocities, "He is Lauderdale County's own." His name lives on at springs, caves, and roads throughout North Alabama and parts of Tennessee. In later years he was given a reservation of land in the eastern part of the county where he lived. Following his death, in 1807, several Cherokees continued to live here. One of these men, mistakenly believed to be Doublehead, guided some of the troops across the Tennessee River during the Creek War. One man recalled:

> "Some of the troops were ferried across the Tennessee River at Ditto's Landing; a large number forded the river near the mouth of Blue-Water, on Muscle Shoals. Doublehead, an Indian, was guide..."[7]

As Doublehead was dead at this time, the Indian guide was undoubtedly one of the Cherokees living here. As Doublehead's descendants seem to be legion, the Indian guide might possibly have been his son. One writer says that two of his daughters married Colberts. Another of his daughters is said to have married John Hough, an early settler in Lauderdale County.

Muscle Shoals is the name that was given to the almost continuous chain of obstructions in the river, beginning at the wide shallows at Elk River Shoals, then followed fifteen miles of rushing, tumbling water known as Big Muscle Shoals, with a fall of 85 feet. Big Muscle Shoals, which stretched about 37 miles, was the worst stretch of the river. Between Big Muscle Shoals and Little Muscle Shoals there was a comparatively smooth stretch of three miles. Further down river were Colbert Shoals and Bee Tree Shoals.[8]

The Shoals prevented navigation of the river and until conquered by the Tennessee Valley Authority in this century obstructed to some degree the progress of this section. Those who can remember the Shoals testify to what an awesome sight the rocks and waters presented. Once seen the Shoals were never forgotten.

Arthur T. Isom, a soldier of the War of 1812, crossed the river on his way South during that war. Sixty years later a friend would write:

> "The writer is reminded of a conversation which he once had with Esquire Isom, then of Mt. Pleasant, while we were crossing the Tennessee River on a bridge over Muscle Shoals, at a place called Bellview, near the mouth of Blue Water. This bridge was 2,250 yards long, and built on trestles, which were secured to the rock bottom by sills and bolts, but owing to some deficiency in the plan or work, a mile of it fell down and was never rebuilt. The water at this place was very shallow, the rock bottom being visible all the way across.
>
> "Esq. Isom, who was with Jackson in the march to New Orleans in the War of 1812, pointed out the ford below the bridge, where the army crossed, and related many incidents and accidents in the crossing. Horses and riders were sometimes submerged by plunging into a deep hole between the rocks and several horses were left in the river with their feet and legs fastened in the crevices of the rocks. This place is the first crossing above Bainbridge, and some twenty or twenty-five miles above Florence."[9]

About 1800 an angry dispute arose between the United States Government and the authorities as to the ownership of the territory between latitude 31° and 35°. This dispute was carried on until April 1803 when commissioners were appointed. The decision of this commission was an agreement whereby the United States should have the territory by paying $1,250,000 to the State of Georgia. Immigration into the Tennessee Valley was spurred by this agreement.[10]

Georgia still had interests in the area as late as 1810. An obituary for a man who died in Lauderdale County reads: "Died--a few days ago at Tennessee River, Capt. James M'Carrol, principal surveyor for the Georgia Company, at Doublehead's Reserve."[11]

Settlers were in Lauderdale County before the Indians had formally deeded their lands to the United States. It has been estimated that 4,000 or 5,000 intruders were in the Chickasaw territory alone in 1810. In the period 1809 to 1811, soldiers at Fort Hampton (located on Elk River) were sent out to drive all settlers off the Indian land.

The absence of records makes it impossible to know who the earliest settlers in Lauderdale County and around Florence were.

Some authorities place Richard Rapier as the first. Some give the honor to Christopher Cheatham. Jonathan Bailey, for whom Bailey Springs was named, came to this area as early as 1810. Parson Kelough, John Webb, and John Johnson were in the county early.

Charles Sharp came from Petersburg, Virginia, in 1818. It was his son David A. Sharp for whom Sharp's Mills was named.[12]

Charles Littleton, Revolutionary Soldier, came to Lauderdale County, after a brief settlement in Giles County, Tennessee. He left Tennessee because his stock multiplied so quickly and he needed more land. His granddaughter, Mrs. W. W. Casey, wrote of his settlement when she was an old lady in 1910:

> "Charles flock increase so fast thought it best to move to Lauderdale County, Ala., 16 miles northwest from Florence, this is a rocky barony country but a great place to raise stock wild pea grew all over the wood, the grap

too grew very tall the climate is mild and the stock only needed a little salt and that is all the attention thar was necessary for them. When a child I have oftain seen the wild dear feeding a long with the cattle wild Turkey were numerous they in drove, wild flower of all collors and sorts a bound as far as the eye could see. The shrub honey suckle grew in low places in the hills and perfumed the woods. The huckle berry also grow on bushes in damp places, they are a small black berry...

"Here Charles Littleton entered a tract of land from the Government built commodious and comfortable house also provided houses for his negroes, then opened a large farm with Cypress Creek running through it. The water is clear can see the fish small and great swimming a round over the rocky bottom...

"He owned three negroes born in Africa, Sylva, Chief's daughter, three black marks on each cheek; Pony (Pomp?) her cousin, Jim a neighbor boy... her grandmother sent them to gether sticks to make a fire and the pale faces was hid in the wood and caught them. David Henderson bought them they were naked..."

She also remembered her grandfather as being a bald-headed man who sang to his grandchildren. He died March 28, 1848, at the age of 105 years.[13]

The late Robert Dyas wrote in 1923, "March 12, 1818, may be properly called the birthday of Florence. On that day the founders of this town met in Huntsville and formally organized the Cypress Land Company...The trustees appointed were General John Coffee, James Jackson, Thomas Bibb, Leroy Pope, John Childress, Dabney Morris, and John McKinley. The represented a 'numerous association of respectable, opulent and enterprising individuals.'"[14]

The Cypress Land Company purchased 5,515 acres of land lying on the north side of the Tennessee River for $85,235.24. Among the stockholders were James Madison (President), Andrew Jackson (President-to-be), Thomas Childress, Thomas Bibb, General John Brahan, Dr. John R. Bedford.

The trustees of the Cypress Land Company had the town and lands surveyed and early in April 1818 began advertising that the first sale of lots would be held on July 22, 1818, and continue for several days.[15]

The Cypress Land Company had offices in a building on Tennessee Street in Florence, where the Tennessee Valley Bank stood in 1923. The building burned on December 14, 1827, and all the records destroyed. General John Coffee had made a private record of the original land sales. The early buyers, lot numbers, and prices paid are as follows:

1	Joseph Royal	$ 289	12	William Stockard	600
2	Joseph Royal	180	13	John Chisum	500
3	James Gadsden	290	14	William Hunter	515
4	J. Donelson to J.H. Smith	300	15	Thos. N. Elliman	555
5	John Asher	255	16	David Craig	605
6	James Gadsden	350	17	Jonathan Estill	500
7	James Gadsden	350	18	Jonathan Estill	505
8	John Pate	305	19	Jonathan Estill	315
9	John Read	610 (?)	20	Jonathan Estill	400
10	John illegible	???	21	Waddy Tait	360
11	William Kid	550	22	Waddy Tait	400

23	Waddy Tait	565	80	Richard Rapier	1000	
24	Waddy Tait	505	81	John McKinley	870	
25	Benj'n B. Jones	300	82	Patrick McGuire	1050	
26	John W. Walker	275	83	Patrick McGuire	2100	
27	John W. Walker	300	84	Hugh Campbell	1600	
28	James Madison	300	85	Jas. G. Burney	1600	
29	John W. Walker	100	86	Edward Bradley	2600	
30	John McKinley	150	87	William Kelley	1405	
31	John McKinley	130	88	Chapman Manly	850	
32	John W. Walker	110	89	William J. Adair	500	
33	Hugh Campbell	195	90	John W. Clay	875	
34	Hugh Campbell	200	91	Sarah Hanna	555	
35	Hugh Campbell	200	92	Francis Kemper	495	
36	Hugh Campbell	185	93	Jas. H. Weakley	600	
37	Thos. G. Percy	315	94	John Childress	525	
38	Thos. G. Percy	310	95	Henry Minor	400	
39	Jas. Madison	390	96	Henry Minor	400	
40	Thos. G. Percy	300	97	John McKinley	175	
41	James Madison	490	98	John McKinley	280	
42	James Madison	485	99	John McKinley	180	
43	James Madison	600	100	John McKinley	135	
44	James Madison	400	101	Abraham Mentzer	300	
44	James Madison	400	102	Ben B. Jones	350	
45	Jesse Wharton	400	103	Ben B. Jones	295	
46	Taylor, Winston and Foote	515	104	John Craig	315	
47	Thos. J. Percy	715	105	Thos. G. Percy	410	
48	Jesse Wharton	800	106	Samuel Whorton	445	
49	Thos. Bruce	670	107	Jesse Wharton	600	
50	Jas. Mitchell	700	108	Samuel Craig	600	
51	John Brahan	775	109	John R. Bedford	700	
51	John Chisam	715	110	Horace Philpot	815	
53	John Chisam	705	111	Horatio Philpot	1300	
54	John Brahan	60	112	Waddy Tait	1200	
55	James Gadsden	400	113	Samuel Craig	2605	
56	James Gadsden	425	114	Wm. Dixon & Co.	2995	
57	James Gadsden	340	115	Jas. Madison	2325	
58	James Gadsden	280	116	Elihu S. Hall	2600	
59	Gen. Andrew Jackson	300	117	Calvin W. Easton	1200	
60	Gen. Andrew Jackson	300	118	John H. Hanna	1100	
61	Jas. Gadsden	295	119	John McKinley	1200	
62	Jas. Gadsden	250	120	John Craig	1175	
63	John Donelson	220	121	Malcolm Gilcrist, J. J'son	3500	
64	Jas. Jackson	200	122	Robeson and Read	3000	
65	John W. Walker	200	123	Oliver C. Porter and Co.	2680	
66	J. Donelson to J. H. Smith	270	124	George Coulter	3070	
67	Ben B. Jones	300	125	Wm. R. and D. W. R'dale	810	
68	John Coffee to J. Brahan	335	126	Joseph Royal	705	
69	Gen. Andrew Jackson	350	127	Wm. J. Adair	505	
70	Malcolm Gilcrist	420	128	Almerin Holley	460	
71	Thos. Bibb	700	129	J. Donelson	285	
72	Jas. Benham	405	130	Jas. Jackson	260	
73	Jas. Benham	700	131	J. Donelson to J. H. Smith	235	
74	Samuel Whorton	1900	132	Joel Rice	200	
75	Presley Ward and Co.	3250	133	Joseph Royal	165	
76	Daniel McKinley	1100	134	Jas. Madison	195	
77	John Brahan	1130	135	John Donelson	280	
78	Richard Rapier	3000	136	Thos. Gerrad	390	
79	Phillip J. Scudder	1050	137	Wm. J. Adair	450	

#	Name	Amount	#	Name	Amount
138	Moses White	505	196	Wm. H. and D. W. R'dale	1010
139	Hugh Campbell	550	197	John Coffee	700
140	Eli Hammond	705	198	George Martin	855
141	George Martin	1690	199	George Martin	710
142	William Easton	915	200	John W. Walker	515
143	Eli Hammond	2315	201	Ferdinand Sannoner	315
144	Elihu S. Hall	3000	202	John McKinley	295
145	J. H. Hanna to J. L. A's'tg	2300	203	John McKinley	160
146	Ben B. Jones	1450	204	John Donelson	190
147	John Leak	1050	205	Archibald Fuqua	300
148	Patrick McGuire	1370	206	Jas. L. Armstrong	320
149	S. Hazard and Co.	1105	207	Jas. L. Armstrong	605
150	Thos. G. Percy	875	208	Jas. Jackson	505
151	Joseph Coleman	1525	209	Ben B. Jones	900
152	S. Hazard and Co.	1800	210	Ben B. Jones	1345
153	Jas. Manning	2310	211	George Coulter	1550
154	Jas. M. Gobson	1010	212	George Coulter	1130
155	John H. Hanna	700	213	Caleb S. Manley	1075
156	Philip Scudder	1150	214	T. C'ldress and S. Hanna	1120
157	Jackson and Alexander	870	215	T. C'ldress and S. Hanna	3005
158	J. Jackson and Alexander	500	216	Taylor, Winston, Foote	2000
159	John McKinley	500	217	Tavern Lots	
160	Jas. Madison	675	218		
161	John R. Bedford	665	219	Waddy Tait	1020
162	Thos. Gerrad	470	220	John Braham	1505
163	John Childress	360	221	John Overton	800
164	John H. Gibson	500	222	Jas. Manning	600
165			223	John H. Gibson	625
166	College Square		224	John Overton	605
167			225	Jas. M. Gibson	515
168			226	John Overton	500
169	J. Jackson and John C'fee	385	227	Milinton Childs	300
170	J. Jackson and J. C'fee	225	228	Jas. Madison	500
171	Jas. Madison	400	229	John Coffee	650
172	Jas. Jackson and J. C'fee	365	230	Ben B. Jones	430
173	John R. Bedford	395	231	Christopher H. Price	550
174	Joseph T. Ellis	300	232	Ben B. Jones	605
175	Allen Morris	500	233	John McKinley	405
176	John R. Bedford	560	234	Jas. Madison	450
177	Edward Ward	690	235	John R. Bedford	235
178	Jas. Madison	665	236	Jas. Madison	300
179	Waddy Tait	970	237	Jas. Sample	305
180	Benj. B. Jones	700	238	Waddy Tait	225
181	Jasan Hopkins	760	239	Waddy Tait	200
182	J. C. McLemore	550	240	Jas. Madison	200
183	Wm. J. Adair	530	241	Jas. Madison	170
184	Ben. B. Jones	890	242	Jas. Madison	120
185	Lazarus Maddox	900	243	Waddy Tait	145
186	John A. Gibson	720	244	Jas. Jackson	185
187	Jas. Manning	765	245	Jas. Madison	280
188	Jas. Madison	775	246	John Mathews	280
189	Daniel Right	1205	247	John McKinley	495
190	John H. Hanna	1500	248	John McKinley	500
191	Jas. Manning	204	249	Archibald Fuqua	380
192	John McKinley	1000	250	Archibald Fuqua	395
193	Leroy Pope	1520	251	Jas. Manning	400
194	Jas. Jackson and Co.	2000	252	John McKinley	310
195	Jas. Jackson and Co.	1300	253	Jas. Jackson	120

254	Jas. Jackson	285	280	John R. Bedford		2800
255	Daniel McKinley	75	281			
256	Lazrus Maddox	265	282			
257	William Kelly	300	283	John McKinley		3000
258	Moses White	210	284	John McKinley		1490
259	Jas. Madison	410	285	J. Jackson, John Mc'ley		1425
260	John McKinley	350	286	Willie Barrow		1470
261	John R. Bedford	805	287			
262	Jas. Manning	1410	288			
263	John McKinley	2500	289	Presley Ward and Co.		1350
264	John R. Bedford	2000	290	Jas. Madison		1210
265	Christopher Rob'son	2000	291	John McKinley		295
266	Jas. G. Burney	1310	292	John McKinley		810
267	John McKinley	700	293	Jas. Madison		825
268	Jas. Madison	1000	294	John McKinley		705
269	Thos. Bibb	1420				
270	Thos. Bibb	805				
271	Thos. Bibb	815				
272	Thos. Bibb	1155	(List published in Muscle Shoals News,			
273	William Ward	760	11 Nov. 1923.)			
274	Archibald Fuqua	590				
275	Allen Morris	500				
276	Allen Morris	620				
277						
278						
279						

At the publication of this list in 1923, Mrs. Mary Coffee Campbell, granddaughter of General John Coffee, made identifications of some of the names on this list:

"Among the descendants of James Jackson are Judge J. J. Mitchell, Misses Helen Hunt, McCullough, and Jennie Jackson, and Mrs. Kate Lassiter, all of Florence. The grand-daughter of General John Brahan is Mrs. Mattie Patton Weeden, who until the last few years was a resident of Florence.

"The descendants of Malcolm Gilchrist are Mrs. D. L. Martin of Florence, and the large Gilchrist connection in Courtland. Mr. James Benham is represented in Florence today by his grand-daughter Mrs. W. L. Reeder, and Mrs. Henry Moore. His great grand-daughter Mrs. Willie Benham Reeder Bond perpetuates part of his name.

"Sarah Hanna was a sister of James Jackson and settled 'Ardoyne'; her descendants live in New Orleans. James Weakley was the head of one of the most hospitable homes in Florence, which was located where the home of Mrs. R. L. Glenn now stands. He was a brother of General Samuel Weakley, whose descendants are Mrs. N. W. Milliken, Miss Jem Weakley of Florence, Mrs. Annie Anglin, and Mr. Harvey Weakley of Huntsville.

"The descendants of John Bedford are also the Weakleys and Burtwells. The grandson of Mr. W. H. Ragsdale is Mr. Bradford Ragsdale of this city. The descendants of Mr. Joel Rice are Mr. Turner Rice, Mr. Lester Norvell, and the late Mr. S. D. Rice, of Florence.

"Mr. Archibald Fuqua has many descendants in this county, among them are the Westmorelands. Among the descendants of James Sample are Miss Mattie Sample and Mrs. Darby who live on Jackson highway.

"The direct descendants of Gen. John Coffee are Mrs. Mary C. Campbell of Florence, Mrs. Heilner, the widow of the late Admiral Heilner of the United States Navy, Mr. Andrew Jackson Coffee of San Francisco, California; Mrs. McDougal, widow of the late Commodore McDougal of San Diego, Messrs Robert and Alex Dyas, formerly of Nashville, Miss Anne Nye of Florence is a great niece of General Coffee.

"General Andrew Jackson bequeathed his Florence property in the children of his comrade in arms and very dear friend General John Coffee."

Some of the lots in the original sale can be identified today. Lot 279, was located on the river bank, near the present railroad bridge. Ferry privileges went with this lot. Another list gives the buyer of this lot at John J. Winston--and the price at $10,100.

Lot 84 was bought by Hugh Campbell for the Presbyterians. Later lots 335 and 372 were purchased for the Methodists and the Baptists. Moses White paid $505 for a lot which has been described as the jail lot, and is possibly lot 138 of this list.

Samuel Craig, who appears as a buyer on the list, lived in the northern part of the county on the Military Road. He had lived in Maury County before he came to Alabama and an acquaintance wrote of him:

"Samuel Craig in 1813 had a log cabin built in woods near Grinders' Stand on Natchez Trace for a dry goods store to 'secure the Indian trade.'

"...Samuel Craig (came to Maury County) in 1810 or 1811, a merchant. Married Miss Gordon had several sons and daughters names not remembered, as he left here early and settle in Ala. on Shole Creek 9 miles north of Florence and kept a public house..."[16]

(Samuel Craig's log home in Maury County, built 1816, was only torn down in 1967.)

Many of the buyers on the list never lived in Lauderdale County, but only bought land for investment or speculation. Out-of-county buyers included: Waddy Tait of Huntsville; Leroy Pope (called "The Father of Huntsville"); John Childress of Tennessee (related to Mrs. James Knox Polk); Patrick Maguire of Maury County, Tennessee; John C. McLemore, great land owner of Tennessee; John Overton of Tennessee; and John Donelson of Tennessee. The last-named man possibly lived for a brief time in North Alabama.

Among the buyers will be found the name of George Coulter (sometimes Coalter), a lawyer. He had lived in Maury County, Giles County, and Lincoln Counties, Tennessee before coming to Alabama. He was admitted to practice law at different times in those counties. In Florence he built in 1820 his fine home "Mapleton". He will be found practicing law later in Mississippi when he was one of the defense lawyers in 1837 when Mercer Bird, a free mulatto, was on trial for the murder of Joel S. Cameron, partner of Governor McNutt of Mississippi.[17]

James G. Burney, one of the buyers, is believed to be the identical man of the same name, who lived in Huntsville, Alabama, and in the 1830s was a leading advocate in Alabama for the abolition of slavery.

Ferdinand Sannoner, on the list, was a young Italian engineer, who laid out the town of Florence, under the direction of General John Coffee. He was the one who gave the city the name Florence. Hunter Peel, also an engineer, assisted Sannoner in his work. Peel was granted two lots for his services as assistant.

Dr. John R. Bedford, one of the original buyers, was involved innocently in one of the exciting episodes of early Lauderdale County history. An account of the "other" Dr. John Bedford follows:

> "In the year 1823, a man answering the description of Dr. Hamilton made his appearance in Florence, Ala., calling himself Dr. John Bedford, and announced himself to the Gazette as a practitioner of medicine and surgery. There was at the time four regular physicians in Florence, all in good repute as they were considered sufficient for the place. Dr. Bedford was advised by the good citizens to remove to a new settlement called the Big Spring, which was destitute of medical men and sometimes was very sickly...He soon located at that place. His entrance was made welcome by the inhabitants of the village. There was in the village a beautiful young lady of rare accomplishments and refined education who soon ensnared the willing heart of the Doctor; she possessed an estate worth about $20,000, which of all things, most delighted the heart of our hero. He addressed her, she consented, the preliminaries were soon settled but before the knot could be tied, business of importance called him to Nashville. On his return home, he unluckily stopped at Florence, to visit those kind friends, whose advice he had made his fortune. Whilst dining at the Florence Inn, a man from Kentucky, took his seat at the table, who instantly recognized Dr. Bedford, to be his old friend Mr. William Talbot of Lexington, Ky., a professor of art and mystery of cord waining. The Kentuckian was delighted to meet him, inquiring very solicitiously after his health, and observed, that but a week since, he had the pleasure of calling on his wife, and family, at Lexington; who he assured him, were all well. The Doctor was so confounded, protested the gentleman was mistaken in the person and declared most vehemently that he would prosecute him if he dared to utter such falsehoods.

> "The Kentuckian was not easily moved by such threats, and continued to reiterate what he had previously stated. The confusion of the Doctor was so great, he could not finish his dinner, but hastily departed to institute a suit against the man who had uttered such outrageous libels; and that was the last seen of him by the citizens of Florence.

> "In the meantime Dr. Bedford repaired to Big Spring, where he borrowed a carriage with horses and a negro servant of a gentleman into whose good graces he had initiated himself, telling him that a person in Tennessee had sent for him to operate in case of lithotomy, which tendered it important that he should depart post haste. Since then, the inhabitants of Big Spring have not been honored by a visit from Dr. Bedford nor has the gentleman heard of his carriage, horses, or negro.

> "The Kentuckian stated that he and Bedford, who had a wife and two children, were employed in the same shop more than a year, when the former was discharged, in consequence of his ignorance of the trade, and consequently inability to perform the duties assigned to him; and that since his departure he had frequently heard of his practising medicine by authority of a patent right which he had purchased from a Dr. Thompson of Boston.

> "It was ascertained that Bedford came to Lexington in the year 1818, assuming the name of Talbot, bringing with him his wife and her mother, Mrs. Jackson, who were formerly of Alexandria, D. C., that Miss Jackson brought him an estate at the time of her marriage in negroes and other property, amounting to about $30,000, which he had

squandered away, and then abandoned her in a land of strangers. From the description of the man and the notoriety of his character, there can be no doubt that Dr. James Hamilton, alias John Randolph Bedford, alias C. Gallop, is the same Dr. Bedford who flourished at Big Spring, and the same William Talbot, cordwainer, who fled from Kentucky."[18]

After the organization of the county, William S. Fulton became the first judge of the Lauderdale County Court. Fulton was also the first postmaster and editor of the first newspaper, the Florence Gazette, and later Governor of the Territory of Arkansas.

The first court was held at "Col. Puler's place," located east of Cypress Creek and near the creek. Within a short time commissioners were appointed to contract for building a courthouse. Nathan Vaught of Maury County, Tennessee, who is said to have built the courthouse, wrote in his memoirs:

"Mr. Pursell went down to Lauderdale Co., Alabama, to the sale of the lots in the town of Florence and contracted with the commissioners to build the Cort House in Florence. When he returned he wished me to wind up buisness here as fast as I could and go down and take charge of the Cort House at Florence. This was done and about the 1st of Oct. in this year 1821 I was ready and packed to move down. He had been down the 2nd time having things arranged and the building commenced. He returned home sick with fever from exposur at knight after some Runaway Negroes he never was up any more died on the 22d of Oct. 1821...

"I was ready to move down but his sudent death stoped things very short. While he was sick he sent for Mr. James Walker (they had been quite intimate) and requested should he die to take charge of his estate and wind up his affars. Mr. Walker promised him to do so but after he died Mr. Walker refused to do so or have anything to do with the estate but he requested that I should go down & look after the cort house contract..."[19]

From this record it appears that the construction on the first house of justice in Lauderdale County was started by James Pursell, and completed by Nathan Vaught.

This building was "two tall stories" with thick walls. The total cost was $5,700, for which the county paid $2,500 in money and the other $3,200 was paid in land located two miles from Florence.[20]

A painting of the original courthouse, by Oscar Lewis, is in the present courthouse in Florence. From this painting the original building was of ante-bellum style, with a broad veranda and eight columns supporting a portico. A tall steeple or cupola with clock surmounted the structure. On the right of the building was a small brick building which housed the county treasurer's office.

This building stood until 1899 when it was demolished and a new courthouse constructed. According to tradition, the same foundation and columns were used in the second courthouse.

Within two years after the sale of lots by the Cypress Land Company, the population of the county was 4,763. By 1830 the population had more than doubled, being 10,781. Of this number 7,960 were free whites, 3,795 were slaves, and 26 were free persons of color.

Within months after the first sale of lots, businesses were being conducted at Florence. The first advertisement, located so far, was by Richard Rapier and Company, advertising in the Alabama Republican on April 10, 1819, that "The Barge

General Jackson to be at Florence next month."

Two years later Anne Royall would be in Florence and write:

> "Florence is one of the new towns of this beautiful and rapid rising state. It is happily situated for commerce at the head of steamboat navigation, on the north side of Tennessee river, in the county of Lauderdale...Florence is to be the great emporium of the northern part of the state...it has a great capital and is patronized by the wealthiest gentlemen in the state... Its citizens, bold, enterprising, and industrious--much more so than any I have seen in the state...
>
> "Many large and elegant brick buildings are already built here...and frame houses are putting up daily. It is not uncommon to see a framed building begun in the morning and finished by night...
>
> "Florence is inhabited by people from almost all parts of Europe and the United States; here are English, Irish, Welch, French, Dutch, Germans, and Grecians. The first Greek I ever saw was in this town. I conversed with him on the subject of his country, but found him grossly ignorant. He butchers for the town, and has taken to arms a mullatto woman for a wife. He very often takes an airing on horseback of a Sunday afternoon, with his wife riding by his side, and both arrayed in shining costume..."

A few days later she wrote of some of the citizens of Florence:

> "The principal gentlemen of wealth are General Coffee, James Jackson, Esq., Major McKinley, and Messrs Simpson and Gaither. Of these J. Jackson is said to be not only wealthy, but the wealthiest man in the state..."[22]

Coffee and Jackson were admired all throughout the area. Everything these two men did seem to be of interest. The number of bales of cotton they raised would be found even in Tennessee newspapers of the period and one writer said:

> "The manner in which those gentlemen are said to have prepared their crops, entitles them to much credit, and we hope they will in the enhanced price, which their cotton will command be handsomely compensated for the laudable example they have set the community..."[23]

Violence appeared in Lauderdale County early. Although possibly this is not the first murder, it is one of the few documented in newspapers of the time:

> "A dreadful homicide was committed on Thursday, 15th inst. (April 1822)... Mr. Rhea, one of the best and ablest pilots of the Muscle Shoals, was killed at Lamb's Ferry by a stranger, an old man to appearance, upwards of 70 years of age. It seems that this old man and Mr. Rhea had a quarrel some ten or fifteen years ago, and having met by accident at the foot of the shoals, some abusive language passed between them. Rhea returned to Lamb's ferry and on the next day the old man followed and having borrowed an axe, went to the house where he found Rhea asleep, immediately applied the axe to his neck and severed his head from his body. This is one of the horrible cases, concerning which it is not proper to express an opinion, as the wretched and unfortunate individual who perpetrated the deed is now in custody of the law, and will be soon called upon to answer for this alarming offence...Florence Gazette."[24]

In December 1822 Florence was hit by the first tornado of record. "Considerable damage" was reported.[25]

On April 12, 1823, the steamer "Thomas Jefferson" arrived at Florence and deposited her load. The next day, Friday, the steamer started for the opposite side of the river with a large party on board. About fifteen feet from shore, the ship struck a stump and sank within four hours. No lives were lost. The owners announced plans to raise the steamer "in a few days."[26]

Andrew Jackson was a popular man in Lauderdale County. In June 1823 a reporter wrote: "About 500 citizens of Lauderdale County gathered at the courthouse last Saturday. Andrew Jackson was nominated for president. Five hundred votes were cast, 300 for Jackson..."[27]

His appearances in the Shoals area were usually great events, climaxed by public dinners. The Nashville Whig, 10 Sept. 1825, recorded:

"On a recent visit to Florence, Alabama, dinners were given in Florence and Tuscumbia for General Jackson..."

Another account is more specific:

"The citizens of the town of Florence...understanding that General Jackson was in the neighborhood, invited him to public dinner on Thursday, the 30th August (1825). The general accepted the invitation, and between fifty and sixty citizens sat down to an elegant dinner at the Florence Hotel. Colonel Peter F. Armistead presided, assisted by Samuel Craig, esq. A great many patriotic toasts were drunk..."[28]

By 1826 there were two newspapers in Florence: the Florence Gazette, and the Florence Register and Public Advertiser. The latter was published by Archibald B. Hubbard and edited by Dr. Shadrack Nye.

An issue for September 9, 1826, of the Register is extant. One public notice is of interest. "Messrs J. M. Martin and Co. are men without honor," advertised Samuel Bryan and Robert Sherrod. Numerous testimonials to their character were included.

D. Lowe, in the same paper, advertised that "Argile Campbell is a lawyer to beware of...worse than a swindler."

Other advertisements included William L. Yarbrough in the "Color Business"; Thomas B. Huling, groceries; Bell Tavern operated by J. W. Byrn.

Notice was given that Edward S. Carey, one of the proprietors of the Florence Register, had died and his interest in the newspaper had been purchased by John Craig.

A Florence Gazette for Feb. 22, 1827, has the following advertisements: D. Low, leather goods; M. Clarke, merchant; Ezra Webb, Jr., groceries; a new horse ferry boat, formerly the Florence Ferry, run by Matthew Neal. James Lasseter had a two story frame house on Pine Street for rent or sale. George Coalter announced that he "will continue to practice in the county" although his law partnership with James Irvine had been dissolved.

Jacob Ellinger was settling the estate of Joseph Bigger; Duncan McIntyre was settling the estate of Malcomb McIntrye, deceased. The estates of Colonel William Lyon and Doctor John S. Young were being settled.

Nicholas Davis wished to "rent out his plantation, five or six miles below Florence." E. Shuffield offered to rent his tavern on the military road "one mile from Blue

Water known as Anderson Johnson's old place."

Patrick Andrews announced that he was proprietor of the Florence Hotel, formerly run by David Fulton.

Notice was given that Thomas H. Alsup had died in Lauderdale County leaving a widow, Margaret, and the following children: Sarah, age 13; James, age 10; Orlena, age 8; Eliza, age 5; and Margaret,1.

By August 4, 1827, "Public Advertiser" had been added to the name of the Florence Register and the editor was William B. Wallace. Merchants in Florence included at this time: George Boggs, Jr., James J. Hanna, Buchanan and Sproule, Abraham Fox, and Baylis E. Bourland.

Lawyers advertising were John A. Chambers and William B. Wallace. The latter also had an announcement that he would sell negroes. A. M. Payne and Co. was a cotton spinning factory, known as Sweet Water Factory, which was located one mile east of Florence.

Dr. J. H. Woodcock and Dr. William H. Harrington had advertisements in this issue. Dr. George Hill announced that he had located one mile west of New Meeting House, and one mile west of the road leading from Florence to Waterloo.

William B. Cobb advertised that his wife Mary had left him on the 9th with a man named Godfrey Peters and that she took two of his children with her, Elizabeth Catherine, age 5, and Mary Jane Cobb, no age given.

There was a $300 reward offered for "a boy by the name of Charles Boyden, 22." Announcement was made of the death of Lucinda Harriet, age one year five months, infant daughter of William Koger.

Many forgotten pieces of Lauderdale County's history will be found in the minutes for the commissioners court of the period. In December 1829 Leptha Bearn was appointed overseer of a road leading from "Nashall's old field" to Lexington. James Hood was permitted to make a change in the Reserve Road. Felix Grundy Martin, "a poor orphan", was under the charge of the court. The court allowed George Smith the sum of $4 for the maintenance of William Daughty; Elizabeth Saddles received $10 for the care of Thury Roberts, another poor orphan boy; and Edie Richardson got $25 for taking care of Parthena Coody, "a poor child." John Donaho was allowed $4 with which to purchase a hammer "to break rocks at the butmet of Shoal Creek bridge." The hammer was to belong to the county.[29]

Bailey Springs came into notice in the 1820s, although most authorities usually give the date 1831, sometimes 1834, for the date Jonathan Bailey acquired the land. Caroline O'Reilly Nicholson (wife of U. S. Senator A. O. P. Nicholson, Tennessee) visited the area in 1829 and wrote many years later:

> "I have a vivid and pleasant memory of a trip made with my father to Ala. My cousin Betsy Witherspoon went with us. We traveled in our carriage and spent the night at Simington's, the half-way house between Columbia and Florence. At the latter place we visited my father's Irish friends, John Simpson and General Coffee. Then we went nearly to Bailey's Springs to visit my aunt, Mrs. Samuel Craig, who had moved there seeking to restore her health by drinking the celebrated water. I remember that old man Bailey brought a wild turkey, which he shot nearby as an offering to her guests, and I have not forgotten what a savory dish it made. We went over to Tuscumbia to attend conference, which was in session there, and were most hospitably entertained in their cabins by the Cockerells, who were preparing to build on a large scale..."[30]

CHAPTER II

The noted Alabama historian, Thomas M. Owen, Jr., did some research in the inns, taverns, and hotels of Lauderdale County. He wrote:

"In the original plan of the land company was the 'Tavern.' A large brick building, two stories in height, which was started in 1819, and completed in 1820. Its location was at the corner of Court and Limestone streets, facing west, and the house now occupied by Dr. James Simpson (colored) stands just about where the middle of the building was.

"A cedar tree now marks what was then the south corner of the structure, and anyone desirous of seeing it may find it if they care to walk down parts of the brick sidewalk, laid 107 years ago, which was in front of the wall and porch, and there also remains parts of the original corner wall.

"This was the first hotel in Florence. It was sold at auction at the second sale of the land company's lots in 1823."

This hotel was destroyed by Federal troops during the Civil War. Owens also wrote that there had been another hotel built a year or so later, but he had been unable to learn anything about it.

The next hotel of prominence, according to Owen, was the "Florence" which occupied "the space on which Stutts Drug Company and Ezell-Young have their stores..." This hotel, according to James Simpson, was burned in 1844.

The old National hotel, also known as Crow's hotel, was the leading establishment for a number of years. It was located on East Tennessee Street, faced north and cornered on the first alley east of Court Street, extending half way to the corner of Seminary Street. This hotel was of wood with a large porch which covered the sidewalk. "Old residents stated that they remember the old hand bell when rung could be heard most all over town." The hotel was operated by James M. Crow. It was pulled down to make place for McCluskey's livery stable. A Mr. Harrison was the manager at the time of demolishment.

The late James Milner stated that "during the Franco-Prussian war he went with his father down to this hotel and that Capt. McFarland, the largest man in town, was on the counter reading the messages from the Memphis Commercial, relative to the war."

Situated opposite what is now Milner's Drug Store on Court Street was the Campbell Hotel, which burned in the early seventies.

"When the firm of McAllister and Irvine went into bankruptcy, the building which had housed their store and the former business of John Simpson became the property of the family of Robert Kernachan. It was remodeled by them into a hotel and for many years was under the management of a man by the name of Harrison. It was first known as the Exchange and later as the Commercial. A part of the property is still in the possession of the Kernachan estate at the corner of Court and College streets."[1]

Research by recent historians has established that the old Lambeth House on the corner of Hermitage Drive and Seminary Street was possibly the first inn in the county. It was known as Pope's Tavern, and at some time called Wayside Inn (not to be confused with an inn of the same name in the eastern part of the county.) In 1967 the Chamber of Commerce set up a Lambeth Home Committee for restoration of the house.[2]

During the "Boom" of 1888, a large store building on Court Street, opposite the courthouse, was remodeled into a hotel for the accommodation of speculators and others who flocked into the area. This place, according to Owen, was known as the "Florence."

The outer walls of a large frame hotel were built in East Florence when development of that area was begun. "But this hotel was not completed inside. If it was, I have not been able to find anyone that ever was on the inside of it."[3]

The city of Florence built on the old Hotel Negley corner a building which cost $15,000. The plan was to have the finest city hall in the entire south, but the plans of the city council fell through. This building was remodeled and became the Jefferson hotel. The hotel later became the property of Major A. G. Negley, cousin of Major General James S. Negley. He had owned it only a short time when it was destroyed by fire. He rebuilt the hotel on the foundation of the original hotel.[4] The Negley Hotel was torn down in 1966.[5] (When General Negley died in 1901, an article in the Florence Herald recorded: "General Negley was the first Union general that entered Florence and is remembered by many of the older citizens for his kind and considerate treatment of our people."[6])

The Hooks House was another hotel in Florence's history, being built in 1906. This interesting old structure was destroyed by fire in November 1966.[7]

Another hotel, which closed in 1967, was the Reeder Hotel located on West Tennessee Street. The older section of this hotel was built in the early 1900s. Its first use was as a livery stable run by J. Will Paulk. On the upper floor was a large mule pen, where mule auctions were held. This was thought to be the first concrete block building in Florence. When the livery business ceased, the auction room was used as a boarding house. On the first floor Fred Fago operated a scrap iron business. The newer section of the hotel building was built in 1917 by the Reeder Estate. It was later leased by Tom Carson, who ran it during World War I and for a number of years following. In 1940 the building was purchased by Clyde Anderson and L. S. Caine. The first Florence-Lauderdale County Public Library was housed in the dining room of the hotel in the 1940s while the library building was being constructed.[8]

At the time of the closing of the Reeder Hotel, it was said that there were only two hotels remaining in the cities of the Muscle Shoals area.

A ferry was established at Florence about where the railroad bridge is today. The landing on the south side became known as South Florence. Two dates, 1817 and 1818, have been found for the establishment of this ferry.

It is known that from about 1820 to 1827, George Cockburn was owner of one-half interest in the southern portion of the ferry. James Jackson and John McKinley with the Cypress Land Company owned the ferry on the north side. The income for the ferry was considerable for the time--said to be $6,000 annually.[9]

Cockburn is worthy of some notice. He had been connected with the ferry business prior to coming to Lauderdale County, when he had settled by the river in Columbia, Tennessee. Nathan Vaught, who knew him, wrote:

> "This Fery house was at the River at the north east margin of Town. This house was a one and half story high with 2 rooms and a large open Hall between the saim above stars and a very Rough Concern built of very Rough Logs and it was a very Rough place in deed. All kinds of wickedness indulged

this place. This house was put up late in 1806 or quite early in 1807 by a Mr. Geo. Cockburn (pronounced Coburn). He had no family and was a man of very bad morals. He was the owner of the Fery for a long time..."[10]

This was written of Mr. Cockburn's character during his Tennessee residence, and it is reasonable to assume that his like establishment in North Alabama might have enjoyed the same notoriety. When he disposed of his Maury County properties, he was described as being of Lauderdale County, Alabama.

Violence continued in the 1830s. In February 1830 the commissioners court held an inquest "over the body of William G. Allen, deceased." In August of the same year John C. Ferguson was paid $6 for "man found dead in Elk River." Samuel Burney was paid $10 for holding the inquest. Prisoners at this time were kept in irons, and there is record that Charles Mainier was paid for "ironing prisoners." Lewis Edwards served as the jailor of Lauderdale County.[11]

One of the greatest scoundrels of the period made in appearance in Florence in the 1830s--John A. Murrell:

TOM BRANNON INTERVIEWED

"The arrest of this famous desperado (Murrell) makes an interesting page in the history of his life; and as the principal party to that arrest still lives, an account from his own lips, and perhaps for the first time the only stenographic interview ever had and published with the well-known Negro Tom Brannon, is here published.

"Knowing that "Uncle Tom", as he is familiarly called, had something to do with the arrest of John A. Murrell, he was sought and found upon the streets of Tuscumbia. After making myself known, and in response to certain questions put to him, a brief synopsis of his life was given, in which he stated that he was born near Nashville, Tenn.; that he was 80 years of age; was a slave of a man named Kinney Brannon, who afterwards sold him to Abraham Rix, of Alabama.

"I asked him to tell me all that he knew about John A. Murrell, and the facts connected with the stealing and selling of himself by the said John A. Murrell, which led to his arrest. His reply was: "Murrell never stole me; he tried hard; I was too sharp for him.

"Several questions were asked him, but he seemed to be in no talkative humor, and it seemed as if the interview was going to prove a failure. He did not like the idea of telling his story away from home, and wanted me to go there, which was quite a distance, and as a last resort I went. When we reached his humble home he seemed to feel easier, and by permitting him to tell his story in his own words and way I soon had a large and complete stenographic report of the facts which led to the arrest and incarceration of John A. Murrell, the reckless "Negro trader."

"When asked when was the first time he ever saw Murrell, he replied that he did not know, as Murrell wore so many different disguises that he would not have known him had he seen him, but that the first time that Murrell made himself known to him was on a moonlight night. 'At the time I was living with Mr. James Irvine, an attorney-at-law at Florence. Saw Murrell at the gate, and was offered a drink of brandy by him which was accepted.'

"'I went,' said Uncle Tom, 'to the edge of town in the bushes, and he gave me another drink of brandy. He said, 'Tom, you are not going to go with me.'

"'I said, 'Yes, sir, I am.' He shoved me into the bushes and cussed me; then he said, 'Tom, I am not mad with you. Will you go with me." I said, 'Yes, sir.'

"He wanted me to strike for him.'"

"'What do you mean by striking?'

"'Means to get Negroes out so he could steal them. Said he had a room at Polk's tavern (in Florence on the Square); I told him I wanted to go to bed and would see him the next night.

"'I went home to Mr. Irvine's; I failed to meet him the next night, and never saw him again after that for a year or more, when I was driving a four-horse wagon on the Nashville and Florence Road. I was driving pretty fast one day after dinner when I saw Murrell and two others playing a three-handed game of cards; think that it was seven-up. Murrell "hollered" to me and came up to the top of the hill, and said, 'Hello, my man, where are you going?' I told him I was going up the hill to get some wood. He said: "Go on you d____." He was cussing me 'cause I didn't stick to promise to meet him; he knowed me. I did not see Murrell after than for a year or two.

"'I was working with Mr. James Sample, a brick mason; he had two of Murrell's brothers working with him, learning the trade. A Negro named Randall Campbell also worked there. Randall and one of the Murrell brothers fell out, and Randall ran away, going back to his master. He was sent back to Mr. Sample by Mr. Campbell; as he was returning he was met by John A. Murrell at the Cypress Creek bridge. Murrell told Randall to tell me to come down there. There were two men with Murrell; Granger was the name of one, I think, and Webster Stewart the other. The man had horses, and Murrell rode in a carryall, carrying the provisions. Randall came to my house, called me and says, 'Tom, I want to see you.'

"'Says I, 'What do you want?'

"'He said come and I will tell you. He said: 'Mr. John A. Murrell is at the bridge, and told me to come up here and get you, and for us two to come down there. He gave me $7 (seven dollar bills on the Bank of Decatur) and wants us to go down to the baker's shop and get lightbread enough for their supper, and for us to have the rest, and divide it 'twixt us.'

"'I looked at it, and said: 'What does this mean I never seed the man; how is it he wants to do such a favor for me? I am living as happy as I can live.' I began to reason with Randall; told him that we were doing as well as we could. 'Let's go over and have him taken up; he is to do us a great deal of damage.' Randall agreed with me.

"'There was a protracted meeting going on at the white folks' Methodist Church at that time. We went down there to tell Mr. Bill Garrett, the County Court Clerk, about Murrell. On the way there Randall said: 'Tom, let's don't have him taken up.'

"'I explained again to him, and he agreed with me again.

"'I went to the church and whispered to Mr. Garrett; he was sitting in the amen corner. Says Mr. Garrett, 'Take the money and go down and get the bread and we will get up some soldiers.'

"'We done so.'

"'Garrett said, 'Come on here, boys, I want to tell you how to catch them fellows.'

"'Me and Randall walked very fast.'

"Garrett's plan was for Randall to take the bread and go to the bridge and stop and then to tell Murrell and his company to come over, that the boys were waiting for them. Randall took the bread and went over. He told Murrell and his company to get out, that the guards were after them. Mr. Garrett hurried me back to tell the soldiers to hurry up. The soldiers went across the bridge, the two men straddled their horses and put out, but Murrell was with the carryall and was taken. He was carried to Florence and was put in jail.

"While lying in jail at Florence a sheriff from Jackson, Tenn., arrived and carried him to that state, where he was wanted for some crime. There he was tried and convicted and sentenced to the State prison for ten years. And thus ended, in a sense, the life of this notorious criminal.

"For the important part that Randall played in his arrest he says he received $100, while Randall Campbell was given a good whipping." [12]
(Note: the Randall in the first sentence above is believed to be a typographical error and should possibly be Tom Brannon instead.)

William L. McDonald wrote in the Sesquicentennial edition of the Florence Times, 9 June 1968: "Until recent years the big tree that stood alongside Waterloo Road was pointed to by oldtimers as the place where Murrel was caught."

Murrell's career in crime has been greatly disputed by historians in recent years. Some argue that he was not as infamous as he has been branded, and that Virgil Stewart had exaggerated his crimes. One who knew Murrell wrote in 1877: "Murrell was a great robber and chief of banditi, and he was not believed by those who had known him long and well to be the red-handed murderer as painted by Virgil A. Stewart, betrayed for money, and by many believed to be a member of the clan. A highly colored life of Murrell was written to make money. It was a success, and made Murrell famous in the annals of vice and crime and his betrayer has left behind the heritage of a dubious name and doubtful fame."[13] A recently discovered issue of the old newspaper the Tennessee Democrat for 1844 tells of Murrell's deathbed confession, which considerably alters some aspects of his career.

In 1833 the mothers of North Alabama were considerably concerned by rumors spreading over the area. Little Caroline H. Bullock had been "stolen". The story was that she had been "blacked as a slave and sold" as she had completely disappeared. Later when her body was found, drowned, in a creek near Courtland, the kidnapping scare was thought to have been unfounded.[14]

On November 13, 1833, people in the area were frightened by the famous meteor storm. Many thought that the end of the world had come. During this time, 10,000 meteors per hour were visible. People were aroused from sleep by the bright flashes. The shooting stars were described as "falling from the sky like snowflakes."[15] This was an event long remembered, and some say is the origin of the phrase "Stars Fell on Alabama," later used as a book title.

A fight of some local interest took place in August 1834 when a shooting match was held at Arnett's Store on the Huntsville Road. A difficulty between William Kendrick and Moses Tomlinson arose and Kendrick stabbed Tomlinson with a knife. It was reported that "Kendrick has kept out of the way of the law" since the fight.[1]

In this decade the Indians were sent to Oklahoma. Heretofore the Indians had been a commonplace sight on the streets of Florence. James Simpson would write about this time:

"I was born in Florence in 27 (1827) and but a lad of ten years when the Indians went to Oklahoma an can but dimly recall the man George Colbert who was then Chief of the Chickasaw Nation. He was tall and slender and handsome with straight black hair that he wore long which came well down to his shoulders. His features were that of an Indian but his skin was lighter than that of his tribe. He wore the dress of a white man of his day and always appeared neat and clean. He frequently ate dinner at my fathers in Florence. The building now known as the Commercial Hotel was my father's store and he had a reputation among the Indians as being an honest and just man and as a consequence of the Indian trade Colbert often crossed the river in canoes with 30 or 50 of his tribe to purchase goods in Florence. The Indians seemed to enjoy roaming over the store looking at everything. They wore buckskin clothes of their own making. Some of them wore feather head dress."[17]

In 1834 Nicholas M. Hentz and his wife Caroline Lee Hentz moved to Florence, where they lived nine years, conducting Locust Dell Academy. She kept a diary during her residence here. In this she revealed several interesting bits of local history. Some of the patrons of the school were free in their criticism of the teachers and the school. We learn that "Mrs. Weakly suggested that her daughter Harriet's poor progress was the result of her teachers' negligence." And that, "Mrs. Gray and Mrs. Asher were ungrateful and vindictive." A "Miss S- A-" often repeated idle gossip and made unjust assertions. "Miss B" was described as "a sour, vinegar old maid."[18]

At one time some of the girls at the school were discovered "coming out of Mitchells." The students, it seemed, had been selling some of their best clothes for food. The girls were scolded for their actions, and Mrs. Hentz wrote: "Mr. H. actually box'd M. K.'s ears, a thing he never did to a big girl in his life before." M. K. was a member of the Kernachan family, "a family of Scotch descent who lived on a fine old plantation ten miles from Florence and sent four daughters to Locust Dell--Maria (who was grown), Ann Eliza, Matilda, and Mollie. 'These four girls came in a carriage ever Monday morning and returned on Friday evening, the carriage coming for them.'"[19]

Mrs. Hentz wrote of one Fourth of July celebration in Florence: "At eleven the people thronged to the new Methodist church...to hear Judge Weakley read the Declaration of Independence in a clear, deliberate manner. Mr. E. Markes delivered an eloquent & animated address..."[20]

In 1836 another Indian war broke out and a company of soldiers left for the fight. Mrs. Hentz wrote:

"(February)25th. A great assembly in town. Men assembled for drafting a company to go on to Florida...A sufficient number of soldiers have volunteered. We hear the strains of martial music, we hear occasionally the cannon roar. The pupils have subscribed to purchase a standard--Mr. Hentz has brought the materials from town...

"26th...Composed some lines for Matilda Kernachan to recite in presenting the banner...

"March 1st...Rain, then large flashes of drifting snow...Two o'clock the sun began to shine and we rode, through a deluge of mud, to the new Methodist church, where the ceremony was to be performed. There were between two or three hundred people there--Matilda delivered my poetical address very finely, Mr.

Hentz and myself holding the banner over her head...I hope to see the flag once more unstained with blood.

And later:

"May 24...The people collected in town to draft a number of soldiers to go out against the Lower Creeks, who are beginning their depredations in the lower part of the state. Col. Gillespie called and invited the whole school to go to the field & witness the scene...The sun poured down burning rays so we did not linger long--Only nine volunteers before we left the field, but afterwards they plied them well with whiskey & they came briskly out of the ranks, more than the adequate number."[21]

After nine years in Florence the Hentz family moved to Tuscaloosa. She became a novelist of some note and several incidents which happened in Florence were used, thinly disguised, in some of her books. She died in 1856 in Florida.

A brief look at the marriage records of the 1830s reveal many names familiar in the annals of the county. Peter R. Flake married Elizabeth White on December 27, 1836; Charles Gookin married Sarah M. Brocchus on September 3, 1838; John Lamb married Ann Houston on November 1838; Jordan Moore married Sarah D. Viser on January 17, 1839. (Moore was a well known Methodist minister.) Patrick Andrews married Harriet Asher on May 26, 1832, with W. P. Kendrick officiating. Calvin Terrell married Matilda Threet on October 30, 1835 with S. Young officiating.

In October 1839 it was reported that the Tennessee River at Florence was lower than any living man had ever seen it before. "The ferry boat crosses with difficulty and droves of horses ford it with ease."[22]

In this decade work on the Muscle Shoals Canal was underway: "Muscle Shoals Canal work going strong...600 hands employed on canal from Campbell's Ferry to Lamb's Ferry." The end result was to be, it was hoped, navigation for six months of the year.[23]

By 1840 another newspaper was flourishing in Florence---Florence Enquirer, edited by R. H. Madra. An issue for August 22, 1840, still exists. In this particular issue it was announced that "James Jackson died Monday...age 58...native of Ballebay County Monaghan Ireland...came here 22 years ago."

Richard D. Roy, age 29, had "died on the 19th inst...native of King William County, Virginia, member of Methodist Church, member of the Alabama guards." And Major John Cockrill "died Tuesday, the 12th, of congestive fever."

Advertisements were for Willett & Trisler, cabinet makers; Dr. William C. Crow, located in Old Drug Store next to Pope's Hotel; the "Old Florence Drug Store"; Irvine and Company, sellers of Kentucky whiskey; Levi Todd's store on Main Street. Todd also had another advertisement for "Todd's Southern Anti-Bilous Pills", which he had used for many years.

N. H. Rice was the second lieutenant, commanding the Alabama Guards. B. Nelson was the proprietor of the Florence Jockey Club and he announced that the races were to begin October 28, 1840.

Locust Grove, "former home of John Donohoo," located nine miles east of Florence on the Huntsville Road was to be sold by Samuel R. Garner.

There was also an advertisement for the Planter's Hotel, located on Railroad and Main Street in Tuscumbia, under the management of John L. McRae.[24]

In the November 1840 election Lauderdale County voted overwhelmingly for Martin Van Buren.[25]

The Globe Factory of Martin and Cassity, near Florence, was destroyed by fire in 1844. It had been described as one of the most extensive in the South and was not insured. The loss was thought to be $15,000. "It supplied a large portion of the country with the best cotton fabric and afforded employment to nearly 150 persons." The owners were able to rebuild.[26]

Marriages of interest for the 1840s included, among many others: James Kyle to Sarah M. Croft on 19 June 1842; Johnson Kackelman to Margaret Kuffner on March 5, 1847, performed by Felix Johnson, M. G.; John Kackelman to Barbary Ect on Dec. 16, 1847, by Felix Johnson, M. G.; William S. Lanier to Margaret D. Snipes on Oct. 21, 1844; Ferdinand Sannoner to Margaret Bigger on Nov. 2, 1848, by J. Harrison, M.G.; Jonathan Wooten to Martha Whitten on June 9, 1843; Peter Whitten to Sarah Ann Locklayer on June 15, 1846; David E. Whitten to Malinda A. Faires on March 14, 1848; Lewis S. Marks to Mary Ann E. Marks on April 17, 1849; Stewart Pool to Sarah Rieves, July 3, 1845; Joshua Paulk to Eliza Pinkston on Feb. 3, 1848; Benjamin Rose to Mary Snyder on August 16, 1846; John A. Rovier to Susan Young on Nov. 14, 1849, performed by W. B. Edwards, M. G; John P. Threet to Mary Waldrip on March 9, 1845; Leonard Stutts to Parilee Story on June 8, 1848; Leonard Stutts to Martha Robertson on March 22, 1848.

A Florence Gazette for 18 July 1846 reveals that V. M. Benham at this time was running the Florence Inn. Estates being settled were for William E. Dupre, deceased. George Hopkins, being settled by Salena Hopkins; the Henry Smith estate, of Sweetwater, being settled by James Carruthers; the estate of Jacob Herald being settled by Eunicy Herald.

W. P. F. Darby, who lived 15 miles out of Florence, had "posted" a horse. J. A. Engle and S. B. Hudson had a shop "nearly opposite the post office." J. M. Conner, dentist, had a room at the Franklin House. J. L. Sloss was a "fashionable tailor", and Stewart and Hyde ran an "emporium of Fashion." B. P. Karsner advertised that he was a commission merchant and grocer. L. P. and R. W. Walker were lawyers. Falk and Sands were merchants. O. H. Hughes, Master of the Monedo, announced that the steamer was on the Tennessee River. Z. P. Morrison advertised that he wanted 10,000 cow tails.

The Florence Apothecary and Drug Store was run by Robert L. Bliss whose "Family residence is on Tennessee Street on the hill west of the court house, long known as the residence of Dr. H. Woodcock."[27]

Throughout these years the papers carried many advertisements for runaway slaves:

STOP THE RUNAWAY

"Left my plantation on the night of the 20th of March, a negro man named Henry; said boy is about 25 years of age, 6 feet high or upwards, and weighing 170 pounds--and rode off a clay bank horse shod all around about 14½ hands high, black main and tail, with a black streek from the wethers to the tail, the left eye out; said boy is black or rather of light copper color. A liberal reward will be given to any person that will lodge said boy in jail, so that I can get him.
John Williams, Lauderdale Co., Ala."[28]

These advertisements were usually accompanied by a rude cut of a negro in a "fleeing posture" and in some instances with a stick across the shoulder, on the end of which was a small bundle tied up in a bandana.

Whenever runaway slaves were caught and put in jail elsewhere, advertisements were also placed to notify the owners:

> COMMITTED - To Jail the 29th August 1847, a negro man who calls his name William, 6 feet ½ inch high, weighs 176 pounds, dark complexion, has very long hair, and is about 25 or 6 years of age and speaks very slow when spoken to, and says he belongs to Buck Weakly, who resides in Florence, Alabama, and that he runaway about the 1st of August 1847 from Florence.
> James W. Gamblin, Jailor
> Maury County, Tennessee."[29]

The late Judge J. J. Mitchell once made a talk on "Historic Homes of Florence," in which he briefly made this statement: "In the late 1830s or early 1840s a Leminosky, one of Napoleon's marshalls, came to Florence as a refugee."[30]

It appears that if Lemenski were a refugee from anything, it was possibly his wife. While he was being lionized in Florence, she was wildly advertising in newspapers over the Mid-South for information about him:

> "Charles Rodolph Lemenski left wife three months ago in Princeton, Kentucky, saying he would return in three weeks, but she lost sight of him. She now is living in Columbia, Tennessee. Mr. L. employed himself in lecturing on history of Poland."[31]

The principal means of out-of-town transportation was still the coaches. A stage line ran from Florence to Savannah, operated by Chaffin & Gullett of Savannah, which advertised their fine Troy coaches for this run.[32] Tom Douglas & Co. ran coaches from Nashville on Monday, Wednesdays, and Fridays to Florence.[33] Price & Hough operated a four-horse coach line which ran from Columbia, Tennessee, to Tuscumbia, which carried passengers and mail. This line ran "with perfect regularity."[34]

The first telegraph reached Florence about 1848. In December 1847 Harvey M. Watterson of Nashville, Tennessee, (later famous as the editor of the Louisville Courier), received the contract to erect the telegraphic lines from Nashville to Florence. He raised his capital by means of subscriptions from the public.[35]

The Mexican War was the only conflict during this decade. Little has been preserved about Lauderdale County's part in this war. "Three companies of Alabama volunteers embarked on the 9th inst. at Tuscumbia, headed direct for the seat of war," was the only notice found. Presumably some of Lauderdale County's young men were in this group.[36] Some Lauderdale County men known to have fought in this war included Robert G. Bail, Francis M. Moore, Lewis M. Moore, William B. Wright, and Bolivar W. Knight.

In 1845, James Milner, native of Yorkshire, England, came to America and settled in the county. He became one of the pioneer woolen manufacturers in the state, establishing his woolen mills on Cowpen Creek in the county. His son Joseph Milner, also born in England, went to the California gold fields in 1849 by way of the Santa Fe trail. It is said "His efforts as a gold seeker were reasonably rewarded." He remained out west for four years before he returned to Florence where he established the Milner Drug Store, which has enjoyed an uninterrupted existence ever since.[37]

When the census enumerators, Matthew Wilson and Hiram Kennedy, took the census of the county in 1850, they were required to list a real estate evaluation for each property owner. The majority of the people owned less than $1,000 in real estate.

Those who were "considerable" property owners were:

Thomas J. Foster	$ 80,000	Horis Summerhill	7,840
Mary Coffee	10,000	Harden Perkins	13,000
Sarah Jackson	10,000	Moses White	5,000
Turner S. Foster	20,000	William Koger	11,550
Mary Hood	18,000	Jerenath Beckwith	20,000
James Martin	7,000	Neal Rowell	35,000
Alexander D. Coffee	15,000	James Stewart	12,000
Thomas Langford	12,000	Nathan Boddie	17,000
James W. Francis	12,000	Moses Wood	6,000
Miss Mary Houston	15,000	E. B. Donalson	9,000
Wyatt Collier	14,520	William H. Key	20,000
R. T. Kernahan, Jr.	10,593	John Peters	34,000
James Noel	6,450	Henry D. Smith	43,040
Edmund Noel	6,000	A. F. Bracken	23,000
Margaret McIntyre	4,000	James P. Williams	7,500
G. W. Foster	61,000	Josiah Hawkins	7,220
James Simpson	20,000	George Armstead	24,000
Levi Todd	10,000	Hugh McVey	9,432
L. P. Walker	10,000	Thomas Simpson	20,000
Thomas Kirkman	80,000	James Owen	28,000
Catharine Probasco	20,000	John Williams	13,000
John Simpson	48,640	David Williams	12,000
Hugh Benford	10,000	Sterling Nance	5,000
George Simmons	5,000	Sarah Ingram	8,000
Jonathan Bailey	10,000	John S. Wilson	12,000
Matthew Wilson	8,000	Robert M. Patton	30,000
Robert McCoriston	6,000	Joseph Hough	10,000
Isam R. Leath	4,000	Thomas White	5,000
Joseph L. Sloss	5,000	Thomas Crow	6,000
Neander Rice	5,200	Martin Harkins	12,000 [38]

(Note: Spelling as was found on census.)

The enumerators were also required to make a list of all persons who had died in the county, ending June 1, 1850. Only the list kept by Hiram Kennedy was available. Those who had died within the past year in Lauderdale County were:

Name	Age	Place of Birth	Month of Death
Baby (female, no surname)	1/12	Ala.	Dec.
Hamill, Mary E.	22	Ala.	Jan.
Gates, Bradford	30	Tenn.	Feb.
Beaners, Margaret	42	Tenn.	Jan.
Baby (female, no surname)	1/12	Ala.	Feb.
Trusedale, Eleanor	72	S.C.	Nov.
Trusedale, Hollinsworth	72	S.C.	June
Infant (female, no surname)	3/12	Ala.	March
Sagers, Jousan	38	Tenn.	March
Penny, Delilah	45	N.C.	March
Hill, Martin	51	N.C.	Sept.
Herrin, Lucinda	31	Tenn.	Aug.
Hill, James H.	9/12	Ala.	July
Ellis, Benjamin	7	Ala.	May
Buttler, Sarah A.	20	Ala.	Sept.
Trobock, Nancy	66	Tenn.	Sept.
Stamps, Franklin	12	Ala.	Sept.

Weston, Samuel H.	2	Ala.	Jan.
Whitehead, William K.	31	Ala.	May
Wood, Thomas	52	S.C.	Aug.
Falks, William	45	Tenn.	Oct.
Westmoreland, Robert	3	Ala.	Aug.
Briggs, Sarah	25	Ala.	Sept.
Cox, Monroe	1	Ala.	March
Brown, Darkie	6	Ala.	Sept.
Lanier, B. (female)	1	Ala.	Nov.
Neely, Thompson	45	S.C.	Sept.
Shoemaker, Alonzo B.	11/12	Ala.	Aug.
Olliver, Matilda	2/12	Ala.	Sept.
Golston, James	24	Ala.	Jan.
Oldham, William	10/12	Ala.	Nov.
Cooper, Sarah	42	Va.	June
Patrick, P.	10/12	Ala.	Sept.
Landmond, William	45	Ala.	Sept.
Landmond, Matilda	35	Ala.	Oct.
Ingram, Benjamin	70	Va.	Sept.
Vaden, Joseph	44	Ga.	April
Faye, Essy	36	Tenn.	May
Thompson, John	10	N.C.	May
Stuart, Duncan	70	Scotland	Feb.
Allen, William E.	6/12	Ala.	March
Murphey, Elizabeth	30	unknown	Sept.
Quail, Dr.	50	unknown	July
Raily, Doctor	50	unknown	August
Clarke, Dr.	40	unknown	July
Barker, Francis (female)	2	Ala.	May [39]

Sometime during this period Henry Donahoo was a constable of Florence. He was remembered as "an interesting character." He wore a queue, was a great story teller, and had come here from North Carolina.[40]

Bailey Springs flourished during this time. Advertisements appeared in newspapers all over Tennessee and Alabama. For the accommodation of visitors coaches were run directly to the springs. A coach left Columbia, Tennessee, every Tuesday, Thursday, and Saturday during the season.[41] As the medicinal benefits of Bailey Springs became known, physicians began sending their patients to use the water, some even coming from as far as St. Louis, Cincinnati, and Louisville. By 1853, the number of health-seekers had multiplied beyond Bailey's ability to accommodate them. He continued to conduct his resort, however, until his death in 1857. The list of notables was impressive. "Ex-Governor Collier of Alabama died Wednesday at Bailey's Springs where he had gone to obtain relief from an attack of jaundice."[42]

In 1858, the Springs and surrounding property were purchased by A. G. Ellis for $35,000. On August 3, 1859, the Florence Gazette reported: "One hundred arrivals, not counting servants, were reported for the week of July 17 at Bailey Springs. They amused themselves with music, bowling, whist and cricket."[43]

An interesting communication for 1855 involves one Charles L. Wheler, "editor of the American Democrat, Know-nothing newspaper, recently started at Florence, Ala... He absconded last week following an expose in the Athens Post. An infamous liar, an unprincipled scoundrel, and a blackhearted Freesoiler and Abolitionist."[44] Research has so far failed to reveal what black secrets were exposed by the Athens Post about this short-lived newspaper and its editor.

On Sept. 11, 1854, a petition was presented to the Florence City Council by George W. Foster, William B. Wood and Edward O'Neal for the removal of LaGrange College to Florence.[45] Considerable hard feelings arose about the removal of the school. As the Florence school was denied the use of the name LaGrange, it was chartered as the Florence Wesleyan University, and went by this name until after the Civil War.

In 1850 the population of Florence was registered by the United States census enumerator as 802. In 1857, a local census revealed that the population was 1,444. There were nine lawyers, two dentists, four doctors, and about fifty other business establishments in Florence. Mayors for this period included George W. Snned, Alexander Wood, W. F. Hawkins, and John A. Smith.[46]

B. P. Joiner, writing in 1901, disputed the fact that the first telegraph lines were run to Florence in 1848. He wrote that these lines were established in 1854, under the operation of Capt. Billy Taylor. There was much skepticism about the lines and many of the wires were cut down and destroyed. "Some people believed that they took all the electricity out of the clouds and kept it from raining..."[47]

When Joiner moved to Florence in 1851, "There were no business houses at that time north of the Court House on the west side of Court Street...In 1851 there were no railroads in the county and a telegraph or telephone line hadn't yet been dreamed of. Goods were shipped to Florence by steamboat and hauled to Huntsville by wagons.

In 1857 one of the pioneers left Florence. Ferdinand Sannoner moved to Memphis. Until about 1917, Wilson Park in downtown Florence was known as Sannoner Park in his honor. It was renamed Wilson Park when Woodrow Wilson signed the bill locating Wilson Dam in this region.[48]

Some marriages for this decade included Francis M. Whitten to Margaret A. Faires, 21 Nov. 1851; Jesse W. Brooks to Olive E. Kennedy, 23 Nov. 1857; Isaac N. Crow to Sarah Jane Miller, 23 Jan. 1853; Pleasant J. Hough to Amanda Ray, 10 March 1853; Toliver R. Garrett to Susan Davis on 19 Dec. 1851, by J. McCorkle, J.P.; Charles E. Littleton to Rebecca Jane Reader on 1 May 1850; Noble R. Ladd to Caroline C. F. Knight on 18 Dec. 1851.

The mills flourished at this time. By 1850 Globe Factory was earning large profits for its owners. The mill, it is said, operated 1,600 spindles and 46 looms, upon which 80,000 yards of cloth were produced weekly.[49] Martin, Weakley and Company were so successful by 1858 they had three mills in operation, employing 800 people.[50]

James Martin, senior partner of the Globe Mill, writing in 1858, described the efforts by the Globe Company to elevate the poor whites and make them useful to society. By the factory's large operation and output, the 800 employees "have virtually added to the wealth of the country...This enables them to live a much more comfortable life, and by constant employment, enables them to make much more useful and better citizens. We had among them twenty-five marriages during the 1st twelve months...We have a day-school, a Sunday-school, well attended, and a church for their benefit, and in this way hope to benefit them, while we benefit ourselves."

By 1860 Florence and Lauderdale County were entering a period of prosperity with bright prospects for further economic development. These prospects were blighted by the Civil War. But as Richard W. Griffin would write in 1956, "Yet the human resources trained in the ante-bellum period provided the nucleus for eventual recovery after the end of Reconstruction."[51]

CHAPTER III

Perhaps the darkest period in the history of Florence and Lauderdale County, Alabama, was that of the mid-nineteenth century when the country was divided in a fierce and bloody Civil War. This chapter, which will be presented in chronological form, will not be concerned with the vital issues of that conflict, but with the events which affected the county. Sources will follow each item, and come from diaries, newspapers, official records, and miscellaneous sources. All items marked "O.R." come from the Official Records of the Rebellion, published by the U. S. Printing Office, and all are from Series I, unless otherwise indicated.

January 1860 - (Florence Gazette, 18 Jan. 1860)
The Old Florence Hotel "which cost the Cypress Land Company $35,000, has been a pile of ruins almost since the days of Old Dick Burrus has passed to the hands of Robert Elliott" who will restore it...Gazette was edited by S. G. Barr. Advertisements for A. M. Hannay, Tailor, and Robert Howell, boot maker. Notice that the estate of Thomas Simpson of Second Creek near Waterloo will be sold...Eliza A. Jones, widow of William E. Jones, settling his estate...Administration notice for George R. Lybrook...Benjamin H. Slayden has been declared a lunatic and William R. Chisholm directed to sell slaves belonging to Slayden.

January 1860 - (Florence Gazette, 25 Jan. 1860)
James W. Stewart, administrator, will sale negroes belonging to Mary W. Noel, deceased.

April 1861
Franklin White, 22, died on the 16th of consumption...Joshua J. Crittenden, guardian for Molly Coffee, makes settlement as guardian. (Florence Gazette, 17 April 1861) The Lauderdale County Dragoons, under Robert McFarland, to hold grand parade on the 20th...The Campbell House, or Marshall House, is now closing and all those who owe bills are requested to pay up...Letter to the editor chastises the paper for always praising the rich and their sons and never saying anything good about the poor people, whose sons are also enlisting in the service of the Confederacy. (Ibid, 18 April 1861, an extra.) James W. Stewart was elected captain of the Silver Grays. The Home Guards are called to meet at the Masonic Hall. (Ibid, 24 April 1861.)

May 1861
S. G. Barr editor of the paper...On the 27th of April there was war meeting at Wesleyan and the ladies gave flag to the Lauderdale County Volunteers. R. M. Patton presided at the meeting. Mrs. Coffee came on stand and unfurled the banner, which features the seven-starred flag of the Confederacy...Henry Sample is the captain of the Florence Blues. (Florence Gazette, 1 May 1861)

June 1861
The Lauderdale Rifles (or Co. D, 9 Alabama Infantry, left June 3, 1861 for Richmond, Virginia, and went into battle on July 14, 1861. When war was over, they walked 600 miles back to Alabama. Captain I. B. Houston headed the company.[1]

July 1861
James Hendrix, known as Uncle Jimmy, at the age of 64 enlisted in Confederate Army and was wounded at First Manassas. He was a pioneer of Lauderdale County and a native of South Carolina. (History of Alabama, by A.B. Moore, III, page 478.)

November 1861
Letter from Tuscumbia, Ala., dated 22 Nov. 1861, addressed to Hon. J. P. Benjamin, Secretary of War, from S. D. Weakley, chairman, and James E. Saunders, Secretary of Committee:

"The undersigned were sent from North Alabama and Northeast Mississippi to the military commander at Columbus, Ky., to inquire if the defense of the Tennessee River were safe, and to know if we could aid them in any manner. The answer from General Pillow, now commanding there, after conferring with General Polk, was that they were as good as the time allowed and the means afforded would permit, but that they were unsafe, and the force on that flank of the army resting on the river insufficient; that there was danger of the enemy ascending the Tennessee River and burning the railroad bridge across it just above Fort Henry and separating our army at Bowling Green from that at Columbus, and, of destroying the Mobile and Ohio and the Memphis and Charleston Railroads, for it is only 18 miles from the Big Bend of the Tennessee to their junction at Corinth.

"The undersigned then determined to make an effort to improve the works on that river, and send 5,000 volunteers, with their own guns to garrison them. General Pillow, to facilitate the work, appointed General Weakley, our chairman, a volunteer aide-de-camp, and specially charged him with the organization of the force; Mr. William Dickson, quartermaster, and Mr. John T. Abernathy, commissary for the force to be raised for this purpose. They are gentlemen of large wealth, patriotic and energetic. And, moreover, General Pillow authorized Col. Thomas J. Foster to raise a regiment, to be armed with their own guns, for twelve months.

"We shall proceed immediately to raise their volunteers. We propose to organize a company of old men, armed, in each county in North Alabama, for 40 days. Our reason for this is that they are not only in general better marksmen than the generation now growing up, but the very fact of gray-headed men moving to the field will give an impetus to volunteering which we need just now; and besides very many of these old men will have their negro men laboring on the works, and their presence would be satisfactory to themselves and useful in furthering them. The volunteers liable to do military duty will be enrolled for 12 months.

"From Columbus we requested the Governor of Alabama to ask the Legislature to pass a law for the purchase and impressment of arms similar to the one enacted in the State of Tennessee, and presume it has been done before this time...

We hope we may have your approval of these arrangements for the public defense. The bonds of Mr. Dickson, as quartermaster, and Mr. Abernathy, as commissary, will be sent, with sureties worth a very large amount under this date..." (O.R. VII, pages 692, 693.)

Tuscumbia, Ala., 23 Nov. 1861 "To our fellow citizens of North Alabama and North Mississippi. The undersigned were sent as delegates from a number of counties in North Alabama and Tishomingo Co., Miss., to the camp at Columbus, Ky., to inquire of the military authorities there if they considered the defense of the Tennessee River safe; and, if not, to tender material aid to make them so...We had several interviews with General Pillow, now commanding the department in consequence of an injury to Maj. Gen. Polk from the bursting of a gun...

"We propose to raise a regiment of men past middle life to serve during the emergency, but the younger men will be enrolled for 12 months. The whole force we must arm with shot-guns and rifles, with which a strongly-fortified position can be defended as perfectly as with musket and bayonet.

"William Dickson of Franklin Co. has been appointed quartermaster and John T. Abernathy of Lawrence Co. commissary...If our people at home were convinced, as we are, that a deadly struggle for our homes and property is impending, that the enemy in a few days will put forth his whole strength for our subjugation, they would rally en masse for the public defense. Col. Thos. J. Foster of Lawrence is empowered by General Pillow to raise a regiment...(signed) Samuel D. Weakley, James E. Saunders, Thos J. Foster, David Deshler, William Dickson, Wm. Cooper, B.B. Trousdale. (O.R. VII, page 694)

January 1862
Soldiers Aid Societies have been formed in Lauderdale County. There is an Oakland Society and a Florence Society, of the latter Mrs. M. L. Cassity is president and Miss H. R. Foster, secretary...The original map of Florence is lost and the city offers a reward for its recovery. (Florence Gazette, 8 Jan. 1862)

On January 30, 1862, D. C. Buell wrote: "Two new gunboats, one old one, and 500 troops on one transport up the Tennessee River can shell out Fort Henry, destroy the bridge, run up the river to Tuscumbia, and the troops can land and destroy two or three bridges near the river along there...I believe the Conestoga or Lexington run over the Muscle Shoals..." (O.R., VII, page 573)

February 1862
Fort Henry surrendered Feb. 6, 1862.
On Feb. 9, 1862, W. O. P. Johnson, telegraph operator, notifies General Leonidas Polk: "Mr. Powers, the operator at Tuscumbia, informs me that the enemy took possession of the telegraph office in Florence and found out nearly everything that was passing over the line before he was informed of their having landed. He then immediately disconnected the Florence line from his office, and cut them off. They had operators and instruments with them. They informed the citizens of Florence that it was their intention to return in a day or so with a force sufficiently large to take and hold their position at that place; that it was not their intention to harm the citizens who would willingly submit and to those who were loyal to the United States." (O.R., VII, a, page 867.)

On Feb. 10, 1862, Lieut. Commander S. L. Phelps, U.S. Navy, on U. S. Gunboat Conestoga reported: "Soon after the surrender of Fort Henry, on the 6th instant, I proceeded in obedience to your orders up the Tennessee River with the Tyler, Lt. Com. Gwin; Lexington, Lieut. Com. Shirk and this vessel...Soon after daylight on the 8th we passed Eastport, Miss., and at Chickasaw, farther up, near the State line, seized two steamers, the Sallie Wood and Muscle, the former laid up, the latter freighted with iron destined for Richmond and for rebel use. We then proceeded on up the river, entering the State of Alabama, and ascending to Florence, at the foot of the Muscle Shoals. On coming in sight of the town three steamers were discovered, which were immediately set on fire by the rebels. Some shots were fired from the opposite side of the river below. A force was landed and considerable quantities of supplies, marked "Fort Henry". were secured from the burning wrecks. Some had been landed and stored. These I seized putting such as we could bring away on board our vessels and destroying the remainder. No flats or other craft could be found. I found also some of the iron plating intended for the Eastport..." (O.R. VII, page 153)

The Florence Gazette of 12 Feb. 1862 reported that there was great excitement in Florence and that two steamboats were leaving. The steamer Dunbar was now on the "Gundle Ford." R. F. M. Lindsey expressed his thanks to the people of Florence for their help at the Florence hospital.

On the same date, Feb. 12, Lt. Com. Phelps made another report: "We have returned to this point from an entirely successful expedition to Florence at foot of the Muscle Shoals, Alabama. The rebels were forced to burn six steamers and we captured two others, beside the half-completed gunboat Eastport. The steamers burned were freighted with rebel military stores. The Eastport has about 250,000 feet of lumber on board...captured 200 stand of arms and a quantity of clothing and stores, and destroyed the encampment of Colonel Drew at Savannah, Tennessee. Found the Union sentiment strong." (O.R., VII, page 153.)

On February 18, 1862, Brigadier General Daniel Ruggles wired from Florence: "Shall I entrench and defend the crossings at Florence and Decatur?" (O.R., VII, page 891

Two days later, Ruggles, who was in charge of Confederate forces at Corinth, noted that gunboats had passed Hamburg at 10 a.m. on way to Florence, and he wired his troops: "Take immediate measures to protect Florence..." (O.R., VII, 894)

P. T. Beauregard in turn wired Ruggles on the 24th: "...hold in observation the landing on the Tennessee River opposite a place called Waterloo." (O.R., VII, 907.)

William Gwin, Lieutenant, on the U.S. Tyler made a report on the 23rd to Flag Officer Foote, U. S. Navy: "I am happy to state that I have met with an increased Union sentiment in South Tennessee and North Alabama. I saw few Mississippians. In Hardin, McNairy, Wayne, Decatur, and a portion of Hardeman, all of which border upon the river, the Union sentiment is strong, and those who do not express themselves openly loyal are only prevented by their fears of the military tyranny and coercion which is practiced by marauding bands of guerrilla companies of cavalry...

"I concluded to take...some fifty sharpshooters, as I could accommodate them on board the Tyler. I was not able to accomplish the destruction of Bear Creek Bridge (my great desire), as I found that the rebels had sent immediately after our first ascent of the river, a large force--1,000--to this bridge, and some 3,000 or 4,000 to a station called Iuka, 3 miles from the bridge. Learning that a large quantity of wheat and flour was stored in Clifton, Tenn...I landed there and took on board about a thousand sacks.

"Union men can now begin to express their loyal sentiments without fear of being mobbed, especially along the banks of the river...I feel confident that a regiment of Home Guards could be raised in ten days. Savannah is in good striking distance of Eastport, Miss., which is the nearest point over Bear Creek, as well, as some extent of trestle work, which, if destroyed, together with a part of the Mobile and Ohio road at its junction with the Memphis and Ohio Railroad, will cut the Southern Confederacy almost in two.

"I brought down under arrest a man named William P. Poole, who has been active in oppressing Union men in his community. I have warned the inhabitants of the different towns of the river that I would hold secessionists and their property responsible for any outrages committed on Unionists in their community..." (O.R. VII, 421)

March 1862
By the 6th of March large numbers of Confederate troops were reported at Eastport, across from the Waterloo, Ala., area. (O.R. X-2, 40.)

On the 18th of March, General Albert S. Johnston, C.S.A., was at Decatur and he wired Col. B. H. Helm at Tuscumbia: "Make silent preparations to burn the Florence Bridge as soon as the enemy's gunboats may pass Eastport or the enemy approach Florence from the north side of the river..." (O.R. X-2, 338)

Florence Gazette, 19 March 1862: Heavy rains reported. Bridge over Cypress Creek swept away, as well as one over Shoal Creek. Two bridges over Bluewater Creek, one on Lexington Road, and one on Huntsville Road washed away. Two hundred twenty bales of cotton of Baugh, Kennedy and Company were swept away from the factory on Shoal Creek. Grist mill belonging to Martin Weakley and Co. on Cypress Creek was washed away.

April 1862
Battle of Shiloh fought on April 6 and 7, 1862.
Florence Gazette, 9 April 1862: Election for probate judge and superintendent of education to be on May 5. S. B. Hudson, sheriff, announces that votings places will be at Taylor's Spring, Ingram's Crossroads, Rodgersville, Mitchell's, Lexington, Stutts', Blackburn's, Rawhide, Gravelly Springs, Waterloo, Spain's,

Oakland and Florence.

An application, dated March 4, 1862, published in this paper. John H. Rapier applies to court for the emancipation of his slaves, Lucretia, Rebecca, Joseph, Thomas, and Susan. Hearing set for May 12, 1862. (Note: On 1850 census of Lauderdale County, John Rapier, a barber, is listed as a free man of color. This is obviously one of those incidences in which a man of color owned slaves.)

On April 12, Troops under O. M. Mitchell entered Huntsville and by 6 a.m. he reported that the town was occupied. (Another report says April 11.) On the 12th Mitchell's forces seized Decatur and advanced toward Florence and Tuscumbia. The bridge at Florence was burned. (O.R. X-2, 108) On the 17th he reported that "On Sunday, 13th, advanced cautiously upon Tuscumbia and Florence and found the enemy had burned the railroad bridges. These were repaired and reconstructed... From deserters we learn that the enemy had burned just in advance of us the bridge at Florence across the Tennessee.." (O.R., X-2, 111.)

By April 22, the gunboats reached Tuscumbia Landing and two days later Mitchell's line extended to Tuscumbia. J. B. Turchin was put in command at Tuscumbia and he was unloading stores just above Florence on the north side of the river. (O.R. X-2, 124.)

On April 27, Mitchell reported that his cavalry outposts extended to Florence, but that the entire region was flooded by the backwaters of the river. (O.R.X-2, 137) He reports again that "Our officers and soldiers have been to Florence...the Florence Bridges burned." (O.R., X-2, 133)

May 1862
By the first of May Mitchell boasted, "...all of Alabama north of the Tennessee River floats no flags but that of the Union." (O.R., X-2, 156)Three days later he would write, "The negroes are our only friends, and in two instances I owe my own safety to their faithfulness. I shall very soon have watchful guards among the slaves on the plantations bordering the river from Bridgeport to Florence and all who communicate to me valuable information I have promised the protection of my Government." (O.R. X-2, 162)

On the 4th of May the name P. D. Roddey, Captain of the Tishomingo Rangers, first appears in the records of this area. Before the war was over, he would earn the title of the Defender of North Alabama. (O.R., X-2, 487)

"Guerrilla warfare has been inaugurated along my entire line, and we are attacked nightly at bridges and outposts," Mitchell would complain on the 10th of May from his headquarters in Huntsville. (O.R., X-2, 180) These particular guerrillas were possibly regular Confederate troops who had been sent into the area. The Texas Rangers, under Col. John A. Wharton, were at Lamb's Ferry on this date, and he reported that Helm's Cavalry was also on the north side of the Tennessee River. (O.R., X-2, 509)

On May 13, General J. S. Negley marched from Pulaski, Tennessee, to the Tennessee River. A member of the Union Army wrote later: "The Confederate pickets were driven in, and gave the alarm to the forces in the town of Rogersville, who fled in every direction. A portion of the cavalry pushed on to Lamb's Ferry on the Tennessee River and fired upon a boatload of the enemy as they were crossing the river, killing several men and horses. Once over the river, the rebels opened fire upon the Federals, but were soon dispersed by Federal Artillery, and fled hastily beyond gun range. A ferry-boat on the north side of Tennessee River was destroyed and Negley pushed to Florence and to Cheatham's Ferry, 15 miles below, destroying the water-craft as he proceeded. He also arrested all the cotton and woolen goods manufacturers and all the iron-founders near Florence who had supplied the Confederate army and exacted heavy bonds and their parole of honor. He also levied taxes on prominent secessionists, and on one occasion ordered his aide-de-camp to ride many miles out of the way to pay, some the funds thus raised, to a widow who had been robbed by guerrillas...He returned to Columbia, Tennessee, on the 20th." (Army of the Cumberland, page 95.)

Troops under Negley entered Florence on May 16, 1862. (O.R., X-2, page 206)

On the battlefields in Virginia, Captain Gillis of the Calhoun Guards died, after being wounded in the arm, on May 22. He left a wife in "dear old Lauderdale," whom he had married only one week before starting for Virginia.[2] Jack Harrell, who was in Company D, 9th Alabama, was wounded on May 30 around Richmond.[3]

On the 31st of the month General H. W. Halleck ordered the steamer Robb to Florence to see if any of the Confederates were in that area. On this day, the 35th Indiana Volunteers, who had been there only two days, left Rogersville. (O.R., X-2,232,288)

June 1862.
The obstruction of the shoals in the river was of concern to the Federal leaders. Some thought that it would be possible to get over the shoals. Finally, on June 2, Halleck wired D. C. Buell: "All the rivermen say no steamer we have can possibly run over the shoals..." (O.R., X-2, 243) By the middle of the month Halleck reported that the railroad was repaired east to Tuscumbia and that the Federal troops were working on the line from Tuscumbia and Decatur. (O.R., XVII, 1, 12.) The activities of the Northern forces were being closely watched by the Confederates. On June 19, from "In the Woods, 2½ miles from Buzzard Roost" Capt. L. E. Hill,C.S.A., reported that the U. S. Army was building a floating bridge at Florence, and that Smith's division was at Cherokee Station. He had observed that on the 18th the train went up loaded with provisions and ammunition. (O.R., XVII-1, 611)

In Virginia the battle of Frayser's Farm was fought in June. Company D, 9th Alabama, sent 28 men into battle, and only seven survived. Ansel Newsom was shot through the foot and shoulder. John Craig was shot through the body and hip. Ed Till was mortally wounded in his side, with two broken ribs. John McMurray was shot through the thigh. Billy Dickey was killed, as were Wesley Turnley, Jim Mathews, John C. Phillips, John D. Phillips, and John Childress. When John Childress fell, shot through, he said, "I am killed, tell Ma and Pa goodbye for me."[4]

At the Battle of Gaines Mill on June 27th, Company H, 4th Alabama Infantry had several casualties--Billy Oakley, Capt. Armstead, Tommy Westmoreland. Young Billy was carrying the regimental colors into battle and as he moved forward in the charge, Capt. Heslop Armstead paused long enough to say, "Go it, my Billy." The same cannon ball killed them both.[5]

Daniel Jones, Perkins Pool, Clayborne Thrasher, and Moses Perkins were casualties of Company D, 9th Alabama Infantry, at Gaines Mill. Jones was shot through the lungs and lingered until the next day. Thrasher was "cut almost entirely in two" by a cannon ball which struck him just above hips. Captain James M. Crow was wounded by a cannon ball while he was carrying the regimental flag. Lt. Wilson was shot in hand as he raised his repeater to fire his last barrel. Marion Young was shot through the ankle. John Beauchamp was shot in the shoulder.[6]

George W. Phillips, son of Wilson and Nancy McPeters Phillips, was killed in the fighting around Richmond, possibly Frayser's Farm. (Moore, II, 264)

July 1862

On July 7 the Florence City Council announced that no more tax money could be paid in Confederate money. On the same day, the city treasurer said that he could not give his annual report. Federal soldiers had entered his office and scattered the records. (Florence Times, 1 May 1966, quoting 1840-1867 city minutes.)

D. C. Buell's sixth division had reached Tuscumbia, Alabama, on the 23rd of June, but Buell made his headquarters near Florence, on the south bank of the river. "Yesterday a foraging party from Gen. Garfield's brigade discovered distinct traces of the whereabouts of a lot of 1000 bales of cotton which had been subscribed by a noted Secessionist of the Southern Confederacy. Capt. Ralph Plumb, Quartermaster, reported the facts to Gen. Garfield, commanding, and the same has been forwarded to Buell..." (Nashville Union, 9 July 1862. Note: Garfield was James Garfield, who later became President of the United States.)

On the 22d General G. H. Thomas at Iuka reported that a store house and other property had been burned and destroyed at Waterloo. (O.R., XVI-2, 201)

In an article "Guerrillas on the Tennessee": "We learn from Capt. McDouglas of the Belle Creole which boat arrived from the Tennessee river yesterday that bands of rebel guerrillas have made their appearance at various points on the Tennessee River. On the 22d inst., a cavalry company entered Waterloo and destroyed in the vicinity 110 bales of cotton and 5 gin houses..." (Nashville Union, 30 July 1862)

August 1862
On the 6th of this month Col. J. K. Mizner was at Tuscumbia, with Michigan troops. General Morgan, also at Tuscumbia, was ordered to seize all cotton, repair the railroad bridges, and to take the negroes of the neighborhood to work on railroad, also "Notify inhabitants within reach of your lines that any words or actions hostile to the Government will oblige you to treat the parties as enemies..." (O.R., XVII-1, 154)

On the 8th of August, the Nashville Union carried this notice:

TRAITOR CLERGYMAN ARRESTED

"On Sunday, the 26th ult., a large number of Union officers attended Old School Presbyterian Church of the Rev. Dr. W. H. Mitchell at Florence, Alabama. So many of them were present that they constituted a majority of the congregation. After the usual opening hymn, the minister asked the congregation to unite in prayer, when, to their utter astonishment the reverend traitor prayed for Jeff. Davis, for the success of the Confederate arms, and for the attainment of the independence of the Confederate people. The Union men were greatly indignant at this gross insult, but remained standing until the prayer was concluded, when they all left the church. After he had commenced his sermon, Col. Harlan returned to the church, walked up to the pulpit, arrested the preacher, and delivered him, in compliance with the orders of General Thomas to a detachment of cavalry, which immediately conveyed him as a prisoner to Tuscumbia."

In the latter part of August, General W. S. Rosecrans wrote: "I have no doubt that the poverty and destitution of the mountaineers in North Alabama is such that we could raise a large force for border service...I think the measure should be promptly taken in hand, or the people will be driven by want into brigandage..." (From Iuka, O.R. XVII-1, 191.)

December 1862

On Dec. 6, 1862, John E. Moore wrote James A. Seddon, Confederate Secretary of War, from Florence: "In behalf of the good people of North Alabama, I take the liberty of calling your attention to their exposed condition, and that an order from you of a force adequate to their protection would be hailed with intense satisfaction and delight. They have no very good reason to apprehend an approach of the enemy in very large force, as points such as Chattanooga, Vicksburg, &c, of a strategic nature will be likely to engage more particularly their attention; but that frequent raids upon our beautiful valley will be often attempted, as herefore, there can be no doubt. We are, however, advantageously situated to resist these, had we a brigade of infantry to act in conjunction with the two regiments of cavalry already stationed for our defense.

"It is unnecessary to relate to you the innumberable instances of pillage and robbery to which the people of North Alabama have already been subjected. Suffice it to say that they have been almost ground into the very dust by the tyrants and the thieves.

"In this connection, permit me respectfully to call your attention to the claims of Colonel O'Neal, of the 26th Alabama, to the appointment of brigadier-general, and to say, further, that it would greatly subserve the interests of the country, and especially of this section, to have him in command of the forces for the protection of North Alabama. He possesses military skill and experience in an eminent degree. An early devotee of the rights of his section, he hesitated at no sacrifice in its behalf; was one of the first to relinquish a lucrative practice of his profession (of law) to engage for the war as a soldier, and bears honorable scars received upon the memorable battlefields of Richmond. I must say of him that he is popular as a statesman, an orator, and a patriot." (O.R., XX-2, 442)

On the 10th of December Union scouts were reporting that "Bragg moving to Florence... rebels have 6,000 to 8,000 men on east side of Tennessee from Duck River to Florence." (O.R., XVII-1, 398.)

General G. M. Dodge announced on the 13th that Colonel Sweeny, operating out of Corinth, struck the outpost of the Confederates at Cherokee, 300 strong, and pursued them for five miles, fighting all the way, until they met with Colonel Roddey, who drove the Union forces back. Roddey fell back toward Decatur, then crossed the river to Florence about the 14th. Roddey had at Florence, according to Union reports two flatboats, "good ones", and two small steamers, that had been fitted up in the last two months. "He (Roddey) is repairing boats at that place all the time, and his men say that he intends to make a raid down the river as soon as water will permit. His force is over 2000. He has telegraphic, but not railroad, communication with Bragg. Roddey burned all his camps after fight with Sweeny, and also the fine covered bridge across Little Bear Creek..." (O.R., XVII, 1, 54.)

The Florence Gazette, which suspended operation in spring, resumed in December. (Florence Gazette, 31 Jan. 1863)

January 1863

Citizens of Florence appealed to the Confederate Secretary of War in a letter written on the 6th: "...would respectfully make known to you that they have been greatly oppressed by the ravages of the Federal army during the past year; their property destroyed, wantonly and vindictively; the privacy of their homes invaded; citizens carried off, ill-treated, and imprisoned; their slaves carried off in very large numbers, declared free, and refused the liberty of returning to their owners, when, in many instances they desired to do so.

"These and many other outrages of a similar nature reduced to poverty many of our

our citizens who before abounded in wealth. But this was not the worst. The tyranny of the officers and men intimidated the people of the country, and had a tendency to make them submissive to a power they had not the means to resist or repel. This past experience, of oppression and insults, makes the citizens of this part of the State apprehensive. They believe that should the Confederate army now in Middle Tennessee, be obliged to fall back, this country will be again overrun by maruading parties of the Federal army, more incensed against the local population than before, and nothing will save the people from ill-treatment but a general exodus to some remote district, there to suffer by starvation.

"The late conscription has left us without men, except the infirm and the aged. Women and children are now the chief population, and upon them will fall the fury of the enemy, incensed and maddened by late defeats, and unrestrained by their officers...We appeal to you for protection...(signed) N. H. Rice, Charles H..Fant, James Irvine, R. W. Walker, James W. Stewart, B. T. Kansner, John Simpson, M. Harkins, H. C. Wood, William Hough, George W. Kansner, Robert V. Foster, J. B. Simpson, B. F. Foster, S. C. Posey, M. P. Asher." (O.R. XX-2,442)

A Federal report, dated January 7: "A man from Florence reports that Roddey has raised the steamboat Dunbar sunk by U. S. gunboats last winter and is trying to fix up her engines...Kirby Smith crossed river here last week. (O.R.XVII-1, 543)

Thomas House, a member of Sloss' cavalry company, "accidently shot himself in neck while at home...buried in City Cemetery." (Florence Gazette, 10 Jan. 1863)

In partial answer to the appeals from the citizens of the area, Secretary of War Seddon announced on January 20 that an engineer "has been sent to examine the shoals in the Tennessee River with a view to placing obstructions at that point if practicable. The Department believes that you have no reason to fear General Grant' movements..." (O.R., XX-2, 502)

General Dodge, U.S.Army, instructed Col. E. W. Rice to assist the gunboats and send all the force necessary if possible to Tuscumbia and "get the battery at that place.. Can do damage to Roddey..." (O.R., XXIII-2, 8)

Local elections were still being held in Lauderdale County and V. M. Benham was candidate for the office of probate judge. (Florence Gazette, 31 Jan. 1863)

February 1863
Dodge noted on the 11th that General Earl Van Dorn's advance was at Burleson in Franklin County and would probably head for Eastport. The next day Van Dorn's troops were reported at a point twelve miles south of Burleson on the Russellville and Cotton-Gin Road. Dodge reported that his cavalry were all in the mountains, and that Roddey "with all the mounted robbers in the country" has crossed the Tennessee River and working north. "I have scouts at Florence and Decatur," Dodge concluded. (O.R. XXIII-2, 62)

Major General C. S. Hamilton wired General Rosecrans about Van Dorn, "A gunboat at Florence would stop him." S. A. Hurlburt informed Rosecrans, "I have requested a gunboat to be pushed to Florence." And finally on the same date, Feb. 13, Rosecrans wrote Capt. A. M. Pennock, "Please send two gunboats up the Tennessee as far as possible to clean out everything at least as far as Florence. Van Dorn with a cavalry force will probably try to cross at Eastport or Florence." (O.R., XXIII-2, 63)

"Van Dorn is crossing at Florence. About 2000 men and six guns are at Waynesborough waiting for him," G. M. Dodge reported on the 16th. "We have annoyed Van Dorn and taken some 50 prisoners from him. He has not yet all across the river..." (O.R., XXIII, 2, 73)

Stopping Van Dorn's crossing seemed to have been the consuming interest of the Federal officers at this time. On the 18th, Brigadier General Robert B. Mitchell in Nashville notified Rosecrans, "Van Dorn is crossing the Tennessee River at Bainbridge, Florence, and Seven Mile Island. It will take him two days to cross. Am directing Lt. Fitch to send two gunboats." (O.R, XXIII-2, 74)

Rosecrans then wire Dodge in Corinth: "Fitch with four gunboats starts up the Tennessee today. If you have any...infantry...you had better send them to Hamburg to meet the boats." (Feb. 18, O.R., XXIII-2, 76)

And finally:

"Five of our (U.S.) gunboats reached Florence on the 22d of Feb., landed and destroyed a ferryboat there. Some of the boats proceeded to Bainbridge at the foot of the shoals, and destroyed the ferryboats there also. The rebel steamer Dunbar escaped over the shoals. Late that evening the Union cavalry dashed into the town. Here they were met and repulsed by about 30 of Major Baxter's battalion. Falling back, they reached their main body, consisting of the 10th Missouri, 5th Ohio, two batteries of Illinois, one company of Mississippi, and one of Alabama, all cavalry with a battery of mounted howitzers, the whole numbering from 800 to 1200 men. The rebels were in turn repulsed but the orderly of the Union commander was killed and several others wounded. The Union forces now nearly surrounded the rebels, and took six prisoners, driving the rest out of town. The rebel accounts say that our troops then plundered the town, and threw into prison all who remonstrated.

"Colonel Corwin, the Yankee commander, took up his quarters at the residence of Dr. L. Chisholm. Colonel Florence M. Corwin, of the 10th Missouri, is from St. Louis, and the forces were the 1st brigade of Gen. Frank Blair's division. Col. Corwin made an assessment of sums of from $500 to $5,000 upon the property of the wealthy rebels. When the Yankees left they took with them 50 bales of cotton, all the mules and horses they could find and 60 negroes. One hundred and fifty prisoners in all were captured by the expedition. At Frankfort they arrested the Confederate treasurer and tax collector and took from them several thousand dollars. (Nashville Dispatch, 23 March 1863)

A letter written by North A. Messenger, editor of the North Alabamian, published at Tuscumbia, found its way into the hands of the editor of the Nashville Dispatch. Messenger, who signed the letter "Colonel", was called by the Dispatch editor "a renegade from the Free States":

"Early on Sunday morning the 22d Feb., five Yankee gunboats came up the Tennessee river; they did not land at Tuscumbia landing, but proceeded on up to Florence & Bainbridge, at the foot of Muscle Shoals, and destroyed the ferryboat at that place. The Confederate States steamer Dunbar had been lying at Bainbridge for some time, but had taken advantage of the high water and gone over the shoals, where the gunboats could not follow. About 3 o'clock the gunboats all went down the river, without making any attempt to land, or showing any warlike disposition except giving three cannon shot at a party of little boys on this side of the river.

"Late in the evening when the excitement caused by the gunboats had in a great measure subsided, the rattle of small arms and the galloping of horses, announced the arrival of the Yankee cavalry. There was at this time about 30 of Baxter's battalion in town; about 16 of them were quietly feeding their horses, and getting supper at their barracks on Main Street; the balance were scattered over town. At the first alarm, these sixteen men got into line, Baker, (Baxter being absent), telling them to stand firm, that it took more than one Yankee to stampede his men.

The advance guard of the Yankees, about 60 men, charged upon these 16 men, our boys gave a yell and galloped to meet them, the Yankees turned and fled as fast as their horses could carry them; our boys pursued them back a mile, until they met the main body of the enemy, consisting of the 10th Missouri, 5th Ohio, two battalions of Illinois, one company of Mississippi, and one of Alabama cavalry, with a battery of mounted howitzers, in all about 1,200 men, some estimate about 800. The enemy fired several volleys and charged in turn, our boys falling back slowly until they were about to be flanked, when they retreated hastily into town; here they made a short stand killing the orderly of the Yankee Commander, and one or two others.

"By this time the Yankees, guided by renegade Alabamians, had got the remaining few of our boys nearly surrounded; but they made a desperate effort, and broke through the enemy's ranks and escaped. We lost six men taken prisoners, but not a man was killed or wounded on our side. It was now dusk, and the enemy did not pursue beyond the suburbs of the town. The wagons, tents, and camp equipage of Baxter's battalion were saved, having been sent out in the morning when the gunboats appeared."

The letter then gives a dreadful account of outrages committed upon fences, shrubery, etc., and says, "You have had Mitchel and Turchin with you; compared to Cornyn (Col. F. M. Cornyn, 10th Missouri Cavalry) and his set, they were angels."

Here is a fascimile of several writs that were served upon citizens of the town and neighborhood:

"Headquarters 1st Brigade, Maj. F. P. Blair's Division, Tuscumbia, Ala. Feb. 23, 1863. The U. S. Government having ordered assessments to be made upon the wealthy citizens of the States now in rebellion against said Government, I have ordered an assessment upon your property to the amount of ____ dollars, payable immediately.

"You are therefore commanded to pay over to Major W. H. Lusk, Paymaster of this Brigade, the above sum, or the same will be collected from you at the sacrifice of your property. (signed) Florence M. Cornyn, Colonel, 10th Missouri Cavalry."

"The lowest assessment that I have heard of under the edict was $500, the highest $5,000. One gentleman, Mr. Wm. Warren, for failing to pay his assessment, was carried off.

"To our inexpressible relief the scoundrels left town on Wednesday afternoon, taking with them about 50 bales of cotton, all the mules and horses they could find, and about as many negroes as they could force off, about 60 in all. They took the plantation teams to haul their cotton. Owing to the bad roads, they left 14 bales of cotton between town and the mountains and I understand they were compelled to leave much more further on; which they burnt. The enemy came through Frankfort to which place they came on the Fulton Road..." (Nashville Dispatch, 27 March 1863)

A dispatch from Memphis about this time wrote on Feb. 11: "Union men of North Alabama and Mississippi are being forced into rebel army and are fleeing...Men from 40 to 60 years of age are being conscripted. Union men in North Alabama are hiding out in the woods and caves rather than to be conscripted. Over 1,000 Union men from Mississippi and Alabama made way to Dodge in Corinth. Some of their families were sent for. A regiment of Union men forming at Corinth, already there are six full companies.

"Abraham Kennedy and J. A. Mitchell of Hackeldo (Hackelboro) settlement, Monroe Co., Alabama, have been hung by rebels for Union proclivities. Mr. Hallbrook and daughter of same county have been shot. Hector Lewis, an immediate neighbor of above, of suspected Union proclivities was hunted down and captured. The houses of J. A. Palmer, Worley Williams, and other Union men, were burned over their families' heads. Mr. Peterson living at head of Bull Mountain was killed for his Union sentiments. Two women of Tulcumbia (Tuscumbia) were torn to pieces by bloodhounds. One hundred families driven out of Alabama reached Corinth on foot without food or clothing. Some were old men of 80 years..." (Nashville Union, 18 Feb. 1863)

Rosecrans announced tersely on Feb. 27, "General Dodge's cavalry has captured Tuscumbia with 200 prisoners and a quantity of stores, and are in pursuit of their scattered forces." (O.R., XXIII-2, 90)

March 1863
Dodge wrote on March 3 from Corinth: "All the cavalry, Partisan Rangers, and mounted parties in Alabama and Georgia have been concentrated and ordered to join Van Dorn and Wheeler. A portion of them have crossed the Tennessee already near Huntsville...One battery of artillery (four guns) crossed at Decatur last week to join Johnston. A heavy cavalry force crossed at Decatur to south side of river by steamer Dunbar to cut off many forces..." (O.R. XXIII-2, 100)

At this time it was also announced that the source of supply and forage for Hardee's C.S.A. Corps came from North Alabama, Giles and Maury Counties, Tennessee. (O.R., XXIII-2, 764)

Henry J. Sims of Tuscumbia, who must have served as a Union informer, reported that Warren's Company was about 14 miles south of Tuscumbia and he thought "they are guerrillas." (Nashville Union, 4 March 1863)

On March 4, 12,000 to 15,000 Union troops left Corinth for Florence. They were transported by one ironclad and six transports. (O.R., XXIII-2, 674)

By the 18th of the month "all the country from Perryville (Tenn.) to Florence is overflowed." (O.R. XXIII-2, 150) Steamers were being sent up and down the river to prevent any crossings by Confederate troops. On the 28th Colonel P. D. Roddey and his regiment of Alabama cavalry were ordered out of Tennessee back to North Alabama to the Tennessee River where he was to relieve Brigadier General S. A. M. Wood. On the 31st Roddey reported he had his men in movement toward the river. (O.R. XXIII-2, 728.) On the 29th Rosecrans said he wanted 2,000 Union troops sent from Nashville by boat up the Tennessee River to Florence. They were to be moved by gunboats. (O.R. XXIII-2, 188)

April 1863
On the 1st from Corinth, Dodge wrote Rosecrans: "Enemy rebuilding all bridges from Savannah east and from Florence north and are increasing forces...three gunboats went up river today. In Wayne and Lawrence Counties (Tennessee) there are several bodies of cavalry, and at or near Mt. Pleasant (Tennessee), there is quite a large force." He also said the Confederates were building a large number of boats in several of the larger creeks. (O.R. XXIII-2, 200)

Leroy Fitch, commander of gunboats on the river, reported to Dodge on the 1st from the U. S. S. Lexington: "From trip to Florence found many of enemy's cavalry near Tuscumbia Landing, not enough water for this boat to get over Coulter's Shoals, so sent a couple of light boats above...Within a few hundred yards of Florence have found enemy in considerable force with a small battery..." (O.R. XXIII-2, 201)

Dodge would write on April 2 that the gunboats Lexington, Silver Lake, and Robb shelled the rebels "out of Florence Tuesday...They destroyed the cotton factories this side of Florence and report about 2000 rebels in that vicinity."(OR XXIII-2,203

By the 3rd it was believed that the gunboats did not silence the batteries at Florence, so Dodge was ordered to move to Tuscumbia. He would have to bridge Little and Big Bear Creeks in order to do so. (O.R., XXIII-2, 206)

Dodge's scouts, who left Florence on April 3, reported that from Decatur to Florence at every ferry they (the C.S.A.) were building a large number of flats and that several were already finished. "At Florence they have 50 men at work building flats. General Wood at Florence with battery and one regiment of infantry; at Waterloo, Col. Debugee's (Dibrell's ?) regiment of cavalry; at Tuscumbia Dodge's (?) cavalry, Colonel Harrison's command have one battery at Bear Creek..." (O.R. XXIII-2, 223)

Ellet's Marine Brigade was sent to the Tennessee River at this time to cooperate with Dodge, as it was important that U.S. gunboats be able to cruise the river from the mouth of Duck River up to Tuscumbia. (O.R. XXIII-2, 223) One writer says that Ellet's brigade was formed to fight the guerrillas that lurked along the banks of the river.

Rosecrans planned to land a force at Florence, "attack and take that place, while, with a heavy body of cavalry, he penetrates Alabama, north of Tennessee River, and gets into Johnston's rear, wrote General Dodge on the 4th. "At the same time I am to strike and take Tuscumbia, and, if practicable push my cavalry to Decatur, destroy the saltpeter works, and the Tuscumbia and Decatur railroad, which they have just finished, and take all the horses and mules in that country to prevent them from raising any large crops. To do this, I propose to move simultaneously with General Rosecrans, throw all my cavalry suddenly across Bear Creek, capture the ferries, and hold them until my infantry and artillery arrive, and then immediately force my cavalry as far toward Tuscumbia as possible and secure the crossings of Little Bear..." (O.R. XXIII-2, 215)

Rosecrans himself wrote of his plans: "I propose to send 1,700 men...land at Eastport...march on Tuscumbia, whip the rebels out of the valley..." (O.R. XXIII-2 215)

On the 13th Dodge scouts reported that all along the Tennessee River there was great activity in building flat boats and collecting forage between Florence and Decatur. (O.R. XXIII-2, 235)

Edmund D. Patterson, fighting in Virginia, made a note in his diary on April 10 about the conditions back home in Lauderdale County: "The Union Heroes burned only fourteen (houses) in my section of the country, on their last visit, and did it without loss of a man as they had only women and children to contend with. They were only private residences..."[7]

Fitch reported on the 16th that his boats could not get over Coulter's Shoals and that the river was rising slowly. Admiral Porter finally advised him to "Go down the river as it falls...ascend as it rises." (O.R. XXIII-2, 251)
By the 17th the Confederate forces in the area were: Col. Dibrell, with 900, at Tuscumbia Landing; Col. Josiah Patterson with 1000 at Florence; Col. M. W. Hannon with 1800 at Tuscumbia; Roddey's old regiment with 800 at Tuscumbia Landing; Baxter Smith with 350 located about 10 miles east of Tuscumbia Landing; Col. Hampton with 300 at the same place; W. R. Julian with 300 at Grey's; Smith with 100 at Big Bear Creek. Between Courtland and Tuscumbia there was one brigade of infantry under Colonel Wood. There were five pieces of artillery at Florence and six at Tuscumbia. All waiting for Dodge when he arrived from Corinth. This information had been collected by Dodge's spies in North Alabama. (O.R. XXIII-2, 245)

On the 20th Roddey at Tuscumbia reported that an Union army was landing at Eastport, "which they burned on the 19th." (O.R. XXIII-2, 778)

In April 1863 Confederate General Van Dorn moved toward Florence, and forced Dodge to fall back to his fortifications.

May 1863

On the 7th of this month Alfred W. Ellet, Brigadier General of the Mississippi Marine Brigade reported, "I have returned from an attempt to ascend the Tennessee River a second time. The water is too low for me to get above the mouth of Duck River." (O.R., XXIII-2, 314.)

By the 21st General Rosecrans would receive word "A force is crossing at Muscle Shoals." (O.R. XXIII-2, 351.) General Dodge would also report "a force of heavy trains crossing at Muscle Shoals and crossing at Brown's Ferry." (Ibid, 358.)

On the 26th Dodge informed Rosecrans: "My cavalry will cross the Tennessee tonight at Hamburg and push east to Waynesborough and Florence and attack enemy; also destory all mills, forage, etc...I understand that all the cavalry on that side of the river have been ordered to Columbia and that all moving that way. Two regiments of Roddey's forces crossing at Florence last Friday." (O.R. XXIII-2, 364)

In the fighting around Fredericksburg, Virginia, Charley Sharpe, Company D, and Josiah Whitten, Company D, were killed. Tom Harmon was shot in the head, the ball entering his face just at the side of his nose, below the eye, and lodging in the back of the head. Jim Edwards received a bad gash across the top of his head.[8]

Cornym came back to Florence the last of this month. Dodge reported on June 1: "Cornym took Florence Thursday. Found Roddey there and whipped him...also (learned that some trains crossed Muscle Shoals a week ago." (O.R. XXIII-2, 381) Hurlbut reported: "Cornym from Corinth crossed at Florence last week; surprised Roddey, killed and wounded 60, captured 100...burned the cotton factories and recrossed with trifling loss." (Ibid, 382)

John Collins, one of Burton's scouts, made a report: "Federals left Corinth and on north side of river crossing to Florence. Roddey crossed at Florence and met enemy...skirmishing all day Thursday and until Sunday a.m. U. S. troops burned factory and other buildings at Florence." (O.R., XXII-2, 857.) (Burton was a Confederate scouting group.)

On July 29 a note from William H. Sinclair, Assistant Adjutant General, from Winchester, Tennessee, had some interest for this area: "Turchin was relieved this morning. Good!" (O.R. XXIII-2, 567)

Throughout the remainder of the year the Muscle Shoals area was the scene of many small skirmishes between the troops of both sides. In the winter of 1863 the so-called night of horror took place at Sweetwater Plantation when Federal troops raided that plantation and robbed the Patton family.

On January 9, 1864, General Dodge in Pulaski made note: "Lt. Col. Phillips at Athens...Major Falconnet has system of couriers from our lines." He also wrote that Falconnet was to be married to Miss Mary Burtwell on the 16th. (O.R. XXXII-2, 404.) Phillips, a Federal soldier, had paid court to Miss Burtwell while he had been in Florence. According to tradition, Phillips received under a flag of truce a piece of the wedding cake.

In February 1864, Duncan Cooper and his "guerrillas" were in the area. Cooper's group was in reality a regularly organized Confederate group of partisan rangers, headed by a nineteen-year old colonel. Federal officers branded them as guerrillas nevertheless. Captain A. J. Kelly, of this group was killed at Bainbridge: "A citizen of Wayne county has brought us the story that Capt. A. J. Kelly, or as he was familiarly called, "Rick Kelly," of Dunc Cooper's guerrillas, was killed near Bainbridge, eight miles above Florence, a few days since. Kelly had crossed from the south bank of the Tennessee river with a detachment of ten men, when seeing three Federal soldiers standing near the door of an adjacent house, he charged upon them, but instead of only three being there, twenty soon emerged, and firing upon Kelly's squad, mortally wounded him and killed all but one of his party...He was the brains of the "Cooper Battalion." (Nashville Union 17 Feb.1864)

A court martial held about this time also had some interest for the Florence area. "The court martial which tried Lt. Col. W. D. Bowen for killing Col. Florence M. Cornym of the 15th Missouri Cavalry at Corinth last August, acquitted him." (Nashville Union, 13 Feb. 1864)

About the 16th of the month Dodge noted there was a steamer on the Tennessee River running from Eastport to Waterloo dealing in cotton, salt, sugar, coffee, and gold. "A relative of Roddey is on boat and has his protection." The steamer was later identified as the S. C. Baker. (O.R. XXXII-2, 405, 406)

In later years W. D. Hamilton would write: "In April, 1864, I received an order from General Sherman through General Granville M. Dodge, to take my command to Florence, Alabama, and from that point as headquarters to continue the patrol of the Tennessee river, obtaining subsistence from the surrounding region and to exhaust the supplies found in that locality.

"The valley of the Tennessee for miles both above and below Florence was a very fertile district, and had been General Forrest's unfailing source of supplies for his cavalry in their raids upon the Union forces in Tennessee.

"We took only two days rations and a fair supply of sugar and coffee, and moved down to Florence, established our camp two miles below the town on Cypress Creek on the plantation of Captain Coffee, whose fine home could be seen in a grove of trees on an eminence above the creek. I had given instructions that while the men and horses were to fare liberally, the different plantations should be allowed their real needs. So that we came to be looked upon simply as one of the burdens of a cruel war; and they met the inevitable without complaint like a high=spirited people.

"Captain Coffee invited me to his house, and my acquaintance with him and his family was interesting and pleasant. They had only one child, Mary, and a sweet little girl of about ten years; and we soon became great friends. One day when I called, I found her sitting by her mother plaiting rye straw from a bundle on her knee. "What are you doing, Mary?" I asked. "I am trying to make a hat." "What for?" I asked. "Why, for myself," she said. "If you will give me some straw, I will help you." I drew up a chair and sat down beside her; she gave me a bundle of straw and we went gayly to work. It took us several afternoons to finish that hat and we had great fun over it. "After all," she said, "The only way to get a new hat is to make one, for the cruel Yankees won't let the ships bring us any."

"I returned to Florence in the spring of 1889. Most of the middle age men were Confederate soldiers and I never received more cordial greetings. I came to the conclusion that I happened to be here at a time when a little kindness went a long ways. A new generation had come and I was one of the traditions of their childhood. The boys and girls stood around whispering to each other. "There is the 'Good Yankee.'"

"I was introduced to Mr. Campbell, president of the bank, whose wife the daughter of Captain Coffee on whose place I had my camp. A carriage drove up, occupied by a lady with a twelve year old boy at her side. Mr. Campbell began an introduction to which I paid no attention, but reaching her my hand said, "What became of that hat?" With a laugh she asked, "Do you remember that hat?" I told her I could never forget it. She then introduced me to her son who was just about the age she was, when she and I were engaged in the hat business.

"Mrs. Campbell sent out invitations to a dinner party given in my honor, where I had the pleasure of meeting a number of my former friends. The company spent the time as a "Committee of the Whole" discussing the war and its results. A number of young people were under the lead of Mrs. Campbell's son, who asked that I should tell Yankee stories. I told him I would, if he would tell some Rebel stories. He said he would, and the contest was quite amazing..." (Two Views of Florence, Col. W. D. Hamilton, Florence Times, n.d., in Lauderdale County folder, Alabama State Archives.)

And in another letter, dated 26 May 1913, Hamilton wrote W. P. Camper, editor: "In the spring of 1864, I, with the 9th O.V. Cavalry of which I was Colonel, was stationed about a month near Martin, Weakley & Co.'s Cotton Mills on Cypress Creek, within two miles of Florence with orders from General Sherman to guard the Tennessee River against the enemy, who had captured part of the scouting force of my regiment one night two weeks before, while encamped on the Jack Peters plantation below town.

"My orders were to prevent further raids in that locality and to exhaust the resources which had been furnishing supplies for General Forrest and his men. While here I made the acquaintance of the families of W. H. Key, Captain Coffee, Mrs. Collier, Patton, and others. On my second visit, 25 years afterwards, I had the pleasure of meeting a number of old friends, and quite a number of new ones, among whom were the ex-Confederates Dr. J. C. Conner, who married Mr. Key's oldest daughter; Mr. W. P. Campbell, who married the daughter of Captain Coffee; and Captain Patton, son of Governor Patton.

"Since the war I have spent a good deal of my active life in the South and I am writing at the request of my old comrades, my 'recollections of a cavalryman during the Civil War.' (Two Views of Florence, by Col. W. D. Hamilton, Alabama State Archives.)

Some of the activities, which Col. Hamilton mentioned, will be found in the Official Records for this period:

On April 5, James H. Clanton wrote Governor T. H. Watts from Whitesburg, Alabama: "Would that I had a trumpet tongue to tell every man and woman in Alabama the outrages of the Yankees on the other side of the river. They spare neither age, sex, nor condition. Some time since they cursed and caused Governor Chapman's little son, four years old, within the hearing of his aged mother, for (child-like) wandering back to his native home out of which the family had just been turned to make way for a negro regiment. They threatened to strip Mrs. Robert Patton of Florence in search of money, and commenced to do so in the presence of her husband, but she drew from her bosom a purse with $2,000 and gave it to them. God Assist us!" (O.R. XXXII-2, 751)

Richard Rowett of the 7th Illinois and 9th Ohio at Florence wrote on the 23rd of April: "Received communication from Major Murphy complaining that Thrasher with his men are committing many depredations and asking that Thrasher be ordered to report to him. Citizens make frequent complaints of the depredations committed by Thrasher's men..." (O.R. XXXII-2, 460)

General Dodge answered immediately: "This man Thrasher you speak of I know nothing about. He is not in my command, nor ever has been. You better inform Major

Murphy. He must belong to the State troops. Any of his men committing unauthorized depredations will be arrested if they come within your jurisdiction..." (O.R. XXXII part 3, 460)

John W. Estes, Lt. Col., Chief Provost-Marshal, C.S.A., had written from Mt. Hope, Alabama, on April 14: "The tory raids in the mountains are becoming less frequent, and it is very evident that their main object in these raids is plunder, not caring a whit whom they rob...Small squads of Yankees are encamped from Florence to Athens, say 50 to 150 in a squad...Colonels Jackson and Ives with 100 men each, crossed the Tennessee River on the night of the 12th, a few miles below Florence, and surrounded a camp of 48 Yankee cavalry, killed four and captured 42, a whole company, and all their officers, only two escaping. They also captured and brought to this side of the river about 65 good horses, saddles, and all the arms of the company. Colonel Jackson lost one man killed, none wounded. The company belonged to the 9th Ohio Cavalry, and was on detail duty gathering up beef-cattle. They had collected about 250 head, all of which were turned out and scattered..." (O.R. XXXII-3, 782-3)

R. W. Walker wrote from Tuscaloosa on the 14th of April: "Mrs. Walker and other persons just out from Florence bring most deplorable accounts of the condition of things in Lauderdale County. The town is constantly infested either by Yankees or tories. It is hardly an exaggeration to say that every good horse in the county has been taken off, and a very large proportion of the slaves. The communication between Nashville and Florence is interrupted, and a good many citizens of Florence have recently been to Nashville. They all concur in the statement that very heavy re-enforcements have been passing through Nashville daily...Seven thousand Yankee infantry, just from Vicksburg, landed at Waterloo last week, and passed through Lauderdale County on their way to Chattanooga or Huntsville. One brigade passed through Florence the day before Mrs. Walker left home; the remainder of the force took the upper road..." (O.R. XXXII-3, 824)

P. D. Roddey had some complaints which he expressed in a letter to Confederate General S. D. Lee on April 26, writing from Hillsborough, Alabama. "To guard against imposition I would suggest that all scouting parties and secret-service men sent to this section be ordered to report to these headquarters, and that they also be accredited...I think this precaution very important--as an instance, a party of Federals just before the last raid into this section, dressed as Confederates and purporting to be from Forrest's command, passed unmolested and unsuspected through the country and gathered all the information they desired. The same party returned afterward with the raiders.

"Much complaint is made of a Lieutenant Harvey, commanding a party of 50 or 60 men, purporting to be sent here by General Armstrong. From all the information in my possession, he had authorized the illegal seizure of private horses for his command. As all the citizens have been nearly stripped of all their stock, and as they are willingly and cheerfully doing all in their power to support an army by raising produce, and as it is impossible for an army to be supported if their stock is taken from them, and as there is nothing in the impressment act that can be so construed as to allow the seize of private property...I have...ordered the arrest of Lieutenant Harvey...I forward to you, in charge of couriers, Philip Henson, who has been represented to me for the last twelve months as a spy for the Federals. My authorities are the most reliable men who were in my service, and who never failed to give me correct information--who are undoubted. They have reported to me constantly during that time that valuable information has been given by Henson to the Federals. He has papers, but I do not deem them sufficiently satisfactory to permit him to pass through my lines...I believe firmly that the said Henson is a spy, and has been in the service of and the pay of the Federals all that time..." (O.R. XXXII-3, 829)

James Jackson, Colonel of the 27th Alabama regiment reported to Roddey on the 25th, "Two (enemy) regiments now in Lauderdale County, viz, 9th Ohio and 7th Illinois. The 9th Ohio has one company at mouth of Elk River, one company at Ben Taylor's, and one at David Williams' and one at Bainbridge; the remainder of the regiment is at Cheatham's Ferry. The 7th Illinois has two or three companies at Bailey's Springs; report say this evening that they are moving to Wright and Rice's and Florence; one company at Waterloo, remaining in lower part of the county..." (O.R., Ibid, 830)

W. D. Hamilton in command of the 9th Ohio Volunteery Cavalry reported to General Dodge on the 17th of the same month: "I have sent Major Williamson to take command of the men sent to the mouth of Elk River, giving him your orders. He will connect with the 7th Illinois, who patrol down to the mouth of Cypress Creek, joining my patrols, who patrol as far as Eastport. The enemy are sometimes seen patrolling opposite Florence, Cheatham's Ferry, and along the river. A reliable man whom I saw today says that they talk of crossing and trying to capture our patrols. I have sent Mr. Harris over today, who will learn what is to be known as to their movements. I think there is no heavy force near here; Johnson's and Jackson's regiments, I think, are all; they probably do not exceed 400 or 500 men. From letters captured, dated March 17, it seems that a forward movement into Tennessee is in preparations...I think their patrols are watching their own deserters more than anything else. One came over yesterday, and I have made arrangements with a man on the other side to send them over as fast as they come. He says the woods are full of them, but they are afraid to venture. I learn that there are some boats and a flatboat on the other side in some of the inlets. I have directed Mr. Harris to ascertain and get the deserters to bail them out and bring them over if possible, also to learn where Jackson is encamped. If practicable, I intend visiting him some night. The neighborhood has sent a delegation to wait upon you in relation to the protection of their property. I find many of them in rather a destitute condition, some of them quite so. I think our men have not used proper discrimination in their levies. The officers are not sufficiently careful to follow the instructions received. I think generally the greatest evils arise from the latter course. Since my arrival I have returned a number of animals taken by men before I came, and a number of others I would return if they had not been sent off..." (O.R. XXXII-3, 389-90)

Richard Rowett, U. S. Colonel, reported from Bailey's Springs on April 18: "The citizen (Thompson) whom I sent to the south of the river a few days since has just returned. He went from Tuscumbia to LaGrange, Ala.; he reports that Jackson's command (27th and 35th Alabama Mounted Infantry), with Moreland's and Wines' (Warren's?) battalions of cavalry, in all about 1200 men, moved from Russellville, Ala., on Saturday morning. They reported that they were going to bring on an engagement at Decatur. Everything has left the Valley of Tuscumbia but Colonel Williams' (?) battalion (cavalry), who are stationed at Tuscumbia and patrolling the river, assisted by a great many citizens. He could not hear anything of Forrest..." (Ibid, 429)

On the 7th of May, Rowett noted: "Roddey crossed both above and below Florence this morning. His force about 5,000. I fought him two hours, but found myself nearly surrounded, and after losing a great many men, fell back on the Rawhide road. The enemy followed as far as Rawhide, when I think they struck toward the Nashville and Decatur Railroad. I am now moving toward Lawrenceburg..." At the time of his report Rowett was then two miles southeast of Lawrenceburg. (O.R. XXXIX-1, 13)

On the 17th Rowett was back in Florence and reported that "he met the enemy, under Captain Johnson at Centre Star, 14 miles this side of Florence, and whipped him and drove him across the Tennessee River, capturing 35 prisoners...(Ibid,16)

The guerrillas were operating at this time. On May 10 the bands "of Hays and Davis, were from thirty to forty in number. Captain (H. K.)McConnell (71 Ohio) drove them from ten to fifteen miles, with 16 men, to the southwest (of Winchester, Tenn.) If Roddey's cavalry should be moving in this direction his probable route will be by Lexington..." (O.R. XXXIX-1, 15) This Hays is possible Burt Hays, noted bushwhacker, who flourished about this time.

Young Joe McMurray, fighting with Alabama troops in Virginia, received word from home that the "Federals" took the rings from his sister's fingers and earrings from ears, besides cursing and abusing her.[9] These Federals were quite possibly bushwhackers, who often posed as Union soldiers.

In July, Dolph Owens and John D. Chandler were killed in the fighting around Petersburg, Virginia. Edmund D. Patterson was thrown into prison at Fort Delaware about this time, and while there met Billy Casey, also in prison.[10]

Stephen A. Jordan, in the 9th Tennessee (Biffle's) Cavalry kept a diary while in service. When his group came into North Alabama, he made the following entries:

Oct. 6, 1864 - Passed Raw Hide, camped on Tenn. River.

Oct. 7, 1864 - ...I was on guard today, command crossing the river at Oats Ferry.

Oct. 8, 1864 - Ala. 9th Reg. & 9th Battalion, 4th Tenn. crossed slough got onto an island several miles in length but narrow. Gen. Forrest was here this evening. The command commenced crossing river this evening. Co. G on picket running up & down the slough. Remained on picket.

Oct. 9, 1864 - ...Stayed on the island last night & today. Saw two Yankees was in 100 yards of them. Large force of Yankees going down the river today.

Oct. 10, 1864 - ...Crossed the river & eat a big bait. Camped at Cherokee, fighting at Chickasaw...

In the fall Confederate troops began to assemble in North Alabama in preparation for General J. B. Hood's big push into Tennessee. The Federals kept close watch.

Colonel George Spalding, 12th Tennessee Cavalry, U.S.A, wrote on September 29: "At daylight (Sept. 21) I moved on military road toward Florence (from Lawrenceburg). Learning that about 1,000 rebels held a mill known as Howell's I proceeded to said point on the 23d instant, being fired on once during the night of the 22d instant by a party of Colonel Biffle's (Roddey's) command. Before I arrived at the mills the rebel force had withdrawn, no one knowing to what point. From thence I proceeded to Squire Wilson's, military road, six miles northeast of Florence. I had heard through the country that Forrest was to cross the river near Florence. My movement toward Wilson's was for the purpose of ascertaining the truth of the said report. The moment I struck the military road I captured three wagons, belonging to Forrest's train and five of his men. At this point I ascertained that Forrest had crossed the Tennessee River on the 21st with 8,000 men and eight pieces of artillery..." (O.R. XXXIX-1, 536)

General Forrest reported of his activites: "With my troops I moved down the river to Ross' Ford, or Colbert's Shoals, and forded with little difficulty. The artillery and wagon trains were safely and rapidly ferried over and joined the main body of command five miles west of Florence. The command encamped at Florence, having crossed the river and traveled about 25 miles during the day. On the morning of the 22d (Sept.) I moved in the direction of Athens, Ala. At Shoal Creek, six miles east of Florence, I was joined by General Roddey's troops, under the command of Col. William A. Johnson, who had been previously ordered to cross the river at

Bainbridge and to join me at this place...After moving on to Masonville, I halted and ordered up the wagon train for the purpose of furnishing Col. Johnson's troops with ammunition and rations..." (O.R. XXXIX-1, 542)

Forrest continues: "On the 4th (Oct.) I halted 18 miles from Florence. On the 5th I reached Florence. Here I found the river, which my troops forded two weeks previous, swollen by recent rains. The enemy was reported advancing on the Athens road I ordered Col. Windes, of Gen. Roddey's command, to Shoal Creek with his regiment, and to hold him in check while my troops were crossing. The boats at Bainbridge were ordered down to the mouth of Cypress, at which place many of my troops were ferried over; but the next morning, the enemy making his appearance in Florence, the boats were dropped still lower down the river. The winds had made the river so rough that it was hazardous to ferry it, but the boats made regular trips day and night. But the enemy were pressing upon my rear, which was greatly endangered. At this juncture I ordered all troops on the north side of the river, with the exception of one regiment, to mount their horses and swim them across a slough about seventy yards wide to a large island, which would afford them ample protection and from which they could ferry over at leisure. Colonel Wilson was ordered to remain with his regiment and to skirmish with the enemy, and thereby divert his attention until the other troops reached the island. This strategy was successful. Every man reached the island in safety." (Ibid, 547)

Federal General Rousseau reported on October 7: "I am now twelve miles north of Florence on the military road on my way to Florence...I am satisfied that a large portion of Forrest's forces are still this side of the Tennessee River..." Another reported that "General Rousseau was at Blue River, on old military road, ten miles north of Florence..." (O.R. XXXIX-1, 625, 624). On October 8, Rousseau wrote "I am out with my forces on the reserve road, or road to Colbert's Ferry, and am at Sampson's plantation, about eight miles from Florence." (Ibid, 625) And finally, the Federals reported: "Forrest has escaped us; he crossed at Pride's Ferry, ten miles below Florence, on the 5th, leaving Florence himself about 2 p.m. that day." (Ibid, 631)

The official journal for the Second Division of the Federal Army has the following entries:

October 4 --Division marched to Rogersville, crossing Elk River, distance, 19 miles. Headquarters at Mr. Bouron's house. It rained hard all the latter part of the day. No enemy seen.

October 5 --Rainy morning. Division moved early. Stopped for dinner on Blue Water Creek; camped for night on Shoal Creek, seven miles from Florence. Headquarters at Mr. John Alexander's house.

October 6 --Cavalry outpost driven in during the night...Cavalry started for Florence but were driven back at Mrs. Huff's house...The line moved steadily on to Florence where we ascertained Forrest had crossed the night before; headquarters not changed. Captain from 2nd Michigan reported Rousseau 25 miles on Shoal Creek on the Federal Road.

October 7 --At Florence by dark, where we met Generals Rousseau, Johnson, and Steedman; some Confederates reported down the river.

October 8 --Rousseau and his troops all started down the river; division remained in camp. Captain Orr started a mill grinding corn. General Morgan and staff rode out to Cypress Creek Oct. 9.

October 9 --(Sunday) General Morgan, Capts. Wiseman, Race, and Lt. Prosser visited Jackson's Ferry where the First Brigade crossed in August 1862.

October 10--Division moved at 6 a.m...marched 19 miles...camped Second Creek; headquarters at Moses Ingram's house.

October 11--Division moved at 6 a.m...camped on Six-Mile Creek; headquarters at Mr. Pierre Farrer's house...(then on to Athens)(O.R.XXXIX-1, 633)

Lt. Col. James W. Langley, 125 Illinois Infantry, remembered the activity thus: "...It was with little difficulty that a reconnaissance was pushed through to Florence, as it was afterwards ascertained that the enemy opposing our progress thither amounted to only about 150 men. We reached the town at 1 p.m. and then learned certainly what we already began to suspect, that Forrest had escaped across the Tennessee River. At 3 p.m. we returned to Shoal Creek, reaching there about sundown. On the following morning the entire command, with the division, returned to Florence and went into camp on the southeast side of town, where we remained three days. Up to this time...it rained heavily every day, rendering the roads from Athens to Florence very muddy, besides swelling the numerous streams to their banks. These streams we were compelled to ford, with the exception of Shoal Creek, which had a good bridge. The men were drenching wet, adding greatly to the weight of their loads, and their sleep, though sound, was the sleep of exhaustion and afforded them but little rest; besides, many were barefoot and footsore. Those who fell sick by the wayside were left in houses to the care of the citizens, as we had no means of transportation. The citizens, as far as I was able to learn, uniformly treated our sick soldiers with a great deal of kindness..."(Ibid, 644)

By October 25th Biffle's Cavalry was back in Lauderdale County, and Stephen Jordan wrote:

Oct. 27, 1864--I remained in camp. Gen. Hood's army reported at Decatur.

Oct. 30, 1864--Remained in camp. Infantry crossing River.

Nov. 1, 1864 --...Hood's Army crossing river at Florence.

Nov. 2, 1864 --Carter's Reg. moved to Tuscumbia, got to camp late at night.

Nov. 3, 1864 --Camp at Tuscumbia. I remained in camp until evening then went to Florence. Very unwell. Stayed with Dr. Brock.

Nov. 4, 1864 --Remained at Dr. Brock's...

Nov. 8, 1864 --...Improving, able to go to the table. Army remains here. Forrest reported to have captured 14 boats in river, 10 transports, 4 gunboats. Review of Gen. (Stephen D.) Lee's Corps today.

Nov. 10,1864--...Eat dinner with Mrs. Louisa Bates, remained in Florence. Gen. (Frank) Armstrong's Brigade had a fight at Foster's Factory, lost two killed, several wounded...

Nov. 16, 1864--Florence, Ala. Cloudy & rainy. Day of Thanksgiving & prayer. Heard a sermon by Rev. McFerrin.

Nov. 18, 1864--Rainy & sloppy. Army crossing river today.

Nov. 19, 1864--Rainy. Brigade left Florence, went about eight or ten miles on Wayland Springs Road...

In all Hood's army spent three weeks in North Alabama, plagued by one difficulty after another. He was prevented from getting his supplies by a ten mile gap in the railroad near Corinth, Mississippi. The heavy rains prevented repair on the railroad. Even though a pontoon bridge had been thrown across the river, the rain, heavy and continuous, had caused the river to rise. After Lee's Corps had successfully made it across the river and gone into camp at Florence, the bridge was partly submerged. The approach roads were muddy and impassable. Forrest had been delayed by his destructive raid around Johnsonville, Tennessee.

On November 13 Hood himself crossed the river, but more rain delayed further troop crossings. It was not until the morning of November 21, that Hood's great invasion army was able to move out of Florence.[11]

Stephen D. Lee recalled: "On the night of the 29th I received orders to cross the Tennessee River at Florence, Ala. By means of pontoon boats, two brigades of Johnson's division were thrown across the river two miles and a half above South Florence, and Gibson's brigade of Clayton's division, was crossed at South Florence. The enemy occupied Florence with about 1,000 cavalry and had a strong picket at the old railroad bridge. The crossing at the point was handsomely executed and with much spirit by Gibson with his brigade of Louisianaians...The distance across the river was about 1,000 yards. The troops landed, and after forming charged the enemy and drove him from Florence. The crossing was spirited and reflected much credit on all engaged in it. Maj. Gen. Ed Johnson experienced considerable trouble in crossing his two brigades because of the extreme difficulty of managing the boats in the shoals. He moved from the north bank of the river late in the evening with one brigade (Sharp's Mississippi), and encountered the enemy on the Florence and Huntsville road about dark. A spirited affair took place, in which the enemy were defeated, with a loss of about 40 killed, wounded and prisoners. The enemy retreated during the night to Shoal Creek, about nine miles distant. The remainder of Johnson and Clayton's divisions were crossed on the night of the 30th and on the morning of the 31st Stevenson's division was crossed on Nov. 2..." (O.R. XXXIX-1, 811)

The Journal of Brigadier General Francis A. Shoup, C.S.A., has the following entries:

Nov. 11--Army headquarters were established last afternoon one mile south Tennessee River, Florence.

Nov. 12--The repairs on the pontoon bridge were finished this evening and it is now in good condition. Scouts report the enemy evacuated Rome and destroyed all their supplies...

Nov. 13--Army headquarters were established at Florence on the north side of the Tennessee River at 10 a.m. Cheatham's corps, with artillery, wagon trains, &c, crossed the river during the day and went into camp on Waynesborough road.

Nov. 14--Army headquarters at Florence. General Forrest arrived here this morning and was serenaded by the Tennesseans in the evening, to which he responded in a very encouraging speech. General Hood also made some remarks. Stewart's corps has not yet crossed the river. The supply train and cattle have been crossing today. (O.R. XXXIX-1, 808)

W. J. Worsham of the 19th Tennessee Infantry, Strahl's Brigade, recorded: "We started out from Florence early in the morning of November 21st, one of the coldest days of the winter, in rain, sleet, and snow. The wind blew almost a hurricane in our faces and, with the snow, was almost blinding. All day long we plodded through this storm, so slow we could hardly keep warm. Late in the evening we halted for the night, passing it without rest or comfort to our weary and cold bodies. We had gone only about twelve miles..."[12]

Many years later Col. R. H. Lindsay, of the 16th Louisiana Infantry, wrote an account of the capture of Florence. This prompted a correction by Lieut. John A. Dicks, who had served in Company E, 4th Louisiana Infantry:

"Col. Lindsay will pardon me for correcting his failing memory, in justice to the many other veterans who took an active part in the capture of Florence, other than the 16th Louisiana. I was at the time a lieutenant in Company E, 4th Louisiana Battalion, Col. John McEwing, under the command of our senior captain T. A. Bisland. All our field officers were then in hospitals, from wounds received in the Dalton-Atlanta campaign.

"I was in the third or fourth pontoon boat launched into the Tennessee River in that memorable affair. The attachment of troops engaged in the capture of Florence consisted of a detail from several if not all the regiments of the beloved Gen. R. L. Gibson's Louisiana Brigade. I believe that Col. Lindsay had command of the detachment, and the balance of his detailed account is vividly correct...Florence was garrisoned by a part of the 10th Federal Cavalry, and they were totally ignorant of the whereabouts of Hood's Army. Our division (Clayton's) had been a day or so in the vicinity of Florence, but across the river. The crossing of our troops under the fire of our artillery was a grand sight to those looking on...We had, however, more than four pontoon boats. In each boat there were nineteen men, two being sharpshooters, and in the bow, firing as skirmishers.

"Our propelling power consisted of paddles made hurriedly from fence pickets and boards from houses near by. A section of Cobb's Battery and some other Napoleon guns formed our artillery, and were masked on the bluffs near the piers of the destroyed railroad bridge. The Yankee garrison occupied an old brick warehouse near the river bank. Some of our men had strolled up and engaged the enemy in conversation, and deceived them as to the whereabouts of Hood's Army; and they were well fooled, for they seemed ignorant of all danger, leisurely lolling about the old house, some in shirt sleeves, others sitting quietly on the river bank, talking with the "Johnny Rebs." At a given signal our masked battery opened fire. The pontoons were launched, and were soon in line of battle like a genuine fleet of naval vessels. Every shell fired seemed to go direct to its mark with fuse properly cut, bursting in or close about the warehouse. Like bees from a hive, the Yankees went running in all directions. They thought not of firing at us.

"When we landed a line of battle was formed with skirmish line in front, and up Todd's Hill (as Col. Lindsey calls it) we went, and in less than one hour the Yankees were miles in the rear of Florence, except such as captured; and the town, with all its pretty women was ours. I was commanding one of the picket posts when, about dark, up came a Dutchman in blue, who had evidently been foraging, for on the pommel of his saddle were the forequarters of a fat mutton. In his broken English he inquired, "Vat droops are dem on de picket line?" When answered, "Company E, 4th Louisiana Battalion," he wheeled his horse to run, but was soon pierced in the back by four or five bullets, and came to the ground. His horse ran a short distance and stopped to graze by the roadside. We soon had horse, mutton, etc. I ate some of "dose mutton" with keen relish. Our only casualty in the capture of Florence was in the death of one of Austin's Battalion sharpshooters, killed by one of our own shells bursting short of the intended range. A piece struck the poor fellow in the back."
(Confederate Veteran, Volume 5, 1897, page 214)

The late John Johnston recalled crossing the Tennessee River during the fall operations of the Confederate Army:

"We soon reached the Tennessee River at the Colbert Shoals. Here the river spread out about a mile wide and was shallow, and ran over a wilderness of rock with a sort of rush that made the water foam. The water was quite swift and the bottom was interpersed with numerous holes or deep places, into which a horse's front or hind foot would be liable to step and bring horse and rider out of balance, and cause them to be swept down the stream.

"Led by a guide, we entered into the river without halting, and soon a long line of slow cautious moving horsemen were stretched from one side of the river to the other. Fortunately, the most of us got over safely, but a few men and horses were submerged and swept some distance downward, though I do not remember that any horses or men were drowned.

"Sometimes the water would reach our horses' knees, and probably in the next step, it would be deep enough to swim...The Tennessee River is still rushing and foaming over the rocks at Colbert Shoals--as it has been doing for centuries past--but the great majority of the host that crossed it that day have long since passed over that other river, whose waters are never crossed again..." (The Civil War Reminiscences of John Johnston, Tennessee Historical Quarterly, March 1955, 43-44.)

Hood's army came back to Lauderdale County following their disastrous defeat at Nashville in December. The retreat was covered by the cavalry troops under the command of General Forrest. Isaac Nelson Rainey wrote of the retreat:

"We reached the river which was very high at night, a dark night. The infantry had already crossed over on the pontoon bridge, and most of our cavalry. I regret I cannot remember where this bridge was; I think, however, at Bainbridge.

"Gen. Jackson, staff and escort, were among the very last to cross. A regiment of cavalry was left to hold the enemy back; we could hear the firing as we went over. It was a scarry passage. The night was very dark, the black, rushing, rearing current only a few inches under us. My young mare was in terror of the strange proceeding, but I led her along I talked to her and succeeded in soothing her. We had hardly gotten to the other bank when the small detail of men left for the purpose succeeded in cutting the ropes, though under a charge by the enemy. The chain of pontoons swung along the bank on our side without the loss of a boat..." (The Civil War Experiences of I. N. Rainey, privately published, 1965.)

The Federals had expected the Confederate troops to head for the river and on December 20 had sent ten gunboats up the Tennessee. These attempted to cross the Muscle Shoals but were unable to do so. (Nashville Union 8 Jan. 1865)

Reports from the pursuers were published in the Nashville papers:

"Below Lexington the rebels diverged from the Lamb's Ferry road and struck the river at Bainbridge, 9 miles above Florence, where the great body of their army passed over. A few detached companies and stragglers may have ferried or forded over at Lamb's or Cheatham's Ferry below Florence, but no considerable body of men escaped by these roads.

"Forrest defended himself to the last with the greatest determination. To him Hood is indebted for his escape. Forrest was compelled to abandon on the river bank about 150 supply wagons.

"Once on the other side of the river the rebels did not want to fight. A few of the pontoons, they got away though the greater part of them, were cut loose and floated away down the river. They were in great part mere wooden scows, though a few of them which they had to bridge Duck River were regular pontoons.

"From Bainbridge he (Hood) moved off southwesterly and is supposed to be presently somewhere south of Corinth..." (Nashville Union, 5 Jan. 1865)

Another report:

"We have again lost the Army of Tennessee. It is somewhere in the vicinity of the Tennessee River and may have crossed that stream ere this." (Nashville Union, 4 January 1865)

Later in January, Will A. McTeer, adjutant of the 3rd (U.S.) Tennessee Cavalry wrote:

"On the night of the 31st of December we came up with Hood's pontoon train near Russellville and burnt it. It did seem like a pity to burn them, they were so fancy, all had some fancy names: Emma, Julia, Becky Sharpe, but they were considerably scorched the last I saw of them." (Nashville Union 24 Jan. 1865)

The bushwhackers were being active as the Confederates were leaving the county. A letter, written 9 Sept. 1865, reveals that Newton Scott was "murdered by a straggling gang of guerrillas at his home in Lauderdale County, Ala., in January 1865." (From letter in Columbia Daily Herald, 19 May 1963. This family had been particularly hard hit by the war. John L. Scott had been killed at the second fight at Fort Donelson in February 1863. James Scott died in 1861, and his youngest son Martin Van Burn Scott died at Jackson, Mississippi, in November 1862. Levi J. Scott had died in prison at Camp Morton in June 1862.)

Roddey came back into the area and did his best to protect the people. In February it was reported that "About three weeks ago Roddy had several bushwhackers and murderers executed by martial law near Moulton, Ala. Some straggling soldiers robbed a widow and burned her house and are now under sentence of death." (Nashville Union 4 Feb. 1865)

In January and February 1865, troops under the command of Major General James H. Wilson began concentrating in the western part of Lauderdale County. The cantonment stretched from Gravelly Springs to Waterloo and by March 27,000 men were said to be stationed here. These troops left on March 22, going South to Selma. The goal was the destruction of the Confederate arsenal at that place. The war was over for this section.

The guerrilla and bushwhackers continued to operate, and one of the most horrible events of the war took place on Sunday, April 30:

THE MASSACRE NEAR BAILY'S SPRINGS, ALABAMA

"We have the particulars of a horrible massacre at the residence of Mr. John Wilson near Baily's Springs, Alabama...It appears that five men called at the residence of Mr. Wilson, six miles from Florence after night and demanded admittance, which was refused them. The inmates of the house were Mr. Wilson, an old man upwards of 75 years of age, Harvey Wilson, his nephew, and young

Foster, son of Judge Foster of this city, who were armed and prepared to defend themselves.

"The men outside then stated that they were soldiers from Eastport who had been out on a scout and were returning, tired and hungry. Upon this Mr. Wilson ordered that they be admitted. As soon as the door was open, they sprang in and disarmed the inmates. They then demanded of Mr. Wilson to tell where his money was, which he refused to do. They threatened to kill him if he did not tell. He replied that they could easily do that and it would make but little difference as he had but a short time to live. Mr. Wilson, still refusing to tell where his money was, was severely beaten by a portion of the men, the others having secured young Wilson and Foster. Still refusing they stripped him and laid him upon a lot of books which they had torn up and thrown upon the hearth. They then set fire to the paper which burned the old man severely but they still failed to extort from him where his money was. They then beat him again until young Wilson and Foster saying that they would kill him, begged him to tell where his money was. After considerable importunity from these young men, he told them that they would find $160 in silver under the front steps.

"Those engaged in torturing him then went out and found the money as directed. Coming in they found the old man dying. The leader of the gang then deliberately shot young Wilson through the breast, killing him dead. He then aimed at young Foster and just as the pistol fired, the latter made a motion of the body which saved his life, the ball having entered and passed through his left arm and lodging in the body; from which it was subsequently extracted. Young Foster fell on his face and feigned death, having the presence of mind enough to know that that was his only hope of escape with his life.

"In the meantime the overseer (Mr. Tweedy) who lived some distance off, hearing the noise, ran to the relief of his friends and was shot dead as he approached the door. After the murderers left, young Foster crawled out to a shed in the yard where he stayed until morning. He was then found and taken to the residence of his uncle (Mr. McAlister) in Florence where his wound, which is not thought of as dangerous was properly cared for.

"That evening the murderers returned to Mr. Wilson's and inquired of the negroes if all the men had been killed and were informed that all except young Foster were killed and that he had been taken to Florence. They appeared at the residence of Mr. McAlister that night and sought to kill young Foster and did fire three shots at Mrs. McAlister, who was discovered near a window in an upper chamber, but fortunately they missed her. We are gratified to learn that no ladies were killed or injured at Mr. Wilson's. Money was the object of the murderers." (Nashville Dispatch, 13 May 1865)

A correspondent who signed his name "Duke" wrote a further account which was published in the Nashville Union on 18 May 1865:

"Noticing an account in one of the Nashville papers of the murder of Mr. Wilson and two or three other persons, near Florence, Alabama, by a gang of bushwhackers, I send you an account of the capture and execution of a part of the cut throats, by a scouting party from the 8th Michigan cavalry, which left this place some ten days ago, under the command of Captain John H. Riggs.

"Arriving in the vicinity of Florence, and getting some little information from the citizens of their whereabouts, and all the particulars of the diabolical murder, the Captain set out to entrap them. It seemed difficult at first to get any trace or clue to their hiding places, and for a time it looked discouraging, but perseverance and shrewdness finally triumphed and two of the most noted of the gang were captured--John Campbell and Charles Oliver. Both of these individuals--or fiends in human form--at the breaking out of the war joined the rebel army and after the occupation of the State by our troops deserted the rebels and joined the Federal army, and, finally deserted and went to bushwhacking, robbing, and marauding in connection with a band of fifteen more desparadoes. Campbell lives in Florence, and his family is said to be one of the first in the place though of secesh proclivities. Oliver lives in the vicinity of Florence and is also of respectable parents.

"After their capture, Capt. Riggs instituted an examination of the affair, and the citizens in and about Florence, were called in to give in evidence for or against them. The testimony produced showed them to be the most hardened villains, and cold blooded murderers on God's footstool. Not only did they commit murder for the sake of plunder, but for personal gratification. Several instances were brought up in the evidence where they had ravished defenceless women, knocking them down in the most brutal manner if they resisted.

"A bright mulatto girl, almost white, testified that Oliver knocked her down with the butt of his pistol and then ravished her. She exhibited the bruise on her head which had not yet healed.

"After the evidence was all given in the Captain and all the officers present decided that they were guilty of the crime of murder, robbery, and rape, and ordered that they should be shot without any further ceremony.

"They were conducted one mile out of town on the military road, under a guard in charge of Lieuts. J. S. Cline and Michael Doyle, and were there executed in the manner ordered.

"Before the execution and when they saw that their fate was determined, they confessed their guilt. They claimed that they were with the party that murdered Wilson, but did not do the deed themselves. They acknowledged being implicated in more crimes than the evidence convicted them of and felt that they deserved death. They were caused to kneel down, when the fatal command was given, "make ready," "take aim," "fire," and their souls were ushered into eternity. Their bodies were turned over to the citizens for burial, and our boys again went in pursuit of more of the gang. Two others, Francis Gibson and Tom Brydges were killed. Captain Riggs being unable to find any more of the cut throats, and as his time to report back here had expired, he returned. Today Lt. Col. W. L. Buck goes out with 200 men, and will remain at Florence sometime to rid the country of these desperadoes. The country in that vicinity has been under the complete control of this gang of outlaws for a long time, and the people are praying for Federal troops to protect them. The state of things there is certainly discouraging to those peaceably inclined, and every effort ought to be made to give the people an opportunity to establish civil law. The only way to deal with these outlaws is to execute them on the spot."

Research by reputable historians confirms that Campbell and Oliver, although they did not actually kill the Wilsons (John W. and Matthew H.) that they were both members of the party that night. Some give the honor of murder to a man named Tom Clark, and some to Tom Thrasher. This is a period in the county's history worthy of more study than can be recorded in this work.

At the time of the Wilson murder, these outlaws were supposed to have made a grand raid on various citizens in Florence including John "Dutch" Kachelman, Joseph Milner, John McAlister, Dr. Hancock, Simon Forch, Dr. Hargraves, and Billy Wade.[13]

Conditions became so bad that Captain Risden D. DeFord (Company H, 6th (U.S.) Tennessee Cavalry), stationed at Pulaski, was ordered to Shoal Creek, Alabama, "for the purpose of hunting down numerous outlaws who infest that country."[14]

Clem Hammond of Lauderdale County received ten years at hard labor for being a guerrilla and for robbery. He was received at the military prison in Nashville on May 16.[15]

Early in 1865 "peace" meetings had been held throughout the state. The local groups were called the "Union" or "Loyal League," and were composed of deserters, tories, and other "renegades." The Freedman's Bureau, supposedly a labor and employment bureau, was also established during this year. At first the Union authorities conducted the bureau, but after the surrender of the Confederate troops, the management was given to loyal Union men or "carpetbaggers". Conditions became so unbearable under the influence of these two organizations that some sort of regulatory group seemed necessary. Out of this bitterness came the Ku Klux Klan. (Early members of the group called it Kuklux Klan.)[16]

The Florence Journal, under the ownership and editorship of David R. Lindsay, flourished after the war. An issue of June 20, 1866, remains. From this paper we learn something about the business life of Florence at the time. Andrew Brown owned Brown's Jewelry Store, which was located in the old building formerly occupied by A. M. Hannay. Thomas J. Fry advertised as a local undertaker with a cabinet shop opposite the jail--whose residence was in the jail.

Information was offered, via an advertisement, for those interested in the death and burial of any Alabama soldier, or other prisoner of war, at Camp Douglas, Illinois.

Lawyers were S. J. Matthews (at Lexington, Ala.), Alexander McAlexander (office in White Building west of the courthouse), James and J. B. Irvine (office west of the courthouse), E. A. O'Neal (west of public square), Robert McFarland (office in White Building), and Thomas Allan Jones (office in building occupied by B. F. Karsner, north of courthouse).

Carlotta Billiard Saloon, owned by Warson and Petty, was located in the alley back of the Journal office.

M. P. Asher announced that he was with James Brock and son--dry goods, hides, beeswax, tallow, cornmeal--located opposite and east of the courthouse. R. A. Ellis had a boot shop four doors south of the Campbell Hotel.

J. Brahan Patton was the agent for the Central Mining and Petroleum Company, who prospected for minerals and petroleum.

Dry goods were sold at the general store of John Harrison in South Florence. Ward and Hartman had a boot shop in the small brick building located immediately below the courthouse. Wilcox and Hedden operated the Florence Book and Music Store on the west side of Court Street, next to the Campbell Hotel. Drugs were sold at No. 9 Main Street, opposite the Campbell House, by Smith and Burtwell--a firm composed of Alexander H. Smith, S. Hardy Smith, and James Burtwell. Joseph Milner also advertised his drug store.

Greek and Hyde were commission merchants located in the Gookin Warehouse at the river and had for sale corn, food, guns, and furniture.

Ellis & Company were again advertising the summer watering place Bailey Springs.

Grocers included Hester and Wood, located at the old drug store of Wood and Stewart, next to Patton, Weems & Co. Powers and Lansford sold dry goods and groceries at the stand formerly occupied by Hillman and Hancock, opposite and east of the courthouse.

In September, 1866, the body of William Lang, German peddler, was found murdered on the plantation of Mitchell Malone. Robbery was thought to have been the motive. The peddler had been long overdue in Florence when a search was made for him.[17] Jonathan J. Paulk married Amanda Austin on August 22, 1866.[18]

Lauderdale County registers were appointed in June 1867, of loyal Union men and at least one man of color: Claiborne Wesson, Samuel Hyde, and John Rapier, the latter listed as a free man of color in 1850.[19]

In July 1867 the Union League was flourishing in the county and had held a large meeting at the College Grove. Someone tore the flag down from in front of the store of Tenge & Hyde, and desecrated the banner. An indignation meeting was held because the flag had been removed from the Freedman Bureau.[20]

In October the following delegates were sent from Lauderdale County to the State Convention, by Military Order 76: James W. Stewart and James T. Rapier, negro. James Rapier had been born in 1840 in Florence and studied law. He was the representative to the 43rd Congress from 1873-75.[21] He had been educated by his white father--in Canada.

In March 1867 the most disastrous flood of recorded history paralyzed the Tennessee Valley. This flood cut off communications and railroads, washed away bridges, destroyed mills and an estimated million bushels of corn. The flood crest reached Chattanooga on March 11, and continued on into Alabama. The river was reported to be "ten miles wide" near the mouth of Duck River in Tennessee.[22]

The lot of the former Federal soldier was not easy in postwar North Alabama. One such soldier was murdered in the dining room of the Franklin House in Tuscumbia in March 1868 in front of forty diners by Robert Kernahan, described as "of Florence." Kernahan, who was intoxicated, was an ex-Confederate soldier and regarded as a "desperate and dangerous man." He drew a revolver and shot Collins near the heart.[23]

Gossip about the legality of his marriage disturbed William T. Pennington, whose marriage had been performed by a "marrying squire" in the southern part of Maury County, Tennessee. Pennington, a former Federal soldier, came to Tennessee to be married after the war. Finally, after much talk, he wrote:

       State of Alabama, Lauderdale County
       Sept. the 11th, 1869

Mr. M_____
Dear Sir: I Seat my selph to Wright you A Few lines, To inform you that I and famly is Well, hoping these Few lines ma Come Safe to hand and Find you and your famly in good health.

...thare has ben a general talk here that I am living With my Wife With out being married To her, and is goying To return me for the Same, and I Shal of cours Stand mi ground.

I Want you if you please To rite A letter to Mr Wm Lucus To Certify him of of my being legally and according to Law and get the citizens of the village to assign it.

I am pretty certain that it Will Settle the Question; but provided it does not I shal Be oblige to have you and Mr. William G. Duke Summonded as my Witnesses to certfy the same.

You Will direct your letter to Mr. William Lucus, Waterloo, Alabama.
(signed) William T. Pennington[24]

On December 13, 1867, Robert Miller Patton of Lauderdale County was inaugurated as Governor of Alabama. Patton, a conservative old-line Whig, was "swept into the governor's chair by a vote almost as large as the combined votes of his opponents" in an election held by the Constitutional Convention in 1867. He served until 1868 when his administration was ended by a decree of Congress.[25]

CHAPTER IV

In 1870 the population of Florence was 2,003. The new year was only a few days old when North Alabama was electrified by the "double murder" of two nephews of General Gideon J. Pillow at LaGrange in Colbert County. This tragedy is still remembered as the Pillar murder.

An account of the time follows:

"Just before going to press we have learned from a trustworthy gentleman who lives in the neighborhood of Leighton, Ala., a true statement of the facts connected with the murder of Granville and William Pillow. Granville was in his own house, alone, when he was first shot. He went to a neighbor's, Horn's, and after sending for a doctor, he told Horn that his murderers had given their names before the shooting as Hugh Phillips and Granville Spangler. Young Horn, on his way for the doctor, met some disguised men, to whom he told all that Granville had said. The maskers asked if Mr. Pillow had given any names, and receiving an affirmative answer, they went immediately to old Mr. Horn, or Horner's, and waited about an hour for Mr. Pillow to die. They then went in and drove everybody out of the house, and though Mr. Pillow was unconscious and probably dying, they shot him in the breast, killing him instantly. Granville talked to Mr. Horn, about the shooting until he could not speak and then wrote down the balance. This paper the murderers destroyed. Young Phillips was engaged to be married to a young lady near Lagrange to whom he acknowledged he had helped to murder Granville, but that he had been urged and instigated to it by influential parties of the neighborhood. The young lady went to Mr. Pillow's funeral next day, and told on her lover. Spangler was also at the funeral, and getting alarmed he and Phillips fled the country. One of the murderers came back after daylight, and stayed with the corpse. He it was that carried the dispatch to Leighton, and sent it to Mrs. Pillow at Columbia, telling her that her sons had been killed.

"William Pillow was doubtless killed on the same night and by the same party that murdered Granville, but nothing positive is known, except that he was found in a sink-hole, shot all to pieces, and with the throat-latch of a bridle around his neck. Everything goes to show that Mr. William Pillow must have reached home just as his brother Granville was shot, and recognizing the murderers, they left their first victim, pursued him. He was shot in the back, and must have made a desperate struggle for his life. Public sentiment is very strong against one or two persons in the neighborhood, and some fear is felt that there will be some lynching done."[1]

There was some attempt on the part of the radicals at this time to link this murder with the Kuklux Klan, but the evidence was against this. Robbery appears to have been the motive.

Advertisements for Bailey Springs were again appearing in newspapers throughout the area:

"The proprietors of this Watering Place take pleasure in informing their friends and patrons that they have completed their arrangement for the comfort and enjoyment of their guests, and that the Hotel is now open for their reception.

"The efficiency of these waters in cases of Dropsy, Scrofula, Dysepsia, diseases peculiar to females, Chronic Diarrhea, and all diseases of the SKIN and KIDNEYS is too well established to need comment.

"A good band will serve the Ballroom, and the tables will be supplied with the best the country affords, while the fishing in Shoal Creek, and the hunting in the surrounding woods, offer their usual attractions to visitors.

"Route, via Memphis and Charleston Railroad, to Florence, Ala., thence by Capt. J. T. Farmer's Stage Line, nine miles to the Springs. Terms: $15 a week, $50 a month. For descriptive pamphlet, circular, or information, concerning special diseases, address Ellis & Co., Proprietors, H. M. Moody, M. D., Resident Physician."[2]

Some were disappointed, however, in their quest for good health: "Colonel Samuel P. Walker died at Bailey Springs where he had gone for his health. He was a leader of the Democratic party in Shelby County, Tennessee, and nephew of President Polk."[3]

A "Marriage Romantique" claimed the attention of the people in Florence in the fall of 1870, when Narcissa Weakley eloped with William Milliken:

"Old folks are the most unwise folks in the world to manage a love affair. They invariably make their daughters love a young fellow, by objecting, hating, persecution, and making a martyr of him. Capt. Millican, of Paducah, Ky., fell in love with Miss Mary Narcissa Weakley, daughter of Gen. Weakley, a millionaire of Florence, Ala. The old gentleman opposed the match. Capt. Millican, who served gallantly through our late war, went to Florence a week or so ago, and referred the old gentleman to any merchant of Paducah, as to his character, but he was inexorable. Finally, Millican's friend stole the young lady across the Tennessee River, where Millican attempted to procure a license. But the laws of Alabama would not let a license be issued unless the parents were willing or the young lady was 21 years old.

"They dared not go back to Florence, so the runaways came on to Tennessee, whose mild laws allow a couple to be married with as much freedom as Chicago permits them to be cut asunder. Capt. M. first thought of going to Nashville before he married, but while passing through our beautiful country, he remembered that his army friend, Jas. B. Childress lived here, and that determined him to stop and be married at Columbia. Sure enough, he found that gentleman, and what is more, very willing and able to assist him. Col. L. D. Myers was consulted as to the laws of Tennessee on the subject of marriage, who soon assured them that the marriage could take place according to law.

"The young lady being a devout church woman wanted Rev. Beckett to perform the ceremony. Mr. Beckett was loth to marry a runaway couple, but finally his objections were overruled by kind and fatherly considerations, and he determined to unite the two young people in the holy bonds of matrimony at St. Peter's church. The only thing now lacking was, who should give the bride away, Mr. Childress or the gentleman who stole her? It was decided that the man that stole her had the most right to give her away, and it was so done. The happy bridegroom immediately telegraphed to the bride's Father what had happened."[4]

A canal around the shoals in the river were still of concern in the 1870s. A surveying party of twenty men from Chattanooga, with two flatboats loaded with supplies, came into the area in June 1871 to survey the canal route from Brown's Ferry to Florence around the shoals. Editorial comments of the time were: "It is a shame to our country and a disgrace to its legislation that this important work should be so long neglected. There is not another stream of its size in the civilized world of so little use to navigation. It drains one of the richest and most fertile and productive sections in the country."[5]

In March 1876 a small pox scare originated from Florence. A colored man, who led the blind wood-sawyer from the Muscle Shoals area all over the region, became sick in Middle Tennessee and died. The rumor got out that he died of small pox.[6] People were considering "shotgun quarantines" against anyone from North Alabama. Finally, M. D. Long, who was surgeon on the Muscle Shoals canal at this time, wrote from Covington, Lauderdale County, denying that the small pox was raging there. This letter calmed those who had been afraid of an epidemic being spread.[7]

Plans for the Centennial were being set in motion in 1876. All the cities and states were going to send items to be displayed at this grand celebration of the first hundred years of the United States. The centennial was to be held in Philadelphia. When a woman at Florence "gave birth to a baby which had two large and distinct faces and a lump on the back of its head resembling a chignon," there were those who thought it should be sent for exhibition. The child was stillborn and the "attending doctor said it had brains enough for six grown men." He paid the mother $20 for the body and "sold it to another doctor for $500." The latter actually planned to send it to the exposition.[8]

In 1878 a yellow fever epidemic broke out in Memphis. In the first two weeks more than 25,000 people fled and sought refuge elsewhere. The disease spread into North Alabama and made its appearance in Florence. The first report of the disease was dismissed as an alarm and an unidentified writer wrote from Florence:

"I have not believed at anytime that yellow fever could be propagated at this place. It has been one of the most healthy places in the United States. All the sickness, or nearly all, that we have had this summer was caused by a slough on this side of an island in the Tennessee, made recently in order to clean out the one side of the river. Some think it is the pond, near where the most of the sickness has been and is now...The nurse who was sent from Memphis said it was not yellow fever...There was quite a panic after Dr. Saunders pronounced it yellow fever. Dr. Saunders' eyesight is not good..."[9]

Despite these comforting assurances, the disease proved to be yellow fever. W. M. Wood was chosen secretary of the local relief committee and he reported on October 12 "Thirty-two cases of yellow fever on hand." He made a call for money for the destitute, for medicine, and for coffins.[10]

By October 16 five additional cases were reported at Florence and some deaths, among those who died was Miss Nora Rice.[11] By October 18, when the epidemic began to subside, there had been 38 deaths. Four nurses were sent to Florence by the Howard Association, the contemporary Red Cross which had been organized about 1857 among clerks in a New Orleans store. (Their work was financed by gifts.) The total deaths for Florence at the end of the epidemic were 42 in number--19 white, 23 colored.[12]

One section in the Florence City Cemetery has a number of burials for victims of this epidemic. The stone of the Reverend Joel W. Whitten has "died of yellow fever October 20, 1878--a martyr to his Christian fidelity". Many of the victims were never marked.[13]

The Florence Gazette was still the leading newspaper in the 1880s. An issue for February 28, 1880, adds to the story of the times. Among the deaths were:

"Died near Centre Star, Miss Martha Jones, of pneumonia on Sunday.
"Died in Colbert's Reserve on Monday, Mac Coburn, son of John Coburn.
"Killed on Section 8 on Muscle Shoals Canal last week, Dow McWilliams, age 16...foot caught in car and terribly mutilated..."

Marriages were recorded for Billy Williams to Mary F. Matheny, and H. F. Blalock to M. L. Cox. There was a non-resident notice in the case of Anthony Garrett vs Lucy Garrett.

The court had decided that John Mayfield should not have a new trial and he was to be hanged on March 7. This issue gave no details of Mayfield's crime.

Advertisements were for: Morrison and Chisholm, undertakers, located on Main Street next door and north of Whitten's; L. C. Hudson, grocer; C. B. Eldred, Florence Marble Works; Baylis B. Shane & Thomas B. Ingram, boots, shoes; T. E. Brown, proprietor, Carlotta Saloon; Samuel A. Diehl, tailor, located over the store of Samuel L. Young; Andrew Brown, watchmaker & jeweler on Main Street; J. R. Price, book store, one door north of Milner's; Dr. Wm. M. Price, proprietor of Price's Book Store; A. J. Walker, dealer in dry goods; James D. Saunders, sign painter; George W. Karsner, dictator of the Pioneer Lodge No. 247, Knights of Honor; Miss B. M. White, dressmaker; W. T. Whitten, tax collector.

The grand jury was announced and the members were W. M. Pratt, James R. Hamm, James Hancock, A. Brown, James McPeters, J. G. Hines, H. C. Hyde, T. B. Killen, John D. Nance, J. M. Cunningham, C. S. W. Paulk, W. E. Warren, W. C. Davidson, Jasper Parker, P. M. Broadfoot, J. J. White, T. H. Peeden, and H. Richardson.

Mrs. Bettie L. Jones had received letters of administration for the estate of J. O. Jones, deceased.[14]

On Friday afternoon, March 11, 1881, about 3 o'clock, Alexander G. Smith, who was U. S. Army paymaster for the Muscle Shoals Canal, was stopped by three masked horsemen "about two miles from Florence" and robbed of $5,200--$500 in gold, $4,500 in 50s, 20s, and smaller currency, and $200 of Paymaster Smith's own money. This successful broad-daylight hold-up was the work of two of America's most renowned outlaws--Jesse and Frank James. Their partner was "Wild Bill" Ryan, alias Tom Hill. The robbers forced Smith to accompany them for about ten miles, where they abandoned him in unfamiliar country. He wandered all night through the thick forest in the hilly, sparsely populated area, and on Saturday about noon stumbled into camp on Bluewater Creek. In February 1884, Frank James, under heavy guard, was brought back to Alabama to stand trial for this bold robbery. The trial was held in Huntsville. James was found "not guilty".[15]

In 1883 the streets of Florence were lit by gas lamps. There were 39 to 40 lamps in town and Simon Simpson was the city lamplighter, who kept the lamps trimmed and burning.[16]

In June 1886, William Sherrod, W. B. Wood, and possibly others formulated the idea of the "Florence Boom" which reached its peak about 1889. Industry flourishing during this period included, among others, the Florence Land, Mining Co., W. B. Wood Furnace Company, Florence Coal, Coke & Iron Co., several railroad interests, William H. Brundige & Co., iron machinery, Florence Cotton Compress, Florence Wagon Factory, Florence Wood-Ware Works.

A letter from Florence during this period:

November 21, 1888

Dear Lynch,
I have been here and out in the country about fifteen miles for four weeks and I can say that I have found every one social and pleasant, and have spent a charming time. My business has allowed me time to be in a certain degree social...The past week I spent four days with three other boys at the home of Mr. W. C. Keys, and we all had a royal time hunting and various other amusements which came to hand.

Tuesday night one of Florence's leading druggists came out to participate.

Florence is growing fast and with no unlooked for hindrance will be a city in a short while. Where was wild uncut thickets seven months ago, now are builded large brick manufacturing buildings and in operation; several other enterprises are in the course of construction and will be in operation in a short while which will swell the population to about 8,000 souls...I think Florence is the coming city of the south as to manufacturing.

King cotton holds sway now and commands a good price--$9\frac{1}{4}$ to 9.2.10 (?) and the streets are blockaded from day to day with wagons from the country bringing it in and lots of it is sold on the river which never comes to town. I have looked at cotton in all stages until I am almost tired of it...

Yellow fever was at Decatur during the fall. We will bring some disinfectant or preventative with us when come up or we will be contaminated...I saw a potato at Smithsonia which weighed $6\frac{1}{4}$ and a turnip at Woodlawn weighing $7\frac{1}{2}$ pounds. How is that for the poor lands of Alabama?...
St. E.[17]

Edward Asbury O'Neal, Florence lawyer, was elected Governor of Alabama in 1882, and re-elected in 1884. He was considered a most forceful man and had been a brilliant soldier during the Civil War, rising in three years from private to brigadier general. "He was alert and fearless and a notable campaign orator."[18]

In 1890 the population of Florence was 6,012, as compared with 1,359 in 1880. The "boom" had at least accomplished some measure of growth.

In 1893 at least three papers flourished--the Florence Herald, Florence Times, and the Florence Gazette. It is not known if the Florence Banner were still in publication at this time or not--there are only issues for the 1880s for this paper. Some items of interest for the period:

<u>Florence Herald</u> -- 7 Sept. 1893
R. T. Killen of Greenhill has a 36 year old gander. J. J. Moore is president of the Greenhill Academy.

<u>Florence Herald</u> -- 14 Sept. 1893
Mrs. W. E. Temple died Saturday...T. D. Pruitt has moved to Florence from Pruitton.

<u>Florence Times</u> -- 25 March 1893
Wash Strickland of Spain threw his child against the walls of the house...He is a man of unsavory reputation and not the first time in trouble with the law...child was five years old.

<u>Florence Times</u> - 2 Sept. 1893
John Dewberry died Wednesday.

<u>Florence Gazette</u> -- 7 Sept. 1893
Thomas W. Steele of Tuscumbia found not guilty. He had been charged with killing Thomas W. Goodwin on May 13, 1892...It was announced that there were 1400 school age children in Florence.

<u>Florenze Gazette</u> - 14 Sept. 1893
Editor: Isaac S. Barr. George W. Seawright advertises that he is a boot and shoe maker; Sam Greenhill announces that his boot and shoe shop is located on Mobile Street...Mrs. Leelia Temple, daughter of Dr. L. P. Young of Mississippi died on Saturday and buried in City Cemetery.

Negro cow thieves have been captured at South Florence.

Florence Gazette - 21 Sept. 1893
George W. Foster died September 15 in Robinsonville, Mississippi, age 49 years and nine months. He was born December 12, 1843 and came to Florence when he was five years old. He was known as "Wash" Foster and had been a Confederate soldier. He was buried in the City Cemetery.

On Friday the home of J. M. Ellis on Tennessee Street was robbed...Charley Key (colored), age 20, was arrested for stealing $135 from John D. Wade...Robert L. Glenn had married Miss Mamie Hayes in "a brilliant wedding in Monroe, La."

The editor wrote: "It would be a God-send if something could be done to induce the loafers in Florence to go to the country and go back to cotton."

Florence Gazette - 5 October 1893
Twenty of the best citizens of Tuscumbia were arrested last week for gambling... John Kernachan is erecting a steam and corn mill and cotton gin at Bainbridge.

Many deaths for the period were caused by the open fires of the homes when clothes would catch fire at the open grates. Mrs. Jane Pool burned to death at Cloverdale in April 1893 when her clothes caught fire. Her husband was deaf and did not hear her screams for help.

The old Lauderdale Hotel burned in December 1894.[19] Home and building fires were particularly disastrous. "The Hawthorne House at Florence burned on February 5, 1897, owned by A. H. Hovey of Springfield, Mass."[20] "Wagon Factory at Florence is burning." The damages were believed to be $27,000.[21] This fire was despite the existence of the factory's automatic sprinkler system, fire house, and own fire brigade.[22]

In 1894 the beginnings of a Florence institution were announced:

"Ben Rogers, Jr., left Friday for New York to buy goods. He will open a Racket Store at Florence."[23]

And,

"B. A. Rogers, Sr., and family arrived in this city last week to make this their home and are keeping house on Poplar Street."[24]

The Confederate monument was erected in 1897 in the intersection of Court Street and Tennessee Street. This spawned a local controversy. Some argued that the correct place was in the City Cemetery. Others wanted it on the courthouse lawn as it was an impediment to traffic. The latter group was victorious and the statue was moved to the courthouse lawn. When the new courthouse was erected, the statue was moved a third time.[25]

The Spanish-American War in 1898 was the shortest and, perhaps the most decisive in the history of the country. There were only 114 days of actual fighting, and the United States emerged from this war as one of the colonial powers. "All soldiers who go to Cuba are to be tagged" read the announcement and the "dog tag" came into being.[26] Each soldier was to wear a small aluminum tag around his neck. This tag was to be stamped with a number, the letter of his company, battery, and regiment. Many men from Lauderdale County served in this war. Among these were Robert Brown, Andrew J. Sharp, Henry J. Moore, and others, whose names were not available.[27]

The local Firenze Club was organized in the 1890s, about 1895. Some of the early members of this literary club were Mrs. A. B. Camper, Mrs. W. P. Campbell, Mrs. G.H. Smith, Mrs. Emmet O'Neal, Mrs. S. J. Price, and Mrs. Lucy Humphries. One outgrowth of this club's early work was the old Southern Library. This library was formed about 1890 and at first occupied a room in the basement of the courthouse. Later the library had a room at the Florence States Teachers College's Bibb Graves Hall. When the local public library was organized, the books were given to the new library.[28]

Marriage records for this decade include names of numerous people familiar to present residents: Weaver Fuqua to Mary Cunningham, 28 July 1897; A. A. Jackson to Ollie D. Earnest, 13 Feb. 1898; Charles Fielder to Mary Morris, 21 December 1898; Alex Locker to Flora Beckus, 14 Feb. 1899; W. D. Moomaw to Lula Young, 26 March 1899; Joseph D. Moomaw to Lizzie D. Townsley, 28 May 1899; Jordan Nipper to Sallie Carter, 19 Dec. 1897; Heslip Armstead to Margaret Parker, 28 March 1886; and George Armistead, colored, to Callie Vaughn, colored, 19 August 1899.[29]

In December 1899 John B. Weakley was elected to a second term as mayor without any opposition. Aldermen and their wards were R. L. Bliss (1), Hugh Boyle (2), Andrew J Smith (3), P. A. Patrick (4), B. B. Garner (5), T. J. Phillips (6), and C. A. Sullivan (7).[30] At this time the old city administration announced that it had reduced the city's indebtedness $20,000, opened several new streets, improved other streets, retired the old city script, erected two new school houses, and placed the fire department on a firm basis.[31]

Porter Hughes, a young farmer in the county, forged an order for $9 on firm of Jackson & Douglas, and was arrested and taken to a jail in Athens. A Lauderdale County deputy went after him and while they were at depot waiting for a train, Hughes escaped. He was recaptured.[32]

Philadelphia Furnace was put into blast on November 25, 1899, and was reported to be the largest in the state.[33]

C. S. W. Paulk, who owned a powder gourd of 1776, brought the relic into to town for the people of Florence to see.[34] An exciting event of December 1899 was a fight in the rear of Milner's Drug Store between Lewis Bibb, 17, son of Professor Lockhart Bibb, and a clerk in the store, and Bob Buckingham, the colored porter. Bibb cut the porter's throat and split one of his ears in two. Bibb was arrested.[35]

By 1900 the population of Florence was 6,478.

On January 9, 1900, William B. McClure, probate judge, died. In his term the cornerstone of the second Lauderdale County courthouse had been laid.

In November 1901 the first automobile was seen on the streets of Florence, and the sight created "a great sensation". The memorable date was November 27, 1901. The owner of the car was a drummer from Decatur, who "entertained the crowds on the streets by maneuvering his machine in a very skillful manner."[36]

This year also saw the completion of the Florence sewerage system under the direction of City Engineer A. G. Negley. The contractor for the work had been Thomas Crowe.[37]

Dr. Lee Fowler Duckett came to Florence to practice medicine in 1901, although he had been in the county practicing since 1896--coming from Wayne County, Tennessee.[38] Orlan Benton Hill was sheriff of Lauderdale County this year and served until 1907. His term was extended by a special act of the Legislature.[39]

In January 1902 the first free delivery of mail was started. Letters could be sent for two cents at this time and postal cards, one cent.40

One of the worst floods in the history of the county occurred on March 28, 1902. Bridges on Cypress Creek, the Gunwaleford and Waterloo bridges, were washed away. Two bridges over Shoals Creek on the Huntsville and Military Roads were demolished by the high waters. The Huntsville Road bridge over Bluewater Creek, Butler Creek Bridge near Pruitton were destroyed. The trestle work on Second Creek at Waterloo was moved about two feet. The bridge on Little Cypress Creek on the Rawhide Road was damaged slightly. The steel approaches to the bridge over Bluewater Creek at Hostler's Mill was wrecked and damage estimated at $400.41 Other damages for this time included:

> "Charlie Paulk lost fifty sheep during the high water...Sharp's Mill was totally destroyed--parts of it were seen at different places on the creek. Big Cypress Creek was six feet above the highest known water mark; little Cypress five feet above high water mark...Jim Sharp lost two yearlings. Sheep had to be put in the loft of John Reeder's barn and the family had to leave home. Bretherick's Mill was also destroyed. T. B. Killen on Bluewater Creek near Greenhill suffered the loss of crib and corn and his family had to leave home. The abutment of a bridge on the Lexington road was also washed away...It was stated that flood waters were 10 feet above the floor of the Waterloo bridge..."42

The Florence Iron and Coal Company was organized in 1902 by Henry J. Moore. This firm began with a capacity of 15 tons a day and within 25 years had increased to 40 tons.43 In this year Joseph P. May, former captain in the Hungarian army, moved to Florence.44

In April 1903 Dr. W. J. Callaway moved to Florence and began his practice.45

In July 1905 an affray at Rogersville was a topic of the day:

> BULLET IN HEAD--Florence, Ala., July 31.--A difficulty which came near ending fatally occurred yesterday at Rogersville, a small hamlet, 25 miles east of Florence. Olim Grissom and Edgar Thornton, two farmers about 21 years old, were the combatants.
>
> Five weeks ago Grissom ran away with and married a sister of Thornton despite the objections of the Thornton family, and since then trouble has been expected by the friends of the two men, Thornton having sent threatening messages to Grissom. Sunday the two men met for the first time since the marriage, some two hundred yards from Mt. Bethel Church, where the Lauderdale County Sunday School Convention was in session. After a few hot words they engaged in a fist fight in which Thornton came off victor.
>
> There were no witnesses to the affair and the two tell conflicting stories as to what happened after Thornton let Grissom up from the ground where he had him down. Thornton, in what he supposed to be a post-mortem statement, said that as he arose Grissom pulled his pistol and shot him. After the affray Grissom fled.46

In August 1906 it was announced that the Florence Synodical Female College was to be pulled down to make way for a new $50,000 post office building.47 This college had been established at Florence in 1847. Only one of the original buildings remains and is now used as the Elks Home on East Tombigbee Street.

In 1906 young Henry A. Bradshaw came to Florence and joined the law firm of Ashcraft and Bradshaw. He practiced law until the outbreak of World War I when he retired to enter the service of the Red Cross and served overseas. Following the war he returned to Florence and resumed his law practice.48

In March 1907 a lynching at Florence created considerable excitement:

> On March 24, 1907, a mob estimated at between 200 to 300 men mobbed and killed Cleveland Hardin, a negro, who attempted to outrage Mrs. B. F. Rice on Friday before. He was captured one mile below Florence on the Tennessee River. He admitted his guilt but never said anything more. He was brought before Mrs. Rice who identified him and then fainted. She was revived and asked what she wanted done to him. She said to do anything they wanted and fainted again.
>
> A large part of the angry crowd was for burning him, but Mr. Rice said shoot him. He was taken one mile from the Rice home, tied to a tree. Mr. Rice, with a Winchester rifle, fired the first shot. This was followed by a fusillade. It was estimated 1,000 bullets were in his body. The body was left tied to a tree.
>
> The sheriff of Lauderdale County had tried to get the crowd to surrender the negro, but the crowd refused.49

Only ten years before the Lauderdale County sheriff's department and the city police had come under something of a cloud of distrust and suspicion. Items such as "The Florence Standard Journal says the sheriff of Lauderdale County has been drinking too much whiskey and also asks that two city policemen be investigated for immorality and official prostitution."50 And a few days later, "Three houses of ill fame in Florence in southeast part of city declared public nuisances and must get out in ten days."51 Jail escapes happened rather frequently: "Pomeroy Chambliss, who was arrested a few days ago by officer James White in Florence, was released on Wednesday night by unknown parties who had key to jail."52 Such items as these were no longer being found, to any great extent, after the turn of the century.

In June 1907 Judge Charles P. Almon of Lauderdale County made what became known as Judge Almon's Goose Decision throughout the state:

> June 14.---Judge Chas. P. Almon of the Lauderdale County Circuit Court has been called upon to decide a knotty problem and one which has never before been raised in any State in the Union. Seven turkeys owned by M. F. Jackson were killed on the track of the Louisville & Nashville Railroad a few miles north of Florence and the owner brought suit against the road for $10 damages. The question was raised as to whether a turkey is an animal or an obstruction in the same sense of the statute, which required the alarm whistle to be sounded and brakes put down and every possible means employed to stop the train when "an animal or other obstruction" appears on the track. A somewhat similar case was cited by the defense and the opinion of Judge Wilkes of the Tennessee Supreme Court read in which three geese were run over by a railroad train. The decision in question recites that "birds have wings to move them quickly from places of danger and it is presumed they will use them; a violent presumption in the case of a goose--an animal which appears to be loth to stoop from its dignity to escape a passing train. But the line must be drawn somewhere and we are of the opinion that the goose is the proper bird to draw it."

Judge Almon in his decision avoided the dangerous point as to whether turkeys and "animals or obstructions" as contemplated in the statute and gave the verdict in favor of the defendant on the ground that the plaintiff did not show recklessness or common law negligence on the part of the defendant.[53]

The caves, mounds, and Indian sites throughout the county have long provided entertainment for those who have some interest in digging and exploration. Doublehead Cave in the eastern portion of the county has been periodically examined and explored through the years, although J. N. McCarley, in his brief memoirs, was convinced that Doublehead never worked this cave as was thought. His opinion was based on statements by people who had lived near the old chief.[54] J. H. Simpson was a well known treasure hunter of Florence and in May 1908 news of his work was reported:

> Last Saturday J. H. Simpson, who has been engaged for some time in a search for hidden treasure in the numerous caverns in the bluffs of the Tennessee River opposite Florence, had been digging in a room of a cave that ran far back underground, and laid his pick down in the glare of the lamp to remove dirt, and the pick disappeared! The diggers thought they were nearing the site of an old Indian treasure and an old Indian spirited their pick away. In all his searches he has found only one ancient piece of pottery complete--but many broken ones.[55]

In 1912 the United States made some settlements of claims dating from the Civil War. Two claims from Lauderdale County were among those settled in January 1912: Gravelly Springs Baptist Church received $725, and the Waterloo Missionary Baptist Church, $615.[56]

Emmett O'Neal of Florence served as Governor of Alabama from 1912 to 1916, and according to historians was "one of the best executives Alabama ever had." He had been education at the Florence Wesleyan University and the University of Alabama. His legal training was received in his father's law office and after he was admitted to the bar he became a full partner. He was the first governor to occupy the "Governor's Mansion" in Montgomery. Under his leadership there was considerable growth and expansion in the public school system of Alabama; he inaugurated rural school libraries; and he created the state highway commission.[57] He was described as a master of oratory, whose flaming speeches were convincing and sincere, and as a man personally incorruptible and high-minded.[58] He was the son of Governor Edward Asbury O'Neal, and they were the only father and son governors in the history of Alabama.[59]

In December 1913, Henry J. Willingham, native of St. Clair County, came to Florence to be president of the college and served for many years.[60] He had a long and distinguished career in the field of education in Alabama.

C. W. Ashcraft was mayor of Florence from 1910 to 1912. After the outbreak of World War I he was in charge of the Red Cross relief work here.[61]

In 1917 William R. Harrison was superintendent of the Florence City Schools. He left and was followed by Flavius Thompson Appleby, native of Marshall County, Tennessee, who moved to Florence in this year.[62]

On April 4, 1917, the United States declared war and a large military force began to be assembled. William F. McFarland served as chairman of the Lauderdale County Draft Board and headed several Liberty bond drives.[63] James Carroll Roberts, grandson of James Roberts, one of the county's early settlers, acted as Government Appeal agent for the county during the war.[64]

The most important event at home during this war was the construction of Wilson Dam and the adjacent nitrate plants. Construction gave employment to many and brought many new residents into the county. In October 1918:

> U. S. Nitrate No. 2, largest of its kind in America, was put into operation at noon on October 26, and will begin operation on the first. Nitrate of munitions will be produced within sixty days. Work was severely handicapped by labor shortage and a severe influenza epidemic. Even so, the contractors completed the nitrate construction in 65 days ahead of schedule. Construction, totaling $40,000,00, began eight months ago. Over 20,000 mechanics and laborers have been employed.
>
> The plant was turned over to Lt. Col. Fred H. Wagner, ordnance department of the army, who pressed the button to turn on the current into the great electric furnace. No. 1 is now under construction.[65]

The local papers were full of deaths from the great "flu" epidemic of this year:

> Mrs. Ed Bivens died October 11, flu, survived by husband and 13 year old son...Mrs. Sid Dabney died 21 October...Mrs. Rollie Green died October 19...[66] Emmet Hurst died October 8, age 9 years 10 months...Infant of Mr. and Mrs. Nora Hill died October 20...Bessie Vickery, age 9, died...Matilda Eveleen Clemmons, daughter of Mr. and Mrs. Alex Clemmons died October 17, was sick only nine days, age 1 year 8 months...Neil Wisdom, 19, died October 20 of Spanish influenza and pneumonia...Tommie Taylor died October 25 of Spanish influenza and pneumonia...James Stevenson died October 18 of Spanish influenza and measles...[67]
>
> Baby daughter of Mr. and Mrs. Bob Lawson died October 23...[68] Lillie Atkinson died November 12 of influenza and pneumonia...Leslie L. Goodman died November 9 of influenza and pneumonia...Bob Lawson died November 8...Pat Muse died October 29...[69] W. L. Reeder died November 18.[70]

William S. Eastep was mayor of Florence during this trying period--having started his term on October 1, 1918. He recalled in later years that when he became mayor Florence did not have a "foot" of paved streets, no "sanitary" schools, inadequate waterworks, and an inferior fire department. He was proud that under him 28 miles of streets had been paved, two fine schools erected, a fine filtration system for the water department installed, and the fire department had been modernized. He was the grandson of Solomon Eastep, former postmaster at Waterloo.[71]

The war was over on November 11, 1918, and the months following were busy and active ones for Florence. In February 1919 the city planted the "Victory Oaks" on city property and became the first county in Alabama to honor in any way the heroes of World War I. May 8, 1919 was the official Victory Day in Florence and was celebrated by a parade. Army aviators were in town and performed breathtaking aerial stunts. Army tanks were on display and fired salutes.[72]

On Robert E. Lee's birthday in January 1919, Mrs. A. D. Coffee gave a flag to the State Normal School. It was unfurled by a color guard from the U. S. Nitrate Plant No. 2.[73]

On January 29, 1919, Jess Darby shot Jack Broadfoot. The shooting took place in front of the livery stable on West Tombigbee Street. Darby had driven up in a buggy and Broadfoot threw a brick at him. Darby immediately fired at him twice and hit him in the left side of the forehead and right lung. Trouble was said to be over Broadfoot's divorced wife, who was Darby's sister.[74] In this same month Lester Staggs was sentenced to prison for 32 years for the murder of Ed Gentry.[75]

In March 1919 Mrs. A. D. Coffee "donated a magnificent sum for the purpose of furnishing and equipping a hospital." The City Commission "prevailed" upon her to allow the hospital to be called "Eliza Coffee Memorial Hospital". The city also announced that it had acquired a building of the Florence Land Company on Tuscaloosa Street "originally constructed for a hotel" for hospital purposes.[76]

The will of the late Mrs. Henry B. Lee was being hotly contested by her relatives in March 1919. She had left her property to a nephew, and another relative Mrs. Florence Fonville claimed Mrs. Lee was not sane at the time she signed the will.[77] About this same time T. Vaughn and E. A. Arnett were arrested for violation of Section 12 of the Selective Service Act. F. E. Weaver was the proprietor of the Jefferson Hotel. Karl Tyree of Clifton, Tennessee, "has accepted a position with the First National Bank".[78] Booker Barnett, 35, married Miss Hunt, 18, and immediately following the ceremony he was arrested and charged with disorderly conduct by the bride's father.[79]

In June 1919 Deputy Sheriff J. H. Hill shot and killed Gilbert Rutherford at Beckham's Landing on the Tennessee River. Gilbert and his brother Henry had taken a boat belonging to Hill and gone across the river.[80]

Two theaters, which long served the public in Florence, were opened in September 1919. The Princess Theater opened on Labor Day. It cost $75,000, and its seating capacity was 1,200.[81] The Majestic Theater, which also opened early in this month, was managed by a Mr. Nisbet. This theater featured the "great Wurtlizer organ".[82] Before this time the theater patrons had been entertained at a local playhouse called "The Theato".[83]

The cornerstone of C. M. Brandon School was laid on August 15, 1919.[84]

In this year Robert W. Drane organized the Muscle Shoals Supply Company to take over the concessions and operate the concessions for the U. S. Engineering Department at Wilson Dam. The Drane, McFarland Supply Company took over the concessions at the Nitrate Plant No. 2 for the U. S. Ordnance Department.[85]

In December 1919, General Pershing visited Muscle Shoals. He was given an ovation on his arrival.[86]

The population of Florence in 1910 had been 6,689. By 1920 it had grown to 10,529.[87]

CHAPTER V

Wilson Dam was the name authorized in 1919 for the new dam, then designated at Dam No. 2. The work was under the direction of the War Department and the construction was by the Corps of Engineers, U. S. Army, with all employees, except common laborers, hired under Civil Service Employment regulations. Six cofferdams were proposed.[1] The dam was not completed until 1925. By 1967 200 million persons had visited the dam. The dam was declared a National Monument by the Department of Interior.

As the Muscle Shoals complex had been started during a time when the United States was preparing for war, by 1922 the project was idle. Henry Ford made an offer for the facilities as early as 1921, and another offer in May 1922. He proposed that a corporation would be formed with a capital stock of $10,000,000, which would be controlled by himself. This company would complete the dams under construction and power-houses. This corporation would then lease the dams and power facilities for a hundred years. Ford's offer seemed reasonable when compared to an offer by the Alabama Power Company. The offer, however, was met with strong opposition from business men who did not care to see Ford acquire control of the Muscle Shoals area and its large potential power capacity. A major spokesman for Ford in Congress was Edward B. Almon. He expressed a hope on many occasions for Ford's proposal being accepted.[2]

Alabama's Congressmen saw the Ford plan as a beginning for the people of the Tennessee Valley and believed economic and social growth would be brought to the area. Ford's plan was rejected.

In 1922 James I. McClure was elected probate judge of Lauderdale County.[3] On Court Street some of the business establishments were Milner's Drug Store, Rogers Department Store, J. W. Stutts Drug Store, Eastep Insurance Agency, Douglass Shoes, and the Eat Cafe. About this time the International Civitan Club was organized and James C. Roberts was the first president.[4]

In 1923 Henry Alexander Cathey, a Republican, replaced M. W. Camper as postmaster in Florence. He was also credited with being a leader in the establishment of Wilson School and helping to influence the State Highway Department to construct the Chisholm Road.

Cherry Cotton Mills flourished in the twenties. Miles W. Darby was general manager and treasurer. By 1927 these mills employed 225 operators running 10,000 spindles and manufacturing cotton yard. N. C. Elting served as president and Turner Rice as Vice-President.[6]

The Florence Pilot Club was chartered in 1925 with a membership of twenty-three. This group furnished milk for the children at Patton Elementary School, helped with hospital projects, sponsored a Girl Scout Troup, and in 1945 pioneered the Lauderdale County March of Dimes.[7]

In this decade the museum at the local college had its beginnings, when Percy Dyer, a history teacher, donated a collection of old papers, letters, and autographs of famous people. Later Mrs. Susan K. Vaughn, using this initial donation as a nucleus, assembled a collection of historical articles and objects which were displayed in a room at Bibb Graves Hall at the college. Miss Martha Porterfield served as curator for a number of years and under her direction the museum was moved to the ground floor of Rogers Hall, the old Foster home. Mrs. Bess McCrory became curator in 1962. Some of the items from the college museum have been placed on display in recent months in the Lambeth House and the Indian Mound museum.

The Tennessee Valley Historical Society held its organizational meeting on November 15, 1923, in response to a request from Frank R. King of Leighton. The name was selected by a committee composed of A. H. Carmichael, Dr. W. H. Blake, Frank R. King, J. W. Milner, Judge E. B. Almon, Mrs. E. P. Rand, and Mrs. J. H. Nathan. Mr. King was the first president.[8]

J. W. Milner, whose name appears in the organizational members of the historical society, was honored by Florentines when they presented him with a silver cup for his services in connection with the Jackson Highway. Mr. Milner chose as a personal project, about 1910 or 1912, the establishment of the old Jackson Military Road as a national highway. He worked and talked his project until local people were saying "Jim Milner is going nuts about the Jackson Highway." Through his efforts an organization was formed and eventually influenced Congress to pass a bill in 1916 designating the road as the Andrew Jackson Military Highway, with provisions for its development and maintenance.[9]

One of the first subdivisions of Florence was developed in the twenties--Hawthorne Heights, now the area around Hawthorne Street.[10]

In 1927 Dr. W. J. Calloway was president of the Lauderdale County Medical Association.[11] In April Drs. W. J. and C. L. Mayo, whose names are famous in the field of surgical science, visited Florence. They arrived by yacht from Chattanooga. They were welcomed by local doctors, W. J. Calloway, A. A. Jackson, H. M. Simpson, L. T. Young, and B. F. Riley.[12] Thomas David Cloyd was a member of the local society and came to practice in Florence in 1923. He had served as a first lieutenant in World War I. He became well known for his diagnostic skill and internal medicine.[13]

The Industrial Corporation of Florence was active in seeking new industry for the city in 1927. Stock was sold, about $100,000, and this raised the necessary funds to purchase the land and build the buildings for the then Gardiner-Warring Knit Underwear Company. This plant furnished employment for hundreds of people, mostly women, during the years following. The property was leased to the company for a number of years with an option to buy. After several years, the company did purchase the plant. When the original investment had been retired, the Florence Industrial Corporation dissolved.

Some members of this old corporation were: O. C. Hackworth, local banker; Mr. Frederickson, realtor; Dr. Wright, doctor and realtor; A. B. Staten, banker and realtor; Robert W. Plowden, realtor; E. L. Deal, agricultural agent; John D. Weeden, realtor; R. T. S. Johnson, insuror; Bill Conner, realtor; Jewett T. Flagg, industrialist; M. J. Carter, realtor; W. S. Eastep, mayor of Florence; K. T. Tyree, banker; G. S. Taylor, realtor; John Kennedy, realtor; W. M. Richardson, lumberman and builder; R. C. Redd, lumberman; J. S. Robison, developer; Earl Jackson, insuror; Charles Curry, realtor; Zack Christian, realtor; Tom Phillips, banker and merchant; W. L. Foy, financier; Mr. Montgomery, realtor; Sam U. Hardie, insuror; and Fred Hill, oil dealer.[14]

In 1928 the conditions at the college, then called Florence State Normal, were reported as crowded. Expansion was needed at this time. Local citizens were urged to pass a bond issue so that the Normal would receive $630,000, needed for construction.[15]

By 1930 the population of Florence was 11,729. The area was in the grip of the depression. Stewart L. Udall would describe the area: "The Tennessee Valley, once rich in timber and petroleum, had been depleted. In no other region of the United States were there more families on relief or with lower incomes. In 1933 this area had become one of the most depressed areas in the country. The silt-choked waters of the Tennessee River rushed unchecked through counties and states where few farmers had electricity."[16]

On May 18, 1933 the act creating the Tennessee Valley Authority was approved.[17] "Florence went wild," an oldtimer recalled. In 1963 when President John F. Kennedy visited the area on the celebration of the 30th anniversary of TVA, he said, "It gave life to a measure which had been vetoed on two previous occasions. But in reality, it was only a beginning."[18]

The prosperity of the Muscle Shoals area can be dated from this time. TVA not only provided jobs for many in the various programs and projects, but it attracted industry to the region.

In 1933 T. S. Stribling won the Pulitzer Prize for his novel, "The Store," which used Florence as its locale. He was threatened with libel after its publication and it is said he agreed to contribute $500 to the lawsuit. The publicity did his book no harm, in fact, if anything increased the interest of many. The book was the story of miscegenation and climaxed by a lynching of an illegitimate mulatto son of Colonel Miltaides Vaiden, the leading citizen of Florence in the book. Vaiden supposedly began his climb to the top by stealing a load of cotton. Many of the scandals of Florence were said to have been thinly disguised in the book, although Stribling always denied that he used anything other than Florence as its setting. However, his leading character gave rise to names for cats, dogs, and other pets through the county. Many Florentine people remember a cat named Colonel Vaiden or a dog named Miltaides in the past.

The new economic era brought growth in many ways. One notable event, 1936, was the burning of the mortgage on the Elks Lodge building. Members who gathered to celebrate were Aubrey Ethridge, Clyde Anderson, Jones, John Robinson, David Harrison, Will Eastep, Dr. G. D. Ingram, O. W. Duke, Bulla May, C. L. Tardy, Charles Haley, Will Conner, J. E. Morris, Doc Robinson, Charles Thomas, Cletus McWilliams, Joe Liles, Frank Cobb, Ray Blakeley, Marcy Darnell, Herschel P. Anderson, Gus McKee, Elbert Burns, J. B. McClure, W. L. Foy, Mr. Atkinson, Homer Reeder, L. M. Douglass, E. E. Beck, Floyd Jackson, Father Alfred, Bill Barnett, Jones Reeder, Jeff Smith, Alex George, and Jim Kilburn.[19]

The Muscle Shoals Service League was organized in March 1934 with thirty charter members. From the beginning its main work has been helping crippled children. The group sponsors an annual Apple Annie Day to raise funds for its work.[20]

Construction on Pickwick Landing Dam began in 1937. As many as 2,400 workers were employed on the dam, and 1,600 more on clearing operations in the lake area. Pickwick Lake was formed when the dam was completed and the waters of the Tennessee River were impounded. The inundation of the lowlands between Florence and Waterloo changed the landscape and rerouted roads.[21]

The American Legion Home on South Court Street was opened to the public in 1939 and became a center for community activities before and during World War II.[22] O'Neal Bridge was also opened to traffic in this year. For a time it was a toll bridge.[23]

In 1940 the population of Florence was 15,043, and the area was beginning a period of growth and devolpment. The construction of Reynolds Metals Aluminum Company was started, and the Muscle Shoals area became one of the nation's most important aluminum centers.

Within ten years after the passage of the TVA act, the Tennessee River was harnessed and "put to work". There were over 700 miles of navigable streams, 200,000,000 trees had been planted in the uplands, and dams provided abundant cheap power.[24]

Early in 1941 the nation began preparing for another war. In January 1941 the local unit of the National Guard was mobilized and sent into the army. The group, Company F, 151st Engineers, built bridges, hospitals and troop processing posts, and cleared mine fields. They were sent to Alaska early in the war. The company commander was Frank Crowe. Frank Marks was the first sergeant, and William Henry Cromwell was the battalion commander.25

Some of the members of this group were: John Clopton, Howard Moomaw, Robert Kershaw, Roland Romine, Robert Masterson, W. T. Hale, James T. Rhodes, Paul Worley, Frank Lamprecht, B. B. Weinbaum, Carl Murphy, Woodrow Thrasher, Leon Rye, John Morgan, A. P. Richardson, H. L. Hendrix, H. B. Jackson, A. B. Richardson, W. H. Rigby, L. C. White, C. R. James, A. L. Rickard, A. M. Brown, Paul Rickard, A. J. Sharp, M. B. Dunn, James D. Busby, E. W. Crowe, L. J. Doss, L. J. Nix, Adrian Vernon, Peck Cauthen, James W. Rhodes, H. L. Bishline, Granville May, Harry Blaylock, R. L. Behel, B. J. Grimes, Howard Marks, Allen E. Fulmer, W. A. Blair, William A. Parrish, W. F. Chisholm, and G. T. Rickard.26 (Complete muster roll not available.)

On December 7, 1941, came the unforgettable shock of the bombing of Pearl Harbor, a catastrophe which began in horror and ended in triumph. In the next four years American fighting men would be sent all over the globe in a war of seemingly limitless scope. Some of the boys from Lauderdale County were sent to the European front to a continent ravaged by Adolf Hitler. Others went to the dreadful jungles and barren atolls of the Pacific.

The following are entries selected at random from a diary kept in Florence during World War II. The diarist was a freshman in the fall of 1941 at Florence State Teachers College and a lifelong resident of the city. (A few names have been deleted. It might come as a surprise to a certain Florence resident that he had been suspected as a spy at the outbreak of the war.)27

Monday, Dec. 8, 1941 - We had a special assembly today at Wesleyan Hall. _____ predicted that before the spring the Japanese will bomb this area. He is confident of that...Some of the boys were missing from school today. I've heard that everyone is rushing to join up...

December 9, 1941 --...School has been rather disjointed this week. The damage at Pearl Harbor was pretty bad...

December 11, 1941 -- Well, today we declared war on Italy and Germany. Guess we will take on the whole world next. Some soldiers from Camp Forrest have been sent down and stationed at the dams to prevent sabotage. They search cars before letting them across Wilson Dam..._____ thinks _____ is a spy...says there are all sorts of mysterious goings and coming at his house at all hours of the day and night. She says she has heard him say treasonous things against the U. S. She thinks the FBI is watching his house...

Dec. 12, 1941 -- ...Soldiers from Camp Forrest are at Wilson Dam. Everyone takes a ride across the dam just so they can have their car searched and come home and tell what the soldiers did when their car was searched...The soldiers are quartered in some old barracks at the dam--right below the Wilson Dam Club House.

Dec. 13, 1941 -- ..._____ of the _____ Church says the Japs planned it (the attack) for Sunday a.m. because most of the soldiers and sailors would be nursing hangovers from the Saturday night before. This points out the evil of drink...

Dec. 20, 1941 -- Newspaper headline pasted in diary: WAKE HOLDS; JAPS BOMB CAVITE.

Dec. 25, 1941 -- Lots of folks getting married...The Japs have landed 200,000 troops in the Philippines...

Jan. 10, 1942 -- _____ insists _____ is a spy. People are getting carried away. _____ jumped an unsuspecting Chinese who came into ____ ____ Store recently and was going to tear the dirty Jap apart...

Jan. 15, 1942 -- The Japs have invaded Burma. They are out to conquer the world, I think...

Feb. 22, 1942 -- ...The Coast Guard has taken over the dams now and the soldiers have returned to Camp Forrest. One of the Coast Guards...is... quite wealthy. A lot of Mamas have set their caps for him for their daughters...

April 9, 1942 -- Bataan in the Philippines has fallen to the Japs...The Civil Air Patrol has been organized...

April 27, 1942 -- The fourth registration for selective service was held today. All male citizens between the ages of 45 and 64, inclusive, had to register--even Uncle Mac!! Surely the war isn't going to have to take men of this age...

June 10, 1942 -- The Germans announced the destruction of a whole town today for punishment...Lidice in Czechoslovakia...

July 1, 1942 -- All males in age bracket of 18 and 19 had to register June 30...

August 1, 1942 -- _____ swears up and down that _____ is an enemy agent...She says someone is also watching his house...

August 9, 1942 -- ...went to Edgewater Beach today...A fierce battle has been raging at Savo Island...

Sept. 6, 1942 -- Today we drove...to Courtland to see the old Saunders home--an ante-bellum mansion in decay... The man on the place let us go all the way through it. There were a couple of armoires still in the place--even plates on the kitchen table...drove out to see the Forks of Cypress, also deserted, and for sale...

March 22, 1943 -- This gas rationing is the worst thing to come out of the war... There is a USO in Sheffield--headed by J. V. McBride....The Florence National Guards are in Alaska of all places...

May 12, 1943 -- ...The Germans have been defeated in North Africa...

July 25, 1943 -- Mussolini has resigned!...Seems as if we have been afraid of Benito and what he might do all my life...

Sept. 21, 1943 -- Fewer boys on campus this term...

Nov. 11, 1943 -- Tonight was the Sigma Tau Delta banquet at Basil's Cafe. Dr. Luitpold Wallach was the speaker and he spoke endlessly on James Joyce and his works...The Marines have finally taken Bougainville...

Nov. 26, 1943 -- The Germans are taking the Belgium Church bells to be melted down for arms...

Nov. 29, 1943 -- School as usual. War continues.

Dec. 1, 1943 -- There are supposed to be something like 25 airplanes missing from Courtland (Air Base)...Some people say it is sabotage...

Dec. 21, 1943 -- We went to Mary Elizabeth Lanier's wedding to Cliff Marshall today at First Methodist Church. He is in Navy...

Jan. 1, 1944 -- Let us hope the New Year shapes up better than last. Col. Walter W. Gross is the new commanding officer at Courtland...

Jan. 19, 1944 -- ...This man shortage can get no worse surely...

Feb. 18, 1944 -- Tonight there was a school dance at the gym...Our troops have landed on a place called Eniwetok...

April 2, 1944 -- Today was Palm Sunday. The palms at Trinity Church were in memory of R. Y. McClain...

April 24, 1944 -- Don "Country" Montgomery and Leonard Trapp, local soldiers, on campus today.

June 17, 1944 -- Cowpuncher Threet was killed on D-Day...We bomb Japan yesterday our first time since the Doolittle raid in 1942...

July 10, 1944 -- The civilian suicides are quite horrible (in South Pacific)-- entire families, hand in hand, jumping off cliffs, mothers cutting the throats of their children...

July 18, 1944 -- Don "Country" Montgomery died July 8 in England of a fractured skull...William Turner Phillips is a prisoner of war in Germany. He is a lieutenant...Something like 20,000 Japanese were killed in the fighting at Saipan.

July 25, 1944 -- _____ got married recently. She has been trying since 1941... We have taken Tinian.

Sept. 15, 1944 -- Miss Sparks is running me ragged with The Flor-Ala...People who drink a lot of coffee and like sugar are in a bad fix...The rayon hose are terrible things and most of us go bare-legged...The shoe rationing has hurt me. (Note: In reference to the Flor-Ala, the diarist served briefly as editor-in-chief.)

Oct. 24, 1944 -- Marvin Olive has been declared dead by War Department. He was reported missing in action on Oct. 4...sent overseas July 14, 1944...As his plane went down he was helping a comrade. Other fliers who saw the plane go down wrote they saw at least one member of the crew parachute to safety, and it is thought that he did not have time to leave the falling plane...

Nov. 13, 1944 -- We all went to Helen Theroux's wedding to Joe Jones at the Methodist Church...

November 18, 1944 -- We all journeyed to St. Florian to attend Odette Rasch's wedding to Frank Howard...

Nov. 21, 1944 -- Mrs. Barley was buried today...She was a fine person...

Dec. 28, 1944 -- The fighting in Leyte is over...

March 16, 1945 -- Iwo Jima is ours!...We are still bombing Tokyo...Ludendorff Bridge still stands...

March 30, 1945 -- Virginia Schmidlkofer, Lucia Mason, and Natalie Sharp left for Waves today...

April 12, 1945 -- I was sitting in my room doing homework when I heard "Miss" Susie Butler come out her back door calling in great distress. She had been listening to her radio when a special announcement was made. Beloved President Roosevelt was dead--cerebral hemorrhage... (Note: Mrs. Robert Butler)

April 17, 1945 -- Mr. William Milliken died today...Weakley descendant...

April 22, 1945 -- There is a horrible cigarette on the market--no one likes it, but it is always available. It is Pinehurst. I think it has wood shavings in it... The 7th Army crossed the Danube today...

May 3, 1945 -- We all went wild today. The German armies are beginning to surrender...We got a holiday from the rest of our classes...

May 16, 1945 -- The I.R.C. banquet was tonight at Basil's Cafe. Mr. Van Boskirk, whom everyone adores, was the speaker...

June 9, 1945 -- It is sure nice for the war to be going our way...According to the papers, Courtland is to be closed...

July 6, 1945 -- Bob Johnson was killed at Fort Jackson yesterday. He was a lieutenant in the 28th Tank Battalion. A land mine exploded after he removed a delayed action safety pin and the bomb exploded immediately. Fragments entered his head near his eye...

July 15, 1945 -- Our warships are shelling the Japanese shores for the first time..

August 6, 1945 -- Today the American Air Force dropped a bomb on Hiroshima in Japan. A bomb--the like of which has never been on this earth before. From this bomb a whole city was destroyed--close to 100,000 killed...

August 9, 1945 -- We dropped an atom bomb on Nagasaki...They say that this bomb kills everything for miles from the center...

August 13, 1945 -- This is the big day. Graduation from college...split infinitives and dangling participles and all...Governor Chauncey Sparks was the speaker--and he spoke and spoke and spoke and spoke...

August 14, 1945 -- How to describe a day when an entire city goes wild? The Sirens began blowing this afternoon. The radio said Japan had surrendered. The war is over!!...Everyone congregated on Court Street--I mean there was a mob! Laughing, hugging, kissing, shouting, drinking. I think everyone was happy.

Jimmy Gilbert started a snake dance that went all the way down Court Street-- at least two blocks long. A car could not drive down Court Street for the people. People did not know what to do, so they went to town.

It was a wild, wild day.

Sept. 2, 1945 -- At 9:04 World War II ended. It had lasted 1,364 days, 5 hours, and 44 minutes from the attack on Pearl Harbor on Dec. 7, 1941...

In the back of this diary is memorandum entitled "They Won't Come Back." The following are listed: Cowpuncher Threet (killed D-Day); Milton Littrell (shot down over Germany); Tommy Campbell (shot down over Germany); Sonny Lucas (shot down in CBI); Country Montgomery (died in England); "Peg" Douthitt (killed at Okinawa); Jack Douthit (killed in France); Marvin Morgan; Lynwood Glazier (shot down at Guadacanal); Willie Lee Threet; Perry Lee Roden (killed in States); Marvin Olive (shot down over Germany); and Bob Johnson.

From 1942 to 1964, E. F. Martin was elected to the city commission six times, and each time served as Mayor. During this period he was defeated twice. In 1948 E. F. Yielding was elected, and in 1954 Walter Harrison won. In 1964 Martin was appointed sheriff by Gov. George Wallace, filing a vacancy left when former Sheriff Roy Call resigned to became U. S. Marshal.28

In 1947 provisions were made at the college whereby A. B. and B. S. degrees could be given in courses of study other than teacher training.29 By 1948 enrollment at Florence State Teachers College had reached 1,500. The school was the third largest state supported college in Alabama.30

Early in March 1948, plans were announced for the construction of a new high school, to be located on the 25-acre Kernachan tract.31 In this same month the first theater, Norwood Theater, was opened by Dan Davis and H. L. Bobo. Construction was also started on a new theater for downtown Florence, the Shoals. The Norwood Theater burned in August 1968.32

In May 1948 one of the largest fires in several years consumed the A&P building on Court Street. The damage was estimated at $50,000.

In January 1949 the Lauderdale-Florence Public Library was opened in a handsome new structure on North Wood Avenue.33

In May 1948 a serious epidemic of rabies swept the county. Many dogs had to be destroyed. George Hobbs of Florence was instrumental in the organization of the Lauderdale County Humane Society, which grew out of this epidemic. The initial meeting was held on Dec. 11, 1950. On Jan. 15, 1951, the group became a permanent organization and received its charter. In 1956, John Hauerwas became the shelter superintendent of this group.34

By 1950 the population of Florence was 23,879. Thanksgiving Day of this year was remembered as being a sunny and mild day, but during the night snow fell, preceding what was to be known as the Great Ice Storm of 1951, and one of the most severe winters within memory.

In 1956 provisions were made for the establishment of a program of graduate study in education, leading to a Master of Arts degree at the college. A graduate division was organized and inaugurated in 1957. In 1957 the State Legislature changed the name to Florence State College.

In March 1958, Florence's most famous son, W. C. Handy, "The Father of the Blues," died at the age of 84 years. He had been born in Florence on November 16, 1873, the son and grandson of a Methodist preacher. His original homeplace was demolished in 1956 during clearance work for Handy Heights. The logs from the home were saved, however, and in 1968 the Florence Chamber of Commerce initiated a project for the restoration and reconstruction of the Handy home as a shrine to the famous composer.35

In June 1958, Miss Ethel Pearson became the regional librarian of the Muscle Shoals Regional Library, which had its headquarters in Florence.36

By 1960 the population of Florence was 31,649, and in 1968 it is estimated at 40,000.

On May 18, 1963, on the 30th anniversary of TVA, President John F. Kennedy visited the Muscle Shoals area, and was greeting by a large and enthusiastic crowd.

On June 6, 1965, the new Lauderdale County Courthouse was formally opened to the public. The cornerstone had been placed on February 27, with members of the Florence Lodge No. 14, F & AM, participating. Members of the county court at this time were Probate Judge Estes R. Flynt; J. Lambert Richardson, D. S. Belew, L. C. Simmons, and Andy White. Other county officials at this time were: Robert Hill, circuit judge; Emmett Roden, circuit judge; W. L. Almon, circuit colicitor; Doyle R. Young, chairman, public building authority; John R. Barnes, county court judge; E. F. Martin, sheriff; Lavern Tate, deputy circuit solicitor; Charles Edgar Young, circuit court clerk; Weaver Fuqua, tax collector; B. P. Lovelace, Jr., tax assessor; Elbert L. Daly, register in chancery; and Allen Thornton, superintendent of education. The new building cost $2,189,400, and was financed without additional taxes. The Confederate Monument was moved from the old public square to a new position in front of the new seat of justice.37

The old Lauderdale County jail, located on Pine Street, was torn down in 1965.

In January 1966, the area was paralyzed by a 9-inch snow which fell on the 29th. In March of this year Jerry Dwayne Lee, U. S. Marine, was killed in action in Vietnam. Before the year would end, Roger J. Bryant, also a marine, was dead in Vietnam, and Robert Lee McCaig was killed in the same theater of war.38 In November, Sergeant Paul O. Brown was killed in Vietnam where he had been stationed. Violent deaths for the year included Aden Lee Coleman, who made a fatal jump from O'Neal Bridge; Cora Lee Darby, who was fatally wounded by her husband; a Florence colored minister who was killed by Dewey Armstead, who was in turn killed by the church secretary; Major Ben W. Stutts, who had been held captive by North Korean Communists, lost his life in small plane crash in Georgia.39

In June 1966, the Forks of Cypress was struck by lightning and burned to the ground. Only the majestic columns of James Jackson's old home were left standing.

In this year C. Hewlett Jackson resigned as manager of the Chamber of Commerce after 23 years of service. He was followed by Jim Odum as manager.39

R. W. Weaver was appointed the new fire chief for the City of Florence.40 In this same year Rufus G. Hibbett retired as superintendent of the city schools.

In January 1967 the employment in the Tennessee Valley area reached 2 million for the first time. During this year the Florence post office was burglarized, with a loss estimated at $100,000. On October 25, a tornado struck Florence, and fifteen houses were demolished, Harlan School damaged, and other houses and crops damaged.41

During 1967 Don Michael was killed in Vietnam; and George T. Mangrum of Rogersville died of wounds in Vietnam. The oldest resident of Florence, Dock McDaniel, age 112, died October 3.

In other events of the year, Jesse Richardson was on trial for rape; Ralph Murphy, 36, was sentenced to thirty years in prison for rape of his 13 year old niece; Gene Darby was found guilty of the murder of his wife; and J. D. McDonald, Florence insurance agent, was arraigned on twelve counts of embezzlement.42

The Florence-Lauderdale Coliseum was the scene of a KKK rally in June 1967, and Robert Shelton, Imperial Wizard of the United Klans of America attended.43

In 1967 Trinity Episcopal Church began construction of a $201,000 addition to the church building. The record books of the church reveal that Episcopal servies were initiated in Florence by "a Mr. Wall" in 1824. The parish was organized on October 15, 1836, and admitted to the Alabama diocese in April 1837. The first services held in the present building were on Easter Sunday in 1895.44

The new addition on Trinity Church was dedicated in January 1968 and named Mullen Hall in honor of E. G. Mullen, who had been minister there for 25 years at the time of the dedication.[45]

In March 1968 plans for the expansion of the First Presbyterian Church were announced.[46] This church was erected in 1824, although a lot was purchased in 1818 from the Cypress Land Company. A frame building originally served the congregation. "Through the years the church has undergone several extensive alterations but essentially has maintained its original form," wrote the compilers of "Historic Muscle Shoals" in 1962.[47]

On July 13, 1968, a Sesquicentennial Parade was held in Florence, celebrating the 150th "birthday" of the city. The Indian Mound and Museum were opened to the public during this observance. The restored Lambeth Home had been opened about a month earlier.[48]

On Florence's 150th anniversary, the city commission is Ben Craig, Mayor; Bill Mapes and Tom L. Watkins, commissioners; and James E. Wilson, City Clerk.[49]

Florence is described by its boosters:

> "...We are the medical and educational center of North Alabama and our 58 churches of every denomination assure you of one in your immediate neighborhood. Being the home of Florence State College, our schools are a source of pride...kindergarten through college without leaving home.
>
> "For evening relaxing we have a daily newspaper (The Florence Times, edited by Louis Eckl), 2 radio stations, a TV station, a weekly newspaper (The Florence Herald), and a public library with over 107,000 volumes! (By June advertisement changed to 2 weekly newspapers.)
>
> "Florence has one of the finest employment records in the country, with 61 manufacturing establishments...With its almost 400 retail stores, 425 service establishments and miscellaneous shops, you'll find everything you need...
>
> "Three of the finest golf courses, city and club maintained tennis courts, miles and miles of the country's most beautiful beaches and waterways, carpet golf courses, riding stables, and bowling alleys...We have the world's finest fresh water fishing!..."[50]

This brochure ends with these words:

> "Before going anywhere to live, check with us."

ADDENDUM

Letter from George Colbert:

Tennessee River, Nov. 27, 1812

Sir:
On the evening of the 25th of this month I was inform by some of the travellers that there was parcels of Creek Indians at Bear Creek drinking, that they inform Joseph Underwood, that they were creeks   if I ever felt any agitation in my mine I felt that night to think that Capt Underwood would suffer anything of the kind, so next morning soon I set of to see if it was possible, but as it happen, I found to the contrary, and Underwood denigh of ever teling any body & no creeks have been there, but when the news get to the settlement will grow bigger, but I corddially assure you no such thing, however if we should see any in this contry we will tell them to go home & if they dont go we immediately give your notice

       I am Dear Sir yr friend
       Brother Geor Colbert
Directed to Genl Isaac Roberts near Columbia, Tennessee.

(Note: This letter was postmarked Franklin, Ten., Dec. 2d, 1812. A handwritten note attached says the letter was sent up Natchez Trace to Franklin to be mailed. This letter in possession of descendants of Isaac Roberts in Columbia, Tennessee. Word had reached Middle Tennessee at this time that the Creeks were in North Alabama, coming north on a raid. Middle Tennessee soon had several thousand men in arms awaiting the Creeks. Isaac Roberts, a Militia General, had sent inquiries to North Alabama to see if the Creeks were there. This letter from Colbert is in answer to the inquiry.)

Notes from interview with Albert "Pike" Riley, on July 25, 1906, by Frank H. Smith. "Father's family lived 4 miles east of Columbia in 1844; moved in 1845 to the Shoal Creek Cotton Mills, 9 miles north of Florence, Ala., on Military Road, lived there till 1864, fall or winter...Cotton Mills a large concern...Business very successfully conducted. About 40 families working in Cotton Mill that had nice cottages. Concern also ran large farm in Shoal Creek Valley, and saw mill, and grist mill.

"Tolls from grist mill almost supplied wants of employees. Large store well stocked with everything to eat or wear. All kinds of whiskies, brandy, wines, &c. Good whiskey there before the war 18¢ gallon. Church and free school for employees. Employees white, but few negroes. Immense water power. Cotton Mill large ___ story, brick, well built.

"Factory proper surrounded by tall paling fence enclosing about 5 acres, with everything kept in apple-pie order. Cotton generally procured from Florence, hauled by wagons 9 miles, excellent road, except on bad hill getting out of Shoal Creek valley.

"Gen. Dodge had a large body of Federal troops there in 1863. One of his wagons was sent to Florence; broke down on the big hill south of the Factory. Wagon was propped up and men were working underneath. Unknown guerilla fired into the crowd, wounding one of the soldiers under wagon. This was in afternoon. Dodge placed guards around enclosure of Factory, allowing all within to get out. Next morning wounded soldier died. Dodge burned everything in the enclosure, and the saw- and grist-mill about ___ o'clock. None of the mill hands mistreated by

Federals.

"Guerillas did not range much about the factory, but further west between there and Tenn. river. The company had big stock of cotton yarns on hand—all burned. The mill was not rebuilt after war, they built big Factory at Tuscaloosa, Ala."

Interview with Ben T. Martin by Frank H. Smith, about 1906:
"Hugh Woolard died of measles at Danville, Tenn. River, just before Fort Henry fell. Nursed by Wm. Carrol Martin (father of Ben T.). W. C. Martin and Wash Rushton of Co.__ 48th Tenn. made Hugh's coffin before death. Remains put on a slow boat. The "Dunbar" passed. Remains transferred to it. They could not accompany remains so they put Masonic marks on the coffin. Wm. C. Martin was a mason. When boat reached Florence, Ala., Masons there were notified and they gave Hugh Woolard Masonic burial. Remains never removed. Masons at Florence notified Wm. C. Martin of his burial there."

A Civil War Letter:

My Dear Son:
If ever there times to try men's souls, these are the times. Bereavement, affliction, separation from loved ones—these all are not enough to fill our cup of sorrow. To cap the climax we are now surrounded by fiends in human form.

On last Sunday, five gun boats landed at Florence, bringing cavalry and infantry. The men that was left at Tuscumbia by Roddie to protect the valley, took the artillery and left with all possible speed for Decatur, burning all the bridges behind them, Fosters among the rest. Capt. Hampton's company, with a dozen or two of Van Dorn's command, are endeavoring to organize, to show some resistance, but the creeks are now swimming, and if it were possible to induce the men to return with the artillery, there is now no way of getting it back on this side of the creek, and the prospect is good for it keeping up for a length of time, at least till the Yanks have finished the already begun work of laying waste the valley. They say they are from the Vicksburg slaughter pen and they intend making the valley pay heavy damages. They say they are collecting U. S. war tax—the people are in a panic, and it is difficult to hear what is going on, but will tell you what I know is reliable. C. McKiernan paid them $1,000, old man Carlock $1,300, Mrs. W. Davidson, $300. They demanded $1,000 in gold of old man Alexander, he told them he did not have it, they then carried off every mule, horse, and about all the Negroes he had left.

They are taking all the wagons and mules and all the cotton they can carry off, driving off the cattle, sheep and laying waste wherever they go. They do not consult the Negro now, they force him into ranks wherever they meet him. They overtook C. Abernathy carrying his bacon out, took him and his overseer prisoners, and 11 of his Negro men. It is impossible to find out what they are doing, they have not been here and I pray they may never be able to get here. What I am to do if they do come I can't tell. I have had Martin to scatter the cotton on the river hills and I have secreted some of our bacon, but if the Negroes are disposed to inform on me, it will be worse than if I had done nothing.

I tell you, it is a gloomy time. Every one seems to think the finishing stroke is now being made to ruin the valley. Not a thing doing towards farming, nor will be done as long as the Yanks are here, and they may be for months.

There has been more rain in the last 10 days than I ever saw before in that length of time. There is more water in the cellar, by far than ever was before. I have not had a word from you since your uncle Amzie wrote my cousin Will. You can imagine my anxiety for you, my son, that is all. I should have looked for Jimmie back soon, if it had not rained so much, with some news from you. I wrote you two weeks since, have heard nothing from Miss E--your sister E. wrote to her but has received no reply as yet--we have had no mail, no news for two weeks. God grant that you may keep well and serve Him as well as your country, is the prayer of

        Your
         Ma.

(This letter was published in Florence Times, 2 March 1961, and contributed by K. W. Morrison of N. Poplar Street in Florence, who identified the writer as his great grandmother. The letter was written to one of her sons.)

Nathan Vaught manuscript:
"John W. Leymaster, 80 odd, now lives in Lauderdale County, Alabama, blacksmith. Came to Maury County (Tenn.) 1808-09; married Miss Alman..."

"Benjamin French first came to Alabama in 1808 from Warren County, Kentucky, and settled on Limestone Creek, 9 miles east of Athens in 1808. He remained there several years and then settled on Elk River. Finally he moved to Rogersville, in Lauderdale County, where he died in 1840 over 90 years of age. He had served as a soldier in the American Revolution. He brought five sons with him--Jerry, Jessie, Samuel, Benjamin, and Amos, and six daughters, Milly, Jane, Ann, Polly, Sallie, and Frances." (page 13, Early History of Limestone County, by R. A. McClellan, 1881)

FOOTNOTES

CHAPTER I

1. Albert Burton Moore, "History of Alabama and Her People," 1927, I, 103.
2. Peter A. Brannon, The Tennessee State Line, Alabama Historical Quarterly, Vol. 18, 412.
3. Note in R. Y. McClain papers.
4. Albert V. Goodpasture, Indian Wars and Warriors of the Old Southwest, 1730-1807, Tennessee Historical Magazine, Vol. 4, 121.
5. Ibid, 121, 124.
6. Ibid, 258.
7. Columbia Herald and Mail (Columbia, Tenn.), 1 June 1877.
8. Donald Davidson, The Tennessee, The Old River, Vol. I, 284.
9. Columbia Herald and Mail, 19 March 1875.
10. Alabama Historical Quarterly, 1956, Vol. 18, 309.
11. Western Chronicle (Columbia, Tenn.) 17 Nov. 1810.
12. Moore, II, 282.
13. Memoirs of Mrs. W. W. Casey, Kenton, Tenn., January, 1910, in Tennessee State Library and Archives.
14. Muscle Shoals Sunday News, 11 Nov. 1923.
15. Ibid.
16. Nathan Vaught, Youth and Old Age, manuscript, unpublished, 11, 71. A copy of this manuscript in Tennessee State Library and Archives.
17. Dunbar Rowland, Encyclopedia of Mississippi History, 1907, I, 348.
18. Independent Gazette (Franklin, Tenn.), 3 Oct. 1823.
19. Vaught, 16, 17. (James Walker was brother in law of President James K. Polk.)
20. Garrett, History of Lauderdale County, Alabama, 1964, 50.
21. Royal, Ann, Letters from Alabama, 143. ("Memphis Down in Dixie," 68, describes her: "Mrs. Ann Royal, a notorious old hag who gloried in the name of Ann Royal and harried Congressmen with her Black Book." She was considered one of the most extraordinary women of the age, certainly one of its most brilliant reformers.)
22. Ibid, 146.
23. Independent Gazette (Franklin, Tenn.) 13 April 1822.
24. Independent Gazette, 11 May 1822.
25. Independent Gazette, 28 Dec. 1822.
26. Independent Gazette, 24 Apr. 1823.
27. Independent Gazette, 6 June 1823.
28. Niles Weekly Register, XXIX, 65, in William L. McDonald papers.
29. Commissioners Court Minutes 1829-1837, 4, typescript in Alabama State Archives.
30. Maury (Tenn.) Democrat, 1 Mar. 1894.

CHAPTER II

1. Thomas M. Owen, Jr., "Many Florence Taverns," clipping from Florence Times-News in Lauderdale County folder, Alabama State Archives.
2. Florence Times, 15 June 1967.
3. Owen, "Many Florence Taverns."
4. Ibid.
5. Florence Times, 28 July 1966.
6. Columbia Herald, 23 August 1901, quoting the Florence Herald.
7. Florence Herald, 24 Nov. 1966.
8. Florence Times, __ Oct. 1967, in Mary T. Sharp Clippings.
9. Nina Leftwich, Two Thousand Years at Muscle Shoals, reprinted 1965, 42, 79.
10. Vaught, 46, 47.
11. Commissioners Court Minutes, 36, 35, 43.
12. Nashville Banner, 23 Nov. 1930.
13. Columbia Herald and Mail, 13 April 1877.
14. Western Weekly Review (Franklin, Tenn.) 31 March 1833.
15. Time Magazine, 18 Nov. 1966.
16. Columbia (Tenn.) Observer, 8 August 1834.
17. Guy Braden, The Colberts and the Chickasaw Nation, Tennessee Historical Quarterly, Sept. 1958, quoting Frank R. King papers.
18. Rhoda Coleman Ellison, Caroline Lee Hentz's Alabama Diary 1836, Alabama Review, Oct. 1951, 260, in William L. McDonald papers.
19. Ibid, 261.
20. Ibid, 265.
21. Ibid, 266, 267.
22. Columbia Observer, 24 Oct. 1839.
23. Western Weekly Review (Franklin, Tenn.) 3 May 1833.

24. Florence (Ala.) Enquirer, 22 August 1840.
25. Columbia (Tenn.) Observer, 19 Nov. 1840.
26. Richard W. Griffin, Cotton Manufacture in Alabama to 1865, Alabama Historical Quarterly, 1956, 291.
27. Florence Gazette, 18 July 1846.
28. Columbia (Tenn.) Beacon, 9 April 1847.
29. Columbia Beacon, 3 Sept. 1847.
30. Judge J. J. Mitchell, Historic Homes of Florence, address delivered 12 Jan. 1921 to Florence Rotary Club in William L. McDonald papers.
31. Columbia Beacon, 26 Nov. 1847.
32. Columbia Beacon, 3 Sept. 1847.
33. Columbia Beacon, 12 March 1847.
34. Columbia Beacon, 28 May 1847.
35. Columbia Beacon, 3 Dec. 1847.
36. Columbia Beacon, 21 May 1847.
37. Moore, II, 277.
38. 1850 Census of Lauderdale County, National Archives, Washington, D.C.
39. 1850 Mortality Schedule in Raymond Y. McClain papers.
40. J. J. Mitchell, Historic Homes.
41. Democratic Herald (Columbia, Tenn.) 18 June 1853.
42. Democratic Herald (Columbia, Tenn.) 1 Sept. 1855.
43. Advertisement handbill.
44. Democratic Herald (Columbia, Tenn.) 13 Oct. 1855.
45. Florence Times, 1 May 1966, in Mary Threet Sharp Clippings. (All Florence newspapers of 1960s come from this collection of historical clippings.)
46. Florence Times, 1 May 1966.
47. Florence Times, 3 July 1965.
48. Florence Times, 21 June 1948.
49. Griffin, 292.
50. Ibid, 293.
51. Ibid, 304.

CHAPTER III

1. John G. Barrett (ed.) Yankee Rebel, The Civil War Journal of Edmund DeWitt Patterson, 1966, 4-6.
2. Ibid, 23.
3. Ibid, 24.
4. Ibid, 58.
5. Ibid, 35.
6. Ibid, 35.
7. Ibid, 97.
8. Ibid, 101.
9. Ibid, 111.
10. Ibid, 125, 192.
11. Stanley Horn, Tennessee's War, 1965, 283.
12. Ibid, 283.
13. Maurice Pruitt, Bugger Saga, unpublished manuscript.
14. Civil War Centennial Commission, Tennesseans in the Civil War, I, 333.
15. Nashville Dispatch, 16 May 1865.
16. E. C. Betts, Early History of Huntsville, Ala., 1909, 102, 104.
17. Florence Journal, 5 Sept. 1866.
18. Lauderdale County marriages in Raymond Y. McClain papers.
19. Daily State Sentinel (Montgomery, Ala.) 13 June 1867.
20. Florence Journal, 11 July 1867.
21. William Letford, Notes on the Reconstruction in Alabama, unpublished. (Mr. Letford kindly let me see his manuscript still in preparation.)
22. Florence Times __ March 1967.
23. Nashville Republican Banner, 31 March 1868.
24. Columbia Herald, 17 Sept. 1869.
25. Moore, I, 573.

CHAPTER IV

1. Columbia Herald, 21 Jan. 1870.
2. Columbia Herald, 24 June 1870.
3. Columbia Herald, 11 Nov. 1870.
4. Columbia Herald, 7 Oct. 1870.
5. Columbia Herald, 30 June 1871.
6. Columbia Herald and Mail, 26 March 1876.
7. Columbia Herald and Mail, 24 March 1876.
8. Columbia Herald and Mail, 26 May 1876.
9. The Daily Memphis (Tenn.) Avalanche, 13 Oct. 1878.
10. Ibid.
11. The Daily Memphis Avalanche, 16 Oct. 1878.
12. The Daily Memphis Avalanche, 18 Oct. 1878.
13. Tombstone inscription of Joel Whitten in Florence City Cemetery; in 1930s this section was pointed out to writer as the yellow fever section.
14. Florence Gazette, 28 Feb. 1880.
15. Birmingham News Magazine, 9 May 1954.
16. Florence Banner, 20 March 1883.

17. Maury (Tenn.) Democrat, 29 Nov. 1888.
18. Moore, III, 630.
19. Florence Herald, 27 Dec. 1894.
20. Nashville Banner, 6 Feb. 1897.
21. Nashville Banner, 7 Jan. 1897.
22. Florence Herald, 14 Oct. 1897.
23. Maury Democrat, 13 Sept. 1894.
24. Maury Democrat, 17 Jan. 1895, quoting the Florence Herald.
25. Nashville Banner, 1 May 1897. (A later date has usually been given for the dedication of this statue. The statue, however, was in Florence on this date and the Confederate Memorial Association of Florence had until May 10 to make up their minds where they wished the statue to be placed.)
26. Dixon Merritt, The History of Wilson Co., Tenn., 1961, 366.
27. Moore, II, 269, 282.
28. Florence Times, 18 Dec. 1966.
29. Lauderdale County Marriages in Raymond Y. McClain papers.
30. Nashville Banner, 5 Dec. 1899.
31. Nashville Banner, 12 Dec. 1899.
32. Ibid.
33. Nashville Banner, 15 Dec. 1899.
34. Ibid.
35. Nashville Banner, 19 Dec. 1899.
36. Oscar D. Lewis, "Past 65 Years Have Seen Many Changes," 1966, Florence Herald clipping.
37. Ibid.
38. Moore, II, 319.
39. Ibid, II, 286.
40. Lewis, "Past 65 Years..."
41. Florence Herald, 28 March 1902.
42. Florence Herald, 4 April 1902.
43. Moore, II, 269.
44. Moore, II, 276.
45. Moore, II, 280.
46. Columbia Herald, 4 August 1905.
47. Birmingham Age Herald, 25 Aug. 1906.
48. Moore, II, 263.
49. Columbia Daily Herald, 25 Mar. 1907.
50. Nashville Banner, 27 Feb. 1897.
51. Nashville Banner, 4 March 1897.
52. Nashville Banner, 10 April 1897.
53. Columbia Daily Herald, 15 June 1907.
54. McCarley manuscript in Lauderdale County folder in Alabama State Archives.
55. Nashville Banner, 5 May 1908.
56. Maury Democrat, 18 Jan. 1912.
57. Moore, III, 737.
58. Ibid, I, 929.
59. Historic Muscle Shoals, 43.
60. Moore, III, 256.
61. Ibid, II, 193.
62. Ibid, II, 144; III, 64.
63. Miscellaneous note in R. Y. McClain papers.
64. Moore, II, 184.
65. Nashville Banner, 27 Oct. 1918.
66. Florence Herald, 24 Oct. 1918.
67. Florence Herald, 31 Oct. 1918.
68. Florence Herald, 7 Nov. 1918.
69. Florence Herald, 21 Nov. 1918.
70. Florence Herald, 5 Dec. 1918.
71. Moore, II, 180.
72. Florence Herald, 8 May 1919; 27 Feb. 1919.
73. Florence Herald, 23 Jan. 1919.
74. Florence Herald, 30 Jan. 1919.
75. Florence Herald, 1 Jan. 1919.
76. Florence Herald, 20 March 1919.
77. Ibid.
78. Florence Herald, 20 March 1919.
79. Florence Herald, 27 March 1919.
80. Florence Herald, 12 June 1919.
81. Florence Herald, 14 Aug. 1919.
82. Florence Herald, 4 Sept. 1919.
83. Florence Herald, 25 Feb. 1915.
84. Florence Herald, 14 Aug. 1919.
85. Moore, II, 251.
86. Florence Herald, 18 Dec. 1919.
87. Figures in Lauderdale County folder, Alabama State Archives.

CHAPTER V

1. Florence Times, 25 Feb. 1968.
2. Ibid.
3. Moore, II, 272.
4. Ibid, II, 184.
5. Ibid, II, 359.
6. Ibid, II, 256.
7. Clipping in Mary Threet Sharp Clippings, no date.
8. Tennessee Valley Historical Society program 31 Jan. 1965.
9. Florence Times, 21 June 1948.
10. Moore, II, 265.
11. Ibid, II, 280.
12. Florence Times, 12 April 1927.
13. Moore, II, 288.
14. Clipping in Mary Threet Sharp Clippings, no date.
15. Florence Times-News, 6 Jan. 1928.
16. Stewart L. Udall, The Quiet Crisis, 1963, 141.
17. Tennessee Historical Quarterly, Dec. 1943, 326.
18. Address of John F. Kennedy--program distributed by Tenn. Valley Authority.

19. Florence Picture, 18 Oct. 1967.
20. Florence Times, 29 Oct. 1967.
21. Florence Times, 8 Jan. 1968.
22. Diary of Raymond Y. McClain.
23. Ibid.
24. Udall, 141.
25. Florence Times, 28 Jan. 1968.
26. Ibid.
27. Writer's personal diary, 1941-1943, 1944-1945.
28. Florence Times, 6 June 1965.
29. Miscellaneous clipping in Mary Threet Sharp Clippings.
30. Florence Times, 10 June 1948.
31. Florence Times, 2 March 1948.
32. Florence Times, 18 Aug. 1968, 12 Jan. 1968.
33. Florence Times, 9 Jan. 1949.
34. Florence Times, 18 July 1965.
35. Florence Times, 25 Aug. 1968, 8 Sept. 1968.
36. Florence Times, 26 June 1958.
37. Souvenir folder of Lauderdale County Courthouse given at dedication of new building.
38. Florence Times, 1 Jan. 1967.
39. Ibid.
40. Ibid.
41. Florence Times, 1 Jan. 1968.
42. Ibid.
43. Ibid.
44. Florence Times, 23 Sept. 1927.
45. Florence Times, 19 Jan. 1968.
46. Florence Times, 26 March 1968.
47. Historic Muscle Shoals, 35.
48. Florence Times, 11 June 1968; 20 June 1968.
49. Florence Times, 25 Feb. 1968.
50. Florence Times, 25 Feb. 1968, 9 June 1968.

ADDENDUM

Sources cited with each entry.

1850 CENSUS

Free inhabitants in District 1 in the county of Lauderdale, state of Alabama enumerated by me in October 1850: M. T. Wilson, assistant marshall. Column headings: Name of every person whose usual place of abode on the first day of June 1850 was in this family; age; birthplace; occupation; other information recorded which might be of interest.

Household 1
James Howie	33	S. C.	Overseer
Annie "	33	Tenn.	
Andrew "	11	Ala.	
Mary "	9	Ala.	
Sarah "	7	Ala.	
Marthy Ann "	5	Ala.	
Nancy Ann "	3	Ala.	
John "	1	Ala.	

Household 2
William Ward	43	Va.	Carpent.
Amanda "	31	Ala.	
Susan "	10	Ala.	
Samuel "	8	Ala.	
Virginia "	6	Ala.	
Annie "	3	Ala.	
James Letsinger	25	Tenn.	"
Marion Love (male)	22	Ala.	"
Elias Grimes	21	Tenn.	"
Robert Bailey	21	Ditto	Florist
Wm. A. Watkins	19	Ala.	"
Robert Do	16	Ala.	*
James Adkerson	11	Ala.	

Household 3
Thomas Massey	64	S.C.	Farmer
Jane "	60	S.C.	
Elizabeth "	21	S. C.	
Elizajane '	18	Ala.	

Household 4
George Grimes	47	N.C.	Farmer
Hetty	47	S. C.	
Caroline	25	Ala.	
William	22	Ala.	Ass't
Nancy	20	Ala.	
Polly	18	Ala.	
Misouri (female)	16	Ala.	
Hetty 2nd	14	Ala.	
Eliza	12	Ala.	
George 2nd	10	Ala.	
Peter	7	Ala.	
Chapman Hough	25	Ala.	S.Teacher

Household 5
Abner Beard	30	Va.	Farmer
Esther	27	Tenn.	
Levi Spinkes	9	Ala.	
James ---	4	Ala.	

*learning trade

Household 6
Nathaniel Smith	31	N.C.	Farmer
Eliza Smith	31	Tenn.	
Levy ? (Jery?)	9	Ala.	(7??)
Mary Ann	6	Ala.	
James	3	Ala.	
Josephus	1	Ala.	

Household 7
Nimrod House	36	S.C.	Farmer
Permentney (?)	23	Tenn.	
William	12	Tenn.	
James Monroe	2/12	Ala.	
Enoch Brewer	40	N.C.	Farmer
Jane	48	S.C.	
Sanders	18	Tenn.	Ass't
Elizajane	15	Ala.	
Riley	14	Tenn.	
Anjaline	12	Tenn.	
John	10	Tenn.	
Mary	8	Ditto	
George	6	Ditto	
Henry Brewer	16	Ditto	Ass't
Lusindy Cantrell	8	Ala.	

Household 9
Allen Howell	32	Ditto	Farmer
Larinda	33	Tenn.	
John Wilson	8	Ala.	
Jonathan Bailey	7	Ditto'	
Mary Francis	5	Ditto	

Household 10
Mary Howell	55	Va.	Farmer
Willis	21	Ala.	Ass't
John	19	Ditto	Miller
Amanda	13	Ditto	
William Sloss	25	Do	Physician

Household 11
Ransom Howell	37	Tenn.	Miller
Eliza	33	S.C.	
William	16	Ala.	Student
Joseph	15	Ala.	
Martin Van Buren	14	Ala.	
John Randolph	9	Ala.	
Ann Eliza Wilson	3	Ala.	

Household 12
Jasper Smith	34	unknown	laborer
Cassy Ann	22	Ala.	
George Washington	5	Ala.	
Presley Harden	10/12	Tenn.	

Household 13
Name	Age	Origin	Occupation
Wilford Curtice	45	Ky.	Shingler
Nancy Curtice	35	Unknown	
Caroline	19	Alabama	
Leanah	17	Ala.	
Daniel	15	Ala.	
Thomas	14	Ala.	
Murrell (male)	12	Ala.	
Rody	10	Ala.	
Mary	8	Ala.	
James	7	Ala.	
John	4	Ala.	
Anne	1	Ala.	

Household 14
Name	Age	Origin	Occupation
Thos. W. Clemmons	43	Tenn.	Farmer
Zilthy	37	N.C.	
Isema (male)	16	Tenn.	Ass't
Caroline	15	Tenn.	
Elizajane	12	Ditto	
Aaron	9	Ditto	
Millissa	7	Ala.	
Marion	5	Ala.	
Jasper	4	Ala.	
Thomas 2nd	2	Ala.	

Household 15
Name	Age	Origin	Occupation
Williamson Clemmen	19	Tenn.	Laborer
Matilda	18	Miss.	

Household 16
Name	Age	Origin	Occupation
Peter Moone (Moore?)	60	Va.	Taylor
Lucy	50	Ditto	
Peter 2nd	20	Alabama	Ass't
Elias	18	Ala.	Student
Elizabeth	16	Ala.	
Charles	13	Ala.	

Household 17
Name	Age	Origin	Occupation
Susan Norwood	60	N.C.	Carding & Spinning
Thompson Roberson	23	Tenn.	Woodchooper
Narsissa	21	Ala.	

Household 18
Name	Age	Origin	Occupation
John Briant	42	N.C.	Farmer (Meth.)
Milla	40	Tenn.	
William	18	Ditto	Ass't
Mary	16	Ditto	
Jefferson	13	Ditto	
Marion (male)	11	Ditto	
Allen	10	Ditto	
Nathaniel	7	Ditto	
John	3	Ditto	
Nunsutts (male)	11/12	Ala.	
William Olliver	27	Tenn.	Shoem'kr

Household 19
Name	Age	Origin	Occupation
Andrew Dyer	24	Tenn.	Carp'ter
Margarett	20	Ditto	
Thomas	2	Ala.	
William	6/12	Ala.	

Household 20
Name	Age	Origin	Occupation
Ivy Lawson (male)	55	Georgia	Farmer
Margarett	53	N.C.	
Martin van buren	19	Georgia	Ass't
Temperance	16	Tenn.	
Frances Marion (Male)	14	Alabama	
Jasper	10	Ala.	
Elizabeth	8	Ala.	
Newton	7	Ala.	

Household 21
Name	Age	Origin	Occupation
Joseph Hardwick	30	Ala.	Farmer
Nancy	28	N.C.	
Anne	4	Ala.	
Francis	2	Ala.	

Household 22
Name	Age	Origin	Occupation
James Hendrix	44	Ala.	Farmer
Nancy	34	Ala.	
Starling (male)	17	Ala.	Ass't
Lusinda	14	Ala.	
Paskil (male)	12	Ala.	
Dennis	10	Ala.	
Malissa	9	Ala.	
Pinkney	7	Ala.	
John	5	Ala.	
Sarah	4	Ala.	
Wiley	1	Ala.	
Hannah Wesson	72	Virginia	

Household 23
Name	Age	Origin	Occupation
John Anderson	60	Ireland	Farmer
Ellender	56	S. C.	
Polly Nail	26	S. C.	
Laura Anderson	18	S. C.	
Ellender 2nd	16	S. C.	
Samuel Nail	7	Ala.	
John Do	4	Ala.	
Levi H. Sport	19	Tenn.	Asst.

Household 24
Name	Age	Origin	Occupation
Wm. R. Anderson	32	S. C.	Farmer
Mary	28	Ala.	
Lodoska	12	Ala.	Farmer
John	8	Ala.	
Margarett	5	Ala.	
Malinda Anderson	3	Ala.	
Thomas	2/12	Ala.	

Household 25
Name	Age	Origin	Occupation
James E. Anderson	30	S. C.	Farmer
Catherine	27	Ala.	
Nancy	8	Ala.	
Leander	5	Ala.	
John	4	Ala.	
Sarah	1	Ala.	
Lusinda Heffington	23	Tenn.	

Household 26
Name	Age	Origin	Occupation
Wm. B. Ollive	26	N.C.	Farmer
Feby jane	34	Ala.	
John Randolph	6	Tenn.	

continued

Household 26 continued
William	4	Ala.	
Huguriah	1	Ala.	

Household 27
John Blackhard	33	Tenn.	Farmer
May Ann	26	Ala.	
Lawson Freeman	32	Unknown	Ass't
Wm. Blackhard	10	Tenn.	
Thomas	9	Tenn.	
John	6**	Tenn.	
Mary	11/12	Ala.	

Household 28
Wm. Reynolds	30	Ala.	Farming
Amanda	22	Tenn.	
Marthy	2	Ala.	
Empress	11/12	Ala.	

Household 29
Willis Archer	45	Ga.	Smithing
Mary	44	Ditto	
Eliza	19	Ditto	
William	17	Ditto	Striker
Selby (male)	15	Ala.	
Sarah	12	Ala.	
Annie Mary	9	Ala.	
Caroline	6	Ala.	
Marthy	4	Ala.	

Household 30
William C. Bailey	39	Tenn.	Farmer
Nancy	29	Ala.	
Elizabeth	10	Ala.	
Ann Eliza Wilson	8	Ala.	
Richard H. Clay	6	Ala.	
Thomas Wilson	5	Ala.	
James ---	1	Ala.	

Household 31
Hughriah Reynolds	21	Tenn.	Farmer
Mary	18	Ala.	
Elender (Female)	2/12	Ala.	

Household 32
James M. Reynolds	27	Ala.	Farmer
Polly Ann	24	Tenn.	
Alexander	2	Ditto	

Household 33
Hugh Reynolds	55	N. C.	Farmer
Elizabeth	50	N.C.	
Wesley	21	Ala.	Asst.
George	18	Ala.	Asst.
Joseph	16	Ala.	Do
Pinkney	14	Ala.	
Winston	12	Ala.	
Elizabeth 2nd	10	Ala.	
Randolph	8	Ala.	

Household 34
Thomas McBride	60	Tenn.	Farmer
Nancy	50	Ditto	

**Milton, male, age 4, omitted by mistake.

Household 35
Joseph Moss	27	Ala.	Farmer
Margarett	25	Ala.	
Thomas	7	Ala.	
Mary	1	Ala.	

Household 36
Washington Campbell	23	Tenn.	Farmer
Mary jane	19	Ala.	
Mary 2nd	2	Ala.	
William	9/12	Ala.	
Alexander Campell	20	Tenn.	Ass't

Household 37
William Howell	48	Tenn.	Farmer
Lucretia	46	Tenn.	
Sarah	24	Ditto	
Nancy	22	Ditto	
Catherine	22	Ditto	
James	20	Ditto	Ass't
Levi	18	Ilinoise	Ass't
Polly	13	Tenn.	
Phillip	11	Ditto	
Permelia	8	Ditto	
William 2nd	5	Ala.	
Isabella	5	Ala.	
Salena	3	Ala.	

Household 38
William Carter	61	Va.	Farmer
Narsissa	31	N.C.	
James	18	Tenn.	Ass't
William 2nd	16	Tenn.	Student
Nancy	14	Tenn.	
Amous	12	Tenn.	
Matilda	10	Ditto	
Mary	8	Ala.	
John	4/12	Ala.	

Household 39
Ellison Hardwick	25	Ala.	Carp'ter
Rachel	20	N.C.	
Richard	3	Ala.	
Sarah	4/12	Ala.	
Sarah Ollive	60	N.C.	
James	23	N.C.	Florist

Household 40
Daverson Kirklin	27	Ala.	Farmer
Elizabeth	22	Ala.	
Sarah	6/12	Ala.	

Household 41
John Liles	60	Unknown	Farmer
Mary	59	S. C.	
Amous	30	S. C.	Carp'ter
Mary 2nd	18	S. C.	
Abigall	18	S. C.	
Marion (male)	16	Ala.	Student

Household 42
Thomas Liles	32	S.C.	Farmer
Rebecca	38	? Ala.	
continued	12	Ala.	

C-3

C-4

Household 42 continued
Orlena Liles (female) 12 Ala.
Elizabeth   11 Ala.
Nancy   9   Ala.
John Simpson   8   Ala.
Charles   5   Ala.
Julious Ceaser)   2   Ala.

Household 43
William H. Wilkes   36   Va.   Farmer
Mary C.   37   Ky.
John E.   12   Ala.
James R.   10   Ala.
Joseph P.(?)   7   Ala.
William G.   6   Ala.
Mary jane   5   Ala.
Levi O.   3   Ala.
Andrew Jackson   11/12 Ala.

Household 44
Alexander Auston   54   S. C.   Farmer
Sarah   44   N.C.
Sinthia   65   S.C.

Household 45
Joseph Kirklin   60   S.C.   Farmer
Mary Kirklin   60   S.C.
James N.   25   Ala.   Asst.
Richard   21   Ala.   Asst.
Enoch   18   Ala.   Asst.
Mary 2nd   14   Tenn.
Marthy Ann   11   Ala.
Rufus   9   Ala.

Household 46
James Clark   73   Va.   Farmer
Nancy   73   Ditto
Nancy Bond   40   Tenn.
Betty   18   Tenn.
Mahaley   14   Ala.

Household 47
Joel Harder   42   Tenn. Farmer
Mary   42   Ditto
James   18   Ditto Asst.
Kasiah   16   Ditto
Elizabeth   13   Ditto
Matilda   10   Ditto
Rachel   8   Ditto
John   6   Ditto

Household 48
Robert Kirklin   32   Va.   Farmer
Mary   30   S.C.
Misouri   9   Ala.
Mary Ann   8   Ala.
William   7   Ala.
Joseph   4/12 Ala.

Household 49
William Shelton   60   Virginia Carp'ter
Sarah   57   Ditto
Polly Ann   32   Kentucky
Elizabeth   22   Alabama
Joseph   19   Ala.   Florist
Kindrick   16   Ala.   Do

Household 50
Hannetta Gwin   29   Ala.
Caleb Do   7   Ala.
Pinkney   4   Ala.
Almarenda   2   Ala.

Household 51
Elizabeth Hendrix 63   S. C.   Farming
William   28   Alabama Asst.
Misouri   29   Ala.
Joseph   6   Ala.
James K. Polk   4   Ala.
Isac   1   Ala.

Household 52
James L. Clark   30   North C. Farmer
Martha   21   Alabama
Sarah   8   Ala.
Sarena   7   Ala.
Elizabeth   5   Ala.
Amanda   4   Ala.
Joseph   2   Ala.
Jonnathan   2/12 Ala.

Household 53
Thomas Clark   29   Ala.   Farmer
Lusinda   23   Ala.
Nancy   6   Ala.
Francis (female)   3   Ala.
William   1   Ala.

Household 54
Powers, Blackburn 54   South C. Farmer
Mary   45   Ditto
Liddy Ann   20   Ala.
Mary Ann   18   Ala.
Elizabeth   14   Ala.
Luvick   13   Ala.
Tamyra   11   Ala.
Malissa   5   Ala.

Household 55
John -- (possibly ditto) 25 South C. Asst.
Caroline   25 Ala.

Household 56
Jesse Blalock   38   South Caro. Farmer
Mary Ann   35   Ditto
William   16   Tenn.
Catherine   13   Tenn.
continued

C-5

Household 56 continued
Anne Eliza Wilson   8   Ala.
Henry Clay   6   Ala.
Jane   4   Ala.
John   2   Ala.

Household 57
John Hunt   30   Tenn.   Laborer
Nancy   28   Ditto
Wesley   10   Ditto
William   9   Ditto
Mary   8   Ditto

Household 58
Mahaley Walker   45   N. C.   Farmer
Nacy (female)   19   Alabama
Andrew Jackson   16   Ala.   Asst.
John Tyler   12   Ala.
Mary   4   Ala.
William   2   Ala.

Household 59
Davey Ostean   50   Georgia   Farmer
Francis (female)   35   S. C.
Luvick   13   Ala.
Josephine   8   Ala.
Nancy   7   Ala.
Eliza   3   Ala.
David   4/12 Ala.

Household 60
Jane Weatherford   23   N.C.   Carding-Spin'g
William   17   Tenn.   Laborer
Thomas   4   Ala.

Household 61
Elizabeth Lyons   50   N.C.
William   30   Tenn.   Shoemaker
Mary   10   Ditto
                         Tenn

Household 62
Andrew Martin   39   Tenn.   Wagonmaker
Feby (Phoebe)   49   Tenn.
George   33   Ditto   None
William   14   Ditto
Gertrude   15   Tenn.
Andrew 2nd   9   Ditto
Phoeby 2nd   4   Ala.

Household 63
Darius H. Butler   53   N. C.   Farmer
Nancy   40   Ala.
Gavin   19   N. C.   Asst.
Diddana (female)   18   Tenn.
Sarah   15   Ala.
Caroline   13   Ala.
Wealthy Boarin   12   Ala.
Margett   10   Ala.
Emily   8   Ala.
Elizabeth   5

Household 63 continued
Benjamin Franklin   1   Ala.
Marquis Lafaitt   1   Ala.
James Daniel   16   Tenn.   Asst.

Household 64
Darius D. Butler   22   N.C.   Laborer
Martha   23   Ala.
Mary   3   Miss.
John   2   Ditto

Household 65
Henry W. Butler   33   N.C.   Farmer
Lethy   23   Tenn.
John   3   Ala.
Bennett   1   Ala.

Household 66
Richard Rice   57   N.C.   Farmer
Elizabeth Rice   57   Va.
Rachel   27   Ky.
George   22   Ala.   Student
James   20   Ala.   None
William   18   Ala.
Sollerman   15   Ala.

Household 67
Lusinda Dillahunty 51   Va.   Farmer
Sally   25   Ala.
Thomas   14   Ala.
Marion Carter (male) 4 Ala.

Household 68
Easter Chisholm   69   Ky.   Farmer
Tolliver L. Do.   38   Tenn.   Asst.
Malissa   35   Tenn.
Hetty   30   Tenn.
Francis (female)   24   Tenn.

Household 69
William Thrasher   53   Va.   Farmer
Rachel   45   Tenn.
Emily   23   Ala.
Malissa   19   Ala.
Kenston (male)   17   Ala.   Student
Hetty (Kitty?)   14   Ala.
James   13   Ala.
Mitchel   10   Ala.
Houston   7   Ala.
John   5   Ala.

Household 70
Horatio Massey   26   N.C.   Overseer
Elizabeth   22   Ditto
Thomas   4   Ala.
Collins   2   Ala.

Household 71
Davy Grisham	39	Tenn.	Farmer
Rachel	47	Tenn.	
Lewis	16	Ala.	
Lusinda	16	Ala.	
Susan Sutton	23	Ala.	

Household 72
Philimon Grisham	50	Georgia	Farmer
Delila	46	Tenn.	
Sarah	26	Ala.	
Elizabeth	24	Ala.	
Andrew Jackson	20	Ala.	Asst.
William	18	Ala.	None
Mary	16	Ala.	
Margarett	11	Ala.	
Marthy	7	Ala.	
Juliar	5	Ala.	
Isabella	2	Ala.	

Household 73
Wilson Tucker	30	Tenn.	Molder
Malinda	32	Ala.	
Annie	25	Tenn.	
William	8	Ala.	
Francis (female)	6	Ala.	
Betty	4	Ala.	
Mary	2	Ala.	

Household 74
Harbord Tucker	23	Tenn.	Molder
Eliza	22	Tenn.	
James	2	Ala.	

Household 75
James A. Johnson	44	Virginia	Mashinest
Elizabeth	36	Ala.	
Frances K.(?)(female)	17	Ala.	
Felix	8	Ala.	
James Wright	26	Ireland	Ditto
William Scott	22	Tennessee	Ditto
Daniel Morison	21	Tennessee	Ditto
John Thompson	19	Ireland	Ditto

Household 76
Thomas Martin	23	Kentucky	Ditto
Catherine	20	Tennessee	
Frances (female)	3	Ky.	
Marthy	6/12	Tenn.	

Household 77
Matilda Bedford	63	N.C.	Farming
Charles	38	N.C.	Physician

Household 78
William Barnhill	57	N.C.	Farmer
Sarah	30	Tenn.	
Everline	18	Ditto	
continued			

Household 78 continued
Caladonia	17	Ditto	Farmer
Matilda	15	Ditto	
Nancy	13	Ditto	illegible
Catherine	11	Ditto	
Mahaley	8	Ditto	
Lusinda	6	Tenn.	
Frances (Female)	3	Ala.	

Household 79
Zadekiah Willett	36	Ala.	Farmer
Mary	23	Ala.	
Mary 2nd	6	Ala.	
William	5	Ala.	
Elizabeth M.	2	Ala.	
Washington Tucker	13	Ala.	

Household 80
James Hutton	56	N.C.	Farmer
Winford	45	Tenn.	
Ellender	20	Ala.	
Martha	18	Ala.	
Addaline	13	Ala.	
Juliar	10	Ala.	
Sarah	5	Ala.	
George Washington	3	Ala.	

Household 81
Artitesa Pig (female)	38	N.C.	Weaving
Ranson	20	Tenn.	Laborer
Martha	18	Tenn.	
Jane	16	Tenn.	
Davis	13	Tenn.	None
Mary	12	Ala.	
Andrew Jackson	10	Ala.	
William	5	Ala.	
Sarah	4	Tenn.	
Margarett	2	Tenn.	

Household 82
John Carr	50	Tenn.	Smith
Margarett A.	23	Ala.	
Elizabeth	18	Ala.	
John	12	Ala.	
Mary	9	Ala.	

Household 83
James W. Rhodes	25	Ala.	Wagoner
Elizabeth	17	Ala.	
Malissa	12	Ala.	

Household 84
Henry Grissom	50	N.C.	Farmer
Dianah	20	Ala.	
William	18	Ala.	Asst.
George	17	Ala.	Student
Hiram (female) ↓	16	Ala.	Do
Henry, Jr.	15	Ala.	
Hiram (male)	14	Ala.	
continued			

Household 84 continued
Parilee (female)   13   Ala.
Columbus   4   Ala.
Henry Rhodes   22   Ala.   Laborer
James Neighbors   23   S. C.   Carp'ter

Household 85
Jonnathan B. Young   32   Tenn.   Millright
Matilda   13   Ala.
Charles   10   Ala.
James   8   Ala.
Julia Ann Young   5   Ala.
Mary Ann   3   Ala.

Household 86
Nathan Neighbors   59? S. C.   Farmer
Lucretia   57? S. C.
Nancy   12   Ala.

Household 87
William Freeman (??) 18   Ala.   Miller
Sarah C.   14   Ala.
Mary Freems(?)   45   S. C.
Jonnathan Rhodes   52   S. C.   Farmer
Mary   44   S. C.
Thomas   20   Ala.   Asst.
Isabella   18   Ala.
Addaline   16   Ala.
Polly   14   Ala.
William   11   Ala.
John   9   Ala.
Polly   4   Ala.
Magdalana   1/12 Ala.

Household 89
Jess Thomas   42   Tenn.   Farmer
Myra   34   Tenn.
Thomas   14   Tenn.
Ann   11   Tenn.
James   8   Tenn.
Mary   5   Ala.
John   4   Ala.
Benton   2   Ala.
Martha Watkins   18   Ala.

Household 90
Joseph Imes   51   N. C.   Farmer
Elizabeth   50   N. C.
Elvira   28   N. C.
Marthy Ann ?   26   N. C.
John   24   Ala.
George W.   20   Ala.   Asst.
Bassle   16   Ala.   Do
Darkus May   65   Unknown   (female)
Mary Watsen   3   Ala.
Household 90 marked "Poor House"

Household 91
William Wassen   31   Ky.   Sawyer
Amanda   23   Tenn.
Sarah   2   Ala.

Household 72
William Calk (?)   42   Ala.   Sawyer
Amelia   28   Tenn.
Amanda   3   Ga.
Ann Eliza   8/12 Tenn.

Household 93
Jiles McBride   39   Tenn.   Farmer
Mary Ann   38   Tenn.
Mary 2nd   16   Tenn.
Thomas   14   Tenn.
John   12   Tenn.
Nancy   10   Tenn.
Ann   8   Tenn.
James   6   Tenn.
Casper   4   Tenn.
Ruthy   2   Ala.
Landers M. Norwood   18   Tenn.   Asst.
James F. Do   15   Tenn.   Do

Household 94
Sterling Hendrix   22   Ala.   Miller
Rebecca   20   Ala.
Leander   1   Ala.

Household 95
Jesse Oakley   34   Tenn.   Farmer
Mary   33   Tenn.
James   8   Ala.
William   6   Ala.
Thomas   1   Ala.
Elizabeth Oakley   64   Virginia
Joshua Bailey   25   Unknown

Household 96
Samuel Martin   55   Ireland   Farmer
Eveline   43   N. C.
Ann   21   Ala.
Matilda   18   Ala.
Malissa   16   Ala.
Emily   15   Ala.
Lewis, Candis   12   Ala.   (female)
Hariett, John (?)   10   Ala.
Andy, Alexander   21   Ala.   Asst.

Household 97
Reddington Barnes   36   S. C.   Farmer
Nicy   36   S. C.
William   12   Ala.

Household 98
John Blanton   72   Virginia   Farmer
Mary   53   S. C.
Ransom   24   Ala.   Asst.
continued

C-8

Household 98 continued				
Martha	17	Tenn.		
Mary 2nd	20	Tenn.		
Jesse	15	Tenn.		
Benjamin	13	Ala.		
Mary Brown	14	Ala.		

Household 99
Dennis ? House ?	56	S. C.	Farmer
Sally	52	S. C.	
Warren ?	22	Ala.	Asst.

Household 100
Bennett ? Gillem	50	Va.	Carp'ter
Nancy	39	Ditto	
Sarah J.	15	Ala.	
Matilda ?	11=	Ala.	
William	19	Ala.	
John	5	Ala.	
George	2	Ala.	

Household 101
John Wesson	30	Ala.	Farmer
Sarah	28	Ala.	
Mary	8	Ala.	
William	6	Ala.	
Amanda	4	Ala.	
Susan	5/12	Ala.	

*Household 102 here - see opposite

Household 103
Joshua Shelton	23	Ala.	Farmer
Mary	24	Tenn.	
Leander P.	a	Ala.	

Household 104
James Smith	41?	Tenn.	Wagon-
Sabera ?	43	Ky.	maker
Martha Ann	22	Tenn.	
William	19	Tenn.	Farmer
Samuel	15	Tenn.	
Lucy	13	Ala.	
Josiah	11	Ala.	
John A.	8	Ala.	
Robert	3	Ala.	

Household 105
Josiah Fowler	35	Ala.	Miller
Mahuldy	25	S. C.	
William	13	Ala.	
Mary E.	10	Ala.	
Juliar Ann	2	Ala.	

Household 106
John Obriand ?	38	Tenn.	Farmer
Ellen	24	Ala.	
James C. O'Briand	13	Ala.	
Dellala A. E. O'Briand	11	Ala.	
William Do	8	Ala.	
Joseph	7	Ala.	
Lucy	1	Ala.	
Sarah Wood	20	Ala.	

Household 107
Owen Obriand	46	Va.	Farmer
?asthi	37	S. C.	
Martha	18	Tenn.	
Levi	16	Tenn.	Asst.
Joseph	12	Ala.	
Louisa	10	Ala.	
Henry	6	Ala.	
Sarah	5	Ala.	

Household 108
B. W. Oneal	36	Ga.	Farmer
Martha Ann	31	Do	
Julia	11	Ala.	
Allice	7	Ala.	
Anne E.	3	Ala.	

Household 109
| Samuel Tilman | 21 | Ala. | Farmer |

Household 110
T. ? P. Bourland	47	Ky.	School teach-er
Rosanah	38	Do	
Winiford	19	Ala.	Farmer
Martha	17	Ala.	
Cinthea	15	Ala.	
Felix Grundy	9	Ala.	
Dallace M.	5	Ala.	

*Household 102
Lorenzo D. Fowler	35	S.C.	Miller
Mary	23	Ala.	
Perrissa A.	8	Ala.	
Wesley W.	6	Ala.	
Mary F.	4	Ala.	
Nancy Ann Elizabeth	9/12	Ala.	

Household 110 continued
Marhsal, W.	3	Ala.	
Mary	1/12	Ala.	
John G. Sport	20	Ala.	Laborer

Household 111
C. L. Pruett	26	Ala.	Farmer
Elizabeth	22	Tenn.	
Warren	1	Ala.	
Mary F.	1	Ala.	

Household 112
Thomas Pruett	67	Va.	Farmer
Elizabeth	63	S.C.	

Household 113
Holman Bird	46	Do.	Carpenter
Elizabeth	37	Tenn.	
Moses	21	"	none(insane)
William	18	"	student
Sarah Anne	14	"	
Mary Anne	12	"	

continued

C-9

Household 113 continued			
Marthey Ann	11	Tenn.	
Harriett	8	Miss.	
Elizabeth	7	Miss.	
Thomas	2	Tenn.	
Daniel	1	Ala.	

Household 114			
James M. Golightly	35	Tenn.	Farmer
Dianah	25	Tenn.	
William	13	Ala.	
Permelia	11	Ala.	
James M.	6	Ala.	
Mary Do	5	Ala.	
Robert	2	Ala.	
Mary Counts	20	Unknown	
James Golightly	77	S. C.	None

Household 115				
Abalom F. Jeans	41	Tenn.	Farmer	
Elizabeth	39	S.C.		
John	18	Ala.	Student	
William	16	Ala.	Student	
Luprisa	15	Ala.	(female)	
Thomas	13	Ala.		
Joseph	11	Ala.		
Absalom 2nd	10	Ala.		
Mary	8	Ala.		
Massey	9	Ala.	(female)	
Marthy	4	Ala.		
Huldy	2	Ala.		
Nancy	10/12	Ala.		

Household 116			
E. G. Phillips	25	S.C.	Farmer
Narissa Ann	21	Ala.	

Household 117				
William Philips	54	S.C.	Farmer	
Jane	53	"		
Massey	35	"	(female)	
Louisa	25	"		

Household 118			
Joseph Beddington	79	S.C.	None
Joseph Phillips	23	Ala.	Farmer
Elizabeth	20	Tenn.	

Household 119			
Thomas K. Stewart	20	Ala.	Laborer
Catharine	24	Ala.	

Household 120				
Thomas W. Young	33	Ala.	Farmer	
Frances	33	S.C.	(female)	
Nancy	10	Ala.		
Thomas	9	~~Ala. Tenn.~~*		
Frances Marion	6	Tenn.	(male)	
Mary E. Young	4	Ala.		

Household 120 continued			
George Fifer	2	Ala.	
William Bennett	8/12	Ala.	
James N. Carr	20	Ala.	Laborer

Household 121			
James Hughs	23	Ala.	Farmer
Sarah	32	Ala.	
Robert T.(P.?)	6	Ala.	
William	5	Ala.	
James	3	Ala.	
Francis A.	1	Ala.	

Household 122				
Elihugh Jeans	30	Ala.	Farmer	
Mary	27	Ala.		
Francis Marion	10	Ala.	(male)	
Martha	8	Ala.		
Matilda	6	Ala.		
Thomas	1	Ala.		

Household 123			
Richard Quaser	47	Ala.	Overseer
Elizabeth	28	N.C.	
Mary	12	Ala.	
Susan	10	Ala.	
Amanda	8	Ala.	
Caroline	6	Ala.	
Alexander	3	Ala.	
Andrew Jackson	11/12	Ala.	

Household 124			
Henry Golightly	72	S.C.	Farmer
Elizabeth	27	Tenn.	
Susan	17	Tenn.	
Samuel	8	Tenn.	
Lurinda	4	Ala.	
George Washington	3	Ala.	

Household 125			
Henry Pruett	29	S. C.	
Eliza	25	Tenn.	
Thomas	7	Ala.	
Henry Clay	5	Ala.	
John	3	Ala.	
Mary	1	Ala.	
Seth Count	15	Tenn.	

Household 126			
Samuel Johnson	28	Ky.	Farmer
Elizabeth	25	S.C.	
Steven	32	Ky.	Ass't
Thomas	30	Ky.	
Rachel Johnson	24	Ala.	
Allen	16	Ala.	None

Household 127			
Elizabeth Littleton	78	Va.	Farmer
Samuel	40	S.C.	Pysician
Eliza Cotton	35	Unknown	

*Marked through this way on census.

Household 128
Jabus Beard	55	Va.	Bats., Farming
Sarah	45	"	
Henry	23	"	Wagon M'kng.
Benjamin	21	"	Physician
Mary	18	"	
Sarah	17	"	
Sophia	15	Ala.	
Martha	12	"	
Emily	11	"	

Household 129
Henry Pruett	50	S. C.	Farming
Malinda	42	Tenn.	
Malissa	19	"	
Manurva (?)	18	Ala.	
John C.	16	"	Student
Oliver H. P.	12	"	
Latitia	14	"	
William	10	"	
Marshal	8	"	
Robert	5	"	
Matilda	2	"	

Household 130
David Littleton	56	S.C.	Farming
Elizabeth	47	Va.	
William	24	Ala.	Ass't
Washington	21	"	"
Robert	18	"	"
John	15	"	
Lusinda	12	"	
Franklin	10	"	
Samuel	8	"	
Rebecca	5	"	

Household 131
James O'Briand	51	Va.	Farming
Elizabeth	40	Tenn.	
George Wash.	22	Ala.	Ass't
Rebecca	21	"	
Oliver	20	"	"
James	14	"	
Polly	13	"	
Samuel	11	"	
Charles	9	"	
Mary Ann	2	"	

Household 132
| Rody Duff | 60 | S.C. | Carding 7 Spin'g |
| Polly | 21 | " | Weaving |

Household 133
| Mary Duckett | 64 | S.C. | Farming |

Household 134
John H. Dewburry	42	N.C.	Farming
Labora	39	Ky.	
William	21	Ala.	Ass't
Louisa	19	"	
Daniel	18	"	"
Luisa (?)	13	"	
Henry	12	"	
Thomas	10	"	
John L.	7	"	
Richard	5	"	
Sarah E.	4	"	
Nancy	2	"	
Patrick Duff	20	"	Laborer

Household 135
John Rhodes	59	S.C.	Farming
Amelia	43	Ga.	
Columbus	23	Ala.	Teacher
William A.	21	"	"

Household 136
Thos. M. Philips	50	Va.	Farming
Mary	50	S.C.	
Elizabeth A.	28	"	
Willian N.	25	Ala.	Ass't
___ A. (male)	23	Tenn.	"
Mary P.	21	"	
Manurvey P.	18	Ala.	
Willis G.	17	"	
Wiley B.	15	"	
Joseph E.	11	"	
Lusinda A. (?)	10	"	
Frances	6?	"	

Household 137
William Stewart	23	Ala.	Farming
Mary	19	Tenn.	
Maderson	1	Ala.	

Household 138
Starling Philips	78	Va.	Farming
Mary	77	"	
Sarah Stewart	48	S.C.	
James L. Ditto	17	Ala.	Ass't

Household 139
Starling W. Philips	29	Tenn.	Farming
Hannah	25	Tenn.	
Mary	4	Miss.	
Nancy	2	Tenn.	

Household 140
John Burnet	39	Va.	Laborer
Ellen	26	S.C.	
Ruben	5	Ala.	
Arabella	3	"	

Household 141
Joshua Polk   25   Tenn.   Farmer
Eliza   19   Tenn.
James   1   Ala.

Household 142
Levi Darby   25   Ala.   Farmer
Nancy   25   Tenn.

Household 143
James A. Fisher   24   S.C.   Farmer
Sarah   21   Ala.
Nancy   3   Ala.

Household 144
Isem Waldrip   54   S.C.   Shoemaker
Mary   48   N.C.
Thomas   18   Tenn.   Student

Household 145
A. P. McDaniel   30   Ala.   Farmer
Francis   21   Tenn.
Sally C.   5   Ala.

Household 146
Persillar Glades   65   S.C.   Seamstress
Anderson   16   Ala.   Student

Household 147
Robert T. McQuerder 37   Ky.   Farmer
Elizabeth   34   S.C.
Sarah   11   Tenn.
Willis   9   Ark.
William   7   Tenn.
George   6   Tenn.
John   4   Ala.
Venson   10/12   Ala.

Household 148
Benjamin J. Randle 68   Va.   Farmer
Martha   49   Va.
William   22   Ala.   Chairmaker
James   19   Ala.   Student
Francis Marion   17   Ala.   Do (Male)
Sarah   15   Ala.
Benjamin   12   Ala.
John   9   Ala.
David   6   Ala.

Household 149
William Rhodes   36   S.C.   Farmer
Caroline   27   Ala.
Matha   8   Ala.
Columbia   6   Ala.   (female)
Nancy   4   Ala.
Mary   2   Ala.
Lusinda   8/12   Ala.

Household 150
John Rhodes   60   S.C.   Farmer
Penelopy   60   S.C.

Household 151
William Cocks   38   S.C.   Farmer
Mary Ann   35   Tenn.
Martha   15   Tenn.
James   13   Tenn.
John   10   Tenn.
George   7   Tenn.
John Wesley   5   Ala.
Mary   3   Ala.
Sarah Ann   7/12   Ala.

Household 1521
Jacob D. Casey   53   S.C.   Farmer
Sarah   29   Tenn.
Zalena   18   S.C.   (female)
William W.   15   Ala.
Charity   9   Ala.
Sarah   7   Ala.
Leander   5   Ala.
Rutitia   3/12   Ala.
Willis Lucust   54   S.C.   Physician

Jacob Duckett Casey, above, born 23 Nov. 1796, died 11 June 1853, buried in Casey Cemetery. He was the son of General Levi Casey and Elizabeth Duckett. He married Charity Whitmire.

William W. Casey, above, born 1834 in Florence, was the third child of Jacob and Charity Casey; he died 27 Oct. 1912. He married 1857 to Josephine A. Westmoreland, daughter of Alfred and Mary Westmoreland of Westmoreland County, Va. He was taken prisoner during the Civil War. On his release he served in the 9th Tenn. Regiment under General N. B. Forrest. (References: "General Levi Casey" by Mrs. Andrew J. Darby, DAR Magazine, April 1960, 277-278; Biography of W. W. Casey in History of Tennessee by Will T. Hale and Dixon Merritt, published 1913.)

Josephine Westmoreland Casey's memoirs, written in 1910, may be found in the Tennessee State Library and Archives, Nashville, Tennessee. She was the granddaughter of Charles and Elizabeth Littleton, and memoirs are based on the teachings and memories of her grandparents.

Household 153
Thomas Farmer	60	N.C. Shoemaker
Elizabeth	58	N.C.
John	30	Tenn. Do
Marion	25	Ala. Do
Martha	21	Ala.
Susanah	20	Ala.
William Darbey	9	Miss.
Richard Do	7	Do

Household 154
Thomas E. Casey	38	S.C. Wagonmaker
Laura Ann	25	Ala.
Ann Eliza	3	Ala.
James M. Sherod	30	Ala. Farmer
Sarah	24	Ala.
Felix	4	Ala.
John	1	Ala.
John Anderson	30	Ala. Shoemaker

Household 155
James P. Oakley	24	Tenn. Farmer
Elizabeth	24	Ala.
Margarett	3/12	Ala.
Rpbert Carr	20	Ala. Ass't

Household 156
John C. Hall	30	Tenn. Farmer
Nancy	21	Do
Mary	3	Ala.
Minda	2	Ala.
Francis	4/12	Ala.

Household 157
Abner Hendrix	68	N.C. Farmer
Margarett	71	Tenn.

Household 158
John N. Cantrell	26	Ala. Saddle m'kr
L. W. Ditto	22	Ala. Ditto

Household 159
John B. Arnold	29	S.C. Farmer
Martha	24	Ala.
Hannah	9	Ala.
Ivy Eli (male)	5	Ala.
Nancy	3	Ala.
James	2	Ala.
Joshua Fowler	25	Ala. Grocery-keeper

Household 160
A. A. Wesmoreland	40	Tenn. Merchant
Mary "	37	Tenn.
Josaphene	12	Ala.
Thomas	8	Ala.
William Duncan	13	Tenn.

(Mary Littleton, born 15 March 1814, married Alfred A. Westmoreland. She was the daughter of Charles Littleton and Elizabeth Henderson; Littleton was soldier in the Revolution.)

Household 161
Benjamin Whitney	47	N.C. Farmer
Mary	46	Do
David	18	Tenn. Ass't
Henry	16	" "
Lusinda	14	"
Elizabeth	12	"
Benjamin H.	9	"
Felix Grundy	4	"

Household 162
Samuel Hendrix	34	Tenn. Farmer
Elender	29	S.C.
Edwin	13	Ala.
Nelson	10	"
James	8	"
Columbia	6	" (female)
Alonso	4	"
Sissaly	2	"
Sparty V. Curtice	16	Tenn. Laborer

Household 163
Henry Darbey	51	S.C. Farmer
Martha	50	Do
Rickard	17	Ala. Ass't
Thomas	11	Ala.
Philip Darbey	75	Maryland Hog Feed
James Kallicutt	40	S.C. Physician
Martha Do	15	Ala.

Philip Darby, married Nancy Davis, served in Creek War, born in Maryland, lived in Union County, S. C. He came to Lauderdale County circa 1816. (From The Darby Family, page 8; copy found in Tennessee State Library and Archives, Nashville.)

Dr. J. D. Calicut married Nancy Littleton, born July 1810. She was the daughter of Charles Littleton, Revolutionary War soldier and his wife Elizabeth Henderson. (Tennessee DAR Roster, page 1022.)

Household 164
William Stags	28	Tenn.	Laborer
Rebecca	31	Ala.	
Parilee	8	"	
Margarett	6	"	
Laura	3	"	
Calafornia	1	"	(female)

Household 165
William Walker	36	Tenn.	Farmer
Susan	19	Ala.	
Sarah	4	"	
Henry	3	"	
George	4/12	"	

Household 166
Thomas Dewberry*	38	Tenn.	Farmer
Elizabeth	25	Va.	
Millard	9	Ala.	
Jabus	7	Ala.	
Thomas	5	Ala.	
Mary	3	Ala.	
Sarah	4/12	Ala.	
Joseph Sport	14	Ala.	

Household 167
Calip Hews	32	S.C.	Farmer
Nancy	30	Tenn.	
Catharine	28	S.C.	

Household 168
Rubin L. Littleton**	45	Ditto	Farmer
Frances	43	Ditto	
Mary	18	Tenn.	
Hannah	16	Tenn.	
William	13	Tenn.	
Simmons (male)	11	Ala.	
Francies (female)	9	Ala.	
Jane	5	Ala.	
Zachariah Taylor	4	Ala.	
Sarah	8/12	Ala.	

Household 169
Charles E. Littleton	22	Tenn.	Laborer
Jane	19	Ala.	

---

*Thomas Dewberry, son of William, married Elizabeth Beard, born near Lynchburg, Va., daughter of Abner Beard. (Hale-Merritt, Volume VII, page 2180.)

Jabus Dewberry taken prisoner at Fort Donelson, died as prisoner of war.

**Rubin Littleton, born 17 Dec. 1805, son of Charles Littleton and his wife Elizabeth Henderson. (Tennessee DAR Roster, page 1022.)

C-13

Household 170
Agnus Reeder (fem.)	50	S.C.	Farming
William	23	Ala.	Ass't
Alminer	6	Ala.	
Rachel	3	Ala.	

Household 171
Lusilla Darbey (fem.)	66	S.C.	Farming
Benjaman	48	Do	Blacksmith
Jacob	19	Ala.	Striker
Margarett	16	Ala.	
Mary	4	Ala.	
Jacob Masters	78	S.C.	None

Household 172
Pulaski Darbey	31	S.C.	Farmer
Nancy	25	Ala.	
Martha	8	Ala.	
Henry	6	Ala.	
Mary Mariah Luiser	4	Ala.	
Nancy 2nd	2	Ala.	
Thomas Smith	18	unknown	Cass'tie..

Household 173
William B. Young	26	Ala.	Merchant
Mary	20	Ala.	
Mary Elizabeth	6	Ala.	
Martha	4	Ala.	
John	2	Ala.	
Jane	11/12	Ala.	

Household 174
James Wallice	27	S.C.	Farmer
Lusinda	33	Ditto	
Thommas	13	Ala.	
William	11	"	
John	9	"	
Harrison	7	"	
Marion	4	"	
Margarett	3/12	"	
Laura A. Roberson	16	"	

Household 175
Alexander Haddock	27	Ala.	Farmer
Mary	23	Miss.	
Thomas	6	Tenn.	
John	5	"	
William	2	"	

Household 176
John B. Wallis	25	Ala.	Cropper
Emily	24	"	
Nancy	4	"	
John	2	"	
James	1	"	
Samuel Wallis	18	"	Student

C-14

Household 177				
Wiley B. Edwards	43	Tenn.	Meth.	Farmer
Ann Jane	36	N.C.		
Benjaman	12	Ala.		
Jarid	10	Ala.		
Mary E.	7	Ala.		
John	5	Ala.		
Wiley 2nd	1	Ala.		

Household 178
Thomas Wallice	55	N.C.	Farmer
Harriso	20	Ala.	Ass't
Samuel J.	17	"	Do
Salenius M.	22	"	Do

Household 179
Alexander McCuin	35	S.C.	Cropper
Malisinda	35	S.C.	
Ellen	14	Ala.	
Sarah	10	"	
John	6	"	
Nancy	2	"	

Household 180
Eghton Grissom	61	N.C.	Farmer
Nancy	50	N.C.	
Henry	23	Ala.	Ass't
Eghton 2nd	21	"	Do
Franklin	21	"	Do
Lewis	19	"	Do
Andy	17	"	Do
Emeline	15	"	
Catharine	11	"	

Household 181
James H. Roberson	29	Tenn.	Farmer
Martha	23	Ala.	
Nancy	6	"	
Richard	4	"	
Rachel	3	"	
Margarett	1/12	"	

Household 182
Andrew Harris	33	S.C.	Farmer
Mary Ann	35	S.C.	
Lucinda	12	Tenn.	
John	6	Ala.	
Amanda	4	"	
Margarett Ann Eliza	1	"	
John Calvin Jackson	12	S.C.	

Household 183
Illijah Fowler	39	S.C.	Farmer
Mary	31	S.C.	
Mary Jr.	15	Ala.	
Margarett	13	Ala.	
Martha	11	Ala.	
continued

Household 183 continued
Columbus	10	Ala.	(male)
Samuel	6	"	
James	4	"	
Richard	2	"	
Susan	3/12	"	
Ebineser Young	17	"	Student

No household 184

Household 185
Jessi Wallice	32	Ala.	Overseer
Culver	32	"	
Mary	14	"	
Sarah	11	"	
Annie	9	"	
William	8	"	
Susan	6	"	
Henry	5	"	
Nancy	3/12	"	

Household 186
Richard Faris	78	S.C.	Farmer
Margarett	60	Ireland	

Household 187
Thos. P. McKnight	53	Ky.	Farmer
Elizabeth	50	Do	
Robert	27	Tenn.	Ass't
Mary	24	Ala.	
Margarett	22	"	
John	19	"	Student
Samuel	17	"	Do
Frances	14	"	
Jennathan Allen	17	"	Laborer

Household 188
Seath Millar	38	N.C.	Farmer
Charlotte	38	S.C.	
Sarah	8	Ala.	
Wiley	6	Ala.	

Household 189
Nathaniel Blasingim	27	Tenn.	Farmer
Matilda	28	Ky.	
Elizabeth	7	Tenn.	
William	5	Ala.	
Catherine	3	"	
George	1/12	"	

Household 190
Andrew Kelley	28	Tenn.	Farmer
Manurvy	23	Ala.	
Sarah	5	Ala.	
Samuel Kelley	3	Ala.	
Hariett	8/12	Ala.	
William Mathena	20	unknown	laborer

C-15

Household 191			
Burel McManus	38	S.C.	Farmer
Mary	37	S.C.	
William Linsley	18	Tenn.	Student
Samuel Tucker	10	unknown	

Household 192			
Philip Darbey	28	Alabama	Farmer
Mary	27	S.C.	
William	8	Ala.	
Elijah	2	Miss.	
Columbus	3/12	Ala.	
Charley Sharp	25	"	Ass't

Household 193			
William N. Scott	33	Tenn.	Miller
Mary	31	"	
Andrew	10	"	
Mary 2nd	7	"	
Sarah	5	"	
Zachariah Taylor	2	Ala.	

Household 194			
Hiram Gailey	35	Ga.	Miller
Ufratus (female)	35	Do	

Household 195			
James Cobb	45	S.C.	Farmer
Mary	42	S.C.	
Margarett	23	S.C.	
John	15	Tenn.	
Elizabeth	13	"	
William	12	"	
Martha	10	"	
Philip	8	Ala.	
James	6	"	
Rickman	3	"	
Mary 2nd	6/12	"	

Household 196			
William Noland	31	Tenn.	Farmer
Catharine	31	N.C.	
James	8	Tenn.	
John	4	Tenn.	
Sarah	5/12	Tenn.	

Household 197			
William Pingston	28	Tenn.	Farmer
Nancy	20	Tenn.	
James	7/12	Ala.	
John Jinnings	24	Tenn.	Laborer

Household 198			
John S. Farr	35	Tenn.	Overseer
Mary Farr	10	Tenn.	
George	8	Tenn.	
Martha	5	Ala.	
James	4	Ala.	
Florence	1	Ala.	

Household 199			
Matthew Pingston	51	S.C.	Farmer
Sina (Lena?)	50	Tenn.	
Peter	17	"	Student
Rebecca	14	"	
Lawson	12	"	
Anderson L.	10	"	
Houston	7	Ala.	

Household 200			
William L. Posey	33	Ga.	Shoemaker
Nancy	27	S.C.	
Elizajane	9	Ala.	
Thomas	6	"	
Martha	4	"	
Sarah	2	"	

Household 201			
Richard Lewis	40	N.C.	Farmer
Martha Ann	27	N.C.	
Mary Ann	8	Ga.	
Rosanah	7	Ala.	
Dianah	5	"	
Andrew Jackson	3	Tenn.	
Benjaman Franklin	1	Ala.	

Household 202			
William Eddings	22	Ala.	Farmer
Martha	21	"	
Mary	2	"	
Nancy	1	"	

Household 203			
Samuel Patton	45	N.C.	Carpenter
Elgiva	40	N.C.	
Martha	22	Ala.	
John	18	Do	Do
Mary	14	"	
Harriett	12	"	

Household 204			
Wesley Mills	55	S.C.	Farmer
Phody	49	N.C.	
Anjalina	18	Tenn.	
Malinda Ann	10	Tenn.	
Tirissa Ann	9	Tenn.	
John	6	Ala.	

Household 205			
Pinkney Dollerson	25	Tenn.	Ass't
Mahaley Dollerson	26	Tenn.	
Amanda	2	Ala.	

Household 206			
John D. Darbey	34	S.C.	Farmer
Sarah	27	"	
Rosanah	11	Ala.	
Ruthy	9	"	
Mary	5	"	
David	3	"	

Household 207
Richard Valentine   23   S.C.   Farmer
Mary   20   Tenn.
Harriett   3   Ala.
John   2   Ala.

Household 208
Benjaman Selby   43   S.C.   Farmer
Mary   33   S.C.
Nancy   16   Ala.
Philip   15   "
James   15   "
Sarah   12   "
Joshua   8   "
Owen   5   "
Thomas   3   "

Household 209
John Sego   60   S.C.   Farmer
Margarett   57   S.C.
Rebecca   33   S.C.
Sally   30   S.C.
John 2nd   25   S.C.   Ass't
Chapman   22   Ala.   Do
William   20   "   Do
Ezra   15   "

Household 210
David Belew   30   Ala.   Farmer
Peggy   21   "
James   1/12   "

Household 211
Mary Hammer   50   S.C.   Poltry
Louiser   28   Ala.
Matilda   26   "
Martha   24   Ohio
Elizabeth   20   "
Rachel   19   Ala.
Kasiah   16   "
Mary   14   "

Household 212
Samuel Grey   51   Ky.   Farmer (?)
Spelman   31   Tenn. (female)
Samuel Grey   14   Tenn.
George Washington   6   Ala.
Thomas Jefferson   4   Ala.
John C. Cahoun   1   Ala.

Household 213
John Cooper   28   Tenn. Farmer
Carmelta   26   Ala.
Wiley   8   Tenn.
Thomas   4   Ala.
William   2   Ala.

Household 214
Thomas Noland   65   Tenn. None
Sarah   60   Tenn.

Household 215
George Ferrel   43   S.C.   Farmer
Mary Ann   36   S.C.
Margarett   18   N.C.
Samuel   16   Ala.   Ass't
Martha   14   "
Thorsy   12   "
Nancy   8   "
John Randolph   2   "
Mary Ann   11/12   "
Lusinda A. Gray   12   "
Manurvey Do   9   "

Household 216
Shelton Scott   27   Tenn. Farmer
Nancy   22   Ala.
Rachel Noland   75   N.C.

Household 217
Thomas Dowdy   20   Ala.   Farmer
Margarett   43   Tenn.
Polly   18   Ala.
Margaett 2nd   16   "
William   12   "
Andrew Jackson   10   "

Household 218
James Dowdy   61   S.C.
Catharine   58   N.C.
Catharine 2nd   28   Ala.
Lavina   16   Ala.
Jerrymyrah   22   Ala.   Ass't
John   19   Ala.   Do
Martha   14   Ala.

Household 219
James T. Dowdy   23   Ala.   Farmer
Margarett   18   Ala.
Mary   32   N.C.

Household 220
Calip Linsley   23   unknown Farmer
Lucy Ann Linsley   32   Tenn.
Nancy   4   Tenn.
Philip   2   Tenn.
Joseph   1/12   Ala.

Household 221
Elijah Young   60   S.C.   Laborer
Martha   21   unknown
("Contrast great" had been written in by
the enumerator by this couple.)

Household 222
Robert Austin   30   Ala.   Farmer
Eliza   27   "
Francis Marion (male)   5   "
Columbus   3   "
Sarah Threete   16   "
Mary Elizabeth Threete   14   "

Household 223
James Valentine   26   S.C. Laborer
Eliza   22   S.C.
Ruel   4   Ala.
William   2   "
James   1/12   "

Household 224
Charles Sharp   55   Va.   Farmer
Matilda Sharp   57   Do
Charles 2nd   21   Ala. Student
Matilda   17   "
Eliza   14   "
David   9   "

Household 225
Philip Linsley   54   Tenn. Farmer
Frances   53   Va.
Silvester   20   Tenn. Ass't
Andrew Jackson   18   "   Do
Aaron   14   "
Robert   11   "
Polly   8   Ala.
John S.   4   "

Household 226
John P. Carr   40   Tenn. Farmer
Martha   37   "
Eliza P.   16   Ala.
Malissa   14   "
Hugh   12   "
Lena   8   "
Thomas   6   "
Margarett   4   "
James   1   "

Household 227
Thos. K. Young   41   Tenn. Farmer
Ardiness (female)   35   Tenn.
Mickle Young (male)   11   Ala.
Benjaman   8   "
Frances   7   "
Mary   5   "
Martha   2   "
Thos. Benton   2/12   "

Household 228
Nathaniel Cobb   24   S.C. Farmer
Martha   22   S.C.

Household 229
James Cr_o_dock   25   Ala. Farmer
Martha   18   "
Josaphine   1/12   "

Household 230
John Aust_o_n   61   Va.   Farmer
Martha   57   S.C.

Household 231
Jesse Y. Aust_e_n   31   Ala. Farmer
Hariett   25   "
Parilee   11   "
Jane   9   "
Robert   7   "
John   8/12   "

Household 232
Alexander Russell   60   S.C. Farmer
Yancy (male)   22   "   Ass't
Alexander 2nd   16   Ala. Do
Joseph   14   "
Caroline   12   "

Household 233
William Coonts*   38   Tenn. Farmer
Salena   30   Ala.
George   12   "
John   9   "
Amanda   7   "
James   4   "

Household 234
George Roach*   66   N.C. Farmer
Lavina   53   S.C.
Edmond   21   Ala. Ass't
Mary   13   "
Richard   10   "
Kiley   6   "

Household 235
David A. Garrett   26   S.C. Farmer
Elizabeth   25   S.C.
Nancy   6   Ala.
Mary   3   "

---

*William Koonce, born Mt. Pleasant, Tenn., married Salena Roach, daughter of George and Vina Roach. (Source: Moore Questionnaire of George Roach Koonce, born 1839, found in Manuscript Section of Tennessee State Library and Archives Nashville. George R. Koonce served in Company B, 9th Tennessee, during the Civil War.

Household 236
John P. Threete*	24	Ala.	Farmer
Mary	25	Ala.	
Thos. W. Threete	4	Ala.	
Sarah	3	Ala.	
Steven Jarman (blind)	80	N.C.	None
Levi Waldrop	19	Ala.	Workman
Joseph Threet	18	"	Student
Susan Waldrep	12	"	

Household 237
Calvin Terrell**	38	S.C.	Farmer
Matilda	32	Tenn.	
John	12	Ala.	
Joseph	11	"	
Pinkney	9	"	
Rickman	8	"	
Sarah	6	"	
Thomas	4	"	
Alford Threete	23	"	Ass't
William	13	"	

Household 238
Catharine Jones	30	S.C.	Farming
John	18	Ala.	Ass't
Mary	14	"	
Samuel	13	"	
Catharine Watson	7	Tenn.	

---

*John Perry Threet, born 18 May 1825, died 29 Oct. 1888; married Mary Waldrop, born 20 March 1823, died 3 July 1910. Thomas W. Threet is believed to be Thomas Weakley Threet.

Joseph Threet is J. J. Threet, born 17 Oct. 1832, died 6 Nov. 1868. He was wounded at Spring Hill, Tennessee, during the Civil War, and died as a result of the wounds received there. He was buried in the La Neave Cemetery. He was brother of John P. Threet, Alford Threet, and William Threet.

**Calvin Terrell married Matilda Threet. She is thought to be buried in the La Neave Cemetery. According to family tradition she died in the middle of the Tennessee River--family on way to Arkansas and she developed yellow fever.

William Threet, born 5 March 1839, died 11 May 1899. His sisters were Liza Threet Austin, Sarah Threet Dowdy, Mary Threet Bevis, and Matilda Threet Terrell. (From family records of Mrs. Mary Threet Sharp, granddaughter of William Threet.)

Household 239
Mary Wallice	42	Tenn.	Farmer
Thomas	19	Ala.	Ass't
Kisiah	21	"	
Robert	15	"	
Mary 2nd	14	"	
John	13	"	

Household 240
William Terrell	22	N.C.	Farmer
Ellender	27	Ala.	
Polly Ann	3	"	
Catharine	1/12	"	

Household 241
William Wallice	23	Ala.	Farmer
Nancy	24	Ala.	
James	7	"	
Thomas	3	"	
Mary	3/12	"	

Household 242
David Dowdy	51	N.C.	Farmer
Mary	45	S.C.	
James Maderson	21	Ala.	Ass't
Sarah	18	"	
William	13	"	
David	11	"	
Mary	7	"	

Household 243
| William Rolin | 77 | N..C. | Farmer |
| Betty | 55 | S. C. | |

Household 244
Moses Clanton	40	S.C.	Farmer
Kisiah	43	"	
James	12	Ala.	
Jessi	11	"	
Caroline	10	"	
Elias	8	"	
Joseph	6	"	
Jerrymyrah	4	"	

Household 245
William McKorkle	27	S.C.	Farmer
Sarah	30	N.C.	
Houston	3	Ala.	
Elizabeth	6/12	Ala.	
James M. Do	74	unknown	none

Household 246
Henry McKorkle	25	S.C.	Farmer
Martha	24	Ala.	
Columbia	2	Ala.	

C-19

Household 247				
Margaret Do	43	S.C.	Farmer	
Thomas	23	Ala.	Ass't	
Joseph	21	"	"	
Mary	16	"		
Margarett	14	"		
William	10	"		
Andrew Jackson	8	"		

Household 248
John McKorkle	40	S.C.	Farmer
Rebecca	37	"	
Mary	16	Ala.	
Elizabeth	14	"	
Thomas	12	"	
John	10	"	
Rebecca 2nd	8	"	
Malissa	4	"	
Martha	2	"	

Household 249
Keet Hold	53	S. C.	Laborer
Francis (female)	45	Ga.	
Matilda	17	Tenn.	
James	14	"	
Elizabeth	9	"	
Polly	2	Ala.	

Household 250
Shelton Scott	30	N.C.
Mary Scott	20	Ala.

Household 251
Daniel Welch	80	S.C.	None
Darkeys (female)	50	N.C.	
William	14	Ala.	

Household 252
John Murphey	49	S.C.	Farmer	
Allice	44	S.C.		
Nancy	21	Ala.		
James	18	"	Ass't	
William	16	"	"	
Polly Ann	14	"		
Francis (female)	12	"		
John 2nd	10	"		
Marion (male)	8	"		
Rebecca	5	"		
William Hankins	30	unknown	none	

Household 253
Thomas Henson	50	S.C.	Whiskey
Mary	45	"	for sale
Benjaman	19	Ala.	Smith
Polly	18	"	
Robert	17	"	
Martha	16	"	
Eliza	14	"	
George	7	"	
Thomas	3	"	

Household 254
John W. Young	33	Tenn.	Wagons
Eliza	24	Ala.	
John W. Jr.	5	"	
James	3	"	
Jackson Jones	35	S.C.	Laborer

Household 255
Ancel Henson	40	Tenn.	Farmer
Martha	44	S.C.	
Jincey	22	Tenn.	
Elizabeth	19	Ilinoise	
Polly Ann	17	Tenn.	
William (note)	16	Tenn.	None
Cynthia	14	Tenn.	
Isem	13	Ala.	
Sarah	11	"	
Margarett	10	"	
Hariett	8	"	
Jessi	5	Tenn.	

(Note: William marked "Deaf, dumb, lame, insane.")

Household 256
James Adams	22	Tenn.	Laborer
Jane Adams	21	"	
William	3	Ala.	
Louiser	4/12	"	

Household 257
John Adams	56	Ga.	Farmer
Frances	46	S.C.	
John 2nd	16	Tenn.	Ass't
Isac	14	"	
Louiser	12	"	
Charlott	9	Ala.	
Joseph	7	"	
Caroline	5	"	
David	3/12	"	

Household 258
Felix Huddleston	33	S.C.	Farmer
Elizabeth	44	Ala.	
Caroline	16	"	
Joseph	14	"	
George	12	"	
Wiley	10	"	
Thomas Jefferson	8	"	
Zachariah Taylor	6	"	
Andrew Jackson	4	"	
Elizabeth	2	"	

Household 259
Thos. Henson	21	Tenn.	Laborer
Mary	22	Ala.	
Samuel	3	Ala.	
John	2	Ala.	

Household 260
Samuel Henson   53 S.C. Farmer
Jane   53   "

Household 261
Thos. C. Jones   46 S.C. Farmer
Mary Ann   33 Ala.
Nancy   12   "
Mary Jane   7   "
Sarah   6   "
John   4   "
William   1   "

Household 262
Abner Scott   40 Tenn. Farmer
Mary   40 Tenn.
Milton   21 Tenn. Ass't
Nancy   20   "
William   19 Ala. Do
Andrew Jackson   15   "

Household 263
Joseph Young   75 S.C. Farmer
Sarah F.   42 Tenn.
Joseph 2nd   13 Ala.
Susan   11   "
Marion   10   "

Household 264
Devenport Lathan 54 S.C. Meth./
Annie   52   "   Farmer
Asbury   31   "   Merchant
James   20 Ala. Clerk
Elizabeth   17   "
George Washington 16 "   Student
Francis Marion   13   "   (male)
Manurvy   12   "
John Harison   9   "
Devenport 2nd   6   "

Household 265
Mary D. Jackson 25 Ala. Farmer
James   6   "
Eliza   5   "
Elizabeth   4   "

Household 266
Josiah Perkins   45 S.C. Farmer
Nancy   40 S.C.
Franklin   19 Ala. Ass't
John   18   "   Do
Foster   14   "
Moses   12   "
Wesley   9   "
Thomas   7   "
Joseph   5   "

Household 267
John Henson   25 unknown overseer
Caroline   23 Ala.
Devenport   2   "
Robert   5/12   "

Household 268
Elizabeth Martin 63 S.C. Farmer
Nancy   23 Ala.
John Green   15   "   Ass't

Household 269
Wesley Williams 35 Ala. Farmer
Hariett   29 S.C.
Elizabeth   8 Ala.
Alexander   9   "
Mary Ann   6   "
Cynthia   4   "
George Washington 3   "
Devenport   1   "

Household 270
Samuel South   20 Tenn. Laborer
Lutitia   19 Ala.

Household 271
John Martin   21 Ala. Farmer
Nancy   21   "
Robert   4/12   "

Household 272
Mary Ward   43 S.C. Spin'g and
Matilda   39 Ga.   Weaving
Isac   20 Tenn. Laborer
Sarah Ann   14 Tenn.
Elizabeth   10 Ala.

Household 273
Hollas A. Talley 18 Tenn. Laborer
Sylvina   16 unknown
(Marked "Married within the year.")

Household 274
Manchester Johnson 60 N.C. Farmer
Molly   63   "
Thomas   35   "   Ass't
Sally   33   "
Annie   26   "
Henry   24   "   Ass't
Daniel   20   "   "
Charles Beckham   7 Ala.
Elizabeth Do   4 Ala.

Household 275
William Pealder 41 S.C. Farmer
Elizabeth   20 Tenn.
William   16 Ala. Ass't
continued

C-21

Household 275 continued			
Thomas	10	Ala.	
Nancy Ann	9	"	
Robert Bruce	7	"	
Kesiah	6	"	
Mary	2	"	
Alabama	1/12		

Household 276
W. J. Hitchcock	32	Tenn.	Carpenter
Rutha	20	Tenn.	
Ransom	11	Ala.	
Mary Jane	10	Miss.	
Sarah	7	"	

Household 277
James Parish	25	Tenn.	Laborer
Martha	4	"	
Elizabeth	2	Ala.	
Catherine Hews	25	Tenn.	

Household 278
John Hough*	45	S.C.	Farmer
Sarah*	46	"	
Amanda Ray	23	Ala.	
Mahaley Davis	42	S.C.	
George Washington	21	Ala.	Laborer

Household 279
Henry Tumblestone	32	unknown	farmer
Darkes	28	S.C.	
Hiram	10	Ala.	
Elizabeth	8	"	
Robert	7	"	
Nancy Jane	6	"	
Thomas Jefferson	4	"	
Andrew Jackson	1	"	
John C. Calhoun	6/12	"	

Household 280
| Elizabeth Turcer | 61 | S.C. | |
| Robert | 22 | S.C. | Ass't |

Household 281
Andrew Hips	46	S.C.	Carp'tr
Margarett	30	Tenn.	
George Washington	13	Ala.	
Andy	10	"	
W. H. Harison	9	"	
Charles	7	"	
Nancy	6	"	
Martha	5	"	
James	1	"	

*Marked "married within the year."

Household 282
John D. Mathas	33	N.C.	Farmer
Nancy	47	N.C.	
William	18	Ala.	Ass't
Emeline	13	"	

Household 283
John Parker	54	S.C.	Farmer
Elizabeth	40	S.C.	
Mary	20	Ala.	
Alexander	18	"	Ass't
Nancy	13	"	

Household 284
Armon Rickman	25	Ala.	Farmer
Rebecca	24	N.C.	
Lucy Do	55	S.C.	

Household 185
David Martin	35	S.C.	Farmer
Mary Ann	34	Ala.	
Rosanah	16	"	
Wiley	14	"	
George Washington	13	"	
Thomas Jefferson	11	"	(twin)
Sarena	11	"	(twin)
Robert	8	"	
Samuel Martin	6	"	
John Wilson	3	"	(twin)
William	3	"	(twin)

Household 286
| Thomas Parish | 35 | unknown | farmer |
| Eliza Ann | 25 | " | |

Household 287
Margarett Spears	60	S.C.	
Calvin	16	Tenn.	Ass't
James P.	8	Ala.	
Mary C.	6	"	
Nancy E.	3	"	

Household 288
Robert Chaney	30	Ky.	Farmer
Sarah	30	"	
Elizabeth	7	Ala.	
Hiram	4	"	
John	5/12	"	
David Do	28	Ky.	Ass't

Household 289
Rachel Price	48	N.C.	Farmer
Milton	21	Ala.	Ass't
William	18	"	"
Martha	16	"	
Mary	14	"	
Samuel	12	"	

C-22

Household 290
Daniel Long   32   Ala.   Farmer
Elizabeth   28   "
Nancy   5   "
James   4   "
Columbia   2   "
James Pool   26   "   Ass't

Household 291
Jonathan Turpin   51   Ky.   Farmer
Polly   53   S.C.
Robert   25   Ky.   Ass't
John   22   "   "
Mary   16   "
Caroline Carter   17   unknown

Household 292
Christopher Price   24   Ky.   Farmer
Lavina   18   "
(Marked "married within the year.")

Household 293
John Price   63   Ky.   Farmer
Isibella   64   S.C.

Household 294
Elizabeth Hutton   28   Ky.
John   10   Ky.
Christopher   5   Ala.

Household 299 (note)
Obediah Waters   23   Ala.   Farmer
Mary Waters   25   Ala.
John   2   "
Sarah   1/12   "
Margarett Balove   8   "

Household 300
Andy Carr   35   unknown farmer
Annie   33   Ala.
George Washington   26   "   Student
Nancy   14   "
John   11   "
Marion (male)   8   "
Wiston   6   "
Daniel   4   "
Martha   5/12   "
Joseph Carr   19   unknown laborer

Household 301
Wilson Whitsett   40   S.C.   Farmer
Elizabeth   38   Ky.
Benjaman   17   Ala.   Ass't
Margarett   13   "
Camby   12   "
Sarah   8   "
Hariett   6   "
Isac   3   "
continued

Household 301 continued
Benjaman Price   65   Ky.   Hog Feeder
Jane Eliza   63   S.C.

Household 302
William Homesley   26   Ala.   Farmer
Caroline   27   "
James   3   "
John   1/12   "
Mary Beloo   10   Tenn.

Household 303
James M. Reynolds   23   Tenn. Laborer
Kesiah   18   Ala.
(Marked "Married within the year.")

Household 304
Jonathan McMurry   43   N.C.   Farmer
Rachel Mc   36   Tenn.
Joseph   13   Tenn.
Mary   9   "
John   8   "
Sarah Emeline Jane   7   "
Patrick   2   Ala.

Household 305
John R. Bedford   30   Tenn. Physician
Addaline   24   Ala.
Matilda   4   "
Ann   3   "
Charles Bedford   2   "

Household 306
Daniel Waters   26   Ala.   Farmer
Addaline   28   "
George Washington   3   "
Levi Norman   2   "
Wm. T. Martin   10   "

Household 307
William Beckham   29   Ala.   Farmer
Manurvey   21   "
(Marked "Married within the year.")

Household 308
George Waters   77   N.C.   Farmer
Nancy   66   N.C.
Wiley Izell   12   Ala.

Household 309
James S. Martin   63   N.C.   Farmer
Margarett   60   N.C.
Elizabeth   23   Ala.
John   20   "   Ass't
Sarah   17   "
Martha Baloo   7   "
James   4   "
Wm. Douglass   20   "   Ass't

Household 310
Andrew Douglas   51 N.C. Bts. Farmer
Mary   51 "
Nathaniel   22 Tenn. Ass't
Mary   18 "
Thomas   15 "

Household 311
Thomas Simpson   59 S.C. Bts. Far-
Polly Ann   40 Ky.   mer
Christopher*   21 Tenn. Ass't
Jane*   18 Ala.
David   19 Tenn. Ass't
Caroline   15 Tenn.
Martha Ann   3 Ala.
John Turner   12 unknown

Household 312
Richard Tagsley   22 Ala. Farmer
Mahuldy   22 "
Sarah   2 "
Emeline Reyborn   16 "

Household 313
Josiah Sperrel   36 Tenn. Farmer
Kisiah   34 "
Mary Elizabeth   15 Ala.
John   23 "
Silus Fealder**   27 Tenn. Constable

Household 314
Archer Cooper   30 unknown Smith
Charlotte   29 Tenn.
Polly Ann   10 "
Betsy jane   9 "
Saby Luiser Ann Wilks Mar 8 "
Rebecca   5 "
Columbia   1 Ala.

Household 315
Delila Short   60 S.C. Poltry
Ellender   31 Tenn.
Rickard   21 "   Laborer
James   14 Ala.
Malinda   3 "

Household 316
Josiah Higgins   39 S.C. Farmer
Charlotte   39 Ala.
Calvin   19 "   Ass't
Catharine   17 "
Marthajane   15 "
Isibella   13 "
Margarett   11 "
Z. Taylor   9 "
Bedford   7 "
Richard   2 "

Household 317
Alexander Higgins   60 S.C. Smith
Isac   17 Ala. Striker

Household 318
John F. Douglass   25 Ga. Farmer
Mary Ann   21 Ala.
Marthajane   1 Ala.

Household 319
John Till   55 Philadelphia F'r
Cameller   44 S.C.
William   21 Ala. Ass't
Rasmus   18 "   "
John   17 "   "
Edwin   14 "
Weekley   13 "
Carter   11 "
Catharine   9 "
James   7 "
Gabriel   4 "
Lusinda Shall   23 "

Household 320
James Webb   46 Ga. Farmer
Edy   44 Tenn. (female)
Thomas   20 Ala. Ass't
John   16 "   "
Elizabeth Webb   15 "
Joseph   12 "
George W.   9 "
Mariah   7 "
Francis Marion   3 "   (male)
James H.   6/12 "
William J. Jordan   18 "   Laborer

Household 321
W. J. Webb   23 Ala. Farmer
Lusinda   20 Tenn.
Joseph K. Behkham   14 Tenn.
Elizabeth Webb   1 Ala.

Household 322
James K. Witherspoon   42 N.C. Farmer
Jane   35 Ireland
Elizabeth   14 Ala.
Charles   12 "
Sarah   9 "
Jane 2nd   7 "
Harriett   5 "
Mary   3 "
George Webb   24 "   Stage Driver

*Marked "married within the year."
**Silas Fielder, died 15 Aug. 1907; buried Fielder Cemetery, Dickson County, Tenn.

C-24

Household 323
Catharine Whitehead	55	Va.	Farmer
Louiser	32	Ala.	
William	30	"	None
Betty Ann	20	Tenn.	
Lusinda	18	Ala.	
Nathaniel	14	"	

Household 324
Saransus Whitehead	23	Tenn.	Overseer
Clark (female)	15	Ala.	
(Marked "married within the year.")			

Household 325
Margarett Tagley	61	Va.	Farmer
John	30	Tenn.	Ass't
Nancy	25	"	
Richard	9	Ala.	
Elizann	6	"	

Household 326
Nathaniel Tibbs	48	Va.	Laborer
Noma (female)	41	S.C.	
Mary	19	Tenn.	
Nathan	17	"	None
Parthenia	12	"	
Andy	7	"	
Elijah	6	"	
Jasper	2	Ala.	

Household 327
Jane Fowler	54	Va.	
William	22	Tenn.	Farmer
James Monroe	20	Ala.	Ass't
Martha	18	"	
Martha Whitehead	34	"	

Household 328
Wm. A. Tibs	21	Tenn.
Saley Catharine	24	"
Maomry (?) Sultanna	4/12	"

Household 329
Brant (?) Dukes	53	S.C.	Farmer
Betsy	41	"	
Robert	1	Ala.	

Household 330
Benjamin F. Green	31	unknown/	
Martha Ann	22	Tenn.	laborer
Manurvey Ann	1	Ala.	

Household 331
William Baner	38	Tenn.	Farmer
Bethenia	36	Ga.	
Alexander	10	Ala.	
John	7	"	
Ann Eliza	5	"	
Martha Ann	3	"	

Household 332
John Brandon	54	Tenn.	Carpenter
Emeline	48	Ala.	
Frances	16	"	
Elizabeth	14	"	
Lusinda	12	"	
James	8	"	
Sarah Jane	5	"	
Charles	4	"	

Household 333
Wm. R. Davis	26	Tenn.	School teach
Lucy	25	N.C.	
Mary	1	Miss.	

Household 334
F. A. Maxwell	30	Tenn.	Carpenter
Latitia	17	Ala.	
Martha	3/12	"	

Household 335
Wm. R. Houston	24	Ala.	Farmer
Mary Ann	65?	S.C.	(illegible)
Mary 2nd	22	Ala.	
Elizabeth	17	"	
John Wilson	16	"	

Household 336
Rhodey Lamb	37	S.C.	Farmer
James	16	Ala.	Ass't
Elizabeth	12	"	
John W. Lamb	10	"	
Sarah	7	"	

Household 337
Thomas M. Long	21	"	Laborer
Juliar Ann	19	"	
Manurvy	2/12	"	

Household 338
John S. Lansford	36	Ky.	Farmer
Annie	24	Ala.	
Milton	26	Tenn.	Ass't

Household 339
Moses Wright	51	N.C.	Farmer
Annie	49	Tenn.	
James	19	"	Ass't
Philip	14	"	
Sarah Ann	11	"	
Mary Ann	8	"	
George T. M.	6	Ala.	
Martha	3	"	

C-25

Household 340			
Drury H. Lane	52	Va.	Farmer
Agnes	46	N.C.	
Henry	20	Tenn.	Ass't
Sarah	18	"	
Elizabeth	16	"	
Sanonah	14	"	
Philip	12	"	
Agnes 2nd	11	"	
Moses	10	"	
Julia Ann	5	Ala.	

Household 341
Richard Long	21	Ala.	Laborer
Matilda	20	Tenn.	

(Marked "married within the year.")

Household 342
William Douglass	48	N.C.	Farmer
Phoeby	47	"	
Thomas	53	Va.	Carpenter
Rhody	18	Tenn.	

Household 343
Agnes Wilson	49	Tenn.	
James	18	Ala.	Student

Household 344
James Wilson	44	Tenn.	Laborer
Sarah	25	"	
Robert	5	Ala.	
Mary	2	"	
John Waldrip	17	"	Ass't

(This entry damaged.)

Household 345
Darling Brandon (male)	28	Tenn.	Workman
Nancy	26	"	
Elizabeth	13	Ala.	
Mary Brandon	5	"	
Julia Ann	3	"	

Household 346
George Murphy	73	Penn.	Farmer
Louisa	70	N.C.	
Betty	33	Tenn.	
Lavinia	6	Ala.	

Household 347
Philip Wilson	72	N.C.	Farmer
Annie	70	"	
Mary Ann Arnold	18	Unknown	

Household 348
Littleton Smith	52	S.C.	Farmer
Susanah	25	Ala.	
John	17	"	
James	14	"	
continued

Household 348 continued
Elizabeth	10	Ala.	
Mahaley (twin)	6	"	
Matilda (twin)	6	"	
Rebecca	4	"	
Henry	3/12	"	

Household 349
John Long	26	Ala.	Farmer
Sarah	21	Ky.	
Alexander	3	Ala.	
Isabeller	1	"	

Household 350
Nancy Smith	55	S.C.	Farmer
Gilbert	25	Ala.	Ass't
Pernissa	16	"	
Perry	14	"	
Collin Overton	22	"	Laborer

Household 351
Caleb Smith	26	Ky.	Laborer
Rachel	25	Tenn.	
John	2	Ala.	

Household 352
William Irey	27	Ala.	Farmer
Liddy jane	30	S.C.	
Samuel	6	Ala.	
Richard	3	Ala.	
Owen	1	Ala.	
Angaline	15	Ala.	

Household 353
Bennett Wood	52	Tenn.	Farmer
Margarett	42	Illinoise	
Sarah	20	Ala.	
Nelson	18	"	(male)
Malissa	16	"	
Benett 2nd	14	"	
John Ford	21	Ky.	Laborer

Household 354
Redman Williams	30	Ala.	Farmer
Ellender	28	S.C.	
Joseph	10	Ala.	
Rutha	5	"	
Isam	4	"	

Household 355
John Burnes	43	S.C.	Farmer
Mary	26	Ohio	
Addaline	8	Ala.	
Caroline	6	"	
Nancy	5	"	
Green	3	"	
Phoebe	1	"	
Abner Swinford	15	Tenn.	Ass't

Household 356
John Dykes   24   S.C. Laborer
Susanna   22   Tenn.
Lusinda (?)   2   Ala.
Jamima   3/12   "

Household 357
James Lamb   55   S.C. Farmer
Peggy   50   "
Martha   25   Ala.

Household 358
Elijah Young   45   Ky.   Ass't
Mary   35   Tenn.
Elizabeth   18   Ala.
Joseph   17   "   Ass't
Caroline   15   "
James   12   "
William   11   "
Devenport   10   "
Bishop   6   "
Mary   2/12   "

Household 359
William Higgins   23   Ala. Farmer
Harriet   22   "
(Married within the year.)

Household 360
John Barkins   46   S.C. Farmer
Rachel   50   "
Hannah   10   Ala.

Household 361
Newton Higgins   30   Tenn. Farmer
Stacey   29   Ga.
James   10   Miss.
Missouri   7   Ala.
John   5   "
Racheal   2   "

Household 362
Ambros Holt   51   N.C. Teacher
Nancy   37   Ga.
Elizabeth   15   Miss.
Martha Ann   11   Tenn.
Rachel   9   "
Perdue   6   Ala. (male)
Joshua   5   "
Abran Junr.   4   "

Household 363
Joseph Sharp   30   Va. Farmer
Emily   23   Tenn.
Charles   6   Tenn.
Hamon (?) (male)   3   Ala.

Household 364
James Brandon   41   Tenn. Do
Margaret   25   Ala.
Matilda   13   "
Rebecca   11   Miss.
William   7   "
John   4   Tenn.
Dennis (?)   1   Ala.

Household 365
Edwin Sharp   42   Va.   Do
Martha   44   Tenn.
James   22   Ala. Ass't
Charles   20   "   "
Elizabeth   17   "
Margaret   13   "
Ruth   10   "
Matilda   7   "
Edwin, Jr.   5   "

Household 366
John Sharp   35   Va. Farmer
Nancy   32   S.C.
Mary   14   Ala.
Sarah   12   Tenn.
Elizabeth   10   "
Carrol (?)(male)   9   Ala.
Martha   7   "
Eliza   4   "
Owen   1   "

Household 367
Robert Sharp   30   Va. Ass't
Elizabeth   25   Ala.

Household 368
Charles Sharp   20   Ala. Ass't
Julia   18   "
Reuben   1   "

Household 369
William W. Jackson   23   Ala. Laborer
Caroline   20   Tenn.
Mary Ann   3   Ala.
William (twin)   4/12   "
Elijah (twin)   4/12   "

Household 370
Jonathan Whitten   55   S.C. Farmer
Jane (?)   43   "
George   15   Ala. Ass't
Mary   13   "
Martha   12   "
Oliver H. P.   11   "
William   9   "
Almira   7   "
Nancy   5   "
Asbury   3   "
Sarah   1/12   "

Household 371
Linsay Clanton   59   S.C. Carp'ter
Malinda   28   "
Martha   13   Ala.
William   10   "
Mary   8   Tenn.
Delila   5   Ala.
Lavinia   3   "

Household 372
John Shewbird   55   S.C.   Wagon-
Darcas   66   "   maker
Jane (twin)   26   "
Moses (twin)   26   "   Do
Ellen   23   "
Marion (male)   9   Ala.

Household 373
Samuel Beasley   80   N.C.   Loom-
Malinda   21   Ala.   maker
Juda   4   "

Household 374
Ransom Shewbird   24   S.C. Laborer
Nancy   24   "
Andrew   5   Ala.
Darcas   3   "
Mary   1   "

Household 375
James Vencin   30   Ala. Shoe-
Glafy (female)   30   Tenn. maker
Nancy   6   "
John   4   "
William   2   "

Household 376
John Shewbird   28   S.C. Farmer
Jane   28   "
Charlotte   4   Ala.
Alsey   1   "

Household 377
Mary Bayless   25   Ga. Spinster
Eliza   3   Ill.
John   1   Ala.
Joseph Garmon   35   Unknown –
                         Loafer

Household 378
Stephen Rieves   60   S.C. Farmer
Eliza   22   Ala.

Household 379
John Lee   22   Ala. Farmer
Carolina   2?   S.C.
William   1   Ala.

Household 380
Asa Rieves   75   S.C. Farmer
William   27   "   Ass't
Elizabeth   25   "
Hariette   10   Ala.
Jacob   9   "
Ellen   7   "
Sarah   5   "
Mary   4   "
Emeline   3   "
John   6/12   "

Household 381
Richard Minton   70   S.C. Laborer
Martha   16   "

Household 382
John Minton   47   ?   Farmer
Sina   47   "
George   22   "   Ass't
Amanda   19   "
William   17   "
John, Jr.   15   "
Isaac   13   Ala.
Richard   5   Ala.

Household 383
Julia Welch   58   Ga.   Farming
Richard   32   Tenn. Shoemaker
Elizabeth   40   S.C.
William   14   Ala.
Mary   13   "
John   11   "
Thomas   10   "
Levi   8   "
Juda   5   "
Elijah Welch   3   "
Richard   10/12   "

Household 384
John McKelvey   24   S.C. Farmer
Sarah   26   "
Martha   2   Ala.

Household 385
Jesse Reaves   42   Tenn. Carpenter
Rhoda   26   "
Martha   15   "
Thomas   12   Ala.
John   10   "
Mary   7   "
Wiley   5   "
Sarah   3   "
Margarett   1   "

Household 386
Peter Moses   72   Penn. Shoemaker
Elizabeth   71   "

C-28

Household 387
Name	Age	Origin	Occupation
John Lee	52	S.C.	Farmer
Amy	52	Va.	
Hanah	18	Ala.	
Juliar	16	"	

Household 388
Name	Age	Origin	Occupation
Aaron Lee	27	S.C.	Farmer

Household 389
Name	Age	Origin	Occupation
Andrew Reaves	60	S.C.	Farmer
Jane	59	"	
Ellen	35	"	
Moses Shewbird	26	"	Ass't
John Towns	11	Tenn.	
Mary	2	Ala.	

Household 390
Name	Age	Origin	Occupation
Aaron Zilander	60	Ga.	Carpenter
Becca	26	"	

Household 391
Name	Age	Origin	Occupation
John McKelvey	50	S.C.	Meth./Farmer
Rebecca	43	"	
William	25	"	Do
Mancy (female)	15	Ala.	
Samuel	12	"	
George	10	"	
Rebecca (twin)	9	"	
Franklin (twin)	9	"	
Jessi (male)	6	"	
Isaac	3	"	

Household 392
Name	Age	Origin	Occupation
James McKelvey	27?	S.C.	Farmer
Lidia	23	Ala.	
John	6	"	
Juliar McKelvey	1	"	

Household 393
Name	Age	Origin	Occupation
Wm. F. Turnley	28	Tenn.	Farmer
Mary	24	S.C.	
John	5	Ala.	
Caroline	4	"	
Sarah	1	"	
James T.	23	Tenn.	
Mary Gilbert	50	S.C.	
Laura	18	Unknown	
Russle Houston	16	Ala.	Do
Pinkney	16	"	Do

Household 394
Name	Age	Origin	Occupation
Simon Kirk	47	Va.	Farmer
Hudley	36	Tenn.	
William	20	Ala.	Ass't
Joseph	17	"	"
Francis (female)	15	"	
Richard	8	"	
Thpmas	4	"	
Zachariah T.	2	"	

Household 395
Name	Age	Origin	Occupation
Moses Whitmire	43	S.C.	Farmer
Nella	33	"	
Sarah	13	Ala.	
William	11	"	
Martha	9	"	
Nancy	7	"	
Francis (female)	4	"	
Ruth	2	"	

Household 396
Name	Age	Origin	Occupation
J. B. Wooten	27	Tenn.	Shoemaker
Rhody	27	Tenn.	
Mary	4	Ala.	
Martha	2	"	
Antha	4/12	"	

Household 397
Name	Age	Origin	Occupation
Robert M. Nelson	37	Tenn.	Do
Mary	30	Tenn.	
Elizabeth	12	Ala.	
John	6	Tenn.	
Lydia	4	Tenn.	
Edward	3	Ala.	
Lutah	1/12	"	
Lydia Norvell	65	N.C.	
R. J. Walker	22	Tenn.	Shoemaker

Household 398
Name	Age	Origin	Occupation
Abrahar Coal	38	Tenn.	Workman
Milley Coal	34	Ala.	
Mary	14	"	
George	12	"	
Wesley	10	"	
John	8	"	
Judy	6	"	
Robert	4	"	

Household 399
Name	Age	Origin	Occupation
Jesse Caroll	30	Tenn.	Farmer
Nancy	31?	S.C.	
Addison	13	Ala.	
Mary	11	"	
John	9	"	
Sarah	8	"	
Catherine	5	"	
Scott	3	"	
Teylor Z.	1	"	

Household 400
Name	Age	Origin	Occupation
John C. Reaves	54	S.C.	Wagons
Rebecca	53	"	
Martha	23	Ga.	
Matthew	21	"	"Lofur" (?)
Amanda	18	Tenn.	
Jane	16	"	
William	10	Ala.	
Henry	16	"	

Household 401
Joseph H. Bratton	25	Tenn.	Laborer
Jane	22	"	
James	2	Ala.	

Household 402
Simon Damrons	53	N.C.	Farmer
Mary	41	N.C.	
Elizabeth	23	Tenn.	
Mary	20	"	
Marthy	18	"	
Benjamin	14	"	
Sarah	11	Ala.	
Abagale	9	"	
Idella	6	"	
Robert	1	"	

Household 403
George Bratton	52	N.C.	Farmer
Mary	46	Unknown	
James	26	Tenn.	Ass't
Rachel	21	Tenn.	
Hugh	24	"	Do
Jane Bratton	23	"	
John	22	"	
Ellen	18	"	
Nancy	17	"	
William	14	"	
Thomas	10	Ala.	
Samuel	8	"	
Mary	4	"	

Household 404
Nicholes Welch	28	Tenn.	Farmer
Elizabeth	27	Missouri	
Juda (female)	9	Ala.	
Mary	7	"	
Rebecca	4	"	
Alzvia	2	"	
Bennett Minten	30	S.C.	Ass't

Household 405
Peter Holmes	46	Do	Smith
Mary	36	Do	
John	21	"	Striker
Elizabeth	18	"	
Caroline	15	"	
Sarah	13	"	
Granville	11	"	
Francis (female)	9	"	
Louisa	6	"	
James	3	Ala.	
William	1	"	

Household 406
Richard Beckwith	48	Va.	Farmer
Priscilla	48	do	
William	25	"	Loafer
Mary	21	"	
Francis (female)	18	"	
Ann	16	"	

Household 407
Israel Cohorn	36	Ala.	Laborer
Martha	30	Tenn.	
William	12	Miss.	
Elizabeth	11	"	
Sarah	8	Ala.	
Mary	5	"	
Reader	4	"	
Rachel	6/12	"	

Household 408
Sarah Young	54	Tenn.	
James	21	Ala.	
Anna Young	17	Ala.	
Parmelia	14	"	

Household 409
William Cohern	83	Ky.	Shoemaker
Mary	79	"	

Household 410
Baylis Bruce	42	S.C.	Do
Elizabeth	38	Ala.	
Pinkney	19	"	"
Samuel	17	"	"
Sarah	14	"	
Obediah	12	"	
Margaret	7	"	
Bayles, Jr.	6	"	
Zachary	3	"	

Household 411
Richard Duckett	53	S. C	Farmer
Mary	41	"	
Martha	18	"	
Lydia	16	"	
David	10	Ala.	
Thomas	8	"	
John	6	"	
Francis (female)	4	"	
Joseph	1	"	

Household 412
Philip J. Iron	59	N.C.	Farmer
Jane	55	Geo.	
Henry Dabbs	14	Ala.	

Household 413
Patrick M. Clark	32	Tenn. Carp'ter
Eliza	27	Ala.
Harriett	12	"
William	11	"
John	8	"
Manurva	6	"
Peggy	4	"
Hetty	1	"

Household 414
William Whittle	38	Tenn. Farmer

Household 415
Henry M. Hort	30	N.C. Farmer
E. D. Watson	30	" Merchant
J. C. Douglass	22	" "
Caroline Heafly	17	Tenn. Clerk
J. H. Heafley	25	N.C. Clerk

Household 416
Noah Rhodes	53	S.C. Farmer
Cothia (female)	35	"
Mary	18	"
Martha Rhodes	18	S.C.
Nancy	16	"
Hezekiah	14	"
Henrietta	12	"
Samuel	6	"
John	4	"
Rebecca	9/12	"

Household 417
Augustus Iron	45	N.C. Machanic
Mary	36	Tenn.
Sarah	13	"
Andrew	11	"
Susan	9	"
Thomas	7	"
John	5	"
Philip	3	"
Mary	2	"
William	5/12	"

Household 418
Richard H. Willott	47	" Farmer
Elizabeth	37	Va.

Household 419
John Young	26	Tenn. Do
Elizabeth	43	Tenn.
Mary	2	Ala.
John Tucker	18	Ky. Ass't

Household 420
James C. Young	30	Ala. Farmer
Mary	27	"
John	7	"
continued		

Household 420 continued
Elizabeth	6	"
Samuel	5	"
Ebenezer	3	"
William	10/12	"

Household 421
Jabez Cannon	50	S.C.	Farmer
Sarah	46	"	
Isaac	18	"	Ass't
Sarah	13	"	
William	11	"	
Hugh	7	"	

Household 422
William Langford	50	S.C.	Do
Gracilla	41	"	
Jacob	18	"	Ass't
Polly	17	"	
Martha	16	"	
Elizabeth	13	Ala.	
Richard Langford	10	"	
Darthnula	9	"	
Drayton	6	"	
Lydia (twin)	4	"	
Harriett (twin)	4	"	

Household 423
Wilson G. Wamble	47	Tenn.	Farmer
Cynthia	43	S.C.	
Rebecca	20	Ala.	
Columbus	19	"	Student
James	16	"	"
Mary	14	"	
Columbia (female)	12	"	
Amanda	7	"	

Household 424
J. R. Rosentall	32	Europe	Merchan
Frances	18	"	
Jacob Rosenthall	30	"	"
Mark Schale (?)	24	"	Clerk
(surname could be Schultz)			

Household 425
Altemont Thompson	40	Ga.	Farmer
Sarah	39	Ky.	
Henry	19	Ala.	
Martha	18	"	
William	16	"	
Amanda	15	"	
Ann	12	"	
John	10	"	
Jefferson	9	"	
Samuel	8	"	
Sarah	5	"	
Mary	4	"	
Louisa	3	"	
Nancy	1	"	

Household 426
| Jesse Rice | 26 | Ala. | Laborer |
| Susanna | 20 | Ala. | |
(Married within the year.)

Household 427
Lewis L. Marks*	56	Va.	Farmer
Mary*	26	Tenn.	
Virginia	23	Va.	
John	21	"	Loafer
(*Married within the year.)

Household 428
A. B. Parsons	51	Va.	Farmer
Elizabeth	43	Ky.	
Eliza Philips	18	Tenn.	

Household 429
Francis Wilkes (male)	30	Va.	Do
Caroline	24	Ala.	
Martha	6	"	
Pinkney	4	"	
Richard	1	"	
Elizabeth Freeman	12	"	

Household 430
William St. Clair	56	Ireland	Farmer
Mary	37	N.C.	
Matthew	22	"	Ass't
Margaret	20	"	
Elizabeth	9	Tenn.	
Nancy	7	"	
Mary	4	Ala.	
William	4/12	"	

Household 431
John Wade	35	Va.	Carpenter
Ann	25	Tenn.	
Andrew	6	Ala.	
Sarah	4	Ala.	
John	1	Ala.	

Household 432
| Ellen Johnson | 50 | Ky. | Spinster |
| James | 20 | Tenn. | Laborer |

Household 433
Martha Howell	61	Va.	Farming
Thomas	28	Ala.	Do
Martha	16	"	
Richd. Clopwell	26	Va.	Laborer

Household 434
J. H. Bracken	39	N.C.	Farmer
Martha	40	"	
Felix	14	"	
Julia	10	"	
Mary	8	"	
continued

Household 434 continued
Nancy	5	"
Sarah	3	"
Joseph	1/12	"

Household 435
Ro. E. Carr	65	N.C.	Farmer
Elizabeth	57	Geo.	
Ann	26	Ala.	
John	17	"	
William	22	"	Ass't
Louisa Hatfield	14	Unknown	
William Freeman	10	Alabama	

Household 436
Jacob Singley	50	???	Farmer
Matilda	48	Geo.	
Amos	24	Ala.	Ass't
Jesse	19	"	"
Mary Singley	16	"	
Francis Marion	17	"	(male)
Samuel	12	"	
John	7	"	
Wilson	5	"	

Household 437
Robert T. Oakley	35	Tenn.	Farmer
Caroline	25	"	
James	4	Ala.	
Charles	1	"	

Household 438
George Singley	38	Ala.	Carpenter
Hariett	26	"	
William	2	"	

Household 439
Claborn W. Wesson	42	N.C.	Farmer
Mary Ann	25	Tenn.	
Elizabeth	19	Ala.	
William	18	"	Ass't
John	15	"	"
Lusinda	14	"	
Mary	12	"	
Martha	10	"	
James	8	"	
Wiley	1	"	
Amy Ivins	72	Va.	

Household 440
Calvin Adkerson	38	N.C.	Shoemaker
Ethelinda	33	Ala.	
Betty	14	"	
James	11	"	
Polly	9	"	
Calvin	5	"	
Joseph	1	"	

Household 441
Robert Watkins   48 Va. Wood Chopper
Phrusey   33 N.C.
Susan   15 Ala.
Thomas   6 "

Household 442
Henson Thrasher   60 Maryland Farmer
Hannah   50 S.C.
John   28 Ala. Millright
Sarah   23 "
Susanah   22 "
Malinda   19 "
Rachel   17 "
Martha   14 "
Claborn Thrasher 12 "
W. H. Harison   10 "

Household 443
James Holland   35 Tenn.   Farmer
Basha   35 "   (female)
Feby   5 "
Jane   3 "
William   1 Ala.
Levin Ross   79 Va.   None

Household 444
James Young   50 S. C.   Farmer
Cornelia   48 "
Mary   26 Ala.
Samuel   23 "   Physician
Virginia   20 "
Drusinda   18 "
Jane   16 "
James   15 "
Elvira   13 "
Ellen   11 "
Edward   9 "
David   5 "

Household 445
William Farmer   56 N.C.   Farmer
Kesiah   43 S.C.
Marthy   22 Ala.
Benjamin Frank.   19 "   Ass't
Henrietta   16 "
Mary J.   14 "
Lucy   11 "
Antamenta   8 "
Sarah   4 "

Household 446
Andrew H. Hipps   46 S.C.   Farmer
Mary   51 "
Sarah   32 "
John   17 Ala.   Ass't
Mary   14 "
Elijah   11 "
James   7 "
William   6 "

Household 447
James M. Proby   62 Va.   Farmer

Household 448
Henry Cimmons   46 N.C.
Mary   45 "
Martha   21 Tenn.
Jane   22 Tenn.
Lucretia Cimmons 16 Tenn.
Demarious   14 "   (female)
Lewis   12 Ala.
Susan   7 "
Z. Taylor   3 "

Household 449
John B. Hipps   25 S.C.   Laborer
Margarett   23 Ala.
Jennett   1 "

Household 450
Thomas Martin   25 Tenn.   Carpenter
Mary   24 "
Jennetta   5 Ala.
John   3 "
Joseph Henry   4 "

Household 451
Ben F. Rhodes   40 S.C.   Farmer
Lusinda   33 "
Columbus   12 Ala.
Leonidas   10 "
Allice   2 "
Alonso   8 "
Georgia (female)   4 "

Household 452
George Herendon   52 N.C.   Farmer
Elizabeth   45 "
William Hips   21 S.C.   Overseer
Margaret Edwards 43 N.C.
Mary   17 Florence, Alabama
Green Lawson   19 "
George Perry   18 Tenn.   Hereland

Household 453
Elizabeth Morgan 64 Ky.   Farming
Ayra (female)   32 "
Amanda   21 Ala.
Tibitha   20 "

Household 454
William Thornton 26 Ala.   Ass't
Elizabeth   26 "
Sarah   4 "
Jefferson Finch   14 "

Household 455
Augustine Harwell	37	Tenn.	Farmer
Susanah	28	"	
James	9	Ala.	
Martha	6	"	
Elizabeth	5	"	
Rebecca	3	"	
Henry	3/12	"	

Household 456
James Richards	38	S.C.	Farmer
Susan	39	Tenn.	
Martha	19	"	
Nancy	16	Ala.	
William	13	"	
Thomas H. B.	12	"	
Julia Ann	8	"	
Samuel	5	"	
Caladonia	4	"	
John	4/12	"	

Household 457
Emily White	52	S.C.	
William	30	Ala.	Farmer
Tempesnce	17	"	
Joseph	12	"	
Elizabeth	28	Tenn.	
James	6	"	
Mary	5/12	Ala.	

Household 458
William Witt	33	S.C.	Farmer
Letty	32	S.C.	
Thomas	4	Tenn.	
Catharine	2	Ala.	

Household 459
Mary Burrass	44	N.C.	Farming
Margaret	24	N.C.	
Martha	22	"	
Rubin	21	"	Ass't
Elizabeth	18	"	
William	16	"	"
Thomas (twin)	14	Ala.	
John (twin)	14	"	
Mary	12	"	
Zenanah (female)	10	"	
Columbus	8	"	
James	6	"	

Household 460
Wm. Armour	29	Tenn.	Farmer
Jane	36	S.C.	
Margarett	18	Ala.	
Andrew	16	Tenn.	
Mary	9	Ala.	
Martha	1	Ala.	

Household 461
Sarah Jackson	35	S.C.	Weaving
Martha	18	"	
Polly	15	"	
William Jackson	9	"	

Household 462
Amanuel Harrison	46	S.C.	Farmer
Sarah	25	Ala.	
Alfred	1	"	

Household 463
Henry Robertson	27	Tenn.	Do
William	3	Ala.	

Household 464
William Anderson	50	N.C.	Farmer
Elizabeth	48	S.C.	
James	19	Tenn.	Ass't
Columbus Waldrep	2	Ala.	

Household 465
Nig Roberson	50	S.C.	Farmer
Elizabeth	46	"	
Thomas	17	Ala.	Ass't
Mary	16	"	
Rachel	12	"	

Household 466
Thomas Shephard	48	Ga.	Farmer
Permelia	41	S.C.	
John	17	Tenn.	Ass't
V. Matilda	15	"	
Clarinda	13	"	
Emily	11	"	
Permelia	9	"	
Thos. Benton	7	"	
Louiser	4	"	

Household 467
Lewis Do	25	Miss.	Farmer
Nancy	23	Tenn.	
William	4	"	
James	2	"	

Household 468
John Casey	62	S.C.	Farmer
Abergale	40	"	
Levi	16	"	"
Martha	14	"	
Samuel	8	"	
Mary	4	Ala.	

Household 469
Philip Harvell	45	Tenn.	Farmer
Polly	44	S.C.	
Benjamin	19	Ala.	"
William	16	"	"
Jane	11	"	

continued

C-34

Household 469 continued
Levi	8	Ala.
Caroline	6	"
Catherine	2	"

Household 470
Harrice Carr	50	S.C.	Wagons
Mary	44	Ky.	
Matilda	23	Tenn.	
Lusinda	21	Ala.	
Joseph	18	"	
Sarah	16	"	
Martha	14	"	
John	12	"	
Emeline	9	"	
Franklin	5	"	

Household 471
Daniel A. Reader	27	S.C.	Physician
Martha	23	N.C.	
Charles	4	Ala.	
Mary	2	Ala.	

Household 472
Thos. W. Waldrep	46	Tenn.	Farmer
Serena ?	37	"	
Eliza	18	Ala.	
William	16	"	Student
Francis (female)	14	"	
Joseph	11	"	
Thomas	8	"	
Rachel	5	"	
James	4	"	

Household 473
Jacob Reader	51	S.C.	Farmer
Sally	50	"	
Rubin	22	Ala.	Merchant
William	21	"	Clerk
Thomas	19	"	None
Mary	17	"	
Rachel	15	"	
Jacob 2nd	13	"	
Sarah	11	"	
Martha	9	"	
Hugh	7	"	

Household 474
Henderson Richards	50	S.C.	Farmer
Sally	30	S.C.	
Jack	18	Ala.	Ass't
Thomas	13	Tenn.	
Hester Ann	11	Tenn.	
Catherine	9	"	
Sarenus (male)	8	"	

Household 475
Wm. H. Farmer	40	Tenn.	Shoemaker
Lavina	40	Ky.	
Martha (twin)	14	Ala.	
Gabrel (twin)	14	"	
Susan	12	"	

Household 476
Joseph Philips	26	S.C.	Farmer
Hester	22	Ala.	
David	2	"	

Household 477
John Wesson	43	S.C.	"
Lavina	21	Ala.	
Margarett	1	"	

Household 478
William Rhodes	46	S.C.	Farmer
Nancy	46	Ga.	

Household 479
Jesse Dewberry	37	Tenn.	Farmer
Margaret	29	Va.	
Sarah	7	Ala.	
Mary Ann	5	"	
Jabus	4	"	
Ester	6/12	"	

Household 480
John Ducatt	57	S.C.	Farmer
Elizabeth	57	"	
Levi	20	Ala.	Ass't
Elizabeth	17	"	
Joseph Nail	32	Miss.	Overseer

Household 481
William Beavers	40	S.C.	Carpenter
Jane	25	"	
Elizabeth	6	Ala.	

Household 482
Maderson Pool	31	Ky.	Farmer
Nancy	37	"	
Mary	12	Ala.	
Perkins	9	"	
James (twin)	8	"	
George W. (twin)	8	"	
Nancy	6	"	
Joseph	4	"	
Stewart	4/12	"	

Household 483
Nancy Pool	52	S.C.	Farming
Perkins	22	Ala.	Ass't
Polly	25	"	
Caroline	20	"	
Hariett	17	"	
Elizabtt	16	"	

Household 484
Stewart Pool   28   Ala.   Farmer
Sarah Pool   24   "
(Married within the year.)

Household 485
Steven Waldrop   31   Ala.   Farmer
Jane   34   "
James   18   "   Ass't
Mary   10   "
William   6   Miss.
Henry   4   "
Elizabeth   3   Ala.

Household 486
Burwell Young   25   Ala.   Farmer
Jane   23   "
James   4/12   "

Household 487
Henry Wesson   45   S.C.   Farmer
Liddy   29   "
William   9   Ala.
John   6   "
Turner S.   4   "
Joseph   2   "
Henry Do   12   "

Household 488
James Beavers   33   S.C.   Farmer
Agnus   44   "
Jane   18   Tenn.
James   15   "
Mary   13   Ala.
Sinthia (twin)   12   "
Richard (twin)   12   "
Jesse   9   "
Agy   6   "
Mikle   3   "

Household 489
William Waldrep   55   S.C.   Shoemaker
Lusinda   18   "
Everline   15   Ala.
Susan   12   "

Household 490
Thos. F. Beavers   31   S.C.   Farmer
Jane   36   "
Thomas   7   Ala.
William   5   "
Calvin   1   "

Household 491
James Beavers   29   S.C.   Farmer
Mary   25   "
John   9   Ala.
Thomas   7   (blank)
Nancy   6   "
Marthy Beavers   1   Ala.

Household 492
James Wesson   30   S.C.   Farmer
Mary   26   Tenn.
Sarah   9   Ala.
Nancy   7   "
Wallice   5   "   (male)
Daniel   1   "
Daniel Cannon   50   S.C.   Teacher

Household 493
Benjamin Burns   49   S.C.   Farmer
Martha   48   "
Josiah   22   Ala.   Ass't
Polly   20   "
Benjamin   18   "   "
Robert   16   "   "
John   15   "
Martha   12   "

Household 494
John Perryman   46   Ky.   Farmer
Martha   44   Tenn.
Alexander   19   Ala.   Student
Samuel   13   "
Martha   11   "
Cornetty (female)   9   "
Emeline   6   "
Columbia (female)   3   "

Household 495
Solleman Pool*   23   Ala.   Farmer
Jane*   23   "
Levi   1/12   "
(*Married within the year.)

Household 496
Jabin Young   35   Tenn. Farmer
Martha   31   S.C.
Sarah   8   Ala.
Mary   6   "
Nancy   3   "
Margarett   2   "
Levi   1   "

Household 497
Jarred Grissom   50   Ga.   Farmer
Susanah   47   "
James   20   Tenn. Student
William   14   "
Nancy Carney   21   Unknown

Household 498
Peter Morison   79   Va.   Farmer
Annie   60   "
Eliza A. Terry   16   Tenn.
Daniel Terry   14   Ala.

Household 499
Miles White   35 N.C.   Farmer
Everline   30 Ala.
Parilee   9   "
Wesley   3   "

Household 500
Warren Wesson   40 S.C.   Farmer
Mary   66 Va.
Martha   30 S.C.

Household 501
Benjamin Wilson   25 Ala.   Farmer
Jane   25   "
(Married within the year)

Household 502
Jerry (?) Burns   37 S.C.   Farmer
Jane   34 Ala.
Mary   12   "
Robert   10   "
Rubin   8   "
Jerry 2nd   6   "
Almarena (female)   1   "
Mary Do   70 S.C.

Household 503
Israel Burns   31 S.C.   Farmer
Caroline   24 Tenn.
Mary   5 Ala.
Elizabeth   4   "
James   2   "
Richard Allen   10   "

Household 504
Elijah Burns   28 S.C.   Farmer
Elizabeth   25 Va.
Robert   4 Ala.
Matilda   1   "
Gabrel B. Allen   11   "

Household 505
Manuel Burns   32 S.C.   Laborer
Mary   38 Tenn.
Drusilla   4 Ala.
Mary Jr.   9   "
Robert   7   "
Rubin   5   "
John   2/12 "

Household 505
Charles Sullivan   56 Va.
Margarett   25 S.C.
Caroline   21 Ala.
Milton Russle   10 Ala.   Student

Household 506
Charles Nichleson 60 Va. Farmer
Sarah   50 S.C.

Household 506 continued
Catharine Nickleson 24 Ala.
Annie   17   "
Ellen   16   "
Amanda   14   "
Henry Clay   13   "
Mary   11   "
Elizabeth   8   "

Household 507
Martha Williams   48 S.C.   Farmer
Maston   19 Ala.
Henry   14 Miss.
Sarah   12 Ala.
Francis Beavers*   16   "   (female)
(*Marked married within the year.)

Household 508
Shelton A. Williams 25 Ala.   Farmer
Juliar   24 S.C.
Josephine   1 Ala.

Household 509
Thos. L. Beavers   61 Va.   Farmer
Isibella   59 S.C.
Susan   17 Ala.

Household 510
John Beavers   26 S.C.   Ditto
Catharine   24 Ala.
Mary   7   "
Samuel   5   "
Martha   4   "
Rosanah   2   "

Household 511
Margaret Baker   66 Va.   Farmer
Rebecca   36 Tenn.

Household 512
Jesse Philips   46 S.C.   Ditto
Mary   37 Ala.
Margarett   19   "
Sarah   16   "
Jesse   14   "
William   12   "
John   8   "
Charles   6   "
Mary   5   "
Rebecca   2   "
Anjellico (female) 83 Va.

C-37

Household 513
A. C. Hunt   26   Tenn.   Farmer
Jantha   26   Ala.
Frances (female)   7   "
Margarett   5   "
John   4   "
Joseph Hunt   3   "
William H. H.   9/12 "

Household 514
Matta. Randle   24   Ga.   Laborer
Frances   19   S.C.
(Marked married within the year.)

Household 515
Ann Smith   39   S.C.   Farmer
William   17   Ala.   Ass't
Elizabeth   15   "
Thomas   13   "
Parilee   10   "

Household 516
Jonnathan Wootten   31   Tenn. Farming
Martha   26   Ala.
Sarah (?)   3   "

Household 517
Lusinda Whitten   50   Va.   Farming
Josiah   17   Ala.   Ass't
Moses   18   "
Polly   15   "

Household 518
John T. Whitten   24   S.C.   Laborer
Martha   19   S.C.
Linsley   1   Ala.   (male)

Household 519
John Wootten   68   N.C.   Farmer
Peggy   55   "
Benjamin   24   Tenn. Ass't
Sarah   22   "
James   10   "

Household 520
Peter T. (S?) Parker 51 Va.   Farmer
Sarah   51   N.C.
Nancy   28   "

Household 521
Lucy B. Thompson   67   N.C.   Farming
William   50   Geo.   None
Lusetta   27   Ala.

Household 522
Thos. W. Thompson   30   Ga.   Farmer
Elizabeth   34   Tenn.
Mary   8   Ala.
Lucy   7   "
continued

Household 522 continued
Tunningham (male)   4   Ala.
Luiser   3   "
Virginia   1/12 "

Household 523
Francis Loveless   57   S. C. Farmer(male
Elizabeth   50   S.C.
Mary   25   Ga.
Joseph   21   Ala.   Ass't
George   18   "   "
James D. Loveless   15   "
Simon   12   "
Lusinda   11   "
Francis M.   9   "
Nancy   5   "

Lauderdale Factory

Household 524
John W. Tennerson   38   Ky.   Physician
Annie   28   S.C.
Cinthia   7   Ala.
Regina   6   "
Sarah Ann   5   Miss.
Catharine   3   Ala.
Abergale   2   "

Household 525
John F. Carson   46   Ky.   Hewing
Greenburry   22   Tenn. Bldg.
Mary   19   "
Sarah   16   "
James   14   "
Jasper   13   "
Catharine (twin)   11   "
Leanah (twin)   11   "
John   9   "
Hugh   5   "
Edy Carson (female) 42   Ky.

Household 526
John W. Riley   50   N.C.   Workman
Lusinda   50   "
James D.   18   "   Realer
John   17   "   Card stripper
Rollin   14   "
Awlston (male)   13   "
Mary   12   "
Albert   11   "
Albin (male)   10   "
Allen   8   "
Lusinda Jr.   7   "
Ann Eliza   3   Ala.
James Gooch   21   N.C.   Baling

Household 527
Sarah Weaver   46   Va.   Cook
Nancy   18   "
continued

Household 527 continued
Mary   15   Tenn.
Thomas   14   "
Robert   13   Ala.
M. T. Greswell   35   Tenn.   Physician
John Sinnett   60   France Watchman
At bottom of page was written "Good Water Power and many canebrakes."

Household 528
Stringer White   39   England Boss Weaver
Mary   38   "
John   16   "   Weaver
Henry   13   N.Y.
Mary   7   Ala.
Robert   4   Ala.
Sarah   2   "
Margaret Shelton   20   England
Thomas Woods   21   Tenn.   Warper

Household 529
William Helton   50   Tenn.   Shoemaker
Sarah   39   "
Rebecca   16   "
Margarett   15   "
Francis (female)   12   "
George Wash.   10   "
Thomas Benton   6   "
Elzera (male)   5   "
Elizabeth Nusum*   18   "
Amanda   12   "
Malila   10   "
William   6   "
Richard Massey*   18   "   Laborer
(*Married within the year)

Household 530
Thomas Whitehead*   21   Ala.   Lizse??
Martha*   21   Tenn.
Sarah Helton   18   "
Jackson Nicholas   19   "   Twisting
Elijah Ham   20   "   Chopper
Marion Smith   25   Ky.   Carpenter

Household 531
Aaron Frankes   37   Tenn.   Sawyer
Lusinda   39   Ala.
Martha G.   16   "
Calafornia   15   "
Anderson   13   "
Elizabeth Arnett   20   Unknown

Household 532
Easter Smith   31   Tenn.   Cook
Peter   14   Ala.
Nancy   12   "
John C. Calhoun   11   "
Julian   10   "
Terry   9   "
George Washg.   4   "   continued

"Growth Poplar, oak, ash; chestnut, ceder" written at bottom of page.
Household 532 continued
James W. T. H. A. G.G.H.E. Smith   1   Ala.
Harison Owen (Wagoner)   25   "

Household 533
James R. Artherton   38   England Boss Weaver
Annie   35   "
Mary Ann   18   "
Thomas   13   "
Frank   3   "

Household 534
Safroney Alexander   41   Ala.   Cook
Mary   22   Va.
Elizabeth*   20   Ala.
James W.   19   "   Laborer
Ferdinand   17   "   "
Thomas   14   "
Annie   8   "
Martha   3   "
Eliza Love   20   England
(*Marked married within the year.)

Household 535
Rebecca Berry   38   Ga.   Cook
John Scott*   19   Ala.   Weaver
Nancy   15   "
William   10   "
Ann Eliza   7   "
Martha Hutton   18   "
Nancy Sparkes   68   Ga.
(*Marked married within the year.)

Household 536
Francis Cockram   45   N.C.   (female)
Jasper   29   "   Laborer
Charity   19   "
Margarett   18   "
William   16   "   "
John   13   "
James   12   "
Elizabeth   9   "
Fanny   7   Tenn.
Jefferson   5   Tenn.
Tansey Briant   23   Unknown ~~Spinster~~
(Marked out in this fashion.)

Household 537
Nancy Joice   48   Tenn.   Cook
John   17   "   Carder
Sally   14   "
Mary   12   Ky.
Allice   10   "
Lemiel   8   "

James West or Welch written at bottom of page--no explanation.

C-39

Household 538			
Rebecca Story	40	S.C.	Cook
Sally	17	Tenn.	
Tennessa Story	15	"	
James	13	"	
Tilman	11	"	
Davy	9	"	

Household 539			
Robert White	43	England	Boss Weaver
Ann	43	"	

Household 540			
James Sikes	48	England	Boss-
Elizabeth	40	Delaware	Spinner
Ann Eliza	12	Ohio	
Mary	10	Ala.	
William	8	"	
Margaret	6	Tenn.	
James	3	"	

Household 541			
James T. Wood	28	S.C.	Laborer
Eliza	24	Ala.	
Moses	5	Tenn.	
Sarah	17	S.C.	
Joseph	16	"	Spinner

Household 542			
John Hardwick	42	Va.	Carpenter
Elizabeth	31	Tenn.	
Joseph	15	"	
Mary	12	Ala.	
Samuel	10	"	
William	8	"	
Frank	6	"	
John	5	"	
Jas. H. Kennedy	22	unknown	laborer

Household 543			
Asarah Davis (male)	39	Va.	Carpenter
Rebecca	35	"	
Elizabeth	15	Tenn.	
Caroline	14	"	
Asariah	12	Ala.	(male)
Martha	10	"	
Samuel	6	"	
Sarah	4	"	
Nancy	2	"	

Household 544			
Wm. Ross	24	Tenn.	Lapper
Margaret	23	N.C.	
William	3	Ala.	

Household 545			
Turner S. Foster	28	Tenn.	Manufacturer
Thos. J. Foster	20	Tenn.	Clerk
George Slaright	19	Ireland	Bookkeeper
John A. Dancy	27	Tenn.	Clerk

End of Lauderdale Factory

Household 546			
G. W. Martin	45	Tenn.	Meth.Farmer
Rebecca	40	S.C.	
Elizabeth	14	Ala.	
Sarah	12	Ky.	
Mary	10	"	
Nancy	8	Ala.	
George	7	"	
Wm. N. Holliman	57	"	None

Household 547			
Mary Coffee	57	Tenn.	Farming
Rachel	24	Ala.	
Catharine	22	"	
William	20	"	Ass't
Joshua	19	"	Student
Andrew Hutchens	11	"	

Household 548			
Sarah Jackson	61	S.C.	Farming
Andrew	35	Ala.	None
Tamutha	25	"	
Martha	9/12	"	
James	28	"	None
Alexander	25	"	None
George	22	"	None
James Kirkman	20	"	None

Household 549			
Harison Wesson	44	S.C.	Overseer
Ellen	31	Ala.	
Leander	14	"	
Martha	11	"	
John R.	8	"	
Rachel	5	"	
Mary	2	"	

Household 550			
Mikle Ollive	49	N.C.	Farmer
Kisiah	49	"	
Mary	23	Ala.	
Martha	12	"	

Household 551			
Antny Ollive	25	N.C.	Overseer
Jonn (male)	22	Ala.	Farmer
James	18	"	Student
William	16	"	"

Household 552			
Thos. Holland	23	Ala.	Overseer
Catharine	24	Tenn.	
William	6/12	Ala.	

Household 553			
Thos. Barnett	61	S.C.	Farmer
Nancy Barnett	45	Tenn.	
William	26	Ala.	Ass't
Sarah	20	"	
continued			

Household 553 continued
Phoebi	18	Ala.	
Thomas	16	" "	
Lucy	11	"	
Henryetta	9	"	

Household 554
Thos. Nail	40	Tenn.	Farmer
Amanda	31	Ala.	
Sarah	14	"	
Eliza	10	"	
James	5	"	
Emeline	2	"	

Household 555
Eliza M. Brown	32	Tenn.	Farmer
Nancy	18	Ala.	
John	16	"	Ass't
William	14	"	
Martha	13	"	
Julia Ann	4	"	
Eliza	2	"	

Household 556
Mary Hood	50	Scotland	Farmer
John	25	Ala.	"

Household 557
Jesse Bradford	37	Tenn.	Overseer
Mary	38	Va.	
Jesse	11	Ala.	
Sarah	8	"	
Marissa	6	"	
James	2	"	

Household 558
Jesse Medum	69	S.C.	Miller
Annie	55	N.C.	
William	18	Tenn.	Laborer
Jesse	14	Tenn.	
Amberis Morgan (male)	21	Unknown	"

Household 559
Thomp. Reader	47	Ditto	Miller
Susan	41	S.C.	
John	18	Ala.	Spinner
William	16	"	"
Duncan	14	"	
Rebecca	11	"	
Washington	9	"	
Susan	7	"	
Z. Taylor	1	"	

Cypress Factory

(Following on pages labeled Cypress Factory.)

Household 560
William Nix	60	Ga.	Wood Chopper
Hannah	49	S.C.	
Mary	20	Tenn.	
Parilee	17	"	
George	15	"	
Madora	12	Ala.	(female)
William	10	"	
John	6	"	

Household 561
Wm. Clark	45	Va.	Warper
Leona	46	Ga.	
James	18	Ala.	Spinner
Eliza (twin)	15	"	
William (twin)	15	"	
Elvira	11	"	
John	9	"	
Lidda Miller	26	England	
Eliza	9/12	Ala.	

Household 562
Manson Rodgers	25	Tenn.	Warper
Nancy	24	Ala.	
William	2	"	
Martha Ray	15	"	

Household 563
Mary House	37	Philad.	
Elizabeth	14	Tenn.	
William	12	"	
Mary	10	"	
Nancy (twin)	7	"	
James (twin)	7		
Sarah M.C.J.E.D.T.	3	"	

Household 564
Mikle Burlison	31	Unknown	Chopper
Ann	41	Tenn.	
Mary	20	Ala.	
Wiley	28	Tenn.	Stocks
Jefferson	21	"	"
John	18	Ala.	Twister
Henry	14	"	
William	13	"	
Martha	12	"	
Sarah	10	"	
Josiah	9	"	
Winiford	6	"	
Ruth	2	"	

Household 565
J. M. Fisher, Jr.*	23	Ala.	Laborer
Samyra Fisher*	26	"	
Elizabeth	13	"	
William	2/12	"	

(*Married within the year.)

Household 566
Thos. Valentine   61   S.C.   Workman
Mary   58   N.C.
Mary Jr.   21   Tenn.
Martha   20   "
Hanna   19   "
Susan   14   "
Elizabeth Hill   21   "

Household 567
James Fisher, Sr. 46   Tenn.   Laborer
Elizabeth   41   Ala.
Elizabeth Jr.   20   "
Malvina   18   "
Henry   16   "   Carder
Martha   14   "
Jabous (male)   12   "
Malinda   10   "
Polly   8   "
Carroll   6   "
Pleasant   5   "
John   9/12 "

Household 568
Comads Rodgers   25   S.C.   Bailing
Kisiah   28   Ala.
Annie Artist   14   "
Isaac Do   8   Tenn.
John   6   "
Jacon (male)   4   "
Thomas   3   Ala.
Jackson   4/12 "

Household 569
Lenord Sibley   50   N.C.   Laborer
Sarah   50   Tenn.
John   32   "   "
Elijah   30   "   "
Mary   19   Ala.
Eliza   17   "
Nancy   15   "
Sarah   10   "

Household 570
Dempsy Brown   50   S.C.   Do
Martha   52   Ga.
David   21   Tenn.   Carder
Samuel   19   "   "
Eliza Brown   18   "
Elias   16   "   Spinner
Martha   12   "
Nancy   13   "
Calidd (male)   9   "
Thomas   7   "
Leander   5   "
Sarah   4   Ala.
Jane Pruett   35   S.C.

Household 571
Andrew Grigery   47   England Weaver
Elizabeth   43   Pennsy.
Elizabeth, Jr.   13   Ala.

Household 572
Wealthy Hill (male) 47 S.C.   Boss Do
Surmicy (?)   49   Tenn.
Mary   10   "
Wm. H. H.   8   "
Russle Coburn   25   "   Blc.Smith

Household 573
Joshua Butcher   40   Ala.   Wagener
Elvira   40   Ky.
Malinda   20   Ala.
Thomas   19   "   Laborer
Felding   18   "   "
Joshua   16   "   "
Samuel   14   "
Gilbert   12   "
Charles   11   "
James   8   "
John   2   "

Household 574
Milla Burrah   36   Tenn.   (female)
Rebecca   21   Miss.
Peter   12   Ala.
Lusinda   10   "
Rebecca   8   "
Calpurney   6   "
James   2   "
Elizabeth Kiddy   36   Ga.

Household 575
J. F. Furgerson   50   Va.   Farmer
Elizabeth   50   Tenn.
Rebecca   27   "
Nancy   25   "
Ellender   16   "
Manurvy Furgerson 14   "
Nimrod   12   "
Ferdinand   11   "
Isebella (twin)   10   "
Caleb (twin)   10   "
Jacob   7   "

Household 576
Marshal J. Do   29   Tenn.   Carder
Elizabeth   22   "
James   1   "

Household 577
Jas. Duncan   56   S.C.   Watchman
Eliza   27   Tenn.
Nancy   1   Ala.

Household 578
Jas. Hillenwward   34 England Spinner
Nancy   21 Tenn.
(Marked married within the year.)

Household 579
Martha Rhodes   42 Ga.
Margaret   17 Tenn.
James   14   "
Susan   13   "
Thomas   12   "
John   9   "
Mary   6   "
Martha   2   "

Household 580
Isebella Briant   42 S.C.
Hanna   24 Tenn.
Winiford   17   "
Mary   15   "
James   14   "
Jane   12   "

Household 581
Henry Reader   20 Tenn. Spinner
Sarah   19 S.C.
(Marked married within the year.)

Household 582
John D. Martin   47 Ky. Carpenter
Lucy   50 Va.
Martha   23 Ky.
Oliver H. P.   19   "   Do
Amanda   16   "

Cypress Factory

Household 583
James Martin   70 Ky. Manufacturer
Tibitha   46 Tenn.
Henry C.   21 Ala. Clerk
James   18   "   Student
Sarah   13   "
Ellen   11   "
Robert   8   "
John Martin   6   "
Charles   3   "
John Grush   25 Maryland Book'per
Joel Nigh   50 N.York   Boss carder
George Dawes (Davis?) 25 Eng.   Boss weaver
George Berkwell   17 Tenn.   Operator
Wm. Gewin   21 Ala.   Do

(James Martin built his first factory in 1839 along Cypress Creek. At the time of Civil War he owned three, with Weakley. Mills were destroyed during Civil War by Federal troops. He re-opened after war and later mills were removed to Barton.)

Household 584
Lewis C. Moore*   50 Ky. Farmer
Atlantic   34 Ala.
Hugh McV.   15   "
John   14   "
Lewis   13   "
Samuel   11   "
James K. Polk   5   "

Household 585
Alexd. D. Coffee**   29 Ala. Manufacturer
Ann Eliza   25   "

Household 586
Elias E. Call   50 S.C. Farmer
Sely (female)   40   "
Nancy   19   "
Caroline   17   "
Delitha   16   "

Household 587
Joab Hines   61 S.C. Farmer
Mary   40   "
Mary 2nd   28   "
Henry   26   "   Ass't
Eliza   24   "
Jacob   21 Tenn. Do
Elizabeth   18 Ala.
Alcy   14   "
Charles   12   "
Elias   9   "

Household 588
Davy Cordle   71 S.C. Farmer
Nancy   47 Tenn.
Charity   22 Tenn.
Nancy   20   "
James   17   "   Ass't
Terry Ann (female)   14   "
Sarah   12   "
William   8   "
Martha   6   "

―――――――――――――

*Lewis C. Moore married Atlantic Pacific McVey, daughter of Hugh McVey, who served six months as ex-officio governor of Ala. They lived at Mars Hill.

**Alexander Donelson Coffee, born 3 June 1821, died 12 May 1901; son of General John Coffee and his wife Mary Donelson. Coffee High School was named in his honor He married 16 May 1844 to Ann Eliza Sloss. His second wife was Mrs. Camilla Madding Jones and by this marriage was the father of Eliza Croom Coffee, for whom the local hospital was named.

Household 589
Bennett Pope   64 S.C. Farmer
Jane   54 N.C.

Household 590
William Powers   39 S.C. Farmer
Rosanah   30 S.C.
Sarah   12 S.C.
John   10 Ala.
Thomas   8   "
Mary   5   "

Household 591
Nathaniel Hews   30 S.C. Farmer
Nancy   23 S.C.
John   5 Ala.
Margaret   4   "
Columbus   2   "
George   1/12 "

Household 592
George Hews   30 S.C. Laborer
Mary   29 S.C.
William   3 Ala.
Mary   6/12 "

Household 593
Wm. Loveless   51 S.C. Farmer
Elizabeth   46   "
Milly Neighbours   63 S.C.
Jinett Roberson   14 Ala.
Ben Rhodes   3 Ala.

Household 594
Mary Loveless   60 S.C.
Margaret   55 S.C.
Rebecca   45 S.C.

Household 595
Hazle Loveless (male) 32 S.C. Farmer
Almyra   30 Ala.
J Ann   8   "
Rebecca   4   "
Rubin   2   "
Lucy Franks   72 S.C.

Household 596
Frances Loveless (f.) 46 S.C. Farmer
John   18 Ala. Ass't
Hazle (male)   17   "   "
George W.   13   "

Household 597
Jesse Cook   37 Ky. Farmer
Nancy   32 Ala.
Martha   11   "
George   9   "
Samuel   6   "
Artemus   3   "
Rebecca   1   "

Household 598
Thos. Skipwith   30 Tenn. Ditto
Manurvy Skipwith   31 Tenn.
Willis   10 Ala.
Marion   9   "
Ann Eliza   7   "
Thomas   3   "

Household 599
George Duncan   40 S.C. Farmer
Jane   37 Tenn.
John   16   "   Student
Nancy   12 Ala.
William   8   "
Leander (twin)   5   "
Ebineser (twin)   5   "
Annie   38 S.C.
Lusinda   13 Ala.

Household 600
Moses Duncan   43 S.C. Farmer
Sarah   44 S.C.
George   22 Ala. Ass't
Martha*   18 Ala.
Robert   16   "   Student
Mary   15   "
Elmira   12   "
Thomas   11   "
James   8   "
Sarah   5   "
Jesse White*   21   "   Ass't
(*Marked married within the year.)

Household 601
Elizabeth Mart<u>n</u>   50 S.C.
Annie   21 Tenn.
James   19 Ala. Laborer

Household 602
Jno. W. Rhodes   29 N.C. Farmer
Manurvy   27 Tenn.
Mary   6 Ala.
Spencer   3   "
Charles   4/12 "

Household 603
Elijah Rhodes   59 Maryland Wagons
Judy   51 S.C.
Thomas   22 Ala. Laborer
Nancy   19   "
Martha   16   "
Ellen   12   "
Leander   5   "

Household 604
Mathius Munn   50 N.Jersey Maskines
Rosanah   50 Ireland
Joseph Munn   25 Ala. Carpenter
Rosanah   20   "
Sarah   18   "

C-43

C-44

Household 605
Peter F. Garner	41	Tenn.	Teacher
Mary	26	Ala.	
Amanda	4	"	
Levi	3	"	
Asburry Martin	19	"	Hereland

Household 606
Samuel Vaughn	60	Va.	Farmer
Nancy	36	N.C.	
Virginia	10	Ala.	
Samuel	7	"	
Pleasant	67	Va.	Overseer
Sarah Armstead	1	Ala.	

Household 607
Isaac Hooper*	25	Unknown	Wagens
Mary*	18	Ala.	
Marissa Brown	16	"	

(*Marked married within the year.)

Household 608
Spencer Rhodes	32	S.C.	Smith
Amanda	32	Tenn.	
Peter	7	Ala.	
Catharine	5	"	
Julia	3	"	
Thos. Ingram	18	"	Student
Joseph Darbey	23	"	Coal Buns (?)

Household 609
John W. Smith	40	Ky.	Farmer
Mary	40	Tenn.	
Elizabeth	17	Ala.	
Ebeneser	12	"	
James	10	"	
George	7	"	
Martha	2	"	

Household 610
Josiah Wingo	36	S.C.	Laborer
Hunt Ann (female)	30	Ala.	
Pernesa	13	"	
Pinkney	10	"	
Susan	8	"	
Sarah	5	"	
Cass (male)	2	"	

Household 611
Lewis Isbell	56	Va.	Farmer
Eliza	50	"	
Fanny	20	"	
Elzab (female)	14	"	

Household 611 (number repeated)
James Waits	49	S.C.	Farmer
Lidda	45	"	
Elizabeth	46	"	
Draton (female)	23	"	Ass't
Martha	19	Ala.	
Benton	18	"	Student
Catharine	16	"	
Carolin (twin)	14	"	
Leonidus (twin)	14	"	
Shelton	6	"	
Permelia	4	"	

Household 612
James Joiner	66	S.C.	Wagins
Elizabeth	60	"	

Household 613
Hiram Joiner	28	S.C.	Laborer
Martha	22	Ala.	
Nancy	2/12	Ala.	

Household 614
Saml. Fowler	39	S.C.	Farmer
Rachel	49	"	
Thomas	13	Ala.	
Columbia (female)	11	"	

Household 615
James Roberson	40	S.C.	Constable
Nancy	68	N.C.	

Household 616
Pugh Houston	47	Tenn.	Physician
Lusinda	43	"	
Butler	19	"	"
Chapman	17	"	Student
James	15	"	
John	10	"	
Benjaman	8	"	
George	4	"	
Easter	2	"	

Household 617
Jones Houston	30	Tenn.	Physician
Elizabeth	24	N. York	
Hanna	5	Ala.	
Mary	2	"	
Josaphine Thompson	13	"	

Household 618
Wm. Wiley	38	S.C.	Carpenter
Frances	33	"	
William	15	Ala.	
Sissily (female)	11	"	
Harison W. H.	9	"	
Jones	6	"	
Stewart Wiley	4	"	
Elizabeth	2/12	"	

Household 619
Name	Age	Origin	Occupation
James Chambers	36	Ireland	Carp'ter
Caroline	26	Ala.	
Andrew	10	"	
George	6	"	
James	5	"	
Elizabeth	2	"	

Household 620
Name	Age	Origin	Occupation
Edwin Winbourn	39	N.C.	Farmer
Sarah	32	Ala.	
John	8	"	
Charles	6	"	
Sarah	5	"	
Mary	3	"	
William	6/12	"	

Household 621
Name	Age	Origin	Occupation
Samuel Croft	50	Va.	Farmer
Jane	50	N C.	
Andrew	15	Ala.	
William	14	"	
Madison	12	"	
Ann	11	"	
Adaline Donalson	22	Tenn.	

Household 622
Name	Age	Origin	Occupation
Roth A. Jenkins	71	N.C.	(Female)
Thos. Mackey	21	Ala.	Laborer
Martha	23	"	
Virginia	3	"	
William	4/12	"	

Household 623
Name	Age	Origin	Occupation
Isaac Arnold	36	S.C.	Farmer
Cynthia	36	Tenn.	
Mary	16	Ala.	
John	14	"	
Martha	13	"	
Louiser	11	"	
William	9	"	
Leander	7	"	
Samuel	5	"	

Household 624
Name	Age	Origin	Occupation
Hugh Bratton	24	Tenn.	Miller
Louiser	20	Ala.	
George	4	Miss.	
John	2	"	
James	3/12	"	

Household 625
Name	Age	Origin	Occupation
Wilson Caroll	43	Va.	Farmer
Nary Carroll	27	Ala.	
George	7	"	
James	5	"	
Ellen	3	"	
Ann W.	1	"	

Household 626
Name	Age	Origin	Occupation
John Haney	50	N.C.	Smith
Susanah	45	"	
Elizabeth	18	Tenn.	
Frances	16	"	
James	14	Ala.	

Household 627
Name	Age	Origin	Occupation
James Third (?)	24	Ala.	Farmer
Ruth	24	Tenn.	
Columbus	13	Ala.	
James	10	"	
Texas Ann	6	"	
Elizabeth	2	"	

Household 628
Name	Age	Origin	Occupation
John Pettypool	50	Va.	Farmer
Susan	46	Tenn.	
Joseph	21	Ala.	Ass't
Martha	19	"	
Eliza	16	"	
Julia	13	"	
John	9	"	
David	4	"	
Rosanah Mosley	47	S.C.	

Household 629
Name	Age	Origin	Occupation
Moses Baskin	30	Tenn.	Laborer
Charity	30	unknown	
Phenz (female)	4	Ala.	(twin)
Jefferson	4	"	"
Henry Foster	26	England	Ditcher

Household 630
Name	Age	Origin	Occupation
Mikle Long	52	Ireland	Farmer
Nancy	50	Ga.	
Lafaett	18	Ala.	Ass't
Jasper	16	"	"
Rebecca	15	"	
Mary	13	"	
Philip	3	"	

Household 631
Name	Age	Origin	Occupation
Thos. Langford	42	Va.	Farmer
Abergale	33	S.C.	
George	13	Ala.	
John	7	"	

Household 632
Name	Age	Origin	Occupation
Wm. Long	27	Ala.	Do
Nancy Long*	18	Tenn.	
George	3	Ala.	

*Beginning with this entry, the sheets were labeled "Town of Waterloo, Ala."

C-46

Household 633
Saml. Wilson   40 Tenn. Farmer
Mary   35 S.C.
Joseph   5 Ala.
Missouri   3 "
Columbia (female)   2 "

Household 634
Hen. T. Webb   37 Ala.   Do
Malissa   36 Ga.
Eliza   19 Ala.
Berry   17 "   Student
Thomas   10 "
David Defore   40 Tenn. Hunter
Lalitia Webb   5 Miss.

Household 635
Elizabeth Webb   71 N.C.
Elizabeth West   14 Ala.

Household 636
O. B. Sullivan*   25 S.C.   Physician
Eliza   22 Tenn.

Household 63_6_ (number repeated)
T. J. McKorkle**   25 Tenn. Merchant
Elizabeth   20 Ala.

Household 637
Tebatha Bradley   46 Ga.   Seamstress
Elizabeth James   30 Ga.

Household 638
Harison Kerningham   36 Tenn. Carpenter
Jane   35 "
Charlotte   8 "
Andrew   6 "
Mary   4 "
A. C. Pickens   36 Ohio   Saddler

---
*Dr. Sullivan was born and reared in the Burcham Valley (Central Heights) area of the county, and moved to Waterloo about 1844 following his graduation from the University of Louisville. After the flood of 1847 destroyed the old town of Waterloo, the town was moved to higher ground and his office was the first building erected at the new site. He had been recently widowed and he married Miss Latham, governess of King family of Leighton. (page 50, Historic Muscle Shoals.)
**McCorkle's Drug Store is the oldest in the county, established 1832, by Thomas T. McCorkle. The middle initial on the census is definitely "J".

Household 639
John Inlow   50   Ga.   Tanner
Margaret   40   Tenn.
James   23   "   "
John   20   "   Shoemaker
Sarah   19   "
Margaret   17   "
Elizabeth   16   "
Cristopher   13   "
Eliza   11   "
Philip   10   Ala.
William   7   "
Richard   5   Tenn.
Joanah   3   Ala.

Household 640
Eph. Homesley   34   N.C.   Laborer
Olliss Homesley   47   Ky.   (female)
Marion (male)   20   Ala.   Laborer
Oletha (female)   11   "

Household 641
Alxd. Cimmons   38   N.C.   Shoemaker
Ellender   18   Ala.
Thomas   6   "
Alxd. Hutchens   39   Tenn. None

Household 642
J. G. Chandler   34   Va.   Merchant
Rachel   20   Ala.
Fanny B.   2   "

Household 643
Jiney Jeams   47   S. C. (female)
James   22   Flor.Ala. Grocery
Mary Pullum   18   unknown

Household 644
J. R. Inlow   22   Tenn. Carpenter
Sally   21   Ala.
William   2   "

Household 645
James Humphrey   45   Va.   Merchant
Sarah   43   Ky.
William   21   "   Farmer

Household 646
John Humphrey   23   Ky.   Clerk
Sarah   20   Ala.
James   3/12 "
George Mincer   46   Ky.   Tanner
Joseph Ott   60   N.York Shoemaker

Household 647 Private Entertainment
Saml. Sanders*   35 England Stage/
Eliza Ann*   30 Tenn.   driver
Isaac Henson   25 Tenn. Boatman
John Owens   28 "   Wagoner
Sylvester Linsley   20 "   Cooper
Ben Henson   19 "   Boatman
Edmond Linsley   18 Ala. Do
Monroe Lolla   11 "
William   9 "

Household 648
Joshua Webb   32 unknown laborer
Rebecca   31 Tenn.
Elizabeth   9 Ala.
Nancy   6 "
Martha   3 "

Household 649
John Beesley   38 Tenn. Boatman
Emeline   30 "
Samuel   7 Ala.
Rachel   3 "
Rebecca Beesley**   4/12 "
Feraby Karry   48 Tenn.

Household 650
Isaac Whitsett   38 Tenn. Farmer
Elizabeth   34 "
William   14 Ala.
James   12 "
Philip   10 "
John   8 "
Samuel   4 "
Isaac   2 "
John Gildon   17 unknown Ass't

Household 651
Danl. Tillar   50 Tenn. Laborer
Rebecca   50 "
Ruby   18 "
Lewis   20 "   Boatman
Rebecca   14 "
Phoebi   12 "
Sarah   10 Ala.

Household 652
Allen McCravin   30 Tenn. Farmer
Charlotte (twin)   20 N.C.
Robert (twin)   20 "   Ass't
Alexander   16 Ala. Do
Martha   19 "
Andrew   15 "
John   14 "
Simpson   12 "

Household 653
Susan Jilton   37 Va.
John   18 Ala. Laborer
James   14 "
Leonidus   13 "
Mary   4/12? "
Mersilla Grey   60 Va.

Household 654
George Staley   45 Penn. Boatman
Marion Ann   37 Tenn.
David   12 Ala.
Rebecca   10 "
Nancy   8 "
Ann   6 "
George   2 "

Household 655
Allen Ivins   68 Va. Shoemaker
Fanny   50 Ky.
Adaline   22 Ky.
(Good lands but subject to overflow)
Stephen Ivins   23 Ala. Boatman
Marissa   13 Ala.
(Note between above entries found at
bottom of the page.)

Household 656
Franklin Taylor   30 Tenn. Ditto
Cinthia   23 Ala.
Lidy Hopson   20 Tenn. Ditto
Leander   27 "   Do

Household 657
Benjamin Williams   79 Va. Farmer

Household 658
Josiah Thomas   49 Ky. Do
Rachel   43 Ky.
Samuel   18 Ala. Ass't
Amous   16 "   Do
Manurvy   13 "
Malinda   8 "
Marion   2/12? "

Household 659
Alfred Thomas   20 Tenn. Laborer
Mary   21 "
William   25 Ala. "
(Alfred and Mary marked married within
the year.)

---
*Married within the year.
**Labeled Tennessee River beginning this entry.

Household 660
Wilson McClain	35	Tenn.	Farmer
Mary	30	"	
Sarah	11	Ala.	
Jane	10	"	
Polly	8	"	
James	6	"	

Household 661
Thos. Black	31	S.C.	Farmer
Mary	31	Tenn.	
Sarah	7	Ala.	
G. W. Shaw*	26	Ala.	Boatman
Sally*	21	Ala.	

(*Married in the year.)

Household 662
Thos. Litchwith	35	Tenn.	Farmer
Isibella	27	Ala.	
Jas. Threet	9	"	
Sarah Burass	9	Miss.	

Household 663
John Lickwith	45	Tenn.	Carpenter
Everline	35	"	
Jane	22	"	
Olly	20	"	
Augustus	12	Ala.	
Christopher	7	Ala.	
Mary	65	Va.	

Household 664
Jesse Husk	62	Va.	Farmer
Winney	60	"	
Julia	22	Tenn.	

(Note: Pine, oak, poplar, ash. This note made at bottom of page)

Rhody Husk	18	Tenn.	
Cinthia	14	"	
Robert	10	"	

Household 665
Jackson Webb	40	Tenn.	Farmer
Nancy	40	"	
Allen	14	Ala.	
Mary	8	"	

Household 666
Abraham Husk	20	Tenn.	Do
Samindivella	24	"	(female)
Aaron	7	"	
James	3	"	

Household 667
Augustus Harwell	32	Tenn.	Do
Susan	39	"	
Perry	8	"	
Jacob	6	"	
Manurvey	4	Ala.	
Daury (male)	1/12	"	

Household 668
Augustus Parker	47	N.C.	Carpenter
Elizabeth	34	Tenn.	
Thomas	15	Ala.	
Samuel	13	"	
James	8	"	
Mary	4	"	
Elizabeth Burns	18	"	

Household 669
John Higgins	27	Tenn.	Farmer
Everline	24	Ala.	
Elizabeth Hopson	18	Tenn.	

Household 670
Elijah Pike	50	Mass.	Blc.Smith
Bathana	26	Tenn.	
Dennis	16	"	Do
Elijah	14	Ala.	
Lewis	12	"	

Household 671
Stephen McCrue	49	N.C.	Carpenter
Elizabeth	40	Tenn.	
Martha	18	"	
Jacob	13	"	
William	10	"	
Vibra	8	"	
Mary	5	"	
Nancy	4	"	
Charles	3	"	

Household 672
| Lewis Black | 52 | S.C. | |

(Narrow bottoms, good lands, but subject to overflow; very hilly.)

Sabrey Black	51	S.C.	
Lewis	20	Tenn.	Ass't
Sarah	19	"	
William	16	"	"
George	14	"	
Mary	10	"	
Nancy	4	"	

Household 673
Wm. Hopson	37	Tenn.	Boatman
Jane	35	"	
Jasper	17	"	Do
Mary	13	"	
Carter	10	Ala.	
Thomas	8	"	
John	6	"	
Sarah	2	"	
Wm. Winfrey	34	unknown	Do
Rbt. Shelton	22	Tenn.	Do

Household 674
Herold Hopson   36   Tenn. Hunter
Mahaldy   21   "
Richard   2   "

Household 675
David Isreal   45   S.C.   Farmer
Nancy   35   Tenn.
Margaret   18   Ala.
Crockett   12   "
Elizabeth   4   "
Polly Ann   1   "

Household 676
James McClain   39   Tenn. Farmer
Shorty (female)   36   "
James   13   Ala.
Nancy   12   "
William   10   "
Mary   8   "
Thursey (female)   7   "
Fountain   4   "
John   1   "

Household 677
Wm. Shelton   60   Tenn. Physician
Nancy   30   "
Sarah   2   "

Household 678
T. J. Owen   38   S.C.   Farmer
George   30   "   Ass't
Fanny   22   Tenn.

Household 679
Thos. Hopson   35   Tenn. Laborer
(Pine oak and poplar; game plenty.)
(Next page is labeled Panther Creek area)
Catharine Hopson   23   Tenn.
Richard   7   Ala.
Elizabeth   5   "
Thomas   3   "
Frances (female)   1   "

Household 680
Saml. Owen   32   Tenn. Farmer
Elizajane   22   "
Frances (female)   1   "

Household 681
John Herold   35   Tenn. Farmer
Harriett   26   Ala.
William   11   "
Andrew   9   "
Rachel   8   "
Daniel   3   "
John   6/12   "

Household 682
Wm. McMahan   46   Tenn. Do
Betty   43   "
Sarah   28   "
William   19   "   "
Andrew   17   "   "
James   14   "
Nelson   12   Ala.
Elizabeth   9   "
Thomas   8   "
Charles   4   "
Mary   1   "

Household 683
Wm. Blakeley   49   S.C.   Carpenter
Darkis   48   "
Sicela   27   Tenn.
Mariah   23   "
Albert   18   "   "
Cinthia   15   "
Leonidus   13   "
Jefferson   11   "
John   9   "
James   3   "
William   1   Ala.

Household 684
Hardy Spain   31   Ga.   Farmer
Martha   22   Tenn.
Walker   1   Ala.

Household 685
Ruffin Spain   68   Va.   Do
Jimmina   65   N.C.
(This Creek the same from it takes its
name.--note by enumerator.)
"P.C." at top of page--Panther Creek.
Household 686
Elizabeth Moore   33   Tenn.
Louiser   10   Ala.

Household 687
Newel Spain*   26   Tenn. Wood corder
Louiser*   17   Ala.
(*Married within the year.)

Household 688
Elbourn Spain*   30   Tenn. Do
Marinda*   26   Ala.
(*Married within the year.)

Household 689
Thos. Lucust	34	S.C.	Farmer
Susan	36	"	
Mary	16	Ala.	
Margarett	15	"	
Louiser	13	"	
Nancy	10	"	
Sarah	8	"	
Jefferson	5	"	
Emily	3	"	
Z. Taylor	6/12	"	

Household 690
Hardy Mathus	50	N.C.	Do
Nancy	39	Tenn.	
James	20	Ala.	Ass't
Malinda	19	"	
John	17	"	"
Margaret	16	"	
Joshua	14	"	
Unicy (female)	12	"	
Benton	10	"	
William	8	"	
Hardy	3	"	
Danl. Tacker	20	Tenn.	Do

Household 691
Thos. H. Brown	36	N.C.	Farmer
Emily	24	Tenn.	
John	5	Ala.	
Welton (male)	4	"	
Robert	3	"	
James	1	"	
Sidney Carter	23	"	Ass't
Joseph Bishop	36	Tenn.	"

Household 692
Isaac Smith	22	unknown	boatman
Sarah	24	Ala.	
Winney	7	"	
William	2	"	
Daniel	2/12	"	

Household 693
Robt. Shaw	45	Tenn.	Farmer
(Panther Creek cont'd)			
Frances Shaw	35	N.C.	
Mary	16	Ala.	
George	14	"	
Benton	4	"	
Houston	2	"	
Jackson	3/12	"	

Household 694
James White	50	N.C.	Boatman
Patsy	30	Unknown	
George	10	Tenn.	
Darlaska (female)	3	Ala.	
J. K. Polk	1	Ala.	

Household 695
Berry Floid	37	Tenn.	Laborer
Elizabeth Floid	30	"	
Margaret	12	"	
William	10	"	
Levi	8	"	
Henry	6	Ala.	
Spencer	4	"	
Frances (female)	1	"	

Household 696
Wm. McManus	44	Tenn.	Farmer
Polly	45	Va.	
Mary	12	Tenn.	

Household 697
Sanders Philips	38	N.C.	Do
Sarah	26	Tenn.	
Elias	11	"	
Amanda	10	"	
Daniel	8	"	
Elizabeth	5	"	
Jackson	3	Ala.	
John	1	"	

Household 698
Jane Loid	55	N.C.	
William	17	Tenn.	Boatman

Household 699
J. L. Waits	43	Ga.	Blc. Smith
Sarah	30	Tenn.	
William	18	"	Student
Catharine	17	"	
Browder (male)	13	"	
Thompson	10	Ala.	
Jane	8	"	
Robert	6	"	
Isebella	4	"	
Mary	2	"	

"P.C."
Household 700
Saml. Carson	26	unknown	Hunter
Perrilla	17	Tenn.	
(Marked married within the year.)			

Household 701
Barthley Pernell	41	Tenn.	Bst. Teacher
Nancy	41	"	
Jacob	20	"	Student
Eliza	17	"	
William	15	"	
Franklin	11	"	
Minus (male)	7	"	
John	3	"	

C-51

```
Household 702                              Household 708
Jacob Tacker        32  Tenn.  Laborer     Marion Emerson      30  Tenn. Meth. Carp'r
Ann                 26   "                 Nancy               30  Tenn.
Wesley               9   "                 Martha               9  Tenn.
Martha               7   "                 William              7  Ark.
Francis (female)     5  Ala.               Marilla              2  Tenn.
John                 4  Tenn.              Columbus          1/12  Ala.
Joshua            2/12  Ala.               Isaac Lucust        65  N.C. Millwright
                                           Martha McKidy       17  unknown
Household 703                              John                 1  Ala.
Andrew Carson       60  N.C.   Farmer
Margaret            56   "                 Household 709
Mary                25   "                 Overton Cartwright  42  Ky.  Shoemaker
Joab                22  Ala.   Boatman     Isebella            36  Tenn.
Margaret            20   "                 Mary                16  Ark.
Jackson             14   "                 John                12  Texas
Eliza                9   "                 Isaac                9  Miss.
Mary Loyd            6   "                 Sarah (twin)         7   "
Carolin              3   "                 Eliza (twin)         7   "
                                           Manurvey             4  Ala.
Household 704                              Elizabeth            3  Ala.
Davy Smith*         24  Tenn.  Farmer
Martha*             18  Ala.               Household 710
Alxd. Patrick       25  Ala.   Ass't       Marion Ingram       23  Tenn. Wood Corder
Easter              19   "                 Olly (female)       20  Tenn.
(*Married within the year.)
                                           Household 711
Household 705                              Charles Ingram      50  N.C.  Farmer
Jon.(Jos.?)L.Smith,Jr.*24 Tenn. Farmer     Margaret            50  Va.
Elizabeth*          17  Tenn.              Martha              21  Tenn.
Etheldrin Madrir    32  Tenn.  Ferryman    Susan               18   "
(*Married within the year.)                Margaret            16   "
                                           Robert              11   "
Household 706
Hamilton Rhodes     38  Tenn.  Farmer      Household 712
Cinthia             31  Tenn.              Gais Qualls         53  Va.   Ditto
Margarett           13  Tenn.              Milla               46  Va.
Andy                 6  Ala.               Mary                23  Tenn.
                                           Louiser             16   "
Household 707                              Nancy               15   "
A. N. Emerson       43  Tenn.  Wagener     Almyra              14   "
Merrilla            49  N.C.               Kitty               12   "
John                18  Tenn.  Do          Rebecca             10   "
Elizabeth           16  Tenn.              Taylor               8   "
Nancy               14  Tenn.              Leander              6   "
**Mary Emerson      11  Miss.              Robert               4   "
Aaron               10  Tenn.
William              7  Tenn.              Household 713
                                           Wm. Lucust          33  Tenn. Ditto
                                           Elizabeth           31   "
**"Pine oak poplar chestnut hilly country" Thos. Lucust         8  Ala.
written on top of page between Nancy and   William              7   "
Mary Emerson.                              Darinda              3   "
```

Household 714
Cravis Johnston	42	Ga.	Farmer
Elizabeth	42	"	
Ann	18	"	
McCrager	16	"	Ass't
Mary	14	Ala.	
John	12	"	
Travis	10	"	
Caladonia	6	"	
Samuel	1	"	

Household 715
Saml. Lembert	46	Tenn.	Farmer
Isebella	48	N.C.	
Nancy	24	Tenn.	
Lusinda	22	Tenn.	
Martha*	21	Tenn.	
Polly	18	Tenn.	
James	15	Tenn.	
Thomas	12	Tenn.	
Sally	9	Tenn.	
John	4	Tenn.	
William	4/12	Tenn.	
Spencer Loid*	19	Tenn.	Ass't

(*Married within the year.)

Household 716
George Magea	29	Ala.	Farmer
Leerer	28	"	
James	8	Miss.	
Elizabeth	3	"	

Household 717
Isaac Swinfoard	42	S.C.	Do
Mary	18	Ala.	
John	11	"	

Household 718
Polly Isreal	30	Ala.	
Lewis	10	"	
George	5	"	

Household 719
George Swinfoard	28	Tenn.	Do
Rebecca	34	"	
Charles	14	"	
Mary	11	"	
Darkus	8	Ala.	
Phoebi	1/12	Ala.	
Samuel Prachard	58	S.C.	None
Rachel	48	S.C.	

Household 720
George Summerhill	21	Ala.	Farmer
Horris (male)	17	"	Ass't
William	15	"	
Jesse Wesmorland	35	S.C.	Carpenter

Household 721
Joel Childress	29	Tenn.	Miller
Malinda	28	Ala.	
Greenburry	9	Ala.	
John	7	Ala.	
James	4	Tenn.	
William	2	Ala.	
Robert Warren	24	Va.	None
Levi Selder	22	Tenn.	None

Household 722
John Swinford	70	S.C.	Farmer
Phoebi	55	"	
Nancy	21	Tenn.	
Martha	14	"	

Household 723
J. B. Swinford	22	Tenn.	Cord Wood
Elizajane	21	Ga.	
John	1	Ala.	

Household 724
James Bankes	40	N.C.	Do
Annie	23	Tenn.	
Eliza	2	Ala.	

Household 725
Nancy Thrasher	48	Tenn.	
Rasmus	21	"	Wagons
William	19	"	Do
Mary	17	"	
Thomas	14	"	
Carnriddy	10	Ala.	
Benjamin	8	"	

Household 726
William Scott	46	N.C.	Farmer
Louiser	26	Ala.	
James	19	"	Ass't
John	16	"	Do
Miles	13	"	
Susana	12	"	
William	9	"	
Jane	3	"	
Allen	2	"	

Household 727
| William Scott Jr.* | 26 | Tenn. | Farmer |
| Elizabeth* | 19 | " | |

(*Married within the year.)

Household 728
| John Lamb | 48 | N.C. | Do |
| Martha | 40 | N.C. | |
continued

"Bumpass Creek Pine oak and chestnut and hickory Iron ore banks and many calybeate springs" written at top of page.

Household 728 continued
Name	Age	State	Occupation
John Lamb	21	Tenn.	Ass't
Polly	19	"	
Jane	17	"	
Martha (twin)	14	"	
Rachel (twin)	14	"	
Mahaley	9	Ala.	
Henry	7	"	

Household 729
Name	Age	State	Occupation
James Scott	23	Tenn.	Farmer
Elizabeth	23	Tenn.	
John	3	Ala.	
Betty	1	"	

Household 730
Name	Age	State	Occupation
John W. Scott*	28	Tenn.	Laborer
Mary*	19	"	

(*Married within the year.)

Household 731
Name	Age	State	Occupation
John Lamb	29	Tenn.	Farmer
Elizabeth	25	Tenn.	
James	7	"	
Nancy	4	Ala.	

Household 731 (number repeated)
Name	Age	State	Occupation
Weathersby Haynes	50	N.C.	Tar Maker
Elizabeth	45	"	
Charity	22	Tenn.	
James*	20	Tenn.	Rosin
Nancy	18	Tenn.	
John	16	Tenn.	Boatman
Darling (male)	12	Ala.	
George	10	"	
Annie	6	"	
Sarah	5	"	
Vicy	1	"	

(*Marked married within the year.)

Household 732
Name	Age	State	Occupation
John Scott	50	N.C.	Farmer
Catharine	21	Ala.	
John	18	"	Assistant
Jerry	16	"	Student
Dexter	14	"	
Rufus	12	"	
Elizabeth	9	"	

Household 733
Name	Age	State	Occupation
Hariett Scott	60	Tenn.	Farming
Jane	19	Ala.	
George	14	"	
Levi	13	"	
James	11	"	
Margaret	10	"	
Thomas	4	"	

"Pine oak chestnut very hill country" written at bottom of page.

Household 735 (no 734)
Name	Age	State	Occupation
Martha Scott	63	N.C.	
Mary Ann	21	Ala.	

Household 736
Name	Age	State	Occupation
Martha Johnson	53	N.C.	Farming
Richard	18	Ala.	Ass't
Letitia	16	"	
Jerry	14	"	

Household 737
Name	Age	State	Occupation
James Adams	29	Ala.	Farmer
Martha	29	"	
Elizabeth	7	"	
Manurvey	5	"	
Malissa	3	"	
William	1/12	"	

Household 738
Name	Age	State	Occupation
John Ray	31	Tenn.	Miller
Lucretia	31	"	
Marion	10	Ala.	
Mary	8	"	
Martha	6	"	
William	3	"	

Household 739
Name	Age	State	Occupation
David Adams	53	Tenn.	Miller
Dicy	47	"	
John	22	Ala.	Do
Joseph	18	"	Student
Betty	12	"	
Isebella	11	"	
Nancy	8	"	
Henry	6	"	
Sally	4	"	
David	3	"	
Tennessee (female)	1/12	"	

Household 740
Name	Age	State	Occupation
Henry Haynes	28	Tenn.	Cooper
Nancy	28	N. York	
John	7	Ala.	
Henry	4	"	
Cristopher	1/12	"	

Household 741
Name	Age	State	Occupation
Martin Palmore	27	Tenn.	Farmer
Nancy	23	"	
Mary	6	"	
Elijah	4	Ala.	
Betty	4/12	"	

Household 742
Name	Age	State	Occupation
Elijah Adams	21	Ala.	Laborer
Malinda	20	"	
John	1/12	"	

Colbert's Reserve

Household 743
| Henry Hanes | 70 | S.C. | Tare? Burner |
| Nancy | 32 | " | |

Household 744
Unus Hurt (male)	35	Tenn.	Coal Do
Lewis	14	"	
Dicy	11	"	
Sally	8	"	
Martha	7	"	
John	6	Ala.	

Household 745
| Caswell Price* | 25 | Ala. | Farmer |
| Polly* | 16 | " | |
(*Married within the year.)

Household 746
Jas. W. Francis	43	Ky.	Farmer
Mary	44	S.C.	
Augustus Bailey*	27	Tenn.	Miller
Laura*	23	"	
Wm. Micher	12	Ala.	
Soleman Freeman	27	Tenn.	Hereland
William	18	"	"
Wm. Young	19	"	"
Buel Brigs	22	"	"
Jno. A. Miller	21	"	"
Wm. G. Tucker	45	Va.	Carpenter
(*Married within the year.)

Household 747
Charles Cockburn	40	N.C.	Blc.Smith
Elisabeth	40	S.C.	
Elijah	18	Ala.	Striker
Harriett	12	"	
Amanda	10	"	
Liddi	7	"	
Lusinda	5	"	
Hadly	3	"	

Household 748
Sarah Franklin	39	Va.	
William	21	Ala.	Teacher
Joseph	19	"	None
Nancy Reyborn	11	"	

Household 749
Jeferson Duncan	26	Tenn.	Shoemaker
Mary	20	Tenn.	
Caroline	1	Ala.	

Household 750
Hanna Jenkins	46	N.C.	Farming
Mack	12	Tenn.	Asst.
Thomas	16	"	Do
Ruth	10	Ala.	
Abner	7	Ala.	

Household 751
Saml. Burns	48	S.C.	Farmer
Eliabeth Burns	47	S.C.	
Robert	22	"	Asst.Farmer
Moses	21	"	"
Thomas	20	"	
James	18	Ala.	
Mary	16	"	
Nancy	13	"	
Benjam	9	"	
Lusinda	8	"	

Household 752
S. M. Dalrumple	43	S.C.	Farmer
Illenissa (female)	29	"	
George	11	"	
Thomas	8	"	
John	5	"	
Nancy	3	Miss.	

Household 753
Miss Mary Houston	29	Tenn.	Farming
" Laura	26	"	Do
Rebecca Williams	40	S.C.	
Ann Bogs	24	Tenn.	
Hanna	3	Ala.	
Emily	2/12	"	

Household 754
E. B. Summerhill	33	N.C.	Farmer
Mary	38	"	
Agnus	12	Tenn.	
William	10	Ala.	
Edward	8	"	
Richard	6	"	
George	4	"	
Elijah	2	"	
Elizabeth	71	N.C.	

Household 755
Wm. Richards	76	N.C.	Do
Nancy	63	"	
Nathaniel	33	S.C.	Blc. Smith
Wesley	23	"	Do

Household 756
| Rubin Do | 38 | S.C. | Overseer |
| Martha | 36 | Tenn. | |

Household 757
Monroe Terrell	25	Ala.	Do
Catharine	23	Tenn.	
James	1	Ala.	

Household 758
Tibitha Do	64	S.C.	Farming
Joseph	18	Ala.	Student
Doctor	16	Ala.	Do
continued

"Good lands - groath poplar oak ash walnut and hickrey and mulbury."

Household 758 continued
James Terrell	14	Ala.
Andrew	13	"

Household 759
Horis Summerhill	48	Va.	Farmer
Permelia	42	N.C.	
Martha	19	Ala.	
Eliza	13	"	
Rebecca	11	"	

Household 760
Seth B. Thomelson	48	N.C.	Overseer
Artiminta	36	N.C.	
Uphraney (female)	13	"	
Rosana	12	Ala.	
Mississippi	10	"	
Thestus (male)	8	"	
Raley (female)	2	"	

Household 751 (note number)
Moses White	57	Va.	Farmer
Francis (female)	46	S.C.	
Washington	23	Ala.	Ass't
Amanda	18	"	
Caroline	16	"	
Elizabeth	13	"	
Franklin	11	"	
David	8	"	
Joseph	8	"	

Household 752
Anderson Caroll	36	Tenn.	Farmer
Lusetta	35	N.C.	
Frank	7	Ala.	
Richard	6	"	
Mary	4	"	
Permelia	2	"	
Marion Holland (male)	21	Tenn.	Ass't

Household 753
Patr. H. Hewett	43	Va.	Overseer
Elizabeth	37	N.C.	
Franklin	11	Ala.	
Elizabeth	9	"	
Robert	8	"	
Frances	6	"	
Sarah	3	"	

Household 754
Harden Perkins	20	Tenn.	Farmer
Louiser	17	Ala.	
Louiser 2nd	1	"	
James C. Reed	20	"	Overseer

Household 755
William Koger*	58	Va.	Farmer
Martha Koger	43	Va.	
Martha	17	Ala.	
Mary	15	"	
Elizabeth	13	"	
Allice	7	"	

Household 766
William Koger	23	Ala.	Physician
Orlena	17	Ala.	
Josephine	4/12	"	

Household 567
Thomas Thrasher	25	Ala.	Overseer
Sarah	22	Ala.	
William	1	"	

Household 768
Jerenath Beckwith	52	Va.	Farmer
Winston	26	Ala.	Ass't
Elizabeth	22	"	
Alexander	21	"	None

Household 769
Wm. H. Jordan	28	Ala.	Meth.Farmer
Sarah	23	N.C.	
William	3	Ala.	
Mary	2/12	Ala.	

Household 770
Jesse Koger	25	Ala.	Farmer
Romelia	17	Ala.	
Relea (female)	1/12	"	

*William Koger's will was dated in 1858. His home was built about 15 miles west of Florence on the Smithsonia-Rhodesville Road, and the house was still standing as late as 1964. Some sources give his wife's name as Mary, but the census for 1850 shows Martha.

William Koger owned Koger Island which consists of about 150 acres in the Tennessee River.

Canaan Methodist Church is located about one mile north and Mrs. Koger was a devoted member of this old church.

(Sources: Historic Muscle Shoals, published by the Tennessee Valley Historical Society, 1962, page 48; William L. McDonald, manuscript, page 13, a copy in Tennessee State Library and Archives.)

Household 771
John Shird	36	N. C.	Overseer
Mary	31	Tennessee	
Henry	9	Alabama	
Leona	8	"	
Frances	6	"	
May Lucy	4	"	
Raby (female)	6/12	"	

Household 772
Robt. Shird	61	N. C.	Farmer
Elizabeth	58	N. C.	
Mack	21	Alabama	Assistant
Andrew	18	Alabama	Assistant

Household 773
Samuel B. Monroe	41	N. C.	Carpenter
Mary	31	S.C.	
Rubin	12	Ala.	
Pugh	8	"	
Mary	6	"	
Josephine	2	"	

Household 773
John Richards	27	S. C.	Carpenter
Sarah	27	Tenn.	
Patrick	13	"	
Eliza Richards	9	"	
David	25	"	Florest
Wm. Holland	20	"	do
Mary	16	"	

Household 777
Neal Rowell	54	Va.	Farmer
Martha	39	N.C.	
Elizabeth	16	Ala.	
Cristopher	15	"	
Ann	12	"	
Virginia	5	"	
Resh Griffet	25	England	Teacher

Note for previous page: Thomas Thrasher married 13 April 1848 to Sarah P. Rice; Lauderdale County marriages.

Dr. Neal Rowell's plantation home was built in the 1830s and called Alba Wood and located on Gunwaleford Road about 12 miles west of Florence. He was born in Wood County, Va., in 1796, and married Martha Ann Cheatham, 1811-1890, daughter of Christopher Cheatham, who operated Cheatham's Ferry. Dr. Rowell died in 1886. (Historic Muscle Shoals, page 48.)

Household 778
Saml. Alexander	25	Ala.	Overseer
Elizabeth	20	Ala.	

Household 779
James Stewart	39	S.C.	Farmer
Mary	32	N.C.	
James	16	Tenn.	Student
Mary	13	Ala.	
John	11	"	
William	9	"	
Edward	5	"	
Lusinda Johnson	30	unknown	
Lutious Lorance	23	Ala.	Teacher

(Florence Gazette, 24 Jan. 1863: Estate of Luceous Lorance being settled by S. B. Hudson.)

Household 780
Ben Wootten	37	Tenn.	Overseer
Hariett	30	S.C.	
Amanda (twin)	13	Ala.	
Mary (twin)	13	"	
Mary Ingram	23	Tenn.	

Household 781
Nathan Body	55	Va.	Farmer
Francis (female)	22	Ala.	
James	20	"	none
Rebecca	18	"	
Nathan	11	"	
Ann Eliza	9	"	

Household 782
Jas. L. Roberts	38	Ga.	Overseer
Sarah	35	N.C.	
Matthew	18	Ala.	none
Mary	15	"	
Robert	13	"	
Martha	7	"	
Henry	4	"	

Household 783
Thos. Nations	38	Ala.	Overseer
Martha	34	Tenn.	
Mary Nations	11	Ala.	
Sarah	10	"	
Robert	8	"	
Martha	7	"	
Thomas	2	"	

Household 781
Moses Wood	50	Va.	Farmer

Household 782
Jas. Hardwick	24	Ala.	Miller
Betty	23	"	
Martha	3	"	
Nancy	2	"	

C-57

Household 783
E. B. Donalson	21	Va.	Farmer
Jas. M. Pearson	28	Ala.	Overseer

Household 784
Wm. H. Key	30	Va.	Farmer
Susan	28	N.C.	
Mary	5	Ala.	
Elizabeth	3	"	
Martha Lane	25	Va.	
James Key	40	Va.	none

Household 785
Wm. E. Parker	32	N.C.	overseer
Sarah	25	Ala.	
Virginia	7	"	
Frances	5	"	
William	3	"	

Household 786
John Peters	48	Va.	Farmer
Temperance Haley	17	N.C.	
Carter Howell	28	S. C.	Overseer

Household 787
Henry D. Smith	47	Va.	Farmer
Martha	42	Va.	
Etheldred	22	N.C.	none
John	20	"	Student
Elizabeth	18	Ala.	
Martha	13	"	
Hanna	11	"	
Henry	9	"	
Caroline	7	"	
Mary	5	"	
Jerry	2	"	
Margaret Salls	10	N.C.	

Household 788
Craney Herold	43	N.C.	overseer
Mariah	35	Ala.	
Dolly	17	"	
James Nations	5	"	
James Herold	8	"	
Charles	5	"	
Mariah	3	"	
Wm. Edwards	19	"	overseer

Household 789
Asbury Hendrix	27	N.C.	do
Jane	23	Ala.	
Margaret	3	"	
Elizabeth	1	"	
Amous S. Daron	25	Conn.	Teacher

John Peters, born 1802, died 1869, son of John and Temple Blance (Temperance) Peters; settled here about 1810, lived 12 miles west of Florence, now L. L. Whitten, Sr. property.

Household 790
Wiett Colliar	58	Va.	Farmer
Jinnetta	45	Scotland	
Clarah	16	Ala.	
Mary	13	"	
Martha	9	"	
Jinnett	7	"	
Allice	5	"	
Catharine	4/12	"	
Juliar Reynolds	22	N. York	

Household 791
Wm. Bradford	30	Tenn.	overseer
Manurvey	27	Ala.	
Mary	4	"	
Richard	1	"	

Household 792
Peter F. Archer	49	Va.	Farmer
Caroline	40	Va.	
Mary	17	Ala.	
Sarah	15	"	
Virginia	13	"	
Martha	11	"	
Clementine	6	"	
Caroline	4	"	
Peter	1	"	
Moses Foster	47	N.C.	overseer
C. F. Jones	30	Va.	do

Household 793
Richman Terrell	25	Ala.	do
Sarah	22	Tenn.	
Ellen	4/12	Ala.	

Household 794
William Lipscomb	28	N.C.	do
Elizabeth	27	N.C.	
James	6	Ala.	
Sarah	4	"	
Samuel	2	"	
Mariah	3/12	"	

Household 795
Mary C. Lorance	52	N.C.	Farming
Andrew	25	Ala.	Ass't
Aseneth (female)	18	"	
Sarah	10	"	

Household 796
Duncan McIntyre	34	N.C.	Farmer
Mary	34	"	
Archer	12	Tenn.	
John	8	"	
Lawrence	6	Ala.	
Andrew	4	"	
Tenny (male)	2	"	
Wm. Bradford	20	N.C.	Ass't
Delana	16	N.C.	

Household 797
Ruffin Burns	32	N.C.	Overseer
Lucy	37	"	
Richard	4	"	
James	2	"	
Robert	6/12	Ala.	

Household 798
Saml. Word	26	N.C.	ditto
Lusinda	17	Ala.	
(Married within the year)			

Household 799
John Gibson	23	N.C.	Ditto
Ann	21	"	
Lusinda	6/12	Ala.	

Household 800
| R. T. Kernahan, Jr. | 23 | Ala. | Farmer |

Household 801
| R. T. Kernahan, Sr. | 56 | Ireland | do |
| John Crodock | 22 | Ala. | overseer |

Household 802
James Noel	70	Va.	Farmer
Mary	56	N.C.	
Samuel	20	Ala.	Ass't
Cornelia	16	"	
John	14	"	
Elizabeth Claiborne	23	"	
William	5	"	

Household 803
| Joseph Hiett | 23 | N.C. | overseer |
| Manurvey | 20 | Ala. | |

Household 804
Richard Faris	38	Ala.	Farmer
Martha	37	"	
William	13	"	
James	10	"	
John	9	"	

Household 805
Jas. Belcher	41	Ky.	overseer
Susan	39	S.C.	
Thomas Belcher	10	Ala.	
William	8	Miss.	
Margaret	7	Ala.	
Annie	6	"	
John	4	"	

R. T. Kernahan, Jr.'s real estate holdings were valued at $10,593, and he was only 23 years old; R. T. Kernahan, Sr., presumably his father, had real estate valued at only $600.

Household 807
Chap. Anderson	48	Tenn.	Farmer
Sarah	38	N.C.	
Frances	15	Ala.	
Henry	13	"	
William	7	"	
Claborn Hiett	17	"	Ass't
Henry Winbourn	30	"	Overseer

Household 808
Thos. J. Irons	40	N.C.	Farmer
Caroline	26	Tenn.	
James*	7	Ala.	
Mary	5	"	
Thomas	2	"	

Household 809
Mitchel Malone**	49	N.C.	Farmer
Susan	34	Va.	
Frances	17	Ala.	(female)
Mitchel	8	"	
Benjamin	5	"	
Ugine	2	"	(female)
Benjamin Carter	31	Va.	Overseer

Household 810
Jno. A. Branch	46	Va.	Farmer
Edmond	21	Va.	Ass't
John	17	"	do
Frances	15	"	
Sarah	13	Tenn.	
Boling	12	Tenn.	
James	10	Ala.	

Household 811
| Wm. E. Jones | 33 | N.C. | Meth. Farmer |
| Eliza | 33 | Ala. | |

Household 812
Lewis Powers	36	S.C.	Overseer
Frances	30	"	
John	12	Ala.	
Joseph	10	"	
Alxd. Powers	8	"	
Frank	5	"	
Susan	3	"	
Statha (female)	2	"	

*James Phillip Irion, born 9 Dec. 1843, son of Thomas and Caroline, married Elizabeth Cannon Branch, born 25 Jan. 1854, granddaughter of Jabez and Sarah Cannon. (Family information from Mrs. Harriet H. Sellers.)

**Mitchell Malone married Susan B. Isbell. They are buried in Florence Cemetery.

C-59

Household 813
Edmond Noel   60   Va.   Farmer
(Lived in bend of river section of
county; donated land for Canaan
Methodist Church. Church is on Smith-
sonia-Rhodesville Road, about 15 miles
west of Florence. Historic Muscle
Shoals, pate 48.)

Household 814
E. B. Thompson   24   N.C.   Farmer
(Member of Canaan Methodist Church;
Captain of Company C, 27th Ala. Infantry,
C. S. A.)

Household 815
R. C. Bumpass   39   S. C.   Farmer
Margaret McIntyre   30   N.C.
Mary   27   Tenn.
Everline   21   Ala.
Catharine Paterson   28   N.C.
Thomas   11   Ala.

Household 816
Temple Turnley   54   Va.   Do
Frances   30   Ala.
(Marked married within the year.)

Household 817
Albert H. Jones   28   Ala.   Physician
Littlebury Underwood 46   N. C. Farmer

Household 818
James Waslston   38 N.C. Meth. Farmer
Lorenah   33 Ga.
Mary   7 Ala.
Turner (twin)   5 "
William (twin)   5 "
Isebella   1 "

Household 819
Turner Walston   66 N.C.   Farmer
Elizabeth   61 Va.

Household 820
William Davis   35 Tenn. Meth. Farmer
Elizabeth   28 Ala.
Amy   2 "

Household 821
A. F. Bracken   40 N.C.   Physician
Elizabeth   32 Tenn.
Thomas   18 N.C.   Student
Elizabeth   6 Ala.
Samuel   1 "

---
*Marked married within the year.

Household 822
Wm. H. Noland   40   Va.   Lt. Navy
Harriett   40   Va.
L. C. Armstead   7   Ala.
Jeseph Tossle   33   Germiny Gardner

Household 823
Wm. Cumptem   60   Va.   Farmer
Sarah Parker   50   Va.
Elizabeth Thomas   36   Tenn.
Harriett   30   "
Thos. Hamons   28   "   Ass't
Parilee   24   Ala.
William Hamons   22   "   Ass't
James Acres   12   "
Sarah   10   "
Allice   8   "
Francis Kemper   77   Va. none (male)

Household 824
Jas. E. Campbell   42   Tenn. Farmer
Aley   43   S.C.
Martha   14   Ala.
Liddi   13   "
Robert   8   "
James   5   "
Mary   3   "
David   1   "
Nancy Fowler   16   "

Household 825
Jas. P. Williams   67   Va.   Farmer
John   20   Ala.   Manager
Frances (female)   15   "
Virginia   11   "
Samuel   8   "
Lucy   7   "

Household 826
Robt. Williams   60   Va.   Farmer
Catharine   48   "
Thos. Roberson   21   Ala.   Manager

Household 827
Stanton Flint*   46   S.C.   Farmer
Julia*   35   "
John   21   Ala.   Ass't
Henry   15   "
George   13   "
Martha   11   "
Benton   9   "
Samuel   7   "
Margaret   5   "

Household 828
Leonidus Wires   35   Tenn. Carpenter
Susan   25   Ala.
Missouri   4   "
Mary   2   "
Sarah   2/12   "

Household 829
Josiah Hawkins   48 Maryland Farmer
Elizabeth   37 "
Edward   3   Ala.
Malinda   1   "
James Weams   18 "   none
Eliza Weams   19 "
Thomas   16 "   Student
Charles   12 "
James   8   "

Household 829
George Armstead   38 Va.   Farmer
Jane   29 "
Mary Frances   17 Ala.
Heslep   12 "
Lewis   8   "
Ellen   4   "
George   2   "

Household 830
Calvin Lipscomb   31 N.C. Overseer
Elizabeth   23 Tenn.
Margaret   4   Ala.
Mary F.   2   "
William   1   "

Household 831
Robert Armstead   41 Va.   Farmer
Lusetta   8   Ala.
George   6   "
Dephtny (female)   5   "
Frances (female)   3   "
Penelopy Nickleson 57 N.C.

Household 832
Isibella Brockass   42 Va.   Farming
Robert   15 Ala.
John   14 "
Peter   12 "
Thomas   10 "

Household 833
Mikle H. Waldrip   45 S.C. Carpenter
Elizabeth   41 S.C.
Amanda   16 Ala.
Martha   15 "
Mary   14 "
Allen   11 "
Thomas   8   "
Preston   5   "
Francis (female)   3   "
Addaline   1   "

Household 834
Jas. L. Brown   30 S.C. Laborer
Emiline   26 Ala.
William   9   "
John   4   "
Mary   1   "

Household 835
Eliza Armstead   50 Maryland Poltry
Sarah   19 Ala.
Louiser   16 "
Mahuldy   14 "
Caladonia   8   "
(All members of this household marked
"M" for mulatto.)

Household 836
Hugh McVey   82 S.C. Farmer
Elizabeth Martin   37 Ala.

Household 837
Manson Rice   52 Va.   Do
Elizabeth   45 Ga.
Martha   20 Ala.

Household 838
Wm. Do   26 Ala. Manager
Mary   20 "
Francis (female)   2   "
Wadsworth   8/12 "

Household 839
John Walston   28 Ala. Meth.Farmer
Ann   24 N.C.
Mary   3   "
Elizajane   3/12 "

Household 840
H. J. Darbey   32 "   Overseer
Lucy Ann   20 "
Henry   6/12 "

Household 841
Jno. C. Goff   31 Tenn. Farmer
Margaret   23 "
Thomas   7   Ala.
Mary   5   Tenn.
George   3   Ala.
Robert Wood   20 Tenn. Ass't
Alyed Thorn (male) 16 "   "

Household 842
John Randle   26 Tenn. Overseer
Dicy   23 "
Thomas   5   "

Household 843
Martha Armstead   60 Va.   Farmer
George (twin)   22 Ala. "None
Mary (twin)   22 "

Household 844
Jonnath Smith   28 Va. Epcle.minste
Ellen   24 Ala.
Virginia   9/12 "
continued

THE TOWN OF FLORENCE

Household 844 continued
Jane Lanier   9 Miss.
Mary   7 Ala.
Martha   5 "
Wm. McKaskle   24 Tenn. Overseer

Household 845
John Faris   25 Ala.   Teacher
Hariett Faris   24 S.C.
Alonso   7 Ala.
Pugh   5 "
Charlotte   2 "

Household 846
John House   32 S.C.   Saddler
Mariah   28 Ala.
Elizabeth   4 "
Abey (female)   2 "

Household 847
Saml. Philips   35 Tenn. Blc. Smith
Martha   23 Ala.
Frances   6 "
Amanda   4 "
Nancy   2 "

Household 848
Stephen Townsly   37 Va.   Carpenter
Sarah   37 Va.
William   15 Tenn.
Lafaett   10 Ala.
Martha   9 "
Amerissa   7 "
Columbus   5 "
Jasper   3 "
Elizabeth Do   61 Va.

Household 849
John Wilkerson   45 Va.   Farmer
Rebecca   40 S.C.
Wesley   24 Tenn. Ass't
Claracy   18 "
Mary   17 "
Hanna   14 Ala.
Oliver   8 "

Household 850
Andrew Arnett   57 N.C.   Farmer
Betty   48 "
Nancy   26 Ky.
Elizabeth   21 "
William   20 "
Susan   17 "
John   15 "
Joseph   14 "
James   9 Ala.
Sarah   5 "

Household 851
John Cackelman*   35 Europe Gardner
Peapula (female)   32 "
John   9/12 Ala.
Adam Lidner   50 Europe Do
Joseph   30 "   "

Household 852
Mary Venness   36 Ky.   Seamstress
George   14 Ala.

Household 853
James Hurt   40 Tenn.   Boatman
Bitty   35 "
Nancy   12 Ala.

Household 854
Henry Lambert   29 Ala.   Do
Margaret   23 Ky.
Malinda   7 "
James   6 "
Nancy   4 "
John   2 Mo.

Household 855
Jas. Brook   56 N.C.   Carpenter
Dicy   58 "
Elizabeth   21 Tenn.
Frances (female)   20 Ala.

Household 856
Letitia V. Sloss   49 Tenn.
James   18 Ala.   Clerk
Thomas   14 "
Robert   12 "

Household 857
F. S. Rutherford   30 N.York Lawyer
Lotitia   20 Ala.
Margaret Woodle   21 Ala.

Household 858
Saml. B. Hudleston   30 Tenn.   Taylor
Mary   26 Ala.
John   9 "
Lewis   3 "
David   2 "
Sarah A. Darbey   24 "
Ebineser   63 Conn.   Shoemaker
Rosana Titus   8 Ala.

---

*John Kackelman lived at the Indian Mound at Florence. At one time his home was on top of the large mound; later he moved his house to one side. He and his wife are buried in the Florence Cemetery.

Household 858
Hennetta Williams   45 Boston
Hennetta   13 Ala.
Thomas   12 "
Margaret Biger   50 Boston

Household 859
Josiah Polock   43 Massach. Tinner
Eliza   38 Va.
Mariah   16 Ohio
Mary Pollock   15 "
Hennetta   11 "
Arletia (female)   9 "
Harriett   4 Ala.
William Ragsdale   21 Ala.   Tinner
Robert Dillan   28 Pitsburg Do
Jas. Andrson   15 Ala.

Household 860
Robt. L. Bliss*   47 England Drugist
Susan   40 Ireland
John   14 Ala.
Sarah   12 "
Robert   7 "
Thomas   5 "
Arther   3 "
Mary Henderson   40 Scotland
Mary Collins   30 Ireland

Household 861
Wm. B. Wood   30 Tenn. Lawyer
Sarah   26 "

Household 862
S. A. Wood**   27 Ala. Lawyer
Lelia   24 "
William   2/12 "

Household 863
J. B. Leftwich   44 Va. Merchant
Ann   41 Tenn.
J. B. Faris   20 "   "
Addaly (male)   18 "   Clerk

―――――――――
*Florence Gazette, 18 July 1846 has an advertisement for the Florence Apothecary and Drug Store operated by Robert L. Bliss, who also advertises "Family residence on Tennessee Street on the hill west of the court house, long known as the residence of Dr. H. Woodcock." Members of this family buried in Florence Cemetery.

**Lauderdale County marriages: Sterling A. M. Wood married Lelia E. Leftwich on 10 April 1849 in Lauderdale County.

Household 864
M. P. Asher   30 Ala. Merchant
Perry   25 "   "
Clarisa   34 "
Mary   20 "
Mary Raglin   9 "
Asher   7 "
William   1 "
Ann Andrews   15 "
Benjamin   17 "   Clerk

Household 865
John S. Kennedy   30 N.C. Lawyer
Mary   26 "
Liddia   5 Ala.
Fagan   4 "
John   2 "
Edward   4/12 "
Edward   20 "   Student
Hiram   14 Miss.
Elias Kennedy   18 Ala. Student

Household 866
L. T. Houston   32 N.York Lawyer
Sarah   30 Ky.
Elizabeth   8 Ala.
Annett   6 "
Hennett Logan   28 Ky.
Mary C. Heslep   15 Ala.

Household 867
R. B. Baugh*   33 Tenn. C.Clerk
Virgina   30 Tenn.
Julia Leftwich   31 "
Emer V. Cassity   5 Ala. (female)

Household 868
Harvey Dillahunty   52 Tenn. Lawyer
Matheland (female)   46 S.C.
Frances   23 Ala.
Charles   18 "   Reading
Harvey   16 "   Student
Samuel   17 "   "
Milla   13 "
Elizabeth   82 N.C.

Household 869
Andrew Thomas   59 S.C. Lv.Stable
Elizabeth   54 Va.
John   29 Tenn. "
James   18 "   "
Elizabeth   16 "
Martha   13 "

―――――――――
*Lauderdale Co. marriages: Richard B. Baugh to Virginia Leftwich on 27 May 1840 in Lauderdale County.

C-63

Household 870			Household 877		
Henry Donahoagh	70	Va. None	B. F. Karner	50	Myld. Merchan
Sarah	67	"	Sarah	38	Va.
			Franklin	24	Ala. Clerk
Household 871			William	18	" Do
Martha Young	35	Ala.	Ann Eliza	15	"
Henry	12	"	Sarah	12	"
Sarah	7	"	Mary	10	"
Samuel	10	"	John	8	"
			Andrew	5	"
			Charles	2	"
Household 872					
M. C. Galleway	30	Ala. Editor			
Fanny	27	Va.	Household 878		
Silus Barr	19	Unknown printer	E. Childress	60	Tenn.(female)
E. J. Cronter	24	Ala. "	Y. A. Gray (male)	20	Ala. Clerk
W. S. Titus	28	" "			
J. B. Barker	13	"	Household 879		
Albert	12	"	Beverly Gray (male) (Mulatto)		Ala. Boatman
Household 873					
Thomas Simpson	53	Ireland Land	Household 880 (HOTEL)		
Elizabeth	48	Scotland Agent	Garret Campbell*	44	N.C. Hotell
John C.	24	Ala. Lawyer	Ann	42	Tenn.
James H.	22	" Clerk	William	14	Ala.
			Garrett	11	"
Household 874			John	8	"
James Owen	57	Ireland lawyer	Martha	4	"
Emily	41	Penn.	Mary Fields	60	N.C.
Franlin	22	Ala. Student	Benj. Abrahams	29	Penn. Dentist
James Jr.	21	"	John Anderson	28	Ohio Furnitur
Emily Jr.	18	"	T. Eubanky	30	N.C. "
Ellen	17	"	Horatio	30	Penn. "
Semour	15	"	Elias Thrasher	28	Ala. "
William	13	"	John W. McAlister	30	Ireland M'cha
Margarett	8	"	Robert Patton	28	" Book'per
Edward	5	"	A. M. Hanna	35	Scot. Taylor
Ellin Boggs	35	Penn.	J. B. Bogs	31	Penn.Capt.Boa
			Jas. D. Belote	28	Tenn.Physicia
			Thomas F. Peters	22	Ala. Barkeepe
Household 875					
Andrew Amnett	66	Va. Carpenter			
Juliar	56	"	Household 881		
Mary	26	"	Jas. T. Hargraves	40	Ga. Physician
Francis (female)	24	Ala.			
Lousana (twin)	22	"			
William (twin)	22	" "			
Juliar Mitchell	7	"			

*Garrick Campbell married Ann Williams on 21 Jan. 1830 in Lauderdale County, Ala. An article from the Florence Times-News in the 1920s, written by T. M. Owen, Jr.: "Situated opposite what is now Milner's drug store on Court street, on the spot where the King Co.'s store now stands a lady by the name of Campbell operated the Campbell hotel. There was a block of frame buildings and this hostelry was in the middle. It was burned in the early seventies." This was based on information furnished by James Milner to Owen.

Household 876		
J. T. Murphy	41	Tenn. Taylor
Concretia	38	N.C.
Virginia	17	Ky.
William	15	Tenn.
Margarett	13	"
Mary	11	Ala.
H. Clay	7	Ala.
Sarah	4	"
Young A.	2/12	"
William Sortin	22	" "
J. A. Mighninger	35	Jaminry "

Household 882
Thos. Matingly	32	D^o Columbia Do	Household 890			
Sarah Walker	28	Va.	Jno. M. Slaughter	51	Va.	Taylor
Thomas	21	Ala. none	Mary	41	N.C.	
Francis (female)	19	"	John	21	"	Do
Sidney Matingly	4	"	George	19	"	Do
Catharine	2	"	Mary	16	"	
			Peter	14	"	
Household 883			William	12	"	
James G. Critenden	31	Tenn. Shoemaker	James	5	Tenn.	
Loucinda	31	Ala.	Z. Taylor	3	Ala.	
Martha	13	"	Matilda Parsons	21	Tenn.	
John	11	"				
James	9	"	Household 891			
Lousinda	8	"	Jno. (?) M. Ellis	37	Tenn.	Shoes
William	6	"	Jmmelia	30	"	
Matilda	4	"	Isaac	11	"	
Hnnetta	1	"	Robert	8	Indiana	
Elis. Hulcy	23	"	Charles	6	Kentucky	
			Henry	4	Ala.	
Household 884			James	3	"	
Julious House	42	N.C. Constable	Nancy	10/12	"	
Eliza	38	S.C.	Jono. McClure	19	"	Taylor
Elias	9	Ala.				
Martha	4	"	Household 892			
Ann Eliza	2	"	Varest Pool	31	Ala.	Stagedri-
Elizb. Reed	15	"	Eliza	29	"	ver
Annah	13	"	Mary	7	"	
			Martha Pool	5	Ala.	
Household 886			William	3	"	
James F. Finn	34	Va. Wagons	James	8/12	"	
Permelia	20	Ala.	Mary Gewin	18	"	
			Household 894			
Household 887			William Cullum	49	Tenn.	Stage-
Saml. W. Barker	38	Tenn. Shoem'kr	Zale (female)	32	Tenn.	driver
Elizabeth	36	"	Cynthia	15	"	
Sarah	12	Ala.	Elizabeth	13	"	
Malinda	10	"	Delanson (male)	10	Ala.	
George	8	"	Ann	7	"	
William	6	"	Martha	5	"	
Lodus (female)	4	"	Mary	2	"	
Andrew J.	2	"				
Louisa	2/12	"	Household 895			
Wm. Mason	30	Tenn. Do	Wm. K. (?) Haze	31	Penn.	Merchant
			Elizabeth	26	Ala.	
Household 888			James	5	"	
W. F. Murphy	22	Ala. Cariages	Sarah	2	"	
Laura	17	Tenn.	Thos. Smith	22	Tenn.	Clerk
Mary	1	Ala.	Thos. Tapp	22	Ala.	Do
			Household 896			
Household 889			Martha Brandon	52	Penn.	
E. B. Martin	39	Main Capt. boat	Martha Pearey	10	Ala.	
Ellin	27	"				
Ellin, Jr.	3	Ala.				
Catharine	2	"				
Eliza	1/12	"				

Household 897
G. W. Foster	42	Tenn. Farmer
Sarah	38	Ga.
Virginia	15	Ala.
Watkins (male)	13	"
Louiser	11	"
Washington	7	Tenn.
Jackson	6	"
Sarah	2	"
James Simpson	23	Ala. Manufacturer
Mary Ann	19	"

Household 898
Jno. T. Burtwell	52	Connet. Capt.-boat
Caroline	40	Tenn.
John	14	Ala.
Isibella	13	"
Mary	11	"
Annie	10	"
James	8	"
Elizabeth	4	"
Lavenia	2	"
Rebecca Cherry	16	Conn.

Household 899
Elizb. Jinkins	58	S.C.
Venson	30	" none

Household 899
Martha Lewis (mulatto)	53	S.C. Washing

Household 900
John Murphy	61	Ireland Tanner
Mary	42	S.C.
John	21	Ala. Do
Eliza	17	"
Edward	14	"
Thomas	12	"
Joseph	10	"
Jackson	5	"

Household 901
Seless Gorden (female)	46	Tenn. Washing
Francis (female)	18	Ala.
(Note: Seless marked "black"; Francis marked mulatto.)		

Household 902
John Rapier (mulatto)	44	Va. Barber
Lucretia (mulatto)	25	Va.
John (mulatto)	14	Ala.
Rebecca (mulatto)	2	Ala.

Household 903
Alexd. Falk	37	Europe Merchant
Catharine	34	"
Sarah	7	N. Orleans
Jmmelia	6	Ala.
continued		

Household 903 continued
Lassar	3	Ala.
Jacob Rosentall	34	Europe Do
James Simmons	22	Ala. Clerk

Household 904
Charles Gookin*	39	Mass. Merchant
Sarah	39	D^C Columbia
Thomas	10	Ala.
Hugh	8	"
Charles	6	"
James	4	"
Eugine (female)	3	"
Thos. Price	21	" Clerk
James	19	" Do
Jane P. Brockass	25	S.C.

Household 905
Walter Glenn	70	Ireland Hardware
Nancy	60	"
Nancy, Jr.	35	Penn.
Walter	26	Ala. Do
John	22	" Carpenter

Household 906
Isaac Williams	30	Ky. Bookkeeper
Mariah	28	Ala.

Household 907
Alxd. Wood	54	Va. Merchant
Mary	54	England
Mary	23	Ala.
Henry Wood	19	" Book clerk
Mariah	16	"

Household 908
W. T. Hawkins	42	Va. Probate-judge
Robert (student)	18	Ala.
Martha	15	"
Mary	13	"
Lucy	11	"
H. Clay	8	"
Wiley	5	"
William	2	"
Mary Mitchel	43	Va.

Household 909
Richard Walthur	27	Ala. lawyer
Mary	22	"
Simpson	1	"
Clifton	12	"
Percy	7	"

*Charles Gookin married Sarah M. Brocchus on 3 Sept. 1838, by J. L. Sloss; Thomas Gookin married Frances Price on "the 18th (Florence Gazette, 24 April 1861.)

Household 910
Edmen Brown	39	Va.	Exchange
Margarett	25	Tenn.	
Thomas	7	Ala.	
Annie	3	Ala.	
James	2	"	

Household 911
Levi Todd	50	Ky.	Physician
Jane	37	"	
Elizabeth	28	"	
Lusinda	24	"	

Household 912
N. C. Goodloe	34	Tenn.	Saddler
Margaret	29	Va.	
Columbia (female)	12	Tenn.	
French (male)	11	"	
Julious	8	"	
May	6	Ala.	
Thomas	5	"	
Martha	3	"	
D. B. Stradford	18	Ala.	Do
A. J. Bates	21	Va.	Do

Household 913
B. A. Oneal	34	Ga.	lawyer
Orlevia	26	Tenn.	
Alfred	9	Ala.	
Rebecca	7	"	
John	5	"	
Julia	3	"	
Mary	6/12	"	

Household 914
Jas. M. Sutherlin	34	Tenn.	Butcher
Louisa	32	Ala.	
James	12	"	
William	10	"	
Z. Taylor	2	"	

Household 915
Henry Seaton	20	Tenn.	Fisherman
Manurvy	24	"	
Parthena	19	"	
William	14	"	
Samuel	10	"	

Household 916
Mary Seaton	48	Ala.	
James Conoway	48	Ga.	Carpenter
John Shelton	14	Unknown	

Household 917
Margaret Anderson	40	Tenn.	Seam-
James	14	Tenn.	stress
Rachel	11	"	
Nancy Moss	24	"	
Sarah	5	"	

Household 918
John Jackson	35	Ala.	
Warder of Jail			
Sarah	21	Tenn.	
John	2	Ala.	
In Jail:			
John Hollerman	24	"	none
James Horn(stealing)	17	Tenn.	Laborer
Abner Spencer (stealing)	40		Shoes

Household 919
Jas. B. Ham	30	Va.	Shoemaker
Lusinda	20	Ala.	
Ausha (male)	12	Tenn.	
Mary	10	Ala.	
Charles	9	"	
William	6	"	
Thomas	4	"	
Richard Glothr	35	"	Sadler

Household 920
L. P. Walker	33	Tenn.	Circt.
Eliza	18	Ala.	Judge

Household 921
Martha Andrews	37	Tenn.
James	13	Ala.
Patterson	9	Ala.
Robert	8	"
Sarah	5	"
Elizabeth Perkins	18	Tenn.
Sarah	16	Tenn.

Household 922
E. H. Eaton (druggist)	33	Vermont
Malinda Eaton	23	N. York
William	2	Ohio
Annie M. Stanten	40	Canada

Household 924
T. J. Kilpatrick	40	S.C.	Teacher
Mary	25	Ky.	
Martha	10	Tenn.	
Louisa	6	"	
H. Clay	2	Ala.	

Household 925
Thos. Kirkman - merchant	50	Ireland	
Elizabeth	41	Tenn.	
Thomas	22	Ala.	Clerk
Samuel	19	"	Do
Sarah	15	"	
Hugh	12	"	
Hunt	10	"	
Mary	8	"	
Jackson	7	"	

Household 926
Catharine Probasco	38	Tenn.
James A. Baker	34	Ala. Lawyer
Caroline	25	"
Mason	11	"

Household 927
Abraham Dean	45	Ohio merch't
Elizabeth	35	S.C.
Frances	8	Ala.
James	6	"
John	5	"
Snoden Hubbert	22	" Bookkeeper
Martha Wayland	20	"
Richard	16	" Clerk
Kiburnia (female)	13	"

Household 928
S. D. Weakley*	38	Tenn. Manu-
Eliza	35	" facturer
John	13	Ala.
Ann	10	"
Sarah	8	"
Catharine	3	"

Household 929
John Simpson - merchant	59	Ireland
Margaret	55	"
John	20	Ala. Clerk
William	19	" Do
Margaret	15	"
Robert	13	"
Hugh Simpson	54	Ireland none

Household 930
James Green	30	N.C. Carpenter
Martha	21	Ala.
William	6	"
James	3	"
Frances (female)	2	"
Thomas	1/12	"
Mariah Ulaid (Nlaid?)	25	"

Household 931
Thos. J. Foster	40	Tenn. Farmer
Jane	30	Ala.
James	7	"
Colman	5	"
Annis	3	"

Household 932
Edmond Kennedy	27	Tenn. Farmer
Catharine	25	"
James	5	Ala.
Thomas	3	"
Nancy	6/12	"
Henry Roberson	21	" Ass't
Susan	15	"
Aaron	16	" Do

Household 933
James Kennedy	50	Tenn. Farmer
Nancy	40	N.C.
William	17	Ala.
Mahaley	13	"
Mary	5	"

Household 934
Thos. Kennedy	24	" Laborer
Jane	20	"
Thomas	2	"

Household 935
Thos. Glidewell	21	Tenn. Do
Sally	20	Ala.
Nancy	2	"
James	2/12	"

Household 936
Martha Neill	49	S.C.
Jane	26	Ala.
Elizabeth	18	"
James	14	"
Rebecca	13	Miss.
Addaline	11	Miss.
Charity	8	Miss.
Mary (continued)	4	Ala.

---

*THE WEAKLEY FAMILY IN AMERICA, by
Francis J. Weakley, published 1904, in Dayton, Ohio, page 31:

Samuel Weakley, son of Robert and Elizabeth Gillespie Weakley, was born 11 Jan 1768, died 30 Oct. 1832, married Sarah Vaughan. Their children included, among others:
1. James Harvey Weakley, born 1798, died about 1855 in New England; married Ellen M. Donegan. They lived in Florence, Alabama.
2. Samuel D. Weakley, born 2 Oct. 1812, died 3 Feb. 1896; married Eliza Bedford in 1836.
3. Sarah Jane Weakley, born 1818, died Dec. 1894, married James H. Webster of Maury County, Tenn.

Nashville Banner, 4 Feb. 1897: Gen. S. D. Weakley dropped dead on the street in Florence, Alabama.

Household 936 continued

Martha	3	Ala.
Francis Null	2/12	"

Household 937
Anderson Stutt	24	Ala. Laborer
Ann	22	"
Sarah	4	"
William	1	"

(Note: although there is no notation on the census record, the census of Florence is believed to be over about this entry.)

Household 938
Marth Lawson	30	Ala.
William	12	"
Margaret	8	"
Joseph	4	"

Household 939
Wm. Kennedy	33	S.C. Do
Malind	32	"
Polly	14	Tenn.
Joseph	10	"
John	8	"
Larena	6	Ala.
Washington	5	"
Obediah	4	"
Elias	3/12	"

Household 940
Matt. Richerson	25	Ala. Do
Mary	13	Tenn.

(Note: these two were marked married within the year.)

Household 941
Nancy Danlton	53	S.C.
James	23	Tenn. Do
Malinda	19	"
Lewis	15	"
Rebecca	22	"
Amanda Dickerson	9	"

Household 942
Nancy Richerson	60	Va.
Clinton	40	Tenn. none

Household 943
Carroll Tucker	28	" Shoemaker
Phoebi	45	"

944
Curtice Kennedy (farmer)	24	unknown
Polly	23	Ala.
William	4	"
Nancy	3	"
Sarah Owens	98	S.C.
Silva Robertson	20	Ala.

Household 945
Polly Curtice	77	S.C.
Kitty Blasingam	40	Ky.
Sarah	20	Ala.
George	6	"

Household 946
Aaron Clemons	35	Tenn. Farmer
Perlissa	29	Ky.
Henry Clemons	13	Ala.
Thomas	12	Tenn.
James	10	Ala.
John	8	"
Rebecca	6	"
Polly	5	"
Adaline	2	"

Household 947
John McGee	25	Tenn. Farmer
Sarah	31	S.C.
Joseph	12	Ala.

Household 948
Wilcoml McGee (male)	19	Ala. Laborer
Catharine	24	Tenn.

(Both marked married within the year.)

Household 949
Bluford Richerson	28	Ala. Do
Milla	27	"
Mary	5	"
John	3	"
Eliza McGee	65	N. Jersey

Household 950
Robert Harwell	34	Miss. Farmer
Louiser	34	S.C.
Margaret	11	Ala.
Isam	9	"
Nancy	7	"
Eliza	5	"
James	2	"
Robert	2/12	"

Notation after household 946, at bottom of original census page: "Northern part of district verry poor and hilly."

C-69

Household 951
Jackson Grisham	26	Tenn.	Laborer
Louiser	31	Ga.	
John	8	Miss.	
Sarah (twin)	7	"	
Margaret (twin)	7	"	
Mary	3	"	
Frances	2/12	Ala.	

Household 952
James Eddleman	27	Tenn.	Farmer
Everline	26	Ala.	
Nancy	7	"	
Jonathan	5	"	
Annis	4	"	
William	2	"	
James	4/12	"	

Household 953
Charles Lawson	25	Ga.	Blacksmith
Rebecca	32	Tenn.	
Margaret	4	Ala.	
Thos. Ham	18	"	Laborer
Ann	20	"	
James	12	"	
John	8	"	

Note at bottom of page: "Hilly, oak, chestnut, very few farms of much value."

Household 954
| James Lawson | 27 | Ga. | Carpenter |
| Sarena | 23 | Tenn. | |
(Marked married within the year.)

Household 955
Berry Rickerson	30	Ala.	Shingles
Jane	30	Ky.	
John	8	Ala.	
Ann E.	6	"	
Nancy	4	"	
Isaac	1	"	

Household 956
John Richerson	63	S.C.	Farmer
Polly	60	"	
Saletha	20	Ala.	
Obidiah	18	"	Ass't

Household 957
Isaac Milner	30	England	
Occupation: Meth. Manufc.			
Joannah	22	N.C.	
Wm. D. Hammar	8	Miss.	

Household 958
James Milner	60	Eng.	Manufc.
Hanna	60	"	
Samuel	20	"	"

Household 959
Dave Kennedy	24	N.C.	Meth.Dc
Julia	24	"	
Joannah	3	Ala.	
John	3/12	"	

Household 960
Jno. Largent	25	Tnn.	Do.
Mary	24	England	
James	4	Miss.	
Sarah	2	"	
Emer	2/12	Ala.	

Household 961
Henry Clemons	36	Tenn.	Farmer
Rebecca	33	Ky.	
James	18	Ala.	Do
Sarah	16	"	
Ann	12	"	
Martha	10	"	
Benjamin	9	"	
William	2	"	

Household 962
Jno. Lawson	33	S.C.	Farmer
Rachel	33	Ala.	
Wm. Ham	21	"	Laborer
Thadeus Lawson	12	"	
H. Clay "	10	"	
Thursday	9	"	
William	4	"	
James	2	"	

Household 963
James Ham	37	Ky.	Farmer
Tennessee	21	Tenn.	
Alfonso	10/12	Ala.	

Household 964
Nancy Harwell	24	Tenn.	
Sarah	7	Ala.	
William	6	"	
Mary	2	Miss.	

Household 965
| Elizabeth McGee | 60 | N.C. | |

Household 966
| John Corhorne | 25 | N.C. | Do |
continued

(Note: Tombstone in Rose Hill Cemetery, Columbia, Tenn.: Isaac Milner, born Stanningly, Yorkshire, Eng., 2 April 1818, died near Columbia, 16 June 1872, "Eloquent minister of M. E. Church, S." Memorial window in First Methodist Church, Columbia, Tenn. has same dates but "Minister of the Gospel 36 years, pastor of this church 2 years.")

Household 966 continued
Margaret   38 Ala.
William   5 "
Jerry   3 "

Household 967
Mss.(?) C. McCammons 46 N.C. Farmer
   (above marked female)
Allis Joice   37 "
Eliza McCluskey   32 S.C.

Household 968
Jansy Hagwood*   21 Miss.   Laborer
Elender*   18 Ala.
Susan Cooker   59 S.C.
(*Marked married within the year.)

Household 969
George Martin   33 S.C.   Farmer
Sarah   25 "
Samuel   4 Ala.
John   2 "

Household 970
William J. Thoma   53 N.C. Do
Sarah   40 Ga.
James   22 Tenn. "
Monroe   21 "   "
Mary   15 "
Louiser   13 "
David   12 "
Margaret   10 "
John   8 "
Susan   6 "
Frank   5 "
Artetia   3 "

Household 971
J. C. Bradley   33 "   Farmer
Rebecca   26 "
Francis (female)   5 "
Jas. Bradley   4 "
David   2 "
Margaret   1 "

Household 972
Jno. Coats   25 Tenn. Farmer
Mary   25 "
William   9 "
Sarah   6 "
Olly (female)   2 "

Household 973
Thos. Ross   40 S.C. Do
Mary   38 "
David   20 Ala. Ass't
continued

Household 973 continued
Francis (female)   16 Ala.
Austin   13 Tenn.
Charles   11 Ala.
John   10 "
Emily   6 "
Sarah   5 "
Henry   2 "

Household 974
Jas. Bradley   57 Va. Farmer
Margaret   57 "
Susan (twin)   28 Tenn.
Jesse (twin)   28 "   Ass't
Permelia   23 "
Calvin   22 "
Amberis   29 "   "
Marion   18 "   "
David   16 "   "
Robert   13 "
Beesley   12 "
Richard   10 "

Household 975
Wm. Liles   45 S.C. Farmer
Joseph Morten   28 Tenn. "
Elizabeth   26 S.C.
William   6 Ala.

Household 976
Charles McCluskey   48 S.C.   Do
Ann   46 "
Carroll   14 Ala.
Moses   13 "
Jerry   8 "
Mary Ross   38 S.C.

Household 977
Rebecca Rickman   48 S.C. Poltre
Caladonia   22 Tenn.
Sarah Bird   18 "
Mary   14 "
Martha   13 "

Household 978
Jas. Dalrumple   22 S.C. Laborer
Rachel   24 Ala.
(Marked married within the year.)

Household 979
Auston Hill   32 S.C. Farmer
Lavenia   33 Ohio
Henry   12 Ala.
Judi (female)   10 "
James   8 "
Claiborn   7 "
William   4 "
Aaron   2 "

Household 980
James Hill   41 S.C. Do
Mary   42 "
Martha   21 Ala.
John   20 Tenn.
Elizabeth   17 "
Rosana   14 "
Gerge   11 "
Ellen   9 "
Julia   6 "
Charles   4 "
William   4/12 Ala.

Household 981
Judi Hill (female) 75 S.C.

Household 982
Rich. Bevis   46 S.C. Do
Nancy   43 "
Elizabeth   19 Ala.
Susan   17 "
James   16 "   Assistant
Caroline   11 "

Household 983
John Hill   40 S.C. Farmer
Susana   37 Ala.
James   18 "   Ass't
Mary   15 "
Elizabeth   13 "
Hiram   11 "
Nancy   9 "
William   7 "
Dority (female)   5 "
Frances   3 "
Tamsey (female) 10/12 "

Household 984
Robt. Strong   22 Tenn. Carpenter
Temperance   19 Ala.

Household 985
John Killin   47 N.C. Farmer
Susan   45 N.C.
Andrew Jack.   18 Ala. Ass't
T. T. Benton   16 "   Do
H. Clay   14 "
Duncan   10 "
Daniel Webster   8 "
Mary   5 "
Robert   4 "

Household 986
Bluford Foster   48 Va. Farmer
Manurvey   30 Tenn.
Martha   13 "
William   10 "
Mary   9 "
continued

Household 986 continued
Susan   8 Tenn.
Constantine (male) 6 "
Julia   4 "
Safronia   2 "

Household 987
Wm. Hill   48 S.C. Do
Nancy   40 Tenn.
Lion   21 Ala. Ass't
Berry   18 "   Do
Julia   14 "
Emmoma (female)   13 "
Hiram   12 "
Jane   10 "
Amanda   7 "
Emery   5 "
Henry   2 "

Household 988
G. B. Hill   49 S.C. Farmer
Nancy   43 Va.
Elizabeth   22 Ala.
Henry   21 "   Ass't
William   20 "   Ass't
Thomas   18 "   Ass't
Elinda   16 "
Sarah   15 "
Mary   13 "
Andrew   11 "
Nancy   8 "
Saludi Hill   7 Ala.
Marsena   4 "
Felix   2 "
Artimissa   1 "

Household 989
Jas. Roberson   28 Tenn. Farmer
Lysinda   24 "
John   5 "
William   3 Ala.
Mary   1 "

Household 990
Tire Do   80 S.C. Do
Dicy   60 "
Tire Jr.   16 Ala. Ass't

Household 991
Archer Do   52 Tenn. Farmer
Sally   52 S.C.
William   19 Ala. Do
Nancy   15 "
David   14 "
Mitchel   12 "
Sabrey   8 "

Household 992
Mills Do   23 Ala. Farmer
Mary   21 Tenn.
Francis (female)   2 Ala.
William   3/12 "

Household 993
Henry Do   21 Tenn. Do
Diana   24 "
Berry   3 Ala.
Marion   1 "

Household 994
Berry Odum   55 N.C. Do
Polly   41 Tenn.
James   24 "   Ass't
Lanisa   13 Ala.
Mary   12 "
Berry   9 "
Amberis   7 "

Household 995
Mills Corhorn   23 Ala. Laborer
Mary   18 "
(Married within the year.)

Household 996
William Do   53 N.C. Do
Sabrey   45 Tenn.
Elizabeth   19 Ala.
Polly   18 "
Nancy   14 "
John   6 "

Household 997
Wm. Corhorn, Jr.   21 Ala. Farmer
Emiline   23 "
(Marked married within the year.)

Household 998
Noel Kendrick   45 Ga. Do
Lucy   43 "
Ellis   18 Ala. Ass't
Milton   15 "
James   12 "
Thomas   9 "
Obidiah   6 "
Amberis (male)   4 "
Mary   1 "

Household 999
James Gest   24 N.C. Farmer
Elizabeth   24 "
William   8 Ala.
Sarah   6 "
Joseph   4 "
Thomas   2/12 "
(James Gist married Elizabeth Richardson on 20 Aug. 1840, by Joseph Guest, J.P. Lauderdale County marriage records.)

Household 1000
Hilary Blasingam   22 Ala. Farmer
Rachel   21 Tenn.
Phoebi   1 Ala.
Mahaly Hefington   18 Tenn.

Household 1001
Sarah Miles   35 S.C. Farmer
Chaney   14 Ala.
James   12 "
Abergale   10 "

Household 1002
Levi Gest   29 Tenn. Farmer
Sarah   32 "
Martha   10 Ala.
Joseph (twin)   8 "
Henry (twin)   8 "
J. K. Polk   6 "
Davy C.   3 "

Household 1003
Sina Do   50 S.C. Do
Joseph   23 Ala. "
John   21 "   "
Washington   17 "   "
Sallabam   19 "
Davy (twin)   12 "
Jackson (twin)   12 "
Sina   11 "
Margaret   10 "
Lafett   8 "

(Note: age of Sina Gist in question, could be either 30 or 50, although the later seems to be correct.

SOLDIERS OF THE WAR OF 1812 BURIED IN TENNESSEE by Mary H. McCown and Inez E. Burns, 1959, page 129: Joseph Gist, born 1789 in N. C., died 9 Feb. 1846 in Lauderdale Co., Ala., married Sinnia Hollis on 24 May 1818 in Lawrence County, Tennessee. She was born 1800 and died 23 Dec. 1853 in Alabama. During the war of 1812 he served as a private in Capt. John Jackson's company, in Colonel William Metcalf's regiment of West Tennessee Militia. His dates of service were 13 Nov. 1814 through 13 May 1815, and it likely that he was in the Battle of New Orleans, 8 Jan. 1815. Sina (or Sinna) Hollis was a member of the Hollis family which had connections with the Hollis and Choate families of Montgomery Co., Maury Co., and Lawrence Co., Tennessee.)

Household 1004
Joseph Roberson   22 Ala.   Farmer
Patty   18 "
(Married within the year.)

Household 1005
Jesse Ham   34 Tenn. Laborer
Eliza   20 "
Mills   5 Ala.
Henry   3 "

Household 1006
William Ham   57 S.C.   Farmer
Milli   56 "
Milli, 2nd   19 Ala.
George   18 "   Ass't
Susana   14 "

Household 1007
James Ham   27 Tenn. Carpenter
Liddi   23 Ala.
Hough Thestus   5 "
William Do   4 "
Mary Ham   4 "
Rachel (twin)   3 "
Francis (twin)   3 "
Winney   1 "

Household 1008
Isam Richerson   57 N.C.   Farmer
Judi   53 "
Lewis   22 Ala.   Ass't
John   17 "   "
Henry   16 "   "
Isam   13 "
William   11 "
James   8 "

Household 1009
Wm. Rickman   21 Tenn. Laborer
Angaline   21 Ala.
(Married within the year)

Household 1010
Jno. Blasingim   46 N.C.   Farmer
Nancy   42 Tenn.
John   19 "   Ass't
Mary   17 "
Isaac   14 "
Lavisa   10 "
George   7 "
Nancy   5 "
William   3 Ala.
James   2 "
Martha Coats   18 "

Household 1011
Andrew Ollive   34 N.C.   Farmer
Charlotte   34 Ala.
Nathaniel Ollive   12 "
William   10 "
Martha   7 "
Annie   6 "
Frances   4 "

Household 1012
John Gifford   30 N.York Farmer
Elizajane   25 Ala.
Missouri   1 "

Household 1013
Matt. McMutrey   67 Ireland Do
Mack   21 Ala.   "
Everline   17 "
Rebecca   14 "
Curtice   10 "
Jesse   9 "

Household 1014
Wm. Stutts   51 N.C.   Bts.Farme
Susana   58 "
John   22 Ala.   Ass't
Safrona   20 "
Martha   15 "
Wm. Roberson   17 "   Do
Leonord Do   74 S.C.   None

Household 1015
Ranson Stutts   26 N.C.   Farmer
Susana   26 "
Elias   8 Ala.
Nancy   7 "
Fereby   5 "

Household 1016
Jesse Gibson (mullato) 67 N.C.   Do
Rhoda (black)   74 "

Household 1017
Samuel Winchester   40 N.C.   Do
Malinda   30 "
George   9 Ala.
James   7 "
Diadema   3 "

Household 1018
Jackson Lawson   22 Ala.   Laborer
Elizabeth   18 "
(Married within the year)

Household 1019
David Foust   46 N.C.   Farmer
Mary   40 "
Margaret   27 "
continued

Household 1019 continued
William	19	N.C.	Do
Lock	10	"	
John	9	"	
Anjaline	6	"	
Alxd. Foust	5	"	
Catharine	3	Ala.	
Mary	2	"	

Household 1020
John McMutrey	34	Tenn.	Farmer
Margaret	28	N.C.	
William	10	Ala.	
Mary	8	"	
John	5	"	
Susan	3	"	
Jane	1	"	
William Do	39	N.C.	Do
Thomas Roberson	16	Ala.	Student
Sarah	12	"	
Polly English	25	"	

Household 1021
H. J. Atwell	37	S.C.	Farmer
Temperance	34	Ala.	
Lewis	16	"	Ass't
Rebecca	15	"	
Julia	13	"	
Mancy	12	"	
Sarah	10	"	
Robert	6	"	
William	1	"	
James Ollive	3	"	

Household 1022
Wilson English	48	Tenn.	Farmer
Elizabeth	41	S.C.	
John	19	Ala.	Ass't
Rachel	13	"	
Agnus	11	"	
James	8	"	
Hiram	6	"	
William	3	"	
Eliza	4/12	"	

Household 1023
Matt McDaniel	33	Tenn.	Blc.Smith
Rhoda	34	"	
Marilla	10	Ala.	
George	9	"	
Matthew	5	"	
Ephraim	3	"	
Rebecca	4/12	"	

Household 1024
Joseph Do	26	Tenn.	Wagons
Jane	21	Ala.	

Household 1025
John McDaniel	58	S.C.	Farmer
Margaret	57	"	
Anderson	28	Tenn.	Carpenter
Lavenia	23	"	
Horris	21	"	Smith
Ottimena (female)	19	"	
John	16	Ala.	None

Household 1026
Duncan J. Smith	60	N.C.	Merchant
Nancy	59	Tenn.	
Polly	22	"	
Nancy	20	"	
Jane	18	"	
John	16	Ala.	Clerk
Susan	13	"	

Household 1027
Amous McDaniel	34	S.C.	Farmer
Nancy	28	Ala.	
William	12	"	
Mary	10	"	
Sarah	8	"	
Spinkes (male)	6	"	
James	4	"	
Carroll	2	"	

Household 1028
Jos. R. Lafan	64	S.C.	Do
Ruth	23	Ala.	
Isaac	20	"	Ass't

Household 1029
Thos. Lafan	21	Ala.	Farmer
Ann	21	"	

(Married within the year.)

Household 1030
Campbell Ross	31	Tenn.	Ditto
Abergale	29	Ga.	
Sterling Pool	19	S.C.	Ass't
James Swinney	24	Tenn.	Do
John Wickes	39	N.York	
(Carpenter)			

signed/ Matthew T. Wilson
    Assistant Marshall.

C-75

The 2d Division, East of the Military Road by Hiram Kennedy

Household 1
Calvin Peton   47 N.C. Farmer
Mary   "   40 "
Monroe   "   18 Ala. Laborer
Devroe   " (male)   15 "   "
Ellender "   13 "
Elizabeth "   8 "

Household 2
J. M. Stephens   38 Va. Boatman
Angeline   "   34 Ga.
James Williams   18 Ala. Laborer

Household 3
Henry Harrison   34 S.C. Farmer
Lydia   "   23 N.C.
William   "   11 Ala.
Caroline   "   7 "
John   "   4 "
Elizabeth "   2 "

Household 4
Aaron Hamill   29 N.C. Farmer
Hugh   "   7 Ala.
William   "   5 "
Frances   "   3 "
Wincey Ann "   10/12 "

Household 5
Richard Bailey   42 Tenn. Farmer
Amelia   "   37 S.C.
(Lauderdale Co. marriages: Richard
Bailey, Jr. married Permelia Harrison
12 July 1829)

Household 6
Nancy Coal   30 Tenn.
Martha   "   11 Ala.
Jane   "   9 "
Sarah   "   7 "
Henry   "   5 "
Samuel   "   3 "
Charity Williams   20 "

Household 7
Little Berry Harrison 75 N.C. Farmer
Little Berry Harrison 32 S.C.   "
Talethia   "   26 Ala.
Luke   "   8 "
Dorinda   "   4 "
Henry Williams   18 " Farmer
Eliza   "   11 "

Household 8
Martha Cross   45 S.C.
Elmira   "   18 Ala.
Benjamin "   19 " Laborer
Martha   "   8 "

Household 9
Shaderic Cross   27 Ala. Farmer
Margaret   "   22 "
Isabella   "   3 "

Household 10
William Ross   27 S.C. Laborer
Hannah   "   25 Ala.
Benjamin "   8 "
Rufus   "   4 "
Elizabeth"   2 "

Household 11
Daniel Archy   45 Geo. Laborer
Jane   "   40 Tenn.
James   "   18 "   Laborer
Eliza   "   14 Ala.
Cynthia "   11 "
Souseanah "   9 "
Sarah   "   6 "
Martha   "   3 "
Ann Cannon   75 N.C.

Household 12
Jackson Brumley   30 Tenn. Laborer
Jane   "   27 "
Thomas   "   7 "
Nancy   "   6 "
William "   4 "

Household 13
Jobe Robertson   45 N.C. Millright
Margaret   "   25 Tenn.
Eilus   "   15 Ala. Laborer
Elizabeth "   4 "
Zachariah "   2 "
James House   32 Tenn. Millright

Household 14
Luke Harrison   61 N.C. Farmer
Elizabeth "   51 "
Marion   "   21 Ala. Laborer
Emily Hamill   25 N.C.
Martha McMahan   14 Ala.
  (above marked deaf and dumb)
Joannah Kennedy   85 N.C.

Note: On the portion of the census listed by Hiram Kennedy, ditto marks were sometimes used for the surnames. This had not been done by Wilson, and sometimes surnames appear to be doubtful.

Household 15
John Harrison   41 Ohio Farmer
Mary   "   35 S.C.
Martha   "   13 Ala.
Willis   "   11 "
John   "   9 "
George Harrison   17 Ga. Laborer
Frances Harrison   15 "

Household 16
John McMahan   44 S.C. Farmer
Margaret   "   27 "
Luke   "   21 Ala. Laborer
William   "   20 "   "
James   "   18 "   "
Elizabeth   "   10 "
John   "   4 "
Robert   "   2 "
John Brewer   24 "   Laborer

Household 17
John Wingo   30 N.C. Miller
Elizabeth   "   20 "
Mary   "   1 Ala.
Amie Wingo   17 N.C.

Household 18
William Twitty   52 S.C. Farmer
Molsie   "   47 "
Mary   "   27 "
George   "   20 "   Laborer
Martha   "   17 "
Lavend   "   15 Tenn.
Eliza   "   13 Ala.
Nancy   "   11 "
Amanda   "   7 "
Charlotte   "   5 "

Household 19
Tillman Harrison   28 S.C. Farmer
Emily   "   30 Ala.
Mary   "   5 "
Johnathan   "   3 "
Dorinda   "   1/12 "
Jackson Twitty   28 S.C. none
  (Jackson Twitty marked idiotic.)

Household 20
Daniel Nunley   50 S.C. Hirdand
Tobetha   "   51 "
Thomas   "   15 Tenn. Laborer

Household 21
Calvin Brewer   21 Ala. Laborer
Delilah   "   17 Tenn.

Household 22
Meloch Waddle (male) 23 Ala. Farmer
Martha   "   23 Tenn.
Elizabeth   "   3 Ala.
Nancy   "   1 "

Household 23
Mahalah White   51 S.C.
William   "   26 Ala. Laborer
Eliza   "   20 "
John   "   17 "   "
Caroline   "   14 "
Robert   "   13 "
Lucy   "   18 Ky.
Mahlah   "   2 Ala.

Household 24
James Smith   67 S.C. Farmer
Sarah   "   46 "
Rebecah   "   24 Tenn.
Washington "   20 Ala. Laborer
Marion   "   15 Ala. "
Monroe   "   12 "
Sarah   "   10 "
Jane   "   8 Tenn.
Benjamin   "   23 "   Laborer

Household 25
W. T. Lanier   30 Tenn. Blc.Smith
Margaret   "   28 "
Mary   "   5 Ala.
Martha   "   3 "
William   "   1 "
(Lauderdale Co. marriages: William Lanier
married Margaret D. Snipes on 21 Oct.
1844.)

Household 26
Newel Motethrop   52 Ct. Carpenter
Rebecca   "   46 S.C.

Household 27
Thomas Cook   28 Tenn. Farmer
Roseanah   "   40 S.C.
William   "   4 Ala.
Anderson Lakey   9 Miss.

Household 28
John Gracey   28 Ala. constable
Sarah   "   23 "
Robert   "   2 "
Mariah   "   5/12 "

Household 29
Samuel W. Barr   46 S.C. Farmer
Silus   "   21 Ala. Laborer
Isaac   "   18 "   Do
Elizabeth   "   16 "
         continued

Household 29 continued
William Barr   12 Ala.
Margaret "   7 "
John   "   5 "

Household 30
Mary Ives   49 N.C.
Shaylor   "   29 Ala. Laborer
Sarah   "   27 "
Amos   "   24 "   "
John   "   21 "   "
Samuel   "   18 "   "
George   "   14 "
Henry   "   10 "
Isabella "   8 "

Household 31
Pheby Best   28 N.C.
James   "   22 Ala. Laborer
Charlote "   19 "

Household 32
Ephraigm Shuffield* 59 S.C. Farmer
Sarah   "   52 "
John   "   16 Ala. Student
Vurinda   "   11 "
Elizabeth "   13 "

Household 33
Arthur Shuffield   32 Ala. Farmer
Mary Ann "   19 "
Benjamin "   4/12 "

Household 34
John Trousdale   48 S.C. Farmer
Nancy   "   24 Ala.
William   "   3 "
John   "   1 "
(Surname could be Trusedale.)

Household 35
Thomas Trusedale   38 S.C. Farmer
Ann Trusedale   30 "
John   "   6 Ala.

Household 36
Philip Snipes**   61 S.C. Shoemaker
Angeline "   21 Tenn.
Ann   "   19 Ala.
Nancy   "   12 "

Household 37
William Basket   71 N.C. Miller
Catharine "   52 S.C.
Hestrian Whiticer 18 N.C. (female)

Household 38
Presley Hardin   33 Tenn. Farmer
Mary   "   31 Tenn.
Lucretia "   6 Ala.
Mary E. Huse   8 "
Mary Williams   64 S.C.
William O. Williams 33 Tenn. Laborer

Household 39
William McMillon   33 Tenn. Overseer
Lucinda   "   30 "
Mary   "   8 "
Ethylinda "   6 "
William   "   2 Ala.

Household 40
Thomas Powers   72 S.C. Farmer
Margaret "   44 Ireland
James Thomas   19 Tenn. Student

Household 41
Zachariah Ellis   24 Tenn. Overseer
Cathey   "   19 Ala.
William   "   2 "
Phoeby (?) "   3/12 "

Household 42
Johnson Trusedale 40 Tenn. Farmer
Jane   "   30 Ala.
William   "   11 "
Martha   "   14 "
John   "   8 "
Sousan   "   5 "
Benjamin "   2 "

Household 43
Elizabeth Cuttingdon 65 Va.
Margaret Marks   39 Tenn.
Julia   "   12 Ala.
Martha   "   2 "

Household 44
Green Fisher   35 Tenn.
Sousan   "   30 "
Benjamin "   10 "
continued

---

*Florence Gazette, 23 Feb. 1827:
"E. Shuffield offers to rent his tavern on military road, one mile from Blue Water known as Anderson Johnson's old place."

**Manuscript in Alabama State Archives by J. N. McCarley: About Snipes the shoemaker "He always lived from hand to mouth." Snipes had several daughters... would make a pair of shoes, sell them, and then drink proceeds, according to the McCarley memoirs.

C-78

Household 44 continued
Mary Fisher	9	Tenn.
Richard "	7	"
Elizabeth "	5	Ala.
Margaret "	3	"
Mary Tutt	27	Tenn.

Household 45
James Douglass	42	S.C. Farmer
Malasiah "	37	Geo.
Melenah "	17	Ala.
Jane "	15	"
William "	13	"
Senalea " (female)	11	"
James "	9	"
John "	7	"
Margaret "	5	"
George "	3	"
Souseannah"	1	"

Household 46
William M. Patton	37	N.C. Overseer
Nancy "	40	Ireland
Martha Lancer	11	Ala.

Household 47
Benjamin Taylor	50	Va. Farmer
Sousin "	45	"
Elizabeth "	15	Ala.
Benjamin "	13	"
Sarah "	11	"
Thomas "	8	"
Sousin "	6	"

Household 48
Christopher Steen	40	S.C. Overseer
Malia (?) "	35	Tenn.
Mary "	15	S.C.
Martha "	11	"
Thomas "	13	"
Elizabeth "	9	Ala.
William "	7	"
Nathan "	3	"
Hannah "	6/12	"

Household 49
| Jesse Brooks | 22 | Tenn. Farmer |

Household 50
Mary Hammin (?)	50	S.C.
James "	21	Ala. Laborer
Martha "	28	"
Sousin "	17	"
William Stuart	4	"

Household 51
Andrew McClary	57	S.C. Farmer
Leander "	52	N.C.
James "	22	Ala. Laborer
Elizabeth"	17	"
Reuben "	16	" Laborer
Sarah "	13	"
Ellen "	7	"

Household 52
George McClary	32	Tenn. Merchant
Sarah "	24	Ohio
Ellen "	2	Tenn.

Household 53
Joseph Jackson	43	Tenn. Farmer
Fanny "	35	"
Jeremiah"	15	"
Elizabeth"	13	Ala.
Ellender "	11	"
Mary "	8	"
William "	6	"
Nancy "	3	"
Sarah "	1/12	Ala.
Jackson Fisher	26	Tenn. None

Household 54
Prudence Crittigdon	45	Va.
Josuah " *	21	Ala. Laborer
Mary "	18	"

Household 55
| Caroline Coffee** | 44 | Va. |
| Jane Night | 18 | Tenn. |

Household 56
| Joshua Coffee | 42 | Va. Farmer |
| Mary " | 6 | Ala. |

---

*Florence Gazette, 17 April 1861: Joshua J. Crittenden, guardian for Molly Coffee, settles as guardian. See young Coffee girl in household 56.

**Caroline Coffee was the daughter of Thomas Coffee and she never married. She raised Jane Knight, daughter of Carlisle Knight. Carlisle Knight was a cousin of the Coffees, his father being a brother to Mrs. Thomas Coffee (Mary Knight.). (See letters in Dyas Collection, Tenn. State Archives; also information furnished by Mrs. Minnie Bulls.)

Household 57
Lewis Hill   41 S.C. Farmer
Mary   "   40 N.C.
James   "   20 Ala. Laborer
Calvin "   18 "   "
George "   16 "   "
Lydia   "   15 "
Lucy   "   13 "
Lewis   "   11 "
Berry   "   9 "
Henry   "   6 "
William "   4 "
Mary   "   1 "

Household 58
Andrew J. McClary   26 Tenn. Farmer
Mary   "   17 Ala.
William   "   3 "
James   "   2 "
Crissey Prentice   45 Tenn.

Household 59
Benjamin Tutt   24 Tenn. Farmer
Jane   "   25 "
Baby   " (male)   2/12 Ala.

Household 60
Dempsey Bull*   35 N.C. Farmer
Catharine "   36 Va.
John   "   15 Ala. Laborer
Frances   "   14 "
Woodson   "   12 "
James   "   10 "
Elizabeth "   8 "
Junius   "   6 "
Catharine "   3/12 "

---

*Dempsey Deans Bulls, died 1874 at Center Star. He married Catherine Jackson, daughter of Stewart Jackson and his wife Elizabeth Coffee. (Elizabeth Coffee was the daughter of Thomas Coffee, 1767-1846 and his wife Mary Knight, c. 1771-1832.)

Dempsey D. Bulls was the father of Franklin B. Bulls, born 1836 at Center Star, died 1894, in Clay Co. Texas. (He is probably the one listed as Frances on the above census record.)

Thomas Graves Coffee (who married Mary Knight) was the oldest brother of General John Coffee.

(Information from Mrs. Minnie O. Bulls, Readley, California, 1965; also see letters in Dyas Collection, Tenn. State Archives.)

Household 61
Jack Philips   62 N.C. Farmer
Souseannah "   50 S.C.
Sally   "   27 Tenn.
John   "   19 Ala. Laborer
Jane   "   16 "
Souseannah "   13 "
Sarenah   "   10 "
Edney   "   7 "
Mason   "   4 "
Benjamin H. Allen   21 " Silversmith
Jane   "   19 Tenn.

Household 62
James French   23 S.C. Overseer
Elizabeth "   15 Ala.
Henry   "   3 Ala.

Household 63
Benjamin F. Crittingtton 30 Tenn. Doctor
Mary   "   25 Ala.
William   "   4 "
Benjamin   "   3 "
Wiley   "   7/12 "
Lemuel Eston   23 Tenn. Blc.smith

Household 64
Hezekiah Call   27 Tenn. Overseer
Caroline   "   24 "
Thomas   "   3 Ala.
John   "   9/12 "

Household 65
John Williams   50 Tenn. Farmer
Meriter   "   41 Tenn.
Simpson   "   24 Ala. Laborer
John   "   18 "   "
Lenorah   "   16 "
Presley   "   13 "
Pheby   "   11 "
Andrew   "   8 "
Benjamin   "   4 "
Robt. T. Catharins   25 Ireland Carptr
Eliza   "   20 Ala.

Household 66
David Williams   21 Ala. Farmer

Household 67
John Skipworth   37 Tenn. Overseer
Manervia   "   28 S.C.
John   "   13 Ala.
Turner   "   11 "
Henry   "   14 Tenn.
Jane   "   2 Ala.

Household 68
Isaac Davis		47	Geo. Farmer
Isabella	"	36	Tenn.
James	"	17	Ala. Laborer
Sulema	"	15	"
Elias	"	12	"
Sarah	"	10	"
Margaret	"	8	"
Mary	"	6	"
Isaac	"	4	"
Edy	" (female)	2	"
Jessee	"	3/12	"

Household 69
William J. Tapp		24	S.C. Merchant
Elizabeth	"	20	Ala.

(Married within the year.)

Household 70
William May		28	Tenn. Farmer
Margaret	"	22	"
Benjamin	"	6	"
John	"	4	Ala.
Sarah	"	2	"
Mary	"	1	"

Household 71
Jasper Smith		56	S.C. Laborer
Mary	"	45	"
Rebecca	"	30	Tenn.
Charles	"	28	" Laborer
Lucinda	"	26	"
Nancy	"	24	"
Margaret	"	19	"
Thomas	"	18	" "
Washington	"	16	" "
Mary	"	15	"
Martha	"	12	"
Franklin	"	9	"

Household 72
George W. Price		34	Tenn. Taylor
Lucy	"	20	"
William	"	7	"
Lafayette	"	2	"
John Stuart		18	" Laborer

Household 73
Wm. M. Smith		28	Tenn. Blcsmith
Caroline	"	23	"
Frances	"	5	"
Robert	"	2	Ala.

Household 74
Wilson Philips		32	Tenn. Farmer
Nancy	"	33	"
George	"	9	Ala.
John	"	7	Miss.
Benjamin	"	5	"
Sarah	"	4	"
Wilson	"	3	Ala.
Baby	" (male)	10/12	"
Wm. McPeters		17	" Laborer
James McPeters		10	"

Household 75
Wm. R. McMahan		39	Tenn. Farmer
Nancy	"	24	Miss.

Household 76
Thomas G. Scags		48	S.C. Saddler
Thomas	"	20	Ala. "
Ann	"	21	"
David	"	18	Tenn. Laborer
John McGaee (?)		22	Ala. "
Bird (male)	"	17	Tenn. Laborer
Malinda	"	14	"
Martha (twin)	"	13	Ala.
Susy Ann (twin)	"	12	"
John	"	16	"
Lewis	"	8	"
Benjamin	"	2	"
Margaret Markham		70	Va.

(Note: impossible to determine the surname for the latter part of this listing; confusing.)

Household 77
Samuel Richardson		42	S.C. Farmer
Mary	"	41	Ky.
Jane	"	20	Ala.
Daniel	"	19	" Laborer
Sarah	"	16	"
Elizabeth	"	15	"
Mark	"	13	"
Gabriel	"	11	"
Edney	"	9	"
Mary	"	7	"
David	"	5	"
Eliza	"	3	"
Sousan	"	1	"

Household 78
Mark Richardson		38	S.C. Farmer
Emily	"	30	Tenn.
Mary	"	6	Ala.
Edney	"	4	"
Benjamin	"	2	"
Willis	"	8/12	"
Edney Richardson		64	S.C.

Household 79
Name	Age	Origin	Occupation
Elias Hughes	34	Tenn.	Farmer
Dorinda "	36	Ala.	
David "	6	Tenn.	
Banester "	4	Ala.	
Elizabeth "	3	"	
Eliza "	2	"	
Sarah "	6/12	"	

Household 80
Name	Age	Origin	Occupation
Abert A. Simmons	30	Ala.	Farmer
Nancy "	30	"	
Rebecca "	5	"	
Wm. Alexander	22	"	Laborer

Household 81
Name	Age	Origin	Occupation
Robert T. Lanier	34	Tenn.	Blcsmith
Mirian "	22	Ala.	
Margaret "	10	Tenn.	
Aaron "	3/12	Ala.	

Household 82
Name	Age	Origin	Occupation
William L. Trousdale	43	N.C.	Farmer
Elizabeth "	30	S.C.	
Elizabeth "	16	Ala.	
Benjamin "	14	"	
Catharine "	12	"	
James "	11	"	
Mary "	8	"	
Samuel "	6	"	
Rebecca "	4	"	
Baby (female) "	1/12	"	

Household 83
Name	Age	Origin	Occupation
Rebecca Crow	65	unknown	

Household 84
Name	Age	Origin	Occupation
William Harmin	40	Ala.	Farmer
Lucinda "	36	Geo.	
Stephen "	14	Ala.	
Eliza "	12	"	
Mary "	9	"	
James "	5	"	
Elizabeth "	4	"	
Julia Young*	29	"	School/teacher
Frances Hamer	10	Miss.	
John Teis	22	Ala.	Laborer

Household 85
Name	Age	Origin	Occupation
Ephraim Gray	30	Ala.	Farmer
Pheby "	30	"	
James "	4	"	
Andrew "	2	"	

Household 86
Name	Age	Origin	Occupation
John McMullen	30	N.C.	Farmer
Catharine "	28	Ala.	
Willis "	2	"	
Edwin "	4	"	

Household 87
Name	Age	Origin	Occupation
William Donohoo	30	Ala.	None
Ann "	30	"	
William "	10/12	"	

Household 88
Name	Age	Origin	Occupation
John L. Rast	34	S.C.	Farmer
Nancy "	34	Tenn.	
Mary "	10	Miss.	
William "	8	"	
John "	6	Ala.	
James "	3	"	

Household 89
Name	Age	Origin	Occupation
Mary Boothe	55	S.C.	
Harriet "	22	Ala.	
Catharine "	21	"	

Household 90
Name	Age	Origin	Occupation
Robert Cook	49	S.C.	Farmer
Mary "	49	"	
Elizabeth "	19	Ala.	
William "	15	"	Laborer
Sidney "	14	"	
Ellender "	12	"	
Martha "	8	"	
Catharine "	6	"	
Wesley "	4	"	

Household 91
Name	Age	Origin	Occupation
Thomas McKey	30	Tenn.	Farmer
Levisey "	26	Ala.	
William "	9	"	
Elizabeth "	4	"	
John "	2	"	

Household 92
Name	Age	Origin	Occupation
James Miller	53	S.C.	Farmer
Sarah "	52	Ireland	
John "	22	S.C.	Laborer
Robert "	21	"	"
Sarah "	18	"	
Mary "	16	"	
Martha "	10	"	

---

*Florence Times, 9 June 1968: Miss Julia Ann Young (27 Oct. 1821-22 Oct. 1906) was Lauderdale County's first school mistress. Her school was a one room cabin, built by Henry Stutts on the Military Road. In 1860 she married Hiram Richardson, who was nine years younger, and also a teacher. He was the son of David and Martha Richardson who came here from Moore Co., N.C., in 1818. Hiram and Julia Richardson helped establish some five Methodist churches in the county.

Household 93
Wm. N. Rast   35 S.C. Wagonmkr
Jane   "   33 "
Margaret "   14 Ala.
William   "   12 "
Sarah   "   10 "
Elizabeth "   7 "
John   "   4 "
Josiah   "   1 "

Household 94
Mary Yancy   60 unknown
Milly   "   27 Ala.
John   "   21 "   laborer
Nancy   "   9 "

Household 95
Silus Petit   44 S.C. Farmer
Mary   "   46 Ireland
Fanny   "   18 S.C.
Margaret "   16 Ala.
Martha   "   14 "
John   "   12 "
Nancy   "   10 "
Rachel   "   8 "
Benjamin "   7 "
James   "   5 "

Household 96
John M. Tapp   43 S.C. Farmer
Frances   "   43 Ireland
Thomas   "   21 S.C. Clerk
Mary   "   19 "
James   "   16 Ala. Laborer
Presley   "   14 "
Vincent   "   12 "
Margaret "   10 "
Frances   "   6 "
Sarah   "   3 "

Household 97
Moses Crow   25 S.C. Laborer
Mary   "   23 Ala.
Martha   "   1 "
Baby   " (male) 2/12 "

Household 98
David Hynemon   55 S.C. Farmer
Jane   "   55 Ireland
Martha   "   24 S.C.
James   "   21 Ala. Laborer
Robert   "   19 "   "
Sarah A. Cox   8 "
Sarah Rodgers   84 Ireland

Household 99
A. Hughes   37 Tenn. Laborer
Nancy   "   27 "
Martha   "   9 "
Elizabeth "   6 Ala.
Mary   "   4 "
Elizabeth Davis   62 N.C.

Household 100
John Curtis   26 Tenn. Laborer
Nancy   "   23 Ala.

Household 101
Stephen D. Cox   26 Ala. School/teacher
Sarah   "   25 "
Lucy   "   1 "

Household 102
Nathan McAphee (black)   53 Ky. Tanner
Priscilla "   (black)   43 Ala.
George   "   (black)   11 "
Elizabeth "   (black)   7 "
John   "   (black)   6 "
Sarah   "   (black)   4 "
Nathan   "   (black)   3 "
America   "   (black)   2 "
Elizabeth Chapman (black) 70 Va.
Martha   "   (black)   16 Ala.

Household 103
William C. Philips 35 S.C. Merchant
Louisa   "   26 "
Sousan   "   10 Ala.
Mary   "   8 "
Nancy   "   6 "
William   "   4 "
Elizabeth "   2 "

Household 104
James Bradshaw   50 Ky. Laborer
Pheby   "   48 "
Sarah Thornton   14 "
William   "   7 "

Household 105
Absolum Barnet   69 Va. Shoemaker
Cynthia   "   50 N.C.
Rebecca   "   18 Ala.
James McGhee   34 "   Laborer

Household 106
Samuel McMillon   32 Tenn. Laborer
Mary   "   34 Va.
Sarah   "   11 Tenn.
Nancy   "   8 "
Henry   "   5 "
William   "   3 "

Household 107
Isaac Crow		46	S.C. Tanner
Mary	"	44	Tenn.
Lucy	" *	20	Ala.
Rebecca	"	19	"
Sousan	"	16	"
James	"	13	"
Isaac	"	11	"
Mary	"	9	"
Rachel Cox		7	"
David Porter *		26	S.C. Tanner
Stephen Cox		4	Ala.
Sarah	"	3	"

(*Marked married within the year. David Porter was also marked "female.")

Household 108
Lucy Cox		58	N.C.
Nancy " (idiotic)		40	N.C.
Elizabeth " (idiotic)		37	N.C.

Household 109
William Tomblin		37	Tenn. Farmer
Rebecca	"	32	S.C.
Moses	"	14	Ala.
Fanny	"	12	"
Frances	"	9	"
Samuel	"	7	"
Isaac	"	5	Ark.
Elizabeth	"	2	Ala.
Benjamin Fisher		58	Tenn. Laborer

Household 110
James McLary		35	Tenn. Farmer
Cynthia	"	29	"
Sarah	"	11	"
Robert	"	9	"
Martha	"	6	Ala.
John	"	4	"
Mary	"	1	"
Joseph York		20	" Laborer

Household 111
Drury Joiner		49	N.C. Farmer
Frances	"	37	Tenn.
Sarah	"	18	Ala.
Rebecca	"	11	"
Margaret	"	2	"
Brantly	"	17	" Laborer
Drury	"	9	"
Eli	"	7	"
William	"	5	"
Benjamin Joiner		22	" Laborer

Household 112
Robert Tidwell (laborer)		35	unknown
Martha	"	35	Tenn.
Elizabeth	"	12	"
Samuel	"	10	"
Leroy	"	8	"
Rickman	"	7	"
Sousan	"	6	"
Thomas	"	4	"
Sarah	"	2/12	Ala.

Household 113
Drury Joiner, Jr.			Ala.
Jane	"		Tenn.
Mary	"		Ala.

Household 114
Charles B. Jones		39	N.C. Farmer
Sarah	"	32	Ala.
Annis	"	13	"
Margaret	"	11	"
Jessee	"	9	"
Mary	"	7	"
Martha	"	5	"
Eli	"	3	"
Tabitha	"	2	"
James E. Joiner		19	" Laborer
William Ray		17	" "

Household 115
Jason Prince		28	S.C. Laborer
Josaphene	"	27	Ala.
William	"	5	"
Zachariah	"	2	"

Household 116
Calwell Hughes		56	N.C. Farmer
Rebecca	"	54	S.C.
Martha	"	23	Ala.
Cynthia	"	20	"
Margaret	"	19	"
William	"	12	"
Washington	"	10	"
Rosannah	"	8	"

Household 117
William H. Parker		55	N.C. Taylor
Margaret	"	55	N.C.
Elizabeth	"	20	Ala.
Jackson	"	15	" Laborer
Amanda	"	13	"
Wesley	"	11	"

Household 118
Denis Holden		39	Ala. Farmer
Matilda	"	28	La.
Elbern	" (male)	8	Miss.
Frances	"	5	"
Sarah	"	3	Tenn.
Matilda	"	9/12	"

Household 119
Joseph Holden   50 Va. Farmer
Rachel   "   44 S.C.
James   "   11 Tenn.
John   "   8 "
Judah   " (female)   6 "
Levi West   23 "   Laborer
Caroline   "   18 "

Household 120
Alexander Stuart   50 N.C. Farmer
Manerva   "   46 S.C.
Eliza   "   25 Ala.
Martha   "   22 "
Mary   "   20 "
James   "   19 "   Laborer
Duncan   "   16 "   "
Marion   "   13 "
Richard   "   10 "
Nancy   "   9 "
Elizabeth "   6 "

Household 121
Alexander Harmin   50 S.C. Farmer
Elizabeth "   50 "
Eliza   "   24 Ala.
William   "   18 " Student
Mary   "   10 "

Household 122
Margaret Alexander   45 Tenn.
William   "   24 Ala. Laborer
Prince   "   22 "
Sarah   "   18 "

Household 123
Larkin Brumley   36 Ky. Farmer
Sarah   "   42 S.C.
William   "   17 Ala. Laborer
Lakin   "   14 Tenn.
Absolum   "   12 "
Hiram   "   10 Miss.
Matthew   "   8 "
Alfred   "   6 "
James   "   4 Ala.
Chaity   " (female) 2/12 "

Household 124
                            maker
Samuel Miller   46 Penn. Wagon-
Darkis   "   23 Ala.

Household 125
Thomas Cautch   46 S.C. Farmer
Charity   "   37 "
Elizabeth "   16 Tenn.
Charles   "   14 "
continued

Household 125 continued
Mary   "   11 Tenn.
Thomas   "   9 "
Catharine "   8 Ala.
Washington "   5 "
John   "   2 "

Household 126
Mayberry White   30 S.C. Laborer
Rebecca   "   26 Tenn.
Mary   "   5 Ala.
John   "   1 "
Martha Kelly   53 Va.

Household 127
Catharine King   44 N.C.
William   "   22 " Laborer
Arnold   "   20 "   "
Stephen   "   18 Ala.
Emeline   "   15 "
Joseph   "   14 "
George   "   11 "
Luke   "   7 "

Household 128
Alexander King   24 N.C. Laborer
Lydia   "   18 "

Household 129
John Cox   42 N.C. Farmer
Mary   "   42 "
Wiley   "   19 " Laborer
Elizabeth "   17 "
Martin   "   15 "   "
Hiram   "   13 "
William   "   11 "
Anderson   "   9 "

Household 130
John Story   28 Tenn. Shoemkr.
Elizabeth "   29 "
Richard   "   7 Ala.
Sarah   "   5 "
Martha   "   2 "

Household 131
William T. Pratt   30 Tenn.
Sarah   "   21 "
Mary   "   3 "
Rebecca   "   1/12 Ala.
Polly Pratt   60 Tenn.

Household 132
William McGhee   35 Tenn. Farmer
Debby   "   33 Ala.
Mary   "   12 "
Nancy   "   10 "
Milly   "   8 "
continued

C-85

Household 132 continued
Rebecca McGhee   6   Ala.
Bartley   "   5   "
James   "   3   "
Sarah   "   2   "

Household 133
Lizzy Ritter   50   N.C.
Catharine "   23   Ala.
Rebecca   "   20   "
Martha   " (twin)   15   "
Hiram   " (twin)   15   " Laborer

Household 134
William C. Thomes   54   S.C. School
Jane   "   34   "   teacher
Wilmot   "   17   Ala.
James   "   14   "
George   "   10   "
Sarah   "   8   "
Frances   "   6   "
Mary   "   4   "
Philadelphia"(female)   1   "

Household 135
Jacob McGhee   26   Tenn.Farmer
Mary   "   22   Ala.
Cynthia   "   1   "

Household 136
James Scags   24   Tenn.Laborer
Caroline   "   20   "
William   "   4   Ala.
Sousan   "   1   "

Household 137
Heton Richardson   32   N.C.Farmer
Jane   "   25   "
Isam (twin) "   7   Ala.
Elizabeth (twin)"   7   Ala.
Emeline   "   5   "
John   "   3   "
Vina   "   1   "
Macom Brookes (mulatto) 45 N.C.Laborer
James Davis   10   Tenn.
                            mkr
Household 138
James Penny (Perry?)   70   N.C.Wagon/
John   "   15   Tenn.Laborer
Nancy   "   14   "
Mary   "   12   "
Eliza   "   10   "
James   "   21   " Laborer

Household 139
Elizabeth Hill   49   N.C.
John   "   25   " Laborer
Mary   "   23   "
Lavina   "   21   "
Catharine "   19   "
Haywood   "   16   " Laborer
Martha   "   15   "
Aimy (female)"   11   Ala.
Lucy   "   8   "
Charlotte "   5   "
Benjamin Foresythe   21   unknown
    /laborer

Household 140
Camel Cross   28   Tenn.Farmer
Sarah   "   22   "
Martha   "   9   Ala.
Arthur   "   7   "
Shederic "   5   "
Balzora (female)"   2   "
Camell (male)   "   6/12 "

Household 141
Tilmon England   31   Tenn.Laborer
Eliza   "   34   "
John   "   11   "
Matilda   "   10   "
Martha   "   8   "
George   "   6   "
James   "   3   Ala.
Margaret   "   10/12 "

Household 142
Squire Herin- carpenter 40 unknown
Mermilly   "   14   Ala.
Arnold   "   9   "
Nancy   "   7   "
Sousannah "   4   "
Mary   "   1   "

Household 143
Phlemon Herin   23   " Laborer
Jane   "   20   "
William   "   3   "
Paret Herin   19   " Laborer

Household 144
Henry Richardson   45   N.C. Farmer
Nancy   "   44   "
Nancy   "   23   Ala.
James   "   20   " Laborer
Rebecca   "   17   "
Turner   "   15   " Laborer
Henry   "   13   "
Sarah   "   8   "
Frances   "   6   "
Martha   "   3   "
Angeline McDoogal   15   Tenn.
Archy McDoogal   12   "

Household 145
James Williams		56	S.C.	Gin maker
Charlotte	"	45	"	
James	"	15	Ala.	Laborer
Milly	"	13	"	
Marion	"	10	"	
Elizabeth	"	7	"	
Jackson	"	5	"	
Talethia	"	3	"	

Household 146
James Hill		54	N.C.	Farmer
Catharine	"	48	"	
Archer	" *	22	"	Laborer
William	"	23	"	"
Martha	"	16	Ala.	
Souseanah	"	14	"	
Jacob	"	13	"	
Nancy	"	9	"	

(*Marked married within the year--no female also marked.)

Household 147
Robert Fowler		42	Tenn.	Farmer
Sarah	"	35	Geo.	
William	"	14	"	
Mary	"	9	Ala.	
Henry	"	6	"	
Thomas	"	2	"	

Household 148
Alfred Hill		25	N.C.	Farmer
Lucinda	"	23	S.C.	
John	"	4/12	Ala.	
Margaret Woods		18	S.C.	
Edy	"	14	"	

Household 149
Thomas Askew		36	Tenn.	Farmer
Elizabeth	"	31	"	
William	"	13	Missouri	
Murrell	" (male)	7	"	
Newton	"	4	"	
Chonado	" (male)	1	Ala.	

Household 150
Hiram Hill		30	N.C.	Farmer
Malinda	"	35	Tenn.	
Thomas	"	8	Ala.	
Murrell	"	7	"	
James	"	6	"	
Quinton	"	5	"	
Davis	"	4	"	
John	"	1	"	

Household 151
Camel Holden		25	Tenn.	Farmer
Elizabeth	"	26	"	
Mary	"	3	"	
Rachel	"	5/12	Ala.	

Household 152
Richard Holden		21	Tenn.	Farmer
Rachel	"	22	"	
Caledona	"	2	"	

Household 153
Wesley Stutts		25	N.C.	Farmer
Perilee	"	20	Ill.	
Mary A. Story		45	Unknown	
Thomas	"	13	Tenn.	

Household 154
Charles Ludkins		34	Va.	Carpenter
Elizabeth	"	32	Tenn.	
John	"	16	Ala.	Student
Martha	"	14	"	
Sarah	"	12	"	
William	"	10	"	
Frederic	"	8	"	
Charles	"	4	"	
Rebecca	"	2	"	

Household 155
William C. Best		27	Ala.	Farmer
Mary	"	25	"	
Charles	"	4	"	
James	"	2	"	
Sarah Gordan		20	"	

Household 156
| Elias Crandford | | 78 | N.C. | Farmer |
| Tobitha | " | 68 | " | |

Household 157
William Crandford		27	Tenn.	Farmer
Lucinda	"	21	Tenn.	
Elias	"	6	Ala.	
Tobithia	"	4	"	
Thomas	"	2	"	
Garrett Neely		21	"	Laborer

Household 158
John Ellis		55	N.C.	Laborer
Nancy	"	42	Tenn.	
Mary	"	23	Ala.	
Richard	"	21	"	Laborer
Sarah	"	19	"	
Oren	"	17	Tenn.	"
Davis	"	15	"	"
Frances	"	13	"	
Sousan	"	10	"	
John	"	5	"	
William	"	3	"	
Rebecca	"	1/12	"	

Household 159
Gabriel Butler   71   S.C. Farmer
Frances   "   51   N.C.
Gabriel   "   20   Ala. Laborer
Frances   "   13   "
Sarah   "   10   "
Abraham Cox   40   unknown, laborer
Charity Pane   29   Ala.

Household 160
Thomas Holley   26   unknown, laborer
Emily   "   28   Tenn.

Household 161
Henry Ingram   38   Va.   Farmer
Mary   "   27   Ala.
Sarah   "   5   "
Mary   "   2   "

Household 162
Anthony Lindy   24   S.C. Laborer
Sarah   "   4   Ala.
Nancy   "   3   "

Household 163
George Ingram*   36   Va.   Merchant
Lucy   "   23   Ala.
Georgenia "   3   "
Sarah   "   2   "
Thomas   "   1/12 "
Moses Ingram   21   "   Merchant

Household 164
Bryant Dean   43   Tenn. Farmer
Emeline   "   40   Va.
Dempsy   "   18   Ala. Laborer
Benjamin   "   16   "   "
Edmond   "   14   "
Nancy   "   10   "
Ermin   " (female) 8   "
Lucy   "   5   "
Baby   " (female) 5/12 "

Household 165
John Trobock   56   N.C. Farmer
Rebecca   "   34   Ala.
Elvina Bacohaw (twin) 16   "
Julena Do   (twin)   16   "
Thomas Do   11   "

Household 166
J. T. Burrow   31   Ky.
  Com. Pres. Preacher, occupation
Mary Burrow   24   Ala.
George   "   1   "

Household 167
Alex. Harvey   63   S.C. Farmer
Jane   "   62   "
John   "   29   Tenn. Laborer
William   "   21   Ala. Do
Patrick Henry   3   "

Household 168
William Heston   32   Tenn. Farmer
Catharine "   34   "
Samuel   "   9   Ala.
Nancy   "   7   "
John   "   5   "
William   "   2   "

Household 169
William Thorngton   33   S.C. Farmer
Sarah   "   34   Tenn.
John   "   8   Ala.
Thomas   "   6   "
Eliza   "   3   "
William Buset   17   "   Laborer
George   "   13   "
Baby   " (male) 3/12 "

Household 170
James Thonngton   34   "   Farmer
Nancy   "   20   "
Margaret   "   1   "

Household 171
Philemon B. White   38   Tenn. Laborer
Alellellitha "   13   Ala.
Martha   "   7   "

Household 172
Samuel Heston   60   S.C. Farmer
Nancy   "   60   "

Household 173
William Prince   45   S.C. Laborer
Mary   "   31   unknown
Delilah   "   17   Tenn.
Matthew   "   16   Ala. Laborer
Gideon   "   14   "
Franklin   "   12   "
Jelethia   " (twin)   10   "
Teletha   " (twin)   10   "
Elizabeth "   2   "
Baby   " (female) 6/12 "

_____

*George M. Ingram married Lucy
Crittenden. (John Trotwood Moore, Tenn.
Volunteer State, Vol. II, page 694.)

Household 174
T. F. Jackson   40 Va.
    Com. Pres. Preacher, occupation
Frances Jackson   38 Va.
Elizabeth   "   15 Tenn.
Castilla   " (female)   14   "
Catharine   "   12   "
Montezuma   " (male)   10   "
Mary   "   8 Ala.
Andrew   "   6   "
Quintevid   " (female)   2   "

Household 175
Isaac C. Whittier   44 Ct. Tanner
Jane   "   31 Tenn.
Hester   "   17 N.C.
Elizabeth   "   10 Ala.
William   "   8   "
Willis   "   6   "
Catharine   "   4   "
Isaac   "   1   "

Household 176
Rufus Henry   38 N.Y. Miller
Nancy   "   45   "
William   "   14 Ohio
George   "   12 Ky.
Julia   "   9   "

Household 177
T. J. Critingdon   28 Ala. Physician
Elizabeth   "   20   "
Idephonde   " (female)   1   "

Household 178
Sampson Lanier*   45 N.C. Farmer
Sarah   "   20 Tenn.

Household 179
John C. Coffee   25 Ala. Farmer

Household 180
Richard Coffee   50 N.C. Farmer
Sarah   "   46 Tenn.
Joel   "   19 Ala. Student
Nimrod   "   13   "
Joshua   "   11   "
Prudence   "   17   "
Mariah   "   15   "
Elizabeth   "   9   "
Sarah   "   5   "

Household 181
Claybourn Coffee*   29 Ala. Shoemaker
Caroline   "   25 Va.
Joshua   "   5 Ala.
Richard   "   2   "

Household 182
John Prat   28 Tenn. Gin maker
Hirum   "   24 Ala.
William "   3/12 "

Household 183
William Butler   55 Ky. Farmer
Margaret   "   44 Tenn.
Eliza   "   24 Ala.
Lee   "   21   "   Laborer
Minah   " (female)   13   "
Martha   "   12   "
Mariah   "   10   "
William   "   5   "

Household 184
Nicholas Jackson   25 Tenn. Laborer
Elizabeth   "   23   "
Ann   "   10   "
Henry   "   8   "
Dothey (?) " (male)   6   "
Joseph   "   2 Ala.
Mary Boyed   80 N.C.
Edward J. Harrison   55 N.C. Laborer

Household 185
Elizabeth Jackson   55 N.C.
Edward   "   18 Tenn. Laborer
Caroline   "   14 Ala.

Household 186
James Tomlinson   50 Ireland Farmer
Elvirah   "   40 Ala.
Joseph   "   23   "   Laborer
Charles   "   20 Tenn. "
James   "   15 Ala.   "
William   "   11   "
Martha   "   6   "
Sarah   "   1   "

*Sampson Lanier married Sarah Adaline Knight on 9 Feb. 1849 in Lauderdale County. (From Lauderdale Co. marriage records.).

*Claiborn Coffee married Cornelia E. Green in Lauderdale County on 17 Dec. 1840. (Lauderdale County marriage records.)

C-89

Household 187			
Vincent Kelly		57	Va. Carp'ter
Edy	"	42	Geo.
Henry	"	20	Ala. Laborer
Jane	"	15	"
Adeline	"	13	"
John	"	12	"
Anthony	"	9	"
George	"	7	"
Andrew	"	5	"
Felix	"	4	"
Benjamin	"	7	"
Martha Thorington		13	"

Household 188				Laborer
James Thomas		35	Ireland /	
Mary	"	30	Ohio	
John	"	14	"	
William	"	12	"	
Hiram	"	10	"	
Mary	"	8	"	
Sarah	"	6	"	

Household 189				
Margaret McCusley		32	Ala.	
Joshua	"	18	"	Clerk
Robert	"	17	"	Laborer
Timmors	" (male)	15	"	Student
Thomas	"	12	"	
Eliza	"	13	"	

Household 190			
John Thorngton		44	S.C. Farmer
Mary	"	33	"
Elizabeth	"	25	"

Household 191				
James Springer		50	Tenn. Laborer	
Mary	"	48	"	
Franklin	"	22	"	"
Jane	"	19	"	
William	"	18	"	"
Marshal	"	12	"	
Lydia	"	5	"	

Household 192				
Bazil Woodbank		50	S.C. Farmer	
Mary	"	47	"	
Sarah	" *	22	"	
Irey	" (male)	21	"	Laborer
William	"	20	"	"
Mark	" *	17	"	"
John	"	15	Tenn!	
Edy	" (female)	13	Tenn.	
Safey	" (female)	12	"	
Mary	" *	9	Ala.	
Smith	" *	3	"	

Household 193			
James McMurry		70	N.C. Farmer
Rebecca	"	65	"

Household 194			
T. Ellis		30	N.C. Overseer
Edney	"	30	"
Rebecca	"	9	Ala.
James	"	7	"
John	"	5	"
William	"	1	Ala.

Household 195			
Mary Moon		50	Geo.
Jane	"	21	"
Lydia	"	18	"
George	" *	20	" Laborer
Elizabeth	" *	19	Ala.

(*Married within the year.)

Household 196				
Thomas Martindale		50	S.C. Farmer	
Rebecca	"	50	"	
Thomas	"	25	"	Laborer
James	"	23	"	"
John	"	21	"	"
Nancy	"	18	Tenn.	
George	"	16	"	"
Cynthia	"	13	"	
Martha	"	11	Ala.	
Joseph	"	9	"	
Sarah	"	7	"	

Household 197				
James R. Alexander		50	Tenn. Farmer	
Ann	"	42	"	
James	"	21	Ala.	Laborer
Jessee	"	18	"	"
George	"	16	"	"
Mary	"	14	"	
Silus	"	12	"	
Thomas	"	10	"	
Elizabeth	"	4	"	

Household 198			
Josiah Page		40	N.C. Farmer
Nancy	"	38	Tenn.
Julia	"	18	Ala.
Thomas	"	14	"
Jonah	"	12	"
James	"	7	"
William	"	2	"

*All marked with * in this household were marked deaf and dumb

Household 199
William Shoulder	27	Ala.	Farmer
Mary "	20	"	
Sousan Lanmon	7	"	

Household 200
J. D. Stamps	45	Geo.	Farmer
Elizabeth "	43	Tenn.	
John "	19	Ala.	Laborer
Thomas "	17	"	"
Martha "	13	"	
Mary "	10	"	
Sarah "	8	"	
Harriet "	6	"	

Household 201
David W. Haraway	27	Ala.	Farmer

Household 202
James Cooper	48	S.C.	Ginmaker
Samuel "	34	Ala.	Laborer
Robert Dickson	23	"	"
Elizabeth Hill (black)	50	Va.	
James " "	22	Ala.	"
Indiana " (mulatto)	12	"	
Elizabeth " "	10	"	
John " "	8	"	
Catharine " "	1	"	

Household 203
William Rodgers	40	Tenn.	Laborer
Mary Ann "	22	"	
John "	6	Ky.	
James "	4	Tenn.	
Elizabeth "	7/12	Ala.	

Household 204
Jane Cooper	50	unknown	
Nancy "	18	Ala.	
Hugh "	16	"	laborer
Annie "	8	"	

Household 205
Jessee Grisham	47	Tenn.	Farmer
Moses "	25	Ala.	Laborer
Eliza "	20	"	
Prudence "	1?	"	
Alley "	15	"	
James "	13	"	
Gracy "	9	"	

Household 206
James Whitehead	54	Geo.	Farmer
Sarah "	35	Tenn.	
George " *	20	Ala.	Laborer
Elzera " *	15	"	
continued			

Household 206 continued
Ellander "	* 16	Ala.	
Jessee "	8	"	
Margaret "	6	"	
Philip "	5	"	
James "	4	"	
Sarah "	2	"	
Baby (female) "	1/12	"	
Green Berry Watson	40	Ky.	Laborer

Household 207
John M. Heston	31	Tenn.	teacher School/
Margaret "	23	Ala.	
James "	4	"	
Margaret "	1/12	"	
Lavina Harrison	22	"	

Household 208
Hosey Baloo	33	N.C.	Laborer
Matilda "	30	Ala.	
John "	15	"	
Rainy "	13	"	
Elias "	10	"	
William "	8	"	
Elizabeth "	4	"	

Household 209
Walter M. Haraway	43	Va.	Farmer
Emily "	39	Va.	
George "	14	Ala.	
John "	12	"	
Benjamin "	8	"	

Household 210
Jacob Whitehead	28	Ala.	Farmer
Elizabeth "	24	Ala.	
Julia "	3	"	
Frances "	6/12	"	
Ruthy Brooks	16	"	
Joseph Watson	15	"	Laborer
Thomas Watson	12	"	

Household 211
Nancy E. Whitehead	28	Tenn.	
Henry "	9	Ala.	
____keal Brooks	21	"	Laborer

Household 212
Andrew J. Grisham	36	Tenn.	Blc.smith
Alley "	28	Ala.	
Bailes "	11	"	
Julia "	8	"	
Winston "	5	"	
Sarah "	4	"	
Jessee "	2	"	

---

*Marked married within the year.

C-91

Household 213
Jessee Baloo		36	Tenn.Laborer
Sarah	"	30	"
Martha	"	14	"
Granllville	"	12	Ala.
Nancy	"	10	"
Amanda	"	8	"
Ruthey	"	5	"
Rethia	" (female)	3	"

Household 214
William Harvey		28	Tenn.Farmer
Elizabeth	"	28	Ala.
Mary	"	3	"
Elmira	"	8/12	"

Household 215
Hugh S. Havey		30	Tenn.Farmer
Eliza	"	28	Ala.
James	"	10	"
Nancy	"	8	"
Eliza	"	5	"
John	"	3	"
Virginia	"	1	"
Robert Brooks		23	Geo.Laborer

Household 216
Tobius Rice		36	Ala.Farmer
Lucretia	"	35	"
William	"	18	" Laborer
Mary	"	16	"
Eliza	"	14	"
George	"	11	"
Anne	"	8	"
Irvine	"	6	"
Martha	"	4	"
Taylor	"	1	"

Household 217
Thomas B. Whitehead		22	Ala.Farmer
Elizabeth	"	19	Ky.
Minor	"	3	Ala.
James Watson		6	"
Sarah	"	3	"

Household 218
Anderson Overby		55	Va.Farmer
Jane	"	61	Ireland
Richard	"	26	Tenn.Laborer
Drury Forgison		17	" Do
Lucinda	"	13	"
Micheal	"	10	"

Household 219
William Overby		30	Tenn.Laborer
Maiah	"	31	"
John	"	8	"
William	"	6	Ala.
Thomas	"	2	"

Household 220
Samuel McCrew		26	Ala. Laborer
Martha	"	25	"
Manerva	"	8/12	"

Household 221
Sion Swiney		44	N.C. Farmer
Mary	"	33	Tenn.
Sion	"	1	Ala.
Lucinda	"	10	Tenn.

Household 222
Robert McCartney		51	Geo. Brickmaso
Elizabeth	"	49	N.C.
Margaret	"	18	Ala.
Robert	"	17	" Laborer
Elisah	" (male)	15	" "
James	"	12	"
Elizabeth	"	10	"
Ann Baugh		8	Ala.
Elizabeth Baugh		11	"
Frances	"	9	"
John	"	6	"
Elisha	"	2	"

Household 223
Alfred McMien		32	Tenn. Farmer
Elizabeth	"	28	S.C.
Charles	"	7	Ala.
Nancy	"	1	"

Household 224
William Wrathers		40	S.C. Farmer
Rebecca	"	43	Do
Charles	"	18	Ala. Laborer
William	"	16	" Do
Martha	"	14	"
Rebecca	"	12	"
John	"	7	"
Samuel (?)	"	5	"
Sarah	"	1	"

Household 225
Sarah Brawley		48	Unknown
Mary	"	24	Ala.
William	"	20	" Laborer
Eliza	" *	21	"
Ellison	"	18	" "
Franklin	"	15	" "
Milly	"	13	"

(*Marked married within the year. Eliza only one thus marked.)

Household 226
Elias Nation		34	S.C. Farmer
Sally	"	44	Tenn.
Martha	"	20	Ala.
Margaret	"	15	"
continued			

Household 226 continued
John Nation   12 Ala.
Eli   "   9 "
Susah   " (?)   6 "
James   "   3 "

Household 227
Pleasant Thompson   25 Ala. Farmer
Mary   "   21 "
William   "   3 "
John   "   8/12 "

Household 228
Samuel Dumey (Darney?) 65 S.C. Farmer
Matilda   "   56 Ky.
Rachel   "   24 "
James   "   17 "   Laborer

Household 229
Samuel Gore   40 Tenn. Do
Nancy   "   33 "
Sarah   "   4 "
James   "   3 "

Household 230
Alexander Gore   26 Tenn. Laborer
Mary   "   20 Ala.
Elizabeth "   8/12 "

Household 231
John Darney (Dumey?) 40 Tenn. Shoemaker
Mary   "   44 "
Levi   "   11 Ala.
Joseph   "   9 "
Sarah   "   8 "
Mary   "   5 "
Franklin "   7 "
Elizabeth "   4 "

Household 232
Andrew Burney   26 Ala. Laborer
Lucinda   "   26 Tenn.
Elias   "   2 Ala.
William   "   10/12 "

Household 233
Martha McMeen   40 S.C.
William   "   26 "   Laborer

Household 234
Alfred Litreal   38 Tenn. Farmer
Lucinda   "   40 N.C.
Frances   "   19 Ala. Laborer
Jesse   "   17 "   "
James   "   16 "   "
Mary   "   11 "
Sarah   "   8 "
continued

Household 234 continued
Elizabeth Litreal   6 Ala.
Lucinda   "   4 "
John   "   3 "
Alfred   "   1 "
Lucinda Literal   18 "

Household 235
Nathan Rice   54 Ky. Stone mason
Harriet   "   48 Va.
Mary   "   27 Ala.
Sousan   "   15 "
Nathan   " (?)   12 "

Household 236
Anderson Lovell   26 Ala. Laborer
Alvey   " (female)26 "
William   "   6 "
Samuel   "   4 "
Hiram   "   5/12 "

Household 237
Samuel Literal   26 Ky. Laborer
Sarah   "   23 "
Eliza   "   2 Ala.

Household 238
William Barnet   70 S.C. Blacksmith
Jane   "   65 "
William   "   25 Ala. Laborer
Hannah   "   22 "
Lucinda   "   28 "
George   "   11 "
Martha   "   8 "
Logan   " (male)   3 "
Elizabeth "   17 "

Household 239
John W. Michal   30 Tenn. Farmer
Sarah   "   22 Ala.
Columbus "   9/12 "
Stuart Fulks   14 "

Household 240
Eliza J. Wood   33 Tenn.
Robert   "   13 Ala.
Sousan   "   8 "
Martha   "   7 "
Randolph "   5 "
Amanda   "   3 "

Household 241
George J. Newton   30 Tenn. Farmer
Nancy   "   26 Ala.
Rebecca   " (twin)   9 "
Ruthy   " (twin)   9 "
James   "   7 "
Baby   " (female)7/12"

Household 242
Samuel Corum		36	Tenn.	Farmer
Jane	"	35	"	
Thorington	"	19	Ala.	Laborer
Catharine	"	18	"	
Charlotte	"	15	"	
Sousan	"	13	"	
James	"	10	"	
George	"	8	"	
John	"	6	"	
Louisa	"	4	"	

Household 243
Sally Hopkins		60	S.C.	
Martindale	"	28	Ala.	Laborer
John	"	22	"	Do
Nancy	"	35	"	
Sarah	"	25	"	

Household 244
Chism Butler		28	Ala.	Farmer
Mary	"	28	Tenn.	
John	"	11	Ala.	
Gabriel	"	9	"	
James	"	6	"	
Chism	"	2	"	

Household 245
Asa F. Barnet		25	S.C.	Farmer
Martha	"	20	Tenn.	
Mahala	"	9/12	Ala.	

Household 246
Joseph Murphey		30	Tenn.	Laborer
Tabitha	"	25	Tenn.	
Elizabeth	"	14	Ala.	
Martha	"	10	Ala.	
Mary	"	8	"	
Cynthia	"	6	"	
Baby	" (female)	6/12	"	

Household 247
Thompson Hannah		35	S.C.	Blksmith
Sebina	"	35	"	
Marthis	"	5	"	

Household 248
William Croney		40	S.C.	Farmer
Sarah	"	33	Tenn.	
William	"	10	Ala.	
James	"	8	"	
Martha	"	6	"	
Margaret	"	4	"	
Rody	"	2	"	

Household 249
Thomas Davis		65	N.C.	Farmer
Hannah	"	51	S.C.	
Elizabeth	"	24	Ala.	
William	"	21	"	Laborer
Matilda	"	18	"	
Cynthia	"	16	"	

Household 250
Irvine Y. Barnette		35	S.C.	Farmer
Mary	"	29	Ala.	
James	"	9	"	
John	"	5	"	
Zekeal	"	2	"	
Mary Fardell		13	"	

Household 251
Bergus Croney		50	S.C.	Farmer
Margaret	"	50	"	
Johnson	"	25	N.C.	Laborer
Bergus	"	23	Ala.	"
Sousan	"	21	"	
Elizabeth	"	18	"	
Noah	"	15	"	"
Nancy	"	13	"	
Annis	"	10	"	
Benjamin	"	8	"	
William	"	5	"	

Household 252
| James Barnette | | 42 | S.C. | Farmer |
| Mahula | " | 43 | " | |

Household 253
Jacob Barnette		60	S.C.	Farmer
Caty	"	50	S.C.	
Selina Hopkins		40	"	
Elizabeth	"	13	Ala.	
Henry	"	2	"	
James Smith		60	S.C.	Laborer

Household 254
Samuel B. Thigpen		24	Ala.	Farmer
Elizabeth	"	24	"	
John	"	2/12	"	

Household 255
Amos Thigpenn		60	N.C.	Farmer
Elizabeth	"	55	S.C.	
Jane	"	27	Ala.	
Green Berry	" (blind)	26	"	none
Joshua	"	22	"	Laborer
Joseph	"	17	"	"
Riley	"	14	"	

C-94

Household 256
William White   30 Ala. Farmer
Eliza   "   30 S.C.
Mary   "   10 Ala.
Levisa   "   8 "
Richard   "   6 "
Jessee   "   5 "
Margaret   "   3 "
Perry   "   1 "

Household 257
Zekeal Barnette   73 S.C. Farmer
Ollive   "   67 "
Lucinda   "   45 "
Parrie   " (female) 36 "
Elvina   "   32 "
Sarah   "   24 "
Warren J. Davis   20 "   Laborer
Amanda   "   17 "
Mary   "   16 "
James McClewer   18 "   "
Elizabeth "   16 "
Frances Barnette   4 Ala. (male)

Household 259
Jacob Cox   54 N.C. Farmer
Selia   "   60 "
Chestly"   30 Ala. Laborer

Household 260
Joshua McKey   27 S.C. Laborer
Elvy   "   22 Ala.
(Marked married within the year.)

Household 261
Robert A. Cox   30 S.C. Laborer
Mahala   "   30 Ala.
Nancy   "   12 "
Sanford   "   10 "
Eli   "   8 "
Isora   " (female) 6 "
Martha   "   4 "

Household 262
Charles A. Cox   26 Tenn. Laborer
Catharine "   26 Ala.
Josiah   "   10 "
Sarah   "   8 "

Household 263
Charles Cox Senr. 85 N.C. None
Sarah   "   70 "

Household 264
A. B. Putman   21 Ala. Laborer
Nancy   "   25 "

Household 265
Nancy C. Fulks   33 Ala.
Mary   "   19 "
John   "   17 " Laborer
Stuart   "   15 "   "
George   "   13 "
James (?) "   7 "
Mahala   "   5 "
Cynthia   "   3 "

Household 266
Meredith Fulks   23 Ala. Laborer
Sousan   "   22 "
James   "   2 "

Household 267
William Beavers   40 Tenn. Farmer
Margaret   "   32 N.C.
Elizabeth "   15 Ala.
Catharine "   14 "
John   "   13 "
Quinton   "   8 "
Mary   "   6 "
Drury   "   4 "
William   "   1 "

Household 268
George W. Thigpen 37 Tenn. Farmer
Elizabeth "   36 N.C.
Lecie (?) " (female)*17 Ala.
Margaret   "   15 "
Bluford   "   14 "
Gilford   "   12 "
Amanda   "   10 "
Mary   "   9 "
Amos   "   7 "
Sarah   "   5 "
George   "   3 "
Selphy   "(female) 1 "
(*Lecie marked married within the year.)

Household 269
John Ray   27 Tenn. Laborer
Elmira   "   19 "

Household 270
George Luney   45 Tenn. Farmer
Lucinda   "   30 "
Mary   "   12 Ala.
John   "   10 "
Joseph   "   8 "
Aveline   "   5 "
Nancy   "   2 "
Joseph Luney   16 "   Laborer

C-95

Household 271
John White		54	Tenn. Farmer
Mary	"	49	Ala.
Anderson Grisworld		5	"

Household 272
Gilford D. King		60	N.C. Farmer
Selfa (female)	"	56	"
Sousan Cox		11	Ala.

Household 273
Burney M. King		26	N.C. Farmer
Matilda	"	24	Ala.
Roenia	"	2	"
Eliza	"	1	"

Household 274
Eliza Kitchens		30	Tenn.
George	"	13	Ala.
Permelia	"	11	"
Mary	"	9	"
Lucy	"	6	"
John Cox		22	Tenn. Laborer

Household 275
William Caugh		52	S.C.
Nancy	"	40	"
Mary	"	16	Ala.
John	"	13	"
Martha	"	11	"
Ann	"	9	"
Thomas	"	7	"
Robert	"	5	"
Ephaim	"	3	"
Caroline	"	2/12	"

Household 276
James Robertson		45	Tenn. Blksmith
Mermia	" (female)	40	Geo.
Martha	"	13	Ala.
James	"	10	"
Dulcena	" (female)	8	"
Lucina	"	6	"
Ludilla	" (female)	4	"
Ozella	"	2	"
John	"	1	"
John McDoogal		21	" Laborer

Household 277
Thomas Springer		58	S.C. Do
Sarah	"	46	N.C.
Samuel	"	21	Tenn. Laborer
Elphraim	" (idiotic)	14	"
Albert	"	11	"
Calvin	"	6	"

Household 278
James M. Philips		25	Tenn. Laborer
Elizabeth	"	26	Ala.
Nancy	"	6	"
Margaret	"	4	"
Mary	"	2	"

Household 279
William Springer		45	S.C. Farmer
A. B. M.	"	27	Ala. Laborer
Eliza	"	22	"
Robert	"	29	" "
Mary	"	25	"
William	"	6	"
Elizabeth	"	2	"

Household 280
Thomas M. Williams		49	S.C. School/teacher
Julia	"	33	Tenn.
Lucy	"	8	Ala.
Nancy	"	6	"
Columbia	"	5	"
Mary	"	4	"
Lafayette	"	2	"

Household 281
John N. Springer		39	S.C. Farmer
Sarah	"	35	"
Jane	"	16	Ala.
Jessee	"	12	"
Sousan	"	11	"
Mary	"	10	"
Mariah	"	6	"
Johathan	"	4	"
Taylor	"	2	"

Household 282
John M. Davis		34	Ky. Merchant
Eliza	"	27	Ala.
William	"	8	"
Mary	"	6	"
Martha	"	2	"
Baby	" (female)	7/12	"
George W. Richardson		23	" Doctor

Household 283
| Gideon Barnette | | 47 | S. C. Farmer |

Household 284
James C. Myrick		59	N.C. Gunsmith
Isam	"	20	Ala. Laborer
Mary	"	21	"
Hiram	"	15	"
Frances	"	13	"
Sarah	"	11	"
Henry	"	9	"

Household 285
Buford T. Allen	35	Tenn. Farmer
Telthie "	27	S.C.
Mary "	10	Ala.
Henry "	8	"
Martha "	6	"
Nancy "	3	"
Thomas Morris	17	" Laborer

Household 286
John R. White	33	Ky. Do
Nancy "	36	Tenn.
James "	6	Ala.
Elizabeth"	5	"
Sousan "	2	"

Household 287
Lucy Loving	60	N.C.
Constant "	24	Ala. Laborer
Ruben "	22	" "

(NOTE: compare this household listing with that of household 352, believied to be the same, although surname is different—the other information seems to be the same.)

Household 288
Henry D. Allen	69	N.C. Farmer
Mary "	65	Do
Martha "	19	Ala.

Household 289
James Estep	40	N.C. Farmer
Winney "	30	Ala.
Elizabeth"	10	"
Solomon "*	8	"
Abraham "	6	"
Isaac "	4	"
Martha "	2	"
Jacob "	1	"
Austin P. Morris	45	Indiana, laborer

Household 290
William C. Mitchell	47	Va. Farmer
Elvina "	30	Tenn.
Frank "	18	Ala. Laborer
Richard "	16	" "
Mary "	3	"

Household 291
Garlandon Estice	34	S.C. Farmer
Catharine "	29	Ala.
Mary "	9	"
William "	5	"

Household 292
Thomas Grisham	52	Geo. Farmer
Mary "	50	N.C.
Martha "	18	Ala.
Rebecca "	16	"
John "	14	"
Thompson"	9	"
Mary "	7	"
Mirah "	5	"

Household 293
William French	27	S.C. Blacksmith
Sarah "	21	Ala.
Benjamin "	3	"
William "	4/12	"

Household 294
F. H. McGwin	31	Tenn. Shoemaker
Margaret "	64	Geo.(?)
Margaret "	18	Tenn.

Household 295
William R. McGwin	39	Geo. Farmer
Elizabeth "	30	Ala.
Mary "	6	"
Sarah "	4	"
Henry "	2	"
Edmund Comer	26	S.C. Laborer

Household 296
| Thomas Davis | 25 | Ala. Do |
| Jane " | 20 | S.C. |

*HISTORY OF ALABAMA AND HER PEOPLE,
Vol. II, page 179: The Eastep family was of Scotch ancestry and first settled in Virginia after coming to the United States. Solomon Eastep, who spent all of his life in the Rogersville community, was born there in 1832 and died in 1908. He conducted a large farm and also held the office of postmaster and was a Confederate soldier during the Civil War. Solomon Eastep was the father of James F. Eastep, born 4 July 1862 at Rogersville, and died 4 July 1911. He married Isabel Williams, born at Rogersville in 1864, died in Florence in 1909. James and Isabel Eastep were the parents of ten children.

Household 297
Jane Davis   50   S.C.
Clayburn "   18   Ala. Laborer
Joseph   "   13   "
Sarah   "   11   "
Louisa   "   9   "

Household 298
William R. Porter   45   S.C. Clerk
Margaret "   45   "
Andrew   "   16   Ala. Student
Sarah   "   14   "
Elizabeth "   11   "
John   "   8   "
William   "   5   "

Household 299
Stephen Harmin   36   Tenn. Farmer
Sarah   "   29   Ky.
John   "   10   Ala.
Elizabeth "   8   "
Mary   "   5   "
Sousan   "   3   "
Sarah   "   11/12 "
Nancy Harmin   82   S.C.

Household 300
Joseph H. Walker   50   Geo. Carp'tr
Mary   "   51   N.C.
James   "   24   Ala. Laborer
John   "   18   "   "
Malicia   "   15   "
George   "   13   "
Elizabeth "   21   "

Household 301
                           Farmer
Anderson McPeters   77   Ireland /
Elizabeth "   50   S.C.
Caroline "   18   Ala.
George   "   16   "   Laborer
William   "   14   "
James   "   9   "
Bales   "   7   "

Household 302
William Davis   26   "   Laborer
Catharine "   18   "
Ruben   "   6/12   "

Household 303
Elisha Shelton   25   "   Farmer
Caroline "   25   S.C.
George   "   6   Ala.
Elizabeth "   4   "
Martha   "   2   "

Household 304   Assessor
J. J. Matthis   36   Tenn. Tax/
Catharine "   30   N.C.
William   "   12   Tenn.
James   "   10   "
Mary   "   8   "
Thomas   "   5   "
Elizabeth "   2   Ala.

Household 305
E. W. Vichars   30   Ala. Farmer
Nancy   "   20   "
William   "   3   "
John   "   2   "
Andrew   "   3/12   "

Household 306
Stephen Shelton   37   Tenn. Farmer
Sousan   "   39   "
Sarah   "   16   Ala.
Nancy   "   13   "
Elizabeth "   12   "
Rebecca   "   9   "
Thomas   "   6   "
Mary   "   4   "
Sousan   "   2/12   "
Franklin Holt   17   "   Laborer
Mary Carter   63   Unknown

Household 307
John C. Hammons   37   N.C. Farmer
Sarah   "   37   Unknown
Josephus "   10   Tenn.
William   "   9   "
Clemens   " *   8   "
Jasper   "   7   "
John   "   4   "
Sousan   "   3   "
Thomas   "   1   "

Household 308
C. H. Clark   54   S.C. Shoemaker
Nancy   "   56   "
Fereby   "   16   Ala.

Household 309
William Hammons   25   Tenn. Farmer
Mary   "   18   Ala.
James   "   2   "
Sarah Hammons   61   N.C.
Matilda Do   27   Ala.

*Nashville Dispatch, 16 May 1865:
Clem Hammond of Lauderdale Co., Ala.,
received 10 years, hard labor, for
guerrillaing and robbing and was
received at military prison.

Household 310
Lightle Robertson   43 Tenn.Farmer
Leander   "   35 "
Mary   "   11 Ala.
James   "   6 "
Amanda   "   10 "
Joseph   "   3 "
Martha Robertson   65 N.C.

Household 311
Zachariah Johnson   65 Do Farmer
Nancy   "   63 Do
Zachariah "   30 Do Farmer

Household 312
N. W. Butler   50 S.C.Doctor
John   "   18 Ky.Student
Aldolphus "   14 "
Risen   " (male)   12 "
Margaret "   10 "
Minor   "   8 "
Daniel Carborn   60 Penn. None
Angeline "   16 Ky.

Household 313
        Smith
William Davidson   31 N.C. Gun/
Matilda   "   30 Tenn.
Leroy   "   6 Ala.
Mary   "   5 "
Hiram   "   3 "
Wiley   "   2 "

Household 314
Jesse L. Herrell   28 Ala.Farmer
Rody   "   25 "
James   "   6 "
Elizabeth "   5 "
Luke   "   3 "
Eldridge "   1 "
Valles R. Hartless (male) 18 Tenn.laborer

Household 315
Rebecca Porter   70 N.C.
Andrew   "   46 S.C.laborer
Mary   "   50 "

Household 316
John Burrow   40 Tenn.Farmer
Roan   "   39 "
William   "   14 Ala.
Joel   "   12 "
James   "   10 "
John   "   8 "
Mary   "   6 "
George   "   3 "
Rebecca   "   8/12 "

Household 317
John Kenny (?)   45 Tenn.Tanner
Jane   "   37 N.C.
Frances   "   16 Ala.
Mary   "   14 "
John   "   13 "
Thomas   "   11 "
Martha   "   9 "
William   "   7 "
Ann Liza "   6 "
James   "   4 "
Davis   "   1 "

Household 318
E. B. Westmoreland   53 Va. Merchant
Lucy   "   44 "
John   "   15 Ala.Student
Virginia "   12 "
Lucy   "   8 "
Eliza   "   3/12 "
John W. Briggs (?)   30 Tenn.Merchant
Ann   "   6 Ala.
Mary   "   4 "
Martha   "   1 "
Nathaniel Leath   24 Ala. Doctor

Household 319
Green Berry Vichars   64 Geo.Shoemaker
Elizabeth "   50 N.C.
William   "   35 Tenn.Laborer
Verdinand "   13 Ala.

Household 320
Hardin Naland   25 Tenn.Laborer
Cynthia   "   24 Ala.
James   "   4 "
Necis   " (female)   3 "
Elizabeth "   8/12 "

Household 321
J. W. McGwin   31 Tenn. Grocer
Frances   "   21 Ala.
William   "   3 "
Wiley   "   2 "
Virginia "   8/12 "

Household 322
George Cox   26 Ala.Merchant
Elizabeth "   18 "
(Married within the year.)

Household 323
John McWilliams   70 N.C. Farmer
Nancy   "   46 Va.

C-99

Household 324			
Samuel McWilliams	30	Do	Overseer
Mary "	25	Tenn.	
Sarah "	5	Do	
Joseph "	2	Ala.	

Household 325
Jesse McMillon	50	Va.	Farmer
Rachel "	45	Do	
Sousan "	28	Tenn.	
Archibald "	27	Do	Laborer
Allen Hunter	25	Ala.	Do
Mary "	24	Do	
Frances "	4	Tenn.	
Jesse "	6/12	Ala.	

Household 326
Lewis Fields	45	N.C.	Farmer
NarCynthia "	35	"	
Sarah "	8	Ala.	
Solomon "	6	"	
George "	4	"	
Lucy "	2	"	

Household 327
John L. White	35	Tenn.	Laborer
Nancy "	35	"	
Gilbert "	6	Ala.	
Elizabeth "	4	Ala.	
Sousan "	2	"	

Household 328
Jepsah W. Crowder	51	S.C.	Farmer
Sousan "	46	N.C.	
Cynthia "	23	Tenn.	
James "	21	"	Laborer
Samuel "	18	"	"
Nancy "	15	Miss.	
William "	14	"	
Julia "	11	"	
John "	9	"	
Martha "	7	"	
Thomas "	4	"	

Household 329
Henry Poteet	28	Ala.	Farmer
Nancy "	22	Tenn.	
Rufus "	1	Ala.	

Household 330
P. N. Todd	36	Tenn.	Farmer
Matilda "	28	"	
Roena "	13	"	
Olza " (female)	10	"	
Nancy "	8	Ala.	
Mary "	6	"	
Samuel "	2	"	

Household 331
A. B. Hammons	29	Tenn.	Farmer
Sabrey "	24	"	
Mary "	8	Ala.	
Orebelle "	2	"	

Household 332
Z. B. Hammons	26	Do.	Farmer

Household 333
J. W. Price	31	Tenn.	Do
Sousan "	26	"	
John "	6	"	
Mary "	4	"	
Emily "	2	Ala.	
Frederic "	1	"	

Household 334
C. D. Porter	51	S.C.	Com.Pres./Preacher
Easter "	54	"	
Eliza "	21	Ala.	
Mary "	19	"	
Nancy "	17	"	
Franklin "	14	"	

Household 335
James G. Porter	35	S.C.	Blacksmith
Elizabeth "	25	Tenn.	
John "	7	Ala.	
Samuel "	5	"	
Norcis Brown (fmle)	20	"	

Household 336
Rachel Springer	60	S.C.	
Alexander "	15	"	Laborer

Household 337
Thomas Williams	70	Va.	Farmer
Elizabeth "	53	Ky.	
Angeline "	23	Ala.	
Emily "	19	"	
Catharine "	16	"	
Matilda "	13	"	
Phones " (female)	10	"	
William Rickman	27	N.C.	Laborer

Household 338
John Shelton	26	Ala.	Farmer
Jane "	26	"	
Talethia "	4	"	
Mary "	3	"	
Madilla "	1	"	
Jane Harwood	60	S. C.	

Household 339
Philip Penny Cup	20	Tenn.	Farmer
Sarah Hammons	86	S.C.	
Elizabeth " (twin)	14	Ala.	
Nancy " (twin)	14	"	
Jachariah Harwood	18	Tenn.	Laborer

Household 340
Hugh Porter	60	S.C.	Farmer
Sarah "	50	"	
Rebecca"	28	"	
Wesley "	22	"	Laborer
John "	19	"	Do
Cynthia"	14	"	

Household 341
Andrew Porter	27	"	Laborer
Frances "	28	Ala.	
Sarah "	5	"	
Mattha "	3	"	
Mary "	11/12	"	

Household 342
Elizabeth Springer	40	N.C.	
Mary "	18	Ala.	
William "	15	Do	Laborer

Household 343
William Johnson	30	Do	Farmer
Sarah "	22	N.C.	
James "	11	Miss.	
Margaret "	8	"	
William "	7	Kansas	
George "	5	Ala.	
Chottler " (male)	3	"	
Thomas "	7/12	"	

Household 344
William Poteet	58	N.C.	Carpenter
Ruthey "	48	Tenn.	
Jane "	23	"	
Elizabeth "	16	"	
Martha "	11	"	
Mary "	7	"	

Household 345
John Sheton	26	Ala.	Farmer
Mary "	24	"	
Louisa "	4	"	
Mary "	3	"	
Baby " (female)	1	"	
Jane Haywood	60	S.C.	
Eliza Watson	13	Ala.	

Household 346
T. S. Springer	35	S.C.	Farmer
Sarah "	37	N.C.	
Allen "	10	Ala.	
Robert "	8	"	
Henry "	6	"	
John "	4	"	
William "	2	"	

Household 347
Nathan Barr	50	S.C.	Laborer
Martha "	40	"	
William "	19	Ala.	Laborer
Ephraim "	17	"	"
Elizabeth"	15	"	
Jessee "	14	"	
Ruben "	13	"	
John "	10	"	
Henry "	8	"	
Edmund "	5	"	

Household 348
Jessee Hammons	28	Ala.	Farmer
Ritta "	21	"	
Sarah "	7	"	
Mary "	3	"	
Elizabeth"	9/12	"	
Harrison Balbo	25	"	Farmer
Catharine "	24	"	
Sarah "	7	"	
Rainy "	3	"	
Juda "	2	"	
Nancy "	1	"	

Household 349
Y.(Z.?) L. Wood	44	"	Farmer
Mary "	40	Unknown	

Household 350
Patan Lovell	39	Tenn.	Laborer
Nancy "	27	"	
Amanda "	17	Ala.	
Thomas "	14	"	
Sarah "	12	"	
Lucy "	10	"	
Polly "	8	"	
William "	6	"	
Frances "	2	"	

Household 351
James Lovell	29	Tenn.	Laborer
Rody "	26	Do	
William"	9	Ala.	
Levisa "	8	"	
George "	4	"	
Ruben "	9/12	"	

Household 352
Lucy Lovell   60 Va.
Constant "   22 "   Laborer
Ruben   "   20 "   "
(Compare this with household 287)

Household 353
John Ridgeway   30 unknown farmer
Caiesy " (female)   25 Ala.
Eliza   "   8   "
Elizabeth "   5   "
Catharine "   1   "

Household 354
Jessee Literal   29 unknown, farmer
Sarah   "   27 Ala.
Mary   "   6   "
Martha   "   5   "
Joseph   "   3   "
James   "   1/10 "
Mary A. Walker   25 Tenn.

Household 355
John Literal   31 Ala. Farmer
Marinda "   25   "
Amanda "   10   "
Joseph "   7   "
George "   5   "
Elizabeth"   4   "
Lucy   "   2   "

Household 356
Isaac McCluskey   35 S.C. Farmer
Martha "   25 Tenn.
William "   8   "
Hugh   "   5   "
Elizabeth"   2   "

Household 357
Samuel Cox   69 Va. Farmer
Ritty   "   68   "
Anderson"   37 Tenn. Farmer
Sarah   "   35 N.C.
Elizabeth"   16 Ala.
William "   14   "
Martha "   12   "
Andrew "   10   "
Melicia "   8   "
Louisia "   6   "
Mary   "   5   "
James Walker   25 Tenn. Laborer

Household 358
Aaron Cox   47 Do Farmer
Nancy   "   44 S.C.
Newton " *   20 Ala. Laborer
Joel   "   14   "
continued

Household 358 continued
Elizabeth "   13 Ala.
Charlotte "   11   "
Elisha   "   9   "
Aaron   "   6   "
Sarah   "   4   "
Virginia "   2   "
(*Marked married within the year.)

Household 359
James Cox   24 Ala. Laborer
Nelly   "   20   "
Newton "   2   "
George " (twin)   1/12 "
Andrew " (twin)   1/12 "

Household 360
George W. Shelton   34 Tenn. Farmer
Lenny   "   33 N.C.
Robert   "   16 Ala. Laborer
Sousan   "   14   "
Elisha   "   12   "
Jessee   "   10   "
Jasper   "   8   "
George   "   6   "
Charity   "   4   "
James   "   5/12 "
Anagal Holt (female) 14   "

Household 361
John Jones   35 unknown farmer
Sarah   "   32 Tenn.
Martha "   7 Ala.
Mary   "   5   "
Elizabeth"   4   "
Neil   "   3   "
Henry   "   2   "
Thomas "   1   "

Household 362
Joel Glassip   39 Tenn. Millright
Julia "   22 Ala.
Clinton"   7   "
Sampson"   5   "
Martin "   3   "
Mary   "   2   "
Rubin Lovell   23   " Laborer

Household 363
Levi A. Glossip   23 Tenn. Do
Orah   "   19 Ala.
Mary   "   4   "
Joel   "   2   "

Household 364
H. W. Williams   51 Va. School/teacher
Mary   "   47   "
Curthbirth "   19 Tenn. Laborer
Thomas "   13 Ala.

Household 365
James Shelton   36 Ala. Laborer
Manerva   "   35   "
Eliza   "   15   "
Crocket   "   12   "
Hardin   "   9   "
Poke   "   4   "
Jacob   "   5   "
Mary   "   1   "

Household 366
William Martin   30 N.C. Blksmith
Nancy   "   28 Geo.
James   "   8 Ala.
William   "   6   "
Gracy   "   5 Tenn.
Nancy   "   3   "
Baby   " (female) 2/12 Ala.

Household 367
Mark Shelton   33   "   Laborer
Emeline   "   30   "
Martha   "   11   "
Laneer   " (male)   5   "
Caroline   "   3   "
Baby   " (female) 6/12 "

Household 368
Samuel Glassep   30   "   Farmer
Elizabeth "   29   "
Eliza   "   13   "
Sarah   "   12   "
Martha   "   10   "
Jasper   "   5   "
William   "   1   "

Household 369
Arthur Forgers   46 unknown/ laborer
Elizabeth "   35 Tenn.
Mary   "   13   "
Baby   " (male)   1 Ala.

Household 370
Hardin Howard   38 Tenn. Laborer
Mary   "   20   "
Thomas   "   21   "   Laborer
Zachariah "   18   "   "
Obediah   "   17   "   "
Martha   "   12 Ala.
Eliza   "   10   "
Elizabeth "   2   "

Household 371
                                  laborer
Elisha Eldridge   35 not known/
Sousan   "   30 Tenn.
Nancy   "   17 Ala.
Franklin   "   14   "
Andrew   "   12   "
continued

Household 371 continued
Sarah Eldridge   5 Ala.
Alfonzo   "   3   "

Household 372
Zachariah Johnson   70 S.C. Farmer
Minor   " (female) 60   "
Richard   "   24   "   Laborer

Household 373
William Brown   54 Geo. Farmer
Mournen   "   57   "
Gracey   "   26   "
James   "   24   "   Laborer
Jessee   "   21   "   "
Sousan   "   18   "
Mark   "   17   "   "
Sarah   "   15   "
Leethia   "   13   "
Mary   "   11   "

Household 374
Samuel Bentley   45 Tenn. Farmer
Ritta   "   40   "
Joseph   "   10   "
Mary   "   8   "
Pressy   "   4 Ala.

Household 375
Cynthia Howard   43 S.C.
Lucy   "   15 Ala.
Acria   " (male)   6   "
Thomas Howard   21   "   Laborer

Household 376
Wesley Brown   46 Geo. Farmer
Charity   "   40 N.C.
Elizabeth "   19 Ala.
George   "   18   "   Laborer
Mary   "   14   "
Sarah   "   12   "
Nancy   "   9   "
Lenora   "   5   "
Alfred   "   3   "
Alexander Brown   22 Tenn. Laborer
James   "   26 Geo.   "
Nancy   "   77 Va.
Julian Nail   82   "   none

Household 377
William H. McCasshity 35 S.C. Farmer
Amanda   "   22 Ala.
John   "   7   "
Frances   "   5   "
Charity   "   3   "
William   "   2   "
Baby   " (male) 3/12 "

Household 378
N. F. Sullivan   57 Va. Shoemaker
Malicia   "   55   "
Nancy   "   14 Tenn.

Household 379
Burrell Ray   40 Tenn. Farmer
Sarah   "   40   "
John   "   17   "   Laborer
Martha   "   15   "
Thomas   "   13   "
Mary   "   11   "
Robert   "   9   "
Sarah (?) "   6 Ala.
James   "   3   "
William   "   3/12   "

Household 380
Booker Foster   55 Va. Farmer
Lucinda   "   46 S.C.
William   "   23 Ala. Laborer
Sarah   "   17   "
Mary   "   18   "
Asa   "   11   "
Martha   "   10   "
Julia   "   6   "

Household 381
Wm. A. Coggen*   25 N.C. Farmer
Cazada   "   *   18 Tenn.
Robert   "   2/12 Ala.
(*Marked married within the year.)

Household 382
Sampson Mize   30 N.C. Laborer
Sarah   "   30 S.C.
James   "   8 Miss.
Martha   "   6   "
Nancy   "   2 Ala.

Household 383
Charles Whitney   76 N.C. none
Nancy   "   69   "

Household 384
David Floyed   60 Ky. none
Rachel   "   45 Ala.
Nancy   " (twin) 13   "
Sealy   " (twin) 13   "
Hiram   "   9   "
Mary   "   7   "
Elizabeth "   5   "
Sarah   "   3   " (?)

Household 385
William Howard   23   " Laborer
Narcissus "   21 Tenn.
Malicia   "   4   "
Patrick   "   2   "

Household 386
Ephraim Jones   31 Ala. Farmer
Martha   "   30   "
Allen   "   12   "
Nancy   "   10   "
John   "   8   "
Kisiah   "   6   "
William   "   2   "
Mirsen (?) Jones   14   "   none
John M. Jones   7   "

Household 387
Jacob Jones   22 Ala. Farmer
Rebecca   "   27   "
Neil   "   10/12 Tenn.

Household 388
Leonard Parten   60 Geo. Farmer
Elizabeth "   52 S.C.
Abigal   "   17 Ala.
Edney   "   14   "
Franklin Wood   16   "   none
Joseph Brookes   3   " (mulatto)

Household 389
John W. Parten   25   " Farmer
Rachel   "   29 Tenn.
Adeline   "   15 Ala.
Elizabeth "   14   "
Columbus   "   9   "
John   "   8   "
George   "   5   "
Martha   "   4   "

Household 390   laborer
John Dobbin   45 not known/
Kissy   "   45 N.C.
Jane   "   22 Ala.
Jasper   "   17   " Laborer
James   "   16   "   "
Nancy   "   12   "
Lucy   "   10   "
Samuel   "   5   "
John   "   1   "

Household 391
Nehemiah Jones   24   " Farmer
Mary   "   28 Tenn.
Ephraim   "   3   "
Stephen   "   11/12 Ala.

Household 392
Bethel Chandler   30 N.C. Farmer
Manerva   "   28 Ala.
Lucretia   "   12   "
Matilda   "   10   "
Mary   "   8   "
continued

Household 392 continued
William Chandler   5   Ala.
John   "   3   "
Baby   " (female) 1/12 "

Household 393
Jason Howard   27   "   Farmer
Nancy   "   28   Tenn.
Stephen   "   3   Ala.
John   "   2   "
Lucy   "   7/12 "

Household 394
Rainy Baloo   48   S.C.
Rebecca   "   47   "
Mary   "   19   Ala.
Henry   "   14   "
Elizabeth"   12   "
Julia   "   11   "
Sousan   "   8   "
Margaret   "   6   "
Winneth   " (female)   1   "

Household 395
John H. Baloo   26   Ala.Farmer
Catharine "   29   "
Sarah   "   6   "
Rainy   "   4   "
Julia   "   2   "
Mulin   " (female)   1   "

Household 396
John T. Sturgant   22   "   Laborer
Ensly   " (female)   21   "
William   "   2   "

Household 397
John C. Sturgant   73   N.C. Farmer
Eliza   "   37   "
Jamima.   "   26   Ala.

Household 398
Thomas Stone   44   N.C.Farmer
Mary   "   43   "
Christopher "   21   Ala.Laborer
Louisa   "   18   "
Francis   " (female)   12   "
William   "   10   "
Mary   "   7   "
John   "   6   "
James   "   5   "
Josephine "   4   "
Thomas   "   3   "
Albert   "   6/12 "

Household 399
Green B. Shelton   23   Ala. none
Alfey   " (female)   23   "
George   "   3   "
Elizabeth "   2   "
Stephen   "   6/12 "

Household 400
Hezekiah Shelton   38   Tenn. Farmer
Mary   "   34   S.C.
Lifus   " (male)   16   Ala. Laborer
James Shelton   14   "
Stephen   "   12   "
Lucy   "   10   "
Leer   " (male)   8   "
Robert   "   6   "
Caroline"   4   "
Nehemiah"   2   "
Hezekiah"   8/12 "

Household 401
Anthony Griffin   40   S.C. Farmer
Mary   "   39   Ga.
Eliza   "   18   Ala.
Joseph   "   14   "
Rebecca   "   12   "
Bluford   "   10   "
Sarah   "   7   "
George   "   4   "
Henry   "   2   "

Household 402
James Harmin   55   S.C. Farmer
Sarah   "   49   Tenn.
Joseph   "   24   Ala. Laborer
William"   22   "   Do
Nancy   "   19   "
Mary   "   17   "
Sarah   "   15   "
Rebecca"   13   "
Lucretia"   9   "
James   "   5   "
Benjamin"   2   "
James White   18   "   Laborer

Household 403
Edwin Daily   50   Va. Cabinet/
Elizabeth "   46   S.C.   maker
Sarah   "   16   Ala.
Sousianah "   12   do
Joseph Daily   20   Illinois, apprentice

Household 404
William D. Caphity (?) 50   S.C. Farmer
Nancy   "   43   "
John   "   18   Ala. Laborer
continued

Household 404 continued
Elizabeth	"	21	Ala.
James	"	16	" Laborer
Starns	" (male)	13	"
Ditous	" (male)	11	"
Harison	"	9	"
Caroline	"	7	"
Mary	"	2	"
Thomas	"	23	" Laborer
Greene	"	26	" "

Household 405
James Wood		72	N.C. Farmer
Martha	"	66	Geo.
Mary	"	23	Ala.
Solomon	"	40	Tenn. Laborer
Nancy	"	39	"
Mary	"	18	"
James	"	16	" "
John	"	13	"
William	"	10	"
Wesley	"	4	"
Ellender	"	3	"

Household 406
Hiram Foust		38	N.C. Farmer
Jane	"	35	Tenn.
Sarah	"	16	"
Mary	"	15	"
Nancy	"	14	"
Newton	"	12	"
George	"	10	"
John	"	8	"
Canzoda	" (female)	5	"
Harrison	"	2	"

Household 407
Joseph Armor		50	Farmer not known/
Lucinda	"	47	Tenn.
Ilsey	"*	17	Ala.
Franklin	"	15	" Laborer
Manon (?)	" (male)	14	"
Nathan	"	13	"
William	"	11	"
Eliza	"	8	"
Mary	"	6	"
Lewis	"	3	"

(*age appears to be 77, but could be 17, which is believed to be correct.)

Household 408
Margaret Anderson	60	unknown
Turnice " (female)	30	Tenn.
John "	10	Ala.
Martha Gilbert	20	Tenn.

Household 409
Joseph Davis	31	Tenn. Laborer
Catharine "	24	"

Household 410
Hosey Baloo		53	S.C. Hatter
Sarah	"	51	"
Monen	" (female)	18	"
William	"	17	Ala. Laborer
Sarah	"	15	"
Calfernia	"	13	"
Isaac Cross White		12	unknown

Household 411
John Davis		45	Tenn. Farmer
Margaret	"	47	"
William	"	12	"
Joseph	"	9	"
Martha	"	8	"
Mary	"	7	"
Samuel	"	4	Ala.
Nancy	"	3	"
Julia	"	3/12	"

Household 412
Larkin Lamour		43	Ky. Farmer
Millie	"	41	Tenn.
Mary	"	22	Ala.
Louisa	"	19	Tenn.
William	"	17	" Laborer
John	"	15	" "
Larkin	"	13	"
Malinda	"	11	"

Household 413
Rody Acres		57	Va.
James	"	24	Ala. Laborer
John	"	22	" "
Franklin	"	17	" "
Nancy	"	19	"
Azel	" (male)	14	"

Household 414
Jessee Prat		60	Va. Farmer
Kessy	"	53	N.C.
Sousan	"	26	Ala.
Fanny	"	22	"
Rebecca	"	19	"
James	"	18	" Laborer
Franklin	"	14	" "
Martha	"	14	"

Household 415
William M. Prat		30	" Farmer
Matilda	"	26	"
Rebecca	"	5	"
Elizabeth	"	3	"
James	"	6/12	"

Household 416
Caroline Porter	40	Tenn.
Malicia Linder	30	Ala.
Elvria " (idiotic)	22	"

Household 417
Samuel Landmon	38	Ala. Farmer
Mariah "	33	"
Lavinah "	11	"
Francis "	9	"
Samuel "	4	"
Elvira "	2	"
Davis Miles- laborer	23	unknown

Household 418
| Robert Smith (black) | 67 | N.C. |

Household 419
Richard Boyce	39	N.C. Farmer
Nancy "	36	Va.
Martha "	14	Ala.
William "	12	"
Eliza "	10	"
Sylva "	7	"
James "	5	"
Leroy "	1	"
Mills Boyce	80	N.C. None

Household 420
William Irvine	73	S.C. Wheel/right
Delilah "	69	"
Robert Ellam	10	Tenn.

Household 421
Thomas York	23	Ala. Laborer
Ruthey "	20	Tenn.
Houston "	9	Ala.
Catharine Harris	18	"
Baby " (female)	7/12	"

Household 422
Wilborn Wilson	24	Tenn. Laborer
Lucinda "	20	"
Alexander "	6	Ala.
John "	4	"
Nancy "	1/12	"

Household 423
William H. Shelton	28	Ala. Laborer
Darkis "	26	"
William "	13	"
Elizabeth "	11	"
Sarah "	9	"
Lifus "	7	"
Nancy "	4	"
Sarah "	2	"
John Holt	13	"

Household 424
Feildon Literal	51	Ky. Farmer
Louisa "	37	Tenn.
John "	21	Ala. Laborer
continued		

Household 424 continued
Joseph Literal	14	Ala.
Ailsey "	13	"
Martha "	8	"
Sarah "	6	"
Amanda "	4	"
Hannah "	2	"
Elisha "	5/12	"

Household 425
Richard Varnal	53	Tenn. Farmer
Artie "	48	S.C.
William "	21	Tenn. Laborer
Lydia "	16	"
Sarah "	14	"
Kissie "	12	"
Sousan "	10	"
Permelia "	6	Tenn.
Furman "	3	Ala.

Household 426
| Mary Fowler | 70 | S.C. |
| Sarah " | 28 | " |

Household 427
John Varnal	22	Tenn. Farmer
Elizabeth "	20	"
William "	1	Ala.

Household 428
James Cursey	48	Va. Carpenter
Hannah "	43	S.C. teacher
Mirum " (female)	19	Ala. School/
Levisa "	15	"
Angeron " (twin)	12	" (female)
Winford " (twin)	12	" (male)
Winfield "	10	"
Jefferson "	8	"
Lemuel "	6	"
Clinton "	5	"

Household 429
George W. Standeford	31	Tenn. Laborer
Mary "	25	Ala.
Elizabeth "	7	"
Sarah "	3	"

Household 430
Moses Estep	66	N.C. Farmer
Eliza "	66	"
Debby "	25	"
Solomon "	15	Ala. Laborer
(Also refer to a note about the Eastep family made a few pages earlier.)

Household 431
John Wilson	30	Tenn. Farmer
Jane "	28	Ala.
continued		

C-107

Household 431 continued		
Herell Wilson	10	Ala.
Charles "	8	"
Sarah "	6	"
Solomon "	4	"
Martha "	2/12	"

Household 432
William Wilson	24	Tenn. Laborer
Gracie "	21	Ala.
Nancy "	2	"
John "	1	"
Millie "	4/12	"
Martha Ellemn	10	"

Household 433
Wilborn Wilson	27	Tenn. Laborer
Lucinda "	28	Ala.
Alexander "	6	"
John "	4	"
Nancy "	1/12	"

Household 434
Nancy Wilson	65	N.C.
Rachel "	21	Ala.
Hiram "	17	" "

Household 435
William Patton	40	Ky. Do
Nancy "	32	N.C.
Moses "	12	Ala.
William "	10	"
Rachel "	8	"
David "	6	"
Jane "	4	"
Debby "	2	"

Household 436
John Anderson	40	Tenn. Farmer
Elizabeth "	30	"
Mary "	18	"

Household 437
Elizabeth Mize	67	N.C.
Martha "	22	Tenn.
Isam "	19	" Laborer

Household 438
Millage Romine	25	Ala. Farmer
Martha "	25	"
Thomas "	6	"
Elizabeth"	4	"
Jessee "	2	"

Household 439
William B. Johnson	21	Ala. Farmer
Sevillea "	34	Tenn.
John Wilson	14	Ala.
Nancy "	12	"
Milly "	11	"
Mary "	9	"
Sarah "	6	"
Rebecca "	5	"
Martha "	3	"

Household 440
Elizabeth Luney	30	Tenn.
William "	14	Ala.
Rebecca "	12	"
Mary "	21	"

Household 441
Boney Donaldson	30	Tenn. Blksmith
Nancy "	20	Ala.
Dozly " (male)	1	"
Mary Dement	60	unknown

Household 442
Blaney W. Wade	27	N.C. Laborer
Mary "	24	Ala.
Calfernia "	4	"
William "	1	"

Household 443
Thomas Standford	62	S.C. Farmer
Charlotte "	50	N.C.
Wesley "	34	Tenn. Laborer
James "	26	" Do
Caroline "	22	Ala.
Joseph "	20	" Laborer
Thomas "	16	" "
Pinkney "	14	"
Lucinda Mize	28	"

Household 444
James H. Linly	25	Ala. Farmer
Lucinda "	25	Tenn.
Malinda "	8	Ala.
Tarthie " (female)	5	"
John "	3	"
James "	6/12	"

Household 445
James Ellum	45	Tenn. Laborer
Elizabeth "	45	Ala.
Virginia "	14	"
Albert "	8	"
Langoda " (female)	7	"
George "	3	"
Margaret "	1	"

Household 446
William Mize		37	Ala.	Laborer
Ruthy	"	44	N.C.	
James	"	14	Ala.	
Elizabeth	"	12	"	
William	" (twin)	10	"	
Henry	" (twin)	10	"	
Margaret	"	8	"	
Isaac	"	6	"	
Nancy	"	4	"	
Sarah	"	2/12	"	

Household 447
John Hughes	26	S.C.	Laborer
Catharine "	23	Ala.	
Thomas "	10/12	"	
Martha House	61	Va.	
Nancy A. Irvine	5	Ala.	

Household 448
John Estep	21	"	Farmer
Sarah "	19	"	
Winney "	6/12	"	

Household 449
Abram Coal	60	N.C.	Farmer
Jemimah "	45	"	
James "	19	Ala.	Laborer
Mary "	15	"	
Ollive "	13	"	
Easter "	10	"	
Solomon "	7	"	
John Prix	41	Geo.	Laborer

Household 451
John Owens	67	Va.	Laborer
Elizabeth "	50	N.C.	
Eliza "	30	Tenn.	

Household 450
| Philip Longe | 55 | N.C. | Do |
| Mary " | 51 | " | |

Household 452
Robert Owens	38	N.C.	Laborer
Rebecca "	29	Ala.	
Eliza "	11	"	
John "	9	"	
Sarah "	7	"	
Frances "	5	Ala.	
Mary "	2	"	
Samuel "	8/12	"	

Household 453
John Johnson	27	Tenn.	Laborer
Jane "	30	Ala.	
Joseph "	8	"	
Lucy "	6	"	
Mary "	2	"	

Household 454
Malinda Johnson	50	Penn.	
John "	29	Tenn.	Laborer
Milanda "	14	Ala.	

Household 455
Nancy Kendrick	35	Ky.	
William "	13	Geo.	
James "	10	"	
Thomas "	8	"	
Rebecca "	6	"	

Household 456
| Alexander Patton | 45 | Ky. | Laborer |
| Elizabeth " | 40 | " | |

Household 457
| Rachel Yearwood | 60 | N.C. | |
| Thomas " | 22 | Ala. | Laborer |

Household 458
| George Pike | 75 | unknown, none |

Household 459
Samuel Porter (black)		70	N.C.	Farmer
Milinda " (mulatto)		40	Tenn.	
Joseph " (black)		18	Ala.	None
Robert "	"	16	"	"
Louisa "	"	14	"	
Elizabeth "	"	12	"	
Pleasant "	"	9	"	
Eli "	"	7	"	
Provia "	"	2	" (female)	

Household 460
David Dement	27	Ala.	Laborer
Frances "	26	"	
James "	9	"	
Laurel "	7	"	
John "	5	"	
Benjamin "	4	"	

Household 461
| Rachel Coal | 60 | Va. | |
| Rody " | ?? | Ala. | |

Household 462
Robert H. Dement	34	Tenn.	Farmer
Benjamin "	24	Ala.	Laborer
Rebecca "	25	"	
Francis Dement (female)	69	N.C.	

Household 463
John Medlock	39	unknown/laborer
Sousianah "	16	N.C.
Mary Morgan	60	unknown

C-109

Household 464
John Stamps	41	Geo.	Carpenter
Armanda "	31	Tenn.	
Mary "	12	Ala.	
Elizabeth "	10	"	
Caroline "	8	"	
Catharine "	7	"	
Mary "	5	"	
William Gates	30	unknown, laborer	
Baby " (male)	1	Ala.	

Household 465
Washington A. Gilbert	33	N.C.	Merchant
Sarah "	27	Ala.	
James "	6	"	
Albert "	4	"	
Adsin (male) "	11/12	"	
Benjamin Bullman	25	"	Carpenter
James Bullman	22	"	"

Household 466
| Thomas Dement | 26 | " | Laborer |
| Rachel " | 22 | " | |

Household 467
John Y. Shoemaker	37	"	Farmer
Rebecca "	33	"	
Martha "	13	"	
Mary "	8	"	
John "	4	"	

Household 468
Mary Shoemaker	51	Tenn.	
Angeline "	21	Ala.	
John "	14	"	
Richard "	12	"	
Sousan "	10	"	
John Campbell	60	Va.	None

Household 469
| James Shoemaker | 23 | Ala. | Farmer |
| Sousiannah " | 20 | " | |

Household 470
James Lambert	39	"	none
Sarah "	35	"	
Joel "	12	"	
John "	10	"	
Mary "	4	"	
Josephine "	1	"	

Household 471
| Prince Willis (black) | 60 | unknown, farmer |
| Martha " (Mulatto) | 40 | " |

Household 472
William Brooks	65	N.C.	Farmer
Mary "	40	Tenn.	
John "	17	Ala.	Laborer
Andrew "	14	"	
Henry "	12	"	
Margaret "	11	"	
Amanda "	4	"	

Household 473
James Romine	23	Ala.	teacher School/
Ann "	22		
James "	8/12	"	

Household 474
Thomas Homes	48	S.C.	Farmer
Sousiannah "	47	N.C.	
Thomas "	18	Ala.	Laborer
Delilah "	14	"	
Tillie "	12	"	
Richard "	7	"	
Harriet "	4	"	

Household 475
Stanmore Goodman	34	S.C.	Plasterer
Parthenia "	33	N.C.	
Sarah "	11	Ala.	
Sousan "	9	"	
Mary "	6	"	
William "	4	"	
Eliza "	11/12	"	

Household 476
John Smith	30	S.C.	Farmer
Cynthia "	25	Ala.	
Peter "	8	"	
Sarah "	6	"	
John "	1	"	

Household 477
Peter Romine*	50	Tenn.	Farmer
Sarah "	49	N.C.	
Zachariah "	20	Ala.	Laborer
Peter "	15	"	"
Sarah "	12	"	
Lucy "	9	"	
Aveline "	7	"	
William Romine	27	"	Farmer
Matelatha "	4	"	
George "	1	"	

*Peter Romine, born ca 1795-96 at Sevier Co. Tenn., died 4 July 1881 near Rogersville. Married 27 Aug. 1818 in Limestone Co. to Sarah Rose, born 1800, died 4 Nov. 1896. Peter Romine was War of 1812 soldier and received pension for his services. (From Peter Romine information compiled by Seymour T. Rose, San Jose, California.

Household 478
Thomas McDonald	25	N.C.	Laborer
Mary "	22	Ala.	
John "	1	"	

Household 479
Andrew J. Romine*	30	Ala.	Farmer
Mary "	25	"	
Sarah "	7	"	
Mary "	5	"	
California "	2	"	
Angeline Rickard	21	"	

Household 480
William Romine*	53	Tenn.	Blacksmith
Mary "	49	Geo.	
Matilda "	24	Ala.	
Eli "	20	"	Student
Mary "	19	"	
Martha "	16	"	
William "	14	"	
James "	12	"	
Bethel "	10	"	
Asenith "	6	"	

Household 481
John L. Romine	21	"	Farmer
Margaret "	21	S.C.	
Mary "	7/12	Ala.	
Margaret Booa	53	S.C.	
Sarah "	22	"	

Household 482
Samuel McMeen	27	Ala.	Farmer
Catharine "	24	S.C.	
John "	6	Ala.	
Martha "	4	"	
Charity "	2	"	

Household 483
Thomas Estep	35	N.C. Farmer
Martha "	38	Tenn.
William "	12	Ala.
James "	10	"
Elizabeth "	9	"
Rachel "	7	"
Martha "	6	"
Margaret "	5	"
Mary "	3	"
Louisa "	1	"

Household 484
Samuel Flanagan	56	Var.	Farmer
J.(?) Ann "	43	Tenn.	
James "	29	Va.	Farmer
Margaret "	15	Ala.	
Nancy "	12	"	
John "	11	"	
Martha "	8	"	

*Andrew Jackson Romine, son of Peter, born 15 Oct. 1820, died 14 March 1912; married 16 Feb. 1841 Maryann Eveline ____(Jones?), born 29 Feb. 1824. They were the parents of 1. Sarah Rebecca (b. 31 July 1843); 2. Maryann Angeline (b. 21 March 1846, died 11 Oct. 1900); 3. Columbia California (b. 21 Sept. 1848); 4. Alfred Huston (b. 9 July 1851, died 15 May 1871); 5. James McAlister (b. 15 March 1854); 6. Roland Rodway (b. 2 Sec. 1856, died 11 May 1900); 7. Rite Rise (b. 27 Apr. 1860); 8. Rose Cherokee (b. 27 Feb. 1863, died 18 Nov. 1863); 9. Frances Eveline (b. 13 Oct.1865, died 2 March 1892); 10. Marion Webster (b. 12 Dec. 1869, died 2 Feb. 1897.)

*William Romine "was one of the youngest sons of Layton Romine and his first wife... when 16 he came to live with his older brothers Sam and Peter in North Ala. He herded cattle for Sam for awhile in Cherokee Co..." (quoting from W. B. Romine manuscript.)

The W. B. Romine manuscript also states that Peter Romine (Household 477, page C-109) is believed to be son of Layton Romine and his first wife, Miss Canterbury, and that their children were: James, Peter, Sam, William, Susan, Molly, and Mary. By his second marriage Layton Romine was the father of Henry, Jane, John, George, Thomas, Raleigh, David, Abel, Tabitha, Rebecca, Betty, Job, Riley, and Jasper.

Cynthia Romine, daughter of Peter Romine, married about 1831 to John Smith. Their listing will be found Household 476, page C-109.

James Wood Romine (Household 473, page C-109) was son of Peter Romine. He married Permelia Ann____. Their children were: James Henry, William, Andrew F., Susan F., Julia A., Albert R., Valzora, and Melissa, and possibly others. (From Peter Romine information compiled by Seymour T. Rose, San Jose, California.)

Household 485
James Ross*   45   unknown, laborer
Martha   "   20   Ala.
Nancy   "   17   "
Benet   "   13   "
Zachariah"   12   "
Samuel   "   10   "

Household 486
A. A. Cahoun   33   Tenn. Tanner
Rebecca   "   28   S.C.
Mary   "   9   Ala.
Easter   "   7   "
John   "   6   "
Charles   "   5   Tenn.
Washington"   3   "
Colleselia"   8/12 Ala. (female)

Household 487
Archibal Baget   35   unknown Farmer
Lelia   "   35   Ala.
George   "   13   "   idiotic
Ann   "   10   "
Caroline "   8   "
Columbus "   6   "
Albert   "   1   "

Household 488
J. C. Greer   45   N.C. Laborer
Ollive   "   53   "
David   "   11   Tenn.
Angeline"   13   "
Ann   "   9   "
Joshua   "   6   "

Household 489
Charles Booa   31   S.C. Farmer
Elizabeth "   27   Ala.
Margaret   "   7   "
Mary   "   5   "
Sarah   "   4   "
Martha   "   1   "

Household 490
P. D. Furkinson   48   Va. Miller
Lucy   "   45   "
Elizabeth "   19   "
Parthenia "   17   Tenn.
Lucinda   "   15   "
William   "   12   "
Catharine "   10   "
Lafayette "   8   "
Mary   "   6   "
James   "   3   "

Household 491
G. S. Chandler   35   Geo. Farmer
Sarah   "   33   "
Rody   "   15   Ala.
William "   12   "
Elizabeth"   10   "
James   "   7   "
Bethel   "   3   "

Household 492
Butler Brown   43   N.C. Carpenter
Mary   "   34   Tenn.
George "   16   "   Laborer
Manerva "   14   Ala.
Mary   "   9   "
Lucy   "   6   "
Jane   "   1   "

Household 493
William L. Olliver   39   Va. School/teacher
Eliza   "   27   Ala.
Julia   "   9   "
Sarah   "   5   "

Household 494
Hugh Benford   60   N.C. Farmer
William "   23   Ala.   "
John   "   12   "
Thomas   "   10   "
Ann Benford   18   Va.
Martha   "   3/12 Ala.

Household 495
Charles Bedingfield 41   Tenn. Farmer
Francis (female) "   41   N.C.
William   " 15   Ala. Student
Stephen   " 13   "
James   " 10   "
John   "   8   "
Andrew   "   2   "
Mary   " 2/12   "

Household 496
James Bedingfield   53   S.C. Farmer
Hannah   "   44   N.C.
Elizabeth"   13   Ala.

Household 497
Charles Bedingfield 30   Ala. Farmer
Cynthia   "   23   "
James   "   2   "
Charles   "   9/12   "
Charles T. Coal   22   "   Laborer

---

*This surname could possibly be Rose, instead of Ross, even though it appeared to be Ross. Men by the names of Bennett Rose and Zachariah Rose were known to have settled in this vicinity, and as the name Bennett and Zachariah appear in this household, it is possible that the surname is correctly Rose.

Household 498
Lewis H. Lanier	30	Ala.	Farmer
Willimina	"	21	"
William	"	3	"
Edrom (male)	"	10/12	"
Ethela Canon		50	Va. (female)

Household 499
James Haulbert	43	N.C.	Farmer
Matilda	"	36	Tenn.
Mary	"	14	Ala.
Martha	"	8	"
William	"	6	"

Household 500
Elizabeth Burrow	60	Geo.
Mary McCoriston	13	Ala.
James	"	7	"

Household 501
Giles Love	70	N.C.	(female)
John	"	30	Ala.	Con.

Household 502
Nancy Standeford	26	Ala.
Millie	"	10	"
John	"	2	"

Household 503
Alexander H. Durey	38	Ky.	Laborer
Martha	"	31	Ala.
Jaremia (female)	"	12	"
Angeline	"	10	"
Ann	"	8	"
Colicita	"	5	" (female)

Household 504
Benjamin Spigall	74	Va.	Shoe & Boot/ maker
Nancy	"	50	Ky.
Elliom	" (male)	29	Tenn. Laborer
Sarah	"	15	"

Household 505
Kelly G. Spigall	34	Tenn.	Shoe & Boot maker
Elizabeth	"	36	"
George	"	12	Ala.
John	"	9	"
James	"	7	"
Palena	"	4	"
Ediom	"	1	" (female)

Household 506
Briggs McLemour	47	Tenn.	Farmer
Mary	"	38	Tenn.
Elizabeth	"	19	"
McLin	"	14	Ala.
Richard	"	12	"
continued			

Household 506 continued
Ann McLemour	11	Ala.
Burrell	"	8	"
Martha	"	6	"
James	"	4	"
John	"	1	"

Household 507
John Chandler	60	Geo.	Farmer
Roda	"	55	"
Mary	"	23	Ala.
Matin	"	20	" Laborer
Lucinda	"	14	"
Elizabeth Coat (black)	10	"

Household 508
B. W. Knight*	26	Tenn. Farmer
Prudence	"	20	"
Robert	"	10/12	Ala.
Thomas Right	16	Tenn. None

Household 509
Joseph Weaver	40	Tenn. Farmer
Isabella	"	35	"
Mary	"	13	Ala.
Thomas	"	11	"
Martha	"	9	"
Josephine	"	3	"
Barnet	"	5/12	"
Thomas Lanier	80	N.C. none
Martin Nelson	23	Ala. Student
Ann Coat (black)	12	"
Isabella Coat (black)	6	"

Household 510
James Foster	54	Illinois /	Farmer
Jane	"	45	S.C.
Harriet	"	19	Ala.
William	"	18	" Laborer
Elizabeth	"	16	"
George	"	13	"
Balus	"	11	"
Lucinda	"	10	"
Ann	"	8	"
Richard	"	8/12	"

Household 511
John Cooper	40	Tenn.	Mill/ wright
Matilda	"	25	Geo.
Mary	"	7	Ala.
Samuel	"	5	"
Roda	"	3	"
Elizabeth	"	2/12	"
Jacob Pricket	30	Geo. none
Margaret Coat (black)	10	Tenn.

*Bolivar W. Knight, son of Carlisle and Almira Shaw Knight. He married Prudence Ann Wells, granddaughter of Thomas and Mary Knight Coffee. In Mexican War.

Household 512
Robert McLemour		55	Ohio	Farmer
Ruthea	"	33	Ala.	
Mary	"	18	"	
Ellender	"	16	"	
Joseph	"	14	"	
Benjamin	"	13	"	
Milly	"	11	"	
Souseannah	"	9	"	
Lafayette	"	7	"	
Nancy	"	2	"	

Household 513
Jane Spenser		55	unknown	
Jane Overby		25	Ala.	
Sevicoa " (female)		4	"	
Charles Maples		20	"	none idiotic

Household 514
___bey Butler (male)	30	N.C.	none
Sarah Bryant	25	Ala.	
Lathey "	11	"	(female)
James "	8	"	
Mary "	5	"	

Household 515
Terry Bradley	62	N.C.	doctor
Lydia "	27	Ala.	
Sarah "	9	"	
Lafayette"	7	"	
Mary "	6	"	
Caledonia"	5	"	
Senecia " (female)	1	"	

Household 516
Hannah Hardy	32	Tenn.	
Jane "	17	Ala.	
Joseph "	16	"	none
Jackson "	12	"	
Caroline"	9	"	
Amanda "	7	"	
Eliza "	5	"	
George "	10/12	"	

Household 517
William Graham	27	Tenn.	Miller
Mary "	19	"	
Catharine"	6	"	
Ann "	5	"	
William "	3	"	
Baby " (male)	1	Ala.	
Rebecca Putet	45	Tenn.	
Caroline "	16	"	

Household 518
William Goad	36	Tenn.
Martha "	24	Ala.
Mary "	14	"
continued

C-113

Household 518 continued
Rebecca Goad		12	Ala.	
Elizabeth	"	10	"	
Martha	"	9	"	
James	"	8	"	
Sarah	"	6	"	
Francis	" (female)	4	"	
Charles	"	2	"	
Richard Luckey		15	"	none

Household 519
Rebecca York		53	Tenn.	
Jessee	"	18	Ala.	Laborer
Joseph	"	16	"	"
Elizabeth Stamper		12	"	
Sarah Johnson		11	"	

Household 520
Gabriel Davis		44	S.C.	Laborer
Mary	"	42	Tenn.	
John	"	18	Ala.	Laborer
Sousan	"	17	"	
Mary	"	15	"	
Caroline	"	10	"	
Eliza	"	6	"	
Thomas	"	3	"	
William Davis		22	"	Laborer

Household 521
Burrell McLemour		80	Va.	Farmer
Nancy	"	58	"	
John	"	28	Ala.	Laborer
David	"	21	"	"
James	"	25	"	"
Martha	"	29	"	
Ann	"	18	"	

Household 522
Henry Marks		27	France	Laborer
Margaret	"	32	Tenn.	
Levi	"	1	Ala.	

Household 523
Thomas Oldham		47	Tenn.	Laborer
Sarah	"	45	"	
Ruthey	"	25	Ala.	
Elizabeth	"	19	"	
Fanthey	" (female)	17	"	
George	"	14	"	
Francis	"	13	"	
John	"	11	Ala.	
Thomas	"	7	"	
Mary	"	5	"	
Joseph Armstrong		24	"	Laborer

C-114

Household 524
William Smith		47	Va.	Laborer
Elizabeth	"	45	"	
John	"	19	Ala.	"
Austin	"	17	"	"
Sarah	"	15	"	
Lucy	"	11	"	
William	"	9	"	
Mary	"	7	"	
Julia	"	2	"	

Household 525
William Fuqua		31	Va.	Farmer
Sousa Ann	"	22	"	
Louisa	"	4	Ala.	
Sarah	"	2	"	
Archibald	"	3/12	"	
David Snoddey		25	"	Overseer

Household 526
John Fuqua		47	Va.	Farmer
Julia	"	32	"	
Ingram	"	14	Ala.	
Mary	"	12	"	
Sarah	"	8	"	
Georgia	"	6	"	
John	"	4	"	
Benjamin	"	1	"	
Thomas Snoddey		24	"	Overseer
Sarah	"	17	"	

Household 527
Johathan Cunningham*		45	S.C.	Farmer
Ollive	"	35	Tenn.	
James	"	10	Ala.	
Johnathan	"	8	"	
John H. Luster		10	"	
Laura	"	8	"	

Household 528
William J. Cunningham			Ala.

Household 519
William S. Stamps		21	"	Farmer
Martha	"	23	"	

Household 530
John West		38	Geo.	Overseer
Elizabeth	"	32	Tenn.	
Catharine	"	10	Ala.	
John	"	9	"	
Nancy	"	7	Ala.	
Mary	"	5	"	
James	"	3	"	
Benjamin	"	1	"	

Household 531
Samuel Howard		47	Geo.	Laborer
Jane	"	47	Ky.	
Robert	"	15	Ala.	"

Household 532
Gray L. Peirce		45	Geo.	"
Nancy	"	40	Tenn.	
Mary	"	13	"	
Thomas	"	10	"	
Franklin	"	9	"	
Nancy	"	8	"	
Washington	"	7	"	
Eliza	"	4	"	
Josephine	"	2	"	

Household 533
Jessee Pierce		24	"	Laborer
Elizabeth	"	23	"	
Nancy	"	2	Miss.	

Household 534
Sterling Nance		42	Tenn.	Farmer
Eliza	"	39	S.C.	
John	"	17	Ala.	Laborer
Elizabeth	"	16	"	
James	"	14	"	
Sterling	"	12	"	
William	"	10	"	
Mary	"	6	"	
Robert Porter		22	S.C.	Overseer
William Scot (black)		35	"	Laborer

Household 535
Gray Dun		58	N.C.	Farmer
Lydia	"	55	"	
Luther	"	21	"	Laborer
Van	"	18	"	"
Poindexter	"	16	"	"

Household 536
Nancy Haraway		60	Va.	
Robert	"	31	Tenn.	Farmer
Senonah Nance (female)		20	Ala.	
Samuel	"	1	"	

Household 537
D. J. Canon		30	Ala.	Farmer
Elizabeth	"	29	"	
Ann	"	4	"	
James	"	2	"	
Baby	" (male)	7/12	"	

*Cunningham Plantation Home located near Center Star Community. A Jonathan McDavid Cunningham married Susannah Polk Taylor after the Civil War. He had served in Company I, 27th Alabama Infantry regiment. (Historic Muscle Shoals, page 58.)

Household 538
Allen Shoulder	40	Tenn.	Farmer
Tabitha "	37	"	
Mary "	10	Ala.	
Carisa " (female)	8	"	
Selia "	7	"	
William "	4	"	
Sarah "	2	"	
Mary Landmon	10	"	

Household 539
Robert Cooper	50	Tenn.	Farmer
Frances "	16	Ala.	
Sousan "	14	"	
John "	12	"	
William "	10	"	
Mary "	4	"	
Julia "	2	"	

Household 540
Thomas Davenport	40	Ireland	Carp'tr
Sarah "	38	S.C.	
Matilda " (twin)	13	Tenn.	
Martha " (twin)	13	"	
Edward "	9	Ala.	
James "	6	"	
Grey "	4	"	
Levi "	2	"	
Harriet "	3/12	"	

Household 541
Abner Barnet	38	Tenn.	Farmer
Sousanah "	24	Ala.	
Mary "	8	"	
Sarah "	6	"	
Eliza "	4	"	
Baby " (female)	11/12	"	
Jasper Ducust	27	Tenn.	Laborer

Household 542
T. J. Gassaway	30	S.C.	Farmer
Elizabeth "	23	Tenn.	

Household 543
J. H. Creamer	31	Geo.	Laborer
Mary "	30	"	
Mary "	9	"	
Harriet " (twin)	6	Ala.	
Sarah " (twin)	6	"	
Alvey " (male)	4	"	
Lucy "	1	"	
Francis Butler (male)	50	Geo.	Laborer

Household 544
Robert Chaim	51	S.C.	Saddler
Margaret "	49	"	
Elizabeth "	20	Ala.	
Martha "	19	"	
continued			

Household 544 continued
Permelia Chaim	15	Ala.	
Bulus "	10	"	
James M. Standford	18	"	Saddler
James Coat (black)	12	unknown	

Household 545
Jacob Fifer	30	Tenn.	Keeper" "10 Alley/
Lucy "	18	Ala.	
Fanny "	8/12	"	

Household 546
George Simons	61	Va.	Farmer
Elizabeth "	51	"	
Perlina "	22	Ala.	
Sylvester " (female)	20	"	
William "	18	"	Student
Nicetter " (female)	13	"	
___dson " (female)	10	"	

Household 547
Ferdinand Sannoner*	26	Ala.	Merchant
Margaret "	24	"	
James Neely	18	"	Clerk
J. N. Beard	21	Tenn.	"

Household 548
___ B. Steardivant	31	Va.	Merchant
Sarah "	22	Ala.	
Mary "	4	"	
J. F. Tate	19	"	Clerk

Household 549
P. A. O. Hankins	40	N.C.	Merchant
Mary "	29	Ala.	
Mariah "	12	"	
Winslow "	1	"	
Simon Brooks	30	unknown	clerk

Household 550
C. W. Haraway	25	Ala.	Merchant
Margaret "	25	Tenn.	
R. M. Coffee	22	Ala.	Clerk

Household 551
Anderson P. Neely	38	"	Farmer
Eliza "	36	"	
James "	18	"	Clerk
Caroline "	14	"	
Elizabeth "	12	"	
Mary "	8	"	
Alex. (?) "	6	"	

*Ferdinand Sannoner married Margaret Bigger, 2 November 1848, by J. Harrison, Minister of the Gospel. (Lauderdale County marriage records.)

Household 552
A. W. Olliver   29   Va. Machinist
Elizabeth "   18   Ala.
William   "   1   "
Sarah Olliver   55   Va.

Household 553
Edward T. Olliver   26   Do Merchant
Martha   "   16   Ala.

Household 554
John Butler   37   Penn. Taylor
Elizabeth "   21   Tenn.
Mary   "   2   Ala.
John   "   1/12   "
Cynthia O'Brian   62   Geo.

Household 555
James Kyle   38   Ala. Doctor
Sarah   "   25   "
Elizabeth "   4   "
Albert   "   1   "
G. M. Baker   21   "   Student

Household 556
Jabez Hicks   50   Tenn. Waggon Ma.
Elizabeth "   58   N.C.
William   "   18   Tenn. Waggon M.
Thomas Hicks   90   N.C. None

Household 557
John Pool   54   Tenn. Shoe & boot
Margaret   "   56   S.C.   maker
Elizabeth"   26   Ala.
Mary   "   15   "

Household 558
William Haraway   33   Tenn. Doctor
Eliza   "   26   Ala.

Household 559
Balus C. Balin   45   Ky. School/teacher
Sarah   "   45   N.C.
Sarah Melton   5   unknown

Household 560
Thomas Brown   35   N.C. Overseer
Sarah   "   35   Ala.
John   "   18   "   Laborer
James   "   8   "
Elizabeth "   5   "
Levica   "   2   "

Household 561
P. M. Haraway   39   Va. Farmer
Caroline   "   30   Ala.
Achilis   "   8   "
Mary   "   5   "
continued

Household 561 continued
Eliza Haraway   3   Miss.
Adeline Donaldson   25   Ala.

Household 562
T. F. Patrick   44   Ky. Stage Contr.
Elvira   "   25   Ala.
Amanda   "   16   Ala.
Sarah   "   13   "
Henry   "   10   "
Margaret   "   7   "
James   "   5   "
Robert   "   3   "
William Arnet   60   S.C. None

Household 563
Joshua James   45   Tenn. Blacksmith
Easter   "   43   "
Sarah   "   18   Ala.
Harriet   "   17   "
Mary   "   16   "
Elvira   "   15   "
Isabella   "   12   "
Richard   "   8   "
Joshua   "   5   "
California "   3   "
Holden Simons   21   Tenn. Blacksmith
Samuel Ramsey   20   Ala. Student

Household 564
Hiram S. Sartin   25   Tenn. Taylor
Elizabeth "   24   Ala.
James   "   2   "
Quin Sartin (male)   13   "
Mary   "   16   "

Household 565
Balus E. Williams   25   "   Carpenter
Virginia   "   24   Tenn.
John   "   6   Ala.
James   "   1   "
F. Leemanah   66   France Cabinet-
                                  maker

Household 566
George W. Martin   42   Tenn. Carpenter
Spotwood   "   10   Ala.
Rush   "   8   "
Balus   "   5   "
Azula Curley (female) 65   Ky.

Household 567
George M. Haraway   45   Va. Laborer
Rachel   "   25   Tenn.
Durett   "   8   "
Samuel   "   4   "
William   "   2   "

C-117

Household 568			
Green D. Davis	27	Tenn.	Waggon M.
William "	6	"	
Jane "	4	"	
Henry "	2	"	

Household 569
Levi Patrick   30 Ky.   Grocer
Rebecca "   20 Ala.
George   "   2   "
Elizabeth Gates   40 Tenn.
William   "   27   "   None

Household 570
Burrell Davis   70 S.C. Farmer
Nancy   "   56 Va.
Sarah   "   26 Ala.
William   "   25   "   Shoemaker
Rebecca   "   19   "
Lucretia "   18   "
Nancy   "   16   "
George   "   14   "
Henry   "   2   "

Household 571
William P. Weathers 45 Tenn. Farmer
Mary   "   45 S.C.
Mary   "   19 Ala.
Martha   "   17   "
Rebecca   "   15   "
James   "   14   "
Samuel   "   11   "
Jessee   "   9   "
Franklin   "   7   "
Balus   "   3   "

Household 572
William Martin   25 unknown, farmer
Frances   "   22 Tenn.
John   "   2 Ala.

Household 573
Elizabeth Castleberry 60 unknown
William   "   25 Tenn. Laborer
Eliza   "   26   "

Household 574
Harrison McMeen   22   "   Laborer
Nancy   "   20   "
Sarah   "   3 Ala.
Josephus "   1   "

Household 575
Arthur Hicks   36 Tenn. Stonemason
Mary   "   30 Ala.
Nancy   "   7   "
Margaret "   6   "
Mary   "   6   "
Martha   "   4   "
Mariah   "   1   "

Household 576
Jackson Swinford   31 S.C. Laborer
Penelofia "   30 unknown
Mary   "   13 Tenn.
Jane   "   11   "
Harriet   "   9   "
John   "   6   "
Catharine "   3   "
Baby   "   3/12 Ala. (male)

Household 577
William Abet   22 Tenn. Laborer
Jane   "   24 S.C.
Nancy   "   6/12 Tenn.

Household 578
James Barnett   55 Va. Shoemaker
Mary   "   50 S.C.
James   "   24 Ala. Laborer
Job   "   22   "   Shoemaker
Keller "   17   "
Samuel "   13   "
Ellender Smith   19   "
Virginia "   2/12   "

Household 579
Jacob Couch   32 Tenn. Stagedriver
Julina "   32   "
Eliza   "   6 Ala.
John   "   4   "
James   "   3   "
Sarah   "   8   "
Baby   " (male)   2   "

Household 580
William C. Boston 37 Tenn. Farmer
Eliza   "   35 Ala.
Hugh   "   12   "
Nancy   "   11   "
Dolly   "   9   "
William   "   6   "
Morris   "   2   "
Sarah   "   2/12   "
Elizabeth Foster   25 Tenn.
Sarah   "   3 Ala.
Sousianah "   8/12   "

Household 581
Hiram Ducust   35 Tenn. None
Franky "   35 Ala.
Mariah "   1/12   "

Household 582
William Staples   62 Geo. Farmer
Nancy   "   57   "
William "   16 Ala. Student
Caroline "   19   "

Household 583
Nicholas Greer		30	Tenn.	Laborer
Nancy	"	29	Ala.	
Wiley	"	9	"	
Mary	"	6	"	
Andrew	"	2	"	

Household 584
James Newgen		46	S.C.	Farmer
Elizabeth	"	36	Tenn.	
William	"	14	Ala.	
James	"	11	"	
John	"	8	"	
Samuel	"	5	"	
Allen	"	2	"	

Household 585
Adam Weaver		50	Tenn.	Farmer
Caroline	"	41	"	
Martha	"	19	Ala.	
George	"	17	"	Laborer
Mary	"	15	"	
John	"	13	"	
Sarah	"	12	"	
James	"	10	"	
Joseph	"	8	"	
Arbella	"	6	"	
Souseannah	"	4	"	
Frances	"	1/12	"	

Household 586
William B. White		36	Ala.	Farmer
Matilda	"	23	"	
Cynthia	"	3	"	
Samuel	"	4/12	"	

Household 587
Samuel Weaver		27	Ala.	Farmer
Mary	"	25	"	
Martha	"	5	"	
Sarah	"	2	"	

Household 588
Clansey Shoulder		70	S. C.	(female)
Solomon Shoulder		22	Ala.	None
John Landmon		19	"	Laborer
Clansy	" (female)	14	"	
William	"	12	"	
Matilda	"	7/12	"	

Household 589
John S. Simpson		45	Geo.	Farmer
Kassy	"	41	Ala.	
John	"	16	Ala.	Laborer
Martha	"	14	"	
Robert	"	11	"	
Riston	"	9	"	
continued

Household 589 continued
William Simpson		7	Ala.	
George	"	4	"	
Amanda	"	2	"	
William McMurry		21	"	Student

Household 590
Sarah Ingram		61	Va.	
Benjamin	"	30	Ala.	Merchant
Joseph	"	25	"	Farmer
Benjamin J. Binford		8	"	

Household 591
Peterson Goodwin		35	Va.	Farmer
Mary	"	30	S.C.	
Sarah	" (idiotic)	11	Ala.	
William	"	10	"	
Mary	"	7	"	
Eliza	"	5	"	
John	"	2	"	

Household 592
Elizabeth W. Jackson		60	Va.	
Caroline	"	26	Ala.	
Belzora (female)	"	22	"	
Caroline Knight*		30	Tenn.	
Elizabeth	"	8	"	

Household 593
Barbary Mathers		42	N.C.	
James	"	17	Ala.	Laborer
Sarah	"	21	"	Student
Mary	"	18	"	

Household 594
Milly Tate		55	S.C.	
John	"	25	Ala.	None
Hiram	"	22	"	Overseer
Franklin	"	18	"	Clerk
Elmera	" (female)	30	"	
Caroline	"	17	"	
Virginia	"	15	"	
Amanda	"	14	"	
Frances	"	7	"	(female)
James Parks		47	Ky.	Carpenter

Household 595
Thomas Covington		35	Ala.	Farmer
Miram	"	22	"	
William	"	7	"	
Mary	"	1	"	

*Elizabeth Jackson was the daughter of Thomas Coffee. Lauderdale Co. marriages show that on 17 April 1842, Caroline C.F. Jackson married Carlisle Knight. She later married, 18 Dec. 1851, to Noble R. Ladd in Lauderdale County.

C-119

Household 596
Joseph Boyd		45	Ala. Laborer
Emily	"	35	"
Robert	"	13	"
Charles	"	10	"
James Harrison		25	Tenn. Laborer

Household 597
A. E. Jackson		34	Va. Farmer
Cynthia	"	23	Ala.
Lucy	" (twin)	6	"
Sarah	" (twin)	6	"
Catharine	"	4	"
Martha	"	2	"

Household 598
John B. White		50	N.C. Farmer
Cynthia	"	43	S.C.
Samuel	"	23	Ala. "
Benjamin	"	14	" Laborer
George	"	13	"
Andrew	"	11	"
Neely	" (male)	2	"
William Barnet		70	S.C. None

Household 599
Philemon White		25	Ala. Farmer
Adeline	"	25	"
Patrick	"	2	"

Household 600
Catherine Vaden		36	Tenn.
Mark	"	11	"
Mary Petigo		25	Illinois

Household 601
Walter West		48	S.C. Farmer
Petress	"	45	" teacher
John	"	21	Ala. School/
William	"	18	"
Margaret	"	12	"
Mary	"	10	"
Sarah	"	7	"
Petress	"	4	"

Household 602
Calvin M. Pitts		34	Ala. None
Mary	"	28	Tenn.
James	"	7	Ala.
John	"	5	"
Mary	"	2	"
Maneva Pitts		32	Ala.
Morgan	"	11	"
Adeline	"	7	"
Elizabeth	"	7/12	"

Household 603
Philemon B. White		40	Tenn. Farmer
Caledonia	"	43	Ala.
Mandana	" (female)	8	"

Household 604
Sherrod White		32	" Farmer
Jane	"	31	Tenn.
Eliza	"	12	Ala.
Nancy	"	10	"
Jane	"	8	"
Alexander	"	6	"
Larges	" (female)	4	"
David	"	2	"

Household 605
Jerome Tate		28	Ala. Laborer
Elizabeth	"	20	Tenn.
Elmira (?)	"	4	Ala.
Jessee	"	1	"

Household 606
| Alexander H. Harvey | | 23 | " Laborer |
| Elender | " | 24 | " |

Household 607
Jessee White		22	" Laborer
Mary	"	21	"
Daniel	"	11/12	"

Household 608
| Margaret White | | 58 | N.C. |
| Margaret | " | 23 | Ala. |

Household 609
Henry Webster		25	unknown, Black/smith
Elizabeth	"	22	Ala.
Mary	"	6/12	"

Household 610
Lucy Barnet		33	Ala. Farmer
Martha	"	30	"
Eliza	"	13	"
Franklin	"	11	"
Zachariah	"	9	"
James	"	7	"
Elizabeth	"	5	"
Ann	"	3	"
Baby	" (male)	1	"

Household 611
Hugh Campbell		35	Tenn. Farmer
Rody	"	20	"
James	"	6	"

Household 612
Nancy A. Harvey		53	S.C.
Elizabeth	"	20	Ala.
Robert	"	18	" Laborer
continued

Household 612 continued
George Harvey   12 Ala.
Franklin "   22 unknown none

Household 613
Sarah Linda   46 S.C.
Nancy "   21 Tenn.
William"   18 " Laborer
Matilda"   15 "
Sarah "   12 "
Elizabeth "   10 "

Household 614
William D. Murphy 35 Va. Shoemaker
Mary   "   34 Tenn.
John   "   11 Ala.
Elvy   "   9 "
Mary   "   6 "
William "   2 "

Household 615
Dewy B. White   39 Tenn. Farmer
Margaret "   40 S.C.
John   "   18 Ala. Laborer
Elizabeth "   16 "
Watts   " (male) 14 "
Benjamin "   12 "
Dury   "   10 "
Margaret "   8 "
William "   6 "

Household 616
Ephraim White   29 Tenn. Farmer
Deana   "   28 "
Miram   "   7 Ala.
Mary   "   6 "
John   "   4 "
Aaron   "   1 "

Household 617
Jackson Hills   35 Tenn. Farmer
Elizabeth "   30 "
John   "   9 Ala.
Robert   "   8 "
Mary   "   6 "
Pelina   "   4 "
Elizabeth "   3 "

Household 618
William B. Taze 35 Tenn. Farmer
Elizabeth "   13 "
Ann   "   11 "
James   "   9 "
Chainy   "(female) 7 "
William "   2 "
A. J. Kindman   25 unknown, laborer
Mary   "   7 Ala.

Household 619
James Jones   33 Ala. Farmer
Pressci "   27 N.C.
Bathany "   11 Ala.
John   "   9 "
Moses   "   8 "
Elizabeth"   6 "
Adeline "   5 "
James   "   4 "

Household 620
John Wilcoxen   52 Ky. Farmer
Lavina "   49 "
William "   24 Ala. Laborer
Isaac   "   22 "   "
Warren "   18 "   "
John   "   12 "
Lewis (?)"   9 "
Daniel "   4 "
Margaret Wilcoxin 22 "
Isaac   "   2/12 "
Hiram   "   20 "   "

Household 621
William Estice Jun. 25 Geo. Farmer
Elizabeth "   25 Ky.
Jane   "   2 Ala.
John   "   1 "

Household 622
William Mealer   25 Tenn. Laborer
Manerva "   21 "
John   "   1 Tenn.

Household 623
Bassil Putman   50 S.C. Laborer
Louisa "   30 "
Samuel "   18 Tenn. "
Sarah   "   14 "
Frances " (female) 13 "
Mary   "   9 "
Neely   " (female) 7 "
Zedie   " (male) 5 Ala.
Nancy   "   3 "

Household 624
Abigel Putman   23 S.C. Laborer
Nancy   "   22 Ala.

Household 625
Thomas Fields   52 N.C. Farmer
Catharine "   52 "
Newton   "   14 Tenn.

Household 626
Lewis G. Fields 22 "   Laborer
Margaret "   17 "

C-121

Household 627
Alexander McKey   27 Tenn. Farmer
Delilah   "   25 Ala.
Mary   "   6   "
John   "   4   "
William   "   1   "

Household 628
Eli Joiner   56 N.C. Farmer
Mary   "   52 S.C.
John   "   18 Ala. Laborer
Mary   "   14   "
Martha   "   11   "
Eliza   "   8   "

Household 629
Moses Joiner   54 N.C. Farmer
Lydia   "   44 S.C.
Mary   "   17 Ala.
Charles   "   13   "
Souseanah "   11   "
Drury   "   5   "
Thorington"   20   "   Laborer

Household 630
Cynthia Ashford   35 Tenn.
Abner   "   19 Ala. Laborer
William   "   17   "   "
Ann   "   12   "
Elizabeth "   8   "

Household 631
Milton Philips   34 Tenn. Farmer
Mariah   "   32   "
John   "   12 Ala.
Milton   "   7   "
Lucinda   "   5   "
Sarah   "   3   "
Cynthia Butler   14   "

Household 632
Gideon Wood   27 S.C. Farmer
Amanda   "   23 Tenn.
William   "   6 Ala.
Sousiannah"   4   "
Newton   "   8/12 "
Hiram M. Woods   16 Tenn. Laborer

Household 633
Robert Philips   37 Tenn. Farmer
Elizabeth "   34 Ala.
Henry   "   10   "
Mary   "   8   "
Nancy   "   6   "
Thomas   "   5   "
Mariah   "   3   "

Household 634
John Wilson   45 Tenn. Laborer
Elizabeth "   29   "
Cynthia   "   17 Ala.
Nancy   "   14   "
Edney   "   11   " (male)
Martha   "   8   "
Margaret "   6   "
Eliza   "   4   "
William   "   2   "
Levica (?)" (female) 8/12 "

Household 635
Samples Jordan   25 S.C. Laborer
Mahala   "   27 Tenn.
Tobetha   "   3 Ala.
Elizabeth"   2   "
James   "   1   "

Household 636
Archibald Hanks   50 S.C. Laborer
Martha   "   30   "
William   "   16 Tenn. "
Matilda   "   13   "
Jane   "   6 Ala.
Julia   "   5   "
John   "   1/12 "

Household 636
Stuart Wilson   38 Tenn. Farmer
California "   24 Ala.
Mary   "   11   "
William   "   9   "
John   "   7   "
Christon "   2   " (male)
Henry Cox   20   "   Laborer

Household 638
Robert Ray   45 Tenn. "
Ellender "   43 N.C.
Melvina   "   21 Ala.
Peter   "   18   "
Lucy   "   16   "
Newton   "   14   "
Melicia   " (?)   12   "
Catharine "   10   "
Hannah   "   8   "
Frances   "   2   " (female)

Household 639
James Wilson   36 Tenn. Farmer
Nancy   "   26 Ala.
Sally   "   8   "
Elizabeth"   6   "
Simpson   "   4   "
Benjamin "   2   "
Eliza   "   6/12 "

Household 640
Robert Wilson   90 N.C. None
Nancy   "   70 "

Household 641
Benet D. Todd   32 Tenn. Farmer
Sabry   "   35 "
Malinda "   10 Ala.
William "   8 Tenn.
Sousan   "   7 "
Licurgus "   5 "
Mary   "   3 "
Taletha Poteet   17 "

Household 642
Matthew Harrison   36 N.C. Laborer
Ellender "   30 "
Sarah   "   1 Ala.
Mermelia Moore   6 "

Household 643
James Estep   36 N.C. Laborer
Winney   "   32 Ala.
Solomon "   11 "
Elizabeth"   12 "
Abram   "   9 "
Josiah   "   6 "
Martha   "   5 "
Thomas   "   2 "
Austin Morris   45 unknown, none

Household 644
Mary Pitts   50 S.C.
Charlotte "   27 Ala.
Jasper   "   18 "   none
John   "   15 "   "

Household 645
Quinton King   31 N.C. Farmer
Elizabeth "   25 S.C.
George   "   8 Ala.
Sarah   "   6 "
Margaret "   4 "
Gilford   "   2 "

Household 646
Hinton King   35 N.C. Farmer
Sarahbeth "   20 "
Selfy   " (female) 1 Ala.

Household 647
Bransom Jones   55 N.C. Farmer
Delania "   45 N.C.
Elizabeth"   24 Ala.
Jessee   "   19 "   Laborer
Branson "   16 "   "
continued

Household 647 continued
Charles Jones   15 Ala. Laborer
Nancy   "   12 "
Michal   "   9 "

Household 648
Leo Jones   28 N.C. Blacksmith
Sarah   "   24 Ala.
Mary   "   3 "
William "   2 "
Jasper Quillen   19 "   Laborer

Household 649
John Crow   39 S.C. Overseer
Frances "   25 Va.
Margaret "   17 Ala.
Elizabeth"   14 "
Lucy   "   11 "
Thomas   "   7 "
Newton   "   5 "

Household 650
Walter Walton (blind) 80 Va. none
Rebecca "   75 "
Robert   "   39 "   Laborer

Household 651   Laborer
Benjamin Ray   70 unknown/
Nancy   "   55 Tenn.
Malinda "   20 "
William "   15 "   Laborer
Mintes   " (female) 13 Ala.
John   "   12 "
Elizabeth"   11 "
Stephen "   9 "
Rody   "   6 "
Nancy   "   4 "

Household 652
Daniel White   36 Ala. Farmer
E___us   " (female) 35 "
Matilda "   13 "
Mary   "   11 "
Margaret "   8 "
Drury   "   6 "
George   "   2 "

Household 653
William C. Thigpen 32 Tenn. Farmer
Mary   "   21 Ala.
Selfy   "   5 "
Sarah   "   3 "
Mary   "   3/12 "

Household 654
Samuel Call   61 S.C. Farmer
Sarah   "   60 "
Ellender"   35 "
Samuel   "   13 "

Household 655
Thomas Alexander	37	S.C.	Laborer
Elizabeth "	37	"	
Hezekiah "	14	Tenn.	
Mary "	13	"	
Rosanah "	12	"	
James "	10	"	
Tobitha "	8	"	
Randolph "	6	"	
Sarah "	4	"	
Samuel "	2	"	

Household 656
Martin Stutts	45	N.C.	Farmer
Mary "	41	Tenn.	
Nancy "	20	Ala.	
Martha "	18	"	
Sousan "	17	"	
Sarah "	15	"	
Elizabeth"	13	"	
David "	11	"	
James "	9	"	
Ann "	7	"	
Mary "	5	"	
John "	2	"	

Household 656
Charles Quillen	48	Tenn.	Saddler
Mary "	45	Ala.	
William "	20	"	Laborer
Jasper "	18	"	"
Isella "	16	"	
Timethea"	14	"	
Jack "	12	"	
Mary "	10	"	
Chesley "	8	"	

Household 658
| Horatio Pettus (palsy) | 76 | Va. | none |
| John French | 18 | Ala. | Laborer |

Household 659
William Pettus	32	Va.	Farmer
Mary "	25	Ala.	
Ann "	7	"	
Henry "	5	"	
Mary "	3	"	
Winston "	3/12	"	

*Florence Gazette, 18 July 1846: Mrs. Mary S. Pettus died on the 9th inst., at Lexington, Ala., wife of Horatio Pettus; mother of sheriff; born in Mecklenburg Co., Va., came to this county in 1819; member of Baptist Church; husband and children survive.

Household 660
Mary McClanahan	70	Ireland	
Jane "	35	Tenn.	
Catharine "	31	"	
Robert "	27	"	Cons.

Household 661
William McClanahan	43	Ky.	Farmer
Mary "	35	Ala.	
Sarah "	13	"	
Mary "	11	"	
John "	9	"	
Martha "	8	"	
Rebecca "	6	"	
William "	4	"	
James "	2/12	"	
James McClanahan	33	Tenn.	Laborer

Household 662
Elizabeth Smith	45	S.C.	
Mary "	24	Ala.	
Henry "	20	"	Laborer
William "	17	"	"
Joshua "	23	"	"

Household 663
J. G. Jones	39	Va.	Farmer
Nancy "	28	Tenn.	
Isaac "	9	"	
Rebecca"	7	"	
Lucinda"	6	Geo.	
Robert "	5	Ala.	
Nancy "	2	"	

Household 664
John Davis	25	unknown, laborer
Elizabeth"	23	Ala.
John "	1	"

Household 665
Horatio Pettus	40	Tenn.	Farmer
Sarah "	38	"	
Mary "	16	Ala.	
Nancy "	14	"	
George "	12	"	
Winston "	10	"	
Emily "	6	"	
Martha "	3	"	
John "	3/12	"	

Household 666
Ruben Brazel   45 Tenn. Farmer
continued

Household 666 continued
Catharine Brazel		34	Ala.
Tobitha	"	13	"
Sousan	"	11	"
James	"	10	"
Frances	"	6	"
Nancy	"	4	"
Andrew	"	2	"

Household 667
Manuel Moore		48	Tenn. Carp'ter
Mary	"	31	"
Sarah	"	16	Ala.
Mary	"	14	"
Robert	"	11	"
Nancy	"	9	"
Margaret	"	7	"
Martha	"	4	"
James	"	7/12	"

Household 668
Jacob Bard		52	Tenn. Laborer
Mary	"	33	Ala.
Margy	"	13	"
Thomas	"	11	"
Alfred	"	9	Miss.
George	"	6	"
Elizabeth	"	4	"
Henry	"	1	Ala.

Household 669
James Ray		54	N.C. Farmer
Nancy	"	37	unknown
Sucinda	"	17	Ala.
Dorinda	"	13	"
Mary	"	9	"
Mirium	"	7	"
Lydia	"	5	"
Isaac	"	3	"
Eliza	"	1	"
James Foster		13	"

Household 670
George W. Green		42	Tenn. School/teacher
Lavina	"	23	Ala.-Tenn.(1)
George	"	2	Ala.
Emily	"	7/12	"
Rebecca Robertson		39	Ky.
Jefferson Hughs		65	Tenn. Laborer

Household 671
Thomas Mitchell		28	Ala. Farmer
Ann	"	24	"
John	"	10	"
Sousiannah	"	6	"
Mary	"	4	"
Allen	"	1	"

Household 672
William Herrell		20	Tenn. Laborer
Ellender	"	25	"

Household 673
Alexander McDoogal		24	Ala. Laborer
Rachel	"	30	"
Nancy	"	5	"
Alexander	"	3	"

Household 674
Thomas H. Kiddy		27	Tenn. Laborer
Louisa	"	23	S.C.
William	"	2	Ala.
Thomas	"	10/12	"

Household 675
Daniel Killen		30	Ala. Farmer
Saluda	"	24	"
James	"	6	"
Thomas	"	4	"
John	"	2	"

Household 676
Asa Herrell		56	N.C. Farmer
Elizabeth	"	52	"
Hannah Pitts		21	Tenn.
James M. Stuart		14	"

Household 677
Peter Bundant		30	" Carpenter
Manerva	"	24	Ala.

Household 678
James Herrell		30	" Farmer
Sarah	"	24	Tenn.
Mary	"	1	Ala.

Household 679
William Bundant		34	Tenn. Laborer
Julia	"	30	N.C.
Louisa	"	13	Tenn.
John	"	10	"
George	"	8	"
Dallas	"	6	"
Martha	"	4	"
Jane	"	9/12	"

Household 680
B. F. Chisholm		30	Tenn. Cons.
Margaret	"	24	Ala.
Rufus	"	3	"
Joseph	"	8/12	"
John Green		22	Tenn. None
Wash Davis (mulatto)		8	"

Household 681
John Chisholm		73	Maryland Stonemason

Household 682
William Garrard   35 Ky. none
Julia   "   34 Tenn.
Alexander"   14 Ala.
John   " (twin) 12   "
America   " (twin) 12   "
Daniel   "   10   "
James   "   7   "

Household 683
Daniel McDoogal   44 N.C. Farmer
Chany   "   44 S.C.
Martha   "   19 Ala.
William   "   8 Tenn.
Harriet   "   7   "
Henry Carr   25 S.C. Stage-
                             driver

Household 684
Elizabeth Holland   88 Va.

Household 685
James Mattocks   85 S.C. none
Sarah   "   38   "
Thomas   "   18   "   "
Ann   "   15   "
Sarah   "   11   "

Household 686   driver
John Gannon   52 N.C. Stage/
Agnes   "   40   "
Jack   "   17 Ala. Laborer
Matilda   "   16   "
Lucinda   "   15   "
Thomas   "   13   "
Louisa   "   9   "
Mary   "   6   "
Nancy Maize   25 Tenn.

Household 687
Augustus McKinney   65 unknown, none
Rebecca   "   60 Tenn.

Household 688
Catharine Stuart   70 Scotland
Christine "   40 N.C.
Mary   "   30 Ala.
Agges   "   28   "
Duncan   "   35 Tenn. Overseer

Household 689
William Estice   52 S.C. Farmer
Elizabeth "   52   "
Jasper   "   27 Geo. Laborer
James   "   21 Tenn. "
Catharine "   15 Ala.
Joel   "   14   "
Martha   "   12 Ala.
John   "   10   "
William McDoogal   11   "

Household 690
Henry Grisham   26 Ala. Overseer
Narcissa   "   19   "

Household 691
Elias Myrick   30 N.C. Farmer
Elizabeth "   24 Ala.
James   "   5   "
Isaac   "   3   "
John   "   1   "

Household 692
John Myrick   26   " Laborer
Adeline   "   20   "

Household 693
H. Y. Mitchell   36 Va. Farmer
Rebecca   "   34 Ala.
John   "   15   " Laborer
William   "   10   "
Elizabeth"   8   "
Lucy   "   5   "
Sousiannah"   4   "
Willis   "   7/12 "
William Hubbard   35 unknown, none

Household 694
Catharine Richardson 73 N.C.
Willis Davis   35 Ala.

Household 695
Robert B. Allen   41 Tenn. Farmer
Melinda   "   38   "
Henry   "   17 Ala. Laborer
Bluford   "   15   "   "
Mary   "   14   "
Nancy   "   12   "
Eliza   "   10   "
Sarah   "   8   "
Emily   "   7   "
Margaret   "   4   "

Household 696
Thomas Crow   36 S.C. Farmer
Mary   "   34 Ala.
Martin   "   3   "
Patrick   "   11/12 "
Julia A. Spain   11   "

Household 697
Charity Posey   52 Geo.
Frances   " (male) 20 Tenn. Laborer
Franklin   "   17   "   "
George   "   14   "

C-126

Household 698
Ruel Garrard   38 S.C. Farmer
Sarah   "   25   "
Louisa   "   4 Ala.
Samuel   "   2   "
Edward   "   1   "

Household 699
William Jones   61 S.C. Farmer
Mary   "   54   "
Lucinda "   17 Ala.
Richard "   13   "

Household 700
John McDonald   24 N.C. Farmer
Catharine "   36 Tenn.
Martha   "   11/12 Ala.

Household 701   (gambler)
Christopher Stutts 35 N.C. None
Charlotte   "   35 Tenn.
Margaret   "   15 Ala.
John   "   13   "
James   "   9   "
William   "   7   "
Lucinda   "   5   "
Mary   "   3   "
Willis   "   1   "
Frances Beavers   18 Tenn.
Leonard Stutts   85 N.C. Stone-
                            mason

Household 702
Kenneth Stutts 33   " Farmer
Elizabeth "   34 Tenn.
Julia   "   11 Ala.
Charlotte "   8   "
Nancy   "   6   "
Leonard   "   4   "
James   "   1/12 "

Household 703
James Dannelley 34 N.C. Carp'ter
Souseannah "   44   "
William   "   18   " Laborer
John   "   16   "   "
Elizabeth "   15   "
Leonard   "   13   "
Dumos   "   12 Ala.
Henry   "   10   "
Mary   "   7   "
Sarah   "   6   "
Swain   "   4   "
Nancy   "   2   "

Household 704
Alexander Dannelly 21 N.C. Laborer
Mary   "   18 Tenn.

Household 705
Walter Dannelly 25 N.C. Con.
Lucinda "   18 Ala.

Household 706
Daniel Rowie   56 N.C. Miller
Mary   "   53 S.C.
John   "   20 Tenn. none
Elizabeth "   18   "
Sarah   "   12 Ala.

Household 707
Barbary Smith   48 unknown
Eliza   "   30 Tenn.
Francis   "   25   "
James   "   18   " Laborer
Margaret "   15   "
Henry   "   12 Ala.
William   "   10   "
Mary   "   6   "
Sousiannah"   2   "

Household 708
David Lancaster 68 N.C.
    Baptist preacher
Nancy Lancaster 65 Va.
Lucy   "   22 Ala.
Samuel "   19   "   Laborer

Household 709
James Roberts   31 Tenn. Overseer
Nancy   "   25 Ala.
Lucy   "   9   "
Martha   "   7   "
Nancy   "   5   "
Sousianah "   1   "

Household 710
John Watkins   43 Va. Farmer
Rody   "   30 Tenn.
Matilda"   11 Ala.
Joel   "   9   "
Jane   "   8   "
Thomas "   7   "
Louisa "   5   "
Selada "   3   "
Annaliza"   2   "
James Dalton   17 Tenn. Laborer

Household 711
Washington Penny 30 N.C. Laborer
Eliza   "   28 Tenn.
Frances " (male) 8 "
Houston "   6   "
Dolly   "   4 Ala.
George   "   3   "
Sarah   "   2   "
Milton   "   1/12 "
Mary E. Hicks   22 Tenn.

Household 712
Name	Age	Origin	Occupation
Jessee Smith	50	Penn.	Farmer
Arminda "	36	Tenn.	
William "	14	Ala.	
Jane "	13	"	
Benjamin "	11	"	
Jacob "	9	"	
Annaliza "	6	"	
George "	1	"	

Household 713
Name	Age	Origin	Occupation
John McCabe	38	Va.	Attorney
Elizabeth "	39	Tenn.	
Mary "	11	Ala.	
Anna "	9	"	
Richard "	6	"	
Elizabeth "	3	"	

Household 714
Name	Age	Origin	Occupation
Josiah Roberts	45	Geo.	Carp'ter
Eliza "	38	Va.	
James "	12	Ala.	
Josiah "	9	"	
Eliza "	7	"	
John "	5	"	
Sarah "	3	"	
Lewis Moore	24	"	Carpenter
Cynthia "	19	"	

Household 715
Name	Age	Origin	Occupation
Catharine Feutral	60	Va.	
Mariah McCan	41	N.C.	
William "	16	Tenn.	Laborer
John "	14	"	
Thomas "	12	"	
Martha "	10	"	
Andrew "	8	"	
Arthur "	7	"	

Household 716
Name	Age	Origin	Occupation
Joseph Step	30	S.C.	Farmer
Elizabeth "	29	Ala.	
Sarah "	10/12	"	
Moses Step	26	Geo.	Laborer

Household 717
Name	Age	Origin	Occupation
Lorenzo D. Ross	21	Tenn.	Do
Cynthia "	22	Ala.	
Robert "	6/12	"	

Household 718
Name	Age	Origin	Occupation
Irvine Ross	26	Tenn.	Shoe/maker
Nancy "	50	unknown	
Marye McElyea	22	Ky.	
James Ashley	20	"	Laborer
William "	19	Ala.	"

Household 719
Name	Age	Origin	Occupation
Johnathan Bailey*	58	Va.	Farmer
Frances "	52	N.C.	
James "	21	Ala.	None
Minirva Ray	20	"	
Margaret Wood	20	N.C.	

Household 720
Name	Age	Origin	Occupation
James N. Karsen	45	Ky.	Farmer
Elizabeth "	57	S.C.	
James N. Karsen	14	Tenn.	
Catharine Karsen	11	"	

Household 721
Name	Age	Origin	Occupation
Ebeneza Karsen	23	Tenn.	Chair/maker
Easter "	18	S.C.	
Jane Derumple	46	"	
Henry "	15	"	none
Wm. C. Feutral	24	N.C.	Chairmkr.
Calvin Karsen	20	Tenn.	none
Rebecca "	21	S.C.	

Household 722
Name	Age	Origin	Occupation
John B. Denison	77	My.	Farmer
Nancy "	70	"	

Household 723
Name	Age	Origin	Occupation
John S. Wilson	60	Va.	Farmer
Ann "	57	"	
Thomas "	22	Ala.	Ass't
John R. W. Foster	3	"	
Turner E. Foster	2	"	

Household 724
Name	Age	Origin	Occupation
Isaac Hunt	39	Ala.	Con.
Martha "	39	Va.	
Elizabeth "	19	Ala.	
William "	16	"	Laborer
Sarah "	14	"	
Nancy "	12	"	
James "	10	"	
Lucinda "	7	"	
Amanda "	5	"	
Frances " (female)	3	"	
Mary "	10/12	"	

Household 725
Name	Age	Origin	Occupation
Thomas T. Abington	38	Ky.	Farmer
Sarah "	32	Tenn.	
Mary "	13	Ala.	
Sidney "	11	"	
Louisa "	8	"	
Martha "	6	"	
Sousianah "	4	"	
Cornelius "	6/12	"	

*Florence Gazette, 18 Apr. 1861. Jonathan Bailey's estate being settled by James J. and Richard A. Bailey.

Household 726
William F. Baldridge	45	Tenn.	Tanner
Elizabeth "	35	"	
Milton "	18	"	Student
James "	15	"	Laborer
Jane "	13	"	
Virginia "	11	"	
Mary "	9	"	
John "	7	"	
William "	5	"	
Alermilla "	3	"	

Household 727
Franklin Lunn	30	S.C.	Tanner
Mary "	24	Ala.	

Household 728
Peter A. Andrew	33	My.	Founder
Isabella "	35	Tenn.	
Amanda (?) "	8	Ala.	
James "	5	"	
Sarah "	4	"	
Isabella "	2	"	
John "	2/12	"	
Johnathan Wooton	21		unknown founder

Household 729
Francis H. Jones	41	N.C.	Farmer
Antonessia "	18	Ala.	
Thomas "	2/12	"	

Household 730
Shephard Rhodes	27	S.C.	Overseer
Nancy "	23	Tenn.	
Jacob "	4	Ala.	
Columbus "	2	"	

Household 731
William Mason	39	Va.	Farmer
Thomas Mason	23	"	"

Household 732
William T. Kendrick	52	Va.	M.E.Preacher
Mary "	47	Tenn.	
James "	14	"	
Rebecca "	12	"	
Henry "	7	"	

Household 733
Matthew Wilson	67	Va.	Farmer
Harriet "	34	"	
Frances "	30	"	

Household 734
James Young	30	Va.	Overseer
Martha "	25	Ala.	
Elizabeth"	6	"	
Martha "	4	"	
continued			

Household 734 continued
Sarah Young	2	Ala.	
Baby " (female)	6/12	"	

Household 735
Priscilla Wilson	65	Va.	
Jane C. F. "	40	"	Farmer
Isaac N. Crow	33	S.C.	Overseer

Household 736
Preston Murphy*	56	Va.	Farmer
Hannah "	35	Geo.	
James " **	20	Ala.	Farmer
Ann " **	16	"	
Lavina "	16	Tenn.	

Household 737
Amos Liles	56	S.C.	Farmer
Elizabeth "	54	"	
Chainy " (male)	20	Tenn.	Laborer
Sarah "	17	"	
Stephen "	14	"	
James Liles**	23	"	Laborer
Sarah " **	18	Ala.	

Household 738
Sidney C. Posey***	47	S.C.	M.E./Preacher
Harriet "	36	Tenn.	
John "	16	Ala.	
Mary "	8	"	
Rachel "	7	"	
Andrew "	1	"	
John M. Miller	24	Tenn.	Overs'r

Household 739
James B. Price	44	Tenn.	Farmer
Frances "	37	Va.	
Isabella "	18	Ala.	
John "	16	"	Laborer
William "	13	"	
James "	11	"	
Isaac "	8	"	
Virginia "	5	"	

_____

**Marked married within the year.

*Preston Murphy is buried in Price Cemetery, off Highway 72 in Florence. His stone reads born 1795, died 1861.

***Sidney Posey, son of Jesse H. Posey; served as county judge at one time; married 14 Feb. 1833 Harriet Calista DePriest, daughter of Dr. Horatio DePriest of Maury County, Tennessee.

C-129

Household 740			
Martha Price		38	Va.
William "		21	Ala. Clerk
James "		19	" "
Nancy "		17	"
Wesley "		14	"
Francis " (female)		10	"
Martha "		7	"
Elias M. Fort		22	Tenn. Farmer
Ann "		24	Va.
Francis "		14	Tenn.
Martha "		12	"
Philex "		2	Ala.

Household 741
Robert M. Patton*	40	Va. Merchant
Jane "	35	Ala.
John "	16	" Student
William "	13	"
Mary "	10	"
Martha "	8	"
Robert "	6	"
Charles "	6/12	"
Martha Pettepool	17	"

Household 742
Washington M. Brandon**	40	unknown/ overseer
Martha "	30	Ala.
Martha "	5	"
Sis "	3	"
Baby (female) "	1	"

---

*Robert Miller Patton, born 10 July 1809, son of William Patton early settler of Huntsville, Ala. In 1829 R. M. Patton moved to Florence and married Jane Locke Brahan, daughter of Gen. John Brahan, in 1832. They made their home in Sweetwater, which still stands on Highway 72 in Florence. He was chosen governor of Alabama by constitutional convention in 1867. According to the Weakley family history, he and his wife are buried in cemetery in Huntsville.

**Washington Brandon, buried in the Florence Cemetery, was the father of Charles M. Brandon, born 1859, died 1898, for whom old Brandon School was named. His daughter Rosa, born 1852, married J. D. Hooks; daughter Mary J. Brandon married James M. Crow.

Household 743
Winston Pettus*	45	Va. Sheriff
Eveline "	36	Tenn.
Ann "	18	Ala.
Horatio "	17	" Laborer
William "	14	"
Harriet "	7	"
Martha "	5	"

Household 744
Philip Forsythe	47	Geo. Farmer
Margaret "	32	N.C.
Jane "	15	Tenn.
Elizabeth "	13	"
William "	11	"
James "	9	"
John "	7	"
Smith "	5	Tenn.
Sarah "	3	"

Household 745
David Brewer	50	N.C. Carpenter
Elizabeth "	45	Tenn.
Nancy "	17	Ala.
Mary "	15	Tenn.
Jacob "	13	"
Rebecca "	10	Ala.
James "	8	"
Joseph "	6	"
Martha "	4	"
Franklin "	3	"
Isaac "	2	"

Household 746
William P. Thorington	25	Tenn. Overseer
Sousiannah "	20	"
Baby " (female)	3/12	Ala.

Household 747
Robert McCoristin	48	Ireland
occupation: Bridge keeper		
John McCoristin	24	Ala. Farmer
Joel "	21	Ala. School- teacher
Robert "	15	" Student
Mary "	13	"
James "	6	"
Elizabeth McConston	19	Tenn.
William "	4/12	Ala.
George Miller	24	Germany
occupation: laborer		

---

*Winston Pettus married Eveline B. Letsinger in Lauderdale Co. on 8 April 1849; he was son of Mary S. and Horatio Pettus.

C-130

Household 748
John Forisythe   53 Geo. Farmer
Rebecca   "   46 Tenn.
George   "   13   "

Household 749
Benjamin Foresythe*   22 Tenn. Farmer
Mary   "   *   21 N.C.

Household 750   Preacher
Johnathan Richardson 25 Ala. M.E./
Elizabeth "   22 Tenn.
John   "   1 Ala.

Household 751
Sylvanus Terrell   30   "   Overseer
Mary   "   28   "
Mary   "   7   "
Nancy   "   5   "
Winston   "   1   "

Household 752
John J. Craig   30   "   Merchant
Mary   "   25 Tenn.
Mary   "   3 Ala.
Ellen   "   2/12 "
John Cackleman   30 Germany
   occupation: laborer

Household 753
Chales C. Lewter   42 N.C. Farmer
Emily   "   27 Va.
John   "   3 Ala.

Household 754
William Posey   30 Tenn. Overs'r
Eliza   "   24 Ala.
Elizabeth "   10   "
James   "   8   "
John   "   6   "
Golson   "   4   "
Lewis   "   11/12 "

Household 755
John Brahan   43   "   Farmer
William Cimmons   18   "   Laborer

Household 756
Thomas White   30 N.C. Overseer
Mary   "   24 Atlantic Ocean
Thomas   "   8 Ala.
James   "   5   "
Buyist   " (female) 3   "
Sarah   "   8/12 "
Monren White (female) 60 N.C.
William White   15 Ala. Laborer

*Married within the year.

Household 757
William H. Crittingtton 33 Tenn. Farmer
Octavo   "   27 Ala.
Benjamin   "   4   "
William   "   6/12 "
Albert Marks   15   "   Laborer

Household 758
George Gaten   33 S.C. Overseer
Molsey   "   34   "
Oremitta   " (female) 11   "
Charlotte "   9   "
Mary   "   7 Ala.
Spencer   "   4   "

Household 759
John Stephens   33 Tenn. None
Annie   "   35   "

Household 760
Elizabeth Caten   35 Ala.
Elva Tutt   30   "
Margaret Tutt   10   "
Baby   " (female) 6/12 "
Thomas Peton   25 Tenn. None
Randolph Estridge   35   " Ferryman

Household 761
Enoch H. Garner   40   "   Farmer
Livanda   "   28 S.C.
Catharine "   10   "
Ellen   "   7   "
Julia   "   6   "
Robert   " (twin)   1   "
Octava   " (twin)   1   "
William Lee   19 Tenn. Student
Catharine Garner   80 Penn.

Household 762
John Cain   56 S.C. Farmer
Margaret   "   44   "
Sarah   "   32   "
Jane   "   30   "
Elizabeth "   28   "
Harriet   "   17   "
Mary Calhoun   4   "
William N. Cain   20 Ala. Student
Franny   "   14   "

Household 763   man
H. J. Boman   55 Tenn. Fisher/
Sarah   "   50   "
Parilee   "   22   "
Martha   "   19   "
Sarah   "   16   "
Mary   "   14   "
Amanda   "   2 Ala.
John Bomun   25 Tenn. Laborer

C-131

Household 764
Ann Hough		45	N.C.
William	"	19	Ala. Farmer
Chapman	"	17	"
Nancy	"	14	"
John	"	11	"
Amos	"	7	"
Ann	"	4	" laborer
William Cork		35	unknown/

Household 765
Anderson H. McMurry	40	N.C. Farmer
Catharine	"	40	"
Caroline	"	9	"
Elmoia	"	8	Ala.
Andrew	"	2	"

Household 766
J. P. Mitchell	28	Tenn. Doctor
Sarah	"	24	"
Allis	"	2	"

Household 767
Jessee Denson	45	S.C. Farmer
Melvina	"	32	Ala.
Nancy	"	15	"
Sarah	"	13	"
Thomas	"	12	"
John	"	11	"
James	"	8	"
Albert	"	6	"
Richard	"	2	"
William	"	1	"

Household 768
| Fanny Williams | 35 | unknown |
| William | " | 8 | Ala. |

Household 769
Henry Musselman	60	Penn. Farmer
Catharine	" *	58	"
Kizanda	"	34	" Laborer
David	"	32	" "
Esenith	"	25	"
Martha	"	22	"

Household 770
John Warden	30	Tenn. none
Elizabeth	"	28	"
Eliza	"	7	Ala.
Hannah	"	2	"

Household 771
Joseph Hough	49	S.C. Farmer
Eliza	"	21	Ala.
John	"	20	" Student
continued

*Catherine Musselman buried in Price Cemetery, born 1793, died 1858.

Household 771 continued
Saletha Hough	17	Ala.
Joseph	"	16	" Student
Nancy	"	13	"
William	"	12	"
Hetty Hough	14	"

Household 772
Thomas Irvine	60	Penn. Laborer
Christian	"	28	"
Parthena	"	23	"
Henry	"	20	" Laborer
Thusood	"	17	"
Martha	"	8	Ala.
Mary	"	6	"
Sarah	"	3	"

Household 773
John B. Graham	38	S.C. Laborer
Martha	"	34	Ala.
Elizabeth	"	12	"
George	"	8	"
Sousan	"	6	"
Martha	"	4	"
Milandge	"	1	"

Household 774
Washington Mobbly	45	S.C. Farmer
Catharine	"	40	"
Mary	"	19	Ala.
Sarah	"	17	"
Elizabeth	"	15	"
Washington	"	13	"
Catharine	"	11	"
Adeline	"	9	"
William Twitty	6	"

Household 795
Alfred Twitty	24	S.C. Laborer
Sarah	"	20	"
Marion	"	5	Ala.
Coresa	" (female)	2	"

Household 776
Jordan Hamm	25	Ala. Farmer
Sarah	"	45	S.C.
Margaret	"	15	Ala.
William	"	13	"
Jeremiah	"	12	"
Ollive	"	10	"
Thomas	"	5	"

Household 777
Jacob Stutts	53	N.C. Gunsmith
Nancy	"	49	"
Wesley	"	23	Ala. Blcsmith
Elizabeth	"	21	"
continued

Household 777 continued
Sarah Stutts	19	Ala.	
Asa "	18	"	Laborer
John "	16	"	"
James "	12	"	
Mary "	10	"	
Nancy "	8	"	
Calvin Key	20	N.C.	Gunsmith

Household 778
Anderson Stutts*	25	"	Laborer
Frances "	19	Ala.	
Sarah "	3	"	
William "	1	"	

Household 779
James W. Lafan	40	S.C.	Carp/tr
Elizabeth "	39	"	
Prissa "	20	Ala.	
Rutha "	18	"	
William "(female.)	15	"	Laborer
James "	10	"	
Hannah "	8	"	
Matthew "	5	"	
John "	3	"	
Isaac "	3/12	"	

Household 780
John Right	21	Ala.	Farmer
Nancy "	20	"	
James "	5/12	"	

Household 781
Bethana Beavers	54	N.C.	
William Right	17	Ala.	Laborer

Household 782
Nicholas Right	56	N.C.	Farmer
Barbary "	51	"	
Mary "	18	Ala.	
Martha "	16	"	
Rebecca "	14	"	
Wesley "	12	"	
James "	9	"	

Household 783
Nicholas Right, Jr.	20	"	Laborer
Lydia "	25	"	
Carrol " (male)	8/12	"	

Household 784
William Gray	26	Tenn.	Farmer
Ann "	27	N.C.	
Rutha "	12	Ala.	
Catharine "	6	"	
Benjamin "	5	"	
James "	3	"	

Household 785
John Gray	30	Tenn.	Laborer
Bethana "	24	Ala.	
Mary "	10	"	
Eliza "	8	"	
James "	5	"	
Elizabeth "	4	"	
John "	2	"	

Household 786
John Sanders	54	Tenn.	None
Rody "	54	"	

Household 787
John McCalahan	41	Geo.	Schoolteacher
Sarah "	32	S.C.	
Eli "	12	"	
Sousannah "	10	"	
Benjamin "	8	"	
Nancy "	6	"	
William "	4	"	
Mary "	2	"	
Levica "	3/12	"	
Eliza Poteet	19	Tenn.	

Household 788
Amos McDonald	21	N.C.	Laborer
Nancy "	18	Ala.	
Amanda "	1	"	

Household 789
John Robertson	38	Tenn.	Farmer
Martha "	30	"	
Jane "	12	Ala.	
Michael "	9	"	
Newton "	7	"	
Sarah "	3	"	
Hulda "	8/12	"	

Household 790
Duncan McDoogal	72	N.C.	Farmer
Margaret "	55	"	
Daniel "	15	Ala.	Laborer

Household 791
Charles W. Thomas	30	S.C.	Farmer
Harriet "	24	"	
John "	3	Ala.	
Benjamin "	1	"	
Mary Wood	19	S.C.	

*Anderson Stutts married Frances Hull on 20 Dec. 1846 in Lauderdale County.

Household 792
William P. Holcum	47	N.C.	Carpenter
Lainy	"	47	Tenn.
Cordelia	"	16	"
Richard	"	14	"
Clementine	"	11	"
Cemerine	"	9	" (female)
A. O. P. Nelson		6	"

Household 793
Richmond Gardener	33	Va.	Farmer
Letha	"	24	Tenn.
Harrison	"	8	Ala.
Sousiannah	"	6	"
George	"	4	Tenn.
Albert	"	1	"

Household 794
Rainy White	27	S.C.	Farmer
Catherine	"	29	Tenn.
Margaret	"	7	"
William	"	5	"
Fountain	"	3	"
James (?)	"	1	"

Household 795
Calvin Garrard	28	S.C.	Farmer
Souseannah	"	31	"
Lucinda	"	8	"
Thomas	"	6	Ala.
Kessiah	"	4	"
James	"	2	"
Rebecca	"	10/12	"
Ceybourn Garrard		24	S.C. Schoolteacher

Household 796
Cymson Campbell	37	N.Y.	Blacksmith
Elizabeth	"	25	Va.
Samuel	"	6	Tenn.
William	"	2	"
Ruthey	"	1/12	Ala.

Household 797
Asa Richardson	30	N.C.	Blacksmith
Flora	"	28	Ala.
Nancy	"	8	"
Mary	"	6	"
Juda	"	3	"
Sarah	"	3/12	"
John Roberson		11	"

Household 798
Martin Harrison	30	S.C.	Farmer
Philadelphi.	"	25	Ala.
James	"	4	"

Household 799
Isam R. Leath	50	Va.	Buck Lager
Elizabeth	"	28	"
Uriah Bell		20	Tenn. Laborer

Household 800
Thomas White	40	N.C.	Gun Press Maker
Lucinda	"	29	Tenn.
Nancy	"	16	Ala.
Henry	"	13	"
William Jeanes		14	"

Household 801
Edward Feutral	28	Ala.	Farmer
Eliza	"	23	Tenn.
Catharine	" (twin)	3	Ala.
William	" (twin)	3	"
Needum	" (male)	1/12	"
Eliza Stuart		24	"

Household 802
George Kennedy	71	N.C.	None
Mary	"	66	"
Thomas Lakey		12	Ala.

Household 803
| Welcom McGhee | 18 | " | none |
| Catharine | " | 22 | Tenn. |

Household 804
William Story	25	Tenn.	Laborer
Martha	"	26	"
John	"	6	"
William	"	4	"
Mary	"	2	"

Household 805
| Nathaniel Watson | 70 | S.C. | Farmer |
| Clary | " | 60 | N.C. |

Household 806
Thomas Hamm	27	Ala.	Farmer
Sarah	"	23	S.C.
Elizabeth	"	6	Ala.
David	"	4	"
James	"	1	"
Levinny (?) Ross		60	S.C. (female)

Household 807
Archibald McDonald	49	N.C.	Gunsmith
Ferriby	"	52	"
Henry	"	24	" Laborer
James	"	17	Ala. "
Willis	"	12	"
Mary	"	9	"

C-134

Household 808
Thomas Strong		47	Va.	Laborer
Lydia	"	32	N.C.	
Edmund	"	19	Tenn.	"
James	"	17	"	"
John	"	15	"	"
Lewis	"	11	"	
William	"	10	"	
Olliver	"	1/12	Ala.	
Mary Loving		7	Arkansas	

Household 809
Martha Richardson		35	N.C.	
Hiram	"	20	"	Laborer
William	"	18	Ala.	
Wesley	"	16	"	
Martha	"	14	"	
Nancy	"	12	"	
Catharine	"	10	"	
Julia	"	8	"	

Household 810
R B Hussey		45	N.C.	Shoemaker
Lucy	"	40	"	
Thomas	"	19	Ala.	Laborer
Mary	"	17	"	
Spinks	"	15	"	"
George	"	13	"	
Nancy	"	11	"	
Lydia	"	9	"	
James	"	1	"	
Williamson	"	5	"	

Household 811
| Abraham McGhee | | 22 | " | Horse trader |
| Mary | " | 20 | Tenn. | |

Household 812
Isiah Curtis		50	S.C.	Shoemaker
Nancy	"	45	Tenn.	
Henry	"	30	"	None
Sousan	"	25	"	
Eli	"	18	"	Laborer
Jasper	"	16	"	
Houston	"	14	"	
Mary	"	6	Ala.	
Josiah	"	4	"	
Baylor	"	1	"	

Household 813
Thomas Key		32	N.C.	Wheelright
Martha	"	30	"	
Mary	"	9	"	
William	"	7	"	
Robartes	"	2	Ala.	

Household 814
Murrell Askew		35	Tenn.	Schoolteacher
Eliza	"	32	Ala.	
Mary	"	6	"	
Ellen	"	4	"	
Isabella	"	2	"	

Household 815
Aaron Askew		60	N.C.	Baptist preacher
Lovey	"	55	"	
Mary	"	30	Tenn.	
Elizabeth	"	20	Ala.	
Moses	"	25	"	Schoolteacher
Lovey	" *	18	"	
William Holden*		22	Tenn.	Laborer

Household 816
Hiram Kennedy		58	N.C.	Gunsmith
Mary	"	58	"	
Hiram	"	17	Ala.	Student
Ollive	"	14	"	
Martha P. Palmer		29	N.C.	
Orlando	"	11	Ala.	
Artemissa	"	9	Miss.	
Winny Curtis		40	Ky.	

Household 817
Enoch R. Kennedy		25	N.C.	M. E. Preacher
Louisa	"	24	Ala.	
Luther	"	4	"	
Martha	"	2	"	

Household 818
James Lewis		50	N.C.	none
Nancy	"	58	"	
Quebec	" (male)	22	"	Laborer
Wiley	"	19	"	Carpenter
Thomas Lakey		12	Ala.	
James	"	10	"	

Household 819
Matthew Shuffield		40	N.C.	Miller
Nancy	"	40	"	
Alexander	"	19	"	Laborer
Mary	"	17	"	
Anderson	"	14	Ala.	
Nancy	"	10	"	
Monroe	"	6	"	
Martha Allen		16	Tenn.	

Household 820
Andrew Hooi		31	Ala.	Overseer
Mariah	"	31	"	
Nancy	"	9	"	
John	"	5	"	
Martha	"	2	"	

*Marked married within the year.

Household 821
Samuel Clarke   32   N.C. Plasterer
Julia   "   33   Geo.
John   "   10   "
William   "   8   Ala.
Sarah   "   5   "
Samuel   "   10/12 "
Sarah Entrican   15   Tenn.
Cynthia   "   13   "
William Lewis   23   Ala. Plasterer

Household 822
Bayler B. Barker 32 Va.   Merchant
Martha Ann "   26   Ala.
Parthenia   "   11   "
Florence Alabama" 6   "
Taylor Robert "   1   "
Henry Sample   ?   "   Brick layer
James   "   20   "   "

Household 823
Joseph L. Sloss 54   Ireland Taylor
Clarissa   "   48   Ohio
Eveline   "   14   Ala.
James January   15   "   Taylor
Jacob Spotwood   30   Penn.   "

Household 824
John A. Smith   43   N.C.   Merchant
Margaret   "   32   Tenn.
Alexander   "   9   Ala.
William   "   6   "
Stulin   "   3   "
Mary   "   4/12 "

Household 825
James M. Stuart 43   Va.   Taylor
Paulina   "   40   Ky.
John   "   21   "   Engineer
Charles   "   18   "   Taylor
Ophelia   "   16   "
Viola   "   9   "
Josephine   "   6   "
James   "   2   "

Household 826
Daniel Harmon   56   Va.   Carriage/maker
Lucy   "   55   "
Albert   "   30   "   Merchant
Augustus   "   28   "   Carriage-maker
Henrietta   "   26   "
Elizabeth   "   23   "
Hiliard   "   20   "   Taylor
Thomas   "   16   "   Clerk
Lucy   "   13   "
continued

Household 826 continued
Sarah Harmon   30   Tenn.
James   "   8   "
Sarah   "   6   "
Allis   "   4   "

Household 827
Andrew Blair   45   Ireland Brick/layer
Mary   "   27   Ala.
William   "   4   "
John   "   2   "
Mary   "   1/12 "
Sarah Farmer   14   "
Thomas Lowry   35   unknown   none

Household 828
John A. Portlock 48   N.C.   Blacksmith
Mahala   "   40   Tenn.
Nancy   "   21   Ala.
Mary   "   19   "
Martha   "   17   "
William   "   13   "
Julia   "   11   "

Household 829
Samuel C. Stafford 31 Tenn. Merchant
Priscilla   "   22 "
Caleb A. Stafford   24 "   Clerk

Household 830
Margaret Thompson 36 Philadelphia
Margaret   "   18 Ala.
Jane   "   8 "
Emily   "   3 "

Household 831
Mary A. Saffarnans* 41 Tenn.
Mary   "   19 Ala.
Ann   "   16 "
Gertru Hannah   5 "
Alexander   "   11 "
Malcom   "   1 "
Sousan M. Saffarnans 22 Tenn.
Amos Shelton   2 Ala.

Household 832
George W. Sneed**   51 Va.   Post Master
Mary   "   51 Tenn.
Alexander   "   20 Ala. Ass't P.M.
Mary   "   16 "
George   "   10 "
Z. P. Morrison   35 Va.   Carpenter
Briget   "   23 Tenn.
Friend   "   10/12 Ala.

*Estate of Mary Saffarans, dec'd, being settled by Robert M. Patton, executor: Florence Gazette, 19 March 1862.
**Mayor of Florence at one time.

C-136

Household 833			Keeper	Household 837	
Thomas Crow	50	Ky. Tavern/	Isaac Price	28 Tenn. Blacksmith
Elizabeth "	36	N.C.	Christian "	24 Scotland (female)
William "	16	Ala. Clerk	Mary "	6 Ala.
James "	15	" "	William "	3 "
Ann Liza "	8	"	William Price	75 N.C. None
David "	5	"	Nancy "	64 "
Martha "	2	"	Amanda "	35 Tenn.

(TAVERN written vertically by the
following names in this household) teacher Household 838

Joseph Hervey	25	Va. School/	Vincent Benham	33 Tenn. Farmer
John S. Weaver	30	Tenn. Grocery	K. J____ " (female)	31 Ala.
William C. Allen	25	Ala. "	Elizabeth"	7 "
Benjamin Weaver	28	Tenn. Shoe & -	William "	4 "
		Boot Maker	James "	3 "
Samuel Gallaway	30	unknown, Shoe-		
		Boot Maker	Household 839	
O. H. Oats	25	Ala. Att. at law	Thomas J. Crow Junr.	33 " Carpenter
William F. Toodd	26	Ky. "	Louisa "	30 Tenn.
Benjamin Andrews	19	Ala. Clerk	Wm. B. Barton	23 Ala. Druggist
Thomas Burnsides	30	Ire. Merchant	Elizabeth "	51 S.C.
William Harvey	35	Ala. Clerk	S. W. Barton	19 Ala. Clerk
Allen Mitchell	28	" "		
James Wooddle	25	" "	Household 840	
A. M. Price	30	unknown, none	John Hooks	33 N.C. Carpenter
John Barr	30	" Taylor	Eliza "	28 Ala.
Valentine West	30	Germany "	Curtis "	8 "
Wesley Mitchell	33	Tenn. Carpenter	Charles"	4 "
James Martin	25	Ala. "	John "	3 "
George Wed	35	unknown, stage-	Mary "	4/12 "
		driver		
John T. Campbell	35	Ala. Carpenter	Household 841	
			James H. Weakley	52 Va. Com. Merchant
Household 834			Ellen "	45 Ireland
Neander H. Rice*	35	Ky. Merchant	Minerva "	50 "
Lucy "	28	Tenn.	Margaret Jenkins	20 My.
Senora "	4/12	Ala.		
William Patton	19	Ireland clerk	Household 842	
Mariah Lester	21	Tenn.	Robert Duckey	56 Va. Carpenter
			Elizabeth "	42 "
Household 835				
W. H. Wilson	27	Tenn. Carpenter	Household 843	
Sousan "	28	S.C.	John Reed	42 Tenn. None
James "	6	Ala.	Letha "	31 "
Robert "	1	"	Sarah "	13 "
			Mary "	9 Miss.
Household 836			Harriet"	7 "
Ferdinand Sannoner**	55	Italy Surveyor	Samuel "	5 "
Frances "	50	Ala.	John "	3 Ala.
Samuel "	13	"		
Franklin "	8	"	Household 844	
Barney Nelson	21	" Clerk	Dolly Johnson	60 Va. (mulatto)
			Nancy Franklin	25 Ala. "
			Ellen "	7 " "
			Sarah "	6 " "
			John "	4 " "
			Mary "	1 " "

*Christian name appeared to be Beander,
but Neander believed to be correct. A
Neander Rice married Penelope C. Sannoner
on 5 Nov. 1844 in the county.
**Buried 4 June 1859 in Elmwood Cemetery
in Memphis; named town of Florence.

Household 845
Milly Dean (black)	70	Va.
Mirah Majors	30	"
Elizabeth Watson	25	Tenn.
Jane Dean (black)	10	unknown

Household 846
James Cox	45	Ky. Painter
Teletha "	31	Tenn.
William "	7	Ala.
Mary "	11/12	"
Frances Cox (male)	73	England

Household 847
Samuel M. Hyde	38	Vt. Taylor
Mary "	25	Ala.
Franklin "	3	"
Francis "	1	"
Frances O. Horrow	18	" (female)

Household 848
| Joseph Worley | 33 | N.C. Ostler |
| Rebecca " | 36 | Tenn. |

Household 849
| William Wood | 68 | Va. Carpenter |

Household 850
| Robert Campbell | 25 | Scotland " |
| Isaac Campbell | 65 | " none |

Household 851
Samuel S. Stebbins	52	Ct. School/ teacher
Louisa "	51	"
Sarah "	24	N.Y.
Sousan "	22	"
Mary Gibbs	22	Mass.

Household 852
William L. Crow	36	Tenn. Carpenter
Sarah "	30	"
John "	10	Ala.
Newton "	7	"
Sousan "	6	"
Sarah "	4	"
Columbia "	10/12	"
Ralston Bare	23	unknown carptr
Samuel Brown	22	Tenn. "
Keira Robberts (male)	21	unknown "
George Roberts	22	" "
June Jackson	26	Ala. Carpenter

Household 853
Marshal Clarke	45	Ireland
Occupation: merchant		
Mary Clarke	37	Ireland

Household 854
Martin Harkins	54	S.C. Merchant
George Kaisner	23	Ala. "
John Harkins	30	S.C. "

Household 855
Matilda C. Powell	26	Tenn.
Elizabeth "	22	Tenn.
William "	4	Ala.

Household 856
James Horne	55	Tenn. Farmer
Martha "	40	N C.
James "	14	Ala.

Household 857
| Eliza Leftwich (mulatto) | 40 | Va. |

Household 858
Elija Brown	40	Tenn. Laborer
Eliza "	21	"
Samuel "	19	" Carpenter
Elizabeth "	13	"
Rufus "	9	"
Newton "	5	Ala.

Household 859
Johnathan Kelly	36	Tenn. none
Ann "	36	"
Mary "	15	"
Samuel "	13	"
James "	10	"
John "	8	"
Martha "	3	Ala.

Household 860
| Fereby Fomby | 35 | unknown |

Household 861
| Ordeal Laster (male) | 34 | Germany laborer |

Household 862
Daniel Oliver	46	England Farmer
Jane "	32	Tenn.
Benjamin "	12	Ala
Genette "	14	"
Mary "	10	"
Frances "	6	"
Hugh "	2	"
Charles "	8	"

Free inhabitants 5,124, signed:
H. KENNEDY

LAUDERDALE COUNTY MARRIAGES

VOLUME I

1820 - 1825

(Note: These marriage records were originally copied from the books in the court house by the late Raymond Y. McClain in 1940. Numbers in parenthesis are the page numbers of the original books.)

Agee, William to Julia B. Henderson	27 July 1822 (97)
Akers, Thomas to Betsy Hamm	27 July 1820 (17)
Allen, James to Sally Kimbel	15 Jan. 1823 (91)
Anderson, James to Margaret Douglas	25 Jan. 1825 (157)
Anderson, Samuel to Rachel Waters	20 Sept. 1824 (148)
Arnold, Davis to Mary Ann Morriss	11 Feb. 1823 (57)
Bailey, Hiram H. to Sarah Anderson	20 Nov. 1820 (15)
Baker, Danny to Phoebe McNeeley	11 Sept. 1821 (23)
Barnes, Davis to Jane Dowdy	28 Aug. 1822 (54)
Barnes, Thomas to Elizabeth Armour	28 Jan. 1823 (62)
Barnes, Washington to Fanny Parrish	20 Mar. 1823 (74)
Barksdale, Miscanda to Mary S. Scruggs	21 Aug. 1823 (89)
Barnett, Thomas to Nancy Williams	15 Dec. 1823 (95)
Barron, John to Elizabeth Wilborn	5 June 1821 (97)
Bauldin (Baldwin?) John to Catherine Harmon	22 Sept. 1822 (65)
Bell, John to Sally Owens	18 Nov. 1822 (53)
Bearden, Thomas to Polly Littlejohn	21 Mar. 1822 (43)
Bivins, Joseph to Rebecca Kendrick	21 Sept. 1823 (110)
Blasengine, John to Sarah Gartine	19 Aug. 1824 (129)
Bowman, Thomas to Sally Johnson	9 Apr. 1823 (79)
Booth, Nathan to Mary Shelby	22 Nov. 1822 (61)
Bradley, Lemore to Rebecca Duberry	13 Dec. 1822 (42)
Brim, Daniel to Hannah Whitaker	20 Sept 1823 (84)
Broadway, Cornelius to Rachel Whitaker	13 May 1823 (82)
Brown, Elijah to Polly Trombaugh	25 Mar. 1823 (122)
Brown, George to Isabel Galloway	14 Sept. 1820 (17)
Brown, Obediah to Sally Cox	27 Nov. 1823 (112)
Brown, Robert to Nancy Hays	27 Apr. 1820 (8)
Brown, William to Jeanne McNeeley	20 Aug. 1822 (9)
Brown, Dickson to Noma (Hana?) McBride	22 Aug. 1822 (48)
Brown, Burnett to Betsy Goings	8 Feb. 1822 (45)
Butler, Thomas F. to Mary E. Ingram	21 Dec. 1824 (148)
Bryant, Needham to Amy Fisher	22 Mar. 1823 (83)
Campbell, David to Nancy McAlister	13 Jan. 1823 (80)
Cantrell, Lenoir to Nelly Thornton	12 Aug. 1825 (121)
Carlisle, Campbell to Eliza Eastep	14 July 1822 (31)
Care, Harris to Mary Young	12 March 1825 (113)
Carr, John to Elizabeth Womack	7 March 1822 (37)
Chesure, Zachariah to Ruthy McBride	5 March 1822 (44)
Clark, John to Polly Yocum	4 March 1822 (43)
Clem, Adam to Sally Williams	25 Jan. 1824 (75)
Coale, William to Penelope Hammonds	25 Nov. 1824 (109)
Cockburn, Harmon to Rachel Prince	5 April 1822 (36)
Cooper, Samuel to Jane Wood	12 March 1824 (147)
Cotter, John to Nancy Beasley	4 March 1824 (131)

Cox, Drury H. to Eliza C. Westmoreland — 12 April 1821 (22)
Craddock, Burrell to Elizabeth Darby — 22 Sept. 1822 (48)
Collins, Thomas to Rachel Beasley — 22 April 1822 (75)
Crawford, William W. to Angeline M. Pryor — 13 March 1823 (76)
Crittenden, Thomas W. to Prudence J. Coffee — 20 April 1820 (12)

Darby, James to Polly Rogers — 9 Feb. 1825 (152)
Davis, Gurley to Patience B. Smith — 8 Jan. 1825 (72)
Davis, Nathan to Amelia McLester — 8 July 1821 (24)
Davis, James to Polly Rice — 2 Feb. 1825 (160)
Dickson, John to Delia Powell — 4 April 1823 (114)
Dickson, John to Tempie Richardson — 10 Feb. 1824 (150)
Doane, John to Patsy Coburn — 21 March 1825 (158)
Dobbins, John S. to Barsheba Adams — 29 July 1824 (151)

Eaves, John to Polly Stewart — 5 August 1823 (59)
English, Abraham to Nancy Sanders — 27 Nov. 1823 (115)
English, John to Elizabeth Huggins — 19 Oct. 1820 (19)
English, Wilson to Sally Humbrell — 19 Jan. 1823 (93)
Evans, David A. to Betsy Bearden — 15 Jan. 1823 (57)
Evans, Jesse to Amy Petty — 10 April 1821 (21)
Ennis, Cornelius to Adessa Graves — 3 June 1821 (21)
Eves, John to Malinda Crum — 7 Feb. 1820 (12)

Farris, Cornelius to Sally Wallace — 9 Aug. 1823 (88)
Farmer, William to Sally Files — 27 April 1820 (1)
Farris, James Alexander to Sarah Jones — 21 March 1823 (77)
Fisher, Benjamin to Charity Cooper — 26 March 1823 (74)
Flent (Flint?) Stanton to Candes Wright — 22 Aug. 1823 (102)
Flerida (Florida) Richard to Betty York — 15 Nov. 1820 (16)
Foster, James to Jane Cooper — 9 Dec. 1823 (144)
Fullerton, Nathan to Margaret Fullerton — 12 May 1823 (87)
Fullerton, Weldon to Sarah Campbell — 9 Oct. 1822 (51)
Fuller, William S. to Matilda F. Howland — 9 Feb. 1823 (63)

Gaines, Ira to Elizabeth Hayes — 11 March 1825 (107)
Garrett, John to Jenny Higgins — 12 Jan. 1823 (92)
Garrett, James to Betty Willett — 9 Oct. 1823 (78)
Garrett, William to Martha Leonard — 25 Dec. 1821 (32)
Gibson, Alexander L. to Sarah Dement — 12 Oct. 1823 (102)
Gibson, John to Sarah Whitehead — 27 May 1824 (161)
Gibson, John to Mary Johnson — 25 Dec. 1824 (137)
Gooding, John B. to Jane McGee — 5 Jan. 1823 (81)
Gibson, Richard to Elizabeth Chandler — 4 Sept. 1823 (96)
Graham, Thomas to Polly White — 27 Jan. 1824 (134)
Gray, John to Nancy Robinson — 5 Nov. 1821 (30)
Greer, James to Susannah Hammon — 2 June 1822 (32)
Greer, Thomas to Elizabeth Fannon — 18 Dec. 1824 (72)
Griffin, Owens to Lucinda Perryman — 2 Sept. 1824 (155)
Griffin, Maccomb to Temperance Williams — 10 May 1823 (76)
Grissom, B. P. to Jane Perryman — 2 March 1823 (81)
Grissom, Jesse N. to Gracey Whitehead — 24 Jan. 1824 (159)
Grissom, Wilson to Christine Smith — 10 April 1825 (162)
Grissom, Philemon to Delia Foiles — 22 Jan. 1821 (57)

Halton, Tilly to Patsy Kirk	15____1821 (25)*
Hamm, John to Sally Terry	30____1822 (31)
Hamm, Buckley to Rosell Martin	5____1822 (44)
Hammonds, Willie to Usley Newton	1____1820 (3)
Hammonds, Howell to Polly Lindsey	24____1820 (1)
Hammersley, Robert to Polly Birgin	5____1823 (62)
Hanna, James J. to Paralee Childress	5____1823 (62)
Hanna, John to Mildred Hamm	23____1825 (146)
Hardin, Calloway to Louise McKinsey	19____1823 (87)
Harmon, Alexander to Elizabeth Arnett	9____1823 (64)
Harley, James to Polly Beardon	17____1825 (141)
Harmon, James to Sally Price	3____1823 (73)
Harden, John P. N. to Sally Lindsey	19____1824 (113)
Haralson, William to Frances Bearding	3____1824 (138)
Harris, Edward H. to Ann D. Allen	9____1824 (128)
Harris, Elias to Catherine Westmoreland	5____1822 (55)
Hatter, Jesse to Sarah Hamm	20____1825 (140)
Hawkins, Henry James to Frances Bailey	14____1822 (40)
Heavington, Archibald to Elizabeth Yocum	17____1823 (71)
Henderson, James to Rebecca Gilbert	8____1824 (137)
Higgens, Michael to Jane Donelson	1____1825 (154)
Hill, John G. to Dicey Martin	4____1823 (108)
Hodges, Granville to Elizabeth Campbell	4____1824 (123)
Hodges, James to Martha Quall	5____1823 (68)
Holland, William to Charity Thomas	9____1824 (126)
Holland, Richard to Polly Markham	9____1824 (119)
Holloday, John to Ruthy Beasley	3____1820 (12)
Holly, Almeria to Hannah Belew	0____1820 (19)
Holly, Julius to Lilly Bailey	____1820 (10)
Hoobs, Herman to Susan English	____1821 (5)
Hood, James to Mary Bailey	____1823 (73)
Hopper, Coburn to Amelia Barnes	____1821 (??)
Howell, William to Lucretia Loid	____1824 (67)
Horn, John to Nancy Poteet	____1824 (111)
Hubbard, Stephen to Nancy Williams	____1824 (149)
Huff, John to Hannah Coburn	____1823 (94)
Huff, Stephen to Mariah Garrard	____1824 (143)
Huggins, James to Elizabeth Robertson	____1823 (92)
Huggins, Philip to Elizabeth English	____1823 (91)
Huggins, Thomas to Nancy English	____1823 (93)
Hurley, Thomas to Rebecca Strawn	____1825 (152)
Huston, Robert to Delia Fannon	____1822 (39)
Ingram, Jones to Nancy Broadway	____1824 (128)
Ingram, John to Amy Whitaker	____1823 (80)
Ives, Amos to Mary Jackson	____1819 (7)
Jackson, William to Margaret Killen	4 March 1822 (41)
Judd, Daniel to Dinah Farray	18 Aug. 1824 (121)
Johnson, Samuel G. to Margaret Springer	21 June 1824 (120)

*The blanks were illegible on the McClain copy of these marriages--waterstained.

Kenemore, Hilery to Alis Pratt   1 March 1825 (157)
Kenemore, Isaiah to Sarah Lamb   13 Jan. 1824 (155)
Kenemore, Wileby to Miranda Shore   3 Jan. 1822 (39)
Kendrick, John to Margaret Brown   27 Nov. 1823 (114)
Killen, John to Susannah Richardson   6 March 1825 (159)
King, Joseph to Mary Wiggins   3 Feb. 1825 (154)
Kirk, Allen to Elizabeth Ross   13 Aug. 1824 (132)
Knight, William to Darthenia Phelps   4 Nov. 1823 (83)
Koger, William to Martha Westmoreland   12 April 1821 (22)

Lackey, Thomas to Nancy Welch   11 Jan. 1821 (25)
Lance, Spencer to Polly Woody   14 Nov. 1821 (29)
Lard, Nathaniel to Elizabeth Weatherly   1 Feb. 1820 (11)
Lenoir, Clement to Mary Atheridge   17 April 1820 (4)
Lester, James to Jane Hearlston   3 Aug. 1820 (20)
Lilly Edward B. to Elizabeth Verona   23 Jan. 1824 (116)
Lindsey, Josiah to Eritely Harder   27 Oct. 1823 (96)
Lindsey, Philips to Frank Sharpe   22 May 1822 (34)
Littlejohn, Peter to Susannah Pettis   21 Feb. 1824 (86)
Littlejohn, Samuel to Rebecca English   15 Jan. 1823 (94)
Long, Michael to Vaney Webb   5 Aug. 1821 (29)
Lowell, John to Catherine Asbell   11 Nov 1822 (40)
Lyon, Micajah to Manervy Henderson   25 Oct. 1824 (136)
Lyon, James L. to Jane Share   21 Dec. 1824 (136)

Mackey, Charles H. to Eliner Bert   5 March 1825 (163)
Martin, Lewis to Betsy Price   25 July 1822 (61)
Martin, James to Amy White   7 Jan. 1825 (161)
Martin, Thomas to Jane Hodges   5 July 1821 (27)
Martindell, George to Agnes Martin   4 Dec. 1823 (113)
Marshall, Lewis to Jane Shelton   29 Dec. 1824 (117)
Matthews, William, Polly Ray   20 Feb. 1820 (9)
Mayfield, James to Jane Kirk   29 July 1820 (11)
Mays, Claiborn to Mary K. Coffee   13 June 1820 (10)
Maxey, Stephen to Polly Collier   24 Feb. 1824 (9)
Mize, Nathan R. to Polly Lowell   1 Feb. 1821 (118)
Morrison, Peter to Polly Young   6 Nov. 1823 (111)
Morrison, Peter to Elander Ann Collison   28 Nov. 1824 (145)
Morrow, Robert to Tiny Brown   14 Sept. 1820 (9)
Myers, Henry to Pharaba Phelps   9 April 1820 (5)

McBride, James to Margaret Harrington   27 Jan. 1824 (110)
McBride, Sherod to Catherine Steward   15 March 1821 (27)
McCarley, Abraham to Polly Looney   9 Feb. 1820 (2)
McCarta, Samuel to Margaret Hill   29 Nov. 1820 (14)
McClarey, John to Mary McDougal   22 May 1822 (98)
McClure, Samuel to Thursian Marshall   23 April 1825 (160)
McCowan, John to Susannah Houlause   9 April 1822 (34)
McFall, John A. to Margaret Clark   9 Jan. 1825 (107)
McKinsey, Alexander to Lucinda Chisholm   11 Dec. 1823 (101)
McMahan, Richard to Tabitha McKinsey   27 Aug. 1824 (170)
McMahan, William to Leah Franks   30 Jan. 1822 (37)
McMickin, Andrew to Eliza Farris   18 Sept. 1823 (60)
McMillan, James to Jane Isbell   20 Aug. 1823 (89)

Nail, Joseph to Elizabeth Walker	20 Oct. 1823 (78)
Norman, Alfred to Anna Bailor	2 Jan. 1823 (67)
Nowland, Perkins to Julia Brown	16 Oct. 1823 (100)
Null, John to Nancy Bossen	18 Nov. 1823 (115)
O'Bryant, Brandon to Rebecca McAllister	27 June 1824 (129)
Odell, James to Jane Marks	3 Aug. 1820 (127)
Owens, Lesa C. to Jane Smith	10 June 1824 (1)
Palmer, Elisha to Anna Weatherly	27 Sept. 1821 (45)
Parker, John to Elizabeth Short	18 March 1824 (133)
Parrish, Nicholas to Anna Files	14 Oct. 1821 (26)
Paulk, Jacob to Elizabeth Rogers	26 Feb. 1824 (142)
Paulk, Jonathan to Betsy Darby	4 March 1822 (35)
Perryman Bidear to Sally Brown	24 April 1821 (28)
Perryman, John to Patsy Waters	14 Aug. 1823 (71)
Phillips, Daniel to Cornelia M. Bumpass	17 Jan. 1824 (126)
Phillips, Mason to Deby Kendricks	13 Feb. 1825 (153)
Pillow, William B. to Emily L. Chisholm	25 Dec. 1822 (54)
Plowman, John to Polly Blockwell	1 Aug. 1821 (24)
Peters (Petes), John to Nancy Young	17 Feb. 1825 (118)
Prince, Edward to Esther Cockburn	12 July 1821 (42)
Quillen, Charles to Polly Joiner	15 July 1824 (127)
Read, James to Jane Norwell	25 Jan. 1824 (142)
Read, Daniel to Martha Lyon	9 Sept. 1823 (86)
Reeves, Joseph to Sally Hendricks	2 May 1822 (35)
Renfro John to Emily Griffin	12 Feb. 1824 (133)
Reynolds, Milledge to Nancy Flatt	29 Sept. 1824 (156)
Reynolds, Isaac to Elizabeth Garrett	2 Jan. 1822 (56)
Rice, Nathan to Harriett Pettus	24 April 1820 (99)
Rice, Manson to Elizabeth Grissom	20 Sept. 1821 (27)
Richardson, Isaac to Mariah Thornton	22 May 1822 (95)
Richardson, Jonathan to Nancy Barnes	29 Aug. 1822 (55)
Richardson, Henry to Nancy McDougal	7 Oct. 1824 (140)
Roberts, Peter H. to Sarah Bailey	27 May 1824 (151)
Romine, William to Polly Callahan	20 Aug. 1821 (99)
Rucker, Wester to Frances Savage	15 April 1823 (76)
Rickin, Richard to Anny Higgins	23 Dec. 1824 (153)
Sabier, Julian to Mary Black	11 Oct. 1822 (51)
Safferans, Peter to Mary Haralson	4 Nov. 1824 (117)
Shares, Robert to Margaret Rogers	11 Nov. 1824 (??)
Shelton, Robert B. to Jane McArley	30 March 1820 (7)
Shoemaker, Thomas to Mary Moon	1 Sept. 1823
Single, Jacob to Matilda Wilkes	5 Nov. 1823 (68)
Smedley, John to Susannah Menster	23 Nov. 1824 (10)
Smith, James A. to Ann Smithers	11 Nov. 1824 (13)
Springer, James to Polly McDonald	24 April 1822 (38)
Springer, Jonathan to Jane Belew	29 March 1824 (12)
Spain, Marshall D. to Hannah Owen	3 April 1825 (158)
Stergeon, Elias to Starberry Kenemore	21 Dec. 1824 (147)
Still, John to Marriah Lancaster	2 Dec. 1824 (118)
Strahan, William to Eliza Miller	20 Nov. 1822 (69)
Starkey, Jesse to Nancy Birdsong	10 April 1823 (71)
Stewart, Allen to Nancy Stewart	29 March 1824 (13)

Stanford, George to Betsy Ann McCallahan   15 July 1821 (?)
Swearingin, William to Polly Brown   14 Nov. 1822 (65)

Tally, Page to Nancy Coats   9 March 1821 (16)
Taylor, James to Nancy Bayley   17 Aug. 1824 (139)
Taylor, Thomas F. to Patience Evans   26 Jan. 1824 (109)
Terry, Francis to Sally Corum   20 Oct. 1824 (156)
Terry, Thomas to Elizabeth Morris   18 Dec. 1823 (101)
Thomas, Josiah P. to Rachel Strawn   28 July 1824 (149)
Thrasher, William L. to Rachel Hoaltsleaver   3 Sept. 1822 (50)
Thornton, Josiah to Franley Duberry   21 Dec. 1823 (144)
Tomlinson, John to Lucretia Harmon   13 March 1822 (41)
Till John to Camilla Bumpass   17 June 1823 (125)
Trout, William to Tamsey Weatherly   12 Nov. 1823 (114)
Tucker, James to Elizabeth G. Mayhew   14 March 1825 (141)
Trainer, William to Betsy Hays   10 Feb. 1822 (45)

Vickers, Green B. to Betsy Lindsey   27 Jan. 1824 (116)

Wallace, John to Dolly Farris   25 March 1824 (131)
Walker, David, Polly Fannon   8 Dec. 1821 (39)
Wamble, Harvey A. to Elizabeth Wilkes   18 Aug. 1822 (49)
Wamble, Lorenzo Dow to Polly Perkins   25 Dec. 1822 (56)
Ward, Brittian to Mary Clem   11 Dec. 1823 (101)
Weatheram, James to Polly Stafford   25 Aug. 1824 (135)
West, Walter to Patience Burnett   25 March 1823 (96)
Westmoreland, E. B. to Lucy Mitchell   25 Dec. 1822 (99)
Weathers, Reuben to Nancy Hardin   19 Sept. 1824 (139)
Welch, John to Martha Cornish   28 Jan. 1823 (82)
Welch, John to Jane South   8 Sept. 1824 (120)
White, John to Cynthia Barnett   19 Dec. 1822 (64)
White, Philemon to Elizabeth Grissom   27 July 1822 (47)
Whitaker, James to Teresa Trouton   12 Jan. 1825 (84)
Willis, Joshua to Martha Hall   15 Sept. 1823 (185)
Wilkes, Phillip to Alsey Morris   13 May 1824 (122)
Wiley, John to Lucy Skaggs   9 Dec. 1822 (60)
Winsted, John to Ruthy Jones   9 Aug. 1821 (23)
Withers, William F. to Katherine Hawkins   30 Oct. 1823 (90)
Williams, Bickner to Martha Phillips   25 Feb. 1821 (18)
Williams, James to Winnifred McCarley   3 Feb. 1820 (3)
White, Carroll to Rosa Nelson   12 Feb. 1824 (142)
Williams, Terry to Martha Garrett   9 Dec. 1824 (107)
Wilkerson, Joel to Rachel R. Scott   23 Dec. 1823 (138)
Wisemer, John to Cynthia Hawkins   27 June 1822 (33)
Wood, Bennet A. to Mary W. Ellis   28 Nov. 1824 (162)
Woods, John L. to Polly Fair   12 Dec. 1824 (135)
Wright, William to Nancy James   22 Feb. 1824 (130)

Yarborough, William L. to Elizabeth Bowman   4 Jan. 1825 (146)
Young, William to Susannah Flint   15 July 1825 (79)

Zachariah, George to Olivia Flanlin   25 July 1823 (69)

End of Volume 1 of Lauderdale County Marriages.

LAUDERDALE COUNTY MARRIAGES

Volume 2

1825 - 1833

Adams, Samuel to Polly Bryant	7 July 1825 (11)
Adams, William C. to Tabitha Adams	13 Jan. 1831 (160)
Adair, William to Mary Rogers	1831 (215)
Allen, John L. to Margaret E. Boyd	5 July 1827 (53)
A____, John to Margaret McDougal	20 Apl. 1829 (86)
Allen, H. J. to Drusilla Hard	24 Oct. 1833 (225)
Alpind, William M. to Polly Ronsey	18 March 1826 (19)
Andrew, Patrick to Harriett Asher	26 May 1832 (188)
Armistead, Anthony P. to Sarah T. Ragsdale	12 August 1829 (101)
Armstrong, Alexander to Nancy Wells	22 Nov. 1832 (245)
Arnold, Ira to Cynthia Hendrix	5 Jan. 1832 (173)
Asher, Alen to Parmelia Jane Andrews	14 July 1831 (195)
Atwell, Hardy to Tempy Hill	17 Feb. 1833 (225)
Bartlett, John L. to Jane Jobe	27 Nov. 1825 (1)
Bond, William to Catherine Goodnight	11 Sept. 1825 (3)
Bourland, John to Martha Simmons	11 Sept. 1825 (4)
Barnes, Starling B. to Martha Ann Mitchell	14 Sept. 1825 (6)
Bumpass, Gabriel to Charlotte Winstead	1 Sept. 1825 (12)
Brown, Gabriel to Patsy Boston	15 June 1825 (13)
Bowman, Joseph J. to Eliza M. Yarborough	25 Jan. 1824 (15)
Baugh, Joseph H. to Unicy Lea	19 April 1826 (21)
Brown, Elijah to Elizabeth Loyd	26 Jan. 1826 (23)
Bryan, Royal to Elizabeth Jenkins	23 Feb. 1826 (32)
Burns, Samuel to Mary Ann Adams	30 Nov. 1826 (35)
Barnett, John to Patsy Jones	31 July 1826 (38)
Brown, Wesley to Charity Hammonds	18 Jan. 1827 (39)
Bourland, Balis to Sarah Brown	6 March 1827 (43)
Binford, John M. to Martha Ann Craig	8 March 1827 (45)
Bailey, John C. to Lucerty H. Burton	17 Jan. 1828 (49)
Bradshaw, William C. to Nancy E. Williams	13 Sept. 1827 (55)
Betterton, Harvey to Nancy Hendricks	25 Feb. 1828 (55)
Bell, Benjamin to Frances Chandler	29 Dec. 1827 (63)
Bruce, Joel to Mary Callahan	27 July 1827 (64)
Bayne, Daniel W. to Elizabeth A. Fuqua	11 Dec. 1827 (65)
Blockwell, William D. to Nancy Gilbert	13 April 1827 (67)
Bibb, Thomas M. to Sophia H. Byrn	9 Aug. 1827 (67)
Brown, Elisha to Mary Jarman	7 Aug. 1827 (68)
Butler, John to Margaret Herston	19 Jan. 1829 (75)
Boyd, Joseph to Pressy Ezell	9 Oct. 1826 (78)
Barnes, Alexander to Sarah Ann Wallace	15 Jan. 1829 (81)
Blasingame, Harvey to Hester Curtis	23 Feb. 1829 (83)
Bedingfield, James to Hannah Speagle	5 May 1827 (84)
Brewer, Davis to Elizabeth McGee	18 Jan. 1827 (86)
Bailey, Richard to Rachel Saunders	9 June 1829 (90)
Brown, Elijah to Rachel Jarman	14 July 1828 (94)
Brown, Shadrack to Emily Drennett	25 June 1829 (96)
Blair, Samuel W. to Margaret H. Blair	7 July 1829 (97)
Bailey, Richard, Jr. to Parmelia Harrison	12 July 1829 (106)

Buchanan, Andrew to Harriett P. Coulter   2 Dec. 1828 (106)
Bidens, Hugh to Harriett Nolen   5 June 1826 (108)
Burges, Elias E. to Rachel Pretihard   9 Oct. 1827 (109)
Brown, Ruffin to Susannah Cheatham   20 Dec. 1828 (111)
Buford, Daniel to Nancy Denton   23 Oct. 1828 (111)
Burrow, William to Frances Waddell   22 Jan. 1828 (103)
Boyles, James to Anny Jones   2 Nov. 1828 (113)
Brown, Thomas to Nelly Hodges   13 July 1828 (116)
Burton, William G. to Elmira Tate   6 July 1830 (141)
Burnes, W. A. to Perlina Cobb   6 Aug. 1830 (149)
Brumley, Augustine to Sally Jones   13 June 1830 (154)
Borerin, Downs, Nancy Phillips   13 Jan. 1830 (158)
Beebe, Justin E. to Anna Belle Buppos   20 Jan. 1831 (160)
Bevis, James to Aggy Waldrop   25 April 1832 (167)
Byrne, John A. to Ann Shoemaker   7 Dec. 1831 (168)
Brannum, David to Malinda Holt   15 July 1832 (170)
Bratton, John to Sarah Flint   21 Dec. 1831 (172)
Bragg, William to Frances Armstead   15 Feb. 1832 (175)
Baughman, David to Ann Stephens   22 March 1832 (177)
Brown, Thomas to Sarah Sherod   15 March 1832 (179)
Burnet, Joseph to Chancy (?) May   22 May 1831 (184)
Bearden, George to Phoebe Newman   1 Oct. 1831 (186)
Byrne, John W. to Mary Virgus   24 April 1831 (193)
Brown, William to Bethany Higgins   18 Nov. 1830 (194)
Butler, Henry to Nancy Phillipps   18 Sept. 1831 (196)
Burns, Barbanus (Barnabus?) to Polly Adams   30 Oct. 1831 (198)
Bourland, Joseph P. to Susan B. Morgan   18 Aug. 1831 (197)
Boyles, Thomas T. to Cinthia Ann Whitten   1 March 1831 (206)
Bond, John to Nancy Clark   8 June 1831 (207)
Burnett, ___? to Malissa Boyles   10 April 1831 (208)
Barnett, Daniel to Elizabeth Jourdon   7 Aug. 1833 (219)
Breemly (Brumley?) Larken to Maretta Short   21 June 1832 (220)
Bell, John J. to Martha Lancaster   20 Dec. 1832 (230)
Barnett, Absolom to Cintha McGee   18 March 1832 (233)
Beavers, Bradley G. to Malvina Keeton   11 Nov. 1832 (236)
Boyd, John to Nancy Wood   10 July 1832 (239)
Bailey, John C. to S___ Moore   17 Jan. 1832 (240)
Blanton, Carter to Elizabeth Webb   24 Dec. 1832 (244)
Brook, William to Mary Maples   26 Oct. 1832   (245)
Bishop, Oliver W. to Margaret Dement   30 Oct. 1832 (246)
Burk, William to Mary Dement   15 April 1833 (263)
Butts, Canagair (?) to Elizabeth <u>Garinger</u> 17 Dec. 1832 (264)

Choate (refer to Shoat marriages)
Cox, Arom to Nancy B. Carter   18 Dec. 1825 (2)
Crum, Peter to Catherine Bearden   4 Sept. 1825 (6)
Campbell, Andrew H. to Nancy Adams   18 Jan. 1825 (7)
Campbell, John M. to Eliza Holt   13 June 1823 (13)
Coburn, Francis to Elizabeth Widner   7 Aug. 1825 (14)
Cooper, William to Nancy Hart   27 Oct. 1825 (21)
Cockburn, Canny to Lucindia Cartrell   15 Jan. 1826 (22)
Campbell, William M. to Mary Ann Glen   23 Feb. 1826 (20)
Cameron, Duncan to Sarah Ann Evans   5 Sept. 1826 (26)
Cocrane, Robert to Elizabeth Lamb   8 Oct. 1826 (28)
Collie, Maynard to Elizabeth Shoat (?)   26___1826 (43)
Cloer, Elisha L. to Matilda Barnett   19 Sept. 1827 (57)

Cable (Coble) Adam to Polly Harris	8 June 1827 (67)
Carroll, William to Eliza Barton	2 Jan. 1827 (83)
Cloer, Elijah to Elizabeth Weathers	5 March 1829 (86)
Cockburn, Whitnul (Whitmel?) to Easter Polk	18 Oct. 1826 (91)
Clore, John to Frances Johnson	28 Mary 1828 (74)
Colier, John to Sally Arnett	5 Aug. 1829 (97)
Caplin, Austin to Liddia Williams	18 June 1829 (108)
Carr, Isaac to May Cooke	27 March 1828 (118)
Cox, Jesse to Susannah Cheatham	9 Oct. 1828 (114)
Chisholm, Alexander G. to Betty Garrard	31 Dec. 1829 (124)
Cook, Robert to Mary Grocy	12 Nov. 1829 (126)
Campbell, James E. to Alsey Reeder	5 Dec. 1830 (128)
Campbell, Garrick to Ann Williams	21 Jan. 1830 (129)
Cartwright, William to Lucy Miles	25 March 1830 (142)
Clark, David to Ruth McBride	21 Jan. 1830 (134)
Cockburn, Charles to Harriett Vance	15 June 1830 (135)
Cook, George to Abitas Dowdy	15 Nov. 1829 (140)
Crawford, Samuel to Elizabeth Blasingame	12 July 1830 (142)
Curtis, Wilford to Nancy Fisher	23 Dec. 1830 (153)
Cox, Charles to Sally Price	13 July 1830 (165)
Coron, Lemuel to Jane Thompson	12 Jan. 1830 (155)
Crews, John to Jane Terry	15 May 1832 (166)
Carey, Benjamin to Phesoba Beasley	15 Sept. 1831 (182)
Clark, James M. to Mary Ann Whitten	11 March 1830 (184)
Creel, John to Nancy Roberson	8 Sept. 1831 (185)
Coburn, Thomas to Betsy Parks	27 July 1832 (215)
Carr, John to Cynthia Carr	4 Oct. 1832 (219)
Cartier, John D. to Ann Clemons	24 April 1832 (221)
Couch, Thomas to Charity Barnett	29 Jan. 1832 (222)
Costell, John to Eliza Guest	17 March 1833 (227)
Copeland, Richard to Martha Lovelace	9 Sept. 1832 (231)
Copeland, Thomas to Elizabeth Patterson	12 Aug. 1833 (259)

Davis, John G. to Nancy Lynch	11 May 1825 (81)
Dowdy, Dravis to Mary Reeves	3 Oct. 1825 (7)
Douglis, John to Constantine Greely	1 June 1826 (20)
Davis, Joseph to Cynthia Williams	17 Aug. 1826 (32)
Davis, Gabrel to Mary McLemore	20 Dec. 1827 (69)
Davis, Kinchen to Mahala Dowdy	5 Dec. 1827 (80)
Donohoa, John to Mary M. Fuqua	15 Nov. 1826 (85)
Despain, John to Margaret Reeder	10 March 1829 (87)
Duberry, John to Deborah Darby	11 Oct. 1828 (92)
Darby, Isiah to Verlinda Jeanes	22 May 1828 (92)
Dance, William E. to Isabella Newman	11 Aug. 1828 (96)
Darrell, R. D. to Nancy Barr	11 Oct. 1829 (105)
Darby, Benjamin to Mary Reader	5 Nov. 1828 (108)
Duncan, Maps to Sally Clark	27 March 1829 (113)
Dement, Ruben to Mary Brown	22 Sept. 1829 (117)
Deane, Bryant to Evelyn Jackson	30 May 1830 (142)
Dement, Josiah to Rebecca Speigle	18 March 1830 (137)
Douglas, James to Malinda Simmons	18 Aug. 1830 (145)
Dority, John to Jane Brown	9 August 1832 (239)
Davis, Isom to Jenny Literal	6 Sept. 1830 (155)
Dillehunty, Henry to B. M. Johnson	14 July 1831 (193)
Dickard, George to Docie Hutchinson	2 Oct. 1831 (158)

Dement, Thomas to Polly Donaldson   16 Feb. 1833 (235)
Darby, James D. to Elizabeth Swearingen   27 Dec. 1832 (242)
Donald, John G. to Jane Brown   20 Jan. 1832 (247)
David, William to Nancy Kibbs   15 July 1833 (257)
Dickey, ? to ? Anderson   12 July 1832 (257)
Dicks, John to Mary Caldwell   9 Sept. 1833 (261)

English, Mathias to Anny Null (Neel??)   10 June 1827 (65)
Edwards, Lewis to Margaret Ijams   18 Sept. 1828 (95)
Ezell, William to Ann Hobbs   6 Oct. 1830 (157)
Ealey, George M. to Anna Robertson   1 March 1822 (179)
Estell, Frederick to Nancy Lea   11 Aug. 1825 (5)
English, Thomas B. to Sarah Brewer   22 Nov. 1831 (202)

Files, James to Polly Willet   7 July 1825 (11)
Farris, Samuel D. to Cossy Wallace   6 July 1826 (34)
Fuller, John to Charity Hickman   15 March 1827 (40)
Fuller, Isaiah to Margaret Douglas   1 Oct. 1827 (59)
Foster, Asa to Sarah Bailes   10 July 1827 (62)
Flemington, John to Margaret Best   27 July 1827 (64)
Fowler, Jeremiah to ____ Penny   1 Feb. 1829 (72)
Fowler, Dennis to Ruth Haygood   22 July 1830 (137)
Follis, Washington to Rebecca Sparks   16 April 1830 (143)
Flake, Silas to Sally Bird   5 August 1830 (149)
Fields, John G. to Mary Deirt   23 August 1830 (154)
Flint, Alex to Nancy Tucker   18 Dec. 1831 (171)
Faires, William to Jane Faires   30 Aug. 1831 (196)
Fields, Fielding to Mary Williams   10 Nov. 1831 (201)
Fowler, H. to Micha Nolen   26 July 1832 (241)
Farmer, William H. to Sarina Thompson   13 Jan. 1833 (?)

Greesham, Benjamin to Nancy Griffin   30 April 1825 (10)
Griffin, Jesse to Sarah Brooks   19 June 1825 (14)
Garrett, Pressley to Elizabeth Littlejohn   22 Dec. 1826 (24)
Grace, John to Rhody Morrison   29 Nov. 1926 (34)
Gibson (Gribson?), James to Nancy Jordon   25 July 1827 (57)
Grayson, Joel to Delia Hooks   12 Feb. 1828 (57)
Garner, William to Martha Pope   18 July 1827 (60)
Grooms, Isaac to Delia Littlejohn   27 Oct. 1827 (60)
Garner, Thomas to Nancy Lyons   30 Jan. 1827 (85)
Griffith, Solomon to Jane Ransom   20 March 1829 (85)
Griffin, Autry to Mary Ann Corum   30 July 1829 (89)
Goode, Holbert to Juliana Bryan   9 Feb. 1830 (137)
Guest, Albert to Elizabeth Richardson   21 Feb. 1832 (195)
Green, Jesse to Nancy Bivins   20 June 1832 (210)
Gray, John to Manerva Lunsford   1 July 1832 (217)
Green, Lewis to Lucinda McDonald   ____ 1832 (221)
Garner, John G. to Mary A. Williams   19 April 1832 (237)
Gray, James to Elizabeth Jones   22 August 1832 (240)
Grisholm, Daniel to Susan Files   30 Oct. 1833 (253)
Grisholm, George to Marian Ann Thornton   20 Nov. 1831 (259)
Greenhow, James to Ersley Bromley   30 Oct. 1832 (260)

Howel, Philip to Mary Wesson	13 Sept. 1825 (3)
Heffington, Barney to Martha Garrett	28 Nov. 1825 (5)
Heffington, Thomas to Susannah Smith	1 Dec. 1826 (6)
Hodges, William to Margaret Satterfield	21 July 1826 (13)
Hayes, Alfred to Avaline McCuluster	18 April 1825 (15)
Holmes, Thomas to Silvey Boyce	22 Feb. 1825 (23)
Hooks, Isaac to Amos (Amy?) Holt	26 June 1826 (26)
Hammons, Henry to Polly Linsoff	7 Sept. 1826 (31)
Holton, William to Ruth Tanner	29 June 1826 (33)
Heardon, George to Elizabeth James	5 Oct. 1826 (37)
Hall, Benjamin F. to Durenda Chisolm	2 Jan. 1827 (38)
Holt, Joseph W. to Martha A. M. Smith	2 May 1826 (46)
Hargrove, John G. to Mary Jones	26 Nov. 1826 (49)
Haygood, George to Susannah Barnes	19 June 1827 (50)
Holleman, William M. to Rebecca L. McVey	9 Oct. 1827 (54)
Higgins, Phillip to Agnes Roberson	30 Dec. 1827 (59)
Hammons, John to Polly Greer	23 Jan. 1828 (63)
Halford, Edward to Margaret Newman	8 July 1827 (66)
Henderson, John B. to Mary Williams	18 Jan. 1829 (81)
Hill, James to Mary McColsky	2 March 1829 (84)
Houston, Ross to Martha A. Bumpus	19 March 1829 (87)
Haygood, George M. to Nancy Armour	27 March 1829 (88)
Hardin, William B. to Ann Holehouse	20 August 1829 (98)
Holt, Jackson to Lidia Jones	15 October 1829 (101)
Howard, Hardin to Harriett Johnson	15 Oct. 1829 (105)
Holt, Hiram to Evelyn Holland	8 June 1828 (106)
Henson, Thomas to Mary Burns	17 March 1829 (107)
Howard, Jesse to Mary Hall	23 Dec. 1828 (107)
Henley, Joseph to Charlotte Stephens	2 June 1828 (115)
Harrison, William to Alexan Skelton	23 Dec. 1828 (112)
Holmes, Ira to Milly Alford	19 June 1828 (115)
Hickman, John to Kath Killen	26 Feb. 1830 (122)
Heathcock, John to Martha Young	28 Jan. 1830 (123)
Howard, Newton to Rita McCaffery	4 Jan. 1830 (130)
Hendrix, Larkin to Elizabeth Huff	31 Dec. 1829 (132)
Holt, John to Patience Jones	29 Oct. 1829 (132)
Hawkins, Wiley T. to Mary Ann Mitchell	23 Nov. 1830 (139)
Houston, Pugh to Lucinda Chisolm	23 Dec. 1830 (151)
Ham, Blessingum to Minerva Berry	23 Dec. 1830 (157)
Harrel, David to Lucinda Day	14 Oct. 1830 (158)
Higgins, Josiah to Chelaty Smith	4 Jan. 1830 (158)
Hendricks, Joseph M. to Nancy Wessin	24 Dec. 1831 (167)
Holt, Edgman to Jane Smith	15 June 1832 (169)
Hendricks, Green L. to ___?___ Arnold	5 Jan. 1832 (173)
Harvey, Burges to Elizabeth Harvey	12 Jan. 1832 (177)
Hill, John G. to Susannah Hodges	27 Aug. 1831 (191)
Haygood, Stephen to Elizabeth Boston	26 Jan. 1831 (192)
Harraway, Walter to Emily Ingram	6 Sept. 1831 (207)
Holbrook, John to Rebecca Ellis	15 Sept. 1831 (209)
Hood, Humphrey to Juda Trout	4 Oct. 1832 (217)
Ham, Sanders to Rebecca LaFen	4 June 1832 (233)
Huzza, Robert to Lucy Laky	4 March 1831 (234)
Hammons, Samuel to Elizabeth Campton	1 Aug. 1833 (252)
Howard, Ranson to Eliza Finell	2 May 1833 (253)
Hail, Galand to Mary Dodd	15 Aug. 1833 (261)
Holt, John C. to Malinda Swearingen	30 Sept. 1833 (262)
Holt, Isaiah to Nancy Lamb	10 Sept. 1833 (263)

Jordan, David to Rebecca Gibson   2 Dec. 1825 (9)
Jinnings, Jesse to Tempie White   21 Jan. 1826 (22)
Jenkins, Chopley (Chessley?) to Elizabeth Johnson 22 March 1827 (45)
Jones, William to Catherine Wallace   17 Jan. 1828 (63)
Jones, Cullender to Serene Garrett   25 Feb. 1829 (72)
Joiner, Drury to Frances Price   19 March 1829 (73)
Johnson, John G. to Lucinda Cleer (Cloer?) 20 March 1820 (83)
Jeaves, Jesse to Sally C. Young   25 June 1829 (88)
Jones, William to Nancy Cotton   26 Nov. 1829 (122)
Jackson, Edward K. to Malinda Bruce   18 Feb. 1830 (125)
Jackson, Peter to Rhody Holmes   20 Oct. 1830 (152)
Johnston, William to Early Springer   7 Oct. 1830 (159)
Jones, Wyate to Sarah Smally   22 July 1831 (171)
Jones, John to Polly Richardson   8 March 1832 (180)
Jenkins, Hanson J. to Polly Ann Willett   5 Oct. 1831 (183)
James, Absolom to Nazarrin Betterton   22 Sept. 1831 (205)
Jones, John S. to Margaret Holt   3 May 1832 (238)
Jones, William to Nancy Dowdy   12 June 1832 (251)

Kinsey, Carter M. to Elizabeth Conrey (Conroy?) 20 July 1825 (8)
Knight, James to Nancy Brown   13 Sept. 1825 (12)
Kidd, John to Mary Gibson   21 May 1825 (33)
Kitchens, George to Amy Dillard   14 Jan. 1827 (41)
Kelly, Vincent to Edith Ramsey   18 Feb. 1828 (58)
Karsner, Benjamin to Sara McCarter   21 June 1827 (68)
King, Robert to Nancy Whitehead   2 Sept. 1829 (102)
Kirkman, James to Mary Jackson   25 Feb. 1830 (123)
Killough, John to Ethel Young   20 April 1830 (140)
Kirkpatrick, James to Polly Davis   13 Nov. 1831 (202)
Keith, Joseph to Margaret Brown   26 Aug. 1832 (208)
Kimbrel, John to Susannah Hobbs   25 June 1833 (253)
Kernard, Charles A. to Mary J Dupree   22 Aug. 1833 (258)

Lutton, Miles G. to Catherine Reed   12 Feb. 1825 (28)
Lassiter, James to Sarah Thornton   13 June 1826 (32)
Laxington, William B. to Betsy Farris   20 Feb. 1826 (34)
Littleton, Reuben to Frances Wadlington   28 Dec. 1826 (35)
Lightfoot, Henry to Elizabeth G. Simmons   25 May 1826 (37)
Lamb, Morgan to Esther Hurley   20 Feb. 1827 (42)
Larkin, Lenore to Emily Adams   5 Sept. 1827 (51)
Littlejohn, Charles to Mary Kimbrell   25 Sept. 1827 (55)
Looney, Claiborne to Margaret Hearon   29 Nov. 1827 (58)
Looney, Martin to Sarah Joiner   10 Dec. 1828 (74)
Lacefield, Martin to Mary White   20 March 1828 (95)
Landham, William to Matilda Sholar   20 Nov. 1828 (111)
Lindsay, Anderson to Patsy Hammonds   13 July 1829 (127)
Lafann, James to Elizabeth McMurtrey   23 Sept. 1829 (128)
Lindsay, Thomas B. to Sarah M. Waddell   23 Dec. 1829 (139)
Looney, Jesse to Polly Welch   26 Aug. 1830 (153)
Litrell, Alfred to Lucinda Hammonds   5 Oct. 1830 (156)
Lindsey, Littleton to Rhody White   14 June 1832 (174)
Lively, James to Sally Wood   13 June 1832 (169)
Looney, George to Elizabeth Hammonds   23 Dec. 1830 (197)
Lasiter, William to Harriett Dillahunty   12 March 1832 (214)
Littleton, Basil to Eliza Palmer   22 Nov. 1832 (226)
Lasiter, William to Katherine Howell   4 Oct. 1832 (237)

Letsinger, James to Eveline B. Ewell	28 Feb. 1833 (234)
Lavington, John to Susan Waldrop	23 Feb. 1833 (250)
Looney, Benjamin to Rutha Clark	20 July 1833 (255)
Morrison, Benjamin to Margaret Collison	30 April 1825 (10)
Mitchell, William G. to Eliza Durrett	19 Nov. 1825 (1)
May, John M. to Elizabeth Paulk	17 Nov. 1825 (3)
Miles, Alexander to Sally Allen	29 Dec. 1825 (28)
Morris, Abraham to Susannah German	14 Dec. 1826 (36)
Mustin, Henry to Hannah Clark	16 Feb. 1823 (46)
Mutrey, William to Edy Norrell	24 June 1827 (52)
Milligan, Charles G. to Nancy Moer	13 Sept. 1827 (65)
Matthews, Hardy to Nancy Thompson	27 July 1827 (69)
Miller, Jacob to Elizabeth Wilder	11 Dec. 1829 (72)
Madlin, Samuel to Elizabeth Staples	20 Jan. 1831 (160)
Miller, Peter to Minerva Jane Davis	18 June 1828 (75)
Marks, Nathaniel H. to Harriett Westmoreland	28 Aug. 1828 (94)
Melton, Samuel to Ann Morgan	29 Jan. 1826 (99)
Miller, Seth to Charlotte Jones	19 Aug. 1829 (102)
Martindale, James H. to Elizabeth Richards	5 Oct. 1829 (102)
Manning, Edward to Sarah H. Whisett	19 Nov. 1829 (110)
Murphy, John to Ally Welch	7 Aug. 1828 (116)
Moore, Stephen B. to Lucy McDougal	23 Dec. 1829 (133)
Mobley, Alfred to Jemima White	8 April 1831 (110)
Moseley, John C. to Elizabeth P. Duncan	26 Aug. 1830 (148)
Mattocks, Charles to Ann Wilkes	2 Sept. 1830 (154)
May, William to Malinda Gardner	26 Nov. 1831 (172)
Menton, Alfred to Betsy M. Peters	12 Jan. 1832 (176)
Merriman, Eli to Rachel Tankersley	22 March 1832 (178)
Maubly, Littleberry to Mahulda (?) Mason (?)	1 March 1831 (190)
Moore, Lewis G. to Atlantic McVey	3 Nov. 1831 (201)
Mockley, Ranson to Susan Crawford	21 Sept. 1831 (204)
Marvel, John to Rachel Miget	1 March 1832 (206)
McBride, David H. to Nancy McBride	7 Nov. 1830 (146)
McCarley, Thomas to Heda Newman	17 Feb. 1830 (147)
McBride, William to Matilda (?) Yocum	18 Dec. 1830 (159)
McBride, Strawn to Margaret Evans	28 Nov. 1830 (161)
McLemore, E. H. to Jane Orrick	15 Feb. 1832 (181)
McClain, Reuben to Rebecca Norris	8 May 1833 (51)
McGinney, Lawrence to Eliza Brown	10 April 1827 (45)
McDougal, Alexander C. to Ruthy D. Cronson	21 Feb. 1833 (214)
McKnight, James to Elizabeth Jackson	21 Aug. 1825 (17)
McLemore, _____ to Ruthy Thornberry	15 Feb. 1832 (165)
McLemore, Briggs to Mary Stegall	18 Sept. 1833 (229)
McCarta, Samuel to Eliza Walls	8 March 1833 (232)
McNeill, Daniel to Jane H. Cunningham	13 Aug. 1832 (238)
McCarty, Andrew F. to Sarah McDougal	10 May 1832 (248)
McKirby, Robert R. to Mary Littrell	10 May 1832 (248)
McRavey, John to Parmelia Newton	4 Feb. 1833 (116)
McDonald, William W. to Aladelphia Jeans	12 Dec. 1831 (175)
Newman, Moses to Polly Gates	8 Jan. 1827 (36)
Nations, Eli to Sally Weathers	7 March 1827 (44)
Norvell, John P. to Eady Gibson	4 April 1827 (103)
Nealy, Nicholas to Peggy Fisher	6 Aug. 1828 (114)
Nolin, Austin to Elizabeth McGarin	28 Aug. 1828 (117)

Nance, Sterling to Eliza Cunningham   9 Feb. 1832 (174)
Nolen, Rufus K. to Mary Winslow   18 July 1831 (189)
Nolen, Berry to Rachel Thomas   18 Aug. 1831 (190)
Nicholason, Charles to Sally Hammons   15 Dec. 1825 (2)

Oldham, Green Lee to Mary Conway   30 Oct. 1827 (80)
Obrient, William to Vashty Richardson   12 April 1832 (189)
Ogdon, Edward to Letitia Hannah   23 July 1832 (220)

Phillips, Gray to Fanny Welch   14 Sept. 1826 (30)
Pettus, Winston P. to Mary Williams   4 Oct. 1827 (49)
Powers, Henry to Rachel Callahan   14 Dec. 1827 (56)
Pricket, Joel to Malinda McNarry   9 Dec. 1827 (64)
Patton, David to Eliza Garrett   3 March 1829 (74)
Payne, Andrew W. to Henrietta M. Wilson   ? 1827 (79)
Price, James B. to Frances Mosin   25 Dec. 1828 (81)
Parker, Adlphis to Sarah Tankersley   17 June 1827 (80)
Powell, Henry P. to Elizabeth Speegle   25 Feb. 1820 (85)
Pickens, L. M. to Martha Farris   2 Feb. 1829 (89)
Paull, Jochin to Mahala Thornton   2 Oct. 1829 (73)
Price, William H. to Martha Mason   20 Nov. 1828 (100)
Polk, Jesse to Mahala Arnold   22 Oct. 1829 (104)
Parson, B. S. to Louis Harkins   22 Jan. 1828 (107)
Peyton, Colvin to Mary Futrell   12 June 1828 (115)
Phillips, Sterling to Sarah Wesson   22 Nov. 1829 (135)
Phillips, Asher to Caroline B. Thomas   20 March 1830 (145)
Porter, John P. to Susan C. Lindley   18 Feb. 1830 (141)
Powers, Moses to Sarah Sholer   21 Nov. 1830 (155)
Plummer, Segmon to Julia Boggs   22 March 1832 (178)
Peters, James M. to Nancy Trousdale   26 Oct. 1831 (204)
Patton, Alexander to Nancy Ann Sherrod   29 April 1832 (223)
Pollock, Jonathan to Nancy H. Knight   ___ Feb. 1831 (227)
Posey, Sidney C. to Harriett C. Dupriest   14 Feb. 1833 (242)

Richardson, Samuel H. to Mary Butler   ___ Feb. 1830 (??)
Redford, Anderson to Sally Baily   25 Dec. 1825 (4)
Rollins, Reuben to Indiah Tacey   4 June 1825 (11)
Ressin, John to Harriett Milton   5 Feb. 1826 (17)
Robertson, Christopher to Tobitha Reeves   26 Jan. 1826 (25)
Rust, Robert to Nelly Howard   4 Jan. 1827 (42)
Richardson, Littleton to Nancy Going   25 Sept. 1827 (50)
Rogers, James M. N. to Lucrety Chandler   19 Aug. 1827 (53)
Roper, James to Edney Jones   15 Sept. 1828 (80)
Robertson, James to Priscilla Darby   9 Feb. 1829 (90)
Rayburn, Ransom to Polly Tankersley   31 April 1829 (91)
Robertson, Robert W. to Martha Welch   8 July 1827 (91)
Richardson, Wiley C. to Jane Truesdale   2 Dec. 1828 (100)
Read, Griffin to Jane Smith   17 Nov. 1827 (104)
Ross, James to Sarah Burns   30 April 1829 (117)
Reese, Washington to Frances Huff   27 April 1829 (118)
Richardson, Thomas to Elliner Richardson   23 Sept. 1829 (126)
Robison, Basil to Elizabeth Anderson   4 Feb. 1830 (130)
Richards, Henderson to Sarah Murphy   1 Nov. 1829 (134)
Rogers, William H. to Martha Lowe   30 April 1830 (146)
Rice, Tobias to Louisa Gilbert   25 Sept. 1830 (146)

Ross, William A. to Grena Mason   5 March 1832 (185)
Rainey, Washington to Jane _____   18 Nov. 1831 (199)
Richardson, Wiley to Elizabeth M. Phillips   16 Sept. 1831 (203)
Rowel, Neal to Martha Ann Cheatham   6 Dec. 1832 (224)
Roach, Abraham to Martha Dupree   1 Nov. 1833 (226)
Reeder, Thomas to Eliza Fowler   30 Dec. 1832 (231)
Richardson, Washington to Betsy Kennedy   7 Oct. 1827 (59)
Rogers, William to Catherine Carrothers   19 July 1831 (241)
Robinson, Thomas to Rosella Willson   20 Sept. 1832 (246)
Rees, Thomas to Mary Hill   19 Jan. 1830 (124)

Skelton, Mark to Elizabeth Howard   21 Sept. 1825 (2)
Stewart, James to Sarah Ann Phillips   15 Dec. 1825 (4)
Springer, Joshua to Thursey Bryant   25 Dec. 1825 (4)
Simmons, George P. to Roan Cook   30 June 1825 (7)
Sute, James to Sealy Scogs   9 Nov. 1823 (17)
Strawn, Green Berry to Rebecca Howell   7 Feb. 1826 (27)
Stuart, George to Rochell Fullerton   21 Jan. 1826 (27)
Simmons, Robert S. to Nancy Smart   6 Feb. 1826 (29)
Simmons, William to Lucy Graham   27 April 1826 (29)
Strawn, Feilding to Nancy Ann Thomas   18 Oct. 1826 (37)
Stacy, Benjamin to Sallie W. Collier   12 Sept. 1826 (39)
Stone, Samuel to Matilda Eaton   26 Oct. 1826 (43)
Springer, Marshall to Elizabeth Johnson   11 June 1831 (208)
Spain, Solomon D. to Syntha Biler   15 Jan. 1828 (47)
Shields, John to Nancy McGee   27 Sept. 1827 (52)
Steele, James to Julia Ann B. Nolen   29 March 1827 (54)
Sharp, Arden to Martha Lamb   26 Jan. 1826 (56)
Smith, John to Susan Rogers   30 June 1827 (60)
Smith, Allen to Susan Richardson   4 May 1827 (62)
Sulivant, Cable to Judith Garden   25 Oct. 1827 (76)
South, Eli to Elizabeth Wilson   6 Oct. 1827 (76)
Smith, Augustine to Ann S. Fuqua   18 Dec. 1828 (77)
Shelburn, Samuel to Nancy Morris   26 Feb. 1829 (88)
Scott, Andrew to Elizabeth Durham   23 June 1829 (98)
Stout, Isaiah to Phebe Weatherly   20 March 1828 (99)
Stutts, Martin to Mary Lancaster   1 Oct. 1829 (100)
Shoat, John to Sarah Brown   15 Oct. 1829 (104)
Springer, Solomon to Matilda Brewer   17 Jan. 1828 (110)
Sessums, Richard R. C. to Lucy Durrett   30 Oct. 1828 (109)
Shelton, Thomas P. to Balinda C. Chambers   7 Aug. 1829 (114)
Stone, Thomas to Rebecca Hammond   3 Dec. 1828 (118)
Standridge, James to Susannah Barr   28 Dec. 1829 (125)
Springer, Dennis to Martha L. Young   26 Dec. 1829 (131)
Stepp, Joseph to Nancy Mears   14 Feb. 1830 (139)
Saunders, Aaron to Sally Daily   2 May 1830 (143)
Scott, Thomas to Rebecca Sparks   11 Aug. 1830 (143)
Spears, George to Jane West   18 Aug. 1830 (144)
Shelton, Robert R. to Rachel C. Sturgeon   26 Aug. 1830 (151)
Scott, Samuel C. to Elizabeth Prtichard   21 Nov. 1830 (151)
Smith, Joshua to Ann L. Moore   28 June 1832 (187)
Smith, Smith to Polly Young   27 Jan. 1831 (192)
Smart, Bennett to Nancy Adams   27 Sept. 1832 (197)
Scott, Joseph E. to Lucy Simmons   9 March 1831 (200)
Sullivant, John to Jane Roach   9 July 1831 (219)
Skeel, Samuel to Mary Ann Bradfield   13 May 1833 (222)

Shelby, Evan to Mary Williams   31 January 1833 (225)
Salovis, Daniel to Martha Cusonberry   13 January 1833 (230)
Smith, Burton to Canahan Visor   28 Feb. 1833 (230)
Skelton, Elijah to Eliza Webb   1 Nov. 1832 (235)
Smith, William F. to Elizabeth Snoddy   22 Feb. 1830 (150)
Smith, Frederick to Ann Phillips   24 Feb. 1833 (250)
Smith, Archibald to Amelia Holt   21 Aug. 1833 (260)
Smith, Thomas D. to Julean Mitchell   ___ Nov. 1833 (258)
Stone, Alfred to Sally Huggins   10 June 1825 (10)
Smith, William W. to Rebecca Simmons   19 Jan. 1830 (135)

Thompson, Samuel C. to Melinda Lakey   20 Aug. 1825 (?)
Trotter, John W. to Elizabeth Weatherford   19 Aug. 1826 (27)
Terry, Joseph to Susannah Miller   14 Jan. 1826 (33)
Thornton, William to Elizabeth Richardson   16 April 1827 (69)
Tolifer, William to Amanda Mitchell   8 Jan. 1829 (74)
Thompson, Samuel to Hariett Ferrel   27 Dec. 1827 (77)
Turbeville, Joseph to Matilda James   17 May 1829 (96)
Tucker, John H. to Elizabeth Cooper   4 Dec. 1828 (144)
Tisdale, Philander to E___ Lyon   3 Dec. 1828 (147)
Tibbs, William to E. Brown   ___ Oct. 1828 (147)
Ticer, James to Sarah Wilder   12 Oct. 1831 (152)
Thompson, Hugh to Margaret Boggs   18 June 1832 (200)
Tubbeville, Edmond to Sarah Pottman   22 April 1831 (209)
Trusdale, William to Elizabeth Crow   ___Sept. 1832 (244)
Taylor, Benjamin to Susan Brooks   1 Oct. 1833 (251)
Turbaville, L W to Frances Newman   _____1833 (?) (262)

Urban, Cooper to Catherine Wise   6 Feb. 1830 (153)

Vaughter Alejena to Mary Robertson   1 Jan. 1830 (150)
Valin, Samuel to Amelia Terass   24 March 1827 (19)
Vitilow, John to Fanny Robison   8 August 1831 (203)
Vamdever, Andrew to Elvirah Fuller   22 Oct. 1833 (228)

Westmoreland, Hartwell to Rhoda Rossin   12 April 1825 (8)
Webb, Richard to Malinda Lockey   5 August 1825 (9)
Wilson, John to Ann Johnson   21 April 1825 (12)
White, Anderson to Polly Davis   3 May 1825 (29)
Warrell, William E. to Eliza Jane Davis   6 May 1826 (30)
Wright, Moses to Anna Wilson   6 May 1826 (30)
Winburn, Richard to Rebecca Lloyd   21 April 1825 (31)
Womble, William C. to Cynthia Ticer   31 Dec. 1826 (35)
Winelow, Thomas to Jane E. Wilson   25 Oct. 1826 (36)
Winsted, John L. to Mary Davis   9 Jan. 1827 (38)
Wilson, Samuel to E. C. Johnson   ___July 1825 (40)
Walker, Archilus to Nancy J. Partin   21 Dec. 1826 (40)
Webb, Richard to Ethelinda Bumpas   30 Oct. 1826 (41)
White, Moses to Frances Brown   22 March 1827 (44)
Whitehead, Alexander H. to Rebecca Whitehead ___Sept. 1827 (47)
Williams, Dave to Rebecca Hill   15 June 1827 (53)
Waddell, Elam to Margaret (?) Campbell   5 April 1827 (54)
Winburn, Jesse to Mary Walker   21 Sept. 1827 (55)

Wade, Joseph W. to Eliza M. Wood	10 Jan. 1828 (62)
Wells, Robert to M. C. Coffee	25 Sept. 1827 (66)
Wilson, John to Elizabeth Hurston	15 Sept. 1828 (73)
Waters, John to Sally Laremore	31 Dec. 1828 (76)
Webb, Berry to Mary Webb	21 Feb. 1828 (78)
Webb, Richard to Nancy White	15 July 1828 (78)
White, Thomas to Elizabeth Jarman	21 April 1829 (90)
Winborn, William to Nancy N. Oden	30 April 1829 (?)
Whitten, Nicholas to Rebecca Murphy	20 April 1830 (92)
Wood, John L. to Susan W. Peters	14 August 1829 (93)
Weathers, William P. to Mary Ann Burney	22 May 1828 (93)
Whitehead, Tobias to Nancy Looney	28 July 1828 (95)
Williams, Henry to Lenora Appleton	15 Jan. 1829 (99)
Wilkes, Jesse to Nancy Robinson	2 Nov. 1828 (100)
Wilson, William to India Clark	5 Oct. 1825 (98)
White, Allen to Margaret Harvey	14 Aug. 1829 (103)
Walls, Risdon to Isabella Barron	29 Dec. 1829 (121)
Whitsett, Wilson to Elizabeth Price	11 Feb. 1830 (124)
Whitsett, William to Permelia Hunter	18 Oct. 1829 (139)
Willis, John W. to Katherine Grissum	13 Oct. 1830 (145)
Wilson, Thomas to Agnes Creel	18 Jan. 1826 (25)
Womble, Lorenza to Patsy Davis	7 Aug. 1830 (148)
Weatherly, Jeremiah to Maria Farris	12 Aug. 1830 (148)
Wilkes, Newman to Elizabeth Carr	21 Oct. 1820 (148)
Winstead, Seth H. to Mary Winstead	12 June 1830 (150)
Whitehead, Joseph to ____ Lacefield	15 June 1830 (151)
Willis, Emanuel F. to Eliza Asher	23 Dec. 1830 (152)
Wood, Isaiah J. to Mary Dixon	18 July 1830 (157)
Womble, Joseph H. to Clarissa Tankersly	30 Dec. 1830 (159)
Whitehead, William to Mary Gilbert	24 Sept. 1832 (165)
Waddell, Joseph P. to Lucinda J. Bryan	5 Jan. 1832 (168)
Walker, Robert to Eliza S. Morgan	22 Nov. 1831 (170)
Wiles, Benjamin to Tempy Hand	6 March 1832 (176)
Wood, Solomon to Elizabeth Dickson	18 Oct. 1832 (180)
Weathers, I. to Rebecca Burney	1 Dec. 1831 (181)
White, Drury B. to Margaret West	2 Oct. 1831 (182)
Wilson, Dennison to Nancy Westmoreland	28 April 1831 (183)

INDEX

Abernathy, John, 27, C-79.
Abet, Jane, C117; Nancy, C117; William C117.
Abington, Cornelius, C127; Louisa, C127; Martha, C127; Mary, C127; Sarah, C127; Sidney, C127; Souseanah, C127; Thomas, C127.
Abraham, Benjamin, C63.
Acres, Allice, C59; Azel, C105; Franklin, C105; James, C59;, C105; John, C105; Nancy, C105; Rody, C105; Sarah, C59.
Adair, Mary, C144; William, 5, 6, C144.
Adams, Barsheba, C139; Billy, C53; Caroline, C19; Charlotte, C19; David, C19, C53; Dicy, C53; Elizabeth, C53; Emily, C149; Frances, C19; Henry, C53; Isaac, C19; Isebella, C53; James, C19, C53; Jane, C19; John, C19, C53; Joseph, C19, C53; Louiser, C19; Malinda, C53; Malissa, C53; Manurvey, C53; Martha, C53; Mary, C144; Nancy, C53, C145, C152; Polly, C144, C145; Sally, C53; Samuel, C144; Tebithia, C144; Tennessee, C53; William, C19, C53.
Adkerson, Betty, C31; Calvin, C31; Ethelinda, C31; James, C1, C31; Joseph, C31; Polly, C31.
Agree, Julia, C138; William, C138.
Akers, Betsy, C138; Thomas, C138.
Alexander, 79; Andy, C7; Ann, C89; Annie, C38; Elizabeth, C38, C56, C89, C123; Ferdinand, C38; George, C89; Hezekiah, C123; James, C38, C89, C123; Jesse, C89; John, 45; Margaret, C84; Martha, C38; Mary, C38, C89, C123; Prince, C84; Randolph, C123; Rosannah, C123; Safroney, C38; Samuel, C56, C123; Sarah, C84, C123; Silus, C89; Thomas, C38, C89, C123; Tabitha, Tobitha, C123; William, C81, C84.
Alford, Milly, C148.
Alfred, Father, 70.
Allen, Ann, C140; Benjamin, C79; Bluford, C125; Buford, C96; Drucilla, C144; Eliza, C125; Emily, C125; Gabriel, C36; H. J., C144; Henry, C96, C125; James, C125; Jonnathan, C14; John, C144; Margaret, C125, C144; Martha, C96, C125; Mary, C96, C125; Milinda, C125; Nancy, C96, C125; Richard, C36; Robert, C125; Sally, C125; C144; Sarah, C125; Telthie, C96; William, 16, C79, C125.

Alman, Almon, Miss, 80.
Almon, Charles, 64, 65; Edward B., 68, 69; W. L., 76.
Alpine, Polly, C144; William, C144.
Alsup, Eliza, 13; James, 13; Margaret, 13; Orlena, 13; Sarah, 13; Thomas, 13.
Amnett, Andrew, C62; Francis, C62; Juliar, C62; Lousana, C62; Mary, C62; William, C62.
Anderson, C147; Catherine, C2; Champ, C58; Clyde, 15, 70; Columbus, C33; Elizabeth, C33, C107, C151; Francis, C58; Henry, C58; Herschel, 70; James, C2, C33, C66, C138; John, C2, C12, C62, C105, C107; Laura, C2; Leander, C2; Lodoska, C2; Malinda, C2; Margaret, C2, C66; C105, C138; Mary, C2, C107; Nancy, C2; Polly, C2; Rachel, C66, C138; Samuel, C2, C138; Sarah, C2, C58, C66, C138; Thomas, C2; Turnic, C105; William, C2, C33, C58.
Andrews, Amanda, C128; Ann, C62; Benjamin, C62, C136; Harriett, C144; Isabella, C128; James, C66, C128; John, C128; Martha, C66; Patrick, 13, C144; Patterson, C66; Permelia, C144; Peter, C128; Robert, C66; Sarah, C66, C128.
Andrson, James, C62.
Anglin, Annie, 7.
Appleton, Lenora, C154.
Appleby, Flavius, 65.
Archer, Annie Mary, C3; Caroline, C3, C57; Clementine, C57; Eliza, C3; Martha, C57; Marthy, C3; Mary, C3, C57; Peter, C57; Sarah, C3, C57; Selby, C3; Virginia, C57; William, C3; Willis, C3.
Archy, Cynthia, C75; Daniel, C75; Eliza, C75; James, C75; Jane, C75; Martha, C75; Sarah; C75; Souseanah, C75.
Armistead, Anthony, C144; Callie, 62; George, 23, 62; Peter, 12; Sarah, C144.
Armor, Ailsey, C105; Eliza, C105; Franklin, C105; Joseph, C105; Lewis, C105; Lucinda, C105; Manon, C105; Mary, C105; Nathan, C105; William, C105.
Armour, Andrew, C33; Elizabeth, C138; Jane, C33; Martha, C33; Margarett, C33; Mary, C33; Nancy, C148; William, C33.
Armstead (see Armistead) Capt., 31; Caladonia, C60; Champ, C58; Depheny, C60; Dewey, 76; Eliza, C60; Ellen, C60; Frances, C58, C60, C145; George, C60; Henry, C58; Heslop, 31, 62, C61; Jane, C60; L.C., C59, continued

Armstead, continued, Louisa, C60; Lusetta, C60; Mahulda, C60; Margaret, 62; Martha, C60; Mary, C60; Mary Frances, C60; Robert, C60; Sarah, C58, C60.
Armstrong, A's'tg, 6; Alexander, C144; Frank, 46; General, 42; J. L., 6; James, 6; Joseph, C113; Nancy, C114; Sarah, C44.
Arnett, Andrew, C61; Betty, C61; E. ...,67; Elizabeth, C38, C61, C140; James, C61; John, C61; Joseph, C61; Nancy, C61; Sally, C146; Sarah, C61; Susan, C61; William, C61.
Arnold, Cynthia, C45; Davis, C138; John, C45; Isaac, C45; Leander, C45; Louiser, C45; Mahala, C151; Martha, C45; Mary, C25, C45; Mary Ann, C138; Samuel, C45; William, C45.
Artherton, Annie, C38; Frank, C38; James, C38; Mary, C38; Thomas, C38.
Asbell, Catherine, C141.
Ashcraft, C. W., 65.
Asher, Alen, C144; Clarisa, C62; Eliza, C154; Harriet, 20, C144; John, 4; M. P., 34, 54; Mary, C62; Mrs., 19; Permelia, C144;Perry, C62; M. P., C62.
Ashford, Abner, C121; Ann, C121; Cynthia, C121; Elizabeth, C121; William, C121.
Ashley, James, C127; William, C127.
Askew, Aaron, C138; Chonado, C86; Ellen, C134; Eliza, C134; Elizabeth, C86, C134; Isabella, C134; Lovey, C134; Mary, C134; Moses, C134; Murrell, C86, C134; Newton, C86; Thomas, C86; William, C86.
Atheridge, Mary, C141.
Atkins, Letty, 66.
Atkinson, Mr., 70.
Atwell, H. J., C74; Hardy, C144; Julia, C74; Lewis, C74; Nancy, C74; Rebecca, C74; Robert, C74; Sarah, C74; Temperance, C74; Tempy, C144; William,C74.
Austen, Harriett, C17; Jane, C17; Jesse, C17; John, C17; Parilee, C17; Robert, C17.
Austin, Amanda, 54; Columbus, C17; Eliza, C17; Francis, C17; Robert, C17.
Auston, Alexander, C4; John, C17; Martha, C17; Sarah, C4; Sinthia, C4.

Bacohaw, Elvina, C87; Julena, C87; Thomas, C87.
Baget, Ann, C111; Albert, C111; Archibal, C111; Caroline, C111; Columbus, C111; George, C111; Lelia, C111.

Bail, Robert, 22.
Bailer, Anna, C142.
Bailey, Amelia, C75; Ann Eliza, C3; Augustus, C54; Elizabeth, C3; Frances, C127, C138; Hiram, C138; James, C3, C127; John, C144, C145; Joshua, C7; Jonathan, c, 13, 23, C127; Laura, C54; Lilly, C140; Lucrety, C144; Mary, C140; Nancy, C3; Permelia, C144; Rachel, C144; Richard, C3, C75, C127, C144; Robert, C1; Sarah, C138, C142; Thomas, C3; William, C3.
Bailes, Sarah, C147.
Baily, Sally, C151.
Baker, 35; Danny, C138; G. M., C116; Margaret, C36; Phoebe, C138; Rebecca, C36; S. C., 40.
Baldridge, , Almirmilla, C128; Elzab, C128; James, C128; Jane, C128; John, C128; Milton, C128; Mary, C128; Virginia, C128; William, C128.
Ballo, (Balbo), Catherine, C100; Harrison, C100; Juda, C100; Nancy, C100; Rainy, C100; Sarah, C100.
Balin, Balus, C116; Sarah, C116.
Baloo, Amanda, C91; Calfernia, C105; Catherine, C104; Elias, C9; Elizabeth, C90, C104; Granllville, C91; Henry, C104; Horsly, C91; Hosey, C105; Jessee, C91; John, C90, C104; Julia, C104; Margaret, C104; Martha, C91; Mary, C104; Matilda, C9; Mulin, C104; Monen, C105; Nancy, C91; Rainy, C90, C104; Rebecca, C104; Rethia, C91; Ruthie, C91; Sarah, C91, C104, C105; Sousan, C104; Winneth, C104; William, C90, C105. (See Ballo, Balbo)
Baner, Ann Eliza, C24; Alexander, C24; Bethenia, C24; John, C24; Martha Ann, C24; William, C24.
Bankes, Annie, C52; Eliza, C52; James, C52.
Bard, Alfred, C124; Elzab, C124; George, C124; Henry, C124; Jacob, C124; Margy, C124; Mary, C124; Thomas, C124.
Bare, Galston, C137.
Barker, Alabama, C135; Albert, C63; Andrew, C64; Bayler, C135; Elizabeth, C64; Florence, C135; Frances, 24; George, C64; J. B., C63; Lodus, C64; Louisa, C64; Martha Ann, C135; Parthenia, C135; Robert, C135; Samuel, C64; Sarah, C64; Taylor, C135; William, C64.
Barkins, Hannah, C26; John, C26; Rachel, C26.
Barksdale, Mary, C138; Miscanda, C138.

Barnes, Alexander, C144; Amelia, C140; Davis, C138; Elizabeth, C138; Fanny, C138; Jane, C138; John R., 76; Martha, C144; Nancy, C142; Nicy, C7; Reddington, C7; Sarah, C144; Starling, C144; Susannah, C148; Thomas, C138; Washington, C138; William, C7.

Barnhill, Caladonia, C6; Catherine, C6; Evaline, C6; Frances, C6; Lucinda, C6; Mahaley, C6; Matilda, C6; Nancy, C6; Sarah, C6; William, C6.

Barley, Mrs., 73.

Barnet, Abner, C115; Ann, C119; Ash, C93; Baby, C115, C119; Eliza, C115, C119; Elizabeth, C92, C119; Franklin, C119; George, C92; Jane, C92; James, C119; Logan, C92; Lucy, C119; Lusinda, C92; Mahala, C93; Martha, C92, C93, C119; Mary, C115; Sarah, C115; Sousannah, C115; William, C92, C119; Zachariah, C119.

Barnett, Absolum, C82, C145; Bill, 70; Booker, 67; Charity, C146; Cynthia, C82, C143, C145; Daniel, C145; Elizabeth, C145; Henryetta, C40; James, C117; Job, C117; John, C144; Keller, C117; Lucy, C40; Matilda, C145; Mary, C117; Nancy, C39, C138; Patsy, C144; Pheobie, C40; Rebecca, C82; Samuel, C117; Sarah, C39; Thomas, C39, C40, C138.

Barnette, Elvina, C94; Frances C94; Gideon, C95; Irvine, C93; James, C93; John, C93; Lucinda, C94; Mary, C93; Ollive, C94; Parric, C94; Sarah, C94; Zekeal, C93, C94.

Barr, Edmond, C100; Elizabeth, C76, C100; Ephraim, C100; Henry, C100; Isaac, 60, C76; Jessee, C100; John, C77, C100; C136; Margaret, C77; Martha, C100; Nancy, C146; Ruben, C100; S. G., 26; Samuel, C76; Silas, C63; Silus, C76; Susannah, C152; Willikm, C77, C100.

Barron, Elizabeth, C138; John, C138; Isabella, C154; Willie, 7.

Bartlett, Jane, C144; John, C144.

Barton, Elizab, C136, C146; S. W., C136; William, C136.

Baskin, Charity, C45; Jefferson, C45; Moses, C45; Phoenz, C45.

Bates, A. J., C66.

Baugh, Ann, C91; Elisha, C91; Elizabeth, C91; Frances, C91; John, C91; Joseph, C144; R. B., C62; Unicey, C144; Virginia, C62.

Baughman, Ann, C145; David, C145.

Bauldin (Baldwin?) Catherine, C138; John, C138.

Bayley, Nancy, C143.

Bayless, Eliza, C27; John, C27; Mary, C27.

Bayne, Daniel, C144; Elizabeth, C144.

Beaners, Margaret, 23.

Beard, Abner, C1, C13; Benjamin, C10; Elizabeth, C13; Emily, C10; Ester, C1; Henry, C1; J. N., C115; Jabus, C10; Martha, C10; Mary, C10; Sarah, C10; Sophia, C10.

Bearden, Catherine, C145; George, C145; Phoebe, C145.

Beardon, Betsy, C139; Polly, C138, C140; Thomas, C138.

Bearding, Frances, C140.

Bearn, Leptha, 13.

Beasley, Judy, C27; Malinda, C27; Nancy, C138; Phesoba, C146; Rachel, C139; Ruthy, C140; Samuel, C27.

Beauchamp, John, 31.

Beauregard, P. T., 29.

Beavers, Agnus, C35; Agy, C35; Bethana, C132; Bradley, C145; Catherine, C36, C94; Drury, C94; Elizabeth, C34, C94; Frances, C36, C126; Isabella, C36; James, C35; Jane, C34, C35; Jesse, C35; John, C35; C36, C94; Malvina, C145; Margaret, C94; Martha, C36; Marthy, C35; Mary, C35, C36; C94; Mikle, C35; Nancy, C35; Quinton, C94; Richard, C35; Rosanah, C36; Samuel, C36; Sinthia, C35; Susan, C36; Thomas, C35, C36; William, C34, C94.

Beck, E. E., 70.

Beckett, Rev., 57.

Beckham, Charles, C20; Joseph, C23; Manurvey, C22; William, C22.

Beckus, Flora, 62.

Beckwith, Alexander, C55; Ann, C29; Elizabeth, C55; Frances, C29; Jerenath, 23, C55; Mary, C29; Priscilla, C29; Richard, C29; Winston, C55.

Beddington, Joseph, C9.

Bedingfield, Andrew, C111; Charles, C111; Cynthia, C111; Elizabeth, C111; Frances, C111; Hanna, C111, C144; James, C111, C144; John, C111; Mary, C111; Stephen, C111; William, C111.

Bedford, Addeline, C22; Ann, C22; Charles, C6, C22; Eliza, C67; John, C22; Matilda, C6, C22.

Beebe, Anna Belle, C145; Justine, C145.

Beesley, Emeline, C47; John, C47; Rachel, C47; Rebecca, C47; Samuel, C47.

Behel, R. L., 71.

Belcher, Annie, C58; James, C58; John, C58; Margaret, C58; Susan, C58; Thomas, C58; William, C58.

Belew, D. S., 76; David, C16; Hannah, C140; James, C16; Jane, C142; Peggy, C16.
Bell, Benjamin, C144; Franklin, C144; John, C138, C145; Martha, C145; Sally, C138; Uriah, C133.
Belote, James, C63.
Belue, see Baloo, Ballo, Balbo.
Benford, Ann, C111; Hugh, C111; John, C111; Martha, C111; Thomas, C111; William, C111.
Benham, Elizabeth, C136; J., C136; James, 5, 7, C136; V. M., 21, 34; Vincent, C136; William, C136.
Bennet, William, C9.
Bentley, Joseph, C102; Mary, C102; Pressey, C102; Ritta, C102; Samuel, C102.
Benton, T. T., C71; Thomas, C17.
Berry, Minerva, C148; Rebecca, C38.
Berkwell, George, C42.
Bert, Eliner, C141.
Best, Charles, C86; James, C86; Margaret, C147; Mary, C86; William, C86.
Betterton, Harvey, C144; Nazarrin, C149; Nancy, C144.
Bevis, Aggy, C145; Caroline, C71; Elizabeth, C71; James, C71, C145; Nancy, C71; Richard, C71; Susan, C75.
Bibb, Sophia, C144; Thomas, 4, 5, 7, C144; William Wyatt, 1.
Bibb, Bibbs, Lewis, 62, Lockhart, 62.
Bidens, Harriet, C145; Hugh, C145.
Biffle, Col. Jacob, 44.
Bigger, Joseph, 12; Margaret, 21, C62, C115.
Biler, Syntha, C152.
Binford, Benjamin, C118; John, C144; Martha, C144.
Bird, Daniel, C9; Elizabeth, C8, C9; Harriett, C9; Holman, C8; Martha Ann, C9; Mary Ann, C8; Mercer, 8; Moses, C8; Sally, C147; Sarah Anne, C8; Thomas, C9; William, C8.
Birdsong, Nancy, C142.
Birgin, Polly, C140.
Bishline, H. L., 71.
Bishop, Joseph, C50; Margaret, C145; Olliver, C145.
Bisland, John, 48.
Bivins, Mrs. Ed, 66; Joseph, C138; Rebecca, C138.
Black, George, C48; Lewis, C48; Mary, C48, C142; Nancy, C48; Sabrey, C48; Sarah, C48; Thomas, C48; William, C48.
Blackburn, Caroline, C4; Elizabeth, C4; John, C4; Libbie, C4; Luvick, C4; Mary, C4; Malissia, C4; Powers, C4; Tamyra, C4.

Blackhard, John, C3; Mary, C3; Mary Ann, C3; Thomas, C3; William, C3.
Blair, Andrew, C135; Gen. Frank, 35, 36; John, C135; Margaret, C144; Mary, C135; Samuel, C144; W. A., 71; William, C135.
Blake, W. H., 69.
Blakely, Albert, C149; Cinthia, C149; Darkis, C149; James, C149; Jefferson, C149; John, C149; Leonidas, C49; Mariah, C49; Sicela, C49; Ray, 70; William, C49. (Note: all C149 numbers should be C49)
Blalock, Ann Eliza, C5; Catherine, C4; H. F., 59; Henry Clay, C5; Jane, C5; Jesse, C5; John, C5; M. L., 59; Mary Ann, C4; William, C4.
Blanton, Benjamin, C8; Carter, C145; Elizabeth, C145; Jesse, C8; John, C7; Martha, C8; Mary, C7; Ransom, C7.
Blasingame, Elizabeth, C146; Harvey, C144; Hester, C144.
Blasengine, John, C138; Sarah, C138.
Blasingam, Hiliry, C72; Phoebi, C72; Rachel, C72.
Blasingham, George, C68; Kitty, C68; Sarah, C68.
Blasingim, Catherine, C14; Elizabeth, C14; George, C14, C73; Isaac, C73; James, C73; John, C73; Lavisa, C73; Mary, C73; Matilda, C14; Nancy, C73; Nathaniel, C14; William, C14, C73.
Blaylock, Harry, 71.
Bliss, Arther, C62; John, C62; R. L., 62; Robert, 21, C62; Sarah, C62; Susan, C62; Thomas, C62.
Blount, John Thomas, 1, William, 1.
Bobo, H. L., 75.
Boddie, Nathan, 23.
Body, Ann Eliza, C56; Francis, C56; James, C56; Nathan, C56; Rebecca, C56.
Bogg, George, 13; Ellen, C63; Margaret C153.
Boggs, Julia, C151.
Bogs, Ann, C54; Emily, C54; Hanna, C54; J. B., C63.
Boman, Amanda, C130; Elizabeth, C143; H. J., C130; John, C130; Martha, C130; Mary, C130; Parilee, C130; Sarah, C130.
Bond, Betty, C4; Catherine, C144; John, C145; Mahaley, C4; Nancy, C4, C145; Willie, 7; William, C144.
Booa, Charles, C111; Elizabeth, C111; Margaret, C111, C112; Martha, C111; Mary, C111; Sarah, C111, C112.

Booth, Mary, C138; Nathan, C138.
Boothe, Catherine, C81; Harriett, C81; Mary, C81.
Borerin, Downs, C145; Nancy, C145.
Boskirk, 74.
Bossen, Nancy, C142.
Boston, Dolly, C117; Eliza, C117; Elizabeth, C144; Hugh, C117; Morris, C117; Nancy, C117; Patsy, C144; Sarah, C117; William, C117.
Bourland, Balis, C144; Bayles, 13; Cinthea, C8; Dallas, C8; Felix, C8; John, C144; Joseph, C145; Martha, C8, C144; Rosannah, C8; Sarah, C144; Susan, C145; T. P., C8; Winford, C8.
Bouron, Mr., 45.
Bowen, W. D., 40.
Bowman, Eliza, C144; Joseph, C144; Sally, C138; Thomas, C138.
Boyce, Eliza, C106; James, C106; Leroy, C106; Martha, C106; Mills, C106; Nancy, C106; Richard, C106; Sylvia, C106; Silvey, C148; William, C106.
Boyd, Charles, C119; Emily, C119; Joseph, C119, C144, C145; Mary, C88; Nancy, C145; Pressy, C144; Robert, C119.
Boyden, Charles, 13.
Boyle, Hugh, 62.
Boyles, Anny, C145; Cinthia, C145; James, C145; Malissa, C145; Thomas, C145.
Bradfield, Ann, C152.
Bracken, A. F., 23, C59; Elizabeth, C59; Felix, C31; J. H., C31; Joseph, C31; Julia, C31; Martha, C31; Mary, C31; Nancy, C31; Samuel, C57; Sarah, C31; Thomas, 59.
Bradford, Delena, C57; James, C40; Jesse, C40; Marissa, C40; Manurvey, C57; Mary, C40, C57; Richard, C57; Sarah, C40; William, C57.
Bradley, Amberis, C70; Beesley, C70; Caledonia, C113; Calvin, C70; David, C70; J. C., C70; James, C70; Jessee, C70; Lemora, C138; Lafayette, C113; Lydia, C113; Margaret, C70; Marion, C70; Mary, C113; Permelia, C70; Rebecca, C70, C138; Richard, C70; Sarah, C113; Senecia, C113; Susan, C70; Tebatha, C46; Terry, C113.
Bradly, Edward, 5.
Bradshaw, James, C82; Henry, 64; Nancy, C144; Pheby, C82; William, C144.
Bragg, Frances, C145; William, C145.
Brahan, John, 4, 5, 6, 7, C129, C130; Jane, C129.
Branch, Boling, C58; Caroline, C58; Frances, C58; James, C58; John, C58; Sarah, C58.

Brandon, Baby, C129; C. M., 67, Charles, C24, C129; Darling, C25; Dennis, C26; Elizabeth, C24, C25; Emline, C24; Frances, C24; James, C26; John, C24, C26; Julia, C25; Lusinda, C24; Margaret, C26; Martha, C64, C129; Mary, C25, C129; Matilda, C26; Nancy, C25; Rebecca, C26; Rosa, C129; Sarah Jane, C24; Sis, C129; Washington, C129; William, C26.
Brannon, Kinney, 16; Tom, 16.
Brannum, David, C145; Malinda, C145.
Bratton, Ellen, C29; George, C29, C45; Hugh, C45; James, C29, C45; Jane, C29; John, C29, C45; C144; Joseph, C29; Louiser, C45; Mary, C29; Nancy, C29; Rachel, C29; Samuel, C29; Sarah, C145; Thomas, C29; William, C29.
Brawley, Ellison, C91; Eliza, C91; Franklin, C91; Mary, C91; Milly, C91; Sarah, C91; William, C91.
Brazel, Andrew, C124; Catharine, C124; Frances, C124; James, C124; Nancy, C124; Sousan, C124; Tabitha, C124.
Breemly, Larken, C145; Maretta, C145.
Brewer, Anjaline, C1; Calvin, C76; David, C129; Davis, C144; Delilah, C76; Elizabeth, C129, C144; Elizajane, C1; Enoch, C1; Franklin, C129; George, C1; Henry, C1; Isaac, C129; Jacob, C129; James, C129; Jane, C1; John, C1, C76; Joseph, C129; Martha, C129; Mary, C1, C129; Matilda, C152; Nancy, C129; Rebecca, C129; Riley, C1; Sanders, C1.
Briant, Allen, C2; Hanna, C42; Jefferson, C2; Isabella, C42; James, C42; Jane, C42; John, C2; Marion, C2; Mary, C2, C42; Milla, C2; Nathaniel, C2; Nunsutts, C2; Tansey, C38; Winefred, C42; William, C2.
Briggs, Ann, C98; John, C98; Martha, C98; Mary, C98; Sarah, 24.
Brigs, Buel, C54.
Brim, Daniel, C138; Hannah, C138.
Broadfoot, Jack, 66; P.M., 59.
Brocchus, Sarah, 20.
Brock, Dr., 46; James, 53.
Broadway, Nancy, C140.
Broak, Dicy, C61; Elizabeth, C61; Frances, C61; James, C61.
Brock, Dr., 46; James, 53.
Brockass, Isebella, C60; Jane, C65; John, C60; Peter, C60; Robert, C60; Sarah, C65; Thomas, C60.
Brockwell, Nancy, C144; Polly, C142.
Bromley, Ersley, C147.
Brook, Mary, C145; William, C145.

Brooks, Beal, C90; Amanda, C109; Andrew, C109; Henry, C109; Jesse, 25, C78; John, C109; Joseph, C103; Macom, C85; Margaret, C109; Marye, C109, C145; Robert, C91; Ruthie, C90; Sarah, C147; Simon, C115; Susan, C153; William, C109, C145.

Brown, A. M., 76; Alexander, C102; Alfred, C102; Andrew, 53, 59; Annie, C66; Bethany, C145; Betsy, C138; Burnett, C138; Butler, C111; Caldid, C41; Charity, C102, C144; Darkis, 24; David, C41; Dempsey, C41; Dickson, C138; E., C153; Edmon, C66; Elias, C41; Elija, C137; Elijah, C138, C144; Elisha, C144; Eliza, C40, C41, C137, C150; Elizabeth, C102, C116, C137, C144; Emiline, C60; Emily, C50, C144; Frances, C153; Gabriel, C144; George, C102, C111, C138; Gracey, C102; Isabel, C138; James, C50, C60, C66, C102; C116; Jeanne, C138; Jane, C146, C147; Jessee, C102; John, C4, C50, C60, C116; Julia, C142; Julia Ann, C4; Leander, C41; Leethia, C102; Lenora, C102; Levica, C116; Lenora, C102; Levica, C116; Lucy, C111; Manerva, C111; Margaret, C66, C141, C145; Mark, C102; Marrissa, C44; Martha, C40, C41 Mary, C40, C41, C144, C146; Mournen, C102; Nancy, C40, C41, C102, C138, C145; Nelly, C145; Newton, C137; Norcis, C99; Obediah, C138; Patsy, C144; Paul, 76; Polly, C138; Rachel, C144; Robert, C50, 61, C138; Ruffin, C145; Sally, C138, C142; Samuel, C41, C137; Sarah, C41, C102, C116, C144, C145, C152; Shadrick, C144; Sousan, C102; Susannah, C145; T. B., 59; Thomas, C41, C50, C66, C116, C145; Tiny, C141; Welton, C50; Wesley, C102, C144; William, C40, C60, C102, C138, C145.

Bruce, Baylis, C29; Elizabeth, C29; Joel, C144; Malinda, C149; Margaret, C29; Mary, C144; Obediah, C29; Pinkney, C29; Samuel, C29; Sarah, C29; Thomas, 5; Zachary, C29.

Bryan, Elizabeth, C144; Julianna, C147; Lucinda, C154; Royal, C144; Sam, 12.

Bryant, Amy, C138; Needham, C138; Polly, C144; Roger, 76; Thursey, C152.

Brydges, Tom, 52.

Buchanan, 13; Andrew, C145; Harriet, C145.

Buck, W. L., 52.

Buckingham, Bob, 62.

Buell, D. C., 28, 31, 32.

Buford, Daniel, C145; Nancy, C145.

Bull (s), Catherine, C79; Dean, C79; Dempsy, C79; Frances, C79; Franklin, C79; John, C79; Minnie, C79.

Bullman, Benjamin, C109; James, C109.

Bullock, Caroline, 18.

Bumley, Absolum, C84; Alfred, C84; Augustine, C145; Charity, C84; Hiram, C84; Jackson, C75; James, C84; Jane, C75; Lakin, C84; Larkin, C84; Matthew, C84; Nancy, C75; Sally, C145; Sarah, C84; Thomas, C75; William, C75, C84.

Bumpas, Cornelia, C142; Ethelinda, C153.

Bumpass, Camilla, C143; Charlotte, C144; Everline, C59; Gabriel, C144; Margaret, C59; Mary, C59; R. C., C59; Thomas, C59.

Bumpus, Martha, C148.

Bundant, Dallas, C124; George, C124; Jane, C124; John, C124; Julia, C124; Louisa, C124; Manerva, C124; Martha, C124; Peter, C124; William, C124.

Buppes, Anna Belle, C145.

Brundige, William, 59.

Burass, Sarah, C48.

Burges, Elias, C145; Rachel, C145.

Burk, Mary, C145; William, C145.

Burlison, Ann, C40; Henry, C40; Jefferson, C40; John, C40; Josheah, C40; Martha, C40; Mary, C40; Mikle, C40; Ruth, C40; Sarah, C40; Wiley, C40; Winford, C40; William, C40.

Burnet, Arabella, C10; Chancy, C145; Ellen, C10; Ruben, C10; John, C10; Joseph, C145.

Burnett, C145; Malissa, C145; Patience, C143.

Buurnette, Caty, C93; Jacob, C93; James, C93; Mahula, C93.

Burnes, Addaline, C25; Caroline, C25; Green, C25; John, C25; Mary, C25; Perlina, C145; Nancy, C25; Phoebe, C25; William, C145.

Burney, Andrew, C91; Elias, C91; James, 5, 7, 8; Lucinda, C91; Mary Ann, C154; Rebecca, C154; Samuel, 16, William, C91.

Burns, Almarene, C36; Barnabus, C145; Benjam, C54; Benjamine, C35; Caroline, C36; Drisilla, C36; Elbert, 70; Elijah, C36; Elizabeth, C48, C54; Inez, C72; Isreal, C36; James, C36, C54, C58; Jane, C36; John, C35, C36; Jerry, C36; Josiah, C35; Lucy, C58; Lusinda, C54; Manuel, C36; Martha, C35; Mtilda, C36; Mary, C36, C54, C144, C145; Moses, C54; Nancy, C54, continued,

Burns, continued, Polly, C35, C145;
Richard, C36; C58; Robert, C35,
C36, C54, C58; Ruben, C36; Ruffin,
C58; Samuel, C54, C144; Sarah, C157;
Thomas, C54.
Burnsides, Thomas, C136.
Burrah, Calpurney, C41; James, C41;
Lusinda, C41; Milla, C41; Peter,
C41; Rebecca, C41.
Burrass, Columbus, C33; Elizabeth,
C33; James, C33; John, C33.
Burrow, Elizabeth, C112; Frances, C145;
George, 87; J. T., C87; James, C98;
Joel, C98; John, C98; Mary, C87, C98;
Rebecca, C98; Roan, C98; William,
C98, C145.
Burrus, Dick, 26.
Burton, Elmira, C145; Lucery, C144;
William, C145.
Burtwell, 7; Annie, C65; Caroline, C65;
Elizabeth, C65; Isibella, C65;
James, 53, C65; John T., C65;
Lavenia, C65; Mary, 39, C65.
Busby, James, 71.
Buset, Baby, C87; George, C87;
William, C87.
Butcher, Charles, C41; Elvira, C41;
Felding, C41; Gilbert, C41; Joshua,
C41; James, C41; John, C41; Malinda,
C41; Samuel, C41; Thomas, C41.
Butler, C113; Adolphus, C98; Bennett,
C5; Caroline, C5; Chism, C93; Cynthia,
C121; Darcus, C5; Diddana, C5; Eliza,
C88; Elizabeth, C5, C116; Emily, C5;
Frances, C87, C115; Gabriel, C87,
C93; Garvin, C5; Henry, C5, C145;
James, C93; John, C5, C93, C98, C116;
C144; Lee, C88; Lethy, C5; Margaret,
C5, C88, C98, C144; Martha, C5, C88;
Mary, C5, C93, C116, C138; C145;
Minah, C88, Minor, C98; N. W., C98;
Nancy, C5, C145; William, C88; Risen,
C98; Robert, 74; Sarah, C5, C87;
Susie, 74; Thomas, C138; Wealthy,
C5; William, C88.
Buttler, Sarah, 23.
Butts, Canagair, C145; Elizabeth, C145.
Byrn, J. W., 12; Sophia, C144.
Byrne, Anna, C145; John, C145; Mary, C145.

Cackelman, John, C61, C130; Peapula,
C61.
Cahoun, A. A., C111; Charles, C111;
Collesselia, C111; Easter, C111;
John, C111; Mary, C111; Rebecca, C111;
Washington, C111.

Cain, Elizabeth, C130; Franny, C130;
Harriet, C130; Jane, C130; John,
C130; Margaret, C130; Sarah, C130;
William, C130.
Caine, L. S., 15.
Caldwell, Mary, C147.
Calhoun, Mary, C130.
Calk, Amanda, C7; Amelia, C7;
Ann Eliza, C7; William, C7.
Call, Caroline, C42, C79; Delitha,
C42; Elender, C122; Elias, C42;
Hezekiah, C79; John, C79; Nancy,
C42; Roy, 75; Samuel, C122;
Sarah, C122; Sely, C42; Thomas, C79.
Callahan, Mary, C144; Polly, C142;
Rachel, C15.
Calloway, Fanny, C63; M. C., C63;
W. J., 63, 69.
Cameron, Duncan, C145; Joel, 8; Sarah,
C145.
Campbell, Aley, C59; Andrew, C145;
Ann, C63, C146; Argile, 12;
Cynson, C133; David, C59, C138;
Eliza, C145; Elizabeth, C113, C140;
Garrett, C63; Garrick, C63; Hugh,
5, 6, 7, C119; Issac, C137; James,
C59, C119; Johnm 52, C63, C109, C136,
C145; Lidda, C59; Margaret, C153;
Martha, C59, C63; Mary, 78, C59,
C145; Nancy, C138, C145; Randall, 17;
Robert, C59, C137; Rody, C119; Ruthy,
C113; Samuel, C113; Sarah, C139;
Tommy, 74; W. P., 40; Mrs. W. P., 41,
62; Washington, C3; Wiliam C63, C145.
Camper, Mrs. A. B., 62; M. W., 68.
Campton, Elizabeth, C148.
Cannon, Ann, C75, C114; Baby, C114;
D. J., C114; Daniel, C35; Elizabeth,
C58, C114; Hugh, C30; Isaac, C30;
Jabez, C30, C58; James, C114;
Sarah, C30, C58; William, C30.
Cantrell, Lenoir, C138; Lusindy, C1;
Nelly, C138.
Caphity, Caroline, C105; Ditous, C105;
Elizabeth, C105; Greene, C105; Harison, C105; James, C105; John, C104;
Mary, C105; Nancy, C104; Starns, C105;
Thomas, C105; William, C104.
Caplin, Austin, C146; Liddia, C146.
Carborn, Angeline, C98; Daniel, C98.
Care, Harris, C138; Mary, C138.
Carey, Edward, 12.
Carley, Benjamin, C146; Phoeba, C146.
Carlisle, Eliza, C138; Campbell, C138.
Carlock, 79.
Carmichael, A. H., 69.
Caroll, Carroll, Addison, C28; Anderson,
C55; Catherine, C28; Frank, C55;
Jesse, C28; John, C28; continued,

Carroll, continued, Lusetta, C55;
Mary, C28, C55; Nancy, C28; Permelia,
C55; Richard, C55; Sarah, C28;
Scott, C28; Taylor, C28.
Carney, Nancy, C35.
Carr, Andy, C22; Ann, C31; C45; Annie,
C22; Cynthia, C146; Daniel, C22;
Eliza, C17; Elizabeth, C6, C31,
C146, 138; Ellen, C45; Emerline, C34;
Franklin, C34; George, C22, C45;
Harrice, C34; Hugh, C17; Henry, C125;
Isaac, C146; James, C9, C17, C45;
John, C6, C17, C22, C31, C34, C138;
Joseph, C22, C34; Lena, C17, Lusinda,
C34; Malissa, C17; Marion, C22;
Margaret, C6, C17; Martha, C17, C22,
C34; Mary, C6, C22, C34, C45; Matilda,
C34; May, C146; Robert, C31; Rupert,
C12; Sarach, C34; Thomas, C17;
Wilson, C45, Wiston, C22; William,
C31.
Carroll (see also Caroll), Eliza, C146;
William, C146.
Carrathers, Catherine, C152.
Carruthers, James, 21.
Carson, Andrew, C51; Carolin, C51;
Catherine, C37; Edy, C37; Eliza, C51;
Greenbury, C37; Hugh, C37; Jackson,
C51; James, C37; Jasper, C37;
Joab, C51; John, C37; Margaret, C51;
Mary, C37, C51; Perrilla, C50;
Samuel, C50; Sarah, C37; Tom, 15.
Carter, Amous, C3; Benjamin, C58;
Caroline, C22; J. M., 69; James, C3;
John C., C3; Mary, C3; Marcy C97;
Nancy, C3, C145; Marcissa, C3;
Sally, 62; Sidney, C50; William, C3.
Cartier, Ann, C146; John, C146.
Cartrell, Lucinda, C145.
Cartwright, Eliza, C51; Elizabeth, C51;
Isebella, C51; Isaac, C51; John, C51;
Lucy, C146; Manurvey, C51; Mary, C51;
Overton, C51; Sarah, C51; William,
C146.
Casey, Abergale, C33; Ann Eliza, C12;
Billy, 44; Charity, C11; Felix, C12;
Jacob, C11; John, C12, C33; Josephine,
C11; Laura Ann, C12; Leander, C11;
Levi, C11, C33; Lucust, C11; Martha,
C33; Mary, C33; Rutitia, C11;
Samuel C33; Sarah, C11, C12;
Thomas, C12; Mrs. W. W., C3; William,
C11; Zalena, C11.
Cassity, Emer, C62; Mrs. M. L, 28.
Castleberry, Eliza, C117; Elizabeth, C117;
William, C117.
Caswell, Gen. Richard, 1.
Caten, Elizabeth, C130.

Catharins, Eliza, C79; Robert, C79.
Cathey, Henry A., 59, 68.
Caugh, Ann, C95; Caroline, C95;
Ephraim, C95; John, C95; Martha, C95;
Mary, C95; Nancy, C95; Robert, C95;
Thomas, C95.
Cautch, Catharine, C84; Charity, C84;
Charles, C84; Elizabeth, C84; John,
C84; Mary, C84; Thomas, C84;
Washington, C84.
Cauthen, Peck, 71.
Ceaser, Julious, C4.
Chambers, Andrew, C45; Caroline, C45;
Elizabeth, C45; George, C45;
James, 13; C45.
Chaim, Bulus, C115; Elizabeth, C115;
Margaret, C115; Martha, C115;
Permelia, C115; Robert, C115.
Chaney, David, C21; Elizabeth, C21;
Hiram, C21; John, C21; Robert, C21;
Sarah, C21.
Chapman, Elizabeth, C82; Martha, C82.
Chambliss, Pomeroy, 64.
Chandler, Baby, C104; Balinda, C152;
Bethel, C103, C113; Elizabeth, C114,
C139; Fanny, C46; Frances, C144;
G. S., C111; J. G., C46; James, C111;
John, 44, C104, C114; Lucinda, C112;
Lucretia, C103, C151; Manerva, C103;
Matilda, C103; Matin, C112; Mary,
C103, C112; Rachel, C46; Roda, C112;
Rody, C111; Sarah, C111; William, C46.
Cheatham, Christopher, 3; Martha Ann, C152;
Susannah, C145, C146.
Chesure, Ruthy, C138; Zachariah, C138.
Cherry, Rebecca, C65.
Childers, Thomas, 4.
Childress, E., C63; Greenbury, C52;
James, C52, C57; Joel, C52; John, 5,
6, 8, 31; Jr., C62; Malinda, C52;
T., 6; William, C58; John (?), C45.
Chisam, John, 45.
Childs, Milinton, 6.
Chisholm, Alexander, C146; B. F., C134;
Betty, C146; Easter, C5; Emily, C142;
Frances, C5; John, C124; Joseph, C124;
Hettie, C5; Dr. L., 35; Lucinda, C141,
C146; Margaret, C124; Millissa, C5;
Paralee, C140; Rufus, C124; Tolliver,
C5; W. F., 71; William, 26.
Chisolm, Durenda, C148; Lucinda, C148.
Christian, Zack, 69.
Cimmons, Alexander, C46; Demarious, C32;
Ellender, C46; Henry, C32; Jane, C32;
Lewis, C32; Lucretia, C32; Martha, C32
Mary, C32; Susan, C32; Thomas, C46;
William, C130; Z. Taylor, C32.
Claiborne, Elizabeth, C58; William, C58.

Clanton, Caroline, C18; Delila, C27; Elias, C18; James, C18, 41; Jesse, C18; Jerrymyah, C18; Joseph, C18; Kesiah, C18; Lavinia, C27; Linsey, C27; Malinda, C27; Martha, C27; Mary, C27; Moses, C18; William, C27.

Clark, Amanda, C4; Betty, C4; C. H., C97; David, C146; Dr., 24; Eliza, C30, C40; Elizabeth, C4; Elvira, C30, C40; Fereby, C97; Hannah, C150; Harriet, C30; Hettie, C30; India, C154; James, C4, C40, C146; John, C30, C135, C138; Jonnathan, C4; Joseph, C4; Julia, C135; Leona, C40; Lusinda, C4; M., 12; Mahala, C4; Manurva, C30; Margaret, C141; Marshall, C137; Martha, C4; Mary, C137, C143, C146; Nancy, C4, C97, C145; Patrick, C30; Peggy, C30; Polly, C138; Ruth, C146; Sally, C146; Samuel, C135; Sarah, C4, C135; Sarena, C4; Thomas, C4; Tom, 52; William, C4, C30, C40, C135.

Clopwell, Richard, C31.

Clay, John, 5; Richard, C3.

Cleer, Lucinda, C149.

Clem, Adam, C138; Sally, C138.

Clemmons, Aaron, C2; Alex, 66; Caroline, C2; Elizajane, C2; Isema, C2; Jasper, C2; Marion, C2; Matilda, 66; Millissa, C2; Thomas, C2; Williamson, C2; Zilthy, C2.

Clemons, Adron, C68; Adaline, C68; Ann, C69, C146; Benjamin, C69; Martha, C69; Perlissa, C68; Polly, C68. Henry, C68, C69; James, C68, C69; John, C68; Martha, C69; Perlissa, P68; Polly, C68; Rebecca, C68, C69; Sarah, C69; Thomas, C68; William, C69.

Cline, Lieut., 52.

Cloer, Elijah, C146; Elisha, C145; Elizabeth, C146; Matilda, C145.

Clopton, John, 71.

Clore, Frances, C146; John, C146.

Cloyd, T. D., 69.

Coal, Abraham, C28; Abram, C108; Charles, C111; Easter, C108; George, C28; James, C108; Jane, C75; Jimimah, C108; John, C28; Judy, C28; Martha, C73, C75; Marcy, C28, C70, C108; Millie, C28; Nancy, C75; Ollive, C108; Rachel, C108; Robert, C28; Rody, C108; Samuel, C75; Sarah, C75; Solomon, C108; Wesley, C28; William, C75.

Coale, Penelope, C138; William, C138.

Coalter, George, 12.

Coats, Ann, C112; Elizabeth, C112; Isabella, C112; James, C115; John, C70; Margaret, C112; continued,

Coats, continued, Martha, C73; Mary, C70; Nancy, C143; Olly, C70; Sarah, C70; William, C70.

Cobb, Elizabeth, 13, C15; Frank, 70; James, C15; John, C15; Margaret, C15; Martha, C15, C17; Mary, 13, C15; Nathaniel, C17; Pertina, C145; Phillip, C15; Rickman, C15; William, 13, C15.

Coburn, Betsy, C146; Elizabeth, C145; Frances, C145; Hannah, C140; John, 58; Mark, 58; Patsy, C139; Russell, C41; Thomas, C146.

Cockburn, Amanda, C54; Canny, C146; Charles, C54, C146; Easter, C146; Elijah, C54; Elizabeth, C54; Esther, C142; George, 15, 16; Hadly, C54; Harmon, C138; Harriet, C54, C146; Liddi, C54; Lucinda, C54, C145; Rachel, C138; Whitnul, C146.

Cockram, Charity, C38; Elizabeth, C38; Fanny, C38; Francis, C38; James, C38; Jasper, C38; Jefferson, C38; John, C38; Margaret, C38; William, C38.

Cockerells, 13.

Cockrill, John, 20.

Cocks, George, C11; James, C11; John, C11; Martha, C11; Mary, C11; Mary Ann, C11; Sarah Ann, C11; Wesley, C11; William, C11.

Cocrane, Elizabeth, C145; Robert, C145.

Coffee, Mrs. A. D., 67; Alexander, 23, C42; Andy J., 8; Ann E., C42; Caroline, C78, C88; Catherine, C39; Clayborn, C88; Edward, C88; Eliza, C42; Elizabeth, C88, C118; Joel, C88; John, 4, 5, 6, 7, 8, 11, 13, C79, C88; Joshua, C39, C79, C88; M. C., C154; Mariah, C88; Mary, 23, C39, 40, C42, C78, C112, C139; Minrod, C88; Mollie, 26, C78; Mrs., C78; Prudence, C88, C139; R. M., C115; Rachel, C39; Richard, C88; Sarah, C88; Thomas, C78, C79, C118; William, C39.

Coggen, Cazada, C103; Robert, C103, William, C103.

Cohorn, Elizabeth, C29, C72; Emiline, C72; Israel, C29; John, C72; Martha, C29; Mary, C29, C72; Mills, C72; Polly, C72; Rachel, C29; Reader, C29; Sabrey, C72; Sarah, C29; William, C29, C72.

Colbert, George, 2, 19, 77.

Coleman, Aden, 76; Joseph, 6.

Colier, John, C146, Sally, C146.

Collier, Allice, C57; Catharine, C57; Clarah, C57; Jennetta, C57; Martha, C57; Mary, C57; Polly, C141; Sally, C152; Wiett, C57; Wyatt, 23.

Collie, Elizabeth, C145; Maynard, C145.
Collins, 54; John, 39; Mary, C62; Rachel, C139; Thomas, C139.
Collison, Elander Ann, C141; Margaret, C150.
Comer, Edmund, C96.
Conner, Bill, 69; J. C., 41; J. M., 21; Will, 70.
Conway, James, C66; Mary, C151.
Conrey, Elizabeth, C149.
Coody, Parthenia, 13.
Cook, Abitas, C146; Artemus, C43; Catharine, C81; Elizabeth, C81; Ellender, C81; George, C43, C146; Jesse, C43; Martha, C43, C81; Mary, C81, C146; Nancy, C43; Roan, C152; Robert, C81, C146; Rosannah, C76; Samuel, C43; Sidney, C81; Thomas, C76; Wesley, C81; William, C76, C81.
Cooke, May, C146.
Cooker, Susan, C70.
Coonts, Amanda, C17; George, C17; John, C17; James, C17; Salene, C17; William, C17.
Cooper, Abraham, C87; Annie, C90; Archie, C23; Betsy Jane, C23; Carmeltia, C16; Charity, C139; Charlotte, C23; Columbus, C23; Duncan, 39; Elizabeth, C112, C153; Frances, C115; Hugh, C90; James, C90; Jane, C90, C138, C139; John, C90, C112, C115; Julia, C115; Matilda, C112; Mary, C112; C115; Nancy, C90, C145; Polly Ann, C23; Rebecca, C23; Robert, C115; Roda, C112; Saby, C23; Samuel, C90, C112, C138; Sarah, 24; Sousan, C115; Thomas, C16; Wiley, C16; William, 27, C16, C115.
Copeland, Elizabeth, C146; Martha, C146; Richard, C146; Thomas, C146.
Cordle, Charity, C42; Davy, C42; James, C42; Martha, C42; Nancy, C42; Sarah, C42; Terry Ann, C42; William, C42.
Corhorne, Jerry, C70; John, C69; Margaret, C70; William, C70.
Cork, William, C131.
Cornish, Martha, C143.
Cornym, 39.
Coron, Jane, C146; Lemuel, C146.
Corum, Catherine, C93; Charlotte, C93; George, C93; James, C93; Jane, C93; John, C93; Louisa, C93; Mary Ann, C147; Sally, C143; Samuel, C93; Sousan, C93; Thorington, C93.
Costell, Eliza, C146; John, C146.
Cotter, John, C138; Nancy, C138.
Cotton, Eliza, C9; Nancy, C149.
Couch, Baby, C117; Charity, C146; Eliza, C117; Jacob, C117; James, C117; John, C117; Julian, C117; Sarah, C117; Thomas, C146.
Coulter, see also Coalter, George, 5, 6, 8; Harriett, C145.
Count, Seth, C9.
Counts, Mary, C9.
Covington, Mary, C118; Miram, C118; Thomas, C118; William, C118.
Cox, Aaron, C101; Arom, C145; Anderson, C84, C101; Andrew, C101; Catherine, C94; Charles, C94, C146; Charlotte, C101; Chestly, C94; Drury, C139; Eli, C94; Elisha, C101; Eliza, C139; Elizabeth, C83, C84, C98, C101; Frances, C137; George, C98, C101; Henry, C121; Hiram, C84; Isora, C94; Jacob, C94; James, C101, C137; Jesse, C146; Joel, C101; John, C84, C95; Josiah, C94; Louisa, C101; Lucy, C82, C82; M. L., 59; Mahala, C94; Malicia, C101; Marlin, C84; Martha, C94, C101; Mary, C84, C101, C137; Monroe, 24; Nancy, C82, C94, C101, C145; Nellie, C101; Newton, C101; Rachel, C82; Ritty, C101; Robert, C94; Samuel, C101; Sanford, C94; Sally, C138, C146; Sarah, C82, C83, C94, C101; Selia, C94; Stephen, C82, C83; Susan, C95; Susannah, C146; Tiletha, C137; Virginia, C101; Wiley, C84; William, C84, C101, C137.
Craddock, Burrell, C139; Elizabeth, C139.
Craft, Andrew, C45; Ann, C45; Jane, C45; Madison, C45; Samuel, C45; William, C45.
Craig, Ben, 77; David, 4; Ellen, C130; John, 12, 31, C130; Martha, C144; Mary, C130; Samuel, 8, 12; Mrs. Samuel, 13; Thomas, 5.
Crawford, Angeline, C139; Elizabeth, C146; Samuel, C146; Susan, C150; William, C139.
Creamer, Alvey, C115; Harriet, C115; J. H., C115; Lucy, C115; Mary, C115; Sarah, C115.
Creel, Agnes, C154.
Crews, Jane, C146; John, C146.
Critenden, Hnnetta, C64; James, C64; John, C64; Lucinda, C64; Martha, C64; Matilda, C64; William, C64.
Crittenden, Joshua, 26; Prudence, C139; Thomas, C139.
Crittigdon, Josiah, C78; Mary, C78; Prudence, C78.
Critingdon, Elizabeth, C88; Idephonde, C88; T. J., C88.
Crittingtoon, Benjamin, C79, C130; Mary, C79; Octave, C130; Wiley, C79; William, C79, C130.

Crodock, James, C17; John, C58; Josephine, C17; Martha, C17.
Croft, Sarah, 21.
Cromwell, William Henry, 71.
Croney, Annis, C93; Benjamin, C93; Bergus, C93; Elizabeth, C93; James, C93; Johnson, C93; Margaret, C93; Martha, C93; Nancy, C93; Noah, C93; Rody, C93; Sarah, C93; Sousan, C93; William, C93.
Cronson, Ruthy, C150.
Cronter, E. J., C63.
Cross, Arthur, C85; Balzora, C85; Benjamin, C75; Camel, C85; Camell, C85; Elmira, C75; Isabella, C75; Margaret, C75; Martha, C75, C85; Sarah, C85; Shairic, C75; Shedrick, C85.
Crow, Ann, C136; Baby, C82; Columbia, C137; David, C136; E. W., 71; Elizabeth, C122, C136, C153; Frances, C122; Frank, 71; Isaac, C83; James, 14, 31, C83, C129, C136, C137; Jane, C128; John, C122; Isaac, 25; Lucy, C83, C122; Louisa, C136; Margaret, C122; Martha, C82, C136; Martin, C125; Mary, C82, C83, C125, C129; Moses, C82; Newton, C122, C137; Patrick, C125; Rebecca, C81, C83; Sarah, C137; Sousan, C83, C137; Thomas, C122, C125, C136, 23.
Crowder, Cynthia, C99; James, C99; Jepsah, C99; John, C99; Julia, C99; Martha, C99; Nancy, C99; Samuel, C99; Sousan, C99; Thomas, C99; William, C99.
Crum, Catherine, C145; Malinda, C139; Peter, C145.
Cullum, Ann, C64; Cynthia, C64; Delanson, C64; Elizabeth, C64; Martha, C64; Mary, C64; William, C64; Zale, C64.
Cumpton, William, C59.
Cunningham, Eliza, C151; J. M., 59; James, C114; Jane, C150; Johnathan, C114; Mary, 62; Ollive, C114; Susannah, C114; William, C114.
Cup, Phillip Penny, C100.
Curley, Azula, C116.
Curry, Charles, C69.
Cursey, Angeron, C106; Clinton, C106; Hannah, C106; James, C106; Jefferson, C106; Lemuel, C106; Levisa, C106; Mirum, C106; Winfield, C106; Winford, C106.
Curtice, Annie, C2; Caroline, C2; Daniel, C2; James, C2; John, C2; Leanah, , C2; Mary, , C68; Murrel, C2; Nancy, C2; Polly, C68; Rody, C2; Sparty, C12; Thomas, C2; Wilford, C2.

Curtis, Baylor, C134; Eli, C134; Henry, C134; Hester, C144; Houston, C134; Isaah, C134; Jasper, C134; John, C82; Josiah, C134; Mary, C134; Nancy, C82, C134; Sousan, C134; Winny, C134.
Cusonberry, Martha, C153.
Cypress Land Company, 4, 10, 15.

Dabbs, Henry, C29.
Daily, Edwin, C104; Elizabeth, C104; Joseph, C104; Sally, C152; Sarah, C104; Sousianah, C104.
Dalrumple, George, C54; Illenissa, C54; James, C70; John, C54; Nancy, C54; Rachel, C70; S. M., C54; Thomas, C54.
Dalton, James, C126.
Daly, Elbert, 76.
Damrons, Benjamin, C29; Idella, C29; Elizabeth, C29; Martha, C29; Mary, C29; Robert, C29; Sarah, C29; Simon, C29.
Dance, Isabella, C146; William, C146.
Dancy, John, C39.
Danlton, James, C68; Lewis, C68; Malinda, C68; Nancy, C68; Rebecca, C68.
Dannelly, Alexander, C126; Dumos, C126; Elizabeth, C126; Henry, C126; James, C126; John, C126; Leonard, C126; Lucinda, C126; Mary, C126; Nancy, C126; Sarah, C126; Souseannah, C126; Swain, C126; Walter, C126; William, C126.
Darbey, Benjamin, C146; Columbus, C15; David, C15; Debora, C146; Elijah, C15; Elizabeth, C148; H. J., C6; Henry, C12, C60; Isaac, C146; James, C147; John, C15; Martha, C12; Mary, C15, C146; Mrs., 7; Nancy, C12, C15; Phillip, C12; Rickard, C12; Rosannah, C15; Ruthie, C15; Sarah, C15; Verlinda, C146; William, C12, C15.
Darby, Benjamin, C13; Betsy, C142; Cora Lee, 76; Ebeneser, C61; Elizabeth, C139; Gene, 76; Henry, C13; Jacob, C13; James, C139; Jess, 66; Joseph, C44; Levi, C11; Lucilla, C13; Lucy Ann, C60; Margaret, C15; Mariah, C15; Martha, C15; Mary, C15; Miles, 68; Nancy, C11, C15; Polly, C139; Priscilla, C151; Pulaski, C13; Sarah, C61.
Darney (?), Elizabeth, C92; Franklin, C92; Joseph, C92; John, C92; Levi, C92; Mary, C92; Sarah, C92.

250

Darrell, Nancy, C146; R. D., C146.
Daron, Amous, C57.
Daughty, William, 13.
Davenport, Edward, C115; Grey, C115;
 Harriet, C115; James, C115; Levi,
 C115; Matilda, C115; Martha, C115;
 Sarah, C115; Thomas, C115.
David, Nancy, C147; William, C147.
Davidson, Hiram, C98; Leroy, C98;
 Mary, C98; Metilda, C98; Mrs. W., 79;
 W. C., 59; Wiley, C98; William, C98.
Davis, Amanda, C94; Amelia, C139; Asarah,
 C39; Asariah, C39; Baby, C95; Burrell,
 C117; Caroline, C39, C113; Catherine,
 C97, C105; Clayborn, C97; Curley,
 C139; Cynthia, C93, C146; Dan, 75;
 Edy, C80; Elias, C80; Eliza, C95,
 C113; Elizabeth, C39, C59, C82, C93,
 C123; Gabriel, C113; George, C117;
 Green, C117; Hannah, C93; Henry, C117;
 Isaac, C80; Isabella, C80; Isom, C146;
 James, C80, C82, C139; Jane, C96,
 C97, C117, C150; Jeff, C32; Jenny,
 C146; Jessee, C88; John, C95, C105,
 C113, C123, C124, C146; Joseph, C97,
 C105, C146; Julia, C105; Kinchen,
 C146; Lecretia, C117; Louisa, C97;
 Lucy, C24; Mahaley, C21, C146;
 Margaret, C80, C105; Martha, C39,
 C95, C105; Mary, C24, C80, C94, C95,
 C106; Matilda, C93; Nancy, C39, C105,
 C117, C146; Nathan, C139; Nicholas,
 C12; Patience, C139; Patsy, C154;
 Polly, C139, C149; C153; Rebecca,
 C39; Ruben, C97, C117; Samuel, C39,
 C105; Sarah, C39, C80; C97, C117;
 Sousan, C113; Sulema, C80; Susan,
 25; Thomas, C93, C96, C113; Warren,
 C94; Wash, C124; William, C24, C59,
 C93, C95, C97, C105, C113, C117;
 Willis, C125.
Daws, George, C42.
Day Luncinda, C148.
Deal, E. L., 69.
Dean, Abraham, C67; Baby, C87; Benjamin,
 C87; Bryant, C87, C145; Dempsey, C87;
 Edmond, C87; Elizabeth, C67; Emerline,
 C87; Ermin, C87; Evelyn, C145;
 Frances, C67; James, C67; Jane, C137;
 John, C67; Lucy, C87; Milly, C137;
 Nancy, C87.
DeFord, Risden, 53.
Defore, David, C46.
Deirt, Mary, C147.
Dement, Benjamin, C108; David, C108;
 Frances, C108; James, C108; John,
 C108; Josiah, C145; Laurel, C108;
 Margaret, C145; Mary, C105, C145;
 Polly, C147; Rachel, C109; continued,

Dement, continued, Rebecca, C108, C145;
 Reuben, C145; Robert, C108; Sarah,
 C139; Thomas, C109, C147.
Denison, John, C127; Nancy, C127.
Denson, Albert, C131; Jessee, C131;
 James, C131; John, C131; Melvina,
 C131; Nancy, C131; Richard, C131;
 Sarah, C131; Thomas, C131; William,
 C131.
Denton, Nancy, C145.
DePriest, Harriet, C128; Horatio, C128.
Derumple, Henry, C127; Jane, C127.
Deshler, David, 27.
Despain, John, C146; Margaret, C146.
Dewberry, Daniel, C10; Elizabeth, C13;
 Ester, C34; Henry, C10; Jabus, C13,
 C34; Jesse, C34; John, 60, C10; Labora,
 C10; Louisa, C10; Luisa, C10;
 Margaret, C34; Mary, C13, C34; Millard,
 C13; Richard, C10; Sarah, C10, C13,
 C34; Thomas, C10, C13; William, C10.
Dickard, Docie, C146; George, C146.
Dickerson, Amanda, C68.
Dickey, ___ C147; Billy, 31.
Dicks, Mary, C147; John, 48, C147.
Dickson, Delia, C139; Elizabeth, C154;
 John, C139; Robert, C90; Tempie,
 C139.
Diehl, Samuel, 59.
Dillahunty, B. M., C146; Carter, C5;
 Charles, C62; Elizabeth, C62;
 Frances, C62; Harriet, C146; Harvey,
 C62; Henry, C146; Lusinda, C5;
 Marion, C5; Martheland, C102;
 Sally, C5; Thomas C5; Samuel, C62;
 Milla, C62.
Dillon, Dillan, Robert, C149.
Dillard, Amy, C149.
Ditto's Landing, 2.
Dixon, William, 5.
Doan, John, C139; Patsy, C139.
Dobbin, Bersheba, C139; James, C103;
 Jane, C103; Jasper, C103; John, C103,
 C139; Kissy, C103; Lucy, C103;
 Nancy, C103; Samuel, C103.
Dodd, Mary, C148.
Dodge, General, 33, 34, 37, 38, 39, 40,
 78.
Dollerson, Amanda, C15; Mahaley, C15;
 Pinkney, C15.
Donahoagh, Henry, C63; Sarah, C63.
Donahoo, John, 13, 20, C146; Henry, 24.
Donald, Jane, C147; John, C147.
Donaldson, Adeline, C116; Boney, C107;
 Dozly, C107; E. B., 23; John, 1, 5, 8;
 Nancy, C107; Polly, C147.
Donalson, Adaline, C45; E. B., C57;
 Mary, C42.
Donelson, Jane, C140.

251

Donohoo, Ann, C81; William, C81.
Dority, James, C146; John, C146.
Doss, L. J., 71.
Doublehead, 2, 65.
Douglas, Douglass, Ann, C23; Andrew, C23; George, C78; J. C., C30; James, C78; Jane, C23, C78; John, C23, C78; L. M., 70; Malasiah, C78; Margaret, C78, C138; Martha, C23; Mary, C23; Melenah, C78; Nathaniel, C23; Phoeby, C25; Rhody, C25; Senalea, C78; Souseannah, C78; Thomas, C23, C25; William, C25, C78.
Douglis, Constantine, C146; James, C146; John, C146; Malinda, C146; Margaret, C147; Thomas, 22.
Douthitt, Jack, 74; Peg, 74.
Dowdy, Abitas, C146; Andrew, C16; Catherine, C16; David, C18; Dravis, C146; James, C16, C18; Jane, C138; Jerrymyrah, C16; John, C16; Lavina, C16; Mahala, C146; Margarett, C16; Martha, C16; Mary, C16, C18, C146; Nancy, C149; Polly, C16; Sarah, C18; Thomas, C16; William, C16, C18.
Doyle, Michael, 52.
Drane, Robert, 67.
Drennett, Emily, C144.
Drew, Colonel, 28.
Duberry, Deborah, C146; John, C146.
Ducas, Franky, C117; Hiram, C117; Mariah, C117.
Ducatt, Elizabeth, C34; John, C34; Levi, C34.
Duckett, David, C29; Elizabeth, C11; Francis, C29; John, C29; Joseph, C29; L. F., 62; Lydia, C29; Martha, C29; Mary, C29; Richard, C29; Thomas, C29.
Duckey, Robert, C136.
Ducust, Jasper, C115.
Duberry, Franley, C143; Rebecca, C138.
Duff, Patrick, C10; Polly, C10; Rody, C10.
Duke, William, 55; W. O., 70.
Dukes, Betsy, C24; Brant, C24; Robert, C24.
Dumey (?), James, C92; Matilda, C92; Rachel, C92.
Dun, Gray, C114; Luther, C114; Lydia, C114; Poindexter, C114; Van, C114.
Duncan, Annie, C43; Caroline, C54; Eliza, C41; Elmira, C43; Ebineser, C43; Elizabeth, C150; George, C45; James, C41; Jane, C43; Jefferson, C54; John, C43; Lucinda, C43;cont'd

Duncan, continued: Leander, C43; Martha, C43; Mary, C43, C54; Mapes, C146; Moses, C43; Nancy, C41, C43; Robert, C43; Sally, C146; Sarah, C43; William, C43.
Dunn, M. B., 71.
Dupriest, Harriett, C151.
Durey, Alexander, C112; Angeline, C112; Ann, C112; Colicita, C112; Jaremia, C112; Martha, C112.
Durham, Elizabeth, C152.
Durrett, Eliza, C150; Lucy, C152.
Dyas, Alex, 8; Annie, 8; Robert, 4, 8.
Dyer, Percy, 68.
Dykes, Jamena, C26; John, C26; Lusinda, C26; Susannah, C26.

Ealey, Anna, C147; George, C147.
Earnest, Ollie, 62.
Eastep, Eliza, C138; Solomon, 66; W. S., 69; William, 66. 70.
Easton, Calvin, 5; Matilda, C152; William, 6.
Eaton, E. H., C66; Malinda, C152; William, C66.
Eaves, John, C139; Polly, C139.
Eckl, Louis, 77.
Edding, Martha, C15; Mary, C15; Nancy, C15; William, C15.
Eddleman, Annis, C69; Everline, C69; James, C69; Jonathan, C69; Nancy, C69; William, C69.
Edwards, Ann Jane, C14; Benjamin, C14; Jarid, C14; Jim, 39; John, C14; Lewis, 16; C147; Margaret, C147; Mary, C14; W. B., 21; Wiley, C14; William, C57.
Eldred, C. B., 59.
Eldridge, Alfonzo, C102; Andrew, C102; Elisha, C102; Franklin, C102; Nancy, C102; Sarah, C102; Sousan, C102.
Ellam, Robert, C106.
Ellemn, Martha, C107.
Elliman, Thomas, 4.
Ellinger, Jacob, 12.
Ellis, A. G., 24; Benjamin, 23; Charles, C64; Davis, C86; Edney, C89; Frances, C86; Henry, C64; Isaac, C64; J. M.,61; James, C64, C89; Jmmetia, C64; John, C64, C86, C89; Mary, C86, C143; Nancy, C64, C86; Oren, C86; R. A., 53; Rebecca, C86, C89, C148; Richard, C86; Robert, C64; Sarah, C86; Sousan, C86; T., C89; William, C86, C89.
Elliott, Robert, 26.
Ellum, Albert, C107; Elizabeth, C107; George, C107; James, C107; Langoda, C107; Margaret, C107; Virginia, C107.

Elting, N. C., 68.
Emerson, Aaron, C51; Columbus, C51; Elizabeth, C51; John, C51; Marion, C51; Marrella, C51; Martha, C51; Mary, C51; Nancy, C51; William, C51.
England, Eliza, C85; George, C85; James, C85; John, C85; Margaret, C85; Martha, C85; Matilda, C85; Tilman, C85.
Engle, J. A., 21.
English, Abraham, C139; Agnus, C74; Anny, C147; Eliza, C74; Elizabeth, C74, C139; C140; Estell, C147; Hiram, C74; James, C74; John, C74, C139; Mathias, C147; Nancy, C139, C140; Polly, C74; Rachel, C74; Rebecca, C141; Sally, C139; Sarah, C147; Thomas, C147; William, C74; Wilson, C74, C139.
Ennis, Adessa, C139; Cornelious, C139.
Entrican, Cynthia, C135; Sarah, C135.
Estell, Frederick, C147; Nancy, C147.
Estep, Abram, C122; Debby, C106; Eliza, C106; Elizabeth, C122; James, C122; Josiah, C122; Martha, C122; Moses, C106; Solomon, C106, C122; Thomas, C123; Winney, C123. (See also Eastep)
Estept, Abraham, C96; Elizabeth, C96; Isaac, C96; Isabella, C96; Jacob, C96; James, C96; John, C108; Martha, C96; Sara, C108; Solomon, C96; Winney, C96, C108.
Estes, John W., 42.
Estice, Catherine, C96, C125; Elizabeth, C120, C125; Garlandon, C96; James, C125; Jane, C120; Jasper, C125; Joel, C125; John, C120, C125; Martha, C125; Mary, C96; William, C96, C120, C125.
Estill, Jonathan, 4.
Eston, Lemuel, C79.
Estridge, Randolph, C130.
Ethridge, Aubrey, 70.
Eubanky, Horatio, C63; T., C63.
Evans, Amy, C139; Betsy, C139; David, C139; Margaret, C150; Jesse, C139; Patience, C143; Sarah, C150.
Eves, John, C139; Malinda, C139.
Ezell, Ann, C147; Pressy, C144; William, C147.

Fago, Fred, 15.
Fair, Polly, C143.
Faires, Jane, C147; Margaret, 25; Matilda, 21; William, C147.
Falconnet, Major, 39.
Falk, Alexander, C65; Catherine, C65; Emmelia, C65; Assar, C65; continued

Falk, continued: Sarah, C65; William, 24.
Fannon, Delia, C140; Elizabeth, C139; Polly, C143.
Fant, Charles, 34.
Fardell, Mary, C93.
Faris, Addaly, C62; Charlotte, C61; Alonzo, C61; Harriett, C61; J. B., C62; James, C58; John, C58, C61; Margaret, C14; Martha, C58; Pugh, C61; Richard, C14, C58; William, C58.
Farmer, Antamenta, C32; Benjamin, C32; Elizabeth, C12; Gabrel, C34; Henrietta, C32; J. T., 57; John, C12; Kesiah, C32; Lavina, C34; Lucy, C32; Marion, C12; Martha, C12, C34; Marthy, C32; Mary, C32; Richard, C12; Sally, C139; Sarah, C32, C135; Serena, C147; Susan, C34; Susanah, C12; Thomas, C12; William, C12, C32; C34, C139, C147.
Farr, Florence, C15; George, C15; James, C15; Martha, C15; Mary, C15.
Farray, Dinah, C140.
Farrer, Pierre, 46.
Farris, Betsy, C149; Cornelia, C139; Cossy, C147; Dolly, C143; Eliza, C141; James, C139; Maria, C154; Martha, C15; Sally, C139; Samuel, C147; Sarah, C139.
Faye, Essy, 24.
Fealder, Silus, C23.
Fenn, James F., C64; Permelia, C64.
Ferguson, John, 16.
Ferrel, Hariett, C153.
Ferrell, George, C16; John, C16; Manurvey, C16; Margaret, C16; Martha, C16; Mary Ann, C16; Samuel, C16; Thorsy, C16.
Feutral, Catharine, C127, C133; Edward, C133; Eliza, C133; Needum, C133; William, C127, C133.
Fielder, Charles, 62; Mary, 62.
Fields, Catherine, C121; Fielding, C147; George, C99; John, C147; Lewis, C99, C120; Lucy, C99; Margaret, C120; Mary, C63, C147; Narcynthia, C99; Newton, C120; Sarah, C99; Solomon, C99; Thomas, C120.
Fifer, Fanny, C115; George, C9; Jacob, C115; Lucy, C115.
Files, Anna, C142; James, C147; Polly, C147; Susan, C147.
Finch, Jefferson, C32.
Finell, Eliza, C148.
Fisher, Amy, C138; Benjamin, C83, C139; Carroll, C41; Charity, C139; Elizabeth, C40, C41, C78; Henry, C41; J. M., C40; Jabous, C41; Jackson, C78; James, C11, C41; John, C41; Malvina, C41; Margaret, C78; continued

Fisher, continued: Martha, C41; Mary, C78;
   Nancy, C11, C146; Peggy, C150; Pleas-
   ant, C41; Polly, C41; Richard, C78;
   Samyra, C40; Sarah, C11, C41; William,
   C40.
Fitch, Leroy, C37.
Flagg, Jewett, 69.
Flake, Elizabeth, 20; Peter, 20; Sally,
   C147; Silas, C147.
Flankin, Olivia, C143.
Flatt, Nancy, C142.
Flemington, Margaret, C147; John, C147.
Flent, Flint, Candes, C139; Stanton, C139.
Flerida, Betty, C139; Richard, C139.
Flint (see also Flent), Alexander, C147;
   Benton, C59; George, C59; Henry, C59;
   John, C59; Julia, C59; Margaret, C59;
   Martha, C59; Nancy, C147; Samuel, C59;
   Sarah, C145; Stanton, C59; Susannah,
   C143.
Flies, Sally, C139.
Floid, Berry, C50; Elizabeth, C50;
   Frances, C50; Henry, C50; Levi, C50;
   Margaret, C50; Spencer, C50; William,
   C50.
Floyed, David, C103; Elizabeth, C103;
   Hiram, C103; Mary, C103; Nancy, C103;
   Rachel, C103; Sarah, C103; Sealy, C103.
Flynt, Estes, 76.
Foiles, Delia, C139.
Follis, Rebecca, C147; Washington, C147.
Fomby, Fereby, C137.
Fonville, Mrs. Florence, 67.
Foote, 5.
Forch, Simon, 53.
Forel, Henry, 68.
Foresythe, Benjamin, C85, C130; Mary,
   C130.
Forgers, Arthur, C102; Baby, C102;
   Elizabeth, C102; Mary, C102.
Forgison, Drury, C91; Lucinda, C91;
   Michael, C91.
Forisythe, George, C130; John, C130;
   Rebecca, C130.
Forrest, General Nathan B., 40, 44, 45,
   46, 48, 49, 50.
Forsythe, Elizabeth, C129; James, C129;
   Jane, C129; John, C129; Margaret, C129;
   Philip, C129; Sarah, C129; Smith,
   C129; William, C129.
Fort, Ann, C128; Elias, C128; Francis,
   C128; Martha, C128; Philex, C128.
Foster, Ann, C112; Annis, C67; Asa, C103;
Ash, C147; B. F., 34; Balus, C112; Blu-
   ford, C71; Booker, C103; Colman, C67;
   Constantine, C71; Elizabeth, C112,
   C117; G. W., 23, 25, C65; George W.,
   C112; Miss H., 28; Harriet, C112;
   Henry, C45; Jackson, C65; continued,

Foster, continued: James, C67, C112,
   C117, C139; Jane, C67, C112, C139;
   John, C127; Judge, 51; Julia, C71,
   C103; Louiser, C65; Lucinda, C103,
   C112; Manurvy, C71; Martha, C71,
   C103; Mary, C71, C103; Moses, C57;
   Richard, C112; Robert, 34; Safronia,
   C71; Sarah, C65, C103, C117, C147;
   Susan, C71; Sousannah, C117; Thomas,
   23, 24, C39, C67; Turner, 23, C39,
   C127; Virginia, C65; Wash, 61;
   Washington, C65; Watkins, C65;
   William, C71, C103, C112.
Foust, Alexander, C74; Anjaline, C74;
   Canzoda, C105; Catherine, C74;
   David, C73; George, C105; Harrison,
   C105; Hiram, C105; Jane, C105;
   John, C74; Lock, C74; Margaret, C73;
   Mary, C73, C74, C105; Nancy, C105;
   Newton, C105; Sarah, C105; William,
   C74.
Fowler, Columbus, C14, C44; Elizabeth,
   C8, C152; Dennis, C147; H., C147;
   Henry, C86; Illijah, C14; James, C14;
   C24, C106; Jane, C24; Jeremiah, C147;
   Josiah, C8; Juliar Ann, C8; Lorenzo,
   C8; Mahuldy, C8; Margaret, C14;
   Martha, C14, C24; Mary, C8, C14;
   C86, C106; Misha, C147; Nancy, C59;
   Nancy Ann, C8; Perressa, C8; Rachel,
   C44; Richard, C14; Robert, C86;
   Ruth, C147; Samuel, C14, C44;
   Sarah, C86; Susan, C14; Thomas,
   C44, C86; Wesley, C8; William, C8,
   C24, C86.
Fox, Abraham, 13.
Foy, W. L., 69, 70.
Francis, James, 23, C54; Mary, C54.
Frankes, Aaron, C38; Anderson, C38;
   Calafornia, C38; Lusinda, C38;
   Martha, C38.
Franklin, Benjamin C5; Daniel, C5;
   Ellen, C136; James, C5; John, C136;
   Joseph, C54; Lafaitt, 65; Mary, C136;
   Nancy, C136; Sarah, C54, C136;
   William, C54.
Franks, Leah, C141; Lucy, C43.
Frederickson, 69.
Freeman, Elizabeth, C31; Lawson, C3;
   Mary, C7; Sarah, C7; Solomon, C54;
   William, C7, C31, C54.
French, Amos, 80; Ann, 80; Benjamin,
   80, C96; Elizabeth, C79; Frances, 80;
   Henry, C79; James, C79; Jane, 80;
   Jerry, 80; Jesse, 80; John, C123;
   Milly, 80; Polly, 80; Sally, 80;
   Samuel, 80; Sarah, C96; William,
   80, C96.
Fry, Thomas, 53.

Fulks, Cynthia, C94; George, C94; James, C94; John, C94; Mahala, C94; Mary, C94; Medrith, C94; Nancy, C94; Sousan, C94; Stuart, C92, C94.
Fuller, Charity, C147; Elvirah, C153; Isaiah, C147; John, C147; Matilda, C139; William, C139.
Fullerton, Margaret, C139; Nathan, C139; Rochell, C152; Sarah, C139; Weldon, C139.
Fullertone, Margaret, C139.
Fulmer, Allen, 11.
Fulton, David, 13; William, 9.
Fuqua, Ann, C114, C152; Archibald, 6, 7, 8, C114; Benjamin, C114; Elizabeth, C144; Georgia, C114; Ingram, C114; John, C114; Julia, C114; Louisa, C114; Mary, 62, C114, C146; Sarah, C114; Sousan, C114; Weaver, 62, 76; William, C114.
Furgerson, Caleb, C41; Elizabeth, C41; Ellender, C41; Ferdinand, C41; Isebella, C41; J. F., C41; Jacob, C41; James, C41; Manurvy, C41; Marshal, C41; Nancy, C41; Nimrod, C41; Rebecca, C41.
Furkinson, Catherine, C111; Elizabeth, C111; James, C111; Lafayette, C111; Lucinda, C111; Lucy, C111; Mary, C111; P. D., C111; Parthenia, C111; William, C111.
Futrell, Mary, C151. (See Fuetral, Feutral, and other spellings.)

Gadsden, James, 4, 5.
Gailey, Hiram, C15; Ufratus, C15.
Gaines, Elizabeth, C139; Ira, C139.
Gaither, 11.
Gallaway, Isabel, C138; Samuel, C136.
Gamblin, James, 22.
Gannon, Agness, C125; Jack, C125; John, C125; Louisa, C125; Lucinda, C125; Matilda, C125; Mary, C125; Thomas, C125.
Garden, Judith, C152.
Gardener, Albert, C133; Elizabeth, C150; George, C133; Harrison, C133; Letha, C133; Richmond, C133; Souseannah, C133.
Garfield, President, 32.
Garinger, Elizabeth, C145.
Garmon, Joseph, C27.
Garner, Amanda, C44; B. B., 62; Catherine, C130; Ellen, C130; Enoch, C130; John, C147; Julia, C13; Levi, C44; Livanda, C130; Martha, C147; Mary, C44; C147; Octava, C130; Peter, C44; Robert, C130; Samuel, 20; Thomas, C147; William, C147.

Garrard, Alexander, C125; America, C125; Betty, C146; Calvin, C133; Ceybourn, C133; Daniel, C125; David, C17; Edward, C126; Elizabeth, C17; James, C125, C133; John, C125; Julia, C125; Kessiah, C133; Lucinda, C133; Louisa, C126; Mariah, C140; Mary, C17; Nancy, C17; Rebecca, C133; Ruel, C126; Samuel, C126; Sarah, C126; Souseannah, C133; Thomas, C133; William, C125.
Garrett, Anthony, 59; Autry, C147; Betty, C139; Bill, 17; Eliza, C151; Elizabeth, C142; James, C139; Jenny, C139; Jesse, C147; John, C139; Lucy, 59; Martha, C139, C143; C148; Mary, C147; Pressley, C147; Sarah, C147; Serene, C149; William, C139.
Gartine, Sarah, C138.
Gassway, Elizabeth, C115; T. J., C115.
Gaten, Charlotte, C130; George, C130; Mary, C130; Molsey, C130; Orenitta, C130; Spencer, C130.
Gates, Baby, C109; Bradford, 23; Eliza, C117; Polly, C150; William, C109, C117.
Gentry, Ed, 66.
George, Alex, 70.
German, Susannah, C150.
Gerrard, Thomas, 5, 6.
Gest, Gist, Guest, Davy C., C72; Elizabeth, C72; Henry, C72; J. K. Polk, C72; Jackson, C72; James, C72; John, C72; Joseph, C72; Lafett, C72; Levi, C72; Margaret, C72; Martha, C72; Salabam, C72; Sarah, C72; Sina, C72; Thomas, C72; Washington, C72; William, C72.
Gerwin, Mary, C64; William, C42.
Gibbs, Mary, C137.
Gibson, Alexander, C139; Ann, C58; Eady, C150; Elizabeth, C139; Francis, 52; James, 6, C147; Jesse, C73; John, 6; Lucinda, C58; Mary, C139, C149; Nancy, C147; R. L., 48; Rhoda, C73; Richard, C139; Rebecca, C149; Sarah, C139.
Gifford, Elizabeth, C73; John, C73; Missouri, C73.
Gilbert, Adsin, C109; Albert, C109; James, C109; Jimmy, 74; John, C105; Louisa, C151; Mary, C154; Nancy, C144; Rebecca, C140; Sarah, C109; Washington, C109.
Gilchrist, Malcolm, 5, 7.
Gildon, John, C47.
Gillem, Bennett, C8; George, C8; John, C8; Matilda, C8; Nancy, C8; Sarah, C8; William, C8.

Gillespie, Col., 20.
Gillis, Capt., 31.
Glades, Anderson, C11; Persillar, C11.
Glassep, Eliza, C102; Elizabeth, C102; Jasper, C102; Martha, C102; Samuel, C102; Sarah, C102; William, C102.
Glassip, Clinton, C101; Joel, C101; Julia, C101; Martin, C101; Mary, C101; Sampson, C101.
Glazier, Lynwood, 74.
Glenn, John, C65; Mamie, 61; Nancy, C65; Mrs. R. L., 7; Robert, 61; Walter, C65.
Glidewell, James, C67; Nancy, C67; Sally, C67; Thomas, C67.
Glossip, Joel, C101; Levi, C101; Mary, C101; Orah, C101.
Glothr, Richard, C66.
Goad, Charles, C113; Elizabeth, C113; Francis, C113; James, C113; Martha, C113; Rebecca, C113; Sarah, C113.
Gobson, James, 6.
Goff, George, C60; John, C60; Margaret, C60; Mary, C60; Thomas, C60.
Goings, Betsy, C138; Nancy, C151.
Golightly, Dianah, C9; Elizabeth, C9; George, C9; Henry, C9; James, C9; Lurinda, C9; Mary, C9; Permelia, C9; Robert, C9; Susan, C9; William, C9.
Golston, James, 24.
Gooch, James, C37.
Goode, Holbert, C147; Juliana, C147.
Gooding, Jane, C139; John, C139.
Goodloe, Columbia, C66; French, C66; Julious, C66; Margaret, C66; Martha, C66; Mary, C66; N. C., C66; Thomas, C66.
Goodman, Eliza, C109; Leslie, 66; Mary, C109; Parthenia, C109; Sarah, C109; Sousan, C109; Stanmore, C109; William, C109.
Goodnight, Catherine, C144.
Goodwin, Eliza, C118; John, C118; Mary, C118; Peterson, C118; Sarah, C118; Thomas, 90; William, C118.
Gookin, Charles, 20, C65; Eugine, C65; Frances, C65; Hugh, C65; James, C65; Sarah, 20, C65; Thomas, C65.
Gorden, Francis, C65; Seless, C65.
Gordon, 8.
Gore, Alexander, C92; Elizabeth, C92; James, C92; Mary, C92; Nancy, C92; Samuel, C92; Sarah, C92.
Grace, John, C147; Rody, C147.
Gracey, John, C76; Mariah, C76; Robert, C76; Sarah, C76.

Graham, Ann, C113; Baby, C113; Catherine, C113; Elizabeth, C131; George, C131; John, C131; Lucy, C152; Martha, C131; Mary, C113; Milandge, C131; Polly, C139; Sousan, C131; Thomas, C139; William, C113.
Grandford, Elias, C86; Lucinda, C86; Thomas, C86; Tabitha, C86; William, C86.
Granger, 17.
Grant, 34.
Graves, Adessa, C139.
Gray, Andrew, C81; Ann, C132; Benjamin, C132; Bethana, C132; Catherine, C132; Eliza, C132; Elizabeth, C147; Ephraim, C81; James, C81, C132, C147; John, C132, C139, C147; Manerva, C147; Mrs., 19; Mary, C132; Nancy, C139; Pheby, C81; Rutha, C132; William, C132; Y. A., C63.
Grayson, Delia, C147; Joel, C147.
Greely, Constantine, C146.
Green, Angeline, C111; Ann, C111; Benjamin, C24; David, C111; Emily, C124; Frances, C67; George, C124; J. C., C111; James, C67; Jesse, C147; John, C20; Joshua, C111; Lavina, C124; Lewis, C147; Lucinda, C147; Manurvey Ann, C24; Martha, C24, C67; Ollive, C111; Mrs. Rollie, 66; Sarah, C111; Thomas, C67; William, C67.
Greenhill, Sam, 60.
Greenhow, Ersley, C147; James, C147.
Greer, Andrew, C118; Elizabeth, C139; James, C139; Mary, C118; Nancy, C118; Nicholas, C118; Polly, C148; Thomas, C139; Susannah, C139; Wiley, C118.
Greesham, Benjamin, C147; Nancy, C147.
Grey, George, C16; John, C16; Mersilla, C47; Samuel, C16; Spelman, C16; Thomas, C16.
Greswell, M. T., C38.
Griffet, Resh, C56.
Griffin, Anthony, C104; Bluford, C104; Eliza, C104; Emily, C142; George, C104; Henry, C104; Joseph, C104; Maccomb, C139; Mary, C104; Nancy, C147; Rebecca, C104; Richard, 25; Sarah, C104; Temperance, C139.
Griffith, June, C147; Solomon, C147.
Grigery, Andrew, C41; Elizabeth, C41.
Grimes, B. J., 71; Caroline, C1; Eliza, C1; George, C1; Hettie, C1; Peter, C1; Polly, C1; Missouri, C1; Nancy, C1; William, C1.
Grisham, Alley, C90; Andrew, C90; Bailes, C90; Elizabeth, C90; Frances, C69; Gracy, C90; Henry, C125; Jackson, C69; James, C90; Jessee, C90; continued,

Grisham, continued: John, C69, C96; Julia, C90; Louiser, C69; Margaret, C69; Martha, C96; Mary, C69, C96; Mirah, C96; Moses, C90; Narcissa, C125; Prudence, C90; Rebecca, C96; Sarah, C69, C90; Thomas, C96; Thompson, C96; Winston, C90.
Grisholm, George, C147; Daniel, C147; Marian, C147; Susan, C147.
Grissom, Andy, C14; B. P., C139; Catherine, C14; Christine, C139; Columbus, C6, C7; Delia, C139; Dianah, C6; Eghton, C14; Elizabeth, C142, C143; Emerline, C6, C14; Franklin, C14; George, C6; Gracey, C139; Henry, C6, C14; Hiram, C6; James, C35; Jane, C139; Jarred, C35; Jessee, C139; Lewis, C14; Nancy, C14; Olim, 63; Parilee, C7; Philemon, C139; Susannah, C35; William, C6, C35; Wilson, C139.
Grissum, Katherine, C154.
Grisworld, Anderson, C95.
Grocy, Mary, C146.
Grooms, Delia, C147; Isaac, C147.
Gross, Walter, 73.
Grush, John, C42.
Guest, Albert, C147; Elizabeth, C146, C147.
Gwin, Almarenda, C26; Caleb, C26; Hannella, C21, C26; Lt. Com., 28; Pinkney, C226; William, 29.

Hackworth, O. C., 69.
Haddock, Alexander, C13; Mary, C13; Thomas, C13; William, C13.
Hagwood, Elender, C70; Jansy, C70.
Hail, Galand, C148; Mary, C148.
Hale, W. T., 71.
Haley, Charlie, 70; Temperance, C57.
Halford, Edward, C148; Margaret, C148.
Hall, Benjamin, C148; Durenda, C148; Elihu, 5, 6; Francis, C12; John, C12; Martha, C143; Mary, C12, C148; Minda, C12; Nancy, C12.
Hallbrook, 36.
Halleck, H. W., 31.
Halton, Patsy, C140; Tilly, C140.
Ham, Alfonso, C69; Ausha, C66; Blessingum, C148; Charles, C66; Elijah, C38; Eliza, C73; Francis, C73; George, C73; Henry, C73; Hough, C73; James, C66, C69, C73; Jesse, C73; Liddi, C73; Lucinda, C66; Manerva, C148; Mary, C66, C73; Mildred, C140; Milli, C73; Mills, C73; Rachel, C73; Rebecca, C148; Sanders, C73; Susan, C73; Tennessee, C69; Thestus, C73; Thomas, C66; William, C66, C69, C73; Winney, C73.

Hamer, Frances, C81.
Hamil, Mary, 23.
Hamill, Aaron, C75; Emily, C75; Frances, C75; Hugh, C75; William, C75; Winey Ann, C75.
Hamilton, C. S., 34; James, 8, 9; W. D., 40, 41, 43.
Hamm (refer also to Ham), Betsy, C138; Buckley, C140; David, C133; Elizabeth, C133; James, 59, C133; Jeremiah, C131; John, C140; Jordan, C131; Margaret, C131; Ollive, C131; Rosell, C140; Sally, C140; Sarah, C131, C133, C140; Thomas, C131, C133; William, C131.
Hammer, Elizabeth, C16; Kasiah, C16; Louisa, C16; Martha, C16; Mary, C16; Matilda, C16; Rachel, C16; William, C69.
Hammersley, Polly, C140; Robert, C140.
Hammin, James, C78; Martha, C78; Mary, C78; Sousin, C78.
Hammon, Eli, 6; Penelope, C138; Susannah, C139.
Hammonds, Clem, 53; Elizabeth, C149; Howell, C140; Lucinda, C149; Patsey, C149; Polly, C140; Rebecca, C152; Usley, C140; Willie, C140.
Hammons, A. B., C99; Clemons, C97; Churity, C144; Elizabeth, C100, C148; Henry, C148; James, C97; Jasper, C97; Jessee, C100; John, C97, C148; Joseph, C97; Mary, C97, C99, C100; Matilda, C97; Nancy, C100; Orebella, C99; Polly, C148; Rella, C100; Sabrey, C99; Sally, C151; Sarah, C97, C100; Samuel, C148; Sousan, C97; Thomas, C97; William, C97; Z. B., C99.
Hemons, Parillee, C59; Thomas, C59; William, C59.
Hampton, Captain, 79; Colonel, 38.
Hancock, Dr., 53; James, 59.
Hand, Tempy, C154.
Handy, W. C., 75.
Hanes, Henry, C54; Nancy, C54.
Haney, Elizabeth, C45; Frances, C45; James, C45; John, C45; Susanah, C45.
Hankins, Mariah, C115; Mary, C115; P. A. O., C115; William, C19; Winslow, C115.
Hanks, Archibald, C121; Jane, C121; John, C121; Julia, C121; Matilda, C121; Martha, C121; William, C121.
Henna, J. H., 6; James, 13, C140; John, 5, 6; Paralee, C140; S., 6; Sarah, 5, 7.
Hannah, A. M., C63; Alexander, C135; Gertu, C135; Letitie, C151; Malcom, C135; Marthie, C93; Sebina, C93; Thompson, C93.

257

Hannay, A. M., 26, 53.
Hannon, M. W., 38.
Haraway, Achilis, C116; Benjamin, C90;
    C. W., C115; Caroline, C116; David,
    C90; Durett, C116; Eliza, C116;
    Emily, C90; George, C90, C116; John,
    C90; Margaret, C115; Mary, C116;
    P. M., C116; Rachel, C116; Samuel,
    C116; Walter, C90; William, C116.
Haralson, Frances, C140; Mary, C142;
    William, C140.
Hard, Drucilla, C144.
Harder, Elizabeth, C4; James, C4; Joel,
    C4; John, C4; Kasiah, C4; Mary, C4;
    Matilda, C4; Rachel, C4.
Hardee, General, 37.
Hardie, Sam, 69.
Harden, John, C140; Sally, C140.
Hardin, Ann, C148; Calloway, C140;
    Cleveland, 67; Louise, C140;
    Nancy, C143; William, C148.
Hardwick, Anne, C2; Betty, C56; Eliza-
    beth, C39; Ellison, C3; Francis, C2;
    Frank, C39; John, C39; Joseph, C2,
    C39; Martha, C56; Mary, C39; Nancy,
    C2, C56; Rachel, C3; Richard, C3;
    Samuel, C39; Sarah, C3; William, C39.
Hardy, Amanda, C113; Caroline, C113;
    Eliza, C113; George, C113; Hannah,
    C113; Jackson, C113; Jane, C113;
    Joseph, C113.
Hargrove, Dr., 53; Mary, C148; John,
    C148.
Hareson, W. H., C32.
Hariett, John, C7.
Harkins, Martin, 23, C137; John, C137;
    Louis, C151.
Harlan, 32.
Harley, James, C140; Polly, C140.
Harman, Tom, 39.
Harmin, Alexander, C84; Benjamin, C104;
    Eliza, C81, C84; Elizabeth, C81,
    C84; James, C81, C104; John, C97;
    Joseph, C104; Lucinda, C81; Lucretia,
    C104; Mary, C81, C84, C104; Nancy,
    C97, C104; Rebecca, C104; Sarah, C97,
    C104; Sousan, C97; Stephen, C97;
    William, C81, C84, C104.
Harmon, Albert, C135; Alexander, C140;
    Allis, C135; Augustus, C135;
    Catherine, C138; Daniel, C135; Eliza-
    beth, C135, C140; Henrietta, C135;
    Hillard, C135; James, C135, C140;
    Lucretia, C143; Lucy, C135; Sally,
    C140; Sarah, C135; Thomas, C135.
Harrawy, Emily, C148; Walter, C148.
Harrel, David, C148; Lucinda, C148.
Harrell, Jack, 31.
Harrington, Margaret, C141; William, 13.

Harris, Amanda, C14; Andrew, C14;
    Ann, C140; Baby, C106; Calvin, C14;
    Catharine, C106; Christian, C140;
    Edward, C140; Elias, C14; Jackson,
    C14; Lucinda, C14; Margaret, C14;
    Mary Ann, C14; Polly, C146.
Harrison, Alexander, C148; Alfred, C33;
    Amanuel, C33; Caroline, C75; Darinda,
    C75, C76; David, 70; Edward, C88;
    Elizabeth, C75; Ellender, C122;
    Emily, C76; Frances, C76; George, C76;
    Henry, C75; J. C., C115, C148;
    James, C119, C133; John, 53, C75, C76;
    Johnathan, C76; Lavina, C90; Little
    Berry, C75; Luke, C75; Lydia, C75;
    Mr., 14; Marion, C75; Martha, C76;
    Martin, C133; Mary, C76; Matthew, C122;
    Parmelia, C144; Philadelphia, C133;
    Sarah, C33; C122; Talethia, C75;
    Tillman, C76; Walter, 75; William, 65,
    C75, C148; Willis, C76.
Harrow, Frances, C136.
Hart, Henry, C30; Nancy, C145.
Hartless, Valles, C98.
Harvell, Benjamin, C33; Caroline, C34;
    Catherine, C34; Jane, C33; Levi, C34;
    Phillip, C33; Polly, C33, William, C33.
Harvey, Alexander, C87, C119; Burges,
    C154; Elender, C119; Elizabeth, C91,
    C119; C154; Elmira, C91; Franklin,
    C120; George, C120; Lieut., 42;
    Margaret, C154; Mary, C91; Nancy, C119;
    Patrick Henry, C87; Robert, C119;
    William, C87, C91.
Harway, Nancy, C114; Robert, C114.
Harwell, Augustine, C33; Augustus, C48;
    Daury, C48; Elizabeth, C33;
    Eliza, C68; Henry, C33; Isam, C68;
    Jacob, C48; James, C33, C68;
    Louisa, C68; Manurvey, C48; Margaret,
    C68; Mary, C68; Nancy, C68, C69;
    Perry, C48; Robert, C68; Sarah, C69;
    Susan, C48; William, C69.
Harwood, Jackariah, C100; Jane, C99.
Hatfield, Louise, C31.
Hatter, Jesse, C140; Sarah, C140.
Hauerwas, John, 75.
Haulbert, James, C112; Matilda, C112;
    Margaret, C112; Mary, C112; William,
    C112.
Havey, Eliza, C91; Hugh, C91; James, C91;
    John, C91; Nancy, C91; Virginia, C91.
Hawkins, Cynthia, C143; Edward, C60;
    Elizabeth, C60; Frances, C140;
    H. Clay, C65; Henry, C140; Josiah,
    23, C60; Katherine, C143; Lucy, C65;
    M., 34; Malinda, C60; Mary, C65, C148;
    Robert, C65; W. F., 25; W. T., C65;
    Wiley, C65, C148; William, C65.

Hayes, Alfred, C148; Avaline, C148; Mamie, 61.
Haygood, Elizabeth, C148; George, C148; Nancy, C148; Ruth, C147; Stephen, C148.
Haywood, George, C148; Jane, C100; Judge, 2; Sousannah, C148.
Haynes, Annie, C53; Charity, C52; Christopher, C53; Darling, C53; Elizabeth, C53; George, C53; Henry, C53; James, C53; John, C53; Nancy, C53; Sarah, C53; Vicy, C53; Weatherly, C53.
Hays, Betsy, C143; Elizabeth, C139; Nancy, C138.
Hazard, 6.
Haze, Elizabeth, C64; James, C64; Sarah, C64; William, C64.
Heafly, Caroline, C30; J. H., C30.
Heardon, Elizabeth, C148; George, C148.
Hearon, Margaret, C149.
Heathcock, John, C148; Martha, C148.
Hearington, Archibald, C140; Elizabeth, C140.
Heffington, Barney, C148; Lucinda, C2; Martha, C148; Susannah, C48; Thomas, C148.
Hefington, Mahaley, C72.
Heilner, Admiral, 8.
Helm, B. H., 29.
Helton, Amanda, C38; Elgera, C38; Elizabeth, C38; Francis, C38; George, C38; Malila, C38; Margaret, C38; Rebecca, C38; Sarah, C38; Thomas, C38; William, C38.
Henderson, Elizabeth, C12; James, C140; John, C148; Julia, C138; Manervy, C141; Mary, C62, C148; Rebecca, C140.
Hendricks, Elizabeth, C148; Green, C148; Joseph, C148; Larkin, C148; Nancy, C144, C148; Sally, C142.
Hendrix, Abner, C12; Alonzo, C12; Asbury, C57; Columbus, C12; Cynthia, C144; Dennis, C2; Edwin, C12; Elender, C12; Elizabeth, C4, C57; George, C88; H. L., 71; Isac, C4; James, C2, C4, C12, 26; Jane, C57; John, C2; Joseph, C4; Julia, C88; Leander, C7; Lusinda, C2; Malissa, C2; Margarett, C12, C57; Missouri, C4; Nancy, C2, C88; Nelson, C12; Paskil, C2; Pinkney, C2; Rebecca, C4; Rufus, C88; Samuel, C12; Sarah, C2; Sissaly, C12; Sterling, C2; Sterling, C4; Wiley, C2; William, C88.
Henly, Charlotte, C148; Joseph, C148.
Henry, David, 1.

Henson, Ancel, C19; Ben, C47; Benjamin, C19; Caroline, C20; Cynthia, C19; Davenport, C20; Eliza, C19; Elizabeth, C19; George, C19; Harrell, C19; Incey, C19; Isem, C19; Isaac, C47; Jane, C20; Jessi, C19; John, C19, C20; Margaret, C19; Martha, C19; Mary, C19, C148; Phillip, 42; Polly, C19; Robert, C19, C20; Samule, C19, C20; Sara, C19; Thomas, C19, C148; William, C19.
Hentz, Caroline, 19; Nicholas, 19.
Herendon, Elizabeth, C32; George, C32; Green, C32; Margaret, C32; Mary, C32; William, C32.
Herin, Arnold, C85; Jane, C85; Mary, C85; Mermelly, C85; Nancy, C85; Paret, C85; Plemon, C85; Sousannah, C85; Squire, C85; William, C85.
Herold, Andrew, C49; Charles, C57; Craney, C57; Daniel, C49; Dolly, C57; Eunicy, 21; Harriett, C49; Jacob, 21; James, C57; John, C49; Mariah, C57; Rachel, C49; William, C49.
Herrell, Asa, C124; Elizabeth, C124; Ellender, C124; James, C124; Mary, C124; Sarah, C124.
Herrold, Eldridge, C98; Elizabeth, C98; James, C98; Jesse, C98; Luke, C98; Rody, C98.
Herrin, Lucinda, 23.
Herston, Margaret, C144.
Heslip, Mary, C62.
Heston, Catherine, C87; James, C90; John, C87, C90; Margaret, C90; Nancy, C87; Samuel, C87; William, C87.
Hewett, Elizabeth, C55; Frances, C55; Franklin, C55; Patr, C55; Sarach, C55.
Hews, Calip, C13; Catherine, C13; Columbus, C43; George, C43; John, C43; Margaret, C43; Mary, C43; Nancy, C13, C43; Nathaniel, C43; William, C43.
Hibbett, Rufus, 76.
Hickman, Charity, C147; Katherine, C148; John, C148.
Hicks, Arthur, C117; Elizabeth, C116; Jabez, C116; Margaret, C117; Mariah, C117; Martha, C117; Mary, C117, C126; Nancy, C117; Thomas, C116; William, C116.
Hiett, Claborn, C58; Joseph, C58; Manurvey, C58.
Higgens, Jane, C140; Michael, C140.
Higgings, Everline, C48; John, C48.
Higgins, Agnes, C148; Bedford, C23; Bethany, C145; Calvin, C23; Catherine, C23; Charlotte, C23; Harriet, C2; Isaac, C23; Isibella, C23, continued:

Higgins, continued: James, C26; Jenny, 139; John, C26; Josiah, C23; Margaret, C23; Martha, C23; Missouri, C26; Newton, C26; Phillip, C148; Rachel, C26; Richard, C23; Stacey, C26; William, C26; Z. Taylor, C23.
Hill, Aaron, C70; Aimy, C85; Amanda, C71; Alfred, C86; Andrew, C7; Archer, C86; Artimissa, C71; Auston, C70; Berry, C71, C72, C79; Calvin, C79; Catherine, C85, C86, C90; Charles, C71; Charlotte, C85; Claiborn, C70; Diana, C72; Dicey, C140; Dority, C71; Elender, C71; Elizabeth, C41, C71, C85, C90; Ellen, C71; Emery, C71; Emmoma, C71; Felix, C71; Frances, C71; Fred, 69; G. B., C71; George, 13, C71, C79; Haywood, C85; Henry, C70, C71, C72, C79; Hiram, C71; Indiana, C90; J. H., 67; Jacob, C86; James, 23, C70, C71, C86, C90, C148; John, C71, C85, C86, C90, C140, C148; Judi, C71; Julia, C71; Mr., 67; Mrs. Nora, 67; Lavinia, C70, C85; Lewis, C79; Lion, C71; Lucinda, C86; Lucy, C79, C85; Lydia, C79; Margaret, C141; Marion, C72; Marsena, C71; Martha, C71, C85, C86; Martin, 23; Mary, C41, C71, C72, C79, C85, C148, C152; Mills, C72; Nancy, C71, C86; Orlan, 62; Rebecca, C153; Robert, 76; Rosana, C71; Saludi, C71; Sarah, C71; Souseanah, C86; Surmicy, C41; Susann, C71; Tamsey, C71; Tempy, C144; Thomas, C71; Tom, 59; Wealthy, C41; William, C41, C70, C71, C72, C79, C86.
Hills, Elizabeth, C120; Jackson, C120; John, C120; Mary, C120; Pelina, C120; Robert, C120.
Hillenwward, James, C42; Nancy, C42.
Hines, Alcy, C42; Charles, C42; Eliza, C42; Elizabeth, C42; Henry, C42; J. D., 59; Joab, C42; Mary, C42.
Hips, Andy, C21; Andrew, C21; Charles, C21; George, C21; James, C21; Margaret, C21; Martha, C21; Nancy, C21; W. H. Harrison, C21.
Hipps, Andrew, C32; Elizabeth, C32; James, C32; John, C32; Jennett, C32; Margarett, C32; Mary, C32; Sarah, C32; William, C32.
Hitchcock, Mary Jane, C21; Ransom, C21; Rutha, C21; Sarah, C21; W. J., C21.
Hoalause, Susannah, C141.
Hoaltsleaver, Rachel, C143.
Hobbs, Ann, C147; George, 75; Susannah, C149.
Holbrook, John, C148; Rebecca, C148.

Hodge, Elizabeth, C140; Grandville, C140; James, C140; Martha, C140; Nelly, C145; Susannah, C148.
Hodges, Jane, C141; Margaret, C148; William, C148.
Holcum, Cemerine, C133; Clementine, C133; Cordelia, C133; Lainy, C133; Richard, C133; William, C133.
Hold, Elizabeth, C19; Francis, C19; James, C19; Keel, C19; Matilda, C19; Polly, C19.
Holden, Caledona, C86; Camel, C86; Denis, C83; Elbern, C83; Elizabeth, C86; Frances, C83; James, C84; John, C84; Joseph, C84; Judah, C84; Matilda, C83; Mary, C86; Rachel, C84; C86; Richard, C86; Sarah, C83; William, C134
Holehouse, Ann, C148.
Holland, Basha, C32; Catharine, C39; Charity, C140; Elizabeth, C125; Evelyn, C148; Feby, C32; James, C32; Jane, C32; John, C140; Marion, C55; Mary, C56; Polly, C140; Richard, C140; Ruthy, C140; Thomas, C39; William, C32, C39, C56.
Holleman, Rebecca, C148; William, C148.
Hollerman, John, C66.
Hollis, Sina, C72.
Holly, Almeria, 5, C140; Emily, C87; Hannah, C140; Julius, C140; William, C87; Lilly, C140.
Holmes, Caroline, C29; Elizabeth, C29; Frances, C29; Ira, C148; James, C29; John, C29; Louisa, C29; Mary, C29; Milly, C148; Peter, C29; Rhody, C149; Sarah, C29; Silvey, C148; Thomas, C148; William, C29.
Holt, Ambros, C26; Amelia, C153; Amos, C148; Amy, C145; Anagal, C101; Edgman, C148; Eliza, C145; Elizabeth, C26; Evelyn, C148; Hiram, C148; Isaiah, C148; Jackson, C148; Jane, C148; John, C148; Joseph, C148; Joshua, C26; Lidia, C148; Malinda, C145, C148; Margaret, C149; Martha, C148; Martha Ann, C26; Nancy, C26, C148; Patience, C148; Perdue, C26; Rachel, C26.
Holton, Ruth, C148; William, C148.
Homes, Delilah, C109; Harriet, C109; Richard, C109; Sousiannah, C109; Thomas, C109; Tillie, C109.
Homesley, Caroline, C22; Eph, C46; James, C22; John, C22; Mary, C22; Marion, C46; Oletha, C46; Olliss, C46; William, C22.
Hoobs, Herman, C140; Susan, C140.
Hood, Delia, C147; Humphrey, C148; J. B., 44, 46, 47, 50; James, 13; John, C40; Juda, C148; Mary, 23, C40.

Hooi, Andrew, C134; John, C134; Mariah, C134; Martha, C134; Nancy, C134.
Hooks, Amos, C148; Amy, C148; Charles, C135; Curtis, C135; Eliza, C135; Isaac, C148; J. D., C129; John, C135; Mary, C135; Rosa, C129.
Hooper, Isaac, C44; Mary, C44.
Hopkins, Elizabeth, C93; George, 21; Henry, C93; Jason, 6; John, C92; Martindale, C92; Nancy, C92; Sally, C92; Sarah, C92; Selina, 21, C93.
Hopper, Amelia, C140; Coburn, C140.
Hopson, Carter, C48; Catherine, C49; Elizabeth, C48, C49; Francis, C49; Herald, C49; Jane, C48; Jasper, C48; John, C48; Leander, C47; Lidy, C47; ,ahaldy, C49; Mary, C48; Richard, C49; Sarah, C48; Thomas, C48, C49; William, C48.
Horn, 56; James, C66, C137; John, C140; Martha, C137; Mary, C140.
Hough, Amos, C131; Ann, C131; Chapman, C1, C131; Eliza, C131; Hettie, C131; John, 2, C21, C131; Joseph, 23, C131; Nancy, C131; Pleasant, C25; Salethia, C131; Sarah, C21; William, 34, C131.
House, Abey, C61; Ann Eliza, C64; Elias, C64; Elizabeth, C40; C61; James, C40, C75; John, C61; Julious, C64; Mariah, C61; Mary, C40; Martha, C64, C108; Nancy, C40; Nimrod, C1; Permentney, C1; Sarah, C40; Thomas, 34; William, C1, C40.
Houston, Annett, C62; Benjamine, C44; Butler, C44; Champman, C44; Easter, C44; Elizabeth, C24, C44, C62; George, C44; Hanna, C44; I. B., 26; James, C44; John C24, C44; Jones, C44; L. T., C62; Laura, C54; Lucinda, C148; Martha, C148; Mary, C24, C44, C54; Pugh, C44, C148; Ross, C148; Sarah, C62; William, C24.
Hovey, A. H., 61.
Howard, Acria, C102; Cynthia, C102; Eliza, C102; Elizabeth, C102, C148, C152; Frank, 73; Hardin, C102, C148; Harriett, C148; Jane, C114; Jason, C104; Jesse, C148; John, C104; Lucy, C102, C104; Malicia, C103; Martha, C102; Mary, C102, C148; Nancy, C104; Narcissus, C103; Nelly, C148; Newton, C148; Obediah, C102; Odette, 73; Patrick, C103; Ransom, C148; Rita, C148; Robert, C114; Samuel, C114; Stephen, C104; Thomas, C102; Zachariach, C102.
Howeel, Carter, C57.
Howel, Mary, C148; Philip, C148.

Howell, Allen, C1; Amanda, C1; Ann Elizabeth, C1; Catharine, C3; Eliza, C1; Francis, C1; Isabella, C3; James, C3; John, C1; Jonathan, C1; Joseph, C1; Katherine, C149; Larinda, C1; Lucretia, C140; Levi, C3; Lucretia, C3; Martha, C31; Martin V. B., C1; Mary, C1; Permentia, C3; Phillip, C3; Polly, C3; Ranson, C1; Rebecca, C152; Robert, 26; Salena, C3; Sarah, C3; Thomas, C31; Willis, C1; William, C1, C3, C140.
Howland, Matilda, C139.
Howie, Andrew, C1; Annie, C1; John, C1; Martha Ann, C1; Mary, C1; Nancy, C1; Sarah, C1.
Hubbard, Archibald, 12; Nancy, C140; Stephen, C140; William, C125.
Hubbert, Snoden, C67.
Hudson, L. C., 59; S. B., 21, 29, C56.
Huddleston, Andrew, C19; Caroline, C19; David, C61; Elizabeth, C19; Felix, C19; George, C19; John, C61; Joseph, C19; Lewis, C61; Mary, C61; Samuel, C61; Thomas, C19; Wiley, C19; Zachariah, C19.
Huff, 45; Elizabeth, C148; Frances, C151; Hannah, C140; John, C140; Mariah, C140; Mrs., 45; Stephen, C140.
Huggins, Elizabeth, C139, C140; James, C140; Nancy, C140; Phillip, C140; Sally, C153; Thomas, C140.
Hughes, A., C82; Banester, C81; Calwell, C83; Catharine, C108; Cynthia, C83; David, C81; Dorinda, C81; Elias, C81; Eliza, C81; Elizabeth, C81, C82; John, C108; Margaret, C83; Martha, C82, C83; Mary, C82; Nancy, C82; O. H., 21; Porter, 62; Rebecca, C83; Rosannah, C83; Sarah, C81; Thomas, C108; Washington, C83; William, C83.
Hughs, Francis, C9; James, C9; Jefferson, C124; Robert, C9; Sarah, C9; William, C9.
Huley, Elis, C64.
Huling, Thomas, 12.
Humbrell, Sally, C139.
Humphrey, James, C46; John, C46; Sarah, C46; William, C46.
Humphries, Mrs. Lucy, 62.
Hunt, A. C., C37; Amanda, C127; Elizabeth, C127; Frances, C37, C127; Helen, 7; Isaac, C127; James, C127; Jantha, C37; John, C1, C137; Joseph, C137; Lucinda, C127; Margaret, C37; Martha, C137; Mary, C5, C127; Miss, 67; Nancy, C5, C127; Sarah, C127; Wesley, C5; William, C5, C37, C127.

Hunter, Allen, C99; Frances, C99; Jesse, C99; Mary, C99; Permelia, C154; William, 4.
Hurlburt, Hurlbut, 38, 39.
Hurley, Esther, C149; Rebecca, C140; Thomas, C140.
Hurst, Emmet, 66.
Hurston, Elizabeth, C154.
Hurt, Bitty, C61; Dicy, C54; James, C61; John, C54; Lewis, C54; Martha, C54; Nancy, C61; Unus, C54; Sally, C54.
Husk, Aaron, C48; Abraham, C48; Cinthia, C48; James, C48; Jesse, C48; Julia, C48; Rhody, C48; Robert, C48; Samindivella, C48; Winney, C48.
Hussey, George, C133; James, C133; Lucy, C133; Lydia, C133; Mary, C133; Nancy, C133; R. B., C133; Spikes, C133; Thomas, C133; William, C133.
Huston, Delia, C140; Robert, C140.
Hutchens, Alexander, C46; Andrew, C39.
Hutchinson, Docie, C146.
Hutton, Addaline, C6; Christopher, C22; Elizabeth, C22; Ellender, C6; George, C6; James, C6; John, C22; Juliar, C6; Martha, C6, C38; Sarah, C6; Winford, C6; Washington, C6.
Huzza, Lucy, C148; Robert, C148.
Hyde, Francis, C137; Franklin, C137; H. C., 59; Mary, C137; Samuel, 54, C137.
Hynemon, David, C82; James, C82; Jane, C82; Martha, C82; Robert, C82.

Ijam, Margaret, C147.
Imes, Bassle, C7; Elizabeth, C7; Elizabeth, C7; Elvira, C7; George, C7; John, C7; Joseph, C7; Marthy Ann, C7.
Ingram, Benjamin, 24, C118; C. D., 70; Charles, C51; Emily, C148; George, C87; Georgenia, C87; Henry, C87; Joseph, C118; Lucy, C87; Martha, C51; Margaret, C51; Marion, C51; Mary, C56, C87, C138; Moses, 46, C87; Ollie, C51; Robert, C51; Sarah, C87, C118; Susan, C51; Thomas, C44, 59, C87.
Inlow, Christopher, C46; Eliza, C46; Elizabeth, C46; J. R., C46; James, C46; John, C46; Joanah, C46; Margaret, C46; Philip, C46; Richard, C46; Sarah, C46; Sally, C46; William, C46.
Irey, Angaline, C25; Liddy, C25; Owen, C25; Richard, C25; Samuel, C25; William, C25.
Iron, Andrew, C30; Augustus, C30; Caroline, C58; James, C58; Jane, C29; John, C30; Mary, C30. C58; Phillip, C29, C30, C58; Sarah, C30; continued,

Iron, continued: Susan, C30; Thomas, C30, C58; William, C30.
Irvine, 14; Christine, C131; Deliah, C106; Ellam, C106; Henry, C131; J. B., 53; James, 12, 16, 34, 53; Martha, C131; Mary, C131; Nancy, C108; Parthenia, C131; Robert, C106; Sarah, 23, C131; Thomas, C131; Thusood, C131; William, C106.
Isbell, Eliza, C44; Elzab, C44; Fanny, C44; Jane, C141; Lewis, C44; Susan, C58.
Isom, Arthur, 3.
Isreal, Crockett, C49; David, C49; Elizabeth, C49; George, C52; Lewis, C52; Margaret, C49; Nancy, C49; Polly Ann, C49; Polly, C52.
Ives, 42; Amos, C77, C140; George, C77; Henry, C77; Isabella, C77; John, C77; Mary, C77, C140; Samuel, C77; Sarah, C77; Shaylor, C77.
Ivins, Adaline, C47; Allen, C47; Amy, C31; Fanny, C47; Marissa, C47; Stephen, C47.

Jackson, A. A., 62, 69; A. E., C119; Alexander, C39; Ann, C26, C88; Andrew, 4, 5, 11, 12, C39, 69, C88; Belzora, C118; C. H., 76; Calvin, C14; Caroline, C26, C118; Castella, C88; Catherine, C79, C88, C119; Cynthia, C119; Dorthy, C88; Earl, 69; Edward, C149; Elijah, C26; Eliza, C20; Elizabeth, C20, C78, C88, C118, C150; Ellender, C78; Evelyn, C146; Fanny, C78; Floyd, 70; Frances, C88; George, C39; H. B., 71; Harry, C88; James, 4, 5, 7, 11, 15, 20, C20, C39, 42, 48, 71; Jenny, 7; Jeremiah, C78; John, C14, C66, C72; Joseph, C78, C88; June, C137; Lucy, C119; M. F., 64; Malinda, C149; Margaret, C140; Martha, C33, C39, C119; Mary, C20, C26, C78, C88, C140, C149; McCuller, 7; Montezuma, C88; Nancy, C78; Nicholas, C88; Olive, 62; Peter, C149; Polly, C33; Rody, C149; Quinteral, C88; Sarah, 23, C33, C39, C66, C67, C119; Stewart, C79; T. F., C88; Tamutha, C39; William, C26, C33, C78, C140.
James, Absalom, C149; C. R., 71; Easter, C116; Elizabeth, C46, C148; Elvria, C116; Frank, 59; Harriet, C116; Isabella, C116; Jesse, 59; Joshua, C116; Matilda, C153; Mary, C116; Nancy, C116; Nazzarine, C149; Richard, C116; Sarah, C116.
January, James, C135.

Jarman, Elizabeth, C154; Mary, C144; Rachel, C144; Steven, C18.
Jeams, James, C46; Jinney, C46; William, C133.
Jeans, Absalom, C9; Aladdphia, C150; Elizabeth, C9; Francis, C9; Huldy, C9; John, C9; Joseph, C9; Lupvisa, C9; Marion, C9; Martha, C9; Mary, C9; Massey, C9; Matilda, C9; Nancy, C9; Thomas, C9; Verlinda, C146; William, C9, C133.
Jeaves, Jesse, C149; Sally, C149.
Jefferson, 12.
Jenkins, Abner, C54; C., C149; Elizabeth, C144, C149; Hanna, C54; Harrison, C149; Mack, C54; Margaret, C136; Polly, C149; R., C45; Ruth, C54; Thomas, C54.
Jeters, Argalus, 1.
Jinkens, Elizabeth, C65; Venson, C65.
Jilton, James, C47; John, C47; Leondas, C47; Mary, C47; Susan, C47.
Jinnings, Jesse, C149; John, C15; Tempy, C149.
Johnson, Allen, C9; Anderson, 13; Ann, C153; Annie, C20; B. M., C46; Bob, 74; Capt., 43; Chottler, C100; Daniel, C20; Dolly, C136; E. C., C153; Ed, 47; Elizabeth, C6, C69, C149, C152; Ellen, C31; Felix, C6, 21; Frances, C6, C146; General, 45; George, C100; Harriet, C148; Henry, C20; J., 5; James, C6, C31, C100; Jane, C108; Jerry, C53; John, 3, 45, C108, C149; Joseph, C108; Letitia, C53; Lusinda, C56, C149; Lucy, C108; Malinda, C108; Manchester, C20; Margaret, C100, C104; Martha, C53; Mary, C108; Minor, C102; Molly, C20; Nancy, C98; R. J.S., 69; Rachel, C9; Richard, C53, C102; Sally, C20, C138; Samuel, C9, C40; Sarah, C100, C113; Sevilla, C107; Stephen, C9; Thomas, C9, C20, C100; J. O. R., 28; William, C100, C107; Zachariah, C98, C102.
Jobe, Jane, C144.
Johnston, 37; A. S., 29; Ann, C52; Caladonia, C52; Cravis, C52; Early, C149; Elizabeth, C52; John, C52; Mary, C52; McCrager, C52; Samuel, C52; Travis, C52; William, C149.
Joice, Allice, C38; Allis, C70; John, C38; Lemiel, C38; Mary, C38; Nancy, C38; Sally, C38.
Joiner, B. P., 25; Benjamin, C82; Brantly, C83; Charles, C121; cont'd

Joiner, continued: Drury, C83, C121, C149; Eli, C83, C121; Eliza, C121; Elizabeth, C44; Frances, C83, C149; Hiram, C44; James, C44, C83; Jane, C83; John, C121; Lydia, C121; Margaret, C83; Martha, C44, C121; Mary, C83; C121; Moses, C121; Nancy, C44; Rebecca, C83; Sarah, C83, C149; Susannah, C121; Thorington, C121; William, C83.
Jones, 70; Adaline, C120; Albert, C57; Allen, 53, C103; Amy, C145; Annis, C83; Bathany, C120; Benjamin, 5, 6; Miss Betty, 59; Branson, C122; C. F., C57; Camilla, C42; Catherine, C18, C149; Charles, C83, C122; Charlotte, C150; Cullender, C149; Daniel, 31; Delania, C122; Edney, C151; Eli, C83; Eliza, 26, C58; Elizabeth, C101, C120, C122, C147; Ephraim, C103; Helen, 73; Henry, C101; Isaac, C123; J. G., C123; J. O., 59; Jackson, C19; Jacob, C103; James, C120; Jesse, C83, C122; Joe, 73; John, C18, C20, C101, C103, C120; Kisiah, C103; Leo, C122; Lidia, C148; Lucinda, C123, C126; Margaret, C83, C149; Martha, 59, C83, C101, C103; Mary, C18, C83, C101, C103, C120, C122, C126, C147; Mary Ann, C20; Mary Jane, C20; Mehemiah, C103; Michael, C122; Mirsen, C103; Moses, C120; Nancy, C20, C103, C122; C123, C149; Neil, C101, C103; Patience, C148; Patsy, C144; Preesasi, C120; Polly, C149; Rebecca, C103, C123; Richard, C126; Robert, C123; Ruthy, C143; Sally, C145; Samuel, C18; Sarah, C20, C83, C101, C122, C149; Serene, C149; Stephen, C103; Thomas, C20, 59, C101; Tebitha, C83; William, C20, 26, C58, C103, C122, C126, C149; Wyatt, C149.
Jordan, David, C149; Elizabeth, C121; James, C121; Mahala, C121; Mary, C55; Rebecca, C149; Samples, C121; Sarah, C55; Stephen, 44; Tebetha, C121; William, C23, C55.
Jordon, Nancy, C147.
Julian, W. R., 38.
Jourdon, Elizabeth, C145.
Judd, Daniel, C140; Dianah, C140.

Kachelman (see also Cachelman), Barbary, 21; John, 21, 53; Johnson, 21; Margaret, 21.
Kaisner, George, C137.
Kallicut, James, C12; Mary, C12.
Kansner, B. T., 34; George, 34.

Karner, Andrew, C63; Ann Eliza, C63;
  B. F., C63; Franklin, C63; John,
  C63; Mary, C63; Sarah, C63; William,
  C63.
Karsner, (see Karner, Kanser, Kaisner,
  and other spellings), B. F., 53;
  B. P., 21; Benjamin, C149; George, 59;
  Sarah, C149.
Karry, Feraby, C47.
Karsen, Calvin, C127; Catherine, C127;
  Easter, C127; Ebeneza, C127; James,
  C127; Rebecca, C127.
Keeton, Malvina, C145.
Keith, Margaret, C149; Joseph, C149.
Kelley, Kelly, Andrew, C14; A. J., 39;
  Adeline, C89; Andrew, C89; Ann, C137;
  Anthony, C89; Benjamin, C89; Edith,
  C149; Edy, C89; Felix, C89;
  George, C89; Hariett, C14; Henry, C89;
  James, C137; Jane, C89; John, C89, C137;
  Johnathan, C137; Manurvy, C14; Martha,
  C84, C137; Samuel, C14, C137; Sarah,
  C14; Vincent, C89, C149; William, 5, 7.
Kelough, 3.
Kemper, Frances, C59.
Kendrick, Amberis, C72; Ellis, C72; Henry,
  C128; James, C72, C108, C128; John,
  C141; Lucy, C72; Margaret, C141; Mary,
  C72, C128; Milton, C72; Nancy, C108;
  Noel, C72; Obediah, C72; Rebecca, C108,
  C128; Thomas, C72, C108; W. P., 20;
  William, 18, C108.
Kenemore, Alia, C141; Hilery, C141;
  Isabel, C141; Miranda, C141; Sarah, C141;
  Starberry, C142; Wileby, C141.
Kennedy, Abraham, 36; Betsy, C152; Catherine, C67; Curtice, C68; Dave, C69;
  Edmond, C67; Edward, C62; Elias, C62,
  C68; Enoch, C134; Fagan, C62; George,
  C133; Hiram, 22, 23, C62, C75, C134;
  James, C39, C67; Jane, C67; Joannah,
  C69, C75; John, C62, C68, C69; John F.,
  75; Joseph, C68; Julia, C69; Larena,
  C68; Liddia, C62; Louisa, C134; Luthur,
  C134; Mahaley, C67; Martha, C134; Mary,
  C62, C67, C133, C134; Milind, C68;
  Nancy, C67, C68; Obediah, C68; Olive,
  25; Olliver, C134; Polly, C68; Thomas,
  C67; Washington, C68; William, C67,
  C68.
Kenny, Ann Liza, C98; Davis, C98; Frances,
  C98; James, C98; Jane, C98; John, C98;
  Martha, C98; Mary, C98; William, C98.
Kernacham, Ann Eliza, 19; Maria, 19;
  Matilda, 19; Molly, 19; R. T., 23;
  Robert, 14;
Kernachin, John, 61.
Kernaham, T. T., C58; R. T., Jr., C58.
Kernahan, Robert, 54.

Kernard, Charles, C149; Mary, C149.
Kernigham, Andrew, C46; Charlotte, C46;
  Harison, C46; Jane, C46; Mary, C46.
Kershaw, Robert, 71.
Key, W. H., 41; William, 23.
Keys, Charlie, 61; Elizabeth, C57;
  James, C57; Martha, C57, C134;
  Mary, C57, C134; Robertes, C134;
  Susan, C57; Thomas, C134; W. C., 59;
  William, C57, C134.
Kibbs, Nancy, C147.
Kidd, John, C149; Mary, C149; William, 4.
Kiddy, Elizabeth, C41; Louisa, C124;
  Thomas, C124; William, C124.
Kilburn, Jim, 70.
Killen, John, C141; Kath C148; Margaret,
  C140; R. T., 60; Susannah, C141;
  T. B., 59.
Killin, Andrew, C71; Daniel W., C71;
  Duncan, C71; Henry, C71; John, C71;
  Mary, C71; Robert, C71; Susan, C71;
  T. T. Benton, C71.
Killough, Ethel, C149; John, C149.
Kilpatrick, H. Clay, C66; Louisa, C66;
  Martha, C66; Mary, C66; T. J., C66.
Kimbel, Sally, C138.
Kimbrel, John, C149; Susannah, C149.
Kimbrell, Mary, C149.
Kindman, A. J., C120; Mary, C120.
Kindrick, Deby, C142; Rebecca, C138.
King, Alexander, C84; Arnold, C84;
  Burney, C95; Catherine, C84;
  Emerline, C84; Eliza, C95; Elizabeth,
  C122; Frank, 69; George, C84, C122;
  Gilford, C95, C122; Hinton, C122;
  Joseph, C84, C141; Luke, C84, Lydia,
  C84; Margaret, C122; Matilda, C95;
  Nancy, C149; Qurnton, C122; Robert,
  C149; Roenia, C95; Sarah, C122;
  Sarahbeth, C122; Selfa, C95, C122;
  Stephen, C84; William, C84.
Kinsey, Carter, C149; Elizabeth, C149.
Kirk, Frances, C28; Hudley, C28; Jane,
  C144; Joseph, C28; Patsy, C140;
  Richard, C28; Simon, C28; Thomas,
  C28; William, C28; Zachariah, C28.
Kirklin, Daverson, C3; Elizabeth, C3;
  Enoch, C4; James, C4; Joseph, C4;
  Marthy, C4; Mary, C4; Missouri, C4;
  Richard, C4; Robert, C4; Robert, C4;
  Rufus, C4; Sarah, C3.
Kirkman, Elizabeth, C66; Hugh, C66;
  Hunt, C66; Jackson, C66; James, 23,
  C39; Mary, 23, C66; Samuel, C66;
  Sarah, C66; Thomas, 23, C66.
Kirkpatrick, James, C149; Polly, C149.
Kitchens, Amy, C149; Eliza, C149;
  George, C95, C149; Lucy, C149;
  Mary, C149; Peremelia, C149.

Knight, Almira, C112; B. W., C112; Bolivar, 22; Carlisle, C78, C112, C118; Caroline, 25, C118; Dorthenia, C141; Elizabeth, C118; James, C149; Jane, C78; Mary, C78, C79, C112; Nancy, C151; Prudence, C112; Robert, C112; Sarah, C88; Thomas, C112.
Koger, Lucinda, 13; William, 13, 23; Allice, C55; Elizabeth, C55; Jesse, C55; Josephine, C55; Martha, C55, C141; Mary, C55; Orlena, C55; Relea, C55; Romella, C55; William, C55, C141.
Koonce, (see also Coontz), George, C17; William, C17.
Kuffner, Margaret, 21.
Kyle, Albert, C116; Elizabeth, C116; James, C21; C116; Sarah, 21, C116.

Lacefield, C154; Martin, C49; Mary, C149.
Lackey, Nancy, C141; Thomas, C141.
Ladd, Caroline, C118; Noble, 25, C118.
Lafan, Ann, C74; Elizabeth, C132; Hannah, C132; Isaac, C74, C132; James, C132; John, C132; Joseph, C74; Matthew, C132; Prissa, C132; Ruth, C74; Rutha, C132; Thomas, C74; William, C132.
Lafann, Elizabeth, C149; James, C149.
Lakey, James, C134; Melinda, C153; Thomas, C134.
Laky, Lucy, C148.
Lamb, Ann, 20; Elizabeth, C24, C53, C145; Esther, C149; Henry, C53; James, C24, C26, C53; Jane, C53; John, 20, C24, C53; Mahaley, C53; Martha, C26, C52, C53, C152; Morgan, C149; Nancy, C53, C148; Peggy, C26; Polly, C53; Rachel, C53; Rhodey, C24; Sarah, C24, C141.
Lambert, Henry, C61; James, C61, C109; Joel, C109; John, C61, C109; Josephine, C109; Malinda, C61; Margaret, C61; Nancy, C61; Mary, C109; Sarah, C109.
Lamour, John, C105; Larkin, C105; Louisa, C105; Malinda, C105; Mary, C105; Millie, C105; William, C105.
Lamprecht, Frank, 71.
Lancaster, David, C126; Lucy, C126; Marriah, C142; Martha, C145; Mary, C152; Nancy, C126; Samuel, C126.
Lance, Polly, C141; Spencer, C141.
Landham, Matilda, C149; William, C149.
Landmon, Clansy, C118; Elvira, C106; Francis, C106; Lavinah, C106; Mariah, C106; Mary, C155; Matilda, C118; Samuel, C106; William, C118.
Landmond, Matilda, 24; William, 24.

Lane, Agnes, C25; Drury, C25; Elizabeth, C25; Henry, C25; Julia, C25; Martha, C57; Moses, C25; Phillip, C25; Sarah, C25; Sanonah, C25.
Lang, William, 54.
Langford, Thomas, 23.
Langley, James, 46.
Lanier, Aaron, C81; B., 24; Edron, C112; Margaret, 21, C76, C81; Martha, C61, C76; Mary, C61, C76; Mary Elizabeth, 73; Marion, C81; Robert, C81; Simpson, C88; Sarah, C88; Thomas, C112; W. T., C76; William, 21, C76, C112; Willimina, C112.
Lankford, Abergale, C45; Dartnula, C30; Draylon, C30; Elizabeth, C30; George, C45; Gracilla, C30; Harriett, C30; Jacob, C30; John, C45; Lydia, C30; Martha, C30; Polly, C30; Richard, C30; Thomas, C45; William, C30.
Lanmon, Sousan, C90.
Lansford, Annie, C24; John, C24; Milton, C24.
Lard, Elizabeth, C141; Nathaniel, C141.
Laremore, Sally, C154.
Largent, Emer, C68; James, C68; John, C68; Mary, C68; Sarah, C68.
Larkins, Emily, C149; Lenore, C149.
Lasiter, Harriett, C149; Katherine, C149; William, C149.
Laster, Ordel, C137.
Lassiter, Kate, 7; James, 12, C149; Sarah, C149.
Lathan, Annie, C20; Asbury, C20; Davenport, C20; Elizabeth, C20; Frances, C20; George, C20; James, C20; John, C20; Manurvy, C20; Marion, C20.
Lavington, John, C150; Susan, C150.
Lawson, Ann, C69; Baby, 66; Bob, 66; Charles, C69; Elizabeth, C2, C73; Francis, C2; Henry, C69; Ivey, C2; Jackson, C73; James, C69; Jasper, C2; John, C69; Joseph, C68; Margaret, C2, C68, C69; Marth, C68; Martin, C2; Newton, C2; Rachel, C69; Rebecca, C69; Sarena, C69; Temperance, C2; Thadeus, C69; Thadeus, C69; Thomas, C69; Thursday, C69; William, C68, C69.
Laxington, Betsy, C149; William, C149.
Lea, Nancy, C147; Unicy, C144.
Leak, John, 6.
Leath, Elizabeth, C113; Isam, 23, C113; Nathaniel, C98; Uriah Bell, C113.
Lee, Aaron, C28; Amy, C28; Caroline, C28; Hanah, C28; Henry, 66; Jerry, 76; John, C28; Juliar, C28; Robert, 66; Stephen, 42, 46, 47; William, C28, C130.
LeFen, Rebecca, C148.

Leftwich, Ann, C62; Eliza, C137; J. B., C62; Julia, C62.
Lembert, Isebella, C52; James, C52; John, C52; Lusinda, C52; Martha, C52; Nancy, C52; Polly, C52; Sally, C52; Samuel, C52; Thomas, C52; William, C52.
Lemenski, Leminosky, 22.
Lenoir, Clement, C141; Mary, C141.
Leonard, Martha, C139.
Lester, Mariah, C136; James, C141; Jane, C141.
Letsinger, Eveline, C129, C150; James, C1, C150.
Lewis, Andrew, C15; Benjamin C15; Hector, 37; Martha, C65; Martha Ann, C15; Nancy, C134; Oscar, 10; Quebec, C134; Richard, C15; Rosnah, C15; Wiley, C134; William, C135.
Lewter, Chales, C130; Emily, C130; John, C130.
Leymaster, John, 80.
Lidner, Adam, C61; Joseph, C61.
Lightfoot, Elizabeth, C149; Henry, C149.
Liles, Abigale, C3; Amous, C3, C128; Charny, C128; Elizabeth, C4, C128; James, C128; Joe, 70; John, C3; Marion, C3; Mary, C3; Nancy, C4; Orleana, C4; Rebecca, C3; Sarah, C128; Stephen, C128; Thomas, C3; William, C70.
Lilly, Edward, C141; Elizabeth, C141.
Linda, Elizabeth, C120; Matilda, C120; Nancy, C120; Sarah, C120; William, C120.
Linder, Elvira, C105; Malicia, C105.
Lindley, Susan, C151.
Lindsay, David, 53; Anderson, C149; Littleton, C149; Rhody, C149; Patsy, C149; Sarah, C149; Thomas, C149.
Lindsey, Betsy, C143; Eritely, C141; Frank, C141; Josiah, C141; Phillip, C141; Polly, C140; R. F. M., 28; R. H., 48; Sally, C140.
Lindy, Anthony, C87; Nancy, C87; Sarah, C87.
Linly, James, C107; John, C107; Lucinda, C107; Malinda, C107; T., C107.
Linsley, Aaron, C17; Andrew, C17; Calip, C16; Edmond, C47; Frances, C17; Joseph, C16, C17; Lucy, C16; Nancy, C16; Phillip, C16, C17; Polly, C17; Robert, C17; Silvester, C17; Sylvester, C47; William, C15.
Linsoff, Polly, C148.
Lipscomb, Calvin, C60; Elizabeth, C57, C60; James, C57; Margaret, C60; Mariah, C57; Mary, C60; Samuel, C57; Sarah, C57; William, C57, C60.

Litchwith, Augustine, C48; Christopher, C48; Everline, C48; Isibella, C48; Jane, C48; John, C48; Mary, C48; Olly, C48; Thomas, C48.
Literal, Ailsey, C106; Amanda, C101, C106; Eliza, C92, C106; Elizabeth, C101; Feildon, C106; George, C101; Hannah, C106; James, C101; Jenny, C146; Jessee, C101; John, C101, C106; Joseph, C101, C106; Louisa, C106; Lucy, C101; Lucinda, C92; Marinda, C101; Martha, C101, C106; Mary, C101; Samuel, C92; Sarah, C92; Sarah, C101, C106.
Litterell, Mary, C150.
Litreal, Alfred, C92; Elizabeth, C92; Frances, C92; James, C92; Jesse, C92; John, C92; Luanda, C92; Mary, C92; Sarah, C92.
Littrell, Milton, 74. (See various other spellings of this name.)
Littlejohn, Charles, C149; Delia, C147; Elizabeth, C147; Mary, C149; Peter, C141; Polly, C138; Rebecca, C141; Samuel, C141; Susannah, C141.
Littleton, Basil, C149; Charles, 3, 4, C11, C12, C13, 25; David, C10; Eliza, C149; Elizabeth, C9, C10, C11, C12, C13; Frances, C13, C149; Franklin, C10; Hannah, C13; Jane, C13; Jim, 3, 4; John, C10; Lusinda, C10; Mary, C13; Nancy, C12; Pony, 3, 4; Rebecca, C10; Robert, C10; Rewben, C149; Rubin, C13; Samuel, C9, C10; Sarah, C13; Simmon, C13; Sylvia, 3, 4; Thomas, C13; Washington, C10; William, C10, C13; Zachariah, C13.
Lively, James, C149; Sally, C149.
Locker, Alex, 62; Flora, 62.
Lockey, Malinda, C153.
Locklayer, Sarah, 21.
Logan, Hennett, C62.
Loid, Jane, C50; Lucretia, C140; Spencer, C52; William, C50.
Lolla, Monroe, C47; William, C47.
Long, Alexander, C25; Columbus, C22; Daniel, C22; Elizabeth, C22; George, C45; Isabella, C25; James, C22; Jasper, C45; John, C25; Juliar, C24; Lafaett, C45; M. D., 58; Manurvy, C24; Mary, C45; Matilda, C25; Michael, C141; Mikle, C45; Nancy, C22, C45; Rebecca, C45; Richard, C25; Sarah, C25; Thomas, C24; Vancy, C141; William, C45.
Longe, Mary, C108; Phillip, C108.
Looney, Benjamin, C150; Claiborn, C149; Jesse, C149; Margaret, C149; continued

Looney, continued: Martin, C149;
Nancy, C154; Polly, C141, C149;
Rutha, C150; Sarah, C149.
Lorance, Andrew, C57; Aseneth, C57;
Lutious, C56; Mary, C57; Sarah,
C57.
Love, Eliza, C38; Giles, C112; John,
C112.
Loveless, Almyra, C43; B. P., 76;
Elizabeth, C37; Frances, C37, C43;
George, C37, C43; Hazle, C43;
J. Ann, C43; James, C37; John,
C43; Joseph, C37; Lusinda, C37;
Margaret, C43; Martha, C146; Mary,
C37, C43; Nancy, C37; Rebecca, C43;
Ruben, C43; Simon, C37; William, C43.
Lovell, Alvey, C92; Amanda, C100;
Constant, C101; Frances, C100;
George, C100; Hiram, C92; James, C100;
Levisa, C100; Lucy, C100, C101; Nancy,
C100; Patan, C100; Polly, C100;
Roda, C100; Ruben, C100, C101;
Rubin, C101; Sarah, C100; Samuel,
C92; Thomas, C100; William, C92,
C100.
Loving, Constant, C96; Lucy, C96; Mary,
C134; Ruben, C96.
Lowe, D., 12; Martha, C151.
Lowell, Catherine, C141; John, C141;
Polly, C141.
Lowry, Thomas, C135.
Loyd, Elizabeth, C144; Rebecca, C153.
Lucky, Richard, C113.
Lucus, Soony, 74; William, 54, 55.
Lucust, Darinda, C51; Elizabeth, C51;
Emily, C50; Jefferson, C50; Isaac,
C51; Louiser, C50; Margaret, C50;
Mary, C50; Nancy, C50;
Susan, C50; Thomas, C50, C51;
William, C51; Willis, C11; Z.T., C50.
Ludkins, Charles, C86; Elizabeth, C86;
Frederic, C86; John, C86; Martha,
C86; Rebecca, C86; Sarah, C86;
William, C86.
Luney, Aveline, C94; Elizabeth, C107;
George, C94; John, C94; Joseph,
C94; Lucinda, C94; Mary, C94, C107;
Nancy, C94; Rebecca, C107; William,
C107.
Lunn, Franklin, C128; Mary, C128.
Lunsford, Manerva, C147.
Lusk, W. H., 36.
Luster, Laura, C114; John, C114.
Lutton, Catherine, C149; Miles, C149.
Lybrook, George, 26.
Lynch, Nancy, C146.
Lyon, William, 12.
Lyons, Elizabeth, C5; James, C141;
Jane, C141; Martha, C142; Mary, C5;
Nancy, C147; William, C5.

Mackey, Charles, C141; Eliner, C141;
Martha, C45; Thomas, C45; Virginia,
C45; William, C45.
Maddox, Lazarus, 6.
Maderson, James, C18.
Madison, John, 4, 5, 6, 7.
Madlin, Elizabeth, C150; Samuel, C150.
Madra, R. H., 20.
Madrir, Etheldrin, C51.
Magea, Elizabeth, C52; George, C52;
James, C52; Leerer, C52.
Maguire, Patrick, 8.
Mainer, Charles, 16.
Maize, Nancy, C125.
Majors, Mirah, C127.
Malone, Benjamin, C58; Frances, C58;
Mitchel(l), C58, 60; Susan, C58;
Ugine, C58.
Maly, Chapman, 75.
Mangrum, George, 76.
Maning, Edward, C150; Sarah, C150.
Manley, Caleb, 6.
Mapes, Bill, 77.
Maples, Mary, C145.
Markham, Margaret, C80; Polly, C140.
Markes, E., 19.
Marks, Albert, C130; Henrietta, C130;
Henry, C113; Howard, 71; Jane, C142;
Levi, C113; Lewis, 21; Margaret, C113;
Mary, C158; Nathaniel, C150.
Marshal, Thursean, C141.
Marshall, Jane, C141; Lewis, C141;
Mary, 73.
Martin, Agnes, C141; Alexander, C7;
Amanda, C42; Amy, C141; Andrew, C5;
Andy, C7; Ann, C7; Asbury, C44;
Ben, 79; Betsy, C141; Catherine, C6,
C64; Charles, C42; D. L., 7; David,
C21; Dicey, C140; Douglas, C22;
E. B., C64; E. F., 75, 76; Eliza,
C64; Elizabeth, C20, C22, C39, C60;
Ellen, C42, C64; Emily, C70; Everline,
C7; Feby, C5; Felix, 13; Frances,
C6, C117; G. W., C39; George, C5, 6,
C21, C39, C70; Gertrude, C5; Harrell,
C7; Henry, C42; J. M., 12; James,
C22, 23, 25, C42, C136, C141; Jane,
C151; Jeanette, C32; John, C7, C20,
C21, C22, C31, C32, C42, C117; Joseph,
1, C32; Lewis, C7, C31, C141; Lucy,
C42; Malissa, C7; Margaret, C22;
Martha, C22, C42; Marthy, C6; Mary,
C21, C31, C32, C39; Matilda, C7; Oliver, C42; Phoeby, C5; Rebecca, C39;
Robert, C20, C21, C42; Rosanah, C21;
Rosell, C140; Samuel, C7, C21, C70;
Sarah, C22, C39, C42, C70; Serena, C21;
Thomas, C6, C32, C141; Tobitha, C42;
Virginia, C31; Wiley, C21, continued:

Martin, continued: William, C5, C21, C22; William Carroll, 79.
Martindale, Agnes, C141; Cynthia, C89; Elizabeth, C150; George, C89, C141; James, C150; Joseph, C89; John, C89; Martha, C89; Nancy, C89; Rebecca, C89; Sarah, C89; Thomas, C89.
Martn, Annie, C43; Elizabeth, C43; James, C43.
Marvel, John, C150; Rachel, C150.
Mason, Grena, C152; Lucia, 73; Mahulda, C150; Martha, C151; Thomas, C128; William, C64, C128.
Massey, Collins, C5; Elizabeth, C1, C5, C38; Eliza Jane, c1; Horatio, C5; Jane, C1; Richard, C38; Thomas, C1, C5.
Master, Jacob, C13.
Masterson, Robert, 71.
Mathas, Emeline, C21; John D., C21; Nancy, C21; William, C21.
Mathena, William, C14.
Matheny, Mary, 59.
Mathers, Barbary, C118; James, C118; Mary, C118; Sarah, C118.
Mathews, Jim, 31; John, 6.
Mathus, Benton, C50; Hardy, C50; James, C50; John, C50; Joshua, C50; Malinda, C50; Margaret, C50; Nancy, C50; Unicy, C50; William, C50.
Matingly, Catherine, C64; Francis, C64; Thomas, C64; Sidney, C64.
Matthis, Catherine, C97; Elizabeth, C97; J. J., C97; James, C97; Mary, C97; Thomas, C97; William, C97.
Matthews, Polly, C141; S. J., 53; William, C141.
Mattocks, Ann, C125; C150; Charles, C150; James, C125; Sarah, C125; Thomas, C125.
Maubly, Mahulda, C150; Littleberry, C150.
Maxey, Polly, C141; Stephen, C141.
Maxwell, F. A., C24; Latitia, C24; Martha, C24.
May, Benjamin, C80; Bulla, 70; Chaney, C150; Darkus, C7; Elizabeth, C150; Grandville, 71; John, C80, C150; Joseph, 63; Malinda, C150; Margaret, C80; Mary, C80; Sarah, C80; William, C80, C150.
Mayfield, James, C141; Jane, C141; John, 59.
Mayhew, Elizabeth, C143.
Mayo, C. L., 69; W. J., 69.
Mays, Claiborn, C141; Mary, C141.
McAlexander, Alexander, 53.
McAlister, John, 53, C63; Mr., 51; Nancy, C138.
McAllister, 14; Rebecca, C142.

McAphee, America, C82; Elizabeth, C82; George, C82; John, C82; Nathas, C82; Priscilla, C82; Sarah, C82.
McArley, Jane, C142.
McBride, Catherine, C141; Casper, C7; David, C150; James, C7, C141; Jiles, C7; John, C7; Joseph, C3; J. V., 72; Landers, C7; Margaret, C144, C150; Margarett, C3; Mary, C3, C7; Matilda, C150; Nancy, C7, C150; Noma, C138; Ruth, C146; Ruthy C., C7, C138; Sherod, C141; Strawn, C150; Thomas, C3, C7; William, C150.
McCabe, Anna, C127; Elizabeth, C127; John, C127; Mary, C127; Richard, C127.
McCaffery, Rita, C148.
McCaig, Robert Lee, 76.
McCalahan, Benjamin, C132; Eli, C132; John, C132; Lavice, C132; Mary, C132; Nancy, C132; Sarah, C132; Sousannah, C132; William, C132.
McCammons, Allis Joice, C70; Miss C, C70.
McCan, Andrew, C127; Arthur, C127; John, C127; Mariah, C127; Martha, C127; Thomas, C127; William, C127.
McCarley, Abraham, C141; Heda, C150; J. M., 65; J. N., C77; John, C141; Mary, C141; Polly, C141; Thomas, C150.
McCarta, Eliza, C150; Margaret, C141; Samuel, C141, C150.
McCarter, Sara, C149.
McCarty, Winnifred, C143.
McCartney, Elizabeth, C91; James, C91; Margaret, C91; Robert, C91.
McCarty, Andrew, C150; Sarah, C150.
McCarrol, James, 3.
McCasshity, Amanda, C102; Baby, C102; Charity, C102; Frances, C102; John, C102; William, C102.
McClain, Fountain, C49; James, C48, C49; Jane, C48; John, C49; Mary, C48, C49; Nancy, C49; Polly, C48; Rebecca, C150; Rewben, C150; Sarah, C48; Shorty, C49; Thursey, C49; Wilson, C48; William, C49.
McClanahan, Catherine, C123; James, C123; Jane, C123; John, C123; Martha, C123; Mary, C123; Rebecca, C123; Robert, C123; Sarah, C123; William, C123.
McClary, Andrew, C78, C79; Elizabeth, C78; Ellen, C78; George, C78; James, C78, C79; Leander, C78; Mary, C79; Reubin, C78; Sarah, C78; William, C79.
McClary (?), Mclary, Cynthia, C83; James, C83; John, C83; Joseph, C83; Martha, C83; Mary, C83; Robert, C83; Sarah, C83.
McClellan, R. A., 80.

McClewere, Elizabeth, C94; James, C94.
McClure, J. B., 70; James, 68; John, C64;
    Samuel, C141; Thurs, C141; William, 62.
McCluskey, Elizabeth, C101; Isaac, C101;
    Hugh, C101; Martha, C101; William, C101.
McClusky, Ann, C70; Carroll, C70; Charles,
    C70; Eliza, C70, C89; Jerry, C70;
    Joshua, C89; Margaret, C89; Moses, C70;
    Robert, C89; Thomas, C89; Timmors, C89.
McColsky, Mary, C148.
McConnel, H. K., 44.
McConston, Elizabeth, C129; William, C129.
McCoristin, James, C129; Joel, C129;
    John, C129; Mary, C129; Robert, C129.
McCoriston, James, C112; Mary, C112;
    Robert, 23.
McCowan, John, C141; Susannah, C141.
McCravin, Andrew, C47; Alexander, C47;
    Allen, C47; C., C47; John, C47;
    Martha, C47; Robert, C47; Simpson, C47.
McCrew, Manerva, C91; Martha, C91;
    Samuel, C91.
McCrory, Bess, 68.
McCrue, Charles, C48; Elizabeth, C48;
    Jacob, C48; Martha, C48; Mary, C48;
    Nancy, C48; Stephen, C48; Vibra, C48;
    William, C48.
McCuin, Alexander, C14; Ellen, C14;
    John, C14; Malissnda, C14; Nancy, C14;
    Sarah, C14.
McCuluster, Avaline, C148.
McDaniel, A. P., C11; Amos, C74; Anderson,
    C74; Carroll, C74; Dock, 76; Ephraim,
    C77; Francis, C11; George, C74; Harris,
    C74; James, C74; Jane, C74; Joseph,
    C74; Lavenia, C74; Margaret, C74;
    Marilla, C74; Mary, C74; Matt, C74;
    Mathew, C74; Ottimena, C74; Nancy, C74;
    Rebecca, C74; Roda, C74; Sally, C11;
    Sarah, C74; Spike, C74; William, C74.
McDonald, Aladelphia, C150; Amanda, C132;
    Amos, C132; Archibald, C133; Ferriby,
    C133; Henry, C133; J. D., 76; James,
    C133; John, C110; Lucinda, C147;
    Mary, C110, C133; Nancy, C132;
    Polly, C142; Thomas, C110; William,
    18, C147; Willis, C133.
McDoogal, Alexander, C124; Angeline, C85;
    Archy, C85; Chany, C125; Daniel,
    C125, C132; Duncan, C132; Harriet,
    C125; John, C95; Margaret, C132;
    Martha, C125; Nancy, C124; Rachel,
    C124; William, C125.
McDougal, Alex, C150; Commodore, 8;
    Lucy, C150; Margaret, C144; Mary, C141;
    Mrs., 8; Nancy, C142; Ruthy, C150;
    Sarah, C150.
McDouglas, Captain, 32.

McElyea, Marye, C127.
McEwing, John, 48.
McFall, John, C141; Margaret, C141.
McFarland, Captain, 14; Robert, 26, 53;
    William, 65.
McFerrin, Rev., 46.
McGaee, Benjamin, C80; Bird, C80;
    John, C80; Lewis, C80; Malinda, C80;
    Martha, C80; Susy Ann, C80.
McGarin, Elizabeth, C150.
McGee, Catherine, C68; Cinthia, C145;
    Eliza, C68; Elizabeth, C69, C145;
    Jane, C139; John, C68; Joseph, C68;
    Nancy, C152; Sarah, C68; Wilcom, C68.
McGhee, Abraham, C134; Bartley, C85;
    Catherine, C133; Cynthia, C85; Debby,
    C84; Jacob, C85; James, C82, C85;
    Mary, C84, C85, C134; Milly, C84;
    Nancy, C84; Rebecca, C85; Sarah, C85;
    Welcom, C133; William, C84.
McGinny, Eliz, C150; Lawrence, C150.
McGown, Mary, C72.
McGuire, Patrick, 5, 6.
McGwin, Elizabeth, C96; F. H., C96;
    Frances, C98; Henry, C96; J. W., C98;
    Margaret, C96; Mary, C96; Sarah, C96;
    Virginia, C98; Willy, C98; William,
    C96, C98.
McIntyre, Andrew, C57; Arthur, C57;
    Duncan, 12, C57; Lawrence, C57;
    Malcomb, 12; Margaret, C59, 23;
    Mary, C57; Tenny, C57.
McKaskle, William, C61.
McKay, Elvy, C94; Joshua, C94.
McKee, Gus, 70.
McKelvey, Franklin, C28; George, C28;
    Isaac, C28; James, C28; Jesse, C28;
    John, C27, C28; Juliar, C28; Lidia,
    C28; Mancy, C28; Martha, C27;
    Rebecca, C28; Samuel, C28; Sarah,
    C27; William, C28.
McKey, Alexander, C121; Delilah, C121;
    Elizabeth, C81; John, C81, C121;
    Levisey, C81; Mary, C121; Thomas, C81;
    William, C81, C121.
McKidy, John, C51; Martha, C51.
McKiernan, C., 79.
McKinley, Daniel, 5; John, 4, 6, 7, 15;
    Major, 11.
McKihney, Augustine, C125; Rebecca, C125.
McKinsey, Alexander, C141; Louisa, C140;
    Lucinda, C141; Tabitha, C141.
McKirby, Mary, C150; Robert, C150.
McKnight, Frances, C14; Elizabeth, C14,
    C150; James, C150; John, C14; Margaret,
    C14; Mary, C14; Robert, C14; Samuel,
    C14; Thomas, C14.

McKorkle, Andrew, C19; Columbia, C18; Elizabeth, C18, C19, C46; Henry, C18; Houston, C18; John, C19; Joseph, C19; Malissa, C19; Margaret, C19; Martha, C18, C19; Mary, C19; Rebecca, C19; Sarah, C18; T. J., C46; Thomas, C19, C46; William, C18, C19.

McLemore, Ann, C112; Briggs, C112, C150; Burrell, C112; E. H., C150; Elizabeth, C112; J., C6; James, C112; John, 8, C112; Martha, C112; Mary, C112, C150; McLin, C112; Richard, C112; Ruthy, C150.

McLemory, Mary, C146.

McLemour, Ann, C113; Benjamin, C113; Burrell, C113; David, C113; Ellender, C113; James, C113; John, C113; Joseph, C113; Lafayette, C113; Martha, C113; Mary, C113; Milly, C113; Nancy, C113; Robert, C113; Robert, C113; Ruthea, C113; Souseannah, C113.

McLester, Amelia, C139.

McMahan, Andrew, C49; Betty, C49; Charles, C49; Elizabeth, C49, C76; James, C49, C76; John, C76; Leah, C141; Luke, C76; Margaret, C76; Martha, C75; Mary, C49; Nancy, C80; Nelson, C49; Richard, C141; Robert, C76; Sarah, C49; Tabitha, C141; Thomas, C49; William, C49, C76, C80, C141.

McManus, Burel, C15; Mary, C15, C50; Polly, C50; William, C50.

McMeen, Harrison, C117; Josephine, C117; Martha, C92; Nancy, C117; Sarah, C117; William, C92.

McMein, Alfred, C91; Charles, C91; Elizabeth, C91; Nancy, C91.

McMickin, Andrew, C141; Eliza, C141.

McMillan, James, C141; June, C141.

McMillon, Archibald, C99; Henry, C82; Jessee, C99; Mary, C82; Nancy, C82; Rachel, C99; Samuel, C82; Sarah, C82; Sousan, C99; William, C82.

McMullen, Catherine, C81; Edwin, C81; John, C81; Willis, C81.

McMurry, Anderson, C131; Andrew, C131; Caroline, C131; Catherine, C131; Elmoia, C31; James, C89; John, C22, 31; Jonathan, C22; Joe, 44; Joseph, C22; Mary, C22; Patrick, C22; Rachel, C22; Rebecca, C89; Sarah, C22; William, C118.

McMurtrey, Curtice, C73; Elizabeth, C149; Everline, C73; Jane, C74; John, C74; Jesse, C73; Mack, C73; Margaret, C74; Mary, C74; Matt, C73; Rebecca, C73; Susan, C74; William, C74.

McNarry, Malinda, C151.

McNeeley, Jeanne, C138; Phoebe, C138.

McNeill, Daniel, C150; Jane, C150.

McNutt, Governor, 8.

McPeters, Anderson, C97; Bales, C97; Caroline, C97; Elizabeth, C97; George, C97; James, 59, C80, C97; William, C80, C97.

McQuerder, Elizabeth, C11; George, C11; John, C11; Robert, C11; Sarah, C11; Venson, C11; William, C11; Willis, C11.

McRae, John, 20.

McRavey, McRaney, John, C150; Parmelia, C150.

McTeer, Will, 50.

McVey, McVay, Atlantic, C42, C150; Elizabeth, C60; Hugh, 23, C42, C60; Rebecca, C148.

McWilliams, Cletus, 70; Dow, 58; John, C98; Joseph, C99; Mary, C99; Nancy, C98; Samuel, C99; Sarah, C99.

Mealer, John, C120; Manerva, C120; William, C120.

Mears, Nancy, C152.

Medlock, John, C108; Sousiannah, C108.

Medum, Annie, C40; Jesse, C40; William, C40.

Mellon, Sarah, C116.

Melton, Ann, C150; Samuel, C150.

Menster, Susannah, C142.

Menton, Alfred, C150; Betsy, C150.

Mentzer, Abraham, 5.

Merriman, Eli, C150; Rachel, C150.

Messenger, North, 35.

Metcalf, Col. William, C72.

Michael, Don, 76.

Michal, Columbus, C92; John, C92; Sara, C92.

Micher, William, C54.

Miget, Rachel, C150.

Mighninger, J. A., C63.

Miles, Abergail, C72; Alexander, C150; Chaney, C72; Davis, C106; James, C72; Sally, C150; Lucy, C146; Sarah, C72.

Millar, Charlotte, C14; Sarah, C14; Seath, C14; Wiley, C14.

Miller, Allen, C136; Charlotte, C150; Darkis, C84; Eliza, C142; Elizabeth, C150; George, C129; Jacob, C150; James, C81; John, C54, C81, C128; Lidda, C40; Minerva, C150; Martha, C81; Mary, C81; Peter, C150; Robert, C81; Samuel, C84; Sarah, C81; Seth, C150; Susannah, C153; Wesley, C136.

Milligan, Charles, C150; Nancy, C150.

Milliken, Capt., 57; N. W., 7; Narcissa, 57; William, 57, 74.

Mills, Anjaline, C15; John, C15; Malinda, C15; Rhody, C15; Tiressa, C15; Wesley, C15.

Milner, Hanna, C69; Isaac, C69; J. W., 69; James, 14, 22, C69; Joseph, 22, 53; Samuel, C69.
Milton, Amanda, C27; George, C27; Hariet, C151; Isaac, C27; John, C27; Martha, C27; Richard, C27; Sina, C27; William, C27.
Mincer, George, C46.
Minor, Henry, 5.
Minten, Bennett, C29.
Mitchel, Eliza, C150; Julian, C153; Mary, C65; William, C150.
Mitchell, 36; Allen, C124; Allis, C131; Ann, C124; Elizabeth, C125; Elvina, C96; Frank, C96; H. Y., C125; J. A., 36; J. J., 7, 22; J. P., C131; James, 5; John, C124, C125; Julian, C63; Lucy, C125; C143; Martha, C144; Mary, C96, C124, C148; O. M., 30; Rebecca, C125; Richard, C96; Robert, 35; Sarah, C131; Sousennah, C124, C125; Thomas, C124; W. H., 32; Willis, C125; William, C96, C125.
Mize, Elizabeth, C107, C108; Henry, C108; Isaac, C108; Isam, C107; James, C108, C103; Lucinda, C107; Margaret, C108; Martha, C103, C107; Nancy, C103, C108; Nathan, C141; Polly, C141; Ruthy, C108; Sampson, C103; Sarah, C103, C108.
Mizner, J. K., 32.
Mobbly, Adeline, C131; Catherine, C131; Elizabeth, C131; Mary, C131; Sarah, C131; Washington, C131.
Mobley, Alfred, C150; Jemima, C150.
Mockley, Sarah, C150; Ranson, C150.
Moer, Nancy, C150.
Monroe, James, 1, C1; Josephine, C56; Mary, C56; Pugh, C56; Rubin, C56; Samuel, C56.
Montgomery, Country, 74; Don, 73; Mr., 69.
Moody, H. M., 57.
Moomaw, Howard, 71; Joseph, 62; Lula, 62; Lizzie, 62; W. D., 62.
Moon, Elizabeth, C89; George, C89; Jane, C89; Lydia, C89; Mary, C89.
Moore, A. B., 26; Ann, C152; Atlantic, C42, C150; Charles, C2; Cynthia, C127; Elias, C2; Elizabeth, C2, C49; Frances, 22; Henry, 61, 63; Mrs.Henry, 7; Hugh, C42; J. J., 60; James, C42, C124; John, 33, C42; Jordan, 20; Lewis, 22, C42, C127, C150; Louiser, C49; Lucy, C2, C150; Manuel, C124; Margaret, C124; Martha, C124; Mary, C124, C142; Mermelia, C122; Nancy, C122; Peter, C2; Robert, C124; S., C145; Samuel, C42; Sarah, 20, C124.
Morgan, Amanda, C32; Amberis, C40; Ann, C150; Ayra, C32; continued,

Moore, continued: Eliza, C154; Elizabeth, C32; John, 71; Marion, 74; Mary, C108; Susan, C145; Tibitha, C32.
Morison, Daniel, C6.
Morris, Abraham, C150; Allen, 6, 7; Alsey, C122; Austin, C122; Dabney, 4; Elizabeth, C143; J. E., 70; Mary, 62; Nancy, C152; Susannah, C150; Thomas, C96.
Morrison, Annie, C35; Benjamin, C150; Bright, C135; Elander, C141; Friend, C131; K. W., 80; Margaret, C150; Peter, C35; C141; Polly, C141; Rody , C147; Z. P., 21, C135.
Morriss, Mary Ann, C138.
Morrow, Robert, C141; Tiny, C141.
Morten, Elizabeth, C70; Joseph, C70; William, C70.
Moses, Elizabeth, C27; Peter, C27.
Mosin, Frances, C151.
Mosley, Elizabeth, C150; John, C150; Rosanah, C45.
Moss, Nancy, C66.
Motethrope, Newel, C76; Rebecca, C76.
Mullen, Rev. E. G., 77.
Munn, Joseph, C43; Mathius, C43; Rosanah, C43.
Murphy, Allice, C19; Ann, C128; Baby; C93; Betty, C25; Carl, 71; Concretia, C63; Cynthia, C93; Edward, C65; Eliza, C65; Elizabeth, C93; Elvy, C120; Francis, C19; George, C25; H. Clay, C63; Hannah, C128; J. T., C63; Jackson, C65; James, C19, C128; John, C19, C120; Joseph, C65; C93; Laura, C64; Lavina, C25, C128; Louisa, C25; Major, 41; Margaret, C63; Marion, C19; Martha, C93; Mary, C63, C64, C65, C93, C120; Nancy, C19; Polly Ann, C19; Preston, C128; Ralph, 76; Rebecca, C19; Sarah, C63; Thomas, C65; Tibatha, C93; Virginia, C63; W. F., C64; William, C63, C120; Young, C63.
Murrell, John, 16, 17.
Murphy, Ally, C150; Elizabeth, 24; John, C150; Rebecca, C154; Sarah, C151.
Muse, Pat, 66.
Musselman, Catharine, C131; David, C131; Esenith, C131; Henry, C131; Kisanda, C131; Martha, C131.
Mustin, Hannah, C150; Henry, C150.
Mutrey, Edy, C150; William, C150.
Myers, Henry, C141; L. D., 57; Pharaba, C141.
Myrick, Adeline, C125; Elias, C125; Elizabeth, C125; Frances, C95; cont'd

Myrick, continued: Henry, C95; Hiram, C95; Isaac, C125; Isam, C95; James, C95, C125; John, C125; Mary, C95; Sarah, C95.

Nail, Amanda, C40; Eliza, C40; Elizabeth, C142; Emeline, C40; James, C40; Joseph, C34, C142; Julian, C102; Polly, C2; Samuel, C2; Sarah, C40; Thomas, C40.
Nance, Eliza, C114, C151; Elizabeth, C114; James, C114; John, 59, C114; Mary, C114; Samuel, C114; Senonah, C114; Sterling, C114, C151; William, C114.
Naland, Cynthia, C98; Elizabeth, C98; Hardin, C98; James, C98; Necis, C98.
Napoleon, 22.
Nathan, J. B., 69.
Nation, Eli, C92, C150; Elias, C91; James, C57, C92; John, C92; Margaret, C81; Martha, C56, C91; Mary, C56; Robert, C56; Sally, C91, C150; Sarah, C56; Susah, C92; Thomas, C56.
Neal, Matthew, 12.
Nealy, Nicholas, C150; Peggy, C150.
Neely, Alexander, C115; Anderson, C115; Caroline, C115; Eliza, C115; Elizabeth, C115; Garrett, C86; James, C115; Mary, C115; Thompson, 24.
Negley, A. B., 62; A. G., 15; James S., 15, 30, 31.
Neighbors, James, C7; Lucretia, C7; Milly, C43; Nancy, C7; Nathan, C7.
Neill, Addaline, C67; Charity, C67; Elizabeth, C67; Francis, C68; James, C67; Jane, C67; Martha, C67, C68; Mary, C67; Rebecca, C67.
Nelson, A. O. P., C133; B., 20; Barney, C136; Edward, C28; Elizabeth, C28; John, C28; Lidia, C28; Lutha, C28; Martin, C112; Mary, C28; Robert, C28; Rosa, C143.
Newgan, Allen, C118; Elizabeth, C118; James, C118; John, C118; Samuel, C118; William, C118.
Newman, Frances, C153; Heda, C150; Isabella, C146; Margaret, C148; Moses, C150; Phoebe, C145; Polly, C150.
Newton, Baby, C92; George, C92; James, C92; Nancy, C92; Permelia, C150; Rebecca, C92; Ruthie, C92; Usley, C140.
Newsom, Ansel, 31.

Nicholas, Jackson, C38.
Nichelson, Nicholson, A. O. P., 13; Amanda, C36; Annie, C36; Caroline, 13; Catherine, C36; Charles, C36, C151; Elizabeth, C36; Ellen, C36; Henry, C36; Penelopy, C60; Sally, C151; Sarah, C36.
Nigh, Joel, C42.
Night, Jane, C78.
Nipper, Jordan, 62; Sally, 62.
Nisbet, 67.
Nix, George, C40; Hannah, C40; John, C40; L. J., 71; Madora, C40; Mary, C40; Parilee, C40; William, C40.
Noel, Cornelia, C58; Edmond, 26, C59; James, 26, C58; John, C58; Mary, 26, C58; Samuel, C58; William, C58.
Noland, Catherine, C15; Harriet, C59; James, C15; John, C15; Rachel, C16; Sarah, C15, C16; Thomas, C16; William, C15, C59.
Nolen, Berry, C151; Harriett, C145; Julia, C152; Mary, C151; Misha, C147; Rachel, C151; Rufus, C151.
Nolin, Austin, C150; Elizabeth, C150.
Norman, Anna, C142; Alfred, C142.
Norrell, Edy, C150.
Norris, Rebecca, C150.
Norvell, Eady, C150; John, C150; Lester, 7; Lydia, C28.
Norwell, Jane, C142.
Norwood, Landers, C7; Susan, C2.
Nowland, Julia, C142; Perkins, C142.
Null, Anny, C147; Francis, C68; John, C142; Nancy, C142.
Nunley, Daniel, C76; Thomas, C76; Tobetha, C76.
Nusun, Elizabeth, C38.
Nye, Shadrach, 12.

Oakley, Billy, 31; Caroline, C31; Charles, C31; Elizabeth, C7, C12; James, C7, C13, C31; Jesse, C7; Margaret, C12; Mary, C7; Robert, C31; Thomas, C7; William, C7.
Oats, William, C136.
O'Brian, Cynthia, C116.
O'Briand, Charles, C10; Dellala, C8; Elizabeth, C10; Ellen, C8; George, C10; Henry, C8; James, C8, C10; John, C8; Joseph, C8; Levi, C8; Louisa, C8; Lucy, C8; Martha, C8; Mary, C10; Oliver, C10; Polly, C10; Rebecca, C10; Samuel, C10; Sarah, C8; William, C8.
Obrient, Vashty, C151; William, C151.

O'Bryant, Brandon, C142; Rebecca, C142.
Odell, James, C142; Jane, C142.
Oden, Nancy, C154.
Odum, Amberis, C72; Berry, C72; James, C72; Jim, 76; Lanisa, C72; Mary, C72; Polly, C72.
Ogdon, Edward, C151; Letitia, C151.
Oldham, Elizabeth, C113; Fanthey, C113; George, C113; Green, C157; John, C113; Mary, C113, C157; Ruthey, C113; Sarah, C113; Thomas, C113.
Olive, Marvin, 73, 74.
Oliver, Benjamin, C137; Charles, 52, C137; Daniel, C137; Genette, C137; Hugh, C137; Jane, C137; Mary, C137.
Ollive, Andrew, C73; Annie, C73; Antny, C39; Feby Jane, C2; Charlotte, C73; Frances, C74; Huguriah, C3; Kisiah, C39; James, C3, C39, C74; John, C2, C39; Martha, C39; C73; Mary, C39; Mikle, C39; Nathaniel, C73; Sarah, C3; William, C3, C73.
Olliver, A. W., C116; Edward, C116; Eliza, C111; Elizabeth, C116; Julia, C111; Matilda, 24; Martha, C116; Sarah, C111, C116; William, C2, C111, C116.
O'Neal, Alfred, C66; Allice, C8; Anne, C8; Ashbury, 65; B. A., C66; B. W., C8; Colonel, 33; E. A., 53, 60; Edward, 20, 65; Emmet, 65; Mrs. Emmet, 62; John, C66; Julia, C8, C66; Martha, C8; Mary, C66; Orlevia, C66; Rebecca, C66.
Orrick, Jane, C150.
Ostean, Davey, C5; David, C5; Eliza, C5; Francis, C5; Josephine, C5; Luvick, C5; Nancy, C5.
Ott, Joseph, C46.
Overby, Jane, C113; Sevicoa, C113.
Overley, Anderson, C91; Jane, C91; John, C91; Maiah, C91; Richardson, C91; Thomas, C91; William, C91.
Overton, John, 6, 8.
Owen, Edward, C63; Ellen, C63; Emily, C63; Fanny, C49; Franklin, C63; George, C49; Hannah, C142; James, 23, C63; Margaret, C63; T. J., C49; Thomas, 14; Semour, C63; William, C63.
Owens, Dolph, 44; Eliza, C108; Elizabeth, C108; Frances, C108; Jane, C142; John, C108; Lesa, C142; Mary, C108; Rebecca, C108; Robert, C108; Sally, C138; Samuel, C108; Sarah, C68, C108.

Page, James, C89; Jonah, C89; Josiah, C89; Julia, C89; Nancy, C89; Thomas, C89; William, C89.
Palmer, Anna, C142; Artemissa, C134; Elisha, C142; C149; J. A., 37; Martha, C134; Orlando, C134.
Palmore, Betty, C53; Elijah, C53; Martin, C53; Mary, C53; Nancy, C53.
Pane, Charity, C87.
Parish, Eliza, C21; Thomas, C21.
Parker, Adolphis, C151; Alexander, C21; Amanda, C83; Augustine, C48; Betsy, C146; Elizabeth, C21, C45, C83, C142; Frances, C57; Jackson, C83; James, C48, C142; Jsaper, 59; John, C21, C142; Margaret, 62, C85; Mary, C21, C48; Nancy, C21, C37; Samuel, C48; Sarah, C57, C59, C142; Thomas, C48; Virginia, C57; Wesley, C83; William, C57, C83.
Parrish, Anna, C142; Fanny, C138; Nicholas C142; William, 71.
Parson, A. B., C31; B. S., C151; Elizabeth, C31; Louis, C151.
Parten, Abagal, C103; Adeline, C103; Columbus, C103; Edney, C103; Elizabeth, C103; George, C103; John, C103; Leonard, C103; Martha, C103; Rachel, C103.
Partin, Nancy, C153.
Pate, John, 4.
Paterson, Catherine, C59; Thomas, C59.
Patrick, Alexander, C51; Amanda, C116; Easter, C51; Elvira, C116; George, C117; Henry, C116; Levi, C117; Margaret, C116; P., 24; P. A., 62; Rebecca, C117; Robert, C116; T. F., C116.
Patterson, Edmund, 38, 44; Elizabeth, C146; Josiah, 38.
Patton, Alexander, C151; Charles, C129; David, C107, C151; Debby, C107; Elizabeth, C151; Governor, 41; Jane, C107, C129; John, C129; Nancy, C78, C107, C151; R. M., 26, 55; Rachel, C107; Robert, 23, C63; Mrs. Robert, 41; William, C78, C107, C136.
Paulk Amanda, 54; Betsy, C142; C. S. W., 59, 62; Charlie, 63; Eliza, 21; Elizabeth, C142, C150; J. W., 15; Jacob, C142; Johnathan, 54, C142; Joshua, 21.
Paull, Mahala, C151; Jochin, C151.
Payne, A. M., 13; Andrew, C151; Henrietta, C151.
Pealder, Alabama, C21; Elizabeth, C20; Kesiah, C21; Mary, C21; Nancy, C21; Robert, C21; Thomas, C21; William, C21.

273

Pearson, Ethel, 75; James, C57.
Pearey, Martha, C64.
Peeden, T. H., 59.
Peel, Hunter, 8.
Peetus, Harriett, C142.
Peirce, Eliza, Franklin, Gray, Josephine,
  Mary, Nancy, Thomas, Washington, C114.
Pennington, William, 54, 55.
Pennock, A. M., 34.
Penny, (Perry?), C147; Delila, C23;
  Dolly, C126; Eliza, C85, C126;
  Frances, C126; George, C126; Houston,
  C126; James, C85; John, C85; Mary,
  C85; Milton, C126; Nancy, C85; Sarah,
  C126; Washington, C126.
Percey, Thomas, 5, 6.
Perkins, Elizabeth, C66; Foster, C20;
  Franklin, C20; Harden, 23, C55;
  John, C20; Joseph, C20; Joshiah,
  C20; Louiser, C55; Moses, C20, 31;
  Polly, C143; Nancy, C20; Sarah, C66;
  Thomas, C20; Wesley, C20.
Pernell, Barthley, C50; Eliza, C50;
  Franklin, C50; Jacob, C50; John, C50;
  Minus, C50; Nancy, C50; William, C50.
Perryman, Alexander, C35; Bulear, C35;
  Columbia, C35; Cornetty, C35; Emeline,
  C35; Jane, C139; John, C35, C142;
  Martha, C35; Patsy, C142; Sally, C142;
  Samuel, C35.
Pershing, General, 67.
Peters, Betsy, C150; James, C151; John,
  23, C57, C142; Nancy, C142, C151;
  Susan, C154; Thomas, C63.
Peterson, 37.
Petigo, Mary, C119.
Petit, Benjamin, C82; Fanny, C82; James,
  C82; John, C82; Margaret, C82; Mary,
  C82; Martha, C82; Nancy, C82; Rachel,
  C82; Silas, C82.
Peton, Calvin, C75; Elizabeth, C75;
  Ellender, C75; Devroe, C75; Mary, C75;
  Monroe, C75; Thomas, C130.
Pettis, Susannah, C141.
Pettus, Ann, C123, C129; Emily, C123;
  Everline, C129; George, C123; Harriet,
  C129; Henry, C123; Horatio, C123, C129;
  John, C123; Martha, C123, C129; Mary,
  C123, C129, C151; Nancy, C123; Sarah,
  C123; William, C123; Winston, C129,
  C151; Winson, C123.
Pettypool, Eliza, C45; David, C45; John,
  C45; Joseph, C45; Julia, C45; Martha,
  C45, C128; Susan, C45.
Peyton, Calvin, C151; John, 1; Mary, C151.
Phelps, Durthenia, C141; Pharada, C141;
  S. L., 28.
Phillips, A. C., 10; Amanda, C36, C61;
  Anjellico, C50; Ann, C153; continued,

Phillips, continued: Asher, C151; Baby,
  C80; Benjamin, C80; Caroline, C151;
  Charles, C36; Cornelia, C142; Daniel,
  C50, C142; David, C34; Deby, C142;
  D. G., C9; Edney, C79; Elias, C5;
  Eliza, C31; Elizabeth, C9, C10, C82,
  C95, C121, C152; Fanny, C151; Frances,
  C10, C51; George, 31, C80; Gray, C151;
  Hannah, C10; Hester, C34; Horace, 5;
  Horatio, 5; Hugh, 56; Jack C79; Jackson,
  C50; James, C95; Jane, C9; John,
  31, C36, C50, C79, C80, C121; Joseph,
  C9, C10, C34; Louisa, C9, C82; Lucina,
  C10, C121; Manurvey, C10; Margaret,
  C36, C95; Mariah, C121; Martha, C16,
  C143; Mary, C36, C82, C95, C121; Mason,
  C79, C142; Milton, C121; Nancy, C10,
  31, C61, C80, C82, C95, C121, C145;
  Narissa, C9; Rebecca, C36; Robert,
  C121; Sally, C79; Samuel, C61; Sanders,
  C50; Sarenah, C79; Sarah, C36, C50,
  C80, C121, C151, C152; Sousan, C82;
  Sousannah, C79; Sterling, C151;
  Starling, C10; T. J., 62; Thomas,
  C10, C121; Tom, 69; Urley, C10;
  William, C9, C10, C50, C82; William T.,
  C73; Willis, C10; Wilson, 31, C80.
Pickens, A. C., C46; L. M., C151;
  Martha, C151.
Pierce, Elizabeth, C114; Jesse, C114;
  Nancy, C114.
Pig, Artitisa, C6; Andrew, C6; Davis,
  C6; Jane, C6; Martha, C6; Margaret,
  C6; Mary, C6; Ransom, C6; Sarah, C6;
  William, C6.
Pike, Bathana, C48; Dennis, C48; Elijah,
  C48; George, C108; Lewis, C48.
Pillow, Emily, C142; General Gideon J.,
  27; Granville, 56; William, 56, C142.
Pingston, Anderson, C15; Houston, C15;
  James, C15; Lawson, C15; Lena, C15;
  Matthew, C15; Peter, C15; Rebecca,
  C15; Sina, C15; William, C15.
Pitts, Adeline, C119; Calvin, C119;
  Charlotte, C122; Elizabeth, C119;
  Hannah, C124; James, C119; Jasper,
  C122; John, C119, C122; Manurva, C119;
  Mary, C119, C122; Morgan, C119.
Plowden, Robert, 69.
Plowman, John, C142; Polly, C142.
Plumb, Ralph, 32.
Plummer, Julia, C151; Segnom, C151.
Polk, General, 27; Easter, C146; James,
  C11; Eliza, C11; James K., 8, 57;
  Jesse, C151; Joshua, C11; Mahala, C151.
Pollock, Jonathan, C151; Nancy, C151.
Polock, Arletta, C62; Eliza, C62; Harriet,
  C62; Josiah, C62; Maria, C62; Mary,
  C62.

Pool, Caroline, C34; Eliza, C64; Elizabtt, C34; Elizabeth, C116; George, C34; Hariett, C34; James, C22, C34, C64; Jane, C35, 61; John, C116; Joseph, C34; Levi, C35; Maderson, C34; Margaret, C116; Martha, C64; Mary, C34, C64, C116; Nancy, C34; Perkins, C34; Polly, C34; Sarah, 2¹, C35; Solle, C35; Sterling, C74; Stewart, 2¹, C34, C35; Varest, C64; William, C64.

Poole, William, 29.

Pope, Bennett, C43; Jane, C43; Leroy, 4, 6, 8; Martha, C147.

Porter, Admiral, 38; Andrew, C97, C98, C100; C. D., C99; Caroline, C105; Cynthia, C100; David, C83; Easter, C99; Eli, C108; Eliza, C99; Elizabeth, C97, C99, C108; Frances, C100; Franklin, C99; Hugh, C100; James, C99; John, C97, C99, C100, C151; Joseph, C108; Louisa, C108; Malinda, C108; Margaret, C97; Mary, C98, C99, C100; Mattah, C100; Nancy, C99; Oliver, 5; Pleasant, C108; Provia, C108; Rebecca, C98, C100; Robert, C108, C114; Samuel, C99, C108; Sarah, C97; C100; Susan, C151; Wesley, C100; William, C97.

Porterfield, Martha, 68.

Portlock, John, C135; Julia, C135; Mahala, C135; Martha, C135; Mary, C135; Nancy, C135; William, C135.

Posey, Andrew, C128; Charity, C125; Eliza, C130; Elizabeth, C130; Elizajane, C15; Frances, C125; Franklin, C125; Galson, C130; George, C125; Harriett, C128, C151; James, C130; Jesse, C128; John, C128; C130; Lewis, C130; Martha, C15; Mary, C128; Nancy, C15; Rachel, C128; S. C., 34; Sarah, C15; Sidney, C128, C151; Thomas, C15; William, C15, C130.

Poteet, Eliza, C132; Elizabeth, C100; Henry, C99; Jane, C100; Martha, C100; Mary, C99, C100; Nancy, C99, C140; Rufus, C99; Ruthie, C100; Taletha, C122; William, C100.

Pattman, Sarah, C153. C151

Powell, Elizabeth, C137;/Delia, C139; Henry, C151; Matilda, C137; William, C137.

Powers, Alexander, C58; Blackburn, C4; Caroline, C4; Elizabeth, C4; Frances, C58; Frank, C58; Henry, C151; John, C4, C43, C58; Joseph, C58; Lewis, C58; Libby, C4; Luvick, C4; Malissa, C4; Mr., 28; Mary, C4, C43; Moses, C151; Rachel, C151; Rosanah, C43; Sarah, C43, C151; Statha, C58; cont'd

Powers, continued: Susan, C58; Tamyra, C4; Thomas, C43; Sarah, C43; William, C43.

Prachard, Rachel, C52; Samuel, C52.

Prat, Elizabeth, C105; Fanny, C105; Franklin, C105; Hiram, C88; James, C105; Jessee, C105; John, C88; Kessy, C105; Martha, C105; Matilda, C105; Rebecca, C105; Sousan, C105; William, C88, C105.

Pratt, Alea, C141; Mary, C84; Polly, C84; Rebecca, C84; Sarah, C84; W. M., 59; William, C84.

Pretihard, Rachel, C145.

Price, A. M., C136; Amanda, C136; Benjamin, C22; Betsy, C141; Caswell, C54; Christian, C136; Christopher, 6, C22; Emily, C99; Elizabeth, C154; Frances, C65, C128, C129, C149, C151; Frederick, C99; George, C80; Isaac, C128, C136; Isibella, C22, C128; J. R., 59; J. W., C99; James, C65, C128, C129, C151; Jane, C22; John C22, C99, C128; Lafayette, C80; Lavinia, C22; Lucy, C80; Martha, C21, C129, C151; Mary, C21, C99, C136; Nancy, C129, C136; Rachel, C21; Mrs. S. J., 62; Sally, C140, C146; Samuel, C21; Susan, C99; Thomas, C65; Virginia, C128; Wesley, C129; William, 59, C80, C128, C129, C136, C151.

Pricket, M., C151; Jacob, C112; Joel, C151; Malinda, C151.

Prince, Baby, C87; Delilah, C87; Edward, C142; Elizabeth, C87; Esther, C142; Franklin, C87; Gideon, C87; Jason, C83; Jelethia, C87; Josaphene, C83; Mary, C87; Matthew, C87; Rachel, C138; Teletha, C87; William, C83, C87; Zachariah, C83.

Prix, John, C108.

Probasco, Catherine, C67.

Proby, James, C32.

Prosser, Lt., 45.

Prtichard, Elizabeth, C152.

Pruett, C. L, C8; Eliza, C9; Elizabeth, C8; Henry, C9, C10; Jane, C8; John, C9, C10; Latitia, C10; Malinder, C10; Manurva, C10; Malissa, C10; Marshal, C10; Mary, C8, C9; Matilda, C10; Oliver, C10; Robert, C10; Thomas, C8, C9; Warren, C8; William, C10.

Pruitt, T. D., 60.

Pryor, Angeline, C139.

Puler, Colonel, 10.

Pullum, Mary, C46.

Pursell, James, 9, 10.

Putet, Carline, C113; Rebecca, C113.

Putman, Putnam, A. B., C94; Abigal, C120; Bassil, C120; Frances, C120; Louisa, C120; Mary, C194, C120; Nancy, C194, C120; Neely, C120; Samuel, C120; Sarah, C120; Zedie, C120.

Quail, Cr., 24.
Qualls, Almira, C51; Gais, C51; Leander, C51; Louiser, C51; Kitty, C51; Mary, C51; Martha, C140; Milla, C51; Nancy, C51; Rebecca, C51; Robert, C51; Taylor, C51.
Quaser, Alexander, C9; Andrew, C9; Caroline, C9; Elizabeth, C9; Jackson, C9; Mary, C9; Richard, C9; Susan, C9.
Quillen, Charles, C123, C142; Chesley, C123; Isella, C123; Jack, C123; Jasper, C122, C123; Mary, C123; Polly, C142; Timethea, C123; William, C123.

Raglin, Asher, C62; Mary, C62; William, C62.
Ragsdale, D. W., 5, 6; Bradford, 7; Sarah, C144; W. H., 7; William, 5, 6; C62.
Raily, Dr., 24.
Rainey, Isaac Newton, 48; Jane, C521; Washington, C152.
Ramsey, Edith, C149; Samuel, C116.
Randle, Benjamin, C11; David, C11; Dicy, C60; Francis, C11, C37; James, C11; John, C11, C60; Martha, C11; Matta, C37; Sarah, C11; Thomas, C60; William, C11.
Ransom, Jane, C147.
Rapier, James, 54; John, 30, 54, C65; Lucretia, C65; Rebecca, C65; Richard, 3, 5, 10.
Rasch, Odette, 73.
Rast, Elizabeth, C82; James, C81; Jane, C82; John, C81, C82; Joshiah, C82; Margaret, C82; Mary, C81; Nancy, C81; Sarah, C82; William, C81, C82.
Rand, Mrs. E. P. 69.
Ray, Amanda, C21, 25; Benjamin, C122; Burrell, C103; Catherine, C121; Dorinda, C124; Eliza, C122; Elizabeth, C122; Ellender, C121; Elmira, C94; Frances, C121; Hannah, C121; Isaac, C124; James, C103, C124; John, C53, C94, C103, C122; Lucretia, C53; Lucy, C121; Lydia, C124; Malinda, C122; Martha, C40, C53, C105; Mary, C53, C103, C124; Minerva, C127; Mintes, C122; Melicia, C121; Melvina, C121; Nancy, C122, C124; Newton, C121;cont'd

275

Ray continued: Peter, C121; Polly, C121; Robert, C103, C121; Rody, C122; Sarah, C103; Stephen, C122; Susinda, C124; Thomas, C103; William, C53, C103, C122; Willie, C83.
Rayburn, Polly, C151; Ransom, C151.
Read, 5; Griffin, C151; Jane, C151.
Reader, Charles, C34; Daniel, C34; Hugh, C34; Jacob, C34; Martha, C34; Mary, C34; Sarah, C34; Sally, C34; Rachel, C34; Rubin, C34; Thomas, C34; William, C34.
Reaves, Aaron, C28; Amanda, C28; Andrew, C28; Ellen, C28; Henry, C28; Jane, C28; Jesse, C27; John, C27, C28; Margaret, C27; Martha, C27, C28; Mary, C27, C28; Matthew, C28; Moses, C28; Rebecca, C28; Rhoda, C27; Sarah, C27; Thomas, C27; Wiley, C27; William, C28.
Redd, R. C., 69.
Redford, Anderson, C151; Sally, C151.
Reed, Annah, C64; Catherine, C149; Daniel, C142; Elizabeth, C64; Harriet, C136; James, C64, C142; John, 4, C136; Letha, C136; Martha, C142; Mary, C136; Samuel, C136; Sarah, C136.
Reeder, Agnus, C13; Almira, C13; Alsey, C146; Duncan, C40; Eliza, C152; Henry, C42; Homer, 70; John, C40, 63; Jones, 70; Margaret, C146; Mary, C146; Rachel, C13; Rebecca, 25, C40; Sarah, C42; Susan, C40; Thomas, C152; Thompson, C40; W. L., 66; Mrs. W. L., 7; Washington, C40; William, C13, C40; Z. Taylor, C40.
Rees, Mary, C152; Thomas, C152.
Reese, Frances, C151; Washington, C151.
Reeves, Joseph, C142; Mary, C146; Sally, C142; Tibitha, C151.
Renfro, Emily, C142; John, C142.
Ressin, Harriett, C151; John, C151.
Reyborn, Emeline, C23; Nancy, C54.
Reynolds, Alexander, C3; Amanda, C3; Elender, C3; Elizabeth, C142; Empress, C3; George, C3; Hugh, C3; Hughriah, C3; Isaac, C142; James, C3, C22; Joseph, C3; Juliar, C57; Kesiah, C22; Marthy, C3; Mary, C3; Milledge, C142; Nancy, C142; Pinkney, C3; Polly Ann, C3; Randolph, C3; Wesley, C3; William, C3; Winson, C3.
Rhea, 11.
Rhodes, Addaline, C6, C7; Allice, C32; Alonzo, C32; Amelia, C10; Amanda, C44; Andy, C51; Ben, C43; Benjamin, C32; Caroline, C11; Catherine, C44; Charles, C44; Cinthia, C51; Columbus, C10, C11, C32, C128; Cothia, C30; Ellen, C43; Elijah, C43; Elizabeth, C6;

Rhodes, continued: Georgia, C32; Hamilton, C51; Henry, C7; Henrietta, C30; Hezekiah, C30; Ino, C43; Isabella, C7; Jacob, C128; James, C6, C42, 71; Jonathan, C6; John, C6, C10, C11, C30, C42, C43; Julia, C44; Leondas, C32; Leander, C43; Lusinda, C11, C32; Magdaline, C6; Malissa, C6; Manurvey, C43; Margaret, C42, C51; Martha, C11, C30, C42, C43; Mary, C11, C30, C42, C43; Nancy, C11, C30, C34, C43, C128; Pentalopy, C11; Peter, C44; Polly, C7; Rebecca, C30; Samuel, C30; Shephard, C128; Spencer, C43, C44; Susan, C42; Thomas, C7, C42, C43; William, C7, C10, C11, C34.

Rice, Anne, C91; B. F., 64; Eliza, C91; Elizabeth, C5, C60, C142; Francis, C60; E. W., 34; George, C5, C91; Harriett, C92, C142; Irvine, C91; James, C5; Jesse, C31; Joel, 5, 7; Louisa, C151; Lucretia, C91; Lucy, C136; Martha, C60, C91; Mary, C60, C91, C92; Mason, C60, C142; N. H., 20, 34; Neander, 23; Nathan, C92, C142; Neander, C136; Nora, 58; Polly, C139; Rachel, C5; Richard, C5; S. D., 7; Senora, C136; Solleman, C5; Susan, C31, C92; Taylor, C91; Tobius, C91, C151; Turner, 7, 68; Wadsworth, C60; William, C5, C60, C91.

Richard, Angeline, C110.

Richards, Caladonia, C33; Catherine, C34; David, C56; Eliza, C56; Elizabeth, C150; Henderson, C34; C157; Hester, C34; Jack, C34; James, C33; John, C33, C56; Julia, C33; Martha, C33, C54; Nancy, C33, C54; Patrick, C56; Ruben, C54; Sally, C34; Samuel, C33; Sarah, C56, C151; Sarenus, C34; Susan, C33; Thomas, C33, C34; Wesley, C54; William, C33, C54.

Richardson, A. B., 71; A. P., 71; Amanda, C153; Asa, C133; Benjamin, C80; Betty, C152; Catherine, C125, C134; Daniel, C80; David, C80, C81; Edie, 13; Eliza, C80; Elizabeth, C80, C85, C130, C147; C152; Elliner, C151; Emmerline, C85; Emily, C8; Flora, C133; Frances, C85, C151; Gabriel, C80; Gideon, C95; H., 59; Helton, C85; Henry, C85, C142; Hiram, C81, C134; Isaac, C142; Isam, C85; J. L., 76; James, C85; Jane, C80, C85, C151; Jesse, 76; John, C85, C130; Johnathan, C130, C142; Julia, C81, C134; Lambert, 76; Littleton, C151; Mark, C80; Mariah, C142; Martha, C81, C85, C134; Mary, C80, C133, C151; continued,

Richardson, continued: Nancy, C85, C134; C142, C151; Polly, C151; Rebecca, C85; Samuel, C80, C151; Sarah, C80, C85, C133; Sousan, C80; Susan, C152; Susannah, C141; Thomas, C151; Turner, C85; Vashty, C151; Vina, C85; W. M., 69; Washington, C152; Wesley, C134; Wiley, C151, C152; Willis, C80, C134.

Richerson, Bluford, C68; Clinton, C68; Henry, C73; Isan, C73; James, C73; John, C69, C73; Judi, C73; Lewis, C73; Mary, C68; Matt, C68; Milla, C68; Obidiah, C69; Polly, C69; Nancy, C68; Saletha, C69; Tempie, C139; William, C73.

Rickard, A. L., 71; G. T., 71; Paul, 71.

Rickerson, Ann, C69; Berry, C69; Isaac, C69; Jane, C69; John, C69; Nancy, C69.

Rickin, Anny, C142; Richard, C142.

Rickman, Angeline, C73; Armon, C21; Caladonia, C7; Lucy, C21; Martha, C70; Mary, C70; Rebecca, C21, C70; Sarah C70; William, C73, C99.

Ridgeway, Caisey, C101; Catherine, C101; Eliza, C101; Elizabeth, C101; John, C101.

Rieves, Asa, C27; Eliza, C27; Elizabeth, C27; Ellen, C27; Emerline, C27; Harriet, C27; Jacob, @7; John, C27; Mary, C27; Sarah, 21, C27; Stephen, C27; William, C27.

Rigby, W. H., 71.

Riggs, John, 51.

Right, Barbary, C132; Carrol, C132; Daniel, 6; James, C132; John, C132; Lydia, C132; Martha, C132; Mary, C132; Nancy, C132; Nicholas, C132; Rebecca, C132; Wesley, C132; William, C132.

Riley, Albert, C37, 78; Albin, C37; Allen, C37; Ann, C37; Awlston, C37; B. F., 69; James, C37; John, C37; Lusinda, C37; Pike, 78; Rollen, C37.

Ritter, Catherine, C85; Hiram, C85; Lizzy, C85; Martha, C85; Rebecca, C85.

Rix (Ricks), Abraham, 16.

Roach, Abraham, C152; Edmond, C17; George, C17; Jane, C152; Kiley, C17; Lavina, C17; Martha, C152; Mary, C17; Richard, C17; Salene, C17.

Roberts, Seira, C137.

Rob'son, Christopher, 7.

Roberson, Aaron, C67; Agnes, C148; Archer, C71; David, C71; Dicy, C71; Henry, C67; James, C71; John, C71; C133; Joseph, C73; Lusinda, C71; Mary, C71; Mitchel, C71; Nancy, C71; C146; Patty, C73; Sabrey, C71; cont'd

Roberson, continued: Sally, C7¹; Susan, C67; Tire, C7¹; William, C7¹.
Roberts, Carroll, 65; Eliza, C127; George, C137; Henry, C56; Isaac, 78; James, C56, 65, 68, C126, C127; John, C127; Joshua, C127; Lucy, C156; Martha, C56, C126; Mary, C56, C153; Mathew, C56; Nancy, C126; Peter, C142; Sarah, C56, C127, C142; Sousiannah, C126; Thury, 13.
Robertson, Amanda, C98; Anna, C147; Dulcena, C95; Christopher, C157; Eilus, C75; Eliza, C33; Elizabeth, C75, C132; Henry, C33; Hulda, C132; James, 2, C14, C44, C95; C98, C151; Jane, C132; Jinett, C43; Jobe, C75; John, C95, C132; Joseph, C98; Laura, C13; Leander, D98; Leonard, C73; Lucinda, C95; Lightle, C98; Ludilla, C95; Margaret, C14, C75; Martha, C14, 21, C95, C98, C132, C151; Mary, C33, C98; Mermura, C95; Michael, C132; Nancy, C14, C44; Narsissa, C2; Newton, C132; Nig, C33; Zella, C95; Rachel, C14, C33; Rebecca, C124; Richard, C14; Robert, C137; Sarah, C74, C132; Silva, C68; Thomas, C33, C59, C74; Thompson, C2; Tobitha, C151; William, C33; C73; Zachariah, C75.
Robeson, 5.
Robinson, Dock, 70; J. S., 69; John, 70; Nancy, C139, C154; Rosella, C152; Thomas, C152.
Robison, Basil, C151; Elizabeth, C151; Fanny, C153.
Roddy, Roddey, P. D., 30, 33, 34, 37, 38, 39, 42, 43, 45, 50, 79. (Sometimes found as Colonel, sometimes General.)
Roden, Emmett, 76; Perry Lee, 74.
Rodgers, Annie, C4¹; B. A., 61, Ben, 61; Camads, C41; Elizabeth, C90; Isaac, C41; Jackson, C41; Jacon, C41; James, C90; John, C41, C90; Kiseah, C41; Mason, C40; Martha, C40; Mary Ann, C90; Nancy, C82; Sarah, C82; Thomas, C41; William, C40, C90.
Rogers, B. A., 61; Ben, 61; Catherine, C152; Elizabeth, C142; James, C151; Lucritey, C151; Margaret, C142; Martha, C151; Mary, C144; Polly, C139; Susan, C152; William, C151, C152.
Rolin, Betty, C18; William, C18.
Rollins, Indeah, C151; Reuben, C151.
Romine, Able, C110; Albert, C110; Alfred, C110; Asenith, C110; Bethel, C110; Betty, C110; California, C110; Cynthia, C110; David, C110; Eli, C110; Elizabeth, C107; Eveline, C109; Frances, C110; George, C109, C110; contd

Romine, continued: Henry, C110; Houston, C110; James, C109, C110; Jane, C110; Jasper, C110; Jesse, C107; Job, C110; John, C110; Julie, C110; Layton, C110; Lucy, C109; Matilda, C110; Martha, C107, C110; Marion, C110; Melelaiha, C109; Melissa, C110; Millage, C107; Molly, C110; Permelia, C110; Peter, C109, C110; Polly, C142; Raleigh, C110; Rebecca, C110; Riley, C110; Rite, C110; Roland, 71, C110; Rodway, C110; Rose, C110; Sam, C110; Sarah, C109, C110; Susan, C110; Thomas, C107, C110; Tibitha, C110; Valzora, C110; W. B., C110; William, C109, C110, C142; Zachariah, C109.
Ronsey, Polly, C144.
Roper, Edney, C151; James, C151.
Rose, Benjamin, 21; Bennett, C111; Capt., 45; Mary, 21; Sarah, C109; Seymour, C109; Zachariah, C111.
Rosecrans, General, 32, 34, 35, 37, 38, 39, 40, 45.
Rosentall, Frances, C30; J. R., C30; Jacob, C30, C65.
Ross, Abergale, C74; Austin, C70; Benjamin, C75; Benet, C111; Campbell, C74; Charles, C70; Cynthia, C127; David, C70; Elizabeth, C75, C133; Emily, C70; Francis, C70; Grena, C152; Hanna, C75; Henry, C75; Irvine, C127; James, C111; John, C70; Levin, C39; Levinny, C133; Lorenzo, C127; Margaret, C39; Martha, C111; Mary, C70; Nancy, C111, C127; Rufus, C75; Robert, C127; Samuel, C111; Sarah, C70; Thomas, C70; William, C39; C75, C152; Zachariah, C111.
Rossin, Rhoda, C153.
Rousseau, General, 45.
Rovier, John, 21; Susan, 21.
Rowel, Martha, C152; Neal, C152.
Rowell, Ann, C52; Christopher, C52; Elizabeth, C52; Martha, C56; Neal, 23, C56; Virginia, C56.
Rowett, Richard, 41, 43.
Rowie, Daniel, C126; Elizabeth, C126; John, C126; Mary, C126; Sarah, C126.
Roy, Richard, 20.
Royal, Joseph, 4, 5.
Royall, Anne, 11.
Rucker, Frances, C142; Wester, C142.
Ruggles, Daniel, 28, 29.
Russell, Alexander, C17; Caroline, C17; Joseph, C17; Milton, C36; Yancy, C17.
Rush, Nelly, C151; Robert, C151.
Rushton, Wash, 79.

Rutherford, F. S., C61; Gilbert, 67;
   Griffith, 1; Henry, 67; Lotitea, C61.
Ryan, Bill, 59.
Rye, Leon, 71.

Sabier, Julian, C142; Mary, C142.
Saddles, Elizabeth, 13.
Saffarnans, Ann, C135; Mary, C135;
   Sousan, C135.
Safferans, Mary, C142; Peter, C142.
Sagers, Jousan, 23.
Salls, Martha, C57.
Salovis, Daniel, C153; Martha, C153.
Sample, James, 6, 7, 17, C135; Henry, 26, C135; Mollie, 7.
Sanders, Elia, C47; John, C132; Nancy, C139; Rody, C132; Samuel, C47.
St. Clair, Elizabeth, C31; Margarett, C31; Mary, C31; Matthew, C31; Nancy, C31; William, C31.
Satterfield, Margaret, C148.
Sannoner, Frances, C136; Ferdinand, 6, 8, 21, 25, C115, C136; Franklin, C136; Margaret, 21, C115; Samuel, C136.
Sartin, Elizabeth, C116; Hiram, C116; James, C116; Mary, C116; Quin, C116.
Saunders, Aaron, C152; Dr., 58; James, 26, 27, 59; Rachel, C144; Sally, C152.
Savage, Polly, C142.
Scags, Ann, C80; Caroline, C85; David, C80; James, C85; Sousan, C85; Thomas, C80.
Schale, Mark, C30.
Schmidlkofer, Virginia, 73.
Scoogs, Sealy, C152.
Scot, William, C114.
Scott, Abner, C20; Allen, C52; Andrew, C15, C20, C152; Ann, C38; Betty, C53; Catherine, C53; Dexter, C53; Elizabeth, C52, C53, C152; George, C53; Harriett, C53; James, 50, C52, C53; Jane, C52, C53; Jerry, C53; John, C38, 50, C52, C53; Joseph, C152; Levi, 50, C53; Lucy, C152; Louiser, C52; Margaret, C53; Martha, C53; Martin, 50; Mary, C15, C19, C20; Miles, C52; Milton, C20; Nancy, C16, C20, C38, C53; Newton, 50; Rachel, C153; Rebecca, C152; Rufus, C53; Samuel, C152; Sarah, C15; Shelton, C19; Susanna, C52; Thomas, C53, C152; William, C6, C15, C20, C38, C52; Zachariah, C15.
Scruggs, Mary, C138.
Schudder, Phillip, 6.
Seaton, Henry, C66; Manurvy, C66; Mary C66; Parthenia, C66; Samuel, C66; William, C66.

Seawright, George, 60.
Seddon, James, 33, 34.
Sego, Chapman, C16; Ezra, C16; John, C16; Margaret, C16; Rebecca, C16; Sally, C16; William, C16.
Selby, Benjamin, C16; James, C16; Joshua, C16; Mary, C16; Nancy, C16; Owen, C16; Phillip, C16; Sarah, C16; Thomas, C16.
Selder, L., C52.
Sellers, Harriet, C58.
Sessums, Lucy, C152; Richard, C152.
Sevier, 1.
Shall, Lusinda, C23.
Shane, Baylis, 59.
Share, Jane, C141; Margaret, C142; Robert, C142.
Sharp, A. J., 71; Andrew, 61; Carrol, C26; Charles, 3, C17, C26; Charlie, 39, C15; David, 3; Edwin, C26; Eliza, C17, C26; Elizabeth, C26; Emily, C26; Frank, C141; Hamon, C26; James, C26; Jim, 63; Joseph, C26; John, C26; Julia, C26; Martha, C26; Margaret, C26; Matilda, C17, C26; Mary, C26; Nancy, C26; Natilie, 73; Owen, C26; Reuben, C26; Robert, C26; Ruth, C26; Sarah, C26.
Shaw, Almera, C112; Benton, C50; Francis, C50; G. W., C48; George, C50; Houston, C50; Jackson, C50; Mary, C50; Robert, C50; Sally, C48.
Shelburn, Nancy, C152; Samuel, C152.
Shelby, Evan, C153; Mary, C138, C153.
Sherman, General, 41.
Shelton, Alfey, C104; Amos, C135; Baby, C102; Balinda, C152; Caroline, C97, C102, C104; Crockett, C102; Darkis, C106; Elisha, C97, C101; Eliza, C102; Elizabeth, C4, C97, C104, C106; Emerline, C102; George, C97, C101; C104; Green, C104; Hardin, C102; Hezekiah, C104; Jacob, C102; James, C101, C102, C104; Jane, C101, C141, C142; Jasper, C101; Jessee, C101; John, C66, C99; Joseph, C4; Joshua, C8; Kindrick, C4; Laneer, C102; Leander, C8; Leer, C104; Lenny, C101; Lifus, C104, C106; Lucy, C104; Madilla, C99; Manurva, C102; Margaret, C38; Mark, C102; Martha, C97, C102; Mary, C8, C97, C99, C102, C104; Nancy, C49, C97, C106; Nehemiah, C104; Polk, C102; Polly, C4; Rabt., C48; Rachel, C152; Rebecca, C97, C102; Robert, 76, C101, C104, C142, C152; Sarah, C4, C49, C97, C106; Sousan, C97, C101; Stephen, C97, C104; Talethia, C99; Thomas, C97, C152; William, C4, C49.

Shephard, Clarinda, C33; Emily, C33; James, C33; John, C33; Lewis, C33; Louiser, C33; Nancy, C33; Permelia, C33; Thomas, C33; V. Matilda, C33; William, C33.
Sherod, James, C12; Sarah, C145.
Sherrod, Nancy, C151; Robert, 12; William, 59.
Sheton, Baby, C100; John, C100; Louisa, C100; Mary, C100.
Shewbird, Alsey, C27; Andrew, C27; Charlott, C27; Darcus, C27; Ellen, C27; Jane, C27; John, C27; Mary, C27; Marion, C27; Moses, C27, C28; Nancy, C27; Ransom, C27.
Shields, John, C152; Nancy, C152.
Shird, Andrew, C56; Elizabeth, C56; Frances, C56; Henry, C56; John, C56; Leona, C56; Mack, C56; Mary, C56; Raby, C56; Robert, C56.
Shirk, Lt. Com., 28.
Shoat, Elizabeth, C145; John, C152; Sarah, C152.
Shoemaker, Alonzo, 24; Angeline, C109; Ann, C145; James, C109; John, C109; Martha, C109; Mary, C109, C142; Rebecca, C109; Richard, C109; Sousan, C109; Sousannah, C109; Thomas, C142.
Sholar, Matilda, C149; Sarah, C151.
Shore, Miranda, C141.
Short, Delila, C23; Elizabeth, C142; Ellender, C23; James, C23; Malinda, C23; Maretta, C145; Rickard, C23.
Shoulders, Allen, C115; Carisa, C115; Clansey, C118; Mary, C90, C115; Sarah, C115; Selia, C115; Solomon, C118; Tibitha, C115; William, C90; C115.
Shoup, Francis, C47.
Shuffield, Alexander, C134; Anderson, C134; Arthur, C77; Benjamin, C77; E., 12; Elizabeth, C77; John, C77; Matthew, C134; Mary, C77, C134; Monroe, C134; Nancy, C134; Sarah, C77; Virginia, C77.
Sibley, Elijah, C43; Eliza, C43 ; John, C43 ; Leonord, C43 ; Mary, C43; Nancy, C43; Sarah, C43
Sikes, Ann Eliza, C39; Elizabeth, C39; James, C39; Mary, C39; Margaret, C39; William, C39.
Simmons (see also Cimmons), Albert, C81; Elizabeth, C149; George, C152; Holden, C116; James, C65; L. C., 76; Lucy, C152; Martha, C144; Nancy, C81, C152; Rebecca, C81, C146, C153; Roan, C152; Robert, C152; William, C152.
Simons, Elizabeth, C115; George, C115; Nicetter, C115; Sylvester, C115; William, C115.

Simpson, Amanda, C118; Caroline, C23; Charles, C4; Christopher, C23; David, C23; Elizabeth, C63; George, C118; H. M., 69; Hugh, C67; J. B., 34; J. H., 65; James, 14, 19, 23, C63, C65; Jane, C23; John, C4, 13, 14, 23, 34, C63, C67, C118; Kassy, C118; Margaret, C67; Martha, C23; Mary, C65; Mr., 11; Polly, C23; Reston, C118; Robert, C67, C118; Simon, 59; Thomas, 23, 26, C23, C63; William, C67, C118.
Sims, Henry, 37.
Sinclair, William, 39.
Single, Jacob, C142; Matilda, C142.
Singley, Amos, C31; Francis, C31; George, C31; Harriett, C31; Jacob, C31; Jesse, C31; John, C31; Matilda, C31; Mary, C31; Samuel, C31; William, C31; Wilson, C31.
Sinnett, John, C38.
Skaggs, Lucy, C143.
Skeel, Mary, C152; Samuel, C152.
Skelton, Alexander, C148; Benjamin, 26; Elizabeth, C152; Mark, C152.
Skepwith, Ann Eliza, C43; Manurvy, C43; Marion, C43; Thomas, C43; Willis, C43.
Skipworth, Henry, C79; Jane, C79; John, C79; Manervia, C79; Turner, C79.
Slaright, George, C39.
Slaughter, George, C64; John, C64; Mary, C64; Peter, C64; William, C64; Z. Taylor, C64.
Sloss, Ann Eliza, C42; Clarissa, C135; Eveline, C135; J. L., 21; James, C61; Joseph, C135; Letitia, C61; Robert, C61; Thomas, C61; William, C1.
Smally, Sarah, C149.
Smart, Bennett, C152; Nancy, C152.
Smedley, John, C142; Sousannah, C142.
Smith, Alexander, 53, 59, C135; Allen, C152; Amelia, C153; Andrew, 62; Ann, C37, C142, C152, C153; Anneliza, C127; Archabald, C153; Armander, C127; Austin, C114; Barbary, C126; Baxter, 38; Benjamin, C76, C127; Caleb, C25; Caroline, C57, C80; Cassy Ann, C1; Charles, C80; Chelaty, C148; Christine, C139; Cynthia, C109, C110; Daniel, C50; Davy, C51; Duncan, C74; Easter, C38; Ebeneser, C44; Ellender, C117; Eliza, C1, C126, C153; Elizabeth, C25, C37, C44, C114, C51, C57, C123; Ellen, C60; Etheldred, C57; Frances, C80; Francis, C126; Frank, 78, 79; Franklin, C80; Frederick, C153; G. G., C38; Mrs. G. H., 62; George, C1, 13, C38, C44, C127; Gilbert, C25; H. A., C38; H. E., C38; Hannah, C57; continued,

279

Smith, continued: Hardy, 53; Henry, 21, 23; C25, C57, C123, C126; Isaac, 80; J. H., 4; Jacob, C127; James, C1, C8, C25, C38, C44, C51, C76, C93, C126, C142; Jane, C74, C76, C127, C142, C148, C151; Jasper, C1, C80; Jeff, 70; Jerry, C51; Jery, C1; Jessee, C127; John, C8, 25, C25, C38, C44, C51, C57, C74, C109, C110, C114, C135, C152; Jonnath, C60; Josephus, C1; Joshiah, C8; Joshua, C8, C123, C152; Juleen, C153; Julia, C114; Julian, C38; Kerby, 34; Levi, C1; Littleton, C25; Lucinda, C8, C114; Lucy, C8, C114; Mahaley, C25; Margaret, C80, C126, C135; Marion, C38, C76; Martha, C8, C44, C51, C57, C76; Martin, C148; Mary, C1, C44, C57, C76, C114, C123, C126, C135; Matilda, C25; Monroe, C76; Nancy, C25, C38, C74, C80; Nathaniel, C1; Parilee, C37; Patience, C139; Pernissa, C25; Perry, C25; Peter, C38, C109; Polly, C74, C152; Presley, C1; Rachel, C25; Rebecca, C25, C76, C80, C153; Robert, C8, C80, C106; Sabera, C8; Smith, C152; Samuel, C8; Sarah, C50, C76, C109, C114; Stulin, C135; Susan, C74, C152; Susannah, C25, C126, C148; Terry, C38; Thomas, C15, C37, C64, C80, C153; Virginia, C60, C117; W. T., C38; Washington, C76, C80; William, C8, C37, C50, C80, C114, C123, C126, C127, C135; Winny, C50.

Sneed, Alexander, C135; George, C135; 25; Mary, C135.

Snipes, Angeline, C77; Ann, C77; Margaret, 21, C76; Nancy, C77; Phillips, C77.

Snoddey, David, C114; Sarah, C114; Thomas, C114.

Snoddy, Elizabeth, C153.

Snyder, Mary, 21.

South, Eli, C152; Elizabeth, C152; Jane, C143; Lutitia, C20; Samuel, C20.

Sortin, William, C63.

Spain, Elbourn, C49; Hannah, C142; Hardy, C49; Jemmina, C49; Julia, C125; Louiser, C49; Marinda, C49; Marshall, C142; Martha, C49; Newel, C49; Ruffin, C49; Solomon, C152; Syntha, C12; Walker, C49.

Spaling, George, 44.

Spangler, Grandville, 56.

Sparks, Chauncey, 74; Pearl, 73; Nancy, C38; Rebecca, C147, C152.

Speagle, Hannah, C144.

Spears, Calvin, C21; George, C152; James, C21; Jane, C152; Margarett, C21; cont'd

Spears, continued: Mary, C21; Nancy, C21.

Speegle, Elizabeth, C151.

Speigle, Rebecca, C146.

Spencer, Abner, C66.

Spenser, Jane, C113.

Sperrel, John, C23; Josiah, C23; Kisiah, C23; Mary, C23.

Spigall, Benjamin, C112; Ediom, C112; Elizabeth, C112; Elliom, C112; George, C112; James, C112; John, Kelly, C112; Nancy, C112; Palena, C112; Sarah, C112.

Spinkes, James, C1; Levi, C1.

Sport, Joseph, C13; Levi, C2.

Spotwood, Jacob, C135.

Springer, A. B. M., C95; Albert, C95; Alexander, C99; Allen, C100; Calvin, C95; Dennis, C152; Early, C149; Ephraim, C95; Eliza, C95; Elizabeth, C95, C100, C152; Franklin, C89; Henry, C100; James, C89, C142; Jane, C89, C95, C142; Jessee, C95; John, C95, C100; Johnathan, C95, C142; Joshua, C152; Lydia, C89; Mariah, C95; Marshal, C89, C152; Margaret, C140; Martha, C152; Mary, C89, C95, C100; Matilda, C152; Polly, C142; Rachel, C99; Robert, C95, C100; Samuel, C95; Sarah, C95, C100; Solomon, C152; Sousan, C95; T. S., C100; Taylor, C95; Thomas, C95; Thursey, C152; William, C89, C95, C100.

Sproule, 13.

Stacey, Benjamin, C152; Sally, C152.

Stafford, Caleb, C135; Priscilla, C135; Polly, C143; Samuel, C135.

Staggs, Lester, 66.

Stags, Calafornia, C13; Laura, C13; Margarett, C13; Parilee, C13; Rebecca, C13; William, C13.

Staley, Ann, C47; David, C47; George, C47; Marion, C47; Nancy, C47; Rebecca, C47.

Stamps, Amanda, C109; Caroline, C109; Catherine, C109; Elizabeth, C90, C109, C113; Franklin, C23; Harriet, C90; J. D., C90; John, C90, C109; Martha, C90, C114; Mary, C90, C109; Sarah, C90; Thomas, C90; William, C114.

Standeford, Elizabeth, C106; George, C106; John, C112; Mary, C106; Milly, C112; Nancy, C112; Sarah, C106.

Standford, Charlotte, C101; Caroline, C107; James, C107, C115; Joseph, C107; Pinkney, C107; continued:

Standford, continued: Thomas, C107; Wesley, C107.
Standridge, James, C152; Susannah, C152.
Stanten, Annie M., C66.
Staples, Caroline, C117; Elizabeth, C150; Nancy, C117; William, C117.
Starkey, Jesse, C142; Nancy, C142.
Staton, A. B., 69.
Strawn, Fielding, C152; Greenberry, C152; Nancy, C152; Rebecca, C152.
Steardivant, Mary, C115; Sarah, C115.
Stebbins, Louisa, C137; Samuel, C137; Sarah, C137; Sousan, C137.
Steedman, 45.
Steel, James, C152; Julia, C152; Thomas, 90.
Steen, Christopher, C78; Elizabeth, C78; Hannah, C78; Malia, C78; Martha, C78; Mary, C78; Nathan, C78; Thomas, C78; William, C78.
Step, Elizabeth, C127; Joseph, C127; Moses, C127; Sarah, C127.
Stephen, Angeline, C75; Ann, C145; Annie, C130; Charlotte, C148; J. M., C75; John, C130.
Stepp, Nancy, C152; Joseph, C152.
Stergeon, Ellis, C142; Starberry, C142.
Stevenson, James, 66.
Stewart, Allen, C142; Catherine, C9, C141; Edward, C56; James, C10, 23, 26, 34, 54, C56, C152; John, C56; Maderson, C10; Mary, C10, C56; Nancy, C142; Polly, C139; Sarah, C10, C152; Thomas, C9; Virgil, 18; Webster, 17; William, C10.
Still, John, C142; Mariah, C142.
Stockard, William, 4.
Stone, Albert, C104; Alfred, C153; Christopher, C104; Frances, C104; James, C104; John, C104; Josephine, C104; Louisa, C104; Mary, C104; Matilda, C152; Rebecca, C152; Sally, C152; Samuel, C152; Thomas, C104, C152; William, C104.
Story, Davy, C39; Elizabeth, C84; James, C39; John, C84, C133; Martha, C84; Mary, C86, C133; Parilee, 21; Rebecca, C39; Richard, C84; Sally, C39; Sarah, C84; Tennessee, C39; Thomas, C86; Tilman, C39; William, C133.
Stout, Isaiah, C152; Phebe, C152.
Stadford, D. B., C66.
Strahl, 47.
Strawn, Fielding, C152; Greenberry, C152; Nancy, C152; Rachel, C143; Rebecca, C140, C152.
Strickland, Wash, 60.

Strong, Edmund, C134; James, C134; John, C134; Lewis, C134; Lydia, C134; Olliver, C134; Robert, C71; Temperance, C71; Thomas, C134; William, C134.
Stribling, T. S., 70.
Stuart, (see also Stewart); Agges, C125; Alexander, C84; Catherine, C125; Charles, C135; Christine, C125; Duncan, C84, C125; Eliza, C84, C133; Elizabeth, C84; George, C152; James, C84, C128, C135; John, C80, C135; Josephine, C135; Manerva, C84; Marion, C84; Martha, C84; Mary, C84, C125; Nancy, C84; Ophelia, C135; Richard, C84; Rochell, C152; Viola, C135; William, C78, C84.
Sturgant, Ensly, C104; Eliza, C104; Jamina, C104; John, C104; William, C104.
Sturgeon, Rachel, C152.
Stutts, Anderson, C68, C132; Ann, C68, C123; Asa, C132; Ben, 76; Charlotte, C126; Christopher, C126; David, C123; Elias, C73; Elizabeth, C123, C126, C131; Fereby, C73; Frances, C131; Henry, C81; Jacob, C131; James, C123, C126, C132; John, C73, C123, C131; Julia, C126; Kenneth, C126; Leonard, 21, C126; Lucinda, C126; Margaret, C126; Martha, 21, C73; Martin, C123, C152; Mary, C123, C126, C132, C152; Nancy, C73, C123, C126, C131, C132; Perilee, 21, C86; Ranson, C73; Safronia, C73; Sarah, C68, C123, C132; Sousennah, C123; Susan, C73; Wesley, C86, C132; William, C68, C73, C126, C132; Willis, C126.
Sulivant, C. J., C152.
Sullivan, C. A., 62; Caroline, C36; Charles, C36; Eliza, C46; Malicia, C103; Margarett, C36; Milton, C36; N. F., C103; Nancy, C103; O. B., C46.
Sullivant, Jane, C152; John, C152.
Summerhill, Agnus, C54; E. B., C55; Edward, C54; Elijah, C54; Elizabeth, C54; Eliza, C55; George, C52, C54; Haris, C55; Harris, C52; Horis, 23; Martha, C55; Mary, C54; Permelia, C55; Rebecca, C55; Richard, C54; William, C54.
Sute, James, C152; Sealy, C152.
Sutherlin, James, C66; Louisa, C66; William, C66; Z. Taylor, C66.
Sutton, Susan, C6.
Swearingen, Malinda, C148.
Swearington, Elizabeth, C147.
Sweeny, Colonel, 33.

Swiney, James, C74; Lucinda, C91; Mary, C91; Sion, C91.
Swinfoard, Abner, C25; Charles, C52; Darkus, C52; Eliza Jane, C52; George, C52; Isaac, C52; J. B., C52; John, C52; Martha, C52; Mary, C52; Nancy, C52; Phoebe, C52; Rebecca, C52.
Swinford, Baby, C117; Catherine, C117; Harriet, C117; Jackson, C117; Jane, C117; John, C117; Mary, C117; Penelofia, C117.

Tacey, Indiah, C151.
Tacker, Ann, C51; Daniel, C51; Francis, C51; Jacob, C51; John, C51; Joshua, C51; Martha, C51; Wesley, C51.
Tagley, Elizann, C24; John, C24; Margaret, C24; Nancy, C24; Richard, C24.
Tagsley, Mahuldy, C23; Richard, C23; Sarah, C23.
Tait, Waddy, 4, 5, 6, 8.
Talbot, William, 8, 9.
Tally, Hollis, C20; Nancy, C143; Page, C143; Sylvina, C20.
Tankerslay, Polly, C151; Rachel, C150; Sarah, C151.
Tankersly, Clarissa, C154.
Tanner, Ruth, C148.
Tapp, Elizabeth, C80; Frances, C82; James, C82; John, C82; Margaret, C82; Mary, C82; Presley, C82; Sarah, C82; Thomas, C64, C82; Vincent, C82.
Tardy, C. L., 70.
Tate, Amanda, C118; Caroline, C118; Elizabeth, C119; Elmeria, C118, C119, C145; Frances, C118; Franklin, C118; Hiram, C118; Jerome, C119; Jessee, C119; Lavern, 76; Milly, C118; Virginia, C118.
Taylor, 5; Billy, 25; Benjamin, C78, C153; Cinthia, C47; Elizabeth, C78; Franklin, C47; G. S., 69; James, C143; Nancy, C143; Patience, C143; Sarah, C78; Sousin, C78; Susan, C153; Thomas, C78, C143; Tommy, 66.
Taze, Ann, C120; Chainy, C120; Elizabeth, C120; James, C120; William, C120.
Teis, John, C81.
Temple, Leilia, 60; Mrs. W. E., 60.
Tennerson, Abergale, C37; Annie, C37; Catharine, C37; Cintha, C37; John, C37; Reginia, C37; Sarah Ann, C37.
Terass, Amelia, C153.
Terrell, Andrew, C55; Calvin, C18, 20;

Terrell, continued: Catharine, C18, C55; Doctor, C54; Ellen, C57; Ellender, C18; James, C54, C55; John, C18; Joseph, C18, C54; Matilda, C18, 20; Mary, C130; Monroe, C54; Nancy, C130; Pinkney, C18; Polly Ann, C18; Rickman, C18, C57; Sara, C18; Sarah, C57; Sylvanus, C130; Thomas, C18; Tibatha, C54; William, C18; Winston, C130.
Terry, Jane, C146.
Terry, Joseph, C153; Susannah, C153; Daniel, C35; Eliza, C35; Elizabeth, C143; Frances, C143; Sally, C140, C143; Thomas, C143.
Thigpen, Amanda, C94; Amos, C91; Bluford, C94; Elizabeth, C93, C94; George, C94; Gilford, C94; Greenberry, C93; Jane, C93; John, C93; Joseph, C93; Joshua, C93; Lecie, C94; Margaret, C94; Mary, C94, C122; Riley, C93; Samuel, C93; Sarah, C94, C122; Selfy, C122; Selphy, C94; William, C122.
Third (?), Columbus, C45; Elizabeth, C45; James, C45; Ruth, C45; Texas Ann, C45.
Thoma (s?), Artetia, C70; David, C70; Frank, C70; James, C70; John, C70; Louiser, C70; Margaret, C70; Mary, C70; Monroe, C70; Sarah, C70; William, C70.
Thomas, Alfred, C47; Amous, C47; Andrew, C62; Benjamin, C132; Benton, C7; Caroline, C151; Charity, C140; Charles, C132; Elizabeth, C59, C62; General G. H., 32; Harriett, C59, C132; Hiram, C89; James, C7, C62, C89; Jess, C7; John, C7, C62, C89, C132; Josiah, C47, C140; Malinda, C47; Manurvy, C47; Marion, C47; Martha, C62; Mary, C7, C89; Myra, C7; Nancy, C152; Rachel, C47, C140, C151; Samuel, C47; Sarah, C89; Thomas, C7, C47; William, C47, C89.
Thomelson, Artiminta, C55; Mississippi, C55; Uphraney, C55; Raley, C55; Rosanna, C55; Seth, C55; Thestus, C55.
Thomes, Frances, C85; George, C85; James, C85; Jane, C85; Mary, C85; Philadelphia, C85; Sarah, C85; William, C85; Wilmot, C85.
Thompson, Altemont, C30; Amanda, C30; Ann, C30; E. B., C59; Elizabeth, C37; Emily, C135; Harriet, C153; Hugh, C153; Jane, C135; Jane, C146; Jefferson, C30; John, 24, C30, C92; Josephine, C44; Louisa, C30, C37; Lucy, C37; Margaret, C135, C153;

Thompson, continued: Martha, C30; Mary, C30, C37, C92; Melinda, C153; Nancy, C30; Ac150; Pleasant, C92; Samuel, C30, C153; Sarah, C30; Sarena, C147; Thomas, C37; Tunningham, C37; Virginia, C37; William, C30, C92.

Thorington, Baby, C129; John, C89; Elizabeth, C89; Martha, C89; Mary, C89; Sousiannah, C129; William, C129.

Thorn, Alved, C60.

Thorngton, Eliza, C87; James, C87; John, C87; Margaret, C87; Nancy, C87; Sarah, C87; Thomas, C87; William, C87.

Thornberry, Ruthy, C150.

Thornton, Allen, 76; Edgar, 63; Elizabeth, C62, C153; Franley, C143; Jefferson, C32; Josiah, C143; Mahala, C151; Mariah, C142; Marian, C147; Nelly, C138; Sarah, C32, C82, C149; William, C32, C82, C153.

Thrasher, 44; Benjamin, C52; Claborne, 31; C32; Cornriddy, C52; Elias, C63; Emily, C5; Hannah, C32; Henson, C32; Hetty, C5; Houston, C5; James, C5; John, C5, C32; Kenslon, C5; Malinda, C32; Malissa, C5; Martha, C32; Mary, C52; Mitchel, C5; Nancy, C52; Ramus, C52; Rachel, C5, C32, C143; Sarah, C32, C55; Susannah, C32; Thomas, C52, C55; Tom, 52; William, C5, C52, C55, C143; Woodrow, 71.

Threet, Cowpunder, 73, 74; Matilda, 20; Mary, 21; Willie Lee, 74.

Threete, Alfred, C18; James, C47; John, C18; Joseph, C18; Mary, C18, C47; Sarah, C18, C47; Thomas, C18.

Tibbs, Andy, C24; E., C155; Elijah, C24; Jasper, C24; Mary, C24; Nathan, C24; Nathaniel, C24; Noma, C24; Parthenia, C24; William, C155.

Tibs, Maomry, C24; Saley, C24; William, C24.

Ticer, Cynthia, C153; James, C153; Sarah, C153.

Tidwell, Elizabeth, C83; Leroy, C83; Martha, C83; Rickman, C83; Robert, C83; Samuel, C83; Sarah, C83; Sousan, C83; Thomas, C83.

Till, Camelia, C143; Cameller, C23; Carter, C23; Catharine, C23; Ed, 31; Edwin, C23; Gabriel, C23; James, C23; John, C23, C143; Rasmus, C23; Weekley, C23; William, C23.

Tillar, Daniel, C47; Lewis, C47; Rhoebi, C47; Rebecca, C47; Ruby, C47; Sarah, C47.

Tilman, Samuel, C8.

Tisdale, Philadner, C153; E.(?), C153.

Titus, Rosana, C61; W. S., C63.

Todd, Benet, C122; Elizabeth, C66; Jane, C66; Levi, 20, 23, C66; Licurgus, C122; Lusinda, C66; Malinda, C122; Matilda, C99; Mary, C99, C122; Nancy, C99; Olga, C99; P. N., C99; Roena, C99; Sabrey, C122; Samuel, C99; Sousan, C122; William, C122.

Tolifer, Amanda, C153; William, C153.

Tomblin, Elizabeth, C83; Fanny, C83; Frances, C83; Isaac, C83; Moses, C83; Rebecca, C83; Samuel, C83; William, C83.

Tomlinson, Charles, C88; Elvirah, C88; James, C88; John, C143; Joseph, C88; Lucretia, C143; Martha, C88; Moses, 18; Sarah, C88; William, C88.

Tossle, Joseph, C59.

Towns, John, C28.

Townsley, Lizzie, 62.

Townsly, Amerissa, C61; Columbus, C61; Elizabeth, C61; Jasper, C61; Lafaett, C61; Martha, C61; Sarah, C61; Stephen, C61; William, C61.

Trainer, Betsy, C143; William, C143.

Trapp, Leonard, 73.

Trobock, John, C87; Nancy, 23; Rebecca, C87.

Trombrough, Polly, C138.

Trotter, Elizabeth, C153; John, C153.

Trousdale, Ann, C77; B. B., 27; Baby, C81; Benjamin, C81; Catherine, C81; Elizabeth, C81; James, C81; John, C77; Mary, C81; Nancy, C77, C151; Rebecca, C81; Samuel, C81; Thomas, C77; William, C77, C81.

Trout, Juda, C148; Tansey, C143; William, C143.

Trouton, Teresa, C143.

Truesdale, Jane, C151.

Trusdale, Elizabeth, C153; William, C153.

Trusedale, Eleanor, 23; Hollinsworth, 23.

Tubaville, Frances, C153; L. W., C153.

Tubberville, Edmond, C153; Sarah, C153.

Tuberville, Joseph, C153; Matilda, C153.

Tucker, Annie, C6; Carroll, C68; Eliza, C6; Elizabeth, C143; C153; Francis, C6; Harbard, C6; James, C6, C143; John, C30, C153; Malinda, C6; Mary, C6; Nancy, C147; Phoebi, C68; Samuel, C15; Washington, C6; William, C6, C54; Wilson, C6.

Tumblestone, Andrew, C21; Darkes, C21; Elizabeth, C21; Henry, C21; Hiram, C21; John, C21; Nancy, C21; Robert, C21; Thomas, C21.

Turcer, Elizabeth, C21; Robert, C21.

Turchin, J. B., 30, 32, 39.

Turner, John, C23.
Turnley, Caroline, C28; Frances, C59;
 James, C28; John, C28; Laura, C28;
 Mary, C28; Pinkney, C28; Sarah, C28;
 Russell, C28; Temple, C59; Wesley,
 31; William, C28.
Turpin, John, C22; Jonathan, C22; Mary,
 C22; Polly, C22; Robert, C22.
Tutt, Baby, C79, C130; Benjamin, C79;
 Elva, C130; Jane, C79; Margaret, C130;
 Mary, C78.
Tweedy, Jr., 51.
Twitty, Alfred, C131; Amanda, C76;
 Charlotte, C76; Coresa, C131; Eliza,
 C76; George, C76; Jackson, C76;
 Lavend, C76; Marion, C131; Mary, C76;
 Molsie, C76; Nancy, C76; Sarah, C131;
 William, C76, C131.
Tyree, Karl, 67; K. T., 69.

Udall Stewart, 69.
Ulaid, Mariah, C67.
Urban, Catherine, C153; Cooper, C153.
Underwood, Joseph, 78; Littlebury, C59.

Vaden, Catherine, C119; Joseph, 24;
 Mary, C119.
Valentine, Eliza, C17; Hannah, C41;
 Harriett, C16; James, C17, C41;
 John, C16; Martha, C41; Mary, C16,
 C41; Richard, C16; Ruel, C17; Susan,
 C41; Thomas, C41; William, C17.
Vamdever, Andrew, C153; Elvirah, C153.
Van Buren, Martin, 21.
Vance, Harriett, C146.
Van Dorn, General Earl, 34, 35, 31, 39,
 79.
Varnal (Varnell), A., C106; Elizabeth,
 C106; Furman, C106; John, C106;
 Lydia, C106; Kissie, C106; Permelia,
 C106; Richard, C106; Sarah, C106;
 Sousan, C106; William, C106.
Vaughn, Nancy, C44; Pleasant, C44;
 Samuel, C44; Sarah, C67; Susan, 68;
 T., 67; Virginia, C44.
Vaught, Nathan, 9, 15, 80.
Vaughter, Alejena, C153; Mary, C153.
Vencin, Glafy, C27; James, C27; John,
 C27; Nancy, C27; William, C27.
Venness, George, C61; Mary, C61.
Vernon, Adrian, 71.
Verona, Elizabeth, C141.
Vichars, Andrew, C97; E. W., C97;
 Elizabeth, C98; Green Berry, C98;
 John, C97; Nancy, C97; Verdinand,
 C98; William, C97.

Vickers, Bessie, 66 ; Betsy, C143;
 Green, C143.
Vilin, Amelia, C153; Sam, C153.
Virgus, Mary, C145.
Viser, Sarah, 20.
Visor, Canahan, C153.
Vitilow, Fanny, C153; John, C153.

Waddell, Elam, C153; Joseph, C154;
 Lucinda, C154; Margaret, C153;
 Nancy, C145; Sarah, C149.
Waddle, Elizabeth, C76; Martha, C76;
 Meloch, C76; Nancy, C76.
Wade, Andrew, C31; Ann, C31; Billy, 53;
 Blaney, C107; Calfernia, C107; Eliza,
 C31, 61; Joseph, C154; Mary, C107;
 Sarah, C31; William, C107.
Wadlington, Frances, C149.
Wagner, Lt. Col., 66.
Waits, Benton, C44; Browder, C50;
 Caroline, C44; Catherine, C44, C50;
 Dorton, C44; Elizabeth, C44; Isabella,
 C50; J. L., C50; James, C44; Leonidas
 C44; Lidda, C44; Martha, C44; Mary,
 C50; Permelia, C44; Robert, C50;
 Sarah, C5; Shelton, C44; Thompson,
 C50; William, C50.
Waldrep, Waldrip, Waldrop, Aggy, C145;
 Addaline, C60; Amanda, C60; Eliza,
 C34; Elizabeth, C60, C35; Everline,
 C35; Frances, C34, C60; Henry, C35;
 Isem, C11; James, C34, C35; Jane,
 C35; John, C25; Joseph, C34; Levi,
 C18; Lusinda, C35; Martha, C60;
 Mary, C11, 21, C35, C60; Mikle, C60;
 Preston, C60; Rachel, C34; Serena,
 C34; Steven, C35; Susan, C18, C35;
 Thomas, C11, C34, C60; William, C34,
 C35.
Walker, A. J., 59; Andrew, C5; David,
 C143; Eliza, C66, C154; Elizabeth,
 C97, C142; George, C13, C97; Henry,
 C13; James, C97, C101; John, 5, 6,
 C5, C97; Joseph, C97; L. P., 21, 23,
 C66; Mahaley, C5; Malica, C97; Mary,
 C5, C97, C101, C153; Nancy, C5; Polly,
 C143; R. J., C28; R. W., 21, 34, 42;
 Robert, C154; Samuel, 57; Sarah, C13,
 C64; Susan, C13; William, C5, C13.
Wall, Rev. Mr., 76.
Wallace, Catherine, C149; Cossy, C147;
 Dolly, C143; George, 75; John, C143;
 Sally, C139; Sarah, C144; William, 13
Wallice, Annie, C14; Culver, C14; Harris
 C14; Harrison, C13; Henry, C14; James
 C13, C18; Jesse, C14; continued,

Wallice, continued:
John, C13, C18; Kisiah, C18;
Lusinda, C13; Marion, C13; Margaret,
C13; Mary, C14, C18; Nancy, C14, C18;
Robert, C18; Salenius, C14; Samuel,
C14; Sarah, C14; Susan, C14;
Thomas, C13, C14, C18; William, C13,
C14, C18.
Wallis, Emily, C13; John, C13; Nancy,
C13; James, C13; John, C13; Samuel,
C13.
Walls, Eliza, C150; Isabella, C154;
Risden, C154.
Walston, Ann, C60; Eliza Jane, C60;
Elizabeth, C59; John, C60; Mary, C60;
Turner, C59.
Walthur, Clifton, C65; Mary, C65; Percy,
C65; Richard, C65; Sampson, C65.
Walton, Rebecca, C122; Robert, C122;
Walter, C122.
Wamble, (Womble?) Amanda, C30; Columbia,
C30; Columbus, C30; Elizabeth, C143;
Harvey, C143; James, C30; Lorenzo,
C143; Mary, C30; Polly, C143; Rebecca,
C30; Wilson, C30.
Ward, Amanda, C1; Annie, C1; Brittain,
C143; Edward, 6; Elizabeth, C20;
Isaac, C20; Matilda, C20; Mary, C20,
C143; Presley, 5, 7; Samuel, C1;
Sarah, C20; Susan, C1; Virginia, C1;
William, C1.
Warden, Elizabeth, C131; Eliza, C131;
Hannah, C131; John, C131.
Warrell, Eliza, C153; William, C153.
Warren, Robert, C52; W. E., 59; William,
36.
Warthon, Jesse, 5.
Washington, George, C21.
Waslston, Isabella, C59; James, C59;
Lorenah, C59; Mary, C59; Turner,
C59; William, C59.
Wassen, Amanda, C7; Sarah, C7; William,
C7.
Waters, Addeline, C22; Daniel, C22;
George, C22; Izell, C22; John, C22,
C154; Levi, C22; Margaret, C22;
Nancy, C22; Obediah, C22; Patsy, C142;
Rachel, C138; Sally, C154; Sarah, C22;
Wiley, C22.
Watkins, Annaliza, C126; Jane, C126;
Joel, C126; John, C126; Louisa, C126;
Matilda, C126; Phrusey, C32; Robert,
C32; Rody, C126; Selada, C126;
Sousan, C32; Thomas, C32, C126; Tom,
77; William, C32.
Watsen, Mary, C7.
Watson, Catherine, C18; Clary, C132;
E. D., C18; Eliza, C90; Elizabeth,
C137; Greenberry, C90; James, C90;
Joseph, C90; Nathaniel, C133; cont'd

Watson, continued: Sarah, C90;
Thomas, C90.
Watterson, Harvey, 22.
Watts, T. H., 41.
Wayland, Kiburnia, C67; Martha, C67;
Richard, C67.
Weakley, 25; Ann, C67; Buck, 22; Catherine, C67; Eliza, C67; Ellen, C67,
C136; Harriet, 19; Harvey, 7, C67,
C136; James, 5, 7, C67, C136; Jem,
7, 27; John, 62, C67; Judge, 19;
Manerva, C136; Martin, 29; Mrs., 19;
Narcissa, 57; S. D., 26, C67; Samuel,
7, 27; Sarah, C67.
Weatheram, James, C143; Polly, C143.
Weatherford, Elizabeth, C153; Jane, C5;
Thomas, C5; William, C5.
Weatherly, Anna, C142; Elizabeth, C141;
Jeremiah, C154; Maria, C154; Phebe,
C152; Tamsey, C143.
Weathers, Balas, C117; Elizabeth, C146;
Franklin, C117; I., C154; James, C117;
Jesse, C117; Martha, C117; Mary, C117,
C154; Nancy, C143; Rebecca, C117, C154
Reuben, C143; Sally, C150; Samuel,
C117; William, C117, C154.
Weaver, Adam, C118; Barnet, C112;
Benjamin, C136; Caroline, C118; F. E.,
67; Frances, C118; George, C118;
Isabella, C112; James, C118; John,
C118, C136; Joseph, C112, C118;
Josephine, C112; Martha, C112, C118;
Mary, C112, C118; R. W., 76; Samuel,
C118; Sarah, C118; Souseannah, C118.
Weavir, Mary, C38; Nancy, C37;
Robert, C38; Sarah, C37; Thomas, C38.
Webb, Allen, C48; Berry, C46, C154;
Edy, C23; Eliza, C46, C153; Elizabeth,
C23, C46, C47; C145; Ethelinda, C153;
Ezra, 12; Frances, C23; George, C23;
H. T., C46; Jackson, C48; James, C23;
John, 3, C23; Joseph, C23; Joshua, C47;
Latita, C46; Lusinda, C23; Malinda,
C153; Malissa, C46; Martha, C47;
Mary, C48, C153, C154; Miriah, C23;
Nancy, C47, C48, C154; Rebecca, C47;
Richard, C153, C154; Thomas, C23,
C46; Vaney, C141; William, C23.
Webster, Elizabeth, C119; Henry, C119;
James, C67; Mary, C119; Sarah, C67.
Wed, George, C136.
Weeden, John, 69; Mattie, 7.
Weems, Charles, C60; Eliza, C60; James,
C60; Thomas, C60.
Welch, Ally, C150; Alzvia, C29; Daniel,
C19; Darkeys, C19; Elizabeth, C27, C29
Fanny, C151; Jane, C143; John, C27,
C143; Juda, C27, C29; Julia, C27;
Levi, C27; Martha, C143, C151; cont'd

Welch, continued: Mary, C27, C29; Nancy, C141; Nicholas, C29; Polly, C149; Rebecca, C29; Richard, C27; Thomas, C27; William, C19.

Wells, M. C., C134; Nancy, C144; Robert, C134.

Wesson, Amanda, C8; Claborn, C31, 54; Daniel, C35; Elizabeth, C31; Ellen, C39; Hannah, C2; Harison, C39; Henry, C35; James, C31, C35; John, C8, C31, C34, C35, C39; Joseph, C35; Lavina, C34; Leander, C39; Libby, C35; Lusinda, C31; Margaret, C34; Martha, C31, C36, C39; Mary, C35, C148; Rachel, C39; Sarah, C8, C35, C148; Susan, C8; Turner, C35; Wallice, C35; Warren, C36; Wiley, C31; William, C8, C31, C35.

West, Benjamin, C114; Caroline, C84; Catherine, C114; Elizabeth, C46, C114; James, C114; Jane, C152; John, C114; Levi, C84; Margaret, C119, C154; Mary, C114, C119; Nancy, C114; Patience, C143; Patress, C119; Sarah, C119; Valentine, C136; Walter, C119.

Westmoreland, 7; Alfred, C11; Catherine, C140; E. B., C98, C143; Eliza, C98, C139; Harriett, C150; Hartwell, C153; Jesse, C52; John, C98; Josephine, C11; Lucy, C98, C143; Martha, C141; Mary, C11; Nancy, C154; Rhoda, C153; Robert, 24; Tommy, 31; Virginia, C98.

Weston, Samuel, 24.

Wharton, John, 30.

Wheeler, 37.

Wheler, Charles, 24.

Whettier, Catherine, C88; Elizabeth, C88; Hesler, C88; Isaac, C88; Jane, C88; Willis, C88; William, C88.

Whitaker, Amy, C140; James, C143; Thresa, C143.

White, Aaron, C120; Adeline, C119; Alelleitha, C87; Alexander, C119; Allen, C154; Amanda, C55; Amy, C141; Ann, C39; Anderson, C153; Andrew, C119; Andy, 76; Mrs. B. M., 59; Benjamin, C120; Bujist, C130; Caldonia, C119; Caroline, C55, C76; Catherine, C133; Cross, C105; Cynthia, C118, C119, C143; Daniel, C99, C122; Darliska, C50; David, C55; Davis, C119; Davy, C120; Deana, C120; Drury, C122, C154; Dury, C120; E., C122; Eliza, C76, C94, C119; Elizabeth, 20, C33, C55, C96, C99, C120, C143, C154; Emily, C33; Ephram, C120; Everline, C36; Fountain, C133; Francis, C55, C153; Franklin, 26; George, C50, C119, C120; Gilbert, C99; Henry, C38, C133; Isaac, C105; J. J., 59; J. K. P., C50; James, C33, C50, 64, C96, C104, cont'd

White, continued: C130, C133; Jane, C119; Jemima, C150; Jessee, C94, C119; John, C38, C76, C84, C95, C96, C99, C119, C120, C143; Joseph, C33, C55; L. C., 71; Larges, C119; Levisa, C94; Lucinda, C133; Lucy, C76; Mahalah, C76; Mandana, C119; Margaret, C94, C119, C120, C122, C133, C154; Marion, C120; Martha, C87; Mary, C33, C38, C84, C94, C95, C119, C120, C122, C130, C149; Matilda, C118, C122; Mayberry, C84; Miles, C36; Moren, C130 Moses, 6, 7, 8, 23, C55, C153; Nancy, C96, C99, C119, C133, C154; Neely, C119; Parilee, C36; Patsy, C50; Patrick, C119; Philemon, C87, C119, C143; Polly, C139, C153; Rainy, C133; Rebecca, C84; Rhody, C149; Richard, C94; Robert, C38, C39, C76; Samuel, C118, C119; Sarah, C38, C130; Sherrod, C119; Sousan, C96, C99; Stringer, C38; Temperance, C33; Tempy, C149; Thomas, C130, C133, C154; Washington, C55; Watta, C120; Wesley, C36; William, C33, C76, C94, C118, C120, C130, C133.

Whitehead, Alexander, C153; Baby, C90; Betsy, C24; Catharine, C24; Clark, C24; Elizabeth, C90; Elzera, C90; Frances, C90; George, C90; Gracy, C139; Henry, C90; Jacob, C90; James, C90; Jessee, C90; Joseph, C154; Julia, C90; Louiser, C24; Lusinda, C24; Martha, C38; Margaret, C90; Nancy, C90; C149; Nathaniel, C24; Phillip, C90; Rebecca, C153; Sarah, C90, C139; Saransus, C24; Thomas, C38; William, 24, C24.

Whitmire, Charity, C11; Francis, C28; Martha, C28; Moses, C28; Nancy, C28; Nella, C28; Ruth, C28; Sarah, C28; William, C28.

Whitney, Chales, C103; Nancy, C103.

Whitsett, Benjamin, C22; Camby, C22; Elizabeth, C22, C47, C154; Harriett, C22; Isaac, C22, C47; James, C47; John, C47; Margaret, C22; Permelia, C154; Philip, C47; Samuel, C47; Sarah, C22, C150; Wilson, C22, C150; William, C47.

Whittaker, Rachel, C138.

Whitten, Almira, C26; Asbury, C26; Cinthia, C145; David, 21; Frances, 25; George, C26; Jane, C26; Joel, 58; John, C37; Jonathan, C26; Josiah, C37, 39; L.L., C57; Linsley, C37; Lusinda, C37; Malinda, 21; Martha, 2, C26, C37; Mary, C26, C146; Moses, C37; Nancy, C26; Nicholas, C154; Oliver, C26; Peter, 21; Polly, C37; continued

Whitten, continued: Sara, 21; Sarah, C26; W. T., 59; William, C26.
Whittle, William, C30.
Whorton, Sam, 5.
Wickes, John, C74.
Widner, Elizabeth, C145.
Wiggins, Mary, C141.
Wilborn, Elizabeth, C138.
Wilcoxen, Daniel, C120; Isaac, C120; John, C120; Lavina, C120; Lewis, C120; Warren, C120; William, C120.
Wilcoxin, Hiram, C120; Isaac, C120; Margaret, C120.
Wilder, Elizabeth, C150; Sarah, C153.
Wiles, Benjamin, C154; Tempy, C154.
Wiley, Elizabeth, C44; Frances, C44; Harison, C44; John, C143; Jones, C44; Lucy, C143; Sissily, C44; Stewart, C44; William, C44.
Wilkerson, Claracy, C61; Hanna, C61; Joel, C143; John, C61; Mary, C61; Oliver, C61; Rachel, C143; Rebecca, C61; Wesley, C61.
Wilkes, Alsey, C143; Andrew, C4; Ann, C150; Caroline, C31; Elizabeth, C143, C154; Frances, C31; Jesse, C154; John, C4; Joseph, C4; Judge, 64; Levi, C4; Martha, C31; Mary, C4; Matilda, C142; Nancy, C154; Newman, C154; Pinkney, C31; Richard, C31; William, C4.
Willet, Polly, C147.
Willett, Ann, C149; Betty, C139; Elizabeth, C6; Mary, C6; Zadekiah, C6; William, C6.
Williams, Alexander, C20; Andrew, C79; Angeline, C99; Ann, C20, C63, C146; Balus, C116; Beckers, C143; Benjamin, C20, C79; Billy, 59; Catherine, C59, C99; Charity, C75; Charlotte, C86; Cynthia, C75; Columbus, C95; Curthbirth, C101; Davenport, C20; David, 23, 43, C79, C153; Eliza, C75; Elizabeth, C20, C86, C49; Ellender, C25; Emily, C99; Fanny, C131; Frances, C36; C59; George, C20, C116; H. W., C101; Harriett, C20; Henrietta, C62; Henry, C36, C75, C154; Isaac, C65; Isabella, C96; Isam, C25; Jackson, C86; James, 23, C59, C75, C86, C143; John, 21, 23, C59, C79; Joseph, C25; Josephine, C36; Julia, C95; Juliar, C36; Lafayette, C95; Leonorah, C79, C154; Liddia, C146; Lucy, C59, C95; Mariah, C65; Marion, C86; Martha, C36; C143; Mary, C20, 59, C95, C101, C147, C148, C151, C153; Maston, C36; Matilda, C99; Meriter, C79; Milly, C86; Nancy, C95, C116, C140, C144; Pheby, C79; Phones, C99; continued,

Williams, continued: Presley, C79; Rebecca, C153; Redman, C25; Robert, C59; Rush, C116; Rutha, C25; Sally, C138; Samuel, C59; Sarah, C36; Shelton, C36; Simpson, C79; Spotwood, C116; Tabitha, C86; Terry, C143; Thomas, 1, C62, C95, C99, C101; Virginia, C59; Wesley, C20; William, C131; Winnifred, C143; Worley, 37.
Willingham, Henry, 65.
Willis, Eliza, C154; Emanuel, C154; John, C154; Joshua, C143; Katherine, C154; Martha, C109, C143; Prince, C109.
Willott, Elizabeth, C30; Richard, C30.
Wilson, Agnes, C25, C154; Ann, C127, C153; Ann Elizabeth, C1, C3; Anna, C153; Annie, C25; Benjamin, C36, C127, Calfornia, C121; Christian, C121; Charles, C107; Col., 45; Columbia, C46; Cynthia, C121; Dennis, C154; E. C., C153; Edney, C121; Eliza, C121; Elizabeth, C121, C152; Frances, C128; Gracie, C107; Harriet, C128; Harvey, 50; Henrietta, C151; Herrell, C107; Hiram, C107; India, C154; James C25; 50, 77, C121, C128, C136; Jane, C36, C107, C128, C153; John, 23, 50, 52, C106, C107, C121, C127, C153, C154; Joseph, C46; Lieut., 31; Levica, C121; Lucinda, C106, C107; Margaret, C121; Martha, C107, C121; Mary, C25, C46, C107, C121; Matthew, 22, 23, 52, C74, C128; Millie, C107; Missouri, C46; Nancy, C106, C107, C121, C122, C154; Phillip, C25; Priscilla, C128; Rachel, C107; Robert C25, C122, C128, C136; Rosella, C152; Sally, C121; Samuel, C46, C153; Simpson, C107; Solomon, C107; Sousan C136; Stewart, C121; Thomas, C3, C127, C154; W. H., C136; Wilborn, C106; Wilburn, C107; William, C107, C121, C154.
Winborn, Nancy, C154; William, C154.
Winbourn, Charles, C45; Edwin, C45; Henry, C58; John, C45; Mary, C45; Sarah, C45; William, C45.
Winburn, Jesse, C153; Mary, C153; Rebecca, C153; Richard, C153.
Winebaum, B. B., 71.
Winchester, Diadema, C73; George, C73; James, C73; Malinda, C73; Samuel, C73.
Windes, Col., 45.
Winelow, Jane, C153; Thomas, C153.
Winfrey, William, C48.
Wingo, Cass, C44; Hunt Ann, C44; Pinkney, C44; Pernesa, C44; continue

Wingo, continued: Sarah, C44; Susan, C44.
Winslow, Mary, C151.
Winstead, Charlotte, C144; John, C153;
    Mary, C154; Seth, C154.
Winsted, John, C143; Ruthy, C143.
Winston, 5; John J., 8.
Wires, Leonidas, C59; Mary, C59;
    Missouri, C59; Sarah, C59; Susan, C59.
Wisdom, Neil, 66.
Wiseman, 45.
Wisemer, Cynthia, C143; John, C143.
Withers, Katherine, C143; William, C143.
Witherspoon, Betty, 13; Charles, C23;
    Elizabeth, C23; George, C23; Harriett,
    C23; James, C23; Jane, C23; Mary, C23;
    Sarah, C23.
Wise, Catherine, C153.
Witt, Catharine, C33; Letty, C33; Thomas,
    C33; William, C33.
Womack, Elizabeth, C138.
Womble (see also Wamble), Clarissa, C154;
    Cynthia, C153; Joseph, C154; Lorenza,
    C154; Patsy, C154; William, C153.
Wood, Alexander, 25, C65; Amanda, C92,
    C121; Bennett, C25, C143; Eliza,
    C39, C92, C154; Elizabeth, C154;
    Ellender, C105; Franklin, C103;
    General, 38; Gideon, C121; H. C., 38;
    Henry, C65; Isaiah, C154; James,
    C39; C105; Jane, C138; John, C25,
    C105, C154; Joseph, C39; Malissa, C25;
    Margaret, C25, C127; Martha, C92, C105;
    Mariah, C65; Mary, C65, C100, C105,
    C127, C143, C154; Moses, 23, C39,
    C56; Nancy, C105, C145; Nelson, C25;
    Newton, C121; Randolph, C92; Robert,
    C60, C92; S. A. M., 37; Sally, C149;
    Sarah, C8, C29, C39; Solomon, C105,
    C154; Sousan, C92, C154; Sousannah,
    C121; Thomas, 24; W. B., 59; W. M.,
    58; Wesley, C105; William, 25, C105,
    C121, C127; Y. (Z?) L., C100.
Woodbank, Bazil, C89; Edy, C89; Irey,
    C89; John, C89; Mark, C89; Mary,
    C89; Sofey, C89; Sarah, C89; Smith,
    C89; William, C89.
Woodcock, H., 21, C62; J. H., 13.
Wooddle, James, C136.
Woodle, Margaret, C61.
Woods, Edy, C68; Hiram, C121; John,
    C143; Lelia, C62; Margaret, C86;
    Polly, C143; S. A., C12; Sarah, C62;
    Thomas, C38, C62; William, C62.
Woody, Polly, C141.
Woolard, Hugh, 79.
Wooten, Amanda, C56; Antha, C28;
    Ben, C56; Benjamin, C37; Hariett, C56;
    J. B., C28; James, C37; continued,

Wooten, continued, Jonnathan, 21, C37;
    Martha, 21, C28, C37; Mary, C28, C56;
    Peggy, C28; Rhody, C28; Sarah, C37.
Word, Lusinda, C58; Samuel, C58.
Worley, Joseph, C137; Paul, 71; Rebecca,
    C137.
Wrathers, Charles, C91; John, C91; Martha,
    C91; Rebecca, C91; Samuel, C91;
    Sarah, C91; William, C91.
Wright (see also Right), Anna, C153;
    Annie, C24; Canda, C139; Dr., 69;
    George, C24; James, C24; Martha, C24;
    Mary C24; Moses, C24, C153; Nancy,
    C143; Phillip, C24; Sarah, C24;
    William, 22, C143.

Yancy, John C82; Mary, C82; Millie, C82;
    Nancy, C82.
Yarbrough, Eliza, C144; Elizabeth, C140,
    C143; William, 12, C143.
Yearwood, Rachel, C108; Thomas, C108.
Yielding, E. F., 75.
Yocum, Elizabeth, C140; Matilda, C150;
    Polly, C138.
York, Betty, C138; Jessee, C113; Joseph,
    C113; Rebecca, C113; Ruthey, C106;
    Thomas, C106.
Young, Anna, C29; Ardiness, C17; Baby,
    C128; Benjamin, C17; Bishop, C26;
    Burwell, C35; Caroline, C26; Charles,
    C7, 76; Cornelia, C32; Davenport, C26;
    David, C32; Doyle, 76; Drusinda, C32;
    Ebeneser, C14, C30; Edward, C32;
    Elijah, C16, C26; Eliza, C19;
    Elizabeth, C13, C26, C30, C128;
    Ellen, C32; Elvira, C32; Ethel, C149;
    Frances, C9, C17; Henry, C63; Jabin,
    C35; James, C7, C19, C26, C29, C30, C32
    C35, C128; Jane, C13, C32, C35; John,
    12, C13, C19, C30; Jonnathan, C7;
    Joseph, C20, C26; Julia, C81; Julia,
    C7; L. D., 60; L. T., 69; Leelia, 60;
    Levi, C35; Lula, 62; Margaret, C35;
    Marion, C20, 31; Martha, C13, C16, C17,
    C35; C63, C128, C148, C152; Mary, C9,
    C13, C17, C26, C30, C32, C35, C138;
    Mary Ann, C7; Mikle, C17; Nancy, C9,
    C35, C142; Parmelia, C29; Polly, C141,
    C152; S., 20; Sally, C149; Samuel, C30,
    C32, C63; Sarah, C20, C29, C35, C63,
    C128; Susan, C20, 21; Susannah, C143;
    Thomas, C9, C17; Virginia, C32;
    William, C13, C26, C30, C54, C143.

Zachariah, George, C143; Olivia, C143.
Zilander, Aaron, C28; Becca, C28.

www.ingramcontent.com/pod-product-compliance
Lightning Source LLC
Chambersburg PA
CBHW030545080526
44585CB00012B/268